An Introduction to
Child Development

SAGE was founded in 1965 by Sara Miller McCune to support the dissemination of usable knowledge by publishing innovative and high-quality research and teaching content. Today, we publish over 900 journals, including those of more than 400 learned societies, more than 800 new books per year, and a growing range of library products including archives, data, case studies, reports, and video. SAGE remains majority-owned by our founder, and after Sara's lifetime will become owned by a charitable trust that secures our continued independence.

Los Angeles | London | New Delhi | Singapore | Washington DC | Melbourne

An Introduction to
Child Development

Thomas Keenan, Subhadra Evans & Kevin Crowley

3rd
Edition

Los Angeles | London | New Delhi
Singapore | Washington DC | Melbourne

Los Angeles | London | New Delhi
Singapore | Washington DC | Melbourne

SAGE Publications Ltd
1 Oliver's Yard
55 City Road
London EC1Y 1SP

SAGE Publications Inc.
2455 Teller Road
Thousand Oaks, California 91320

SAGE Publications India Pvt Ltd
B 1/I 1 Mohan Cooperative Industrial Area
Mathura Road
New Delhi 110 044

SAGE Publications Asia-Pacific Pte Ltd
3 Church Street
#10-04 Samsung Hub
Singapore 049483

Editor: Luke Block
Development editor: Colette Wilson
Production editor: Imogen Roome
Copyeditor: Audrey Scriven
Proofreader: Sarah Bury
Indexer: Silvia Benvenuto
Marketing manager: Alison Borg
Cover design: Wendy Scott
Typeset by: C&M Digitals (P) Ltd, Chennai, India
Printed and bound in Great Britain by
Ashford Colour Press Ltd

© Thomas Keenan, Subhadra Evans and Kevin Crowley 2016

First edition published 2001. Reprinted 2008

Second edition published 2009. Reprinted 2010, 2014

This edition published 2016

Library of Congress Control Number: 2015948966

British Library Cataloguing in Publication data

A catalogue record for this book is available from
the British Library

ISBN 978-1-4462-7401-9
ISBN 978-1-4462-7402-6 (pbk)

MIX
Paper from
responsible sources
FSC
www.fsc.org   FSC® C011748

At SAGE we take sustainability seriously. Most of our products are printed in the UK using FSC® papers and boards.
When we print overseas we ensure sustainable papers are used as measured by the PREPS grading system.
We undertake an annual audit to monitor our sustainability.

This book is dedicated to Holly who has taught me more about children than I'll ever discover on my own.
Thomas Keenan

To Kaia and Bodhi, sparks of splendour and masters of mischief. Thank you for being patient and for sharing your stickers with me.
Subhadra Evans

To Amy and Ioan who continue to provide me with the most practical of introductions to child development.
Kevin Crowley

Contents

5 The Biological Foundations of Development II: The Developing Brain   115

SECTION III   THE DEVELOPMENT OF PERCEPTION, COGNITION AND LANGUAGE   137

6 Perception   139

About the Authors

Tom Keenan Thomas Keenan is currently a professor in the School of Academic & Liberal Studies, Niagara College in Niagara-on-the-Lake, Ontario, Canada. He is also an adjunct member of the Department of Psychology, Brock University. He is a developmental psychologist with interests in children's theory of mind, sarcasm & irony comprehension, and music.

Subhadra Evans completed her PhD in Developmental Psychology at the University of Canterbury in New Zealand. She is a lecturer in Child Development and Health Psychology at Deakin University in Melbourne, Australia, where she also researches mind/body medicine and parent child relationships in the context of chronic pain.

Kevin Crowley holds a BA and MA in Applied Psychology from University College Cork and a PhD in Psychology from Royal Holloway, University of London. He is currently a senior lecturer in Psychology at the University of South Wales where he teaches courses in Child Development and Research Methods. His research interests include early reading development, bilingual language and literacy development, and play and learning in the Early Years.

Publisher's Acknowledgements

The publishers would like to extend their warmest thanks to the following individuals for their invaluable feedback on the Second Edition and comments on draft material for the Third Edition.

Henk Boer, HAN University of Applied Science

Jesper Dammeyer, University of Copenhagen

Geraldine Davis, Anglia Ruskin University

Martin Doherty, University of East Anglia

Margriet Groen, Radboud University

Justine Howard, Swansea University

Mariëtte Huizinga, VU University Amsterdam

Carien Lubbe-De-Beer, University of Pretoria

Sarah McGeown, University of Edinburgh

Deborah Odell, University of Suffolk

Berit Overå Johannesen, Norwegian University of Science and Technology

Guided Tour

This feature provides an overview of the content covered in the chapter and outlines what you will learn in the course of reading it.

Key Concepts in orange

Words appearing in **orange** throughout the text indicate key concepts that you should understand, remember and be able to explain after reading the chapters.

Point for Reflection boxes: these are designed to help you stop and think about what you have been reading and consider the subject matter more deeply.

Research Example boxes

These boxes focus on specific pieces of research: from landmark studies to cutting-edge journal articles or experiments. These place the subject matter in real-life contexts, and demonstrate the diversity and rigour of the kinds of research being pursued in this field.

Chapter Summary

The chapter summary reviews the main concepts and issues covered in the chapter to reinforce the key learning aims.

Glossary

Located at the end of each chapter, this allows you to look up important terms and concepts introduced in the chapter quickly and easily.

TEST YOUR KNOWLEDGE

These multiple-choice questions help you to check your understanding of the chapter contents and revise for exams.

Suggested Reading

This feature contains a brief outline of key books, reports and additional articles which you may find helpful if you wish to learn more about a particular topic.

$SAGE edge™

Visit the SAGE edge website at **https://edge.sagepub.com/keenan3e** to find a range of free tools and resources that will enhance your learning experience.

SAGE edge for students provides a personalized approach to help you accomplish your coursework goals in an easy-to-use learning environment. It features:

- **Interactive quizzes,** which allow you to test your knowledge and give you feedback to help you prepare for assignments and exams.
- **Free access to scholarly journal articles**, chosen to deepen your knowledge and reinforce your learning of key topics.
- **Weblinks,** which direct you to relevant resources to broaden your understanding of chapter topics and expand your knowledge.
- A **flashcard glossary**, which features terms from the book, as an ideal tool to help you get to grips with key concepts, terms and revise for exams.
- **Author-selected videos,** to give you deeper insight into select concepts, building on context to foster understanding and facilitate learning.

SAGE edge for lecturers supports teaching by making it easy to integrate quality content into a rich learning environment. SAGE edge lecturer resources for this book include:

- **Instructors manual**, which outlines the key learning objectives covered in each chapter.
- **PowerPoint slides**, featuring figures and tables from the book, which can be downloaded and customized for use in your own presentations.
- **Testbanks**, containing questions related to the key concepts in each chapter can be downloaded and used in class, as homework or exams.

Preface

Background

Developmental psychology is a vibrant and rapidly growing field of psychology that seems, with each passing year, to become more and more exciting, comprehensive and, ultimately, more challenging. And this excitement, this challenge, is not something that is only felt by developmental psychologists themselves! The findings of developmental psychology continue to fascinate the media, to inform educators and assist in the creation of sound educational policy, to aid in the development of government policy that is designed to maximize population health and well-being, and to help parents in their attempts to better understand, raise, and interact with their own children. Students of developmental psychology today will find themselves faced with a growing body of information, most of which they can never hope to truly master due to the ever widening scope of the field. In large part, this is because of the nature of the study of developmental psychology as a field of scientific inquiry. As David Buss (1995) has pointed out, developmental psychology can be thought of as an approach that one takes to some field within psychology. That is, a developmental psychologist is fundamentally interested in understanding change across the life span in some domain of development such as thinking and reasoning, emotion, personality, social understanding, or language. As a consequence, most developmental psychologists end up specializing within a given area of development after their undergraduate and postgraduate training. This specialization reduces the burden somewhat, but it is still the case that many developmental psychologists feel a strong need to keep abreast of theoretical and methodological innovations in the field as a whole in addition to their own areas of specialization, especially as an awareness of these innovations tends, in many cases, to lead to important developments within a given domain of inquiry.

Developmental Psychology Today

The rapid growth of developmental psychology is readily observed in the large number of textbooks devoted to laying out the fields of developmental psychology and child development and by the number of courses in university undergraduate and postgraduate programmes and college diploma offerings that focus on the growth and development of children from infancy through to old age. Typical courses in developmental psychology found in many psychology programmes will include titles such as: *An Introduction to Developmental Psychology*, *Child Development*, *Adolescent Development*, *Adult Development*, *The Psychology of Aging*, *Life-span Development*, *Research Methods in Developmental Psychology*, *The Psychology of the Family*, and so on.

In addition to these courses, there are a large number of societies devoted to supporting and distributing research on child development and developmental psychology. Most countries have their own societies to support developmental psychology. In the UK, the British Psychological Society established the Developmental Psychology Section in 1980 (see www.bps.org.uk/dps). In the USA, developmental psychology is represented within the American Psychological Association as Division 7 (see www.apa.org/about/division/div7.html) and child development is represented more specifically by The Society for Research in Child Development (see www.srcd.org), which lists some 5,500 members from around the world. In Canada, there is a developmental section of the Canadian Psychological Association (see www.cpa.ca/sections/developmental), in Australia, the Australasian Human Development Association (www.ahda.org), and in Europe, there is the European Association for Developmental Psychology (www.eadp.info). These societies work to support, develop and disseminate research on developmental psychology and organize conferences and workshops that support these activities.

There are a large number of international journals that support the dissemination of research related to developmental psychology and child development. There are too many journals supporting developmental research to provide a full list here, but a sampling of some of the top journals (and journals which you may find useful in your own studies on child development) include: *Child Development, Developmental Psychology, Human Development, The British Journal of Developmental Psychology, Developmental Review, Developmental Science, Applied Developmental Science, The European Journal of Developmental Psychology, The Merrill Palmer Quarterly, The Journal of Applied Developmental Psychology*, and *Developmental Psychopathology*. Remember, this list is just a small sample of some of the journals available, and developmental research is regularly published in other major journals, such as *Psychological Bulletin, Psychological Review*, and *Psychological Science*.

Individuals with a background in developmental psychology or child development will work within a variety of professional fields. Many of those interested in child development will also go on to become researchers in the field, working in universities as academics or in centres devoted to research on child development, such as the National Institutes of Mental Health (www.nimh.org) in the USA. Others with a background in child development will often choose to work more directly with children, entering fields such as teaching, early childhood education, and paediatric nursing, or will become social workers or clinical psychologists who may work with children facing difficulties.

The Structure of the Text

One of our goals in writing this book was to provide you with a brief but comprehensive survey of some of the key issues and findings in the field of child development. The text is divided into five sections, with each section containing a number of chapters. Section I, *Introduction, Theories and Methods*, is made up of three chapters. Chapter 1 is intended to provide you with a background to the study of child development by locating the field as a branch within the study of developmental psychology, by highlighting the principles which guide the study of development from a life-span approach, and then by introducing you to some important concepts and key issues within the contemporary study of child development. Chapter 2 surveys a number of theories, both those which are historically significant and modern theoretical developments that are relevant to the study of child development. Chapter 3 addresses the issues surrounding how developmental psychologists actually go about the business of conducting research on children's development.

Section II, *The Biological Foundations of Development*, examines children's physical growth and motor development as well as the nature of interactions between genes and the environment and the implications for development (Chapter 4). In Chapter 5, 'The Developing Brain', we describe the development of the brain and central nervous system and how the brain's development is critical to understanding child development. Section III is entitled *The Development of Perception, Cognition and Language*, and contains four chapters addressing each of these topics. Chapter 6 focuses on perceptual development, particularly the rapid development of our senses. We see that infants are born with a remarkable and rapidly developing ability to make sense of their world over the first few months of life. Chapter 7 addresses theories of cognitive development while Chapter 8 looks at the development of specific cognitive processes such as memory, attention and problem solving. Section 3 concludes with Chapter 9, 'The Development of Language and Communication', in which we cover various theories of language development and the growth of communicative abilities throughout infancy and childhood.

Section IV, *Emotional, Social and Moral Development*, contains chapters on emotional development (Chapter 10), social development (Chapter 11) and moral development (Chapter 12). In Chapter 10 we study emotional development, looking at the course of emotional development, emotional control, the development of an attachment to caregivers and, finally, the concept of temperament. In Chapter 11, the concept of social development is introduced. Chapter 11 explores the growth of social relations, the nature and functions of play, how conceptions of friendship change with age, the importance of peer acceptance, and the role of an understanding of minds in social behaviour. Finally, in Chapter 12, the study of moral development is taken up through an examination of key theories of moral development and moral reasoning, the development of empathy, prosocial behaviour and distributive justice, and the development of aggressive behaviour.

In Section V, *Applied Human Development*, we examine the nature of psychopathology in childhood in Chapter 13, 'Developmental Psychopathology'. This chapter examines the unique approach to psychopathology taken by developmentalists and explores some of the more common disorders of childhood, including anxiety, depression, and attention deficit disorder. The chapter also looks at the factors that place some children at greater risk of developing psychopathology, as well as factors that promote resilience in the face of adversity.

How to Use This Book

As you move through the book, you should notice that throughout the chapters some words appear in orange type. These words indicate key concepts that you should understand, remember and be able to describe. A useful method to enhance your ability to remember the meaning of these terms is to think through the definition carefully and then re-cast it in your own words. It can also prove very helpful to associate new terms with examples from the text that you can illustrate the meaning in a more concrete fashion. Within each chapter there are text boxes that focus on a specific piece of research. We have chosen these examples to illustrate the diversity and rigour of the kinds of research being pursued in the field of child development. Each chapter also has a number of reflection points. These are questions encouraging you to 'stop and think' about what you have been reading. Some of the questions will encourage you to think about your own personal experiences in relation to the subject matter being covered. Other questions will ask you to consider how material in previous chapters might also be useful in understanding the current chapter. We have also included one or two images in each chapter to reinforce some of the salient points being made about development. Each chapter also contains a glossary – a list of these important concepts – which should allow you to look up terms quickly and easily. Each chapter ends with a brief multiple choice test that will allow you to quickly test your memory for the material you have just read. Finally, each chapter ends with some suggestions for further reading, articles or chapters that you may find helpful if you wish to learn more about a given topic.

I

INTRODUCTION, THEORIES AND METHODS

The Principles of Developmental Psychology

1

Chapter Outline

LEARNING AIMS

At the end of this chapter you should:

- be able to articulate the principles of a life-span developmental approach
- be able to explain the different meanings of *development*
- be familiar with and able to describe the key issues in the study of child development
- be familiar with the major historical approaches to understanding child development
- be aware of the evidence relevant to both sides of these issues

Introduction

The world abounds with budding psychologists. The fact that you are sitting down right now reading this text suggests that you may be one yourself. At the least, you are likely to be interested in understanding yourself or any number of other people, including your parents, siblings, friends or even children in general. How can we best gain insight into our own and our family members' past actions and predict their future behaviour, emotions and cognitions? The field of psychology, in general, and developmental psychology, in particular, is concerned with these very questions. We hope, through reading and studying this text, you will gain greater awareness of a number of important psychological questions, including how we develop and grow as a fetus from the very beginning, to how children learn about moral behaviour, and what happens when things go wrong with typical development. As you will discover, there are still many unanswered questions, but we are increasingly expanding on the knowledge of previous generations of psychologists. Perhaps you will become one of the very scientists working so hard to fill in the gaps of our knowledge about human development.

Life-span developmental psychology is the field of psychology which involves the examination of both constancy and change in human behaviour across the entire life span, that is, from conception to death (Baltes, 1987). Table 1.1 below shows the age periods that child development is typically divided into. Developmental psychologists are concerned with diverse issues, ranging from the growth of motor skills in the infant to the gains and losses observed in the intellectual functioning of the elderly. The goal of study in developmental psychology is to further our knowledge about how development evolves over the life span, developing a knowledge of the general principles of development and the differences and similarities in development across individuals. The range of topics comprising the study of modern psychology is vast, and encompasses sub-areas as diverse as social psychology, comparative psychology, the study of learning,

Table 1.1   Age periods for the study of child development

Period	From–to
Prenatal period	Conception to birth
Infancy and toddlerhood	Birth–2 years
Early childhood	2–6 years
Middle childhood	6–11 years
Adolescence	11–18 years
Early adulthood	18–25 years

neuropsychology, abnormal psychology, and cognitive psychology. However, the study of development is possible *within* each of these areas. Thus, in one sense, developmental psychology can be thought of as an *approach* that one takes to the broader study of psychology (Buss, 1995).

This text focuses on a relatively narrow portion of the life span, specifically the time development between conception and adolescence. This area of study is known as the study of **child development**. Understanding children is important in its own right and also has the potential to significantly inform us about the nature of human development. By studying the earlier forms of behaviour and the changes which behaviour undergoes, we can gain a better understanding of the 'end product', that is, adult behaviour. While this text focuses specifically on children's development, the wider principles of life-span developmental psychology (which we discuss shortly) apply as equally to this area as they do to the study of development across the life span.

What is 'Development'?

When we speak of **development**, what in fact are we referring to? One frequently used definition refers to this as *patterns of change over time which begin at conception and continue throughout the life span*. Development occurs in different domains, such as the *biological* (changes in our physical being), *social* (changes in our social relationships), *emotional* (changes in our emotional understanding and experiences), and *cognitive* (changes in our thought processes). Some developmental psychologists prefer to restrict the notion of development only to changes which lead to *qualitative* reorganizations in the structure of a behaviour, skill or ability (Crain, 2000). For example, Heinz Werner (1957) argued that development refers only to changes which increase the organization of functioning within a domain. Werner believed that development consisted of two processes: **integration** and **differentiation**. Integration refers to the idea that development consists of the integration of more basic, previously acquired behaviours into new, higher-level structures. For example, according to Piaget (1952), a baby who learns to successfully reach for objects has also learned to coordinate a variety of skills, such as maintaining an upright posture, moving their arm, visually coordinating the position of their hand and the object, and grasping the object under an integrated structure called a *scheme*. New developments build on and incorporate what has come before.

Differentiation refers to the idea that development also involves the progressive ability to make more distinctions among things, for example, learning to adjust one's grasp to pick up small objects (which requires the use of the fingers and fine motor control) versus larger objects (which only requires closing the hand around the object and less fine motor control). Werner defined development as a combination of these two processes of integration and differentiation: he saw development as a process of increasing hierarchical integration and increasing differentiation. Of course, Werner's view of development is by no means universally accepted within developmental psychology. Many developmentalists argue that anything which evidences change over time is relevant to the study of development (Crain, 2000). Thus, this debate remains a tension within the study of human development.

As we have just seen, we can identify different domains within which development occurs. However, can you think of the ways in which development in one domain might also impact on developments in another?

The Study of Child Development: A Brief History

Developmental psychology emerged as an area of study early on in the history of psychology. Charles Darwin, the founder of evolutionary theory, was an early pioneer in the study of children. Darwin (1877) kept records about the development of his own infant son, and used the data he collected to understand human development in light of the theory of evolution by natural selection. Darwin's work and a host of similar records of children's development – known as *baby biographies* – were among the first studies of human development and the source of many modern ideas about children's development (Charlesworth, 1992). Baby biographies were often criticized for their emotional and biased descriptions of children, yet it is also recognized that many of the early baby biographers, such as William Preyer, set extremely high standards for observing and recording behaviour accurately (Cairns, 1998).

One of the first developmental psychologists was the American psychologist G. Stanley Hall. Hall's research in child development focused on questions such as *what do children know when they go to school?* In an early paper entitled 'The Contents of Children's Minds on Entering School' (Hall, 1891), Hall used questionnaires and interviews to assess what children knew: information that can be potentially of great use to teachers. Hall (1904) also published on adolescence, describing adolescence as a time of *sturm und drang* (or storm and stress). In short, Hall believed emotional turbulence and conflict were a normative part of adolescence, a view which today is not widely confirmed by research (Steinberg, 1990).

In Canada, a significant event in the history of developmental psychology was the appointment of James Mark Baldwin to the faculty of the University of Toronto in 1889 (Green, 2004). Baldwin was a pioneer in the area of mental development, studying topics ranging from imitation to intentionality (see Chapter 11 for further discussion of intention and the child's theory of mind). Another major development in Canada was the opening of the St George's School for Child Study in 1926, headed by the developmental psychologist William Blatz. Blatz was famous for his study of the Dionne quintuplets, a group of five sisters (Blatz, 1938).

The psychologist John B. Watson (1928) took a very different approach to child development from Hall and other early pioneers. Watson argued for the primacy of environmental influences on children's development. In short, his view was that all development was ultimately the result of learning. Watson pioneered the study of learning mechanisms and contributed greatly to modern learning theories. He is also famous, or perhaps infamous, for his Little Albert experiment (described in Research Box 2.1). In contrast, Arnold Gesell took a position that was the opposite of Watson's. Gesell (1925) believed that development was the result of our genetic endowment, a view that is known as **maturation**. Gesell focused on describing the *norms* that characterized children's development, concentrating on *when* children typically acquire a given behaviour (such as walking) and the extent to which many behaviours are affected by environmental influences such as practice or training.

The study of children's development has also been greatly influenced by the work of a group of prominent twentieth-century psychologists, laying the foundations for the field of developmental psychology as it exists today. Jean Piaget (1896–1980) took an *organismic* approach to cognitive development, arguing that it was the development of mental structure within the child's mind that determined how that child understood the world. Under Piaget's view, cognitive development is a constant dance between the way in which a child's cognitive structures shape their view of the world, and the need for that child's cognitive structures to adapt or change in light of new information or learning. The interplay between these two processes leads to a continual reorganization of knowledge into knowledge structures that are better adapted to the world.

In contrast to Piaget's work, the Russian psychologist Lev Vygotsky postulated a sociocultural theory of cognitive development (Vygotsky, 1978). Vygotsky argued that a child's cognitive development occurred within the context of *social* interactions with more experienced members of that child's culture, making cognitive development a truly social process. Children build on their innate perceptual and memory skills and acquire the *mental tools* of their culture, such as language and number, as well as the symbol systems that allow them to manipulate and reflect on these tools. For Vygotsky, understanding children's development was a matter of understanding children's acquisition of these mental tools (Rogoff, 1990).

Broader changes within the field of cognitive psychology during the 1960s had an important influence on the study of children's cognitive development. The study of *information processing*, or how information is taken in and flows through a child's cognitive system causing various outputs or responses, was an important influence on developmental psychologists interested in children's thinking (Klahr & Macwhinney, 1998). Information processing psychologists most often focus on how children take in or encode information from their environment, how they represent it to themselves, and how they operate on their representations of knowledge to create outputs or products (Siegler, 1998), like the solution to a math problem or an answer to a question about what Winnie the Pooh will do next.

This review of the history of developmental psychology is by no means full or complete, and the interested student is recommended to pursue fuller accounts of the history of the discipline. However, it will allow us to go on and examine development within a variety of domains while understanding something of the origins of many of the ideas we will encounter.

Principles of Life-span Development

One of developmental psychology's eminent researchers, the late Paul Baltes (1939–2006), articulated a set of principles which guide the study of human development within a life-span framework. Baltes (1987) argued that these principles form a family of beliefs which specify a coherent view of the nature of development. It is the application of these beliefs as a coordinated whole which characterizes the life-span approach. Thus, Baltes often focused on old age in his later writing and research, but he described the issues of ageing – including wisdom, decline and changing relationships – in the context of the entire life span. We have therefore learned about human development in its entirety from his work. In this book, although we focus on development in children, we will similarly take a life-span approach to the study of development.

Baltes (Baltes & Smith) have identified a number of overarching themes with which developmental psychology is concerned. These include studying the similarities in people's development, studying the differences in their development, and examining the degree to which an individual's development is changeable, within an overall cultural context. In addition to these overarching themes, Baltes (1987) has identified a number of more specific principles of development.

The first principle is that *development is life-long*. This belief has two separate aspects. First, the potential for development extends across the entire life span: there is no assumption that the life course must reach a plateau or decline during adulthood and old age. Second, development may involve processes which are not present at birth but emerge throughout the life span. Development is also *multidimensional* and *multidirectional*. Multidimensionality refers to the fact that development cannot be described by a single criterion such as increases or decreases in a behaviour. The principle of multidirectionality maintains that there is no single, normal path that development must or should take. In other words, healthy developmental outcomes are achieved in a wide variety of ways. Development is often comprised of multiple abilities which take different directions, showing different types of change or constancy.

Another principle is that development involves both *gains and losses*. According to Baltes, any developmental process involves aspects of growth and decline. For example, formal schooling increases a child's knowledge base and develops their cognitive abilities, but also restricts their creativity as they learn to follow rules defined by others. These two aspects of growth and decline need not occur in equal strength and, moreover, the balance between gains and losses can change with time.

A fifth principle articulated by Baltes (1987) is that development is *plastic*. Plasticity refers to the within-person variability which is possible for a particular behaviour or development.

For example, infants who have a hemisphere of the brain removed shortly after birth (as a treatment for epilepsy) can recover the functions associated with that hemisphere as the brain reorganizes itself and the remaining hemisphere takes over those functions. Further research on the topic of such *neuroplasticity* will be described in Chapter 5. A key part of the research agenda in developmental psychology is to understand the nature and the limits of plasticity in various domains of functioning.

The sixth principle states that development is also situated in *contexts* and in *history*. Development varies across the different contexts in which we live our lives. For example, social and rural environments are associated with different sets of factors which have the potential to impact on development: understanding how development differs for individuals within these two settings requires an understanding of the differing contexts. Development is also historically situated, that is, the historical time period in which we grow up affects our development.

Finally, Baltes suggested that the study of developmental psychology is *multidisciplinary*. That is, the sources of age-related changes do not lie within the province of any one discipline. For example, psychological methodologies may not be appropriate for understanding factors that are sociological in nature. Rather, an understanding of human development will be achieved only by research conducted from the perspective of disciplines such as sociology, linguistics, anthropology, and computer science.

Image 1A According to Baltes, development is historically situated. Children currently have unprecedented access to technology, representing a distinct normative history-graded influence

© iStock.com/proxyminder

Contextualism in developmental psychology

As we have seen, Baltes (1987) stressed the importance of contextualism to the study of life-span development. In order to create a coherent framework for understanding contextual influences, Baltes proposed a three-factor model of contextual influences on development (Baltes, Reese, & Lipsitt, 1980). The first factor is **normative age-graded influences**. These are the biological and environmental influences that are similar for individuals in a particular age group. Examples of normative age-graded influences are events such as puberty or the entry into formal schooling. A second type of influence is what Baltes referred to as **normative history-graded influences**. These are biological and environmental influences associated with historical periods in time which influence people of a particular generation. For example, the effects of World War II on much of the world's population, or the changes in the structure of government experienced by the people of the Soviet Union during the 1980s, would constitute examples of normative history-graded influences. *Nonnormative life events* are unusual occurrences that have a major impact on an individual's life. The occurrence of these events is relatively unique to an individual and is not tied to an historical time period. Moreover, the influence of these events often does not follow a typical developmental course. Being struck down with a major illness or losing a parent in childhood are examples of this kind of contextual influence. It is important for developmentalists to recognize that explanations of behavioural development are likely to be complex and require consideration of the wide variety of possible influences on a given individual's development.

 Can you think of any examples of nonnormative life events that might have a positive impact on development?

Image 1B Parenting practices vary along cultural norms. In many parts of the world, older siblings help in the care of younger siblings

Source: Monique K. Hilley/Wikimedia Commons

Cultural context

The importance of culture and context to a child's ongoing development is becoming increasingly apparent. Two prominent theorists who we will explore in the next chapter, Lev Vygotsky and Urie Bronfenbrenner, were ahead of their time in proposing theories of human development that accounted for the child's sociocultural influences. However, many of developmental psychology's forefathers failed to acknowledge the impact of culture on child development. Thankfully, we have learnt much from other disciplines concerned with understanding the impact of culture on human behaviour, including anthropology, and the field of cross-cultural developmental psychology is growing.

At times research questions may be universal and seem to apply to all children everywhere, such as having a predisposition to acquire language, but very often characteristics and skills are acquired in a way that varies from one culture to another. For example, almost all children will eventually learn to walk, but the timing and order of motor skill acquisition vary as a result of how mobility is encouraged within a culture. Among the Kipsigis of Kenya, babies typically learn to walk before children in most other countries, and often walk before they can crawl, due to parenting practices of actively encouraging infants to keep upright and bouncing them on their feet (Super, 1981).

Parenting practices consistent with varying cultural norms can have a profound impact on areas as diverse as involvement of fathers in care giving, warmth from and control of mothers, and the role older children play in their younger siblings' care (Whiting & Edwards, 1988).

The effects of culture have a wider reach than simply upon parenting practices. Norms regarding *individualization*, which stresses each individual's achievement and competition among members, versus *collectivist* societies, which focus on the interdependence of those living within a given culture and are less approving of competitiveness, impact many aspects of a child's development. Given the wide-reaching effects of a person's culture on their development, some psychologists, such as Barbara Rogoff, have argued that individual development is inseparable from community (Rogoff, 2003). We explore more about the importance of understanding the role of culture in Research Example 1.1.

Research Example 1.1

A typical developmental study takes place in industrialized, western societies with white, middle-class children. Are these studies likely to apply to children everywhere? Psychologists interested in cultural, economic and geographical influences upon human development are concerned with this very question. And indeed, much research indicates that cultural effects should be taken into account when understanding the social, cognitive and physical developmental processes of a child within a given environment. As we identify below, one developmental principle may not apply to all cultures, and sometimes important differences between collectivist versus individualized nations will need to be considered.

A recent investigation of cultural differences in the impact of parental control on adolescents' psychological functioning found evidence for the importance of considering culture when applying psychological principles to children's development. Parental control is defined as behaviours through which parents excessively control and regulate their children's activities and routines, encourage children's dependence on them as parents, and instruct the children on how to think and feel. High parental control is believed to induce helplessness and generate anxiety and depression in children. However, the effects may be culturally specific. Parental control may be used in collectivist cultures, including many parts of Asia, to maintain harmony in the family, and may be perceived by children as an expression of care and concern, rather than of harshness, as may be the case in more individualized nations.

A research team from Israel and Saudi Arabia recruited 2,884 Arab, Indian, French, Polish and Argentinean adolescents to report on their mothers' and fathers' use of parental control during a conflict, ranging from a score of 5 ('controlling/punishing') to 1 ('accepting/forgiving') (Dwairy & Achoui, 2010). Results revealed that parental control differs across cultures, such that parental control was higher in the eastern than western countries (parents in both France and Argentina applied lower control than all

(Continued)

other countries). Mothers were reported as more controlling than fathers in most cultures, although there was no clear relationship between maternal control and adolescent psychological health in any of the countries. However, the role of fathers showed an interesting cultural interaction; paternal control was associated with adolescent psychological maladjustment in the West, but not in the East. The authors explained the findings in terms of an inconsistency hypothesis, such that parental control does not cause harm to children in authoritarian/collective societies as control in such societies is consistent with the wider culture in which the children live. However, paternal control in the West is inconsistent with the culture's more liberal climate of independence, and may thus be perceived by children as harsh and result in psychological distress in children.

Questions: Are there any other explanations, apart from the inconsistency hypothesis, that might explain the differential impact of control within cultures?

Can you think of reasons why maternal control strategies were not consistently related to child maladjustment as was paternal control?

Important information was missing from the study, including adolescent age and how psychological disorders were assessed. Can you think of how our interpretation of the study conclusions may be impacted by not knowing this information?

Chronological age in developmental psychology

The variable which is most often studied in developmental psychology is *age*. **Chronological age**, the time which has elapsed since a person's birth, is found in many developmental studies. Chronological age is commonly examined in developmental research because performance on any given task strongly co-varies with age. For example, in the study of child development we find more often than not that older children perform at a higher level than younger children on a given task, or that older children use immature strategies less often than do younger children. However, what do age effects mean to us? Are we any better off for knowing that older children score better on a test than younger children?

It is very important to recognize that chronological age does not *cause* development, but simply *reflects* the fact that we have existed for a certain amount of time. In other words, age is a *proxy variable* (Hartmann & George, 1999). By 'proxy variable', we mean that chronological age stands in for other developmental processes we have not measured. When we find a difference between age groups on some variable, all we can say is that there is a performance difference between age groups – what causes the difference is not known unless specific measures are included. Age differences are only a small part of what developmental psychologists examine. The real interest for developmental psychologists lies in examining the mechanisms that cause developmental change and, thus, performance differences between age groups.

Themes and Issues in Developmental Psychology

A number of major themes have emerged in the study of child development, themes which are recurrent across the various domains of study. For example, the debate over whether development is best characterized as driven by biological or environmental factors has guided study within areas as diverse as emotional, social and cognitive development. The same is true for each of the other major themes which we will examine. After you have become familiar with each of the issues described below, you should think about these themes as you read through the following chapters. You should be able to identify where these themes occur when studying the areas of development discussed in the last seven chapters.

Continuity and discontinuity

An important question which continually confronts the researcher in the study of child development is how to best characterize the nature of developmental change. There are two contrasting positions on developmental change. According to those who hold the first position, development is best viewed as a *continuous* process. That is, development is conceived as a process of gradual accumulation of a behaviour, skill or knowledge. In this model, development proceeds in a smooth and orderly fashion, with each change building on previous abilities. In contrast to this perspective, those who hold the second view would suggest that developmental change is best characterized as *discontinuous* in nature. These theorists suggest that behaviours or skills often change qualitatively across time, and that new organizations of behaviours, skills or knowledge emerge in a rather abrupt or discrete fashion. The notion of a **stage** of development is central to discontinuous views of development. A stage of development can be thought of as a particular organization of a child's knowledge and behaviour that characterizes their development at a particular point in time. The movement to a new stage of development means that a qualitative reorganization of previous knowledge or behaviour has taken place. For example, Piaget (1952) believed that between 7 and 11 years of age children's thinking could be described as concrete, in that it is closely tied to the nature of the objects with which they interact. In contrast, during adolescence, thinking becomes more abstract: it is less bound to particular objects and takes into account the possible or hypothetical. It should be clear that these two positions – development viewed as a continuous process or as a discontinuous process – describe development in quite different ways, ways that on the surface are seemingly difficult to reconcile with one another.

Siegler (1998, 2000) has argued that whether a particular aspect of development appears to be continuous or discontinuous in nature depends largely on how we choose to examine development. When we examine the change in a given behaviour at large intervals (e.g. yearly), or in different age groups such as 4 year-olds and 8 year-olds, development will tend to look very discontinuous or stage-like. If we plotted the level of development of some skill over time, the developmental function might look like a staircase, with periods of little change followed by abrupt shifts in the level of performance. In contrast, if we were to examine the behaviour more closely, at smaller intervals, we might find that development took on a much more continuous character. That is, increases in the level of performance would be seen to occur gradually with no abrupt shifts. We would also find that there is great variability in the methods or strategies that children use to solve problems. Siegler's (1998) work on children's learning in the domain of mathematics showed that children often use a variety of strategies in their attempts to learn how to add together two numbers. Because learning to decide which strategies work best takes some time, the shifts between using different strategies are a gradual process. If we plotted the development of strategy use for addition problems, Siegler claims we would obtain a picture quite different from the staircase model described above. Instead, we would see what he calls 'overlapping waves' of development. The waves occur as the variability in strategy use gradually peaks and declines while the overlap between the waves reflects the fact that children use multiple strategies at the same time. Therefore, how we look at development in time has a great deal to do with the picture we obtain.

Sternberg and Okagaki (1989) have suggested that the attempt to characterize development as uniformly continuous or discontinuous has the appearance of an unanswerable question, being based on a false presupposition. Instead, they argue that a better question to ask is 'what are the sources of continuity and discontinuity in development?' In their view, 'either/or' debates are misleading: development has both discontinuous and continuous aspects, and the real question for developmental psychologists is to find out how these differing aspects arise in the course of development.

Stability and change

Another issue which is of importance to developmental psychologists is the issue of **stability versus change**. Simply put, we can ask whether development is best characterized by stability (for example, does a behaviour or trait such as *shyness* stay stable in its expression over time?) or change (could a person's degree of shyness fluctuate across the life span?). Studies of children have often revealed impressive stability over time in aspects of development such as the attachment bond to their parents (e.g. Sroufe, Egeland, & Kreutzer, 1990) or in personality (Caspi & Silva, 1995). Of course, there is evidence which suggests a contrary view, that change is both possible and indeed likely under the appropriate conditions. For example, research on children's temperament (e.g. Thomas & Chess, 1977) raises the possibility that inherited predispositions to react emotionally in certain ways can be altered by their environment, and particularly by the attitudes and behaviours of caregivers. An important aspect of the debate on stability versus change has to do with the degree to which early experiences play a formative role in later development. Freud was one of the first psychologists to emphasize the critical nature of our early experiences for our later development. In his view, how we resolve our sexual and aggressive urges is strongly tied to the nature of our personality as adults. Similarly, Erik Erikson (1963) believed that how we dealt with key issues, such as the development of a warm, caring relationship with our parents or the ability to think and act autonomously, were important determinants of later developments (although, unlike Freud, Erikson made a greater allowance for the different contexts in which children develop). These early theories of human development as well as a great deal of later research suggest that there is a highly stable quality to our development and that our early experience is crucial to this stability. In contrast

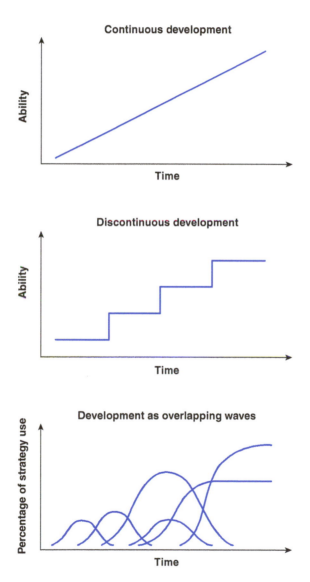

Figure 1.1   Models of developmental change

to this position, researchers who have focused on adult development, such as Baltes (1987), have emphasized that we are malleable throughout the life span and that later experiences are very important to whether development shows stability or plasticity. Baltes argued that too little attention had been focused on those aspects of development which support change, and proposed a methodology for the study of behaviour across the life span which would test the potential for change in behaviour.

A series of studies examining the effects of early experience on children's social, physical and cognitive development was conducted by British psychiatrist Sir Michael Rutter. Rutter (1998) looked at the psychological and physical development of Romanian orphans who had been adopted into British families after the fall of the Ceausescu regime in Romania. The children had been reared in extremely poor conditions in their native country. As a result, a large proportion showed severe problems, including intellectual disability, growth deficiencies and major health problems. Institution records provided data on how long and at what age the children had been placed in an institution. As a result, Rutter et al. were able to examine whether the degree of children's recovery from these early experiences was affected by how long they had been institutionalized. (See Research Example 1.2 for a further discussion of how early deprivation can effect development.)

Research Example 1.2

The Story of the Romanian Orphans

The infants were assessed on their arrival into the United Kingdom (UK) and again a few years after their arrival. A control group of children adopted within the UK was also included for comparison purposes. At the time of their entry into the UK, the Romanian adoptees were very poorly off when compared to developmental norms for children in the UK. They showed deficits on height and weight (more than two standard deviations below the mean) and their cognitive scores indicated that they had scored in the mildly retarded range. When the adoptees were compared among themselves in regard to the length of their institutionalization, a number of important differences emerged. The few adopted children who had been raised mainly in a family environment (experiencing less than two weeks of institutional care) were markedly better off in terms of their physical and cognitive development scores than peers who had spent much longer periods in institutional care. Given the significant deficits in both physical and cognitive development observed in this group, you might reasonably infer that their future prospects were poor.

The long-term follow-up of these children revealed mixed findings. When the Romanian adoptees at age 6 were compared to the control group of children adopted within the UK, a high level of

catch-up growth was observed. Catch-up growth refers to the tendency to rapid recovery with the establishment of normal environmental conditions (as opposed to the privation which caused the initial deficit). In comparison to the control group, the Romanian adoptees showed substantial catch-up growth, attaining similar levels of height, weight and head circumference (although the Romanian adoptees were still on average slightly smaller than the control group). The findings in regard to cognitive growth were similarly impressive. Infants were placed in adoptive families before the age of 6 months similarly to the control group on cognitive measures. Infants placed in families after 6 to 24 months of institutional care showed significant differences in comparison to the control group: the Romanian adoptees scored significantly lower on the cognitive measure, although the mean score was well within the normal range for children of their age. The researchers highlighted the possibility that catch-up growth was not yet complete in this group of children.

However, recent work by the English and Romanian Adoptees Study Team has revealed that the future for some of the children involved may not be so bright. Studies examining a range of functioning at age 11 showed that cognitive functioning and attachment security might still be compromised in these children, and only limited catch-up growth was observed (Beckett, Maughan, Rutter, Castle, Colvert et al., 2006). Analysis of the individual progress of children revealed a great deal of variation: one-fifth of children who spent the longest time in the deprived environment showed normal functioning later (Rutter & the ERA Study Team, 2001), while others did not fare so well and continued to show difficulties. Still other children who showed improvement at age 6 slipped in this growth at age 11. A variety of outcomes were therefore possible for these children.

In short, the results of the studies suggested that, while early experiences can be associated with negative child outcomes, recovery of functioning is still possible. Children's early experiences are not necessarily associated with long-term consequences, but the prognosis for many children may still be poor. These findings showed that children's development can be characterized by both constancy and change. Further research will hopefully identify which factors make this change in deprivation possible.

Maturation versus experience in development: the nature–nurture debate

Of all of the issues which have aroused debate within the study of child development and developmental psychology, the *nature versus nurture issue* has generated the most controversy by far. This may be due to the fact that unlike the other debates we have discussed, the nature–nurture question (as it is often called) focuses on the best explanation for how development takes place. The issue is usually posed as a debate between two positions regarding the relative roles of biological and environmental factors in development. **Nature** refers to the position that our genetic inheritance, through the process of heredity, is the primary influence on development. In contrast, **nurture** refers to the position that the environment (broadly construed as children's experiences, including parenting, education, learning, cultural influences) is primarily responsible for development.

In developmental psychology's past, extreme positions have been taken on the nature–nurture debate. Arnold Gesell (1928) was a strong advocate of the position that the course of our development was largely dictated by genetic factors. Our genetic heritage specifies the set of biological processes which determine the patterns of growth that we observe, which Gesell referred to as *maturation*. Simply put, maturation is the sequence of growth which is specified and controlled by our genes. Gesell used studies of identical twins to study how experience and maturation lead to development (see Chapter 4). His studies compared twins' speed in learning new skills. One twin was given special experience to assist with learning a particular skill while the other twin was given no such experience. Gesell's findings consistently showed that the acquisition of these behaviours was relatively unaffected by the special training, that is, the untrained twin tended to acquire the behaviour as quickly as the trained twin.

In contrast to Gesell's maturationist position, John B. Watson (1928) argued for the dominance of the environment in children's development. Watson believed that genetic factors placed no limits on how environments could shape the course of children's development. Watson was famous for his boast that, given the ability to manipulate the environment to his own standards, he could shape the development of any child: 'Give me a dozen healthy infants, well-formed, and my own specified world to bring them up in, and I'll guarantee to take any one at random and train him to become any type of specialist I might select – doctor, lawyer, artist, merchant-chief, and yes, even beggar-man and thief, regardless of his talents, penchants, tendencies, abilities, vocations, and race of his ancestors' (Watson, 1930: 104). While Watson was never able to make good on his boast, he did show how environmental experiences played a role in shaping children's behaviour through the processes of **classical conditioning**, a type of learning in which a stimulus can come to evoke a response after the repeated pairing of the two stimuli (Watson, 1928).

The positions held by Gesell and Watson regarding the relative roles of maturation and environment on development are essentially extremist positions which are no longer supported in light of current research on child development. Today, most developmental psychologists recognize that nature and nurture both play an important role in development. Rather than discussing nature *versus* nurture, we commonly talk about the interaction between nature *and* nurture. This interactionist view is increasingly held by more than developmental psychologists as the public also recognize the importance of environment and genetics. Research has found that over 90% of teachers and parents accept that nature and nurture are equally necessary for understanding children's behaviour and cognition (Plomin & Walker, 2003). Given the widespread recognition that both nature and nurture play crucial roles in shaping development, the challenge which lies before us today is to examine the interplay between biological and environmental factors, figuring out how they interact to produce developmental change.

The interaction between nature and nurture, of which the new field of epigenetics takes centre stage in current research (we will take this up in greater detail in Chapter 4), has been characterized as being less of an answer to the nature–nurture debate and more a starting point for the study of development (Elman, Bates, Johnson, Karmiloff-Smith, Parisi, & Plunkett 1996). Recent research provides us with more explicit information about the interplay between nature and nurture. Plomin and colleagues (Plomin, DeFries, Craig, & McGuffin, 2001) have shown that children with certain genetic predispositions are more likely to develop problem behaviour. When these children live in abusive environments, they are more likely to be maltreated than children without such difficulties. For abuse to result, a violent environment clearly interacts with children's inherited qualities. Similarly, adoption studies have shown that environmental stress, such as parental separation, is only likely to have a negative effect on children when it is coupled with a genetic risk in children (O'Connor & the ERA Study Team, 2003). Interestingly, recent research has revealed that some genetic 'risks' can result in future positive outcomes when interacting with advantageous environmental factors. Thus, when children who are prone to a high level of negative emotion are raised in harsh environments, they do indeed appear to be at greater risk of developing problems than children with a naturally more easy-going temperament; however, these very same children, when raised in a warm, supportive environment, often surpass their easier-going peers on a number of indicators (Belsky & Pluess, 2009). This notion of *differential susceptibility* will be raised further in Chapter 13.

Another way we can approach the interaction between nature and nurture is by examining the extent to which our biological programming can be altered by environmental influences (Dellarosa Cummins & Cummins, 1999; Elman et al., 1996). The biologist C. H. Waddington (1975) used the term **canalization** to refer to this phenomenon. In other words, is the genetic influence on a particular development robust across varied environments or is it susceptible to change? Highly canalized behaviours are relatively unaltered by changes in the environment. For example, the tendency to acquire a language is a highly canalized development in that it occurs across a wide degree of environmental variation. In contrast, some behaviours are easily modified by environmental factors and are less canalized. Intelligence is a trait which is dramatically altered by environmental variations (e.g. Bronfenbrenner & Crouter, 1983). For example, it is well documented that children who grow up in enriched environments tend to show higher levels of achievement than children growing up in impoverished environments. Studying the relative canalization of different developments has the potential to shed light on the nature of epigenesis.

Our biology is continuously influenced by our environment and our behaviour. At the same time, our experience of our environment is continuously influenced by our biological inheritance. For example, children frequently seek out peers and environments that are suited to their predispositions (Kuczynski, 2003). Trying to divide the causes of behaviour into parts assignable to nature and nurture is futile – nature and nurture are engaged in a continuous, reciprocal interaction. The attempt to separate their influences, as has been done in the past, leads to an over-simplified and incomplete picture of human development.

Glossary

Canalization refers to the extent to which our biological programming can be altered by environmental influences.

Catch-up growth refers to rapid recovery of physical growth (after a period of deprivation) with the establishment of normal environmental conditions.

Child development is the study of development between conception and adolescence.

Chronological age is the time which has elapsed since an individual's birth.

Classical conditioning is a type of learning in which a new stimulus can come to evoke a familiar response after the repeated pairing of the new stimulus with a stimulus which already evokes the response.

Development refers to patterns of change over time, beginning at conception and continuing throughout the life span.

Differentiation refers to the idea that development involves the progressive ability to make more distinctions among stimuli, concepts or behaviours.

Epigenetics is an emerging field within science that explains how environmental factors modify expression of genes.

Integration refers to the idea that development consists of the linking together of more basic, previously acquired behaviours into new, higher-level structures.

Life-span developmental psychology is the field of psychology which involves the examination of both constancy and change in human behaviour across the entire life span.

Maturation is a sequence of growth which is specified and controlled by our genes.

Nature refers to the position on the *nature–nurture issue* that our genetic inheritance is the primary influence on development.

Normative age-graded influences are the biological and environmental influences that are similar for individuals in a particular age group.

Normative history-graded influences are the biological and environmental influences associated with historical periods in time and which influence people of a particular generation.

Nonnormative life events are unusual occurrences that have a major impact on an individual's life. The occurrence of these events is relatively unique to an individual and is not tied to a particular historical time period.

Nurture refers to the position on the *nature–nurture issue* that the environment is primarily responsible for developmental outcomes.

Stability versus change is the debate over whether a particular trait or behaviour is best characterized by stability over time or by change.

Stage is a particular organization of knowledge and behaviour that can be used to characterize a child's level of development at a particular point in time.

TEST YOUR KNOWLEDGE

1. Which of the following is not a principle of life-span development as articulated by Paul Baltes?

   a) Development is life-long
   b) Development involves processes which emerge throughout the life span
   c) Development is multidirectional and multidimensional
   d) Development involves the processes of integration and differentiation

2. What are the contextual influences of development?

   a) Normative age-graded influences, normative history-graded influences, normative life events
   b) Similarities in people's development, differences in people's development, and the degree to which an individual's development is changeable
   c) Normative age-graded influences, normative history-graded influences, and nonnormative life events
   d) The interaction between genes and environment

3. The nature–nurture debate refers to which of the following?

   a) The notion that a child's nature is fixed early on and is caused by their environment
   b) The argument within psychology about whether our behaviour can be explained by inherited causes or environmental causes
   c) Opposing views on whether development is best conceptualized as involving constancy (such as our genetic blueprint) or change (such as we see in different environments)
   d) The suggestion that all creatures within nature should be nurtured

4. Canalization refers to which of the following?

   a) The ridges and furrows that make up the human brain
   b) The attempt to divide behaviour into parts assignable to the environment and parts assignable to our genes
   c) The extent to which our biological programming can be altered by environmental factors
   d) The study of whether development is stable or changeable

ANSWERS: 1–D, 2–B, 3–B, 4–C

Suggested Reading

Baltes, P. B. (1997). On the incomplete architecture of human ontogeny: selection, optimization, and compensation as foundation of developmental theory. *American Psychologist, 52,* 366–380.

Buss, D. M. (2005). *The Handbook of Evolutionary Psychology*. Hoboken, NJ: Wiley.

Butterworth, G., & Harris, M. (1994). *Principles of Developmental Psychology*. Hove: Lawrence Erlbaum Associates.

Want to learn more? For links to online resources relevant to this chapter, interactive quizzes and much more, visit the companion website at **https://edge.sagepub.com/keenan3e/**

Theories of Development

2

Chapter Outline

LEARNING AIMS

At the end of this chapter you should:

- be able to explain the importance and function of theories
- be able to explain the core concepts associated with each of the theoretical positions covered
- be able to define and give examples of the key concepts associated with each of the theoretical positions covered
- be able to compare and contrast the theories, understanding the strengths and the limitations of each theory

Introduction: What is a Theory?

A theory is an interconnected, logical system of concepts that provides a framework for organizing and understanding observations. The function of a theory is to allow us to understand and predict the behaviour of some aspect of the world (e.g. the tendency of an object to slide down an inclined plane or the ability to infer the feelings of a friend from their behaviour). Theories can be either formal or informal: what differentiates formal from informal theories is how explicitly the concepts which make up the theory are made. **Formal theories** take the form of an interconnected set of hypotheses, definitions, axioms and laws, each of which is an explicit concept which fits with or can be deduced from the overall theory (Miller, 2002). Formal theories can be expressed in a variety of ways: using ordinary language; in mathematical form; or sometimes in the form of logical principles. Ideally, a formal theory should be logically consistent and contain no contradictions, fit well with empirical observations (rather than be contradicted by them), be testable, be as simple as possible, and should cover a reasonable range of phenomena (Miller, 2002). In contrast, **informal theories** take a less rigorous form than formal theories; they are often little more than organized sets of intuitions or expectations about our world (these informal theories are often referred to as *implicit theories*). In developmental psychology, we have no formal theories of human development (Miller, 2002), although most theories of child development are somewhat more developed than the intuitive expectations about human behaviour that we all hold. However, we can evaluate developmental theories in terms of how likely they are to develop into formal theories using the criteria for a formal theory.

A good theory must state the range of phenomena it is trying to explain. For example, a theory of intellectual development may include hypotheses about the evolution of the brain or the growth of symbolic abilities, but we would not expect the theory to explain changes in motor ability. Understanding the focus of a theory helps us identify its **range of applicability**, that is, the range of phenomena to which it properly applies. We must also know what **assumptions** a theory is based on. Assumptions are the guiding premises underlying the logic of a theory. For example, evolutionary psychologists take for granted the assumption that natural selection is the only process which can produce changes in the physical structures of an organism over time. In order to properly evaluate a theory, you must first understand what its assumptions are. This is because the assumptions of a theory may be questionable or even incorrect. Assumptions may be influenced by cultural contexts and belief systems, by the sample the researcher was observing, or by the current knowledge base of the field.

Now that we know what a theory is, we can ask 'what do theories do?' First, theories are constructed to organize and interpret our observations of the world and help us identify orderly relationships among many diverse events. They help us to distinguish factors which are central to understanding a given behaviour from factors which are only related in a peripheral way. Our theories give meaning to the facts we discover about the world, serving as a framework within which to interpret facts and integrate new information with previously acquired knowledge. Second, theories guide the acquisition of new knowledge. The statement of a theory should make specific predictions which can be tested. Theories can also cause us to reinterpret knowledge which we have previously acquired; that is, the formulation of a theory may require us to look more carefully at factors we had previously taken for granted or ignored. (For more on the role of theories in the study of psychology, see Haslam and McGarty, 2003.)

According to Miller (1993), theories of human development differ from other theories in a particular way. The critical aspect of developmental theories is a focus on change over time in some particular behaviour or domain of functioning. Miller further argues that any developmental theory should manage three tasks. First, it needs to describe change within a given domain or domains. For example, if one is proposing a theory of emotional development, a good theory would describe what the development of emotion looks like. Second, it needs to describe changes in the relationships between domains. For example, do changes in cognitive functioning give rise to changes in social or emotional functioning? Third, it should explain how the changes in behaviour that have been described take place; that is, what accounts for the transitions between different states of development? Are the observed changes a function of maturation, learning, or an interaction of both? A developmental theory needs a clear description of the mechanisms which guide change.

Now that we have considered what a theory is and what it should provide, let us next examine a selection of theories which are currently used or have previously been important to the study of child development.

Before going on to read about theories of development, think about another possible source of information about development: what is often referred to as 'commonsense' psychology. Can you think of any 'commonsense' views or statements about development? What do you think are the limitations of commonsense explanations of development?

Theories of Human Development

In this section, we review a number of the most important theories of child development. Some of these, such as Freud's psychosexual theory of development, are discussed not because they are currently important to the field of child development, but for their historical value to the discipline. Other theories are examined because of their current importance to the field.

While there are a large number of theories of human development, the search for underlying commonalities across these theories has revealed that all developmental theories can be classified as based on at least one of two philosophical models (Dixon & Lerner, 1998): **organicism** and **mechanism**. These models detail the assumptions about the nature of human development that underlie the various theories which we will review here. Models based on organicism stress the qualitative features of developmental change and emphasize the organism's role in bringing about these changes; that is, organicism focuses on developmental change which is a reorganization based on previous forms and is not simply a change in the quantity of a given behaviour. In contrast, mechanistic theories stress quantitative changes in behaviour and emphasize that factors outside the control of the organism play the major role in developmental change. Of course, not all theories of development are based exclusively on one model as some theories have adopted elements of both mechanism and organicism to explain human development. As we review each of the theories below, see if you can classify the theories discussed in terms of whether they subscribe to organicism, mechanism, or some combination of the two positions.

Another important distinction that can be made between theories is the degree to which they are **contextual**. Many developmental psychologists appreciate that children, and indeed adults, behave differently in different contexts (Magnusson & Stattin, 1998). As you may have noted with your own behaviour, we tend to behave quite differently at home, in the classroom, and with our peers. This differential pattern of functioning applies to the individual's wider context as well. Thus, contextual perspectives commonly take into account a child's broader community and society, and often seek to understand how society and culture impact on that child's development. Contextual approaches may ask questions such as, 'would a child who is difficult to soothe and born into a patient and loving family be less likely to throw temper tantrums later on than the same child born into a hostile or challenged family?' Much of the research on children's temperament (e.g. Plomin, De Fries, Craig, & McGuffin, 2001; Tschann, Kaiser, Chesney, Aikon, & Boyce, 1996) takes such a contextual approach. Bronfenbrenner's bio-ecological model, which we will examine shortly, is a classic example of a contextual approach.

Image 2A Many developmental theories are contextual, appreciating that culture guides children's learning. This mother readies her young daughter to perform a folk dance at the Sarujkund Fair near Delhi in India

© Jeremy Richards/iStock/Thinkstock

Psychodynamic theory

Modern **psychodynamic** theories of human behaviour and development have their roots in the thinking of Sigmund Freud (1856–1939). While there are few psychologists who are strict adherents of Freudian theory (which we discuss below), psychodynamic theories continue to influence many theorists. At their heart, these theories emphasize the belief that forces or dynamics within the individual are responsible for that person's behaviour. In general, psychodynamic theories (although Erikson's work is an exception) are more influential in therapeutic contexts than they are in developmental theory, but they are nevertheless important to know about.

In his theory of human personality, Freud stressed the formative nature of early experience and of biologically-based drives: his belief was that development was the result of a balance being struck between unconscious drives and a conscious need to adapt one's self to the reality in which we find ourselves. Freud (1917) also believed that our personality was made up of three structures: the **id**, the **ego**, and the **superego**. The id is the part of our personality which is made up of instinctual drives. The id operates according to what Freud termed the **pleasure principle**; that is, the id is directed towards maximizing its pleasure in an immediate fashion. Freud believed that the id dominated an infant's behaviour. As we develop and our instincts come into conflict with reality, the ego emerges. The ego works to satisfy our drives but does so in a socially acceptable manner; it attempts to gratify our needs through constructive and socially appropriate methods. For example, the ego redirects aggressive urges such as a desire to lash out physically at another into more socially acceptable forms, such as verbal aggression or vigorous physical play. As the ego operates in this fashion, we begin to internalize the values of our parents and the wider society around us, forming the structure that Freud called the superego. During the preschool years, children accept their parents' values and take these on in the form of their conscience as they apply these standards to their own behaviour. The ego now takes on the role of arbitrating between the id and the superego in an attempt to satisfy both sets of demands. According to Freud, the dynamics of this struggle, occurring during early childhood, sets the stage for our adult personality.

In Freud's view, development is a discontinuous process. Freud postulated five stages of development in his theory of psychosexual development: the *oral*, *anal*, *phallic*, *latency* and *genital* stages. Each stage revolves around the movement of sexual impulses from one **erogenous zone** to the next. In the first year and a half of life, during the oral stage of development, the infant's pleasure is centred on the mouth and involves behaviours such as biting, chewing and sucking as the sources of pleasure. The behaviours infants engage in change during the second year as they enter the anal stage and their pleasure becomes centred on the eliminative function. A potential source of conflict during this stage is a child's desire to immediately expel faeces coming up against their parents' attempts to train them into waiting to use the toilet. The phallic stage, which occurs from about the ages of three to six years, is centred on the genitals and the discovery that their own genitalia provide them with a sense of pleasure. During the phallic stage, Freud believed that children must cope with a sexual attraction to the opposite sex parent, which must eventually be relinquished and replaced by an identification with the same sex parent. This process of identification leads to the latency stage, which lasts until puberty, during which the child suppresses sexual drives and instead focuses on developing social and intellectual skills. Finally, during the genital stage which occurs during puberty, the sexual desires reawaken and the adolescent looks for appropriate peers (instead of family) towards whom they may direct their sexual drives.

Freud's theory was influential in that it focused developmentalists' attention on the role of early experiences in personality formation. It also emphasized a view of development as shaped by the dynamics of the conflict between the individual's biological drives and society's restrictions on the expression of these drives, which many subsequent theorists (such as Erik Erikson) found inspiring. Finally, Freud's theory, notwithstanding the many negative assessments it has faced, has been a rich source of hypotheses about development (Miller, 2002). Despite all of these benefits, his theory has been heavily criticized. Freud focused largely on males (as exemplified by his labelling the second phase of development 'phallic') and neglected to examine issues which might be important to the development of females. In addition, his theory relied mainly on the use of methods such as free association and dream analysis, which make scientific tests of his theory difficult if not impossible. Most tellingly, when his claims have been put to the test, many of the most significant claims have not been supported by empirical tests. Thus, Freud's views do not stand up well to modern psychology's demand for scientific validation.

Psychoanalytic theory has been revised significantly and has spawned many offshoots or schools of thought such as *object relations theory* (Klein, 1952). Modern psychoanalysts emphasize the role of unconscious processes in our behaviour, but place less emphasis on sexual and aggressive instincts and direct more effort into highlighting the importance of early relationships and experiences and an understanding of one's life history.

Psychosocial theory

In contrast to Freud's emphasis on sexual and aggressive drives, Erik Erikson (1902–1990) proposed a theory of development which emphasized the role of social and cultural factors in development. In addition, Erikson's theory did not characterize development as ending with adolescence but proposed a true life-span developmental theory which suggests development continues through to old age.

Erikson (1963) believed that human development could best be understood as the interaction of three different systems: the *somatic* system, the *ego* system, and the *societal* system. The somatic system comprises all of those biological processes necessary for the functioning of the individual. The ego system includes those processes central to thinking and reasoning. Finally, the societal system is made up of those processes by which a person becomes integrated into their society. Thus, Erikson's psychosocial approach focuses on the study of development of the interaction between changes in these three systems.

Erikson (1963) took a discontinuous view of development, believing that each of us progresses through eight stages of development. He viewed the stages as occurring in an orderly sequence and believed that an individual needed to pass through these in order. At each stage, that person is confronted with a unique **crisis**, an age-related task, which they must face and resolve. How successfully an individual resolves each crisis determines the nature of further development: successful resolutions lead to healthier developmental outcomes while unsuccessful or incomplete resolutions lead to less optimal outcomes. In addition, at each stage of development, the accomplishments from the previous stage serve as resources to be applied towards mastering the present crisis or challenge. Each stage is unique and leads to the acquisition of new skills and capabilities.

As noted, Erikson proposed eight stages of psychosocial development: (i) basic trust versus mistrust (birth to 1 year); (ii) autonomy versus shame and doubt (1 to 3 years); (iii) initiative versus guilt (3 to 6 years); (iv) industry versus inferiority (6 to 11 years); (v) identity versus identity diffusion (adolescence); (vi) intimacy versus isolation (young adulthood); (vii) generativity versus stagnation (middle adulthood); (viii) ego integrity versus despair (old age). In what follows, we briefly consider the task of development at each of the eight stages of life proposed by Erikson.

During infancy (*trust/mistrust*), the infant's first task is to develop a sense of trust and a sense of comfort in their caregivers and, eventually, in their environment and in themselves: infants who fail to resolve this crisis in a positive manner may end up mistrusting both themselves and others. During the second stage (*autonomy/shame and doubt*), the infant develops a sense of their independence and autonomy. However, shame and doubt in one's self may arise if the child is forced into activities which they do not choose. In the third stage (*initiative/guilt*), the young child develops a sense of initiative; that is, a desire to master their environment. However, guilt can arise if the child shows too much aggression or is irresponsible. During middle childhood (*industry/inferiority*), children are keen to master intellectual and social challenges but failures may lead to feelings of inferiority and incompetence. During adolescence (*identity/identity diffusion*), individuals strive to discover who they are; that is, to develop a self-identity. Adolescents who fail to adequately explore alternative pathways for themselves or allow their identity to be determined by parents and others may experience confusion about who they are. During young adulthood (*intimacy/isolation*), the task is to achieve a stable and intimate sexual relationship with another person. How well an individual has resolved previous crises (e.g. learning to trust others, making friends and developing social skills) will determine how successful that individual is in achieving intimacy with others: individuals who cannot achieve intimacy are vulnerable to isolation. In middle adulthood (*generativity/stagnation*), the creation of something – whether it is children or something more abstract like ideas or art – becomes the central task. Failing to express one's self in this way can give rise to feelings of stagnation and the feeling that one has no meaningful accomplishments. Finally, in old age (*ego integrity/despair*), we look back and assess our lives. An individual who has resolved previous stages in a negative fashion will tend to look back on their lives with a feeling of despair and gloom, while someone who has been successful will look back on a life well spent and can derive a sense of integrity.

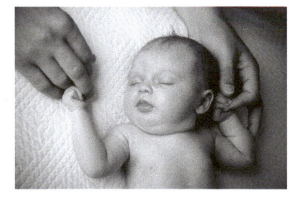

Image 2B During Erikson's first stage of development the infant develops a sense of trust and comfort in caregivers.

Photo credit: Laksmi Greenberg

Erikson's theory of development has been criticized as taking the form of a loosely connected set of ideas which lacks a systematic quality, rather than as a coherent theory of development (Miller, 2002). Concepts such as *generativity* are used in a way that is different from their normal meaning and thus they are somewhat difficult to understand. More problematic is the fact that his theory is difficult to test empirically. Finally, Erikson's theory proposes no specific mechanisms for how development occurs; that is, how a person moves from one stage to the next. It *describes* the roles of factors such as maturation and social forces but fails to clearly state *how* these factors create movement between stages. Despite its weaknesses, Erikson's theory has a number of strengths. One of these was his push to widen the scope of psychoanalytic theory through the integration of social and cultural factors in development. His work has also stimulated research into topics as varied as the relationship between identity development and alcohol consumption in university students (Todd, 2006), and the role of generativity and wisdom in successful ageing (Van Hiel, Mervielde, & De Fruyt, 2006; Warburtin, McLaughlin, & Pinksker, 2006).

Table 2.1 Erikson's eight stages of development

Stage of Development	Age	Crisis
Trust vs. Mistrust	Birth to 1 year	Developing a sense of trust in caregivers, the environment, and one's self
Autonomy vs. Shame and Doubt	1 to 3 years	Developing a sense of one's autonomy and independence from the caregiver
Initiative vs. Guilt	3 to 6 years	Developing a sense of mastery over aspects of one's environment, coping with challenges and assumption of increasing responsibility
Industry vs. Inferiority	6 years to adolescence	Mastering intellectual and social challenges
Identity vs. Identity Confusion	Adolescence (12 to 20 years)	Developing a self-identity, i.e. knowledge of what kind of a person one is
Intimacy vs. Isolation	Young adulthood (20 to 40 years)	Developing stable and intimate relationships with another person
Generativity vs. Stagnation	Middle adulthood (40 to 60 years)	Creating something so that one can avoid feelings of stagnation
Integrity vs. Despair	Old age (60 years +)	Evaluating one's life by looking back; developing a sense of integrity through this evaluative process

Developmental task theory

Many researchers have been influenced by Erikson's psychosocial stages. One notable developmental theorist is Robert Havighurst (1952). He proposed the idea of **developmental tasks**, which are critical tasks that occur at certain periods in our lives. Successful achievement of these tasks leads to happiness and success with later tasks, while not dealing with the tasks leads to unhappiness, social problems and difficulty with later tasks.

Havighurst identified three sources of developmental tasks, and these cover the entire life span. First are tasks that arise from physical maturation, such as learning to walk, talk, or dealing with the changes of menopause during middle age. Second are tasks stemming from personal sources, such as the development of personal values and aspirations, or learning skills for job success. Third are tasks that arise from the pressures of society, including learning the role of a responsible individual. Further, Havighurst identified six major age periods that specific developmental tasks occur within: *infancy* and early childhood (0–5 years): e.g. learning to walk, crawl, talk; *middle childhood* (6–12 years): e.g. learning the physical skills necessary for games, learning to get along with age mates, building wholesome attitudes towards oneself as a growing organism, achieving personal independence; *adolescence* (13–18 years): accepting one's physique and using the body effectively, preparing for marriage and family life, desiring and achieving socially responsible behaviour; *early adulthood* (19–29 years): selecting a mate, learning to live with a partner, rearing children, finding a social group; *middle adulthood* (30–60 years): assisting teenage children to become responsible and happy adults, achieving adult social and civic responsibility, reaching and maintaining a satisfactory performance in one's occupational career; and *later maturity* (61+): adjusting to decreasing physical strength and health, adjusting to retirement and a reduced income, adjusting to death.

As you may have noted from some of the critical developmental tasks listed, Havighurst concentrated on white, middle-class Americans in devising his theory. However, he also recognized that the number of tasks we go through depends on our individual circumstances and the society we inhabit. Some tasks are the same for almost everyone, such as learning to crawl and walk. Other tasks will vary depending on our culture and society: some cultures espouse marriage and employment early, while others approve of a long 'trial' period of education and experience with a partner.

Havighurst has been praised for the practicality of his theory and the recognition of sensitive periods in our lives. For example, knowing that a child is dealing with a critical task for their age (such as learning appropriate behaviour with the opposite sex) allows a parent to be understanding and provide the necessary environmental support and constraints to encourage successful mastery of that task. Despite these strengths, however, Havighurst's theory is not as well known or espoused as some argue it should be.

Behaviourism and social learning theory

Modern behaviourist theory began with the work of John B. Watson (1878–1958). Watson wanted to create an objective science of psychology and he believed that directly observable events should be the focus of study, not hypothetical internal constructs like Freud's *id* and *ego* or the cognitive psychologist's appeal to constructs like *mind*. Watson (Watson & Raynor, 1920) applied Pavlov's principles of **classical conditioning** to children's behaviour. Research Example 2.1 describes one of his most famous research programmes. On the basis of these kinds of findings,

Watson concluded that the environment was the most important factor in child development. He argued that children could be moulded in any direction adults desired if they carefully controlled stimulus–response associations. Watson and his fellow behaviourists eschewed all notions that cognitive processes intervened in the shaping of the individual. In Watson's behaviourism, learning became the key element in explaining development, whereas biological factors were relegated to the sidelines and held to be important only in providing a basic foundation for learned responses.

Another variant of behaviourism was B. F. Skinner's **operant conditioning** theory. According to this theory, the likelihood of a child's behaviour reoccurring could be increased by following it with a wide variety of rewards or **reinforcers**, things such as praise or a friendly smile. Furthermore, Skinner believed that the likelihood of behaviour could be decreased with the use of **punishments** such as the withdrawal of privileges, parental disapproval, or being sent alone to one's room. In other words, reward increases the likelihood of a behaviour reoccurring while punishment decreases the likelihood of it reoccurring. The result of Skinner's work was that operant conditioning became broadly applied to the study of child development.

Research Example 2.1

The Little Albert Experiment

In an attempt to take Pavlov's classical conditioning paradigm to the next level, the behavioural psychologist John B. Watson conducted research to classically condition emotional reactions in people. Perhaps the most famous, or infamous, aspect of his work involved an attempt to classically condition fear in a 9-month-old baby named Albert. Unfortunately for his little subject, Watson was successful. Called the Little Albert Experiment, Watson first exposed Albert to a series of stimuli, including fluffy animals, such as a white rat and a rabbit, as well as other items like masks and burning newspapers. Albert initially showed no fear of the objects. The next time Albert was exposed to the white rat (called a neutral stimulus since he initially showed no fear), Watson made a loud sound by clanging an iron bar behind the infant's head. Albert soon learned to fear the rat, crying and turning his head away from the sight of the animal.

Watson and his colleague, Rosalie Raynor, wrote: 'The instant the rat was shown, the baby began to cry. Almost instantly he turned sharply to the left, fell over on [his] left side, raised himself on all fours and began to crawl away so rapidly that he was caught with difficulty before reaching the edge of the table'. What's more, Albert feared not just the white rat but a variety of other furry objects, including Watson wearing a Santa beard and Rosalie Raynor's fur coat.

Whatever happened to Little Albert after his frightening encounter with Watson was only recently solved. Before Watson could attempt to de-condition the child's fear, Albert's family moved away and all but disappeared. Only recently has it been discovered that poor Little Albert's life took an even more tragic turn; he passed away at the age of 6 from a build-up of fluid in the brain. Also disturbing is the discovery that the condition plagued Little Albert from birth, and that Watson knew about Albert's health problems during the time of the experiment, but intentionally misrepresented his research as a case study of a healthy boy (Fridlund, Beck, Goldie, & Irons, 2012).

The Little Albert Experiment clearly violates ethical considerations when conducting research with children. An ethical committee, which oversees all university research and is required to publish in peer-reviewed journals, would never allow this kind of experiment to occur again. In addition to the ethical and moral issues involved, the recent knowledge of Watson misrepresenting his data shrouds his career and work with doubt.

Activity: List some of the reasons why findings from the Little Albert experiment cannot be generalized to other children.

A variant of traditional behaviourist views on development comes from the work of Albert Bandura (1977, 1989) on **social learning theory**. Bandura believes that the principles of conditioning and reinforcement elaborated by Skinner and others are important mechanisms of development, but he has expanded on how children and adults acquire new responses. Bandura recognizes that, from an early age, children also acquire many skills in the absence of rewards and punishments, simply by watching and listening to others around them, and he has been responsible for an extensive line of laboratory research demonstrating that **observational learning** (often referred to as **modelling**), is the basis of the development of a wide variety of behaviours. In one of his best known experiments (Bandura, Ross, & Ross, 1961) a group of young children watched an adult perform acts of physical and verbal aggression towards a large inflatable doll known as a 'bobo' doll. When these children were left alone with the doll some time later, Bandura observed that they repeated these acts of aggression towards the doll and thus he demonstrated the role of modelling in the development of aggressive behaviour. Subsequent research has also indicated that behaviours such as *helping*, *sharing*, and even *sex-typed responses* can also be acquired in this manner (Perry and Bussey, 1979; Presbie and Coiteux, 1971; Sprafkin, Liebert, & Poulos, 1975). However, children do not imitate everyone around them: they are more selective, being drawn towards models who are warm and powerful and possess desirable objects and characteristics.

Bandura's research continues to influence much of the work in the area of children's and adult's social development (Rubin, Coplan, Nelson, Cheah, & Lagace-Seguin, 1999). Over time, his theory has become increasingly cognitive (e.g. Bandura, 1989, 1992), acknowledging that children's ability to listen, remember and abstract general rules from complex sets of observed behaviour affects their imitation and their learning. In more recent work, his emphasis has been on the development of a sense of **self-efficacy**, beliefs about one's own effectiveness and competence, which guide one's ability to cope with particular situations, such as difficult academic problems at school. According to Bandura, children develop a sense of self-efficacy through observation, watching others comment on their own behaviour and developing standards based on these experiences. Thus, children who are exposed to positive models who demonstrate qualities such as persistence are likely to develop a stronger sense of self-efficacy than children exposed to models that demonstrate less positive qualities like giving up in response to frustration.

A strength of Bandura's social learning theory is its emphasis on particular aspects of the environment, such as the nature of the role models available to children, which can impact on their development. In addition, social learning theory is easily testable (Miller, 2002) as the variables of interest are clearly defined and its hypotheses are stated in a precise fashion. The resultant testing of the theory has led to substantial revisions, such as its increased emphasis on cognitive factors. At the same time, the cognitive model which underlies the theory has been criticized for being poorly worked out in comparison to information processing theories which present detailed models of cognitive processes. Finally, social learning theory has been criticized for not paying enough attention to a wide range of contextual variables which may impact on children's observational learning. While the theory has addressed some contextual variables like the characteristics of models which effect development, other context effects, such as socioeconomic factors, race, sex and education, remain relatively unexplored.

The ethological perspective

Ethology is a perspective on the study of animal behaviour which began to be applied to research on children during the 1960s and continues to be influential today. Ethology is concerned with understanding the adaptive value of behaviour and its evolutionary history. The origins of ethology can be traced to Charles Darwin and his work on evolution, although the modern theory owes its origins to the work of two European zoologists, Konrad Lorenz and Niko Tinbergen. In his theory of evolution, Darwin proposed that we evolved from more simple forms of life through a process called **natural selection**. Natural selection works through the effects of a trait on survival: if a change to our physical structure or behaviour leads to a survival advantage, this change is more likely to be passed on through the genes to the organism's offspring during mating. If the change leads to no advantages, it is less likely to be passed on and the trait will tend to disappear. Thus, only traits which lead to a survival advantage for the organism are passed on. Natural selection is so-called because nature weeds out those individuals who are unfit; in other words, natural selection is the 'survival of the fittest'.

Based on the careful observation of animals in their natural habitats, researchers like Lorenz and Tinbergen noted that many animal species come equipped with a number of behaviour patterns that promote their survival. One of the patterns studied by Lorenz is known as **imprinting**. Imprinting refers to the 'following behaviour' of many species of birds. Imprinting is a behaviour which is acquired extremely rapidly and serves to ensure that offspring will stay close to their mother so as to be fed and protected from predators. While nothing like imprinting seems to occur in human beings, a related concept from ethology has been very usefully applied to the study of child development. In birds such as geese, imprinting occurs during a restricted time period of development known as a **critical period**. A critical period is a time when an organism is biologically prepared to acquire a particular behaviour. For example, using geese, Lorenz found that if the mother goose was not present during the critical period, her goslings would imprint on a moving object which resembled her important features, such as Lorenz himself. Lorenz (1963) showed that a gosling's instinct to follow its mother was not pre-programmed. Instead, the *tendency* to acquire a particular behaviour was programmed but the support of the environment was critical to the acquisition of this behaviour.

Ethologists' observations of a wide variety of animal behaviours have sparked investigations with humans regarding the development of such social behaviours as attachment, dominance hierarchies, aggression and cooperation. For example, Strayer and Strayer (1976) recorded naturally occurring conflicts among preschoolers and found evidence of a stable dominance hierarchy (see Chapter 9), with some children being more dominant and less likely to be aggressed against by other children. Emotion research has also shown that expressions such as joy, sadness, disgust and anger are similar across many cultures, from Brazil to Japan and the United States (LaFreniere, 2000), suggesting there is a degree of universality in such basic emotions. John Bowlby's work on the attachment bond between caregivers and their children was also inspired by ethological theory (see Chapter 8). Bowlby argued that infants had a built-in signalling system to which mothers were geared to respond, a system which is designed to promote nurturance and protective behaviours by the parent.

Are there critical periods in human development? Bornstein (1989) suggested that the term 'sensitive period' is a better descriptor of human development than 'critical period'. According to Bornstein, a **sensitive period** is a window of time in a child's development during which they are particularly responsive to environmental influences. For example, there is a sensitive period for the acquisition of human language which lasts from shortly after birth to early adolescence (see Chapter 9). Learning language is particularly easy for children during this period, but extremely difficult after it. Given the length of time involved for language acquisition, it seems that the notion of a critical period is an inaccurate descriptor of how language-learning takes place. Clearly, the notion of a sensitive period for language provides a more accurate picture of language acquisition.

Ethological theory has been extremely important to the study of child development as regards its methodological contributions to the field (Rubin et al., 1999). Behavioural observations using techniques developed by ethologists are widely employed by researchers studying children. In addition, the emphasis on the evolutionary roots of behaviours has proven to be a key theoretical development within the study of child development. Asking how environmental pressures may have operated to select for a particular behaviour such that, over time, it becomes widely distributed in the species helps us understand the cause of many important behaviours such as attachment behaviour. In addition, concepts such as sensitive periods have been criticized in that they only put off the question of an ultimate explanation for a particular behaviour: more work needs to be channelled into discovering how sensitive periods operate. Finally, looking for the causes of a particular behaviour in our evolutionary history is difficult because we cannot go back in time. The sources of information which are available are not always reliable and often extremely ambiguous.

Evolutionary developmental theory

According to a review of the history of developmental psychology (Dixon & Lerner, 1998), Charles Darwin's theory of evolution has had a profound influence on theories of human development. As we have just seen, evolutionary theory influenced the development of ethological theories of human development. Evolutionary theory has also influenced theories of development as diverse as Freud's psychosexual theory, to information processing theories of cognitive development (Siegler, 1996).

Perhaps not surprisingly, evolutionary theory has come into its own as a theory of human behaviour (e.g. Barkow, Cosmides, & Tooby, 1992). As David Buss argues, 'Any reasonably comprehensive theory of human development must include an account of where people come from, where they are going, and how long they live' (Buss, 1995: 24). In Buss's view, an evolutionary psychological approach to human development has much to offer in the attempt to address these issues.

Geary and Bjorklund (2000) have applied the evolutionary psychology framework to generating an increased understanding of human development. In their view, **evolutionary developmental psychology** is the 'study of the genetic and ecological mechanisms that govern the development of social and cognitive competencies common to all human beings and the epigenetic processes that adapt these competencies to local conditions' (Geary & Bjorklund, 2000: 57). Let's examine this definition more closely. Perhaps the first point of interest is that the consideration of development from an evolutionary framework involves the study of *both* biological factors such as the hereditary transmission of traits from parents to their children *and* the ecology in which development occurs (i.e. environmental effects on behaviour). Development is governed by **epigenetic** processes, that is to say, *interactions* of genes and environments (we will explore this concept more fully in Chapter 4). In this view, genes provide the instructions for guiding the development of observable traits such as height or personality, but that these genetic blueprints are highly sensitive to 'local conditions' – that is, aspects of the environment that may require changes to the genetic blueprints in order for a trait to lead to optimal outcomes.

Research conducted from an evolutionary perspective is growing. Buss (1995) cites a number of instances where an evolutionary developmental framework has contributed to a greater understanding of developmental phenomena. For example, the timing of puberty and the effects of early environments on physical maturation can be aided by an evolutionary analysis. Research using evolutionary theory to guide questions, rather than as an ad hoc explanation, is becoming more common. For example, research with young people from New Zealand and the USA has shown that greater exposure to father absence is strongly associated with risk for early sexual activity and adolescent pregnancy in girls (Ellis, Bates, Dodge, Fergusson, Horwood, Pettit, & Woodward, 2003). Bruce Ellis and his colleagues explain this finding by suggesting that girls detect and internalize information about reproductive behaviours from their parents early in their development. The presence of parents and the quality of their parenting are therefore likely to have a significant effect on a child's sexual understanding and behaviour. As we will discuss later, other research (Moffitt, Caspi, Belsky, & Silva, 1992) demonstrates that ecological factors such as family conflict and the absence of fathers in the household can even have a biological impact by predicting the earlier onset of menstruation in girls. Evolutionary psychology would view the presence of the father during childhood as pushing the child towards a later mating strategy characterized by long-term relationships. In contrast, early father absence may push a child towards an earlier mating strategy marked by early sexual maturation in the form of early menstruation and more short-term relationships (Belsky, Steinberg, & Draper, 1991).

These are just a few examples of the sort of contributions that evolutionary developmental psychology has made to the study of child development. In summary, evolutionary psychology is a very general approach that may shed light on almost any aspect of development that is concerned with understanding the interplay between genetics and environment (Geary, 2006).

The bioecological model of development

A view which has received an increasing amount of attention from developmental psychologists is Urie Bronfenbrenner's **bioecological model** of human development (Bronfenbrenner & Evans, 2000; Bronfenbrenner & Morris, 1998). Bronfenbrenner (1974) is famous for his suggestion that an over-emphasis on laboratory research had caused developmental psychology to become 'the study of the strange behaviour of children in strange situations for the briefest possible period of time'. In contrast to the bulk of developmental research which is conducted in laboratory settings, he has argued that the proper study of development requires one to observe children and adults in their actual environment: most laboratory research misses out on critical information which can only be gained by studying children in natural contexts. In addition, a great deal of laboratory-based research cannot be generalized to the everyday contexts in which humans live and grow (Bronfenbrenner, 1979).

When psychologists examine the effects of the environment on children, that environment is typically construed in a very static and narrow fashion – often as the child's immediate surroundings. In contrast, Bronfenbrenner (1989) views the environment as a dynamic entity which is constantly changing. In his bioecological model of human development, the environment is also conceived in a very wide sense, as a series of nested structures that extend beyond the child's immediate environment (e.g. their home or neighbourhood) to include their school, community, and the social and cultural institutions that impact on their lives. In Bronfenbrenner's model, the individual is the centre of a system which includes four layers, each representing a different aspect of the environment and having a powerful impact on that child's development.

The innermost level is called the **microsystem**. This is the immediate setting in which a child lives and refers to family, peers and school as well as the activities, roles and relationships in their immediate surroundings. In Bronfenbrenner's view, the individual is viewed as an active force, exerting an influence on the people around them and the relationships they have with others. The child is not a passive recipient of others' attention and actions. Thus, within the microsystem, development is often understood in terms of complex, interacting relationships. Long-term bidirectional relationships, such as the relationship between a child and her parents, tend to have a stable and enduring effect on children's development (e.g. Collins, Maccoby, Steinberg, Hetherington, & Bornstein, 2000).

The second level of Bronfenbrenner's model is called the **mesosystem**. This refers to the relationships among microsystems, such as home, school, neighbourhood and child care centre. One could think about the mesosystem as the connections which bring together the various contexts in which a child develops. For example, learning to read may depend not just on activities that take place in school, but also on the extent to which academic learning takes place in the home (Epstein & Sanders, 2002). The African proverb 'it takes a village to raise a child' is accounted for in the mesosystem of a child's life. Bronfenbrenner and Morris (1998) suggested that the best and most complete picture of a child's development will be obtained when they are examined in multiple contexts rather than just in their home or school.

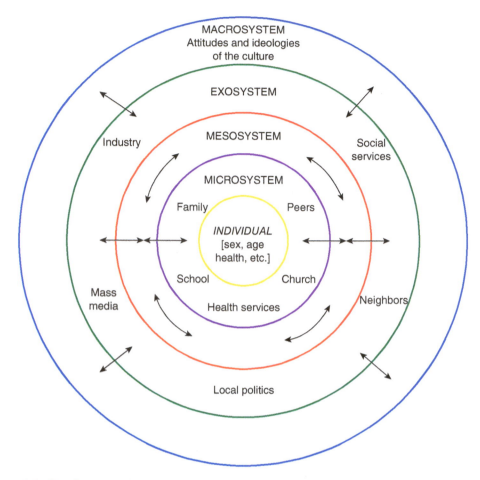

Figure 2.1   Bronfenbrenner's bioecological model of development

Exosystems are broad social settings that provide support for the development of children and adults. These are social settings and institutions that do not directly involve children yet which can have a profound impact on their development. Exosystems include formal settings such as community health services, parks, recreation centres, city government and informal groups such as one's extended family, social support networks, and the workplace. These groups can provide important support for the family such as flexible work schedules, paid maternity and paternity leave, or low cost child care – support that can enhance the development of children. Recent work by the *Growing Up in Australia Project*, a longitudinal study of 10,000 Australian children, has shown that high-quality parental employment conditions that combine family-friendly benefits with security, control and flexibility maximize both parent and child wellbeing (Strazdins, George, Shipley, Sawyer, Rodgers, & Nicholson, 2006). Negative impacts on development can also result when an exosystem breaks down. For example, British research has shown that families who are affected by unemployment, overcrowding and poor social networks show an increased incidence of child maltreatment (Sidebotham, Heron, & Golding, 2002).

At the outermost level of Bronfenbrenner's model is the **macrosystem**. This is not a specific environmental context, but, rather, the overarching ideology, values, laws, regulations and customs of a given culture. Cultural influences can have a powerful effect on children's development. Comparisons made across cultures have the potential to provide very important information about the effects of culture on development.

Bronfenbrenner also included in his model the notion that development occurs in historical time within the model. He called this temporal aspect the **chronosystem**, which involves all aspects of time and how they impact on development. For example, research on the timing of puberty has shown that the age at which this begins can have profound impacts on later development (Jones & Bayley, 1950). Historical events which occur in time also have important effects on development. For example, work by Elder (1974) showed that the economic depression of the 1930s had significant impacts on the lives of children growing up during that period. In these ways and many others, the chronosystem has a powerful influence on development.

Can you think of any examples of 'exosystem' and 'macrosystem' influences on your home life as a child?

Research Example 2.2

Bronfenbrenner's Bioecological Model in Action

Researchers in Ontario, Canada (McDougall, DeWit, King, Miller, & Killip, 2004), have investigated high-school students' attitudes towards other students with disabilities. Given that acceptance by their peers is one of the primary factors in determining whether a young person with a disability will make the transition to adulthood well (Parker & Asher, 1987), such research is extremely important. The Canadian study used a bioecological framework to investigate how school culture and various student interpersonal factors influenced attitudes among non-disabled students towards fellow disabled students. Participants included 1,872 students aged 12 to 16 years of age from 23 high schools. Students were given a variety of questionnaires assessing everything from perceptions of school culture, peer and teacher relationships, social anxiety, and, of course, attitudes towards peers. The good news was that the majority of students held positive attitudes towards students with disabilities. However, 21% of students held slightly below neutral to very negative attitudes. Consideration of bioecological factors allowed the researchers to discover the following interesting information about why some students held positive versus negative attitudes. If the school culture promoted the learning and understanding of all

(Continued)

students rather than social comparison and competition, and if positive student–teacher relationships and high levels of peer support were reported, then attitudes tended to be positive towards students with disabilities. Girls also tended to have more positive attitudes towards disabled peers, as did students who had a friend or classmate with a disability. Although these findings shed light on some important micro- and mesosystem-level factors, it is likely that further research could explore other influential variables within these systems, as well as exo- and macro-level systems. For example, how might reforms dealing with how children with disabilities are educated change people's perceptions? Can you think of other variables within Bronfenbrenner's systems that might change negative attitudes towards students with disabilities?

Life course theory

In a review of his bioecological theory of development, Bronfenbrenner (Bronfenbrenner & Morris, 1998) emphasized the importance of time as a variable which demands the attention of developmental psychologists. Another theoretical orientation which emphasizes the role of time in human development is life course theory (Elder, 1995, 1998). The **life course** refers to a 'sequence of socially defined, age-graded events and roles that the individual enacts over time' (Elder, 1998: 941). According to Elder, our lives are defined in large part by the social context in which we develop. For example, in many western societies parents' conceptions of when it is appropriate for their children to begin dating are changing, partly as our societal expectations for what constitutes normal, age-appropriate experiences evolve.

Life course theory emphasizes the view that human development must be understood in terms of four interdependent principles. First, human lives are situated in an historical time and place. The timing of an individual's birth is an important determinant of the development trajectories they will likely follow. Historical influences can impact on us in different ways. One way in which historical forces impact on us is through **cohort effects**. A cohort is a group of people born at a particular point in time (e.g. 'baby boomers' or 'generation X'). A cohort effect occurs when people from different birth cohorts are differentially impacted upon by some historical event. For example, in his work on the effects of the US economic depression in the 1930s, Elder (1974) showed that younger children were more adversely affected by the impact of the Depression than were older children. Another type of historical effect is called a **period effect**. This occurs when an historical event exerts a relatively uniform influence across different birth cohorts. For example, Elder notes that whatever cause is responsible for the increase in divorce rates over the past four decades, this has affected most birth cohorts in a similar fashion. Finally, in regard to historical time and place, Elder notes that geographical settings are often an extremely important factor neglected in developmental studies, and, furthermore, that time and place are often inextricably linked.

A second key element of life course theory is the idea that developmental studies must pay attention to the timing of lives. Our lives are socially timed in that the way social roles and events are organized has much to do with what is considered normative for a particular age group by the society in which an individual develops. We often ask of ourselves or others, whether we are 'on course' or 'on time' in regard to specific aspects of our development. For example, it is highly likely that our parents worried about whether our academic performance as adolescents was 'normal' relative to that of other adolescents. The social timing of lives can have profound effects on development: consider the woman who puts off having a child until her career is established versus the teenage girl who becomes pregnant. Clearly, this choice entails different developmental pathways for the two women, with each pathway offering opportunities for personal growth, though of different kinds.

Third, life course theory emphasizes that human lives are interdependent or linked to each other. Our lives are embedded in family relationships, peer relationships, romantic relationships, and in various other relationships, such as those we have with our co-workers or classmates. Attachment theory suggests that the quality of the relationship that we form with our primary caregiver in infancy has an impact on later relationships we form with friends and, eventually, with our romantic partners. In turn, our attachment relationship with our own children is affected by the relationship we had with our caregivers. Attachment theory is built on the premise that human lives are linked to each other. Throughout this text we will continue to examine how relationships affect children's development.

Finally, the fourth principle of life course theory is that within certain social constraints, human beings have *agency*, that is, the power to make decisions and change our lives. The social environment places constraints on the kinds of actions that people can take to change their lives. For example, one cannot pursue a career in engineering without the appropriate education, thus, a person's choice of career is necessarily limited by the education they have chosen to pursue. However, although there are constraints, our choices have a high degree of impact on our lives. For example, Rutter and Rutter (1993) note that how we choose to behave with and relate to other people serves to shape and select the environment that we actually experience. In addition, Rutter and Rutter note that planning one's decisions proves to be a protective process in the long term whereas the lack of planning is considered to be a risk factor for poor outcomes. Going back to an earlier example, an adolescent who anticipates engaging in sexual activity and takes steps to obtain contraception reduces not only the risk of an unwanted pregnancy or sexually transmitted disease, but also the risk of embarking on a developmental pathway which may lead to unhappiness.

In summary, life course theory has much in common with theories such as Bronfenbrenner's bioecological theory, with its emphasis on the importance of the various types of environment which impact on development, and with the principles of Baltes's (1987) life-span developmental psychology, which emphasizes the importance of contexts and timing. However, in Elder's view, social environments should be the major emphasis of developmental studies. This differs from the views held by Bronfenbrenner and Baltes, who both place the individual at the centre of their models of development.

Dynamic systems theory

Dynamic systems theories of development emerged out of a growing disenchantment with traditional theories' focus on environmental causes, biological causes, and interactions of biology and environment as explanations of development. A number of researchers have put forward theories which emphasize systems thinking (e.g. Bertalanffy, 1968; Sameroff, 1983; Thelen & Smith, 1994). These researchers have suggested that human beings and their environments can be thought of as a collection of systems, where a system is defined as being composed of a number of elements which are organized in some fashion. A family is a good example of a system. Families consist of a number of elements, such as a father, mother and children. Moreover, the relations of the elements to one another can be described – for example, children normally obey parental rules. However, the behaviour of the family can only be truly understood in systems terms, that is, by considering the interrelations among all of the parts, the family's history, and external influences which may operate to stabilize or destabilize its functioning. In other words, the family's behaviour is more than just the sum of its individual parts.

So then, what is dynamic systems theory? It can be thought of as an integrated system that connects the child's mind, body and social worlds: this system is dynamic, or constantly changing. Moreover, a change in any one part of the system, whether it be growing taller so the biscuit cupboard is now in reach or meeting a new friend, results in a state of flux or change. As a consequence of change, the child must reorganize their behaviour so the system works smoothly again (Spencer & Schöner, 2003). According to a review by Thelen and Smith (1998), dynamic systems theory is a *metatheory*; that is, it is an approach to studying development that can be widely applied to many domains, from areas as diverse as **embryology** (the study of how a fertilized egg becomes an infant), family functioning, and the development of motor skills (Thelen & Ulrich, 1991). However, Thelen and Smith also argue that dynamic systems theory can be employed as a specific theory of how humans gain knowledge via action, perhaps best exemplified in Thelen's work on the development of motor skills.

Thelen and Smith (1998) suggest a metaphor which is useful in understanding the way in which dynamic systems theorists view development. They ask us to consider a fast-moving mountain stream. The stream shows stable patterns in its flow, for example whirlpools, eddies and ripples which occur because of rocks in the stream bed, or waves and spray where the stream bed is shallow and steep. Thelen and Smith argue that no one would explain the regularities in the flow of the stream by invoking a 'grand plan'. Instead, we recognize that the stream shows the patterns it does because of the constraints it operates under. The regularities in the patterns we observe occur because of multiple factors operating simultaneously: the configuration of the stream bed and the placement of rocks, the rate of flow of the water, the erosion of the stream bed. Thelen and Smith suggest that this metaphor of a mountain stream depicts development as truly epigenetic, that is, as constructed by the system's own history, by its current activity, and by the constraints under which the system operates.

How can a dynamic systems perspective be applied to the study of child development? Very often dynamic systems researchers will study children's behaviour during periods of transition (Thelen & Corbetta, 2002). Thelen's own research illustrates how a dynamic systems approach can help us better understand behaviour. For example, it is well known that newborns, when held upright in a standing position, show a stepping reflex. After some time this reflex disappears and later re-emerges. In contrast to theories which postulated that this process was under the control of genetic factors, Thelen and Fisher (1982) showed that the reflex 'disappears' because of changes in other aspects of an infant's physiology. In the case of the stepping reflex, body fat begins to accumulate on the infant's leg, making the leg heavier. However, muscle mass is not added at the same rate, meaning the infant is no longer able to physically lift their leg, and thus the stepping reflex 'disappears'. However, the stepping reflex can be made to reappear by immersing the infant in water from the waist down. The effects of buoyancy act to reduce the weight of the infant's legs and the stepping reflex reappears. In Thelen's view, the best way in which to understand this finding is from a dynamic systems perspective: as changes are made to the system, behaviours are reorganized in a dynamic fashion. The stable patterns previously observed can be brought back by changing the effects of the constraints which altered the behaviour.

Consider another example from the study of infant motor development. Previous theories of motor development have suggested that behaviours such as the development of 'creeping' or 'crawling' are programmed to emerge prior to walking. Thelen and Smith (1998) suggest it is unnecessary to invoke a genetic programme to explain this fact; rather, they suggest that we can think of the development of crawling as a behaviour which is *softly assembled* from previously existing competencies. In other words, a genetic blueprint for crawling does not suddenly emerge and guide the baby towards this behaviour; instead, the infant creates the behaviour based on the constraints under which they operate, plus their goals and desires. An infant may desire a toy which is across the room and intend to move towards it. The state of their neuromuscular system is such that they cannot yet maintain enough balance to walk upright, so the infant employs another solution (crawling) which allows them to make use of the skills they have already acquired. The development of crawling behaviour is a predictable outcome of the infant's desires and its current range of abilities. However, it is not an inevitable solution: some infants develop alternative methods, such as crawling on their bellies or scooting along on their bottoms by using their arms. The development of such alternative strategies depends on an infant's previous history of motor skills and the current state of maturation of their musculature and suggests that crawling is not simply the outcome of a genetic blueprint which dictates development. This illustrates two key points in dynamic systems theory: the existence of *interindividual* differences (e.g. not all children acquire the ability to walk or talk at the same time or in the same manner) and the existence of *intraindividual* differences (e.g. a child may show unique developmental patterns across domains). Piek (2002) even suggests that a child who shows variability in different areas of development may enjoy a better developmental outcome than a child who displays low variability or develops different skills at roughly the same time.

Cognitive Developmental Theories

In regard to the study of cognitive development, there are three theories which have had a dramatic impact on the field. These are Piaget's **cognitive-developmental** theory (e.g. Piaget, 1983), Vygotsky's **sociocultural theory** of development (Vygotsky, 1978, 1986), and the **information processing** approach to cognitive development (Klahr & MacWhinney, 1998; Siegler, 1996). Given that these three theories are primarily theories of cognitive development, we will cover them in more detail in Chapter 7. What follows here is a brief summary of each theory.

Jean Piaget's theory of cognitive development

Jean Piaget (1896–1980) is widely acknowledged as the theorist who has had the greatest impact on research and theory in the field of child development (e.g. Siegler, 1998). Piaget began working in developmental psychology in the 1920s but it was not until the 1960s that his work garnered much attention as it became increasingly available. Piaget's work was largely at odds with the behaviourist tradition that was dominant in North American until the 1960s. Unlike the behaviourists of the day, Piaget did not view children as passive recipients of knowledge whose development was the product of reinforcement or punishment, but, rather, as an active participant in the creation of their own understanding.

Piaget's (1971) theory of development borrowed heavily from the field of evolutionary biology. A central concept in Piagetian theory is the idea that our cognitive structures (i.e. our minds) are *adaptations* which help ensure that our knowledge provides a good 'fit' with the world. Piaget viewed human intelligence as an adaptation which ultimately enhanced our chances of survival. Of course, we know from experience (often, painfully so) that our knowledge does not always match reality perfectly. For example, we often act on the basis of false assumptions, incorrect knowledge, or a partial understanding. Young children's thinking is also rife with misunderstandings about the nature of the world. For example, Piaget noted that preschool children's thinking is often strongly tied to a child's own point of view and fails to consider the fact that another person might have a very different perspective on a situation. According to Piaget, cognitive development is a process of revision: children revise their knowledge to provide an increasingly better fit to reality. Piaget referred to this process as the establishment of *equilibrium* between the child's cognitive structures and the nature of the physical and social world.

Piaget believed that children's cognitive development progressed through four stages. By *stage*, Piaget meant a period of development which is characterized by knowledge structures which are *qualitatively* similar and lead to distinctive modes of thought. In the *sensorimotor stage* of development, lasting from birth to about 2 years of age, the infant thinks about the world through their actions on it. Piaget believed that the basis of our ability to think abstractly is rooted in our ability to act on the world. Eventually, the infant's actions become increasingly organized, leading to the next stage of development, which Piaget termed the *preoperational stage*. The major feature of this stage (which characterizes development from the ages of 2 to 7) is the ability to think using symbolic representations, that is, the child no longer has to act on the world to think but can use symbols and carry out operations mentally. The third stage of development, lasting from 7 to 12 years of age, is the *concrete operational stage*, which is characterized by the increasingly logical character of a child's thinking. Finally, at the *formal operational stage*, the adolescent gains the ability to think abstractly. Unlike the concrete operational child, an adolescent's thinking is no longer tied to concrete reality but can move into the possible or hypothetical.

As mentioned earlier, Piaget's theory has proven extremely influential to the study of children's cognitive development; however, in recent years, the theory has come under increasing criticism. For example, many developmental psychologists are dissatisfied with Piaget's portrayal of the child as a solitary learner and feel that he did not give enough attention to the role of social and cultural factors in children's cognitive development (e.g. Rogoff, 1998). In Chapter 7, we examine Piaget's theory in detail and consider both the strengths and weaknesses of the theory.

Vygotsky's sociocultural theory of development

Like Piaget, Lev Vygotsky (1896–1934) was a firm believer that children actively explored their environment and were influential in shaping their own knowledge. Unlike Piaget, however,

Vygotsky emphasized that a child's social environment was an extremely important force in their development. Vygotsky (1935/1978) believed that it was through social interactions with more experienced and more knowledgeable members of their society – parents, relatives, teachers, peers – that children were able to acquire the knowledge and skills a culture deemed to be important. Thus, according to Vygotsky, development was a social process: social interactions were a necessary aspect of cognitive development.

Vygotsky also believed that children's development followed a particular pattern. Any development occurred at two different levels: children first evidenced development in *interpersonal* interactions which occurred between themselves and other people. Only later did children show evidence of development on an individual or *intrapersonal* level. Vygotsky labelled this shift from development being evidenced on the interpersonal to an intrapersonal level as *internalization*. An example of internalization can be seen in children's self-talk while problem solving. Children take the kinds of dialogues that they engage in with parents or teachers (e.g. '*take your time*' or '*be careful*') while solving problems and talk to themselves while working on problems alone. Eventually, this self-talk is internalized and the child no longer needs to talk out loud.

Finally, Vygotsky noted that parents and teachers tended to interact with children in the context of a teaching task in a particular fashion. Parents tended to adjust their level of interaction dynamically, responding to the child's level of ability, and tried to pitch their teaching at a level that was just outside what the child could do on their own but at a level that was within the child's ability to do with help. Vygotsky believed that parents and teachers worked at a level that was optimal for stimulating children's development. This example highlights Vygotsky's belief that social interactions were critical to children's cognitive development.

Information processing accounts of development

In recent years, an account of cognitive development has emerged which is founded on the analogy between the digital computer and the human mind. Computers are rule-based systems which process information according to a limited and concretely specified set of rules. Information is input into the system and encoded into a form that the computer can manipulate. This information is then transformed via a series of operations into useful output, for example, the solution to an equation. Similarly, the human mind is believed to operate in the same fashion, by encoding information input via our senses and transforming this into useful output. For example, we take in sound waves from the environment and transform this information via a specified set of operations into meaningful sentences. Human beings and computers share other similar features which enhance the strength of this analogy, such as the ability to manipulate symbols or the constraints on information processing caused by memory limitations. According to information processing theorists, the digital computer provides a useful tool for testing theories of cognitive development via the modelling of cognitive processes (Klahr & MacWhinney, 1998).

Information processing theories are useful to the study of cognitive development in that they require a researcher to map out the series of steps which they believe best describes the flow of information through the human mind. This process of mapping information flow adds a degree of precision to these accounts of cognitive development which is generally open to empirical test.

Thus, information processing models are often readily tested and updated on the basis of experimentation. Information processing theories also stress the importance of identifying the mechanisms which underlie developmental change: they do not simply provide a description of change but also model how change occurs. Finally, information processing theories often force us to address the factors that affect development but which previously may not have been considered.

There is a wide variety of information processing models of children's cognition, ranging from models of children's developing ability to perform addition problems (Siegler, 1996; Siegler & Jenkins, 1989) to models of children's learning of the rule for making verbs indicate the past tense in English (Klahr & MacWhinney, 1998). Whereas in the past, information processing theories have been criticized for their lack of attention to cognition in real-world tasks, this trend is changing as newer information processing models begin to address this issue via the modelling of performance on everyday tasks such as reading comprehension.

Table 2.2 Theories of human development

Theory	Organicism vs. Mechanism	Accounts for Contextualism?	Discontinuity vs. Continuity	Nature vs. Nurture
Psychoanalytic Theory	Organismic	No	Discontinuous: emphasizes stages of development which are qualitatively different	Nature (biological drives) and Nurture (role of early experience) both play a role
Psychosocial Theory	Organismic	Yes	Discontinuous: emphasizes stages of development which are qualitatively different	Nurture: age-related social demands are the primary determinants of development
Developmental Task Theory	Organismic	Yes	Discontinuous: emphasizes stages of development which are qualitatively different	Nature and Nurture: some tasks are biologically determined; age-related social demands are the primary determinants
Behaviourism and Social Learning Theory	Mechanistic	Yes	Continuous: increase in learned behaviours is continuous	Nurture: principles of learning are based on environmental contingencies
Ethological Theory	Organismic	Yes	Continuous and discontinuous: learned behaviours increase continuously but critical/sensitive periods may lead to qualitative changes	Nature (biologically based, instinctive behaviours, genetic factors) and Nurture (experience plays an important role in learning) interact

Theory	Organicism vs. Mechanism	Accounts for Contextualism?	Discontinuity vs. Continuity	Nature vs. Nurture
Evolutionary Developmental Theory	Organismic	Yes	Not clearly specified	Nature (genetic factors canalize behaviour) and Nurture (experiences play an important role in shaping behaviour)
Bioecological Theory	Organismic	Yes	Not clearly specified	Nature (individual characteristics) and Nurture (a variety of environmental influences act on the individual)
Life Course Theory	Organismic	Yes	Discontinuous: age-related demands lead to qualitative developmental change	Nurture: social demands and environmental influences play an important role in determining development
Dynamic Systems Theory	Mechanistic	Yes	Continuous and discontinuous: learned behaviours increase continuously with the possibility for qualitative reorganizations	Nature (biological constraints) interact with Nurture (experience in context) to produce developmental change
Cognitive Developmental Theories				
Piagetian Theory	Organismic	No	Discontinuous: emphasizes emergence of stages of development which are qualitatively distinct	Nature (reflexive behaviours and drive for organization) and Nurture (experience with the environment) interact to produce development
Vygotsky's Sociocultural Theory	Organismic	Yes	Continuous: interactions with more competent members of one's culture lead to developmental change in a continuous fashion	Nurture: social interactions with others are the primary influence on development
Information Processing Theory	Mechanistic and Organismic elements	No	Continuous: the development of skills and strategies increases in a continuous fashion	Not clearly specified

Summary

It should be apparent from our brief survey in Chapter 2 that there is a rather large number of theories of human development. Importantly, the theories we cover here are not mutually exclusive: quite often, the theories focus on distinct parts of the life span (e.g. infancy or adolescence) or different domains of development (e.g. emotion or cognition). Our coverage of theories has not been exhaustive but is, in fact, representative of the types of theory which are currently invoked to understand children's development. Developing knowledge of the different theoretical positions is an important task as it will help you better understand the research literature that we cover throughout this book.

Glossary

Assumptions are the guiding premises underlying the logic of a theory.

Chronosystem In Bronfenbrenner's theory, the notion that development occurs in historical time.

Cohort effects A cohort is a group of people born at a particular point in time. Cohort effects events have differential impacts on different birth cohorts.

Contextualism refers to the class of developmental theories which take into account the roles of the broader environment, such as society and culture, in children's development. Contextual approaches also recognize that individuals may behave differently in different environments.

Crisis refers to Erikson's belief that individuals must resolve a series of age-related tasks. How successfully an individual resolves each crisis determines the course of later development.

Critical period is a time when an organism is biologically prepared to acquire a particular behaviour.

Developmental task theory was developed by Havighurst, who suggested there are critical tasks that occur at certain periods in our lives. Successful achievement of these tasks is required for future happiness and success with later tasks.

Dynamic systems theory is a theory of development which suggests that individuals develop within systems. The proper study of development includes a focus on these systems.

Ego In Freud's theory, that part of the personality which works to satisfy instinctive drives in a socially acceptable manner.

Embryology is the study of how a fertilized egg becomes an infant.

Epigenetic processes refer to the interactions of genes and environments.

Erogenous zone is a part of the body which affords pleasure through its stimulation. In Freud's theory, the erogenous zones change with development.

Ethology is a theory of behaviour concerned with understanding the adaptive value of behaviour and its evolutionary history.

Evolutionary developmental psychology is the study of the genetic and environmental mechanisms that govern the development of competencies common to all human beings and the epigenetic processes that adapt these competencies to local conditions.

Exosystems In Bronfenbrenner's theory, the broad social settings that provide support for the development of children and adults but which do not directly involve children (e.g. community health services, parks, recreation centres).

Id is the part of our personality, according to Freud, which is made up of instinctual drives.

Imprinting refers to the extremely rapid acquisition of 'following behaviour' in geese.

Information processing theories are theories of development which focus on documenting how information flows through the cognitive system and the cognitive operations which transform that information.

Life course refers to a sequence of socially defined and age-graded events and roles that the individual enacts over time.

Macrosystem In Bronfenbrenner's theory, the overarching ideology, values, laws, regulations and customs of a given culture.

Mechanism refers to a class of developmental theories that stress quantitative changes in behaviour and emphasize that factors outside the control of the organism play the major role in developmental change.

Mesosystem In Bronfenbrenner's theory, the relationships among microsystems.

Microsystem In Bronfenbrenner's theory, the immediate setting in which a child lives (e.g. neighbourhood, school, family).

Natural selection works through the effects of a trait on survival: if a change to our physical structure or behaviour leads to a survival advantage, that change will be passed on through the genes to the organism's offspring during mating. If the change leads to no advantages, it will not be passed on and the trait will disappear. Thus, only traits which lead to a survival advantage for the organism are passed on.

Observational learning (often referred to as **modelling**) is the acquisition of a behaviour through the observation or imitation of others around one.

Operant conditioning refers to a type of learning where the likelihood of a behaviour reoccurring can be increased by reinforcements and decreased by punishments.

Organicism refers to a class of developmental theories that stress the qualitative features of developmental change and which emphasize the organism's role in bringing about these changes.

Period effects occur when an historical event exerts a relatively uniform influence across different birth cohorts.

Pleasure principle Freud's belief that the id attempts to maximize its pleasure in an immediate fashion.

Psychodynamic theories emphasize the belief that forces or dynamics within the individual are responsible for our behaviour.

Punishments are the consequences of a behaviour that decrease the likelihood of the behaviour reoccurring.

Range of applicability is the range of phenomena to which a theory properly applies.

Reinforcers are the consequences of a behaviour that increase the likelihood of that behaviour reoccurring.

Self-efficacy refers to beliefs about one's own effectiveness and competence to cope with a situation.

Sensitive period is a window of time in development during which an organism is particularly responsive to environmental influences.

Social learning theory is Bandura's theory that the principles of operant conditioning and observational learning are important mechanisms of development.

Sociocultural theory refers to Vygotsky's theory which views development as dependent on a child's interactions with other, more skilled members of the culture.

Superego In Freud's theory, that part of the personality which is the internalized values, standards of a child's parents and culture.

Theories take the form of an interconnected set of concepts used to integrate and to interpret empirical observations. **Formal theories** should be logically consistent and contain no contradictions, fit well with empirical observations, be testable, remain as simple as possible, and cover a defined range of phenomena. **Informal theories** are organized sets of intuitions or expectations about the world, often referred to as *implicit theories*.

TEST YOUR KNOWLEDGE

1. An organismic model of development states which of the following?

    a) Development occurs in all living things
    b) Developmental change happens qualitatively and the individual brings about these changes
    c) Developmental change happens quantitatively and the individual brings about these changes
    d) The environment impacts on the organism to bring about growth and decline

2. In Erikson's psychosocial theory, intimacy versus isolation is the stage concerned with which of the following?

    a) Developing a stable and intimate relationship with a parent and occurs early in childhood
    b) Developing a stable and intimate relationship with a partner and occurs in young adulthood

c) Attachment to important people across the life span

d) The death of those around you in old age

3. Which of the following research areas is studied by dynamic systems theorists?

a) Mapping the brain so that we can understand how brain functioning affects behaviour

b) Personality research to explore which children develop into dynamic adults

c) Understanding how microsystems may interact with the individual's macrosystem to produce development

d) Tracing the development of infants' motor skills to understand whether development in these areas occurs at similar or dissimilar rates

4. Which common analogy illustrates the information processing approach?

a) The flow of a stream

b) A computer

c) A brain map

d) A baby's fear of a white rat

5. In Piaget's sensorimotor stage, which of the following applies to the child?

a) Thinks about the world through their actions on it

b) Develops motor skills through using their senses

c) Makes the mistake of being egocentric about their world

d) Can be likened to a motor in how quickly their senses develop

ANSWERS: 1-B, 2-B, 3-D, 4-B, 5-A

Suggested Reading

Crain, W. (2004). *Theories of Development: Concepts and applications*. New York: Prentice-Hall.

Miller, P. H. (2016). *Theories of Developmental Psychology* (6th edition). New York: Worth.

Want to learn more? For links to online resources relevant to this chapter, interactive quizzes and much more, visit the companion website at
https://edge.sagepub.com/keenan3e/

Research Methodology in Developmental Psychology

3

Chapter Outline

LEARNING AIMS

At the end of this chapter you should:

- understand the importance of research design and methodology to research on child development
- be familiar with the various measurement techniques used in developmental research
- be able to articulate the strengths and weaknesses of different measurement techniques
- understand the relative strengths and weaknesses of controlled experiments, quasi-experiments and non-experiments, and be familiar with the conclusions than can be drawn from each type of study
- recognize research designs specifically geared towards understanding developmental questions and the sort of information provided by each type of study
- be aware of the ethical issues involved in research with children

---

Introduction

In this chapter we examine how researchers who study child development actually go about testing the hypotheses they have formed on the basis of their theories. The study of child development is grounded in the scientific method; that is, developmental psychologists create testable hypotheses on the basis of theory and then develop methods for empirically evaluating whether these hypotheses provide a good fit to the data they have gathered. An important aspect of this method is that observations must be replicable, or able to be duplicated by other researchers. Moreover, research questions should be examined in multiple ways, using different samples of children and different methodologies. When a research question has been thoroughly assessed, researchers can be more confident that they have obtained a valid finding.

Obviously there is insufficient space in this book for a full and detailed treatment of research methods. For a more thorough treatment the reader is referred to the book by Haslam and McGarty (2014) in this series. There are also many texts that deal specifically with research methods in the context of child development (see for example Mukherji and Albon, 2014; O'Reilly, Dogra & Ronzoni, 2013). In this chapter, our focus is on methodological issues that are of particular importance to developmental psychology.

The issues involved in testing research questions in developmental psychology include: the ways in which information about children can be gathered, that is, issues of measurement; different types of investigations, such as case studies, experiments and quasi-experiments; research designs developed specifically to assess developmental questions; issues regarding the reliability and the validity of data; and ethical issues regarding research with young children.

Measurement Techniques: How to Gather Data about Children

Survey methods

One powerful method for gathering information about children is through large-scale surveys. In survey research, a researcher sends out questionnaires or conducts interviews with a **representative sample** of the population of interest (quite often, surveys are conducted at a national level to assess issues that are important to a particular country). A representative sample is one in which the population surveyed resembles the larger population about which data are being gathered. Researchers need to be extremely careful that their samples are representative of the key aspects of the population relevant to the research question. For example, a sample which assessed only children from middle-class homes would not be able to tell us much about the development of the general population which includes children living in poverty and children who are brought up in more affluent areas. In contrast, issues of social class may be less important in the study of questions such as visual development. When a representative sample is obtained, survey methods can provide extremely useful information about important issues in child development.

In one large-scale survey conducted in Britain, the National Child Development Survey, a cohort of all people born in a single week in 1958 was followed. Data were first collected at birth, then when the children were 7, 11, 16, 23, 33, and most recently, 42 years of age. These data have given researchers significant insights into many aspects of British people's health, social, economic and psychological lives. In particular, we can learn about the impact of childhood living conditions on later life. You may remember from Baltes (2006) that a life-span perspective is imperative in understanding development in childhood. For example, the survey has shown that maladjustment in childhood leads to low academic achievement, unemployment and low wages later in life (Fronstin, Greenberg, & Robins, 2005).

Although useful, survey studies are limited in their ability to provide detailed explanations of how the factors surveyed influence child development. They are best suited to revealing broad patterns.

Observational methods

Jean Piaget (e.g. 1926) was a keen observer of children's behaviour. Much of his work on children's cognitive development was informed by careful observations of his own children. In current research, behavioural observation continues to be a powerful method for assessing theories of child development (e.g. Rubin et al., 1999). Observational research can take place in both *naturalistic settings*, such as a playground, day care or classroom, or it can take place in *laboratory settings*, where the experimenter can arrange conditions so as to gain more control over them. Laboratory settings are useful to study behaviour that we may rarely see in real life. One study assessing friendship quality in aggressive and non-aggressive children brought one hundred 10 year-old boys and their best friends into a laboratory where the boys played a range of board and word games. Aggressive boys and their friends behaved as you might expect: they were more likely to ignore the rules, cheat at games and encourage each other to be dishonest. Raters observing the boys also noted the aggressive pairs were more likely to show negative emotions such as anger towards each other (Bagwell & Coie, 2004). This behaviour may have taken a long time to observe and been difficult to capture if the researchers had tried to examine friendship pairs in a naturalistic setting.

In order to be useful to a researcher, observational data must satisfy certain conditions. One such criterion is that the study should allow for gathering an *adequate* sample of children's behaviour. A study which attempted to make generalizations about how children's social competence impacted on their classroom behaviour on the basis of a 10-minute observation of a child in their classroom would be suspect because the researcher would not obtain an adequate sample of the child's classroom behaviour. Most importantly, the data gathered in an observational study must not be influenced by the presence of the observer or observers. In other words, children and other participants in an observational study should not alter or distort their behaviour because they are being observed, so that what is observed is *representative* of their typical behaviour. A group of observers in a classroom who stare at children and continually make notes may cause those children to alter their behaviour, perhaps acting better than they otherwise might! This is an example of children showing **reactivity** to being observed; high reactivity leads to less valid conclusions. Similarly, in laboratory settings, it is important that the situational demands imposed in the laboratory do not exert influences on the behaviour of the participants. For example, factors such as conspicuously placed video cameras may cause parents to interact differently with their children than they might if they were less conscious of being videotaped. As you might guess, it is difficult to overcome these obstacles in observational research. When you read about developmental studies which employ observational methods, it is necessary to ask yourself whether or not the experimenters made adequate attempts to control or account for the presence of the observers or the setting.

In observational studies, the researcher must make some important decisions about the way in which the behaviours that are observed will be recorded, decisions which will be primarily influenced by the researcher's goals for the study. If the researcher is interested in everything that a child does in a given period of time, they may create a **specimen record**, in which everything that happens in a fixed period of time is recorded (Bakeman & Gottman, 1997). Most researchers will specify the behaviours of interest beforehand, so that the observed behaviours can be coded efficiently and quickly. Specimen records are very useful for studies which examine questions about the range of behaviours that children use in a particular situation. For example, researchers interested in how children modulate their emotions while engaged in a challenging task may choose to examine various behaviours which have been identified as being related to the child's ability to modulate their emotion (Rothbart, Ziaie, & O'Boyle, 1992). When the researcher is more specifically interested in how children react to particular events, a technique called **event sampling** may be employed (Bakeman & Gottman, 1997). In this technique, behaviours are measured whenever a particular event occurs. If we were interested in how maltreated children reacted to aggressive behaviours, we could use event sampling to make observations of the children's behaviour whenever an aggressive event occurs. **Time sampling methods** are often used when studying groups of subjects (Bakeman & Gottman, 1997). For example, imagine we want to study incidents of aggression in all of the interactions between a group of brothers and sisters. Using a time sampling approach, we might divide our 60-minute observation into 5-minute chunks or 'windows' and note whether or not particular forms of aggressive behaviour (defined in advance of the study) occur in a given 5-minute window. While this approach makes it easier to study behaviour in groups of subjects such as families and play groups, it leads to a loss of information, such as what happened after an incident or how the other siblings responded.

Laboratory observations are often used when the experimenter wants to ensure that a particular behaviour will be observed and that certain conditions are controlled for. For example, imagine that a researcher wants to examine the reactions of toddlers to brief separations from their mother. One way the researcher could design the study would be to observe the mother and toddler in their home environment. However, there are some problems that might be encountered if this research strategy is selected. For example, it would be difficult to ensure that certain conditions could be met, such as ensuring that the mother behaves in a natural fashion. Also, it may be difficult to arrange equal separations across the participants in the study and to create separations where the infant is free of distractions by other children or pets. By utilizing a laboratory observation procedure, the researcher can create separations that are standardized in length and control for other extraneous variables. The environment can be designed so that the child and mother are relatively unaware that their behaviour is being recorded, for example, through the use of one-way mirrors and hidden microphones. For many of the research questions that researchers would like to ask, the use of laboratory settings is the only way in which meaningful data can be gathered. Also, the use of specialized data collection techniques imposes its own set of requirements on the environment. Techniques that involve recording physiological data, such as the electrical activity of the brain, require an environment that is free of electrical interference that could alter the data collected, and these may also constrain behaviour in important ways. Other techniques require the child to remain focused on a particular stimulus item but also remain immobile for a long period of time. Clearly, when employing such techniques, the use of a controlled setting, which can only be achieved in the laboratory, is desirable.

Researchers have invented some quite ingenious methods for getting around the difficulties posed in their observation of children's behaviour in a natural setting. For example, in a study designed to capture bullying behaviour researchers set up video cameras in classrooms and playgrounds. The observed children also wore small microphones. The results revealed that bullying occurred at rates as high as 2.4 episodes every hour in the classroom and 4.5 episodes every hour in the playground. Moreover, most teachers didn't bother to take the time to stop these episodes. It seems quite possible that without the use of the cameras and microphones, the teachers and researchers would have remained unaware of the true extent of bullying behaviours.

Interviewing children

When many of us want to know something about another person, we simply ask them for the information. Not surprisingly, when we want to know something about children, one of the best methods available is simply to ask them questions. Asking another person for information about themself – which is called *self-report* – can take many forms. One common method is the **clinical interview**, where children are asked to describe their thoughts or feelings about some issue. Clinical interviews differ from other interview formats in that they are conducted in a flexible, open-ended fashion that allows the interviewer to gather as much information about a topic as possible and then follow up on any promising trains of thought the child may express. Jean Piaget (1926) used this method to great effect and was extremely adept at gaining information about young children's conceptions of the world through the clinical interview method. The clinical interview method is very useful in that it allows an interviewer to gather a very large amount of information about a topic in a relatively short time. It is also useful in that the clinical interview method may allow us to obtain information that closely approximates the way in which children really think.

However, getting information from young children presents some difficult problems for an interviewer. First, children's verbal abilities may limit or impede their capacity to understand the interviewer or to express themselves clearly, limiting the usefulness of the information obtained. Second, as Siegal (1991) has argued, because of their difficulties with the social conventions surrounding conversations (see Chapter 7 for a discussion of this issue), young children may fail to understand the interviewer's intention in asking a question and may unwittingly provide unwanted or irrelevant information. Most importantly, clinical interviews may be *inaccurate*. Children's recollections of an experience may be simply incorrect or distorted, or perhaps influenced by a tendency to respond in **socially desirable** ways, that is, the participant may say what they think the interviewer wants to hear. This last point is also applicable to **structured interviews** and to *questionnaire* formats as well.

A structured interview differs from a clinical interview in that each participant is asked the exact same set of questions in the same order. Structured interviews help to avoid the possibility that interviewers may treat individual participants in different ways. They also have the advantage of being more efficient forms of interviews for situations where one's time with a child is short or where their attention span and willingness to talk may be limited. Structured interviews can also be adapted to employ multiple choice responses (e.g. *'Did you feel good or bad about that?'*) or rating scales (e.g. *'Is this description really true of you or just sort of true for you?'*) to help children respond. Of course, structured interviews sacrifice the depth of information that could potentially be obtained by a good clinical interviewer.

Finally, questionnaires are useful methods for obtaining information from older, literate children. In this format, the participant reads through a list of questions and responds in written form or by answering in a specific fashion dictated by the questionnaire format such as *true/false* or *multiple choice*. Questionnaires are useful in that they can be widely distributed at a relatively low cost; however, the lack of personal contact with participants makes it difficult to ascertain whether they are responding in a truthful or socially desirable fashion.

Reports on children by others

Thus far we have considered some of the issues involved in having children report on their own thoughts or feeling about a topic of interest to the researcher. Another common method used in the study of child development is to obtain reports from *third parties*, such as family members, peers, or teachers. It is very often the case that others who are well acquainted with the child can provide very useful information about them. Reports from third parties also have the potential advantage of providing a perspective on the child when viewed in different environments. For example, teachers spend much time with children in a unique and significant context for development: the school environment. For this reason, teachers will be able to provide critical information about children's behaviour in this context. Parents also have the potential to provide the experimenter with information about their children that is unique. An additional advantage in using their reports is that they have also had the opportunity to view children across many different contexts and at different points in time. Moreover, a parent is in a position to discuss their thoughts and feelings about how their behaviours or parenting practices might impact on their child.

Third party reports suffer from many of the same limitations as children's self-reports. For instance, research has shown that parents are often inaccurate in reporting on their children's personality and cognitive abilities (Waschbusch, Daleiden, & Drabman, 2000). Parents also may not be particularly accurate about describing their own parenting practices with a child, or teachers may exaggerate the negative characteristics of children with whom they do not get along well while exaggerating the positive qualities of children with whom they do have a positive relationship. Despite potential problems with third-party reports, these do offer researchers an opportunity to gain valuable information about children. As well, discrepancies between children's self-reports and third-party reports may be an important source of information for the researcher. Even if parents or siblings are not entirely accurate, their views are nonetheless an important part of the child's world (Bugental & Grusec, 2006).

Psychophysiological methods

An increasingly popular means of gathering data about children is through the use of **psychophysiological methods**. These are a diverse set of research methods which have the common feature of measuring some aspect of children's physiological functioning in order to examine how these processes contribute to their behaviour. Psychophysiological methods are also extremely useful in that they can help us identify feelings in very young children or infants who may not otherwise be able to tell us about those feelings. Researchers who use psychophysiological methods can often make strong inferences about which aspects of our physiology – for example, the brain, central nervous system or autonomic nervous system – may underlie the development of some observable behaviour. As you may recall from Chapter 2, researchers interested in developmental neuroscience are concerned with the kinds of question that make use of psychophysiological methods.

Some psychophysiological measures have been designed to measure brain functioning. One potent technique is to record the electrical activity of the brain using an **electroencephalograph**

Table 3.1 Common measurement techniques

Measurement Technique	Strengths	Limitations
Surveys	• Most effective for revealing broad patterns in child development • Researchers are able to provide wide-reaching information about important issues in child development	• Unless the sample is representative of the population, it is difficult to make generalizations about the findings • Limited in their ability to provide detail
Observational methods	• The researcher is able to obtain a sample of natural behaviour • Depending on the goals of the study, researchers can record data in different ways (e.g. event sampling and time sampling) • Laboratory settings can be employed when the researcher needs more control over the environment than can be attained in a naturalistic setting	• Must have an adequate sample of the children's behaviour, which can be time-consuming • Data may be subject to the influence of the observer and the instruments of observation (e.g. video cameras) • It is sometimes difficult to ensure that all relevant criteria are met when employing naturalistic settings
Interviews	• Information is obtained first-hand from the individual • Clinical interviews allow the researcher to gather a large amount of information in a short period of time. Allows the researcher to be flexible and follow promising leads • Structured interviews allow researchers to treat individual children in the same way, and are useful for children with short attention spans • Questionnaires are useful for obtaining information from older, literate children	• Young children may not be cognitively or linguistically advanced to provide information about themselves • Young children may fail to understand the researcher's intention, and provide unwanted information • Children's memory of certain experiences may be inaccurate or distorted • Children may answer in socially desirable ways, and not according to the actual state of affairs (e.g. will tell the researcher what they think the researcher wants to hear)
Third-party reports	• Other people may be able to accurately comment on the child's behaviour • Significant others have an opportunity to view the child at varying stages of development • Provides different perspectives on the child in different contexts (e.g. at home and school)	• Parents and teachers may be biased when reporting the child's behaviour (e.g. negative about a child they consider to misbehave) • Parents and teachers may not remember certain episodes in the child's life • Parents and teachers may also respond in socially desirable ways
Psychophysiological methods	• Help researchers identify feelings in very young children/infants who may be too young to report themselves • Provide some understanding for the ways that physiology and brain development underlie the development of observable behaviour	• Changes in physiological indices (such as heart rate) may be difficult to interpret • The use of psychophysiological methods is inferential (e.g. based on correlations: the researcher makes presumptions about how a child's physiology underlies behaviour) and such inferences are subject to error

(EEG) while a child performs a particular task. An electroencephalograph is a device which amplifies and records electrical activity from the scalp using a number of small electrodes which are temporarily adhered to the scalp. Such methods can provide insight into which parts of the brain underlie performance on some task. In addition, particular aspects of brain activity known as **event-related potentials**, or ERPs (Segalowitz, 1995), can be measured in relation to task performance. For example, Molfese and Molfese (1979) used ERP techniques to show that speech sounds elicit a faster response from the left hemisphere of infants than from the right hemisphere, data which are consistent with the suggestion that the left hemisphere is most responsible for the processing of linguistic stimuli. A study examining brain development in bilingual toddlers revealed that the brain is activated differently for different languages (Conboy & Mills, 2006). In this study, ERPs to words were examined in 19 to 22 month-old English- and Spanish-speaking toddlers. The same words were presented to infants in English and Spanish. Analysis of the ERPs revealed that children's dominant versus non-dominant language resulted in different patterns of neural activity. Thus when children were presented with words from the language that was spoken most at home, there was greater contrast in the brain activity between the right and left hemispheres: conversely, when children were presented with words from their non-dominant language, greater symmetry between hemispheres was revealed. The study also compared bilingual versus monolingual children and found that brain activity was different in the two groups. The use of ERPs in this study allowed for the fine-tuning of our knowledge about language and development.

Another psychophysiological technique which is proving to be increasingly useful in research on child development is **functional magnetic resonance imaging** or **fMRI**. This is a non-invasive technique which allows researchers to detect changes in the blood flow to the brain, using magnetic fields to provide exceptionally clear three-dimensional images of those areas of the brain that are activated during a cognitive task. fMRI techniques have been used to identify the areas of the brain which are activated and presumed to be important to performance on a wide variety of psychological tasks, from memory to computational tasks. Essentially, the device works by measuring changes in blood flow in the brain and recording this information magnetically to produce a computerized image of the brain areas that are activated. In one such study children were asked to perform tasks that involve reasoning about another's mental states (Baron-Cohen, Ring, Moriarty, Schmitz, Costa, & Ell, 1994). The data from this study indicated that the frontal areas of the brain are of key importance to performance on tasks that involve mental state reasoning.

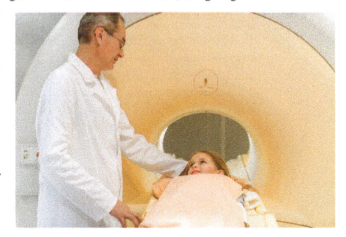

Image 3A One way of collecting data on children is to assess their brain activity through fMRI, which has been used in studies to assess a range of developmental outcomes, from language processing, memory and social comprehension to pain

© iStock.com/skynesher

Another study using fMRI examined differences between children and adults in language processing (Gaillard, Balsamo, Ibrahim, Sachs, & Xu, 2003). The study actually found few differences between adults and children in the location and laterality of brain activity in response to a language processing task. The findings suggest that by 7 years old development of verbal fluency is quite stable. Imaging techniques such as fMRI help researchers to assess which areas of the brain are most likely to underlie cognitive performance, helping us to obtain a better picture of the relationship between brain development and behaviour.

Other psychophysiological techniques have been developed which measure changes in aspects of our physiology. These include measures such as heart rate variability (often referred to as **vagal tone**; Porges, 1991), changes in the electrical conductance of the skin or **galvanic skin response**, and changes in the baseline level of hormones such as *cortisol* (a hormone which is released into the bloodstream in response to stressful events) in the bloodstream after a stimulus event. All of these measures are subject to change in response to stimulation or stress, and provide researchers with good clues to an individual's functioning and psychological state. For example, heart rate is commonly measured to gauge an infant's interest. A stable heart rate indicates the infant is staring blankly at a stimulus and not particularly interested, but a slowing of heart rate indicates concentration and interest. Changes in heart rate are also related to infant emotion, including anger, which shows as an increase in heart rate (Fox & Card, 1999). In a classic study, Joseph Campos and his colleagues used heart rate information to make inferences about the development of depth perception in young infants (Campos, Langer, & Krowitz, 1970). Campos showed that when 1½ month-old infants were placed on a clear glass covering over a deep trench the infants showed a slowing in their heart rate, indicating they perceived the depth of the trench and found it an interesting experience. Physiological differences have also been linked to significant differences in socioemotional development and personality (Kagan, 1998). For example, shy or inhibited children tend to show distinctive patterns of heart-rate variability when compared to children who are rated as less inhibited. Another important area of research that psychophysiological measures have shed light on is the phenomenon of infant pain. This research is examined in more detail in Research Example 3.1 below.

While psychophysiological methods provide the researcher with a powerful means of examining development, they also suffer from a number of limitations. First, changes in physiological indices such as heart rate can be difficult to interpret. A researcher will hope that these indices are changing in relation to the stimulus they have introduced, but there is always the possibility that other factors, such as boredom, anxiety, or even hunger and sleepiness, could alter heart rate as well (Fox, Schmidt, & Henderson, 2000). Thus a researcher using a psychophysiological method must be careful to ensure that such extraneous factors have been controlled. Second, the use of psychophysiological methods is *inferential*. That is, the researcher is measuring a physiological process (such as brain electrical activity) in relation to some behaviour (for example, making a decision about whether a target stimulus is present in a display or not). On the basis of correlations between the physiological data and the behaviour, the researcher makes inferences about how the physiological indices may underlie the behavioural processes. Of course, there is room for error in this procedure. A researcher who observes a specific pattern of brain activity in response to some stimulus cannot be entirely certain how the information has been processed. A third important point is that some children may react to the measures. For example, fMRIs require a child to lie alone in the scanner. Children may then become frightened or fall asleep. Either of these reactions could cause arousal changes in their brain that are not related to the study, thereby interfering with the study findings. However, psychophysiological methods are proving increasingly popular in the study of child development and are helping to provide a better understanding of the relationship between physiology and behaviour.

Research Example 3.1

Babies in Pain

Only recently has the medical world recognized that babies experience pain on a par with older children and adults. For many years, doctors believed that procedures like circumcision could be performed on newborn infants without negative consequences. However, we are now aware that even minor procedures, such as heel sticks (pricking a newborn's heel to extract a sample of blood used to screen for a number of conditions) without analgesia may have adverse consequences. Infants, especially preterm infants, who undergo frequent painful procedures can develop long-term changes to their nervous systems and show greater pain response later in life (Simons, van Dijk, Anand, Roofthooft, van Lingen, & Tibboel, 2003). This has led researchers to search for simple and effective ways that are free from side-effects to reduce newborn pain. As you may imagine, infant pain is not as simple to deal with as adult pain. Adults might pop a pill, but pharmacological interventions can compromise a newborn's delicate system.

Reviews of studies using alternative methods of pain relief have identified that a number of methods, including pacifiers, a small dose of sweet solution, music and holding the infant, can be effective in combating newborn pain (Tsao, Evans, Meldrum, Altman, & Zeltzer, 2007). But how do we know these infants feel less pain than control-group infants who are not given the pain-relief interventions? Newborn babies cannot tell us about their pain. We have to infer this from their behavioural and psychophysiological responses. We can measure behavioural responses such as how much time babies spend crying, or record their facial expressions of sadness and pain. However, interpreting these displays can be difficult, because babies might also cry because they are hungry or cold. This is where physiological measures may be helpful: researchers will often record an infant's heart rate and blood cortisol levels to verify the amount of stress and pain the baby is experiencing. Although information gathered in this way is far from perfect, we can gain a relatively clear picture of infant distress. Such measures may allow us to determine the best method, or combination of methods, to relieve infant pain.

Research Design

When a researcher decides to tackle a particular research question, an issue with which they must come to grips very early is how to design a research project that will give them the best chance of properly examining the question. The researcher's goal is to provide a test of the hypothesis which produces valid results. Researchers will attempt to design their studies so that they can test their hypotheses while controlling for other variables which may potentially provide **validity threats** to the study (Campbell & Stanley, 1963). Validity threats are factors related to the design of experiments which can cause problems with how the data from a study should be interpreted. A discussion of each of the different types of validity threat associated with scientific studies is beyond the scope of this text (but see Haslam & McGarty, 2003). A general distinction can be made between *internal* validity (conditions internal to the study design such as selecting participants from only one kind of background) and *external* validity (whether the study findings can be generalized to other settings and participants). You should think critically about the research you read about and attempt to evaluate this in terms of whether the findings are valid, that is, free of validity threats.

While no experimental design is perfect and entirely free from validity threats, the goal of scientific research is to minimize threats to the validity of one's study in order to provide as adequate a test of the hypotheses as possible. One way researchers meet this goal is to conduct multiple studies, using a variety of research designs and methodologies to test their hypotheses. Findings that stand up across repeated testing are considered both **reliable** and valid. Reliable findings are findings which we are confident could be reproduced again or **replicated**. Research findings which are reliable and valid are the bedrock of psychological science.

Controlled experiments

Controlled experiments are the most powerful form of research designs in terms of their ability to let us make *causal statements*, that is, statements about whether one thing causes another (Hartmann & George, 1999). There are two types of variable in an experimental design: **independent variables** and **dependent variables**. In general, independent variables are variables which are expected or thought to affect other variables (the dependent variables). In controlled experiments, however, independent variables are those variables which are manipulated by the experimenter. For example, imagine a study where two groups of children are observed individually in a play situation with a strange, same-aged peer. The experimenter in this study is interested in whether a child's exposure to aggression will produce aggressive behaviours in the child; thus, the experimenter designs a study in which some children are exposed to an aggressive incident while some others are not. Before the observation period begins, one group of children is exposed to a mock argument between the child's mother and a strange female (an accomplice of the experimenter's). The second group of children simply see the mother and the strange female act normally. Whether or not children are exposed to the mock argument is a variable which is under the experimenter's control and is therefore what we would call an independent variable. In addition, the age and sex of the child are independent variables because these two factors are expected to have important effects on the dependent variable (e.g. boys might be expected to show higher levels of physical aggression than girls).

All children are measured on the dependent variable. The dependent variable is the factor that the experimenter expects to be influenced by the independent variable. In our example, the researcher might choose to measure acts of aggression exemplified by hitting and kicking initiated by the target child during the play session. The researcher could then generate an 'aggression score', such as the number of aggressive acts demonstrated by each target child in five minutes of play with the strange child. In some studies, multiple dependent variables are assessed. In our example, the researcher could measure both physical aggression and verbal aggression.

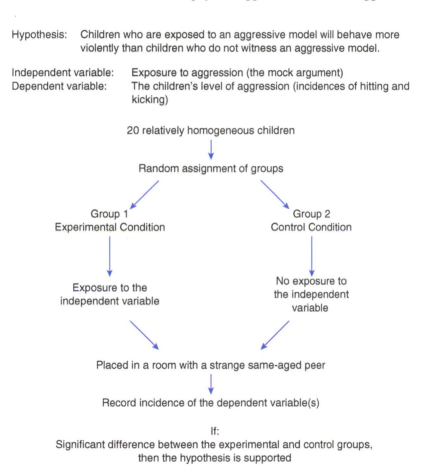

Figure 3.1   The controlled experiment

Children who are assigned to the condition where they receive exposure to the independent variable are in what is called the **experimental condition**. Children who do not receive exposure to the independent variable are part of the **control condition**. Critical to the design of a controlled experiment is that the children in the two groups are assumed to be equal before the study begins. Generally speaking, the best way to achieve this is through the **random assignment** of subjects to the experimental and control conditions. For example, the experimenter might place the names of subjects in a hat and randomly draw 10 to participate in the experimental group and 10 to participate in the control group. Alternatively, the experimenter may flip a coin or use any other method which guarantees that there is no bias in how subjects are assigned to the experimental and control conditions.

When properly conducted, the controlled experiment allows the researcher to make conclusions about cause and effect. Consider our example: if children in the experimental condition show significantly higher levels of aggression when playing with the peer than children assigned to the control condition, the researcher is able to state conclusively that exposure to an aggressive model causes aggressive behaviour in young children (once again, assuming the experiment is properly controlled and within the limits of the statistical techniques used). We provide another example of an experimental design in a classroom setting in Research Example 3.2.

Research Example 3.2

Play and Problem Solving: An experiment in a classroom setting

There has been much interest in researching children's play and how this might contribute to cognitive and social development (this topic will be considered further in Chapter 11). There are many different types of activity that can be classed as play (for example, pretend play, physical play, object play). However, another interesting finding is that the manner in which an activity is presented to children can also influence whether or not the activity is seen as play. Findings from studies such as Ceglowski (1997), Howard (2002) and Karby (1989) have indicated that factors such as the location of an activity (such as whether it takes place at a table or on the floor), whether or not an adult is involved and whether the activity is voluntary or compulsory seem to be important 'cues' that children use to distinguish 'play' from 'non-play' activities. These findings were used by Thomas, Howard and Miles (2006) to set up an experiment to investigate if presenting a task in a 'playful' or 'formal' setting had an impact on children's performance of that task.

The experiment involved a sample of 30 children aged 3 to 5 years-old attending two primary schools in Wales and the task used was a jigsaw puzzle. Initially, the puzzle was presented to each child and the time taken for the child to solve the puzzle was recorded. The jigsaw was then taken apart and the pieces shuffled. Each child was then exposed to the jigsaw again, but this time was allocated to one of two practice conditions: a 'playful' practice condition in which they were *invited* to practise the jigsaw for eight minutes while sitting on the carpeted area of the classroom floor without an adult being present, or a 'formal' practice condition in which they were *instructed* to practise the task for eight minutes while seated at a table with an adult.

Following the practice conditions, the children were then immediately presented with the jigsaw puzzle and the time taken to complete the puzzle was recorded. The children were then presented with the same puzzle one week later and again the time taken to complete the puzzle was recorded. The performance of the 'playful' and 'formal' practice groups was then compared.

At the 'pre-test' phase (before the exposure to the practice conditions), there was no significant difference in the jigsaw completion times between the two groups of children. However, when tested immediately after the practice condition, the children in the 'playful' condition showed a bigger improvement in the time taken to complete the puzzle compared to the 'formal' group, and this difference was statistically significant. At the 'delayed test' phase (when children were tested one week later), this difference between the two groups was still present, with the 'playful' group showing significantly greater improvement in completion times than the 'formal' group.

The results of this study indicate that not only do children make distinctions between 'play' and 'non-play' situations, but also that if a task is presented employing the cues that signal an activity as play, there is the possibility that children may also perform that task more effectively. Given the importance of the use of play in Early Years classrooms, this may have implications for the way teachers present tasks and activities to children, and indicate that rather than classifying some activities as 'play' or 'work', it is the way in which the activity is presented that is most important. Of course further studies will be needed to see if this effect holds for other activities related to the Early Years curriculum, but these types of study do show the potential for the use of play as an educational tool.

Questions: Why was it important to compare the jigsaw completion times of the two groups before exposure to the different practice conditions? Can you identify the *independent* and *dependent* variables in this experiment? Can you think of any controls that would have been necessary to ensure the validity of the results of this experiment?

Quasi-experiments

In contrast to controlled experiments, **quasi-experiments** are investigations where the experimenter has instituted appropriate controls over variables which might influence the results, but is unable to randomly assign participants to experimental conditions (Hartmann & George, 1999). Many developmental studies are not truly controlled experiments because it is impossible to completely randomize the assignment of subjects to conditions when certain variables, such as age, are the variable of interest in the investigation. In other words, when comparing children of different age groups on some variable, the assignment to conditions is obviously dictated by the child's age.

This means that the causal inferences which can be made from quasi-experiments are much less clear than in true controlled experiments (Hartmann & George, 1999).

Can you think of some other examples of research situations that would necessitate the use of a quasi-experimental design rather than a controlled experiment?

Non-experimental designs

Non-experimental designs, often known as **correlational methods**, are research designs in which neither the random assignment of subjects to conditions nor the use of a control group are employed (Hartmann & George, 1999). The goal of non-experimental designs is to inform the researcher about potential relationships among variables or sets of variables. For example, a researcher might wonder whether a child's intelligence is related to their social skills. To answer this question, a researcher could administer measures of intelligence and social skills to a sample of children and look for a statistical relationship between the measures, known as a **correlation**. Non-experimental designs are often known as correlational methods because of the frequency with which this statistical technique is employed, but it is important to note that non-experimental/ correlational designs can be carried out without the use of correlations.

A correlation coefficient measures the strength of relationship between two variables. When two variables are perfectly related, such that an increase in variable X is associated with a predictable increase in variable Y, we say that the variables show a perfect **positive correlation**. Perfect positive correlations are expressed by a correlation coefficient of +1.00. In contrast, when an *increase* in variable X is always accompanied by a completely predictable *decrease* in variable Y, we have an instance of a perfect **negative correlation**, which is expressed by a correlation coefficient of –1.00. When the scores of two variables are completely *unrelated*, there is no correlation, expressed by a correlation coefficient of zero (0.00). Moreover, the strength of a relationship can be assessed by the magnitude of the correlation coefficient: a correlation of .70 between two variables indicates a stronger relationship between them than a correlation of .20.

Getting back to our example, if we found that children's scores on our measures of IQ and social skills showed a correlation of .30, we have evidence that children's intelligence and their social skills are related. There is an important fact to notice here. Note that we do not say 'intelligence *causes* social skills', only that the two variables are associated in a positive fashion. This is because non-experimental or correlational research designs do not allow us to say anything definitive about the *causal* relationship between the variables. This fact is often summed up by the catchphrase *correlation does not equal causation*. Correlation simply tells us that two factors are related, not whether one factor causes the other. In our example, we are unable to ascertain whether intelligence causes the development of social skills, whether the reverse is true (that is, social skills may cause intelligence), or whether the two constructs are caused by some other common factor.

This last possibility is known as the **third variable problem**. A correlation between two variables, X and Y, could be caused by the presence of a third variable Z, which is responsible for

Table 3.2 Research designs – strengths and limitations

Research Design	Strengths	Limitations
Experimental designs	• Allow the researcher to make causal statements about the relationship between two or more variables	• The findings of carefully controlled laboratory experiments may not generalize to real-world settings
Quasi-experimental designs	• Allow the researcher some degree of control • Allow the researcher to take advantage of unique opportunities or natural experiments	• Because assignment to treatment conditions is not random, the ability to make causal statements is weakened
Non-experimental designs	• Allow the researcher to study the relationships among a set of variables • Useful designs for the exploration of new areas and for generating new hypotheses	• These designs do not permit the experimenter to make causal statements about the relationships between variables
Case studies	• Allow for an in-depth examination in a way that is not practical with large groups • Can be set up to provide a quasi-experimental design	• Because assignment to treatment conditions is not random, the ability to make causal statements is weakened • Unable to generalize to the wider population

the relationship between X and Y. For example, reading skill and speed at naming objects might show a positive correlation such that children who are better readers are able to name common objects more quickly than children who are poor readers. However, research has suggested that a third variable, changes in the child's speed of information processing, might underlie the changes in both reading skill and memory span (Kail & Hall, 1994). That is, the faster a child can process information, the faster they can name objects and the better they are at tests of reading skill. One way in which researchers can deal with the issue of a possible third variable relationship is to control for the variable by including measures of it in the study.

Given the limitations of a correlational design in understanding causal relationships, why do researchers use it? The main reason is because many questions cannot be answered with experimental studies. It is often impossible or extremely unethical to divide children into experimental and control conditions. Using our example, we cannot deliberately make children more or less intelligent in order to see whether this impacts on their social skills. Another point to consider is that many researchers are not necessarily interested in questions of causality. For many, documenting patterns or describing developmental pathways through correlational designs is enough.

Case studies

In the other approaches to research design that we have examined so far it is common to focus on groups of children rather than on individuals. This fact may lead you to wonder about the usefulness of studying a single individual. Can we learn anything worthwhile from the intensive study of a single child as opposed to looking at average levels of behaviour or knowledge across groups? **Case study methods** allow the researcher to focus on a single child, looking at their development in an in-depth fashion that is not practical with larger groups. Case studies have been used to examine unusual cases, such as children with rare diseases or exceptional talents in some area. For example, Camras (1994) used a case study methodology to look at the development of emotional expressions in her infant daughter. She created extensive video records of the child which captured emotional expressions produced in a wide variety of situations. Camras's work has proven extremely influential to theorizing on the nature of emotional development and the ties between facial expressions and emotional experience.

Case study methods have also been developed to provide a kind of experimental research design which is particularly useful for studying the effects of interventions on behaviour change. In these **ABAB designs**, the letter A represents a control condition or *baseline phase* of the study where the researcher simply measures the frequency or rate of occurrence of the behaviour they wish to alter. After collecting sufficient baseline information, the second phase of the experiment, the *treatment phase* (represented by the letter B), is begun. During the treatment phase the researcher employs some treatment to each incidence of the target behaviour, often a reward or punishment. The researcher is particularly interested in whether their manipulation has the effect of increasing or decreasing the frequency of the target behaviour in relation to the baseline phase. After some predetermined point in the treatment, the researcher stops implementing the treatment and looks to see whether the behaviour returns to its baseline frequency. Finally, the researcher will then reinstate the treatment, looking to see whether the behaviour increases/decreases in frequency. If the behaviour changes reliably as a function of the treatment, the researcher can be fairly confident that their treatment is effecting change in the target behaviour. Of course, a limitation of the case study method is the inability to generalize to the wider population. Simply because the treatment works with a single child does not mean it will be successful with all children. Another problem is that the target behaviour may not return to baseline levels in the third phase of the study: the behaviour may continue to exist at a different frequency from that of the baseline phase, making it difficult to clearly assess whether the treatment was the cause of the behaviour change. It may also be undesirable or unethical to allow a behaviour to return to baseline levels, for example if the behaviour represents a threat to the safety and wellbeing of the individual or others (for example, in cases of aggressive or self-harming behaviour).

Research Designs to Study Development

Developmental psychologists employ a wide range of research designs to study child development. Given that the goal of developmental studies is most often an examination of change over time in some aspect of behaviour or functioning, research designs which incorporate time as a variable are particularly relevant here. We will examine four such research designs: the cross-sectional study, the longitudinal study, the microgenetic study, and the sequential study. This is only a selection of the full range of research designs used in the study of child development and you should be aware that there are many research designs available (see Schaie, 1965).

The cross-sectional design

One of the most common methods for studying age-related differences in behaviour is the cross-sectional method. In a cross-sectional design, researchers compare groups of children who are of different ages but are studied at the same point in time. For example, we may be interested in the way children develop their notions of what a friend is. Thus, using this design, we would compare conceptions of friendship in children of two or more age groups, for example, 5, 10, and 15 year-olds. A cross-sectional study such as this one would allow us to compare whether or not children's conceptions of friendship change over time. That is, we might find that older children view intimacy as the most important aspect of friendship while younger children see shared interests as defining their conception of friendship (Rubin & Coplan, 1992).

Table 3.3 Research designs to study developmental change

Research Design	Strengths	Limitations
Cross-sectional designs	• Most efficient design for the study of age-related changes in child development. Can be conducted quickly without a need to wait for individuals to change • Useful for studying group differences (as opposed to changes in individuals)	• Unable to address issues about the individual child • Only provides a short-cut to the study of developmental change • Conclusions tempered by the possibility of cohort effects
Longitudinal designs	• Allow the researcher to study individual differences in functioning across time • Useful for identifying developmental pathways • Provide information about important developmental issues such as stability vs. change and the relationship between early behaviours and later outcomes • Identifying whether dependent variables change as a function of age or birth cohort aids in the search for the mechanisms underlying development	• Require a great deal of time and effort (especially large-scale, long-term studies) • Conclusions tempered by the possibility of cohort effects • Developmental change may be confused with practice effects • The attrition of subjects from the sample can make interpreting the results difficult
Time-lag designs	• Allow the researcher to control for cohort effects • Useful as a supplement to longitudinal studies where cohort effects are likely to be a factor	• Unable to address issues about the development of the individual child • On their own, time-lag designs do not address sources of developmental change other than cohort effects
Microgenetic designs	• Allow the researcher to obtain a fine-grained analysis of developmental change • Useful for developing a more complete picture of developmental change which occurs rapidly	• Developmental change may be confused with practice effects

However, the cross-sectional design is only a convenient short-cut to the study of developmental change, and, as you might expect, short-cuts often come with limitations that restrict the conclusions that can be drawn from the findings. For instance, information about how an *individual child* changes is not available from a cross-sectional design. This is because the cross-sectional design only assesses group differences, such as the group of 5 year-olds compared to the group of 10 year-olds or to the group of 15 year-olds. As a consequence, we learn nothing about whether children's early conceptions of friendship influence their later conceptions or how stable conceptions might be over time. Cross-sectional designs also are open to the possibility of cohort effects. In our example above, imagine our 5 year-olds were born in 1995, our 10 year-olds were born in 1990, and our 15 year-olds in 1985. Differences between the three age groups might not reflect developmental differences at all; instead, the differences might be due to the historical time period in which these children were born. For example, children growing up in the 1980s may have experienced different social conditions from those for children growing up in the 1990s, factors which could impact on their conceptions of friendship. While historical effects are not always an issue, they can impact on development and we can't know from cross-sectional studies whether they are an issue in any given study. Interpreting the findings of cross-sectional research requires careful consideration.

Longitudinal designs

In a longitudinal design, a sample of children is observed repeatedly at different points throughout their lives. One clear advantage of longitudinal designs is that they allow us to observe individual differences in functioning over time. Because longitudinal designs allow researchers to follow individuals' (as well as groups') progress, it becomes possible to examine individual patterns of stability and change in the behaviour of individuals. When we have large groups of subjects with clusters of similar variability, we can begin to identify what we call developmental pathways. By developmental pathway, we mean a particular pattern of movement through the life course, evidenced by groups of participants who follow a similar course of development.

While the obvious advantages of longitudinal designs are powerful incentives for researchers to find the resources to design and conduct them, they also have a number of disadvantages. First, they can be difficult to conduct and can take a great deal of time to complete. While short-term longitudinal studies get around this latter point, not all questions are amenable to their use, and require a much longer period of study. Second, longitudinal studies are open to the possibility of cohort effects. Third, practice effects can be an issue in longitudinal designs. Because the participants in a study may receive the same measures on repeated occasions, they may learn how to respond to the measure, meaning that it will not provide an accurate estimate of children's knowledge or abilities. Moreover, practice effects may emerge as children become accustomed to the experimenters; that is, having seen the experimenter on repeated occasions, the child may become more comfortable with them and provide more information than they did initially. Thus, what might seem like developmental change is, in reality, attributable to the child's increasing level of comfort. **Attrition** (or mortality) is another problem faced when designing longitudinal studies. Attrition refers to the tendency for subjects to drop out of a study due to illness, a lack of interest, or other factors such as relocation. Attrition can reduce the power of a study through the reduction in the size of the sample. The effects due to subject attrition can also be more insidious: in many studies, attrition occurs more often among particular groups of subject than in others. For example, imagine that families who are in a lower socioeconomic group are more likely to drop out of a longitudinal study than are families who are in middle or higher socioeconomic groups. This fact could have a dramatic impact on the results of the study, such as reducing the variability in the original sample. In longitudinal studies, it becomes important to assess whether there are detectable patterns among the subjects who drop out of a study.

Microgenetic designs

The **microgenetic design** is a special form of longitudinal study. Microgenetic studies are designed to allow a very fine-grained analysis of developmental change, particularly for behavioural developments which occur rapidly and over a short period of time (Kuhn, 1995). A common feature of all microgenetic studies is that they involve a high density of observations; that is, the researcher looks repeatedly at an emerging development over a short period, trying to measure change in the smallest possible increments. This allows them to form a more complete picture of the development of a given phenomenon. Microgenetic designs are generally short term, lasting from a few days to a few weeks, but this aspect is determined in large part by the nature of the developments the researcher wishes to study. Of course, like longitudinal studies, microgenetic studies are open to the possibility of practice effects and researchers must be careful to check for these.

Image 3B   In this lego building project, this preschooler experiments with constructing a house. When pieces fail to fit, she takes corrective action and proceeds with the task. In a microgenetic design, researchers are able to follow each step of children's decision making to master a challenge, and answer important questions about the steps involved in problem solving

© iStock.com/AnnettVauteck

The time-lag design

A **time-lag design** attempts to control for time of measurement effects, such as historical effects associated with a particular birth cohort. As we have seen, historical factors can have a profound influence on child development. There is an abundance of possible factors which can impact on child development, such as war, disease, economic depressions and booms, the development of technologies such as television or computers, and health-related concerns. In a time-lag study, a researcher is generally more interested in identifying cultural changes which might impact on development rather than in studying the development of individuals. For example, a time-lag study might compare sexual attitudes and behaviours in a sample of 18 year-olds born in 1950 (and thus who were 18 years of age in 1968) to a sample of 18 year-olds born in 1980 (18 years of age in 1998). Such a study would allow the researcher to see how historical factors may have influenced change at the societal level.

A limitation of time-lag designs already noted is their inability to answer questions about the development of individuals. One important use of the time-lag study is as a supplement to longitudinal studies where time of measurement effects or cohort factors may be influencing the outcome. For example, a researcher might want to study the change in the sexual attitudes and behaviours of adolescents as a function of age. However, it would be difficult to be certain that any developments in the sexual attitudes and behaviours observed were not simply the result of changes over time in society's values towards sexuality. By conducting a time-lag study along with the longitudinal study, the researcher would be able to say something about the extent to which these attitudes and behaviours had actually changed, and hence is in a better position to interpret the findings of the longitudinal study.

What method(s) do you think might be appropriate for investigating the following research questions?

1 Comparing two different therapeutic interventions for children suffering from depression
2 Investigating how friends resolve conflicts
3 The effects of bullying on self-esteem in school-age children
4 How early memory skills might predict later school achievement

Ethical Issues in Research on Child Development

A student undertaking the study of child development needs to be aware of ethical issues of relevance to the study of children. Guidelines or standards for conducting ethical research with children have been produced by a number of organizations such as the Society for Research in Child Development (1993) and the American Psychological Association. A number of these principles are summarized in Table 3.4.

The most obvious ethical issue is the need to avoid any *harm* to children who participate in the study. One of the main concerns of a formal ethical review process will be to evaluate the proposed research for any possible harm to the participants. Harm, whether physical or psychological in form, must be avoided as much as is possible. Psychological or emotional harm can include any time the child feels uncomfortable or embarrassed. Some studies will involve procedures that are unpleasant to the child, such as arm restraint procedures which are designed to elicit some negative emotion. Ethics committees must consider whether the costs and benefits of the procedures are justified in relation to the potential of the research to add to our knowledge of child development. If unpleasant procedures are employed, researchers must endeavour to alleviate any negative effects which the participants may experience as much as is possible on completion of the study.

An important right of children involved in research projects is their right to provide consent before taking part in the research. **Informed consent**, that is, an agreement by a participant to take part in a research project based on a full understanding of the nature of the project, what it entails, and its purpose. Children themselves need to be briefed on the study and what will happen to them. They also need to be informed and made to understand that they can withdraw their participation at any time during the experiment; that is, if they become uncomfortable during the experiment, they may refuse to participate further. When children are under 7 to 8 years of age, parents must give informed consent on their child's behalf, as children younger than this may not have the cognitive ability to understand what is being asked of them (Institute of Medicine, 2004). Even children older than this may give consent but not fully appreciate what it means. For example, it is important for children to understand that they can discontinue with the study at any time, but children may continue even if they uncomfortable for fear that they will disappoint an adult or not be sure of the repercussions. Thus it is critical to ensure that the child's parents fully understand the nature of the research if the parents are to act as guardians, safeguarding the child's interests.

All research projects should undergo a formal ethical review process. This means that the research project must be scrutinized by a board of experts whose goal is to ensure that the proposed research project meets the highest ethical standards. Most universities have an ethics committee that oversees all projects conducted under the auspices of the institution. Many hospitals and psychiatric institutions also have their own ethics committees. Finally, it is often the case that research projects submitted to school boards undergo an ethical review by the board's own committee. The net effect of this scrutiny by a group of people trained to evaluate research projects is to head off any potential ethical problems before the project is conducted. If there is any risk to children for which the research project fails to give good reason, then research participants are always the first priority, and the study will be rejected and not permitted to run. Very often, research committees will give researchers additional opportunities to make appropriate changes to safeguard children's rights and the project will be reviewed again until it is sufficiently free from potential harm. In addition to this, many scientific journals in the field of child development now require a statement from the researcher that the project meets ethical guidelines for research in child development and that no ethical principles were violated in conducting the research.

Confidentiality is also an issue. A researcher must maintain the confidentiality of the information obtained from each of the participants in their study. Thus children should know that what they tell researchers will only be used for the study, and not revealed to others. However, researchers may face the difficult dilemma of dealing with a child who reveals information about a situation that may place that child in jeopardy. Should researchers let parents know if their child reports high levels of anxiety or depression on a questionnaire, or reports an incident of sexual abuse? When information comes to a researcher's attention that the wellbeing of a child may be compromised, then parents or other relevant professionals and agencies should be informed.

Other measures should also be in place to maintain confidentiality. For example, information which could identify individuals involved in a project must be removed from their records. In addition, researchers must not publish findings in such a way as to identify an individual child. Finally, the findings of a research project need to be made available to the participants. This should take place in a form that they can understand: generally, this will consist of a report specifically designed for parents, which is made available to them on completion of the project. Researchers also have an obligation to consider the broader ramifications of their findings on social attitudes, public policy and the like. The researcher should give careful consideration to how their findings could be misinterpreted or misused before publication, in order to lessen or avoid the chances of such an event taking place.

The ethics of research into child development is surrounded by much debate. Many child advocates and researchers are calling for more stringent rules governing research with children. Yet other researchers say that if too many rules are imposed, we will no longer be able to ask children to be involved in research, thereby impeding our understanding of children's development. The knowledge acquired through research allows us to help children. For example, knowing about the brain areas involved in language processing may help us in identifying the problems that children who are not developing according to normal standards may have. Ultimately, it is up to individual ethics committees to weigh up the risk-versus-benefit ratio and keep children's research rights in mind when determining whether a study should be given the go-ahead.

Table 3.4 Research with children – ethical standards

No Harm	The child should not be harmed psychologically or physically.
Consent	All children should be informed about the study in a way suited to their comprehension. Children should be informed that they can withdraw, at no penalty, at any time. Assent, i.e. children show agreement although they may not be able to understand the full significance of the research, should be sought. Parents and others responsible for children should be given a full debriefing and if they agree provide signed consent.
Incentives	Children should be compensated for their time; however, incentives must be fair and not exceed the range of incentives the child may normally receive. Children are entitled to these incentives even if they withdraw from the study.
Deception	Certain studies may require holding back information. The researcher must prove that such deception is necessary and justified.
Confidentiality	Records of research should be kept in a way to ensure participants cannot be personally identified. Researchers should also keep in confidence all information obtained from participants. However, if such information reveals the child's wellbeing may be in jeopardy, then parents should be informed to arrange necessary assistance for the child.
Dissemination	Participants have the right to know about the research findings. Results should be presented in a way that children can understand. If a child is too young, a summary of the findings should be provided to the parents.

Find details of the following two influential research studies:

- Rosenthal and Jacobson's (1968) study on the effects of teacher expectations on pupil achievement ('Pygmalion in the classroom')
- Jane Elliott's (1970) 'brown eye/blue eye' intervention which aimed to reduce prejudice in young children (a link to a video of this study is available in the student resources on the companion website)

Do you think these studies would meet the ethical standards demanded of modern studies in child development? Do you think the practical insights gained from these studies might outweigh any ethical concerns?

Summary

A variety of methodologies (e.g. survey, observational and psychophysiological methods) and research designs (e.g. non-experimental and quasi-experimental designs) are employed within the study of child development. Methodology is a fundamental issue in the study of child development, although many students are tempted to devote relatively less time to this topic or skip over it entirely. Sound methods underpin research in this field and without a knowledge of the *hows* and *whys* of these methods, understanding the research which contributes to our knowledge of children is far more difficult.

Glossary

ABAB designs are a kind of experimental research design which is particularly useful for studying the effects of interventions on behaviour change. Baseline measures of a behaviour are obtained, an experimental treatment is introduced, and is then withdrawn and reintroduced.

Attrition refers to the tendency of subjects to drop out of a longitudinal study.

Case study methods are research designs which focus on a single child, looking at their development in an in-depth fashion that is often not practical with large groups.

Clinical interview is a flexible, open-ended interview format that allows an interviewer to gather as much information about a topic as possible and to follow up on any promising trains of thought.

Cohort effects refer to differences which are due to the historical time period in which a cohort of same-aged children was born.

Confidentiality refers to an obligation on the part of the researcher to maintain the confidentiality of the information obtained from each of the participants in their study.

Control condition refers to the condition in an experiment where participants are not exposed to the independent variable.

Controlled experiments are research designs where the researcher manipulates one or more independent variables and measures their effect on one or a set of dependent measures, while controlling for confounding variables.

Correlation refers to a statistical measure of the association between two variables.

Cross-sectional designs are used when researchers compare groups of children who are of different ages but are studied at the same point in time.

Dependent variables are the factor(s) that the experimenter expects to be influenced by the independent variable.

Developmental pathways refer to a particular pattern of movement through the life course, evidenced by groups of participants who show similar patterns of development.

Electroencephalograph (EEG) is a device which amplifies and records electrical activity from the scalp using a number of small electrodes.

Event-related potentials (ERPs) are electrical activity produced by the brain in response to motor or cognitive stimulation.

Event sampling, used in observational research, is a technique where a set of predetermined behaviours are recorded whenever a particular event occurs.

Experimental condition refers to the treatment condition in an experiment where participants receive exposure to the independent variable.

Functional magnetic resonance imaging (fMRI) is a non-invasive technique which allows researchers to detect changes in the blood flow to the brain, using magnetic fields to provide exceptionally clear images of those areas of the brain that are activated during a cognitive task.

Galvanic skin response is changes in the electrical conductance of the skin, a psychophysiological measure.

Independent variables are those variables which are manipulated by the experimenter.

Informed consent is an agreement by a participant to take part in a research project based on a full understanding of the nature of the project.

Longitudinal design is a method where a sample of children are observed repeatedly at various points throughout their lives.

Microgenetic designs are research designs which allow for a very fine-grained analysis of developmental change by using a high density of observations. These are particularly useful for studying behavioural developments which occur rapidly and over a short period of time.

Non-experimental designs (or **correlational methods**) are research designs in which neither the random assignment of subjects to conditions nor the use of a control group is employed.

Practice effects can be an issue in longitudinal designs, as participants in a study may receive the same measures on repeated occasions and may learn how to respond to the measure.

Psychophysiological methods are a diverse set of research methods which have the common feature of measuring some aspect of physiological functioning in order to examine how these processes contribute to behaviour.

Quasi-experiments are investigations where the experimenter has instituted appropriate controls over variables which might influence the results, but is unable to randomly assign participants to experimental conditions.

Random assignment is a quality of experiments where participants are placed in the experimental and control conditions via some random method.

Reactivity occurs when subjects are highly conscious of being observed and can lead to distorted behaviour and less valid conclusions.

Reliable findings are ones that we are confident could be reproduced or replicated.

Replicable refers to the fact that observations need to be able to be duplicated by other researchers.

Representative behaviour In an observational study the researcher should employ methods which do not lead participants to alter or distort their behaviour because they are being observed. We want a sample of behaviour which is representative of a participant's typical behaviour in that situation.

Representative sample is a sample in which the population surveyed resembles the larger population about which data are being gathered.

Socially desirable responding occurs when a research participant responds in a way that they think the interviewer would like, that is, telling the interviewer what they want to hear.

Specimen record is a record of everything that happens in a fixed period during an observational study.

Structured interviews are interview formats wherein each participant is asked the exact same set of questions in the same order.

Third variable problem refers to the fact that a correlation between two variables, X and Y, could be caused by the presence of a third variable Z, which is responsible for the relationship between X and Y.

Time sampling methods are observational techniques where a set of predetermined behaviours are recorded during a particular window of time.

Time-lag designs attempt to control for time of measurement effects such as the historical effects associated with a particular birth cohort.

Vagal tone refers to the variability in heart rate, a commonly used psychophysiological technique.

Validity threats are factors related to the design of experiments which can cause problems with the interpretation of data.

TEST YOUR KNOWLEDGE

1. Which of the following is a representative sample?

    a) A survey method that examines children longitudinally
    b) When the population surveyed resembles the larger population about which data are being gathered
    c) A measurement method for ensuring that all instances of a behaviour are recorded
    d) The group of participants in an experiment who are assigned to the control condition

2. Specimen sampling is which of the following?

    a) Where a set of predetermined behaviours are recorded during a particular window of time
    b) When all of the specimens of one sample of species are observed
    c) When researchers measure all the incidents of a behaviour during a given event
    d) When a researcher is interested in everything that a child does in a given time period

3. Which of the following is not measured in psychophysiological methods?

    a) Change in heart rate
    b) Level of blood cortisol
    c) Electroencephalographs
    d) Duration of gaze

4. A correlation of −0.70 between aggression and social skills in children tells us which of the following?

    a) High levels of aggression are associated with social skills
    b) High levels of aggression cause decreases in social skills
    c) High levels of aggression are associated with fewer social skills
    d) Social skills problems cause aggression

Suggested Reading

Cozby, P. C. (2006). *Methods in Behavioural Research* (9th edition). New York: McGraw-Hill.

Haslam, S. A., & McGarty, C. (2014). *Research Methods and Statistics in Psychology* (2nd edition). Thousand Oaks, CA: Sage.

Miller, S. (2007). *Developmental Research Methods* (3rd edition). Thousand Oaks, CA: Sage.

O'Reilly, M., Dogra, N., & Ronzoni, P. D. (2013). *Research with Children: Theory and practice.* London: Sage.

Want to learn more? For links to online resources relevant to this chapter, interactive quizzes and much more, visit the companion website at **https://edge.sagepub.com/keenan3e/**

THE BIOLOGICAL FOUNDATIONS
OF DEVELOPMENT

The Biological Foundations of Development I: Physical Growth, Motor Development and Genetics

4

Chapter Outline

LEARNING AIMS

At the end of this chapter you should:

- be aware of prenatal development, including the influence of teratogens, labour and birth, and potential birth complications
- be able to describe the developmental course of physical growth and articulate the principles which growth follows
- understand the factors which can influence physical growth and sexual maturation in adolescence
- be able to describe the course of motor development and recognize the difference between *gross* and *fine motor* development
- be able to explain the logic of behaviour genetics, twin designs, and associated concepts such as *heritability*, *niche picking*, and *range of reaction*
- be able to articulate the notion of *epigenetics*

Introduction

Biological influences in development touch on a number of important areas, which is why we have two chapters, 4 and 5, devoted to biological development. In this chapter, we will summarize prenatal development, and examine physical growth across childhood and adolescence, including motor skills in childhood and sexual maturation in adolescence.

The Course of Physical Growth

In comparison to other species, the course of physical growth in human beings is a long, drawn out process. Evolutionary theorists have suggested that our lengthy period of physical immaturity provides us with added time to acquire the skills and the knowledge which are required in a complex social world (Bjorklund, 1997). This suggestion emphasizes the fact that physical growth is not simply a set of maturational processes that operate independent of input from the environment; rather, physical growth occurs within an environmental context. Environments, including factors such as cultural practices, nutrition and opportunities for experience, play an important role in physical development.

Prenatal development

Prenatal development occurs during the nine months or so between conception – the point at which an egg has been fertilized – and birth. As we will explore, our time in the womb can have a considerable impact on our later wellbeing. The nine months of prenatal development can be characterized as involving three periods: (1) the *zygote*, which encompasses the first two weeks of life; (2) the *embryo*, from the beginning of the third week of gestation until the end of the second month; and (3) the *foetus*, the term used to describe the organism from the third month of gestation until birth. The central nervous system undergoes rapid changes during this period, and brain growth is at its peak. The foetus's body parts have developed by the end of the third month, reflexes such as swallowing are present by the fifth month, and it can open and close the eyes by the sixth month. The period between 22 and 26 weeks is called the *age of viability*, as the foetus's systems are sufficiently developed at this point that, if born prematurely, the baby has a good chance of surviving.

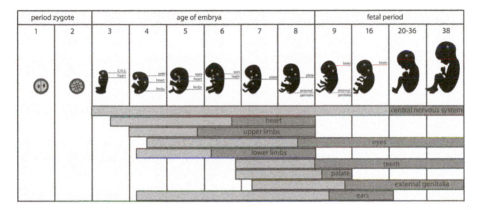

Image 4A   Growth of the human fetus in weeks

© Dragana Gerasimoski/Shutterstock

There are a number of environmental risks to the unborn baby, known as *teratogens*. These teratogens can severely damage a foetus and include a range of agents, from prescription and illegal drugs to the mother's health and stress. The effects of teratogens are dependent on a number of factors, including: *dose response* (longer and more intense exposure leads to more damage); *age* (certain growth periods in the foetus are more critical or sensitive to risk); *biology* (the genetic makeup of the mother and her child play a role; some individuals remain immune to harm); and *combinations* (the presence of many risk factors, such as poverty and poor maternal nutrition, can intensify a teratogen's effect).

Teratogens commonly affect the unborn child's physical health and may cause visible abnormalities, such as a missing limb. Damage can also be delayed or more subtle. For example, high birth weight in baby girls can result in increased risk of breast cancer in later adult life (Vatten, Mæhle, Nilsen, Tretli, Hsieh, Trichopoulos, & Stuver, 2002). It is thought the teratogenic mechanism may be an overweight expectant mother, who releases excess estrogens which promote large foetal size and changes in breast tissue, which may make the baby, when she grows up, more susceptible to breast cancer (Vatten et al., 2002). Moreover, a teratogen can have psychological and *bidirectional* consequences. For example, babies of mothers using cocaine are often born experiencing drug withdrawal, which makes them irritable and less inclined to be cuddled by their mothers. This extra stress can then impact on the mother–child bond, increasing the odds that the child will develop long-term behaviour problems (Ostrea, Ostrea, & Simpson, 1997).

Now you know what teratogens are, let's explore more about what these teratogens look like. Following is a list, by no means exhaustive, of some teratogens.

Legal and Illegal Drugs: In many cases, women take drugs during pregnancy because they do not realize yet they are pregnant, or because they are not aware of the drug's risks. You may be surprised to learn that heavy ingestion of caffeine, including tea and coffee, by expectant mothers has been associated with low birthweight and even withdrawal symptoms in newborns (Klebanoff, Levine, Clemens, & Wilkins, 2002). Heavy use of aspirin in mothers can also lead to low birth weight, lower IQ and poor motor control (Barr, Steissguth, Darby, & Sampson, 1990). These days the general public are more aware of other links, such as alcohol consumption and use of tobacco and cocaine, in pregnancy and foetal problems. The effects of drugs such as marijuana are still being studied, and although the long-term effects are unclear, researchers have noted reduced weight and size and sleep problems in babies and even later attention and memory difficulties in childhood (Fried, Watkinson, & Gray, 2003).

Well-known prescription teratogenic drugs include diethylstilbestrol (DES), which was meant to help prevent pregnant women miscarrying, and thalidomide, an antianxiety and antinausea drug. Both of these prescription drugs resulted in a range of severe foetal abnormalities and are no longer prescribed to pregnant women (Moore & Persaud, 2003). The effects of drugs are often difficult to predict. Such drugs may have severe effects in some children and less of an impact on others. The best policy for pregnant women regarding drugs, whether they are prescription, legal or illegal, is avoidance.

Can you think of some reasons why establishing the effects of specific drugs on prenatal development might be difficult?

Maternal Factors: There are certain characteristics of the mother herself that can result in risk to the child. These include maternal *age* (teenage mothers tend to live in risky environments and neglect their health, while older women may be at greater risk of bearing a Down syndrome child); *diet* (malnourishment caused by famine, poverty or dieting is perhaps one of the biggest threats to foetal development; insufficient nutrition can result in prematurity, physical and neural defects and stillbirth); *disease* (a range of diseases including mumps, rubella, diabetes and STDs can all impact negatively on the foetus); and *stress* (anxiety may lead to miscarriage, a difficult labour and greater need for childbirth anaesthesia – which itself can result in risk). The mother's emotional state is thought to affect a foetus and newborn in a number of ways. Research has shown that a pregnant woman's emotional state can cause biochemical changes that affect the foetus such that foetal levels of stress hormones mirror those of the mother (DiPietro, 2004). The research highlighted in Research Example 4.1 also demonstrates how a mother's behaviour in the form of alcohol consumption can affect childhood depression.

Research Example 4.1

Prenatal Alcohol Exposure and Child Depression

A recent study explored the relationship between a common teratogen – alcohol consumption – and children's mental health (O'Connor & Paley, 2006). We know that maternal alcohol intake is associated with a range of cognitive problems in children, including developmental delays, slowed learning and faulty memory. Physical abnormalities – usually in the head and face region – can also result. Such babies may be diagnosed as having *fetal alcohol syndrome*, a tragic condition caused by drinking during pregnancy. While the cognitive and physical effects of mothers' drinking are well documented, less is known about its psychosocial and emotional effects on children. The authors of this study therefore examined the depressive symptoms of 42 children aged 4 to 5 years-old and their mothers' reported alcohol consumption during pregnancy. Mother–child interactions were also assessed.

The results showed:

- The higher the mother's alcohol consumption, the more depressive symptoms in children and the smaller the child's head circumferences (consistent with fetal alcohol syndrome)
- Child negative affect was associated with less maternal emotional connection
- The results held even when considering the mother's current drinking patterns and current depressive symptoms

The authors concluded that moderate to heavy alcohol exposure is a risk factor for children's later depression, and some of this effect may occur through the impact of a negative mother–child relationship.

While the results are quite compelling, you may want to note that the study involved a correlational design, which limits what we can say about the cause and effect of alcohol consumption. What must the authors do to ensure they can make valid conclusions about the causal relationship between mothers' alcohol intake and children's mental health? (Hint: you may want to turn to Chapter 3.)

Environmental Agents: Radiation has long been known to cause problems in foetal development, which is why pregnant women are no longer given x-rays. Other environmental toxins include lead, mercury, herbicides, pesticides, and even some decongestants (Werler, 2006). A father's exposure to toxins such as radiation, anaesthetic gases or lead can cause harm to the developing foetus. Occupations that involve such exposure can result in men developing chromosomal abnormalities that can lead to their partners miscarrying or giving birth to infants with birth defects (Friedler, 1996). These findings indicate that both parents must evaluate their exposure to teratogens to ensure their baby's safety.

Fetal learning

Research on teratogens clearly shows that the fetus is sensitive to influences in the womb. The fetus is also capable of learning, especially during the last trimester of pregnancy. Research into the early stages of how we start responding to information from our environments is called *fetal origins*. Exciting studies in this field have demonstrated that far from being an inert lump, the developing fetus is an active and dynamic creature responding to and learning from the rich sources of information that filter in through the amniotic fluid and placenta. Such research has demonstrated that developing babies can hear, are sensitive to human voices, and are attracted to the voice of their mother while still in utero. A recent collaborative study between Canadian and Chinese researchers tested 60 women in the final stages of their pregnancy. Mothers were videotaped as they read aloud a poem: half the foetuses heard the recording of their mother, the other half heard recordings of a mother, but not their own mother. The heart rate of foetuses listening to their mothers accelerated, while the heart rates of foetuses listening to a stranger decelerated, indicating they were paying close attention. In other words, the developing babies were trying to figure out who was speaking when they heard the stranger speaking (Kisilevsky et al., 2003). The findings indicate that even before birth we have capacity for attention, memory and sensitivity to language.

Other senses are also being primed for learning. Tastes and smells develop while in the uterus. One study demonstrated that if mothers ate anise flavour while pregnant, their newborns (at days 1 and 4) showed more attraction to an anise-scented cotton swab presented under their noses than infants whose mothers did not consume anise. Obviously the researchers couldn't simply ask the babies and had to rely on behavioural signals, including whether infants moved their heads towards or away from the scent and facial expressions using a well-validated facial configuration measure (which included nose wrinkling, just like in adults) (Schaal, Marlier, & Soussignan, 2000). It is also known that if a mother eats garlic while she is pregnant, the baby will show less aversion to garlic after they are born.

Birth

Labour and delivery represent a significant milestone in the lives of parents and infants. Once babies enter the world, they are exposed to all kinds of stimuli, learning experiences and relationships. However, the process of labour and delivery is an arduous one. Millions of women deliver healthy infants, but birth can be associated with a number of complications. Since the 1970s, when having a baby in a sterile hospital environment was the norm, natural and alternative childbirths have become increasingly popular (Eberhard & Geissbühler, 2000). The father's role in delivery and childrearing has also changed, with many more men today being present at their child's delivery. Research suggests that having a supporter makes the experience of childbirth more positive for women (Mackey, 1995). A study conducted in Greece has shown that a father's attendance at the birth is associated with an increased bond with the infant (Dragonas, 1992).

Despite many women's preference for a home or home-like birth, complications can occur. These include anoxia (a lack of oxygen to the foetus's brain), which can lead to brain damage and even death, and incorrect positioning of the foetus which precludes natural delivery. Male babies are more likely to experience complications, perhaps due to their larger size and the greater pressure on their heads during birth (Berk, 2006). When complications occur, medical intervention is often required. Caesarean deliveries (C-sections), in which the baby is removed through an incision in the mother's abdomen, can be used electively, but are often reserved for deliveries with complications. For normal deliveries, Caesarean births may double both the mother's and infant's complications, including the risk of infection and extended hospitalization, and babies being at risk of breathing problems and reduced short-term responsiveness (Villar, Carroli, Zavaleta, Donner, Wojdyla et al., 2007).

How do we assess the wellbeing of newborns? The most common method for determining how an infant is faring is the *Apgar scoring system* (Apgar, 1953). Medical staff assess the infant's heart rate, respiratory rate, muscle tone, reflexes and skin tone both one and then five minutes after birth. A score of 0, 1 or 2 is given to each of the five signs with a total score yielded. A total score of 7 to 10 indicates a favourable condition, while a score of 4 or less tells medical staff that the infant needs emergency intervention.

Prematurity

The term *premature* is used when a baby is born before the full-term gestational period of 38 weeks. These babies typically have a low birth-weight, often weighing less than 5lbs (compared to a full-term baby, which often weighs 7lbs or more). Premature babies may have to remain in hospital for extended periods as they often cannot survive without assistance. Premature babies may also lag on physical and cognitive development milestones. Although most catch up by the time they are 4 years-old, babies who were born with very low birth weights commonly continue to show deficits (Goldberg & DiVitto, 2002). One study conducted in Norway found that babies born during 28–30 weeks gestation are at particular risk of long-term problems, including a forty-six-fold higher risk of cerebral palsy (a group of disorders that involve various nervous system functions, including perception, cognition and movement), a seven-fold higher risk of autism (see Chapter 13) and a four-fold risk of mental retardation (Moster, Lie, & Markestad, 2008). The later the gestational age, the fewer the risks compared to full-term babies, but even babies born at 37 weeks have comparatively elevated health and cognitive risks. However, the long-term outcomes for premature infants can also be affected by the psychosocial environment in which they are raised, and there is evidence that if they are raised in a stimulating and positive home environment and the parents receive appropriate support from health, education and social services, this can facilitate developmental recovery. Typically, infants raised in such environments have better outcomes in terms of cognitive and motor skills and fewer behavioural problems compared to preterm infants raised in unstable and socioeconomically disadvantaged homes (see for example, Jefferis, Power, & Hertzman, 2002; Robert et al., 1994). Although many preterm births are spontaneous (and these rates are climbing, with limited evidence of why), some are preventable and involve medically inducing labour. Close to 10% of medically induced births before 37 weeks are done in the USA without strong medical reasons, such as complications with a prior pregnancy (Engle & Kominiarek, 2008). This is a critical area that needs addressing in the maternal–child health field.

Patterns of growth

Physical growth does not proceed randomly; instead, it follows orderly patterns known as **cephalocaudal** and **proximodistal development**. The cephalocaudal pattern of development refers to the fact that growth occurs in a head-to-toe direction. For example, two months after conception the human infant's head is very large in contrast to its total height, and by birth this ratio is much smaller as the rate of growth in the rest of the body begins to catch up. Within the head itself the eyes and the brain grow faster than the jaw. These examples illustrate the head-to-toe direction of physical growth. The proximodistal pattern of development refers to the fact that development occurs outwards from the centre of the body. For example, a baby will acquire control over the muscles of the neck and trunk before it acquires control over the fingers and toes.

Body size

Changes in body size are the most obvious manifestation of physical growth. During infancy, the changes in growth are extremely rapid. An example which readily comes to mind is the dramatic changes in height. By 1 year of age infants average a growth of approximately 11 inches (approximately 32.5 cm) over their size at birth (Malina, 1975). Similarly impressive gains are noted in weight. At 2 years of age an infant's weight will have quadrupled since birth. In general, physical developments in height and weight tend to occur very rapidly in infancy, continue at a relatively steady pace throughout childhood, and then slow down towards puberty.

At puberty, there is a marked *growth spurt*, that is, a very rapid increase in size and weight. The pubertal growth spurt varies from person to person in terms of its intensity, its duration and its age of onset. The pubertal growth spurt tends to last around four and a half years, with girls usually showing their pubertal growth spurt around age 11, and in boys the same process beginning at approximately age 13. According to Tanner (1990), girls finish pubertal growth by about age 16 whereas boys continue to grow until approximately 18 years of age; however, in both sexes growth may still take place after the completion of the pubertal growth spurt.

A number of studies have provided evidence that hereditary factors play a strong role in physical growth. Work by Wilson (1986) examining correlations in a variety of physical indices showed that the correlation in height between identical twins was approximately .94 at 4 years of age, and this correlation remained stable after this time. For fraternal twins, the correlation for height was relatively high at birth but became increasingly smaller over time, moving from .77 at birth to .49 at 9 years of age (at which point it became stable). The large and stable correlations observed in identical twins and the smaller correlations observed for fraternal twins suggest that genetic factors play an important role in determining height. Similar patterns are observed for weight as well as for the timing of growth spurts (Wilson, 1986).

Environmental factors in physical growth: nutrition

Of course, genetic factors are unlikely to tell the entire story of physical growth. Growth is highly dependent on our nutritional intake, that is, what kinds of food we eat and how much of them we eat. Height and weight are clearly affected by nutritional intake.

Babies need sufficient food to grow properly, but they also need the correct kind of food. *Breastfeeding* meets a baby's quality of nutritional needs. Although bottled formula attempts to imitate the nutrients in breast milk, research indicates that nothing beats nature's formula. Breast milk provides the ideal balance of fat and proteins, helps ensure healthy growth, provides antibodies that protect against disease, protects against tooth decay (in comparison to babies who fall asleep with a bottle of sweet solution in their mouths), and helps with digestion (Fulhan, Collier, & Duggan, 2003). The benefits of breastfeeding aren't limited to physical growth and health. A recent randomized controlled trial of breastmilk versus formula indicates that breastfed babies are more likely to have higher IQs, better reading comprehension, and general increased cognitive development later in life (Kramer, Aboud, Mironova, Vanilovich, Platt, Matush et al., 2008). Guidelines from health agencies advise exclusive breastfeeding for the first six months and that breast milk is included in a baby's diet for at least one year (Satcher, 2001).

The importance of nutrition is not limited to babies. Eating enough quality food is vital for children of all ages. Studies during World War II showed that the restrictive diets imposed by wartime conditions in Europe led to a general decline in average height, reversing a trend towards increasing height which had been apparent since the end of World War I (Tanner, 1990). However, more than just our height and weight can be affected by nutritional intake: research also indicated that dietary restrictions during the war had an effect on the timing of puberty. Studies of French women showed that **menarche**, the onset of menstruation, was delayed by up to three years (Tanner, 1990).

Cognitive development has also been related to nutrition. For example, *anaemia*, the condition where a person suffers from low levels of iron in the bloodstream, has been associated with a slowing of intellectual development (Pollitt, 1994). A striking example of nutritional effects on cognitive development comes to us from the examination of intestinal worms. Intestinal worms sit in our digestive track and rob us of valuable nutrients which fuel our growth. Watkins and Pollitt (1997) showed that children who have high levels of intestinal worms have reduced performance on psychometric tests of cognitive ability. In some cases, studies have shown that these effects can be quite severe.

Healthy physical growth is not just a product of nutrition. **Psychosocial dwarfism** results from extreme emotional deprivation. Symptoms relate to physical appearance, including short stature and immature skeletal age as well as cognitive and emotional impairments, which are used to differentiate the condition from normal short stature (Voss, Mulligan, & Betts, 1998). Typically, psychosocial dwarfism results when extreme abuse and neglect interfere with the production of growth hormones. When children are removed from the abusive environment, their levels of growth hormone and stature quickly increase.

Recently, a new problem of nutrition has affected industrialized nations. Over-nutrition or childhood *obesity* (a condition in which weight is 30% or more in excess of the average weight) is a growing concern in places like North America, the UK and Australia. It is estimated that nearly 25% of American children are obese (Cowley, 2001). It is likely that weight problems are at least in part due to genetics. The weight of adopted children more closely mirrors their biological than adoptive parents (Stunkard et al., 1986). Environmental factors such as education and family income also play a role; higher education and income are associated with fewer weight problems. This may seem odd given that millions of people in developing countries are starving due to poverty. However, in wealthier counties, the association between income and thinness may be due to luxuries such as health club membership and fat-reduced food. There is also evidence of modelling, with obese children modelling the unhealthy eating of their often overweight parents. Overweight children learn consumption patterns. What parents place in front of children has an enormous impact on children's eating habits. Parents play a role in teaching children what, when and how much to eat (Rozin, 1996). Even by the age of 5, children will eat more when they are given larger portions (Rolls, Engell, & Birch, 2000). The good news is that children can also unlearn eating patterns. If children see their parents eat healthy food and are taught about nutrition, they tend to change their food choices. But such changes must occur early on to be effective. Being overweight is a life-span trend: 80% of children who are overweight will grow up to be overweight adults.

Ironically, the quest for thinness is growing in direct proportion to weight increases in children. Increasingly younger girls and boys have become preoccupied with their appearance. A recent Australian study found that among 5 to 8 year-old children, 60% of girls and 35% of boys wanted to be thinner (Lowes & Tiggemann, 2003). By the time they are 15 years-old, 70 to 80% of girls in the USA have been on at least one diet (Cowley, 2001). This struggle to be thin in the face of so much over-nutrition is associated with eating disorders, including bulimia and anorexia. A thorough discussion of these issues is outside the scope of this text, but eating disorders are affecting ever-growing numbers of young people and represent an important area of study. Girls undergoing puberty appear to be at particular risk.

Hormonal influences

In large part, the physical changes observed at puberty are controlled by **hormones**, a set of chemical substances manufactured by glands and which are received by various cells throughout the body to trigger other chemical changes. The most important of these glands is the **pituitary gland** located near the base of the brain. The pituitary gland triggers changes both directly, via the hormones it secretes into the bloodstream, which act on various tissues to produce growth, and indirectly, by triggering other glands to release different hormones.

The physical changes associated with puberty, specifically **primary sexual characteristics** (growth involving the reproductive organs: the penis, scrotum and testes in males and the vagina, uterus and ovaries in females) and the **secondary sexual characteristics** (visible changes which are associated with sexual maturation, such as the development of breasts in females, facial hair in males, and pubic hair for both males and females) are also controlled through the pituitary gland, which stimulates the release of the sex hormones. In boys, **testosterone** is released in large quantities, leading to the growth of male sexual characteristics, while in females **estrogens** are associated with female sexual maturation. Both types of hormone are actually present in both sexes although in quite different amounts.

Sexual maturation

In terms of sexual maturity, the most important changes to result are **menarche** and **spermarche**, that is, the first menstruation in females and the first ejaculation in males. These two milestones are commonly believed to indicate a readiness to reproduce, although in actuality there is often a short period of sterility which can last about one year in both females and males in which menstruation and ejaculations occur but no eggs or sperm are released (Tanner, 1990).

The factors which determine the timing of puberty are multiple and complex, ranging from genetic determination to the nature and quality of family relationships. Genetic factors are certainly involved in determining when the pituitary gland begins releasing the hormonal signals which begin the physical transformations, but interestingly these are not the sole cause of when pubertal timing occurs for an individual. In young women physical exercise can delay the onset of the physical changes associated with puberty. For example, Brooks-Gunn (1988) found that very few ballet dancers actually had their first menstruation at the 'normal' time. Family factors can also play an important role in pubertal timing. Moffitt, Caspi, Belsky and Silva (1992) found that family conflict and the absence of fathers predicted an earlier onset of menarche. Steinberg (1987) found that an increased psychological distancing between girls and their fathers also predicted an earlier menarche. Ellis and colleagues (1999) showed that the quality of fathers' investment in their daughters was positively associated with the timing of puberty: when fathers had good-quality relationships with their daughters, the onset of pubertal maturation in their daughters came later. Income and nutrition also have an effect on sexual maturation. In poor regions, menarche is generally delayed, while girls from higher-income families in these regions reach menarche up to three years earlier (Allsworth, Weitzen, & Boardman, 2005). Together, these studies highlight the importance of environmental factors in sexual maturation, demonstrating the necessity of examining interactions between genetic and environmental causes in studying development.

Besides examining the questions of when and why adolescents enter puberty earlier or later than their peers, we can ask what effects early or late maturation has on individuals. A classic study by Jones and Bayley (1950; see also Jones, 1965) suggested that early maturation carries distinct advantages for boys but not for females. Jones and Bayley tracked 16 early-maturing and 16 late-maturing boys for a six-year period. Late-maturing boys were characterized as lower in physical attractiveness and masculinity, and were rated as more childish, eager and attention-seeking than early-maturing boys. In contrast, early-maturing boys were character-ized as independent, self-confident, and as making better leaders and athletes. Jones showed that for women (Jones & Mussen, 1958) early-maturing girls were more likely to show social difficulties than late-maturing girls. They were also less popular, less self-confident, held fewer leadership positions, and were more withdrawn than late-maturing girls. More recent research has confirmed and extended these findings. Early-maturing girls tend to have a poorer body image than normally-maturing or late-maturing girls (Brooks-Gunn, 1988), at least in part because the normal weight gains which accompany pubertal maturation violate the cultural ideal for thinness. This trend is exactly the reverse for males: early-maturing boys tend to have a much more positive body image, in large part because many cultures seem to value traits like height and muscularity. Early-maturing boys clearly have a number of advantages compared to late-maturing boys, although recent research suggests there may be more to the story. Early maturing boys report more psychological stress than their later-maturing peers (Ge, Conger, & Elder, 2001) and an increased risk of risk-taking and problem behaviour since they are more likely to associate with older males (Ge, Brody, Conger, Simons, & Murray, 2002).

Behavioural problems have also been associated with early vs. late maturation, particularly in girls. The explanations for these problems seem to reduce to two types. Caspi and Moffitt (1991) argue for a *dispositional account*, believing that it is not early-maturation *per se* that creates problems for girls, but rather, early maturation on top of a previous history of behaviour problems. Their argument is that when stressful events such as early maturation occur, they may highlight dispositional factors (tendencies to behave in a particular fashion, possibly due to genetic factors or previously acquired habits). It is these dispositions which Caspi and Moffitt believe are ultimately responsible for the behaviour problems. In contrast, Graber, Brooks-Gunn and Warren (1995) believe that *psychosocial factors* – factors such as parental warmth, parental approval and the level of family conflict – play an important role in how girls react to early mat-uration. Research from Sweden has tended to support the view that psychosocial factors play a significant role in the effects of early maturation on girls (Stattin & Magnusson, 1990). These researchers found that early-maturing girls tended to have smaller networks of friends, to associ-ate with older friends who often engaged in deviant behaviours, and were more likely to engage in risky behaviours such as smoking, drinking alcohol and sexual intercourse. While the find-ings to date do suggest a risk to early-maturing girls, it is clear that contextual and psychosocial factors play an important role: not all early-maturing girls will experience problems and some early-maturing girls may show very positive developmental outcomes (Brooks-Gunn, 1988).

Motor Development

Human infants start life with very limited motor skills, yet by about 1 year of age they are walk-ing independently. In between birth and learning to walk a great many skills are acquired. What does the course of motor development in infancy look like? Nancy Bayley (1969) provides us with a description of the average age at which infants and toddlers acquire many of the most common motor skills. According to Bayley, infants can hold their heads upright by 6 weeks of age; by 2 months they can roll from their sides onto their back; by 3 months of age they can grasp an object; by 7 months infants can sit alone and begin to crawl; and by 12 months they walk on their own.

Also included in Bayley's work is a description of the age range at which 90% of children achieve a particular skill. For example, while the average infant sits upright alone by 7 months of age, 90% of infants will acquire this skill somewhere between 5 and 9 months of age. Bayley's data highlight a significant fact regarding the variability of motor development: while the sequence of motor development is relatively uniform, progress in the acquisition of motor skills is highly variable. For example, some infants will learn to walk as early as 9 months while others will not take their first steps until 17 months. It is important to remember that individual children will not conform exactly to any description of the average age at which developmental milestones are achieved: some variability is normal and early progress or lack of the same is not a good predictor of the final level of development.

Table 4.1   Selected milestones in motor development

Age	Milestone
6 weeks	Hold head upright while in a prone position
2 months	Roll from back onto side
3 months	Directed reaching for objects
5 to 7 months	Sit without support
9 to 14 months	Stand without support
8 to 12 months	Walk with support
12 months	Use of pincer grasp when reaching
12 to 14 months	Walk alone

A principle known as **differentiation** comes into play when we try to describe the acquisition of motor skills (Bühler, 1930). Differentiation refers to the fact that initially, motor skills are rather global reactions to a particular stimulus – only with time and practice do motor behaviours become more precise and adapted to particular ends. Consider an infant's reaction to having an unwanted blanket placed on top of them. A very young infant might twist and writhe in a random fashion which may or may not achieve the desired effect. Older infants will grasp the blanket and pull it away: they use a more specific, more precise behaviour to accomplish their goals. The principles of cephalocaudal and proximodistal development also apply to the acquisition of motor skills. For example, infants learn to hold their head upright before they learn to sit upright or pull themselves into a standing position.

Maturation vs. experience

The maturation of the neural and muscular systems determines to a large extent when children will acquire a particular skill. Early research on motor skills highlighted a maturationist viewpoint, that is, that development is under the control of inherited programmes that are genetic in origin (Gesell & Thompson, 1929; McGraw, 1935). These researchers were reacting against behaviourists like John B. Watson (see Chapter 2) who believed that motor skills like walking were simply conditioned reflexes. In contrast, maturationists like Gesell and McGraw believed that motor behaviours such as walking emerged according to a pre-programmed genetic timetable.

Gesell devised a simple design to demonstrate the effects of maturation. Using identical twins allowed Gesell to control for biological factors since identical twins share 100% of their genes. One twin would be given extra practice at a particular motor task while the control twin received no extra training. When tested after a period of training, *both* twins showed significant evidence of acquiring the motor skill, not simply the twin who had been given extra practice, as might be predicted (Gesell & Thompson, 1929). Such findings led Gesell to the conclusion that maturation and not experience was the prime factor in determining when children acquire skills.

However, as Thelen (1995) notes, the development of motor skill is not simply the outcome of genetic programming: transactions with the environment must play a crucial role in the timing of motor skill acquisition. Thus, an important aspect of when children acquire a particular motor skill is experience. In contrast to the work of Gesell, opportunities to practise particular motor skills have been shown to promote their earlier appearance (Zelazo, Zelazo, & Kolb, 1972). The acquisition of motor skills also varies across cultures in ways which are not consistent with genetic factors. Some cultures emphasize practices which encourage the earlier or later appearance of a skill. For example, Hopkins and Westra (1988) found that mothers in the West Indies have babies who walk considerably earlier than the average North American infant. West Indian mothers use a particular routine, passed down to them by other members of their culture, which encourages the early development of walking and other motor skills. As this example shows, environments can have important effects on when skills are acquired.

Gross and fine motor development

Bertenthal and Clifton (1998) note that control over one's motor behaviour ranks among the infant's greatest achievements. Psychologists who study the acquisition of motor skills find it useful to distinguish between **gross motor development**, that is, motor skills which help children to get around in their environment, such as crawling and walking, and **fine motor development**, which refers to smaller movement sequences like reaching and grasping. The development of motor skills has implications beyond simply learning how to perform new actions: motor skills can have profound effects on development. For example, researchers have shown that infants with locomotor experience were less likely to make errors while searching for hidden objects (Campos & Bertenthal, 1989; Horobin & Acredolo, 1986). The ability to initiate movement about one's environment stimulates the development of spatial encoding abilities, making hidden object tasks easier to solve. Rovee-Collier (1997) has made a similar point in regard to memory development. She argues that the onset of independent locomotion around 9 months of age marks an important transition in memory development. Children who can move about the environment develop an understanding of locations such as 'here' and 'there'. Because infant memory is initially highly dependent on context – that is, the similarity between the situation where information is encoded and where it is recalled – infants who have experience moving about the environment and who learn to spatially encode information become less dependent on context for successful recall. These examples show that motor development has implications beyond the immediately apparent benefits of crawling or walking.

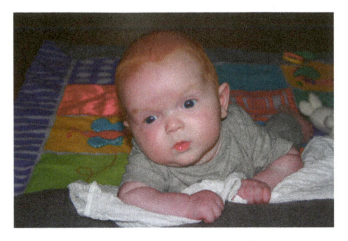

Image 4B Children who can move about the environment develop an understanding of locations

Piaget (1952) argued that the development of reaching and grasping was a key aspect of cognitive development because it formed an important link between biological adaptation and intellectual adaptation. Reaching and grasping are voluntary actions under the infant's control, and as such, they open up exciting new possibilities in their ability to explore their environment. An infant who reaches for and grasps an object in order to explore it pushes their development forward as they engage in processes such as adapting their grip to the size and shape of the object. Piaget argued that these early processes of assimilation and accommodation to objects drove cognitive development in the sensorimotor period.

The development of reaching begins early in life. Newborn infants seated in an upright position will swipe and reach towards an object placed in front of them, a behaviour labelled **prereaching**. These poorly coordinated behaviours start to decline around 2 months of age (Bower, 1982) and are replaced by **directed reaching**, which begins at about 3 months of age (Thelen, Corbetta, Kamm, Spencer, Schneider, & Zernicke, 1993). At this time reaching becomes more coordinated, efficient and improves in accuracy (Bushnell, 1985). According to research conducted by Clifton, Rochat, Robin and Berthier (1994), the infant's reaching does not depend simply on the guidance of the hand and arm by the visual system, but is controlled by **proprioception**, the sensation of movement and location based on stimulation arising from bodily sources such as muscle contractions. By about 9 months of age infants can adjust their reaching to take into account a moving object. However, 9 month-olds are far from expert reachers and a good deal of skill remains to develop.

Once infants begin reaching they also begin to grasp the objects that are the target of their reaches. The **ulnar grasp** is seen when infants first engage in directed reaching. This is a primitive form of grasping in which the infant's fingers close against their palm. The fingers seem to act as a whole, requiring the use of the palm in order to hold an object. Shortly after this accomplishment, when infants can sit upright on their own, they acquire the ability to transfer objects from hand to hand. By around the end of the first year, infants have graduated to using the **pincer grasp** (Halverson, 1931) wherein they use their index finger and their thumb in an opposable manner, resulting in a more coordinated and finely-tuned grip. This allows for the exploration of very small objects or objects which demand specific actions for their operation, such as the knobs on a stereo system, which require turning to the left or right to adjust volume.

Motor development as a dynamic system

You may remember from Chapter 2 that dynamic systems theories stress interactions that make up a complete system. Dynamic systems have been used to understand motor development, by seeing mastery of motor skills as involving a complex system of actions. Thus, different motor skills combine in new and increasingly effective ways. We can understand the combinations that create many motor skills. For example, control of the head and chest allows infants to sit with support; kicking, rocking and reaching combine to allow the infant to crawl; and crawling, standing and stepping combine to produce the ability to walk (Thelen, 1989). Each set of developments unites a number of factors: muscle development, the child's goal and environmental support. Imagine if we lived underwater and how this might affect children's motor skills: it is likely that limbs would develop to support a swimming motion, the child's goal would be to move through water and the environment would support the motion of swimming rather than crawling or walking. A number of elements combine to produce what we call motor skills.

Babies must practise their skills and in doing so they often come up with novel ways around problems, which is why not all infants and children develop the same skills in the same set of ways. For example, some babies do not like to be on their stomachs, and will learn to sit and pull themselves to standing, thereby learning to walk before crawling. Toddlers practise learning to walk for up to six hours a day (Adolph, Vereijken, & Shrout, 2003). That's quite some homework! Through such repetition of movements, new connections in the brain develop to solidify the skill needed to walk.

Cross-cultural research provides further evidence for a dynamic system view of motor skills by showing that opportunity for movement and a supportive environment lead to motor development. For example, mothers in developing countries tend to encourage infant walking at an earlier age than mothers in North America and Britain. One thought is that parents in developing countries place value on their child's physical strength as strength is likely to equate to survival. Thus, in places such as Kenya, mothers vigorously exercise their babies and leave infants sitting alone to explore their environment, providing plenty of time to practise motor skills (Keefer, Dixon, Tronick, & Brazelton, 1991). These infants typically develop the ability to walk early on, often much before children in places such as North America. However, it has also been shown that when mothers of newborns in the United States give their babies practice in a stepping motion, even for a few minutes a day, those babies are more likely to walk early than a control group (Zelazo, Zelazo, & Kolb, 1972).

Together, this research suggests that motor development results from an interaction between nature and nurture. Consistent with a dynamic systems view, it seems that genes provide the basic blueprint for motor skills, but the exact way that motor skills are acquired results from a complex interplay of the brain, body movement and environmental supports.

The development of motor skills beyond infancy

Beyond infancy, not a great deal is known about the development of motor skills. Gallahue (1989) suggests that, beyond infancy, three fundamental sets of motor skills emerge in the child's repertoire. These are *locomotor movements*, which include walking, running, jumping, hopping, skipping and climbing; *manipulative movements*, including throwing, catching and kicking; and *stability movements* (centred on controlling one's body), including bending, stretching, rolling, balancing and walking on one's hands.

The development of motor skills progresses through three stages (Gallahue, 1989). Consider an example such as learning to swing a tennis racquet. Initially, a child tries to execute the motor skill; however, they fail to follow through with the movement. They also fail to engage in any sort of anticipatory movements which prepare them to execute the action. A young child's stroke often looks more like a swipe, barely resembling the straight-armed, locked-wrist style that mature players use. By the second stage, what we might think of as a transitional stage in the development of the skill, children can execute the individual components of the swing more competently; however, they fail to organize the components into a smoothly sequenced whole. At this stage children may adopt a straight arm, start with their racquet well behind their body and follow through, but on any given swing they are unlikely to execute all three of these aspects of an accomplished stroke together. Finally, by the third stage all components of the behaviour are integrated into a coordinated whole. Motor skills continue to improve as related developments in the sensory and perceptual skills, as well as the maturation of the nervous system, take place. However, increased practice will speed children's acquisition of a skilled behaviour.

Genetics

Consider your own siblings or a friend you know who has brothers or sisters: are you or your friend exactly the same as your or their brother or sister? The answer (even if you have an identical twin) is probably 'no'. Siblings share half their genes with each other; that is, half of your genetic material is the same as your brother's or sister's, but these shared genes are not enough to ensure a high degree of similarity. This is because genes interact with the environment to produce observable characteristics such as eye colour, and height or behaviours such as personality and intelligence. When we speak of an individual's **genotype**, we refer to their genetic makeup, that is, the particular set of genes they have inherited from their parents. As a result of development, environments act on individuals to produce their **phenotype**, that is, their observable characteristics.

In our discussion of genetics and human development, we will take for granted that by this point in your career you have acquired an understanding of sexual reproduction and instead will focus on the key genetic aspects of the process. At conception, a single sperm from males unites with the **ovum** or egg from the female to create a fertilized egg called a **zygote**. Sperm and egg are unique cells in that they are the only cells in the human body to carry 23 **chromosomes** (all other cells carry 46 chromosomes). These special cells are known as **gametes**. Chromosomes are a very special chemical structure made up of a series of proteins known as deoxyribonucleic acid or **DNA**. They have a thread-like appearance and are found in the nucleus of a cell. Chromosomes come in 23 pairs; half of these come from the mother and half from the father. The chromosomes carry the **genes** which are the units of hereditary transmission. Genes are sequences of proteins, a part of the DNA molecule. They work by triggering the production of proteins when instructed to do so by environmental signals or by other genes.

Remember that chromosomes come in pairs, one from the father and one from the mother. Thus, a gene on one chromosome has a partner or an alternate form on the other chromosome. This alternate form of the gene is called an **allele**. To further complicate matters, the alleles of a gene from both parents can be similar or dissimilar in their genotype. If the alleles are alike, the child is said to be **homozygous** for the trait coded for by the gene; if the genes are dissimilar, the child is **heterozygous**. Homozygous children will display the trait which is coded for by the genes whereas the relationships between the two alleles will determine how the trait is expressed for heterozygous children. Consider eye colour as an example. The genes which code for eye colour can have different forms, an allele which specifies blue eyes and an allele which specifies brown eyes. If the child's parents both carry the blue-eyed allele, the child will have blue eyes.

The relationships between alleles are described in terms of **dominant** and **recessive** alleles. In some cases, one allele is more powerful or dominant than another and will always express its effects over those of another allele. This is the case for hair colour. The brown hair allele is dominant over the red hair allele. Thus a child who inherits a red hair allele from one parent and a brown hair allele from the other will always develop brown hair. If we represent a dominant allele by **A** and a recessive allele by **a**, then you should recognize that a person could have the following combinations of alleles: **AA**, **Aa**, **aA** and **aa**. These reduce to three patterns: **AA** is homozygous and represents two dominant genes; **Aa** and **aA** are heterozygous and represent combinations where the dominant gene will be expressed; the combination **aa** is again homozygous and represents a person with two recessive genes. In our example of hair colour, this is the *only* combination of genes which would result in a red-haired child. There is yet another possibility which can occur, called **codominance**. Codominance occurs when heterozygous alleles both express their traits with equal force. For example, the blood types A and B are codominant alleles such that a person who inherits the A allele from one parent and the B allele from the other will have the blood type AB.

Many harmful traits coded for by genes are recessive, a fact which has the happy effect of greatly reducing their occurrence in the population. An example of this is the allele for **phenylketonuria** or **PKU**. This is a genetic disorder in which the child is unable to metabolize a protein called phenylalanine, a problem which can lead to brain damage and profound mental retardation. The allele which codes for the normal metabolizing of phenylalanine is dominant while the gene which leads to PKU is recessive. When both parents carry the recessive allele for PKU there is a one in four chance that their offspring will have the disorder (as we described above).

Genes and environments

In contemporary developmental psychology, rarely will one find a psychologist taking up a position that emphasizes either genes or environments as the sole cause of behaviour. Instead, modern psychologists recognize that genes and environments *interact* to shape the course of development.

Research has shown clearly how genetic factors serve to restrict the range of possible courses that development can take, while at the same time we have gained an ever more sophisticated understanding of how environments exert a tremendous influence on development, both supporting and restricting it.

We also know that genes can shape environments. This may strike you as an odd idea, one which violates your intuitive notions of the direction in which biological effects should go. According to the work of Sandra Scarr (1992, 1996; Scarr & McCartney, 1983), genes can have effects on the environment in at least three ways. First, genes can have what Scarr referred to as *passive* effects. Children's environments are most often dictated by parents. Because parents and children share some of their genes, it is not surprising that parents will create a home environment which is supportive of the child's genotype. Consider musical talent. Musical parents will likely have musical children. As a result of their own predisposition, musical parents will create a musical environment for their children. Thus, the parent's efforts provide an ideal environment for the child's genes which code for musical talent to be expressed. Second, genes may have an *evocative* relationship with the environment. This occurs when some trait in the child causes others to react in a certain way which has the effect of strengthening the trait. For example, temperamentally 'easy' babies who smile and act sociably will elicit positive social reactions from others which reinforces the baby's behaviours and ultimately strengthens their genetic predisposition. Finally, genes can affect the environment in an *active* way. This occurs when children seek out environments that are compatible with their genetic makeup. For example, athletically talented children will eventually move towards participation in school sports while musically talented children will join the band. This process, which Scarr (1996) calls **niche picking**, is an active process based on one's genetic predisposition. As Scarr notes, niche picking increases in importance as people move towards adulthood and begin to take increasing control over their own environments. This process may also play a role in explaining why correlations for traits such as cognitive ability show increasing concordance over time.

Can you think of any examples from your own life that might be examples of niche picking? Consider aspects such as your hobbies, sporting activities, school performance or career choice.

As suggested earlier, environments also have profound effects on genetic factors. One way in which this relationship has been conceptualized is through the concept of **range of reaction** (Gottesman, 1963). According to the range of reaction concept, genes do not fix behaviour in a rigid fashion but establish a range of possibilities which depend heavily on environmental circumstances. In a sense, you can think of a person's genotype as placing boundaries on their ability which differ depending on environmental circumstances. For example, if a child is born into an impoverished environment, their genotype may place specific limits on how far their cognitive abilities may develop. This child may show very low ability under impoverished environments and only slightly higher levels of achievement under more enriched environments. In this case, we would say the child has a small range of reaction. In contrast, another child with a different genotype may perform slightly better in impoverished environments but extremely well under an enriched environment. This child would show a much larger range of reaction.

The reaction range concept has been criticized by Gilbert Gottlieb (1991; Gottlieb, Wahlsten, & Lickliter, 1998). Gottlieb suggests that genes play a much less deterministic role than is suggested by the range of reaction concept, which emphasizes the limit-setting effect of genes. He argues that genes and environments engage in a process of *coaction* wherein the relationships between genes, environments and other levels of behaviour, such as neural activity, all mutually influence one another. The influences between any levels are bidirectional, that is, they go both ways. Thus, genes are simply part of a system which are affected by events at other levels of the system.

Behaviour genetics

Thus far we have covered cases of genetic transmission that conform to a simple model where a gene is causally related to a particular trait, such as eye colour. However, most behaviours that are inherited are multifactorial, that is, they have more than one cause. When some trait is affected by more than one gene, geneticists speak of **polygenetic inheritance**. Given the state of genetic research, it is very difficult at this point in time to specify exactly which genes contribute to some trait, but researchers are beginning to make some progress in this regard. More often than not, researchers are only able to specify how important genetic factors are relative to environmental factors in the cause of some particular trait, that is, how much of the variance in a given trait is caused by genetic factors and how much is caused by environmental factors. This area of inquiry, examining the relationship between genetic and environmental factors, is known as **behaviour genetics**.

We know genetic factors play a critical role in human development. For example, researchers have identified a form of a gene which, if present in an individual, increases the risk of developing Alzheimer's disease by a factor of four over the normal population (Plomin, DeFries, McClearn, & Rutter, 1997). Beyond such high-profile cases as a genetic cause for Alzheimer's, behaviour geneticists have shown that genetics play important roles in the development of psychological traits, such cognitive abilities, school achievement, personality, self-esteem and drug use. In the following section we will examine some of the findings from behaviour genetic research.

Heritability

Behaviour geneticists employ a concept known as **heritability** to measure the effects of genetic factors on a trait. Essentially, heritability is an estimate of the relative influence of genetic versus environmental factors. According to Plomin et al. (1997: 79), heritability can be defined as 'the proportion of phenotypic variance that can be accounted for by genetic differences among individuals'. It is estimated by examining the correlations for some trait among relatives and is generally expressed as an *intraclass correlation*, that is, a correlation which can be straightforwardly interpreted as a percentage. In other words, an intraclass correlation of .80 between identical twins for IQ would suggest that 80% of the variance in IQ scores between the twins was due to genetic factors.

Heritability has been criticized as a concept by many authors. Bronfenbrenner (1972) demonstrated that heritability cannot be straightforwardly interpreted as simply an index of genetic causation. In his analyses, Bronfenbrenner shows how environmental factors have a clear impact on the calculation of heritability. While not at all refuting the importance of genetic factors in development, Bronfenbrenner's argument is that heritability should be interpreted as reflecting the capacity of the environment to invoke and nurture the development of a trait. In his critique of research on racial differences in intelligence, Block (1995) questions the common assumption that heritability is simply an index of genetic causation. Block points out that heritability is calculated as a ratio of *genetically caused* variation to *total variation* in some trait. Again, while not refuting the importance of genetic factors in human development, Block's argument is that a characteristic can be highly heritable even if it is not caused by genetic factors. Take a trait such as long hair. Block would argue that in 1950 long hair was caused genetically. That is, in western cultures only women wore long hair, and since women are genetically different from men, the cause of wearing long hair could be construed as genetic. The ratio of genetic variation (sex: men or women) to total variation (women: only women wore long hair) was close to one, indicating high heritability. However, now that variability in who wears their hair long (as both men and women commonly do these days) has increased, the heritability of long hair has decreased. However, neither in 1950 or today is wearing long hair genetically determined in the normal sense. Men did not usually wear long hair in the 1950 due to strong social pressures to conform (i.e. environmental reasons): when the environmental reasons change, so to does the heritability of the trait. While this example may seem frivolous, the point it makes is very important to how we interpret heritability. The student of developmental psychology needs to remember that heritability does not necessarily imply genetic causation.

Epigenetics

Research uncovering the intricate relationship between genes and environment has taken a new, exciting turn of late. While traditional geneticists have examined the interactions of genes and environment upon behaviour, and even the impact of DNA on the individual's environment (such as through niche picking, discussed above), an exciting new question asks whether the environment can actually change a person's genes. It seems the answer is yes, and this emerging field is referred to as the study of *epigenetics*.

How can one's experiences cause permanent genetic changes? In response to certain signals, epigenetic modifications can essentially turn off a region of DNA. This occurs through chemical changes that affect the shape of the particular piece of DNA so that the protein encoded by that gene cannot be made. Furthermore, when cell division occurs and the DNA is copied, the epigenetic changes are copied as well so that all future versions of the cell contain the epigenetic change – thus, permanently changing the genetic makeup. Recent work has revealed that even transient environmental influences can cause long-lasting changes to DNA under this process. Epigenetic influences also explain why identical twins do not always look exactly the same, despite sharing identical DNA.

At this stage, most of the epigenetics research has been done using animal models and we have yet to understand the full range of epigenetic influences on human DNA. Nonetheless, this early research has had profound implications for understanding how impoverished or enriched environments can permanently alter not just the genetic course of the affected individual, but that of their descendants also.

Some of the more interesting findings using animal models examine how when epigenetic modifications occur in sperm or eggs, they impact on future generations. Female mice that spent two weeks of their youth in an enriched environment that included access to a variety of stimulating rat puzzles and toys displayed superior learning skills as adults than rats reared in a regular laboratory environment. Moreover, their pups did too. The pups of the enriched environment rats even showed this advantage when they were raised by a foster mother and did not receive any enriching environmental experiences themselves. It seems the pups were smarter as a result of their mother's rich – albeit briefly so – environment, which was then passed down through epigenetic processes in her DNA (Arai, Li, Hartley, & Feig, 2009). A further landmark epigenetic study is discussed in Research Example 4.2.

It is likely that similar epigenetic mechanisms are at play in the developing human. We know that child maltreatment is associated with a host of problems in adulthood, including anxiety and depression. The association in both rats and humans between persistent behaviours and early life experience suggests that there is some kind of chemical process that serves as a memory of these early life experiences in animals across species (Suderman et al., 2012). There is evidence that through epigenetic processes, early life experiences can alter rat and human DNA as it relates to the stress response (McGowan et al., 2009). Similar to the processes described in Research Example 4.2, early life stress leaves a permanent mark on our genetic makeup, essentially turning on markers of reactivity and increasing an individual's sensitivity to future stress (Labonté et al., 2012). That's not to say the news is all bad. We know from our previous discussion that environments and genes play out in a complex back and forth manner, and just because stress may turn on a stress reactive gene process, this doesn't mean we can't learn coping techniques and ways to adapt later in life. Environments can change our genes, but we also know that genetic information doesn't set our future behaviour in stone.

An additional implication of our DNA's sensitivity to early environmental threat involves seeing the process as an adaptive function. Perhaps we have been shaped to respond to subtle variations in parental behaviour as a forecast of things to come; that is, perhaps in some instances having a reactive stress system 'turned on' from early stress sets up the individual to recognize and survive in a stressful environment (Meaney, 2001). It may be easy to see this in terms of rat survival, such that pups born into stressed, low grooming families grow up to be reactive to stress, vigilant of their surroundings, and perhaps better able to cope and survive in a realistic rat world (one that isn't a safe laboratory) filled with threat and danger and limited food. However, the situation may seem more unfortunate when considering human requirements. Arguably, most of us live in a safe (in relative rat terms) world, one that requires some vigilance for a threat to our survival, but where high reactivity and hypervigilance are associated with unfortunate outcomes, including poor mental and physical health.

We are inclined to think of inheritance as concerning fixed, stable traits written down in the genetic code passed down to us through eggs and sperm at the time of conception. However, these landmark epigenetic studies show us that a mother rat can write information into her pups' DNA in a way that has nothing to do with the traditional way of creating DNA, through eggs and sperm. The mother rat's behaviour actually programmes her pups' genetic material so that they are more likely to succeed in the world they are born into. The epigenetic code provides a level of flexibility in the genome that brings a complex and fascinating level to the field of genetics.

Research Example 4.2

A Mother's Lick

A fascinating study from a group of Canadian scientists has demonstrated the epigenetics of stress (Weaver et al., 2004). This study involved examination of the rates that mother rats licked their pups (the equivalent of human mothers cuddling, stroking or holding their babies). Some rat mothers extensively lick and groom their pups, while others ignore their offspring. Pups that receive attention during the first week of life tend to display calm, non-reactive behaviours, while those that were ignored grow up to be anxious and more prone to disease. The relationship seems straightforward enough, but the mechanics of how this occurs are fascinating. The differences in behaviour reflect different genetic processes at play in the two groups of mother–infant rat pairs. At birth, one of the genes responsible for the body's stress response, known as the glucocortocoid receptor (GR) gene, is highly inactive – or, in scientific speak, it is *methylated*. In the group of sensitive rat mothers, the authors were able to demonstrate that the pups' GR gene demethylated, making the gene more active, and resulting in the pups becoming more relaxed. The opposite was true for the ungroomed pups: these babies did not express the GR gene, and consequently responded poorly to stress. Such tendencies, if left unchecked, persisted, and the pups were more or less anxious as adults depending on whether their mother was a high or low licker.

To directly examine the cause–effect relationship between maternal behaviour and DNA methylation, the scientists performed an adoption study, cross-fostering the rat pups. Biological offspring of low-nurturing mothers were reared by high-nurturing mothers and the results showed they ended up having a similar genetic expression as the normal offspring of high-nurturing mothers, while the converse was true; biological offspring of high-nurturing mothers reared by non-licking mothers resembled the biological babies of the non-licking mothers. The researchers had demonstrated that an environmental condition – maternal care – directly altered the genetic material of an individual.

It may be tempting to think of the high-grooming rats as 'good mothers'. However, as discussed above, this rules out the possibility that early environmental factors provide a forecast for the survival skills babies will need. In fact, both groups of mothers are matching their pups' adult behaviour to likely future conditions. In effect, both the high- and low-licking mothers are preparing their babies for conditions to come.

Research designs in behaviour genetics

Most commonly, heritability is estimated using *twin studies*. In one common twin study design, the correlation on some trait (for example, intelligence) is measured between pairs of **monozygotic twins** and **dizygotic twins**. Monozygotic twins are born of the same fertilized egg, a zygote which has split in half, and thus they share 100% of their genes. Dizygotic or fraternal twins develop in the womb at the same time but are of two different fertilized eggs, and as a consequence they share only 50% of their genes. If one makes the assumption that the environments of identical twins are no different from the environments of fraternal twins, then higher correlations for the trait between identical twins are thought to be the result of their genetic similarity. It is important to note that this conclusion is based on an assumption of equal environments between identical and fraternal twins. Bronfenbrenner (1972) highlighted the reasons why this assumption is problematic. Think for yourself about this issue. Do you think identical twins might be treated differently from fraternal twins in some way? If you bring to mind issues such as parents dressing twins exactly alike or friends and relatives confusing identical twins, then you have identified some of the factors that Bronfenbrenner felt might be problematic for the twin design and which violate the equal environments assumption. Again, while such problems pose issues for how exactly we interpret the findings from behaviour genetic research, they by no means suggest that genetic factors are unimportant determinants of human development.

A large number of behaviour genetic studies have been conducted to examine the heritability of intelligence. A review of many of these studies by Bouchard and McGue (1981) showed that the average correlation between same-sex pairs of monozygotic twins measured for general intelligence was .86. A correlation of .62 was obtained for fraternal twins. Both of these results indicate a substantial effect for genetic factors (although keep in mind the potential interpretative problems discussed earlier). When Bouchard and McGue examined the findings for twins reared apart, the correlation dropped to .72, again, indicating a substantial role for genetic factors. Further work on the importance of genetic factors across the life span has come to the intriguing conclusion that genetic factors become more salient to explaining the correlations between the IQ scores of twins as time goes on. In other words, as age increases so does the correlation for general intelligence between twins (DeFries, Plomin, & Fulker, 1994; Plomin, Pedersen, Lichtenstein, & McClearn, 1994; Plomin et al., 1997). As many of these researchers would note, the findings described above, while indicating a substantial role for genetic factors in the development of general intelligence, also indicate the significance of environmental factors in determining intelligence.

We now briefly consider genetic effects on personality. Behaviour genetic research in the area of personality has suggested that as much as 50% of the personality differences between people are due to genetic factors (Bouchard, 1994). Loehlin (1992) reported evidence of significant genetic effects on two commonly measured aspects of personality: *neuroticism* (emotional instability) and *extraversion* (sociability). Intraclass correlations for identical twins reared together were around .50 for both traits, suggesting a strong link between genetics and personality.

Another trait known as *sensation seeking*, which is comprised of behaviours such as thrill seeking, searching out novel experiences and susceptibility to boredom, showed a correlation of .54 in a sample of identical twins reared apart. Plomin et al. (1997) suggest that there is also strong evidence that a variety of personality disorders, such as schizotypal, obsessive-compulsive and borderline personality disorder, are all at least partially heritable.

Recent research has sought to more fully understand the interactions between genes and environment. This relationship is likely to be more complex than simple formulas or percentages can account for, as shown in the work of Thomas Boyce and Bruce Ellis on stress reactivity. Stress reactivity is the tendency to physically react to psychological stressors (think of a shy person just told he must stand up in front of the class to give an impromptu speech and you get an idea of the extreme end of stress reactivity). Using an evolutionary-developmental model, Boyce and Ellis (2005) suggest that reactivity has genetic and environmental elements; however, a more useful way to look at the equation is to think about how genetic and environmental factors result in the *calibration* of a response system. That is, highly reactive phenotypes (children showing stress reactions) have a biological sensitivity to context. To illustrate, imagine a child born with the genotype to be reactive. If this child is placed in a stressful environment, the odds of the child developing into a calm, socially fearless individual are low. However, if the same child is placed in an environment that is highly protected, a similar sensitivity to stress is likely to result. Thus, for stress reactivity to be high, an individual must be predisposed to stressful environmental influences: exposure to a highly stressful or protective environment then locks in the stressed tendencies. Research has confirmed this theory. Ellis, Essex and Boyce (2005) examined the physiological stress reactions and family life of 249 children. A disproportionate number of children in stressful *and* supportive, low-stress environments displayed high autonomic reactivity (such as high heart rate and stress cortisol levels).

Summary

Perhaps the most noticeable aspect of development is physical maturation and growth. From the moment of conception, the developing baby undergoes enormous physical changes, eventually reaching the near adult size and sexual maturation of adolescence. The course of development doesn't always run smooth, however, and the foetus is at particular risk of damaging and life-threatening influences called teratogens. Genetic and environmental factors, including nutrition and stress, interact over the course of a child's life, leading to individual differences in height, weight and pubertal timing. Another aspect of children's physical development is motor skills, which progress from simple movements such as reaching and grasping in infancy and toddlerhood, to jumping, walking and the mastery of sports in childhood and adolescence. Recent developments in the field of genetics, and particularly epigenetics, sheds light on the complex interplay of DNA and experience in our physical, and also social, emotional and cognitive development.

Glossary

Allele refers to the alternate form of a gene.

Behaviour genetics is the area of inquiry examining the relationship between genetic and environmental factors in development.

Cephalocaudal development refers to the idea that physical growth occurs in a head to toe direction.

Chromosomes are very special chemical structures, found in the nucleus of a cell, which are made up of a series of proteins known as deoxyribonucleic acid or DNA.

Codominance occurs when heterozygous alleles both express their traits with equal force.

Differentiation refers to the fact that, initially, motor skills are rather global reactions to a particular stimulus and only become more precise and adapted to particular ends with time.

Directed reaching describes reaching which has become more coordinated, efficient and has improved in accuracy.

Dizygotic twins develop at the same time but from two different fertilized eggs; otherwise known as fraternal twins.

Dominant refers to the fact that one allele for a trait is more powerful than another and will always express its effects over those of another allele.

Estrogens are hormones that are associated with female sexual maturation.

Fine motor development refers to small movement sequences like reaching and grasping.

Gamete is a reproductive cell, containing only one copy of each chromosome.

Genes are the units of hereditary transmission. A gene refers to a portion of DNA located at a particular site on the chromosome.

Genotype is our genetic makeup, that is, the particular set of genes we have inherited from our parents.

Gross motor development refers to the various motor skills, such as crawling and walking, which help children move around in their environment.

Heritability is an estimated measure of the relative effect of genetic factors on a trait.

Heterozygous a child is said to be heterozygous for a trait coded for by a gene if both forms of the gene are different.

Homozygous a child is said to be homozygous for a trait coded for by a gene if both forms of the gene are alike.

Hormones are a set of chemical substances manufactured by glands that are received by specialized receptor cells throughout the body which can trigger other chemical changes.

Menarche refers to the onset of menstruation.

Monozygotic twins are offspring from the same fertilized egg, otherwise known as identical twins.

Niche picking is an active process whereby one's genetic predisposition leads one to arrange the environment to suit one's disposition.

Ovum is the female germ cell which unites with a male's sperm at conception.

Phenotype refers to the observable characteristics of an organism, created by the interaction of the genotype with the environment.

Phenylketonuria (PKU) is a genetic disorder in which a child is unable to metabolize a protein called phenylalanine which can lead to brain damage and mental retardation.

Pincer grasp refers to a grasp where infants use their index finger and their thumb in an opposable manner, resulting in a more coordinated and finely-tuned grip.

Pituitary gland is a gland located near the base of the brain which triggers physical growth by releasing hormones and controls other hormone-releasing glands via its chemical secretions.

Polygenetic inheritance is said to occur when a particular trait is affected by more than one gene.

Prereaching is a behaviour wherein newborn infants seated in an upright position will swipe and reach towards an object placed in front of them.

Primary sexual characteristics refer to the reproductive organs: the penis, scrotum, and testes in males, and the vagina, uterus, and ovaries in females.

Proprioception is the sensation of movement and location based on stimulation arising from bodily sources such as muscle contractions.

Proximodistal development refers to the idea that physical growth occurs outwards from the centre of the body towards the hands and feet.

Psychosocial dwarfism is the reduction in children's height and weight due to severe emotional deprivation and abuse.

Range of reaction refers to the fact that genes do not fix behaviour in a rigid fashion but establish a range of possibilities which depend heavily on the environment.

Recessive refers to the weaker of two alleles.

Secondary sexual characteristics refer to the visible changes which are associated with sexual maturation, such as the development of breasts in females, facial hair in males, and pubic hair for both sexes.

Spermarche refers to the first ejaculation in males.

Testosterone is a male hormone which is responsible for the production of sperm and for the development of primary and secondary sexual characteristics.

Ulnar grasp is a primitive form of grasping in which the infant's fingers close against their palm.

Zygote is a fertilized egg, created by the union of a sperm and an ovum, signifying the first two weeks of life.

TEST YOUR KNOWLEDGE

1. Which of the following is not a stage in prenatal development?

    a) Zygote
    b) Foetus
    c) Embryo
    d) Teratogen

2. What is the APGAR scale?

    a) A measure of the newborn infant's condition that assesses five signs including heart rate, respiratory rate, muscle tone, reflexes and skin tone
    b) A measure of the newborn infant's condition that assesses five signs including the presence of teratogens, respiratory rate, muscle tone, reflexes and skin tone
    c) A method of determining whether a foetus is at risk of being born prematurely
    d) A type of ultrasound test that determines whether a foetus is a girl or boy

3. Which of the following is not generally involved in the timing of an individual's sexual development?

    a) Nutrition
    b) Relationships with parents
    c) Genetics
    d) Brain lateralization

4. Dynamic systems theories understand the development of motor skills as occurring through a combination of which of the following?

    a) Brain development, the child's present movement possibilities, the goal of the child, and environmental support
    b) Hormones and nutrition
    c) Genetics and environment
    d) Prenatal development, what happens as birth and parental encouragement

ANSWERS: 1–D, 2–A, 3–D, 4–A

Suggested Reading

Malina, R. M., Bouchard, C., & Oded, B. O. (2004). *Growth, Maturation, and Physical Activity* (2nd edition). Champaign, IL: Human Kinetics.

Mayo Clinic (1994). *Mayo Clinic Complete Book of Pregnancy & Baby's First Year*. New York: William Morrow and Company.

Moalem, S. (2014). *Inheritance: How our genes change our lives and our lives change our genes*. New York: Grand Central Publishing.

Thelen, E., & Smith, L. B. (1994). *A Dynamic Systems Approach to the Development of Cognition and Action*. Cambridge, MA: MIT Press.

Want to learn more? For links to online resources relevant to this chapter, interactive quizzes and much more, visit the companion website at **https://edge.sagepub.com/keenan3e/**

The Biological Foundations of Development II: The Developing Brain

5

Chapter Outline

Introduction

In this chapter we will explore the brain's neuroanatomy, from the microscopic level of individual brain cells, to the large structures of the brain, such as the cerebral cortex. It can be argued that all behaviour, thoughts and feelings are rooted in neural events, and consequently that understanding how the brain develops holds the key to unlocking the essential mysteries of human development, including why and how we grow up to learn and behave the way we do.

Moving beyond a description of brain anatomy, we will examine the emerging field of developmental neuroscience, which is concerned with how brain changes across development relate to cognitive and often social and emotional functioning.

Micro-level Structures of the Brain

The brain is made up of a number of different types of cells. **Neurons** are the name given to the nerve cells which send and receive neural impulses (electrical signals) throughout the brain and the nervous system. The average human brain is made up of some 100 billion neurons, each with as many as 15,000 connections to other cells.

The second type of cell which makes up the brain is **glial cells**. These are the cells which provide a number of important, supportive roles. Different kinds of glia are involved in differentiated tasks. Some glia line blood vessels to control which chemical messages are allowed into and out of the brain, others form the brain's defence mechanism by removing foreign matter from dying cells, and yet others have the important task of **myelination**, in which neurons are covered with an insulating layer of *myelin* (a fatty substance) which makes the neuron a more effective transmitter of electrical information (Johnson, 1998). As we will explore, although most myeli-nation happens before age 2, the process is not complete. Some changes continue into adulthood, demonstrating that development is a life-long process (Sampaio & Truwit, 2001).

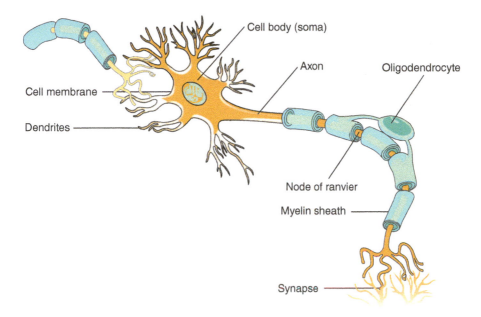

Figure 5.1 The neuron

The neuron itself is made up of **dendrites**, a **cell body**, an **axon**, and **terminal buttons** (see Figure 5.1). The dendrite is that part of the cell which receives signals from other neurons and transmits this information to the cell body. The information collected is then transmitted along the axon to the terminal buttons which send information across the **synapse** (the gap between the terminal buttons of one neuron and the dendrites of another neuron) to other neurons. This transmission across the synapse is carried out by means of special chemical signals known as **neurotransmitters**.

The development of neurons begins during the embryonic period, and most neurons are present by the seventh month after conception (Rakic, 1995). Recall that an average human brain is made up of about 100 billion neurons. This means that neurons are being generated in the brain at the rate of about 250,000 per minute in a process known as **neuron proliferation** (Kolb, Gorny, Li, Samaha, & Robinson, 2003). Neurons which are generated often travel to other locations in the brain, guided by a set of complex and rather extraordinary neurochemical processes known as **neural migration**. The first step in the brain's wiring process occurs well before birth, with the fetus's billions of neurons sending out axons in the beginning stages of neural migration. Some of the first axons must find their way alone, but subsequent axons are guided by the pathways laid down by the earliest axons. Even the early pioneer axons are helped in their navigation through various chemical signals and proteins in the brain, which essentially mark the spot where the axon should find its way to the correct neurons. Once the axon is within reach of its destination, it begins to communicate with surrounding cells to create synapses, thereby setting up the brain's communication channel. It is astounding that all of this begins in the first months of life.

The brain has a peculiar property of overproducing both neurons and synaptic connections between neurons. Such overproduction allows for two possibilities: first, it allows experience to dictate which connections between neurons are kept and which connections are lost, thereby ensuring that the child acquires all of the skills and information required to enable development to take place. Second, the overproduction of neurons and synapses ensures **plasticity** (Segalowitz, 1995). By plasticity, it is meant that the brain can compensate for early damage by either replacing connections which have been lost or transferring functions to other areas of the brain. The available evidence suggests that if brain injury occurs reasonably early in life, the likelihood of recovering the function is good (Fox, Calkins, & Bell, 1994), but the likelihood of recovery is also affected by factors such as the age at which the injury occurs, the severity of the injury, and the quality of the environment in which the child is raised (Anderson, Spencer-Smith, & Wood, 2011). We will further examine the implications of brain plasticity later in this chapter.

While the brain is genetically programmed to overproduce synapses and neurons in the early years, this overproduction is soon curtailed. This thinning of neurons and synapses (Huttenlocher, 1990, 1994; Segalowitz, 1995) is accomplished through two processes: **neuronal death**, in which some neurons are programmed to die, apparently to provide more space for crucial cell clusters, and **synaptic pruning**, in which the brain disposes of a neuron's connections to other neurons. It is thought that as synapses form, as many as 20–80% of the surrounding neurons die (De Haan & Johnson, 2003). According to Huttenlocher (1994), the goal of both processes is to increase the efficiency of transmission between neurons. Essentially, the connections that are used survive, but those that are not die off. We will take up the process of synaptic pruning later to illustrate the processes involved in the study of developmental neuroscience.

Consider how synaptic pruning can be seen as a process that is consistent with Baltes' notion that development involves both loss and gains. In considering this question, you might want to read the relevant section in Chapter 1 again.

Macro-level Structures of the Brain

Thus far we have described the structure of the brain at a micro level. Let us now consider the macro-level structure of the brain. Perhaps the most obvious change in the developing brain is its physical size, as observed by the growth of observable brain structures. At birth, an infant's brain is approximately 400 grams or 25% of the weight of an average adult brain, which weighs in at about 1400 grams (Segalowitz, 1995). By the time the infant is 6 months-old the brain weighs about half as much as an adult brain, and by age 2 it is 75% of the weight of an adult brain (Restak, 1984).

There are various ways of characterizing the structure of the brain, but one influential approach proposed by the brain researcher Paul Maclean (see for example, MacLean, 1990) divides the brain into three regions. The first region is referred to as the **reptilian brain** (as this is the area of the brain most developed in reptiles) and this consists of the *brain stem* and the *cerebellum*. This part of the brain is involved in basic survival and controls processes such as respiration, digestion and excretion. It also helps us to maintain balance and is involved in reflex behaviours. The next region is the **paleomammalian brain** and this consists of a number of structures referred to as the **limbic system**: these are concerned with the experience of emotions and memory. Finally, there is the **mammalian brain** and this part of the brain is formed by the **cerebrum** (see Figure 5.2). The cerebrum itself is made up of two **hemispheres**. These hemispheres are connected by a set of nerve fibres known as the **corpus callosum**. The left and right hemispheres of the brain are anatomically distinct and control different functions (Segalowitz, 1983; Springer & Deutsch, 1993). For example, the temporal lobe, an area associated with language, seems to be larger on the left side of the brain than on the right. However, whether these anatomical differences are related to functional differences remains a question which is open for further research.

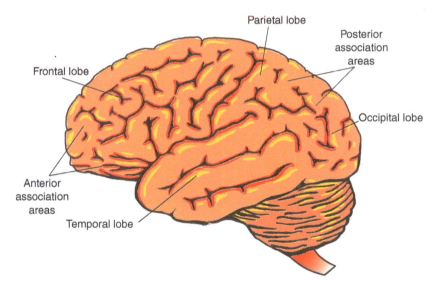

Figure 5.2 The cerebrum

The cerebrum is covered by a layer known as the **cerebral cortex**. This layer of cells is extremely convoluted, giving rise to the distinctive look of brain tissue. The cerebral cortex accounts for approximately 90% of the brain's total number of cells. It is also the most advanced part of the brain, supporting complex functions such as language, vision and motor skills. The cerebral cortex is divided into four main areas called **lobes** and two other areas known as the **association areas**. The four lobes of the brain are known as the **frontal lobe** (which supports planning, organization and other higher mental functions), the **temporal lobe** (involved in language, hearing and smell), the **parietal lobe** (involved in the processing of bodily sensations) and the **occipital lobe** (which is involved in visual processing). The **anterior association area** (located at the front of the brain) and **posterior association area** (located near the rear of the brain) are involved in linking up information from various parts of the brain.

Hemispheric Specialization

One of the most important aspects, and often one of the most misunderstood (Segalowitz, 1983), is the left-right organization of the brain across its two hemispheres. **Hemispheric specialization** refers to the differential functions carried out by the two cerebral hemispheres. Hemispheric specialization begins at birth and the differences between the two hemispheres remain largely the same into adulthood. This belief in the lack of change in the organization of function across the two hemispheres has come to be known as the **invariance hypothesis**. However, as Segalowitz (1995) notes, what will change is what the child is able to do with the information that is processed by the two halves of the brain. Also of note is the fact that the two hemispheres of the brain mature at different rates, with the evidence suggesting that the right hemisphere of the brain matures earlier than the left (Best, 1988). Interestingly, this earlier maturation of the right hemisphere mirrors the growth of functional differences carried out by the two hemispheres (Segalowitz, 1995).

So, what are these functional differences attributed to the left and the right hemispheres? Movement and sensation are each controlled by a single hemisphere. The left side of the brain controls movement and sensation of the right side of the body, while the right side of the brain controls movement and sensation for the left side of the body. The only exception to this pattern is the eyes which send input to both sides of the brain. The left side of the brain is specialized for language processing. In contrast, the right side of the brain is specialized for processing spatial information, music and the perception of faces. The two hemispheres are also believed to be differentially involved in the processing of emotion. According to Davidson (1994), the left hemisphere of the brain is responsible for the expression of emotions associated with approach to the external environment, emotions such as *interest*, *anger* and *joy*. In contrast, the right side of the brain is responsible for processing emotions associated with withdrawal from the environment such as *fear*, *distress* and *disgust*. While the evidence is clear that some functions are associated with a particular hemisphere, it is important to note that the separation of function across the hemispheres is not absolute. For example, a number of studies conducted with individuals who have right brain damage have demonstrated that these people have difficulty processing nonliteral forms of language such as sarcastic speech (Kaplan, Brownell, Jacobs, & Gardner, 1990), suggesting that the right hemisphere may be associated with particular aspects of language processing such as *pragmatics* (Siegal, Carrington, & Radel, 1996).

Lateralization is the term used to describe the processes by which the two halves of the brain become specialized to carry out specific functions. Research in developmental neuropsychology suggests that the lateralization of brain function across the left and right hemispheres is a very complex process. It is likely that brain lateralization isn't as set in stone as many researchers initially thought, for example, there is some evidence that languages learnt in later life might be lateralized in the right rather than left hemisphere (see Research Example 5.1). There is also evidence to show that young children who happen to suffer brain injury can recover a good deal of their loss (Stiles, 2000). It is likely that this occurs in young children because their brains are still developing and the lateralization process is not complete. For example, recall from above that the left hemisphere is associated with language development. Even if a child experiences injury to this hemisphere, almost normal language development is possible (Bates & Roe, 2001). It is known that older adults can also regain some loss after injury (Black, Jones, Nelson, & Greenough, 1998). However, this compensation comes at a cost. Although children with brain damage may be able to recover their language skills, they often show deficits on a wide range of complex tasks later in life. It is likely that when healthy brain regions take over the tasks normally undertaken by damaged brain regions, there is less space for other tasks. Our cerebral cortex is limited: while there is some room for compensation, the brain cannot deal with too much 'crowding' (Huttenlocher, 2002).

Brain lateralization can tell us a great deal about normal as well as abnormal development. Children who have reading disorders, such as **dyslexia**, which is characterized by difficulty reading, often show disruption in lateralization. Children without dyslexia generally process spatial information on the right side of the brain, but children with dyslexia seem to process the same information equally across hemispheres. Their left hemispheres may therefore become overloaded, which results in reading deficits (Banish, 1998). Hemispheric lateralization has also been associated with temperament differences in children. It seems that children who are shy and fearful show greater activity in their right frontal cortex than children not characterized by fear (Henderson, Marshall, Fox, & Rubin, 2004). It is thought that this brain activity indicates high reactivity, as though such children are ever poised to react in a negative manner to stimuli.

Research Example 5.1

Age of Acquisition and Lateralization of Language

While it is generally accepted that it is the left hemisphere of the brain that is specialized for language processing, it has been proposed that this process of lateralization of language is not complete until around puberty (Lennenberg, 1967). Following this claim, a number of researchers have suggested that when a second language is acquired after the maturation of the hemispheres, this might make greater use of the right hemisphere compared to a language acquired earlier in life. A study by Evans, Workman, Mayer and Crowley (2002) looked at patterns of language lateralization in a group of English-Welsh bilingual participants. The participants spoke Welsh as a second language but varied in the ages at which they had learned Welsh.

The participants were aged 15 to 16 years at the time of testing and formed four distinct groups: Group 1 who had learned Welsh prior to 5 to 6 years of age and were raised in a predominantly English-speaking

(Continued)

part of Wales; Group 2 who learned Welsh after 5 to 6 years of age and were also raised in a predominantly English-speaking part of Wales; Group 3 who learned Welsh prior to 5 to 6 years of age and were raised in a part of Wales where both languages were spoken widely; and Group 4 who learned Welsh after 5 to 6 years of age and were also raised in a part of Wales where both languages were spoken widely.

All participants were given a 'split visual field' task in which they were presented briefly with 80 words (40 Welsh and 40 English, shown in a random order). The words were presented in either the left or right side of the screen and the task of the participant was to identify each word as quickly as possible. Words appearing in the left visual field would first reach the right hemisphere, words appearing in the right visual field would first reach the left hemisphere. Hence if language is predominantly lateralized in the left hemisphere, responses should be quicker for words presented in the right visual field as these would reach the language-appropriate hemisphere immediately, whereas words presented in the left visual field would first reach the right hemisphere and the information would need to be transferred to the left hemisphere (via the corpus callosum) for processing to take place, resulting in a delay in response.

Evans et al. used the performance data for English and Welsh words presented to the different visual fields to work out an 'index of laterality' for English and Welsh words. This was a score ranging from +1 (indicating total left hemisphere dominance for visual word recognition) to -1 (indicating total right hemisphere dominance for visual word recognition). They then compared the indices of laterality for English and Welsh in each of the four different participant groups.

The results indicated that all participants were left hemisphere dominant for recognizing English words. However, with regard to Welsh, participants raised in a predominantly English-speaking environment who learned Welsh after the age of 5 to 6 years showed evidence of increased right hemisphere involvement in recognizing Welsh words, compared to children from the same environment who had learned Welsh early in life. However, in the case of children raised in a bilingual environment, there were no differences in laterality scores for Welsh between the children who learned Welsh prior to 5 to 6 years of age or later in life. Both of these groups were left-hemisphere dominant for Welsh as well as English.

The results of this study indicate some support for the notion of a 'right shift' for languages learned later in life, but also indicate that the linguistic environment in which the child is raised can also affect patterns of lateralization. Even if children had not formally learned Welsh in the early years, it seemed to be the case that simply hearing the language being spoken regularly may also have affected the lateralization of that language.

Developmental Neuroscience

In recent years there has been enormous growth in our understanding of how the brain relates to our perceptions, thoughts, feelings, ability to communicate and, ultimately, to our behaviour. This emerging area of brain research has been termed *cognitive neuroscience*. Part of the reason why we have seen so much interest in the area is due to developments in the ability to measure the brain's activity in novel and exciting ways, and hence provide insights into the link between brain activity and our abilities and behaviours. We discussed some of these *neuroimaging techniques* in the psychophysiological methods section of Chapter 3. Perhaps one of the most important and revealing of these techniques is functional magnetic resonance imaging (fMRI) technology, which measures blood oxygen levels in specific brain regions.

The study of *developmental* cognitive neuroscience is possible when we understand how the brain develops all the way from infancy, through to childhood, adolescence and even adulthood. As we will find out, brain development is an ongoing process, and you may be surprised to learn that parts of your brain – particularly the prefrontal cortex – continue to mature well into adulthood. The rest of this chapter will be devoted to exploring and understanding how the brain changes across development. And it does so in some unexpected ways.

Before we continue, it is necessary to note that despite being vulnerable and sensitive in some ways, the brain and indeed much of our development are characterized by a good deal of resilience to internal and external threat. Although there are some ways in which we can foster and support brain maturation in children, for the most part as long as there are no major threats (such as abuse, neglect or a severe underlying genetic disorder; see Research Example 5.2), most brains will develop in just the right way to ensure we are able to learn and adapt to the needs of our environment. We mention this because there are a great many myths and sources of anxiety that have developed along with this area of research. For example, the idea that a certain television programme or toy can increase intelligence in babies has sparked the development of expensive products with little real benefit that are marketed to unsuspecting parents and childhood educators, who can be easy prey in their motivation to do what's best for the children in their care (Twardosz, 2012; Zambo, 2008). In this chapter, we will also explore some of the facts and fictitious notions surrounding what supports and harms brain growth across development.

There are at least three views to understanding how brain changes interact with behavioural development. Johnson (2005) identifies these as the processes of *maturation*, *skill learning* and *interactive specialization*. Maturation refers to the notion that brain development has a direct effect on skill acquisition: to put it simply, the brain grows and this leads to new behaviours. Conversely, the skill learning view assumes the brain is sufficiently developed, and that active training is what leads to the acquisition of new skills or behaviours, such that practice makes perfect. However, it is likely that the relationship between the brain and development is more complex than either of these two views can explain. A third view, of interactive specialization, accounts for the complexity of brain development by suggesting that a specific brain region may begin with a poorly defined function, and that interactions between the environment and how other brain regions develop and connect with each other shape the previously poorly defined regions. This interactive, dynamic relationship seems to capture more of what we know about brain maturation and is consistent with the topics to follow, including the notion of sensitive periods of development.

Research Example 5.2

Exposure to Maternal Depression and Brain Development in Children

There has been much interest in the effects of adverse experiences on brain development and one area of research has focused on the effects of such experiences on the structures of the limbic system. Of particular interest here is a structure called the amygdala, which has been implicated in our ability to process and respond to emotional information, and in particular the safety of our environments. Animal studies have indicated that exposure to stressful events can result in an enlarged amygdala, which is related to increased reactivity to stress. Adults who have been exposed to stressful situations also appear to have larger and more reactive amygdala volumes compared to non-stressed adults. It may have been adaptive to have a larger and more reactive amygdala when exposed to a stressful environment as this may have contributed to an increased readiness to deal with threatening situations, but evidence has shown that an enlarged amygdala is also associated with difficulties in managing emotions and a heightened reactivity to even minor stresses.

A study reported by Lupien et al. (2011) looked at the effects of exposure to maternal depression from birth and amygdala volume in children aged 10 years of age. It is well established that maternal depression is associated with disturbances in caregiving behaviour, with such mothers showing less sensitivity to their infants and increased signs of withdrawn and disengaged behaviours. Children of mothers with depression also tend to show an increased sensitivity to stress later in life. Given this lack of sensitivity in mothers with depression and the increased susceptibility of children of such mothers to stress, Lupien et al. focused on maternal depressive symptoms (MDS) from birth to investigate the association between poor quality caregiving and amygdala volumes in their children.

The participants were children participating in the Quebec Longitudinal Study of Child Development and were 10 years old at the time of testing. Two groups of children were selected from the overall sample, one group who had been continuously exposed to MDS since birth, and a group who had never been exposed to MDS.

An MRI scanner was used to scan the brains of the children and from these scans the amygdala volume of each child was established (correcting for factors such as total brain volume and head size). When the amygdala volumes for the two groups were compared, clear differences emerged. Children exposed to continuous MDS showed significantly higher amygdala volumes compared to the no MDS group.

The results of this study are consistent with results of animal studies and other studies of children exposed to poor quality caregiving, such as children raised in institutional settings (see, for example, Tottenham et al., 2010). These results provide further evidence of how environmental conditions can shape brain development in infancy and childhood.

Synaptic proliferation and pruning

During gestation and the first two years of life, dendrites are busy forming additional branches, resulting in synaptic proliferation and ensuring an ample supply of connections between neurons to relay the vast amount of information that enters the baby's brain. However, as you may recall, the brain creates more synaptic connections than it eventually needs. This process, called synaptic pruning, refers to the way in which neurons that are seldom stimulated lose their synapses. The cerebral cortexes of both human and nonhuman primates initially begin with about two times the adult number of synaptic connections (Huttenlocher & Dabholkar, 1997). Synaptic pruning has been likened to moulding a sculpture from clay. We begin with excess clay, or neurons, and through a delicate process of refining and whittling down what is not needed, we are left with an object of beauty and efficiency. The selective-elimination hypothesis assumes that early childhood involves the overproduction of synapses, and this neuronal activity fine-tunes the structure of individual synapses to determine which will be retained and removed from the brain's circuits (Purves & Lichtman, 1980). Such competition for synaptic survival ensures that each child's brain is appropriately adapted for that child's individual environment. If the brain didn't mould itself in this way, the potentially endless pathways of thinking, learning and behaving would create so much noise we would have a difficult time responding at all. Indeed, recent research in the area of autism has linked this disorder to abnormalities in the process of synaptic pruning, and it appears that a characteristic of the brains of children with this disorder is an *excess* of synaptic connections (Frith & Happé, 2005; Tang et al., 2014). Synaptic pruning thus ensures the brain emerges into a smooth, well-oiled machine with connections that make sense.

It was initially thought that pruning occurred at the onset of puberty and was complete to an adult level during adolescence. However, as we explore below, recent research has shed light on the timing of this process, and it seems that we keep moulding our neurons for a good deal longer than was first thought.

Understanding the timing of the elimination of synapses – and when the process is complete – is an important topic for a number of reasons. First, knowing how far into development this process continues helps us understand the timing of the establishment of cognitive abilities and, thereby, the duration of the window for the best time to acquire new skills, such as learning a language or acquiring mathematical skills. Second, such information provides us with insights into when our personalities shift from developmental mode to a more concrete adult personality. Third, and this relates to Chapter 13 on Developmental Psychopathology, the timing and completion of critical pruning may provide much needed insights into the development of certain neuropsychiatric disorders that mysteriously appear during late adolescence or early adulthood. We saw earlier that abnormalities in synaptic pruning have been linked to autism and evidence also exists for the role of defective synaptic pruning in disorders such as schizophrenia and drug-induced psychoses (Rakic, 1995).

Recent research has confirmed that the process of synaptic elimination extends beyond adolescence, and likely only stabilizes in adulthood. In a large cross-sectional study, synaptic spine density on the dendrites of neurons in the prefrontal cortex was measured in participants aged from newborn to 91 years. The authors found that while dendritic spine density in childhood exceeded adult levels by 2–3 times (evidence for synaptic proliferation) and synaptic spines began to decrease during puberty, it wasn't until around 30 years of age that the researchers saw evidence of stabilization in the overproduction and developmental remodelling of synaptic spines (Petanjek et al., 2011). These findings suggest that the reorganizing brain is sensitive to environmental influences well into adulthood, indicating room for change in cognitive and emotional capacitates beyond childhood. The findings also shed light onto some possible causes and timing of late onset neuropsychiatric disorders such as schizophrenia.

Myelination

While the connections within the neural network become refined and streamlined over time, the actual volume of the brain increases across early development. You may question how this occurs if neurons die off and synapses reduce over time. Approximately half the brain's volume is made up of glial cells, which you will recall are responsible for myelination, the process by which the axons of neurons are covered with an insulating layer designed to increase the neuron's efficiency. You may have heard of the term 'white matter', which refers to the presence of myelinated axons, since myelin is white. Although few neurons are generated in the brain beyond mid gestation (around 20 weeks into the pregnancy), glial cells, or white matter, continue to be generated throughout life and explain growth in brain size even after synaptic pruning has begun.

Myelin is extremely important for the transfer of information throughout the nervous system. It not only plays a role in insulating axons, and hence containing the chemical messages passed from one neuron to another to ensure such information doesn't get lost in the system, it also provides a track along which the regrowth of certain fibres is possible and is thus involved in the process of nerve regeneration (Fancy et al., 2011). Perhaps the greatest example of the importance of myelination for healthy brain functioning is when it fails to do its job efficiently. Many neurodegenerative diseases affecting such basic functions as speech, balance and cognitive abilities, including multiple sclerosis, are related to a loss of myelin. During such demyelination, the conduction of signals along the nerve becomes scrambled, and nerve death can result.

Similar to the story of synaptic pruning, the development of glial cells and myelination may prove to be a rather long tale, beginning early in development and continuing across childhood, adolescence and adulthood. In a recent study, longitudinal white matter development was examined using very sensitive imaging technology called diffusion tensor tractography, capable of measuring factors indicative of myelination and axon density, in participants aged 5 to 32 years-old. Each participant received two scans to examine brain changes over time. For some areas of the brain the changes were complete by late adolescence. However, association fibres connecting the frontal cortex continued to increase in size into adulthood, and this was likely a result of microstructural maturation of white matter (such as myelination). In contrast, grey matter, which consists of neurons and their associated parts, declined with age (Lebel & Beaulieu, 2011). You may recall that the frontal lobes are involved in complex higher-order functions such as planning, attention and inhibition. It is possible that the demanding juggling act of young adulthood, marked by continuing education, employment, independence and growing social and family relationships, is related to this post-adolescence brain growth. It is also why we are increasingly capable of thinking through the consequences of risky behaviour, such as posting that risqué photo on Facebook, as we enter our twenties and thirties. This research pairs nicely with studies showing synaptic pruning across development. It seems that as the brain rids itself of excessive interfering connections, it gains more of the cells responsible for efficiency of information transmission: another example of the intimate relationship between gains and losses.

Neuroplasticity

Understanding developmental brain plasticity, or the brain's ability to change as a result of new experiences over time, is important for at least two reasons. First, in a highly plastic brain, many areas are not yet committed to specific functions, meaning that the brain is highly receptive to learning. Second, plasticity has implications for understanding and ameliorating the effects of brain damage, since a plastic brain can recover some of the lost functions of neural damage. The idea that the brain can continue to renew itself is extremely exciting, and provides hope for those who may have experienced brain function loss. However, it is becoming apparent that while the brain does seem to possess some ability to recover lost functions, there are limits to its regenerative capacities.

Scientists have long known that at birth and during early childhood the central nervous system is malleable. This explains why individuals who have suffered brain injury early in childhood can show recovery of cognitive impairments (Huttenlocher, 2002). In a series of interesting studies, children with brain injuries that occurred before the first 6 months of age were followed longitudinally (Stiles, 2000). Children showed delays in language development until around 3.5 years, but by age 5 had caught up in their language skills. Undamaged brain areas had taken over the language functions. However, the children still showed deficits in a wide range of complex abilities during the school years, including mathematic reasoning. The extent of plasticity seems to depend on a number of factors, including the site of brain damage, amount of brain tissue damaged, skills area and age when the injury occurred. In addition, brain plasticity may come at a cost. A crowding effect seems to occur when healthy regions take over the functions of damaged regions and the brain may overall process information less quickly (Huttenlocher, 2002).

Until recently it was believed that the adult brain diminishes, through disease, injury or just plain old age, with little to no capacity to regenerate. Some exciting recent research has revealed this may not be strictly true. Researchers have demonstrated the presence of neuroplasticity during motor recovery after stroke in adults. Stroke is the term given for the sudden death of brain cells in a specific brain area due to lack of blood flow, often due to blood clots interrupting the normal flow of blood and oxygen to the brain. Following a stroke, injury to brain areas associated with motor functioning can result in spontaneous recovery, such that if the representational brain map of the hand is damaged, functioning can be taken over by a nearby undamaged area, like the region of the brain involved in movement of the shoulder (Cramer et al., 2011). Similar to the findings for brain-damaged children noted above, a related area of the brain compensates for the damaged area. Inter-hemispheric plasticity is also possible, whereby the opposite, undamaged hemisphere has increased activity in relation to movement. Other areas of recovery, such as cognitive and language functioning, have been less studied but similar compensatory mechanisms may apply. Specific therapies can be used to augment the spontaneous brain compensatory processes that occur. Further, targeted therapies can actually result in axons rewiring such that new projections from neurons on the undamaged side of the brain are possible in denervated areas of the brain (Chen et al., 2002). All of this suggests that rather than being set in stone, the adult brain is capable of rewiring itself, and further, that novel treatments are capable of assisting the brain's recovery. It is possible that new, as yet untested, interventions will result in even more advances in the area.

However, certain individuals may be disadvantaged in the extent of their neuroplasticity. As we explored in Chapter 4, preterm-born children commonly experience motor, cognitive and learning difficulties. A recent study has identified that neuroplasticity might offer an explanation as to why prematurity impacts learning and memory so substantially. In this study, collaborators from Australia and Britain compared the motor cortex neuroplasticity of term-born adolescents (born 38 to 41 weeks gestation) with adolescents born early preterm (less than 32 weeks early) and late preterm (33 to 37 weeks). The authors found that compared to both preterm groups, the adolescents born at term showed evidence of greater neuroplasticity in response to brain stimulation. An additional analysis revealed that term-born young adults showed less motor neuroplasticity than the term-born adolescents (Pitcher et al., 2012). The findings suggest a possible neuroplasticity mechanism for some of the challenges faced by individuals born preterm, and also demonstrate the developmental decline in neuroplasticity after adolescence.

Plasticity may involve appropriate stimulation during a sensitive period. We will explore the notion of sensitive periods in development in greater detail in the following section. Despite the hope for persisting neuroplasticity across development, many neuroscientists believe that retraining the brain beyond childhood is difficult and painstaking. It is perhaps advantageous that the brain becomes increasingly limited in its plasticity over time, for if it was so easy to continue reshaping the brain across the life span, we would risk losing what we already have in terms of earlier hard-learned knowledge, memories and skills. Perhaps some rigidity and hard wiring in the brain is not such a bad thing.

Sensitive periods

Sensitive periods are times in an individual's development when experience has a particularly profound impact on neural construction. During this period, it is important that the correct environmental stimuli are present in order to lay down appropriate neural pathways. Failing to have the correct input during a sensitive period can result in 'missing pieces', interfering with future steps in brain development.

Most aspects of brain development are not so constrained. But for certain skills to develop, such as language, appropriate stimulation during a sensitive time is required. Across history, there have been some rare but highly disturbing 'natural experiments', where children were deprived of language. Perhaps one of the most tragic instances of children not receiving appropriate exposure to language during a sensitive period is the case of Genie. Subject to extreme abuse and neglect, Genie is the pseudonym for a child who spent the first 13 years of her life strapped to a potty chair in the bedroom of her parents' home in Greater Los Angeles. Genie was the subject of horrific social isolation and had limited exposure to language. Genie's father beat her for vocalizing and he barked at her like a dog to keep her quiet. Genie's father also forbade his wife and son to speak to her. By the age of 13, when she was discovered by law enforcement authorities in 1970, she was almost mute. Despite receiving intensive therapy and coaching upon her rescue, Genie has limited linguistic abilities to this day. She was able to grasp the meaning of a number of words, but never mastered the rules of grammar so critical to a developed language system (Jones, 1995). A tragic example, Genie illustrates that the acquisition of language is contingent upon sufficient stimulation during a sensitive period. If that period is missed, the complexities and richness of human language may be lost forever.

Fortunately, for most babies and children, sufficient stimulation exists in everyday interactions with caregivers, siblings and the wider world to ensure language development. However, as many of you may have experienced when trying to learn a second language in adulthood, the sensitive period of language acquisition also applies to the particular language we are exposed to. Brain areas that are specialized for understanding language involve different neuronal connections depending on whether a child is exposed to English or French or any other language during the first few years of life. This is why children naturally pick up foreign languages, but the skill becomes so much harder as we grow older. Due to the influence of neuroplasticity, the environment is more likely to shape the activity of axons and synapses earlier in development and during such sensitive periods. In one study, English grammar proficiency was tested in Chinese and Korean immigrants who had arrived in the USA at varying ages. Immigrants who began learning English after age 17 made many simple mistakes on the test, those aged 8–16 when emigrating had varying levels of proficiency, and only individuals who had arrived in the United States before age 7 performed as well

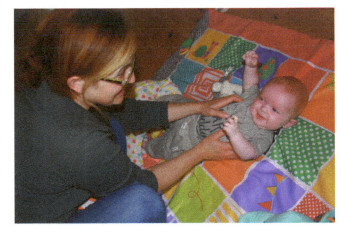

Image 5A   For most babies and children, sufficient stimulation exists in everyday interactions

as native speakers (Johnson & Newport, 1989). Clearly, there appears to be a sensitive period earlier in childhood for acquiring the syntax, or grammar, that makes up a language.

Growth spurts

Timing seems to be crucial for many aspects of development. A recent example of this is a study in which it was reported that the impact of lead, a neurotoxin that affects physical growth such as height and is commonly found in paint used during and before the 1970s, has differential effects depending on the timing of exposure: infants (birth to 24 months) had significantly impacted growth compared to any other age in early childhood, including prenatal exposure (Afeiche et al., 2012). Positive and negative influences appear to differentially affect the brain during periods in which it is growing most rapidly.

Like many other areas of development, brain growth is not smooth and continuous; rather, it occurs in spurts (Segalowitz, 1995). The brain undergoes several growth spurts over the course of its development. Recordings of brain electrical activity as reflected in electroencephalograms (EEG) appear to show correlations between growth spurts and major periods of cognitive development (Fischer & Rose, 1994, 1995). For example, surges in frontal lobe activity that occur during infancy and toddlerhood appear to map onto the emergence of specific abilities: at 3 to 4 months when infants typically reach for objects; around 8 months when they typically crawl and search for hidden objects; at 12 months when they typically walk; and around 18 months when language blossoms (Fischer, 2006). A surge in the production of synapses may account for these brain growth spurts in children under age 2. Indeed, many developmental psychologists and neuropsychologists have drawn connections between developments within the brain itself (changes due to the growth of synapses, synaptic pruning, the development of the frontal lobes and the myelinization of neurons) and cognitive development (Case, 1992; Thatcher, 1994). Case (1992) argued that major stage changes in children's developing cognitive ability mapped onto changes in brain development. While it is tempting to make such leaps, Segalowitz (1995) provides a caveat in doing so, arguing that studying global changes in brain structure is less informative than examining how regional developments in the brain develop to support specific functions.

Recent research has questioned the universal timing of brain growth and underscores the importance of timing in development. Gifted children appear to have asynchronous brain development compared to the brains of typically developing children, as shown by a study conducted by the National Institute of Mental Health and McGill University (Shaw et al., 2006). Children with greater than average intellectual ability demonstrated high neuroplasticity that begins and ends later than average. Increases in synapses within the cortex, which are necessary for high-level thinking, reached their peak at roughly 11 years old in children with high IQs compared to a peak of 7 to 8 years old in children with average IQs. The subsequent pruning phase of cortical development was very rapid in the high IQ group. The authors explain the results as confirming the importance of synaptic pruning, and the importance of timing in the pruning process (which showed a lag for gifted children). The findings also explain why many parents of bright children report that their children display exceptional intellectual abilities one minute, and excessively immature or frustrating behaviour the next minute.

Brain stimulation

We mentioned that most children receive sufficient stimulation from their natural settings to promote appropriate brain growth. In reality, the question of how much stimulation a child needs to promote optimal brain growth is fraught with claims and speculation. While it is true that the brain is particularly sponge-like during the early years and depriving children of rich, caring environments impairs their brain development, it is also true that overstimulation can lead to negative consequences. Much of the cognitive, social and physical advancements we will discuss in the coming chapters occur without babies requiring any special classes, equipment or educational viewing.

Environments that overwhelm a child's developing capacities can in fact lead to that child withdrawing and losing interest in learning. In a rush to promote their children's linguistic and other skills, some parents use vocabulary-based and other educational media with their babies. Recent research has dispelled the notion that screen time provides babies and young children with unique learning opportunities. In fact, overstimulation through exposure to educational programmes leads to babies learning less vocabulary and having lower scores on language skill tests (approximately 10% lower) rather than more. Recent guidelines discourage any use of educational programming for children under 2 years (Brown, 2011). Screen time aimed at infants and young children involves quick edits and is vastly different from the slow-paced, turn-taking communication style adults typically use when speaking to babies. Parents and caregivers have a myriad of inexpensive tools for appropriate stimulation at their disposal: face-to-face time, including reading to infants and young children, singing to them, talking to them and explaining their daily activities, playing with simple toys such as building blocks, outings to the park – these are the kinds of stimulating experiences that the developing brain requires to think, process information and develop language effectively.

Neuropsychological work has made a distinction between **experience-expectant development** and **experience-dependent development** (Greenough, Black, & Wallace, 1987). Greenough, Black and Wallace have shown how neural circuitry is related to environmental events. Some neural circuits require input from the environment in order to begin growing, a process which Greenough et al. refer to as experience-expectant development. During experience-expectant brain growth, the young child's brain depends on and, in fact, has come to expect opportunities to interact with ordinary experiences, including touching, seeing and exploring objects and hearing language. This type of brain development occurs early in life, is maximized by the type of natural caregiver–child interactions mentioned above, and lays the foundation for experience-dependent development. Other types of neural circuit are strongly influenced by the types of environmental input they receive, what Greenough et al. term experience-dependent development. During experience-dependent brain growth, which occurs across development, brain change is the result of specific learning experiences that differ among individuals and within cultures; for example, the brain of an experienced chess player has developed and is wired differently when compared to the brain of a non-chess player. The development of the brain is critically dependent on environmental experience. Brain structures in and of themselves do not cause development. (Similarly, experience with the environment will not produce developmental changes if the brain structures which underlie those changes have not yet matured.) Thus, a theory of cognitive development which attempts to relate changes in brain structure to other developmental changes must also factor in the role of experience in this association. Given that experience is involved, the correlation between brain maturation and developmental change will never be perfect.

Twardosz (2012) and Zambo (2008) point out that there has been much public interest in neuroscience since the 1990s, which they refer to as 'the decade of the brain', and in particular interest in the role of early experiences in promoting brain development. What are the main points from this chapter that you would want to communicate to a parent or Early Years educator in order to foster developmentally appropriate practices with children and avoid misunderstandings about the nature of brain development?

Summary

Acquiring an understanding of our brain and central nervous system is the foundation for understanding other key areas of child development such as language, perception, cognition and emotion. While the study of our biology is important in its own right, it is also tied to development in these other domains and necessary to examine at an early point in our study of children.

Glossary

Association areas refer to two parts of the brain, the **anterior association area** (located at the front of the brain) and the **posterior association area** (located near the rear of the brain) that are each involved in linking up information from various parts of the brain.

Axon refers to the part of the neuron which ends in the terminal buttons.

Cell body is the body of the neuron which contains the nucleus and other structures.

Cerebral cortex is the outer layer of cells which covers the cerebrum. It is the most advanced part of the brain, supporting complex functions such as language, vision and motor skills.

Cerebrum refers to the two interconnected hemispheres or halves of the brain.

Corpus callosum is the bundle of fibres which connects the two **hemispheres** or halves of the brain.

Dendrites are the part of the neuron which receives signals from the other neurons and transmits this information to the cell body.

Dyslexia is a learning disability that appears as a difficulty with written language.

Experience-dependent development is a process which describes how the growth of some types of neural circuit is strongly influenced by the types of environmental input they receive.

Experience-expectant development is a process which describes how some neural circuits require input from the environment in order to begin growing.

Glial cells are the cells which provide structural support to the neurons.

Hemispheric specialization refers to the differential functions carried out by the two cerebral hemispheres. Hemispheric specialization begins at birth and the differences between the two hemispheres remain largely the same into adulthood.

Invariance hypothesis refers to the lack of change in the organization of hemispheric functions from infancy to adulthood.

Lateralization is the term used to describe the processes by which the two halves of the brain become specialized to carry out specific functions.

Lobes encompass the cerebral cortex which is divided into four main areas called lobes and two other areas called association areas. The four lobes of the brain are called the **frontal lobe**, the **temporal lobe**, the **parietal lobe** and the **occipital lobe**.

Mammalian brain In Paul Maclean's model of the brain, this refers to the region that is most highly developed in primates and humans, and encompasses the cerebrum.

Myelination is a process in which the neurons are covered with an insulating layer of *myelin*, a fatty substance which makes the neuron a more effective transmitter of electrical information.

Neural migration is the method by which neurons travel from their origin to their final position in the brain.

Neuron proliferation refers to the rapid generation of neurons during the embryonic period of prenatal development.

Neuronal death is a process in which some neurons are programmed to die, apparently to provide more space for crucial cell clusters.

Neurons is the name given to the nerve cells which send and receive neural impulses (electrical signals) throughout the brain and nervous system.

Neurotransmitters are a special class of chemicals which are released across the synapse by the terminal buttons.

Paleomammalian brain refers to the region of the brain that is most highly developed in mammals and consists of a number of structures called the **limbic system** which are involved in emotional responses and memory.

Plasticity is the reorganizing of neural networks in the brain according to the individual's experience and stimulation.

Reptilian brain refers to the part of the brain consisting of the brain stem and cerebellum which controls basic survival functions such as respiration, digestion, excretion and reflex responses.

Synapse is the gap between the terminal buttons of one neuron and the dendrites of another neuron.

Synaptic pruning is a process in which the brain disposes of a neuron's connections to other neurons.

Terminal buttons are the ends of a neuron which release neurotransmitters across the synapse to be received by other neurons.

TEST YOUR KNOWLEDGE

1. Using the four choices listed below, pick an option that completes this sentence: 'The right hemisphere of the brain is usually associated with _____ while the left hemisphere is associated with _____'

   a) Spatial information/face processing
   b) Spatial information/language
   c) Verbal skills/reading ability
   d) Lateralization/myelinization

2. Synaptic pruning is the process that allows which of the following to happen?

   a) Neural fibres become myelinated as a result of stimulation in the brain
   b) Adults teach children how to garden
   c) New synapses are formed as the result of stimulation by inputs from the surrounding environment
   d) Seldom stimulated neurons are returned to an uncommitted state so they can support the development of future skills

3. Which of the following is the ability of other parts of the brain to take over the functions of damaged regions?

   a) Plasticity
   b) Myelinization
   c) Synaptic pruning
   d) Lateralization

ANSWERS: 1-B, 2-D, 3-A

Suggested Reading

Johnson, M. H. (2011). *Developmental Cognitive Neuroscience* (3rd edition). Oxford: Blackwell.

Want to learn more? For links to online resources relevant to this chapter, interactive quizzes and much more, visit the companion website at **https://edge.sagepub.com/keenan3e/**

THE DEVELOPMENT OF PERCEPTION, COGNITION AND LANGUAGE

Perception

6

Chapter Outline

LEARNING AIMS

At the end of this chapter you should:

- be aware of the distinction between sensation and perception and the reasons why we study perception
- be able to describe the different theories of perception and also explain concepts such as *affordances* and *invariances*
- be familiar with developments in each of the five senses
- understand and describe the different cues which aid in the development of vision
- be able to describe the concept of *intermodal perception*
- be able to think about the development of perception across the life span

Introduction

Psychologists studying perceptual development tend to make a distinction between **sensation**, the act of detecting a particular stimulus event via a sensory system and **perception**, the processes by which we make sense of our sensations. William James (1890), often thought of as the father of American psychology, described the infant's perception of the world as a 'blooming, buzzing confusion'. James believed that newborns (or **neonates**) found the world of sensory stimulation chaotic and argued that perceptual development was required in order for the infant's sensations to become organized and meaningful. In contrast to James's view, perceptual psychologists have learned that infants come equipped with sophisticated abilities that allow them to make much more sense of the world than James would have believed possible. Advances in research methods for studying infant development, such as *preferential looking* and *habituation paradigms*, allow us to better understand the sorts of stimuli that infants are attuned to and how their early perceptual abilities develop.

When studying perceptual development, it is important to keep in mind that there is a close relationship between perception and action. Motor activity provides the infant with key means for learning about the world and stimulates the development of their perceptual capabilities (Bertenthal & Campos, 1987). In turn, as the infant's perceptual skill develops, so too does their motor skill. In short, perceptual activity and motor activity are inextricably linked, each promoting the development of the other (Stein & Meredith, 1993).

Why Study Perception?

Research on infant perception has largely been concerned with two key questions: what can infants perceive at birth and how do their perceptual abilities change over the first few months of life? There are a variety of reasons why it is necessary to answer these questions. Whether infants have adult-like perceptual abilities specified in their genetic inheritance and which develop in a normative manner or whether infants slowly acquire these abilities over time relates to the nature versus nurture controversy. Work on perceptual development has shed light on the relationship between nature and nurture in human development. A second reason for interest in perception and perceptual development is that our capacity for visual, auditory, tactile, olfactory and taste perception enables us to interact with other human beings. Thus their development not only has important implications for our biological growth, it also has a profound effect on our social and cognitive development.

Until relatively recently, the amount of research on infants' perceptual development was limited. Early researchers made the argument that although it would be interesting to study young children's perceptual abilities, it was simply not possible to do so because of the limitations of human infants. However, there has been a recent flurry of activity on perceptual development in infancy, research which has done a great deal to change our image of an infant's perceptual competencies (e.g. Kellman & Banks, 1998). Their perceptual abilities are undoubtedly more impressive than had been previously assumed. John Flavell (1985) suggests three reasons why developmental researchers underestimated the perceptual competencies of infants. First, Flavell argues that there had been an unwarranted generalization from observations of infants' motor abilities to their perceptual abilities. Because on the motor side of their development infants demonstrate incompetence, it has seemed natural to assume a similar level of perceptual incompetence. Second, there has been a strong associationist tradition in both philosophy and psychology that assumes we begin life with very minimal capabilities which are gradually built up through learning. This view of development, prevalent until the early 1960s, contributed to the negative estimation of infants' perceptual skills. Finally, there was a tendency to extrapolate downwards from the findings of poor perceptual skills in years after infancy. The assumption was that, if preschool children showed marked improvement on perceptual abilities, then infants' perceptual capabilities must be very poor indeed. We now know, as a result of a great deal of painstaking research, that infants come equipped with a much higher level of ability than we originally estimated. In what follows, we survey some of these abilities. The rapidity with which infants' perceptual functioning achieves adult levels is very striking in contrast to their development in other domains, such as cognition.

Theories of Perceptual Development

According to Bornstein and Arterberry (1999), theories of perceptual development need to be viewed in light of more general theories about the nature of perception itself. There are two prominent perspectives on perception, which lead directly to the two theories of perceptual development described in this chapter. As we will briefly examine each theory, it should become clear as you read through the chapter that the overwhelming evidence is in favour of *nativist* positions on perceptual development. The very rapid way in which perceptual development occurs suggests that it is, to a large extent, a function of our biological endowment. Even so, learning still occurs, and is central to modern theories of perception.

According to the first view, *nativist theory*, meaningful perceptual structures exist in the world (structures which are independent of how we perceive them). In other words, these structures do not need to be created or constructed from the sensations we receive via our senses; rather, these structures and the information they impart exist independently of us. For those who hold to this view, perception is simply a process of detecting or 'picking up' the information available in these structures (E. Gibson, 1969; J. J. Gibson, 1979). In other words, our perceptual systems have evolved to pick up the information available in the environment. This view, elaborated most articulately by James and Eleanor Gibson, is known as the theory of **direct perception**.

In contrast to this view, other arguments have been put forth that suggest our interpretations of the physical world are not simply constrained by the nature of our perceptual systems. These theorists make the argument that information gained by the organism through transactions with the environment may influence our perception (Bornstein & Arterberry, 1999); that is, our perceptions are often constructions, the result of prior knowledge used to guide our current interactions with the environment in order to interpret immediate experience. Whereas these *constructivist theories* of perception do allow for some innate perceptual abilities, they emphasize that perceptual development is largely the result of a person's interactions with their environment, which lead to the construction of our understanding of the world. Piaget's view of perception is an example of this position.

Table 6.1 Theories of perceptual development

Nativist Theory	
Gibson & Gibson	Perception is a process of picking up information available from structures that are independent of how we perceive them, called direct perception. This process occurs via the exploitation of invariances in stimuli (their unchanging elements), which occurs by interacting with the object through its affordances (properties of a stimulus that allow interaction with it). Perceptual development occurs as the individual absorbs more information from any given stimulus and begins to recognize relationships between stimuli, or compound invariants.
Constructivist Theory	
Piaget	The process of perception is supplemented by the process of perceptual activity, the former being innate and the latter the intellect's correction of initial impressions with reference to previous experience.
Neisser	The individual's previous experience, or the schema the individual applies to a situation, affects perception of affordances. This perception of the environment in turn changes previous knowledge or schemas, which results in further exploration within the environment.

Piaget's theory of perceptual development

Piaget's theory of perceptual development is rather different from other theories of perception in the respect that Piaget believed that perception did not develop, but was 'enriched by the emerging structures of intelligence' (Pulaski, 1980: 108). In his view, it is our intelligence which demonstrates a continual pattern of development (Piaget, 1969).

Piaget's (1969) theory of perceptual development makes a critical distinction between **perception** and *perceptual activity*. For Piaget, perception is the initial and immediate sensory via modalities such as seeing, hearing and touching that occurs when we are exposed to a stimulus. Perceptual activity, by way of contrast, is the 'correction' of our initial impressions by the activity of our intellect (Pulaski, 1980), that is to say, perceptual activity refers to the modification of perception by previous experience.

It is fair to say that Piaget's theory is not so much a theory of perception but instead a theory of the cognitive processes by which infants and children come to interpret perception (Bremner, 1994). Piaget was clear in his belief that perception was dependent on intelligence. Like many modern perceptual psychologists, Piaget believed that perception provided direct knowledge of the environment, however, he made it clear that this direct, perceptually-based knowledge was prone to error (Piaget, 1969). Thus, for Piaget, perception is not the source of our knowledge; rather, knowledge comes from the combined operation of perception and perceptual activity. In other words, knowledge is a product of the whole organism and not simply a product of the sense organs. Given that Piaget's theory of perception is largely a cognitive theory, with a strong focus on the relationship between action or experience and cognitive development, we will consider Piagetian theory further in Chapter 7 on cognitive development, where we take up Piaget's view on the development of knowledge about objects.

Gibson's theory of perceptual development

According to James and Eleanor Gibson, perceptual development is an active cognitive process in which we interact selectively with the array of possibilities afforded to us by the environment (E. Gibson, 1969; J. J. Gibson, 1979). A key concept in the Gibsonian approach to perceptual development is the notion of **affordances**. Affordances are the properties of objects that offer the individual the potential to interact with the object in a variety of ways (E. Gibson, 2000, 2003). Thus, by moving about and exploring their environment, infants come to understand which objects are best grasped, squeezed, tasted or avoided. Knowledge of these affordances allows us to respond to the world with sensitivity, rather than making reactive blunders to every stimulus presented to us. We can perceive affordances by exploiting **invariances** in the visual environment, that is, aspects of the environment which do not change. For example, floors afford walking by virtue of their smooth, continuous and solid qualities, whereas the handle on a coffee mug affords the action of grasping by virtue of its shape and solidity.

Ulric Neisser (1976) suggests that which affordances are perceived is a function of our previous experience, that is, the **schema** we bring to bear on a situation when we first perceive it. A schema is a mental representation or knowledge structure which guides our understanding

Image 6A Consistent with Gibson's notion of affordances, this baby is learning about the properties of his environment through interacting with and selecting aspects of his environment. By exploring through grasping, squeezing and no doubt tasting, he will soon learn that the affordances of grapes include that they are good for eating

© szefei/Shutterstock

of the environment. Our schemas direct how we explore our environment and, therefore, which affordances we pick up from the environment. The information we obtain from the environment causes changes in our knowledge or schemas which direct further exploration, and so on, in a cyclical fashion. According to Neisser, affordances need not be limited to objects like floors and coffee mugs; people afford possibilities for interaction as well. For example, think of facial expressions such as a person's raised eyebrows, wide open eyes and dropped jaw that afford an attribution of a particular mental state, namely surprise.

If, as the Gibsons suggest, perceptual development is merely a process of taking in information that exists in the environment, the question that naturally arises with respect to perceptual development is, simply, 'what develops?' According to Eleanor Gibson (1969), with development, children take more information from a stimulus. With experience, children learn to perceive more information from a set of stimuli, both about individual objects and about the relationships between objects. Gibson (1979) refers to the perception of relationships among stimuli that specify more complex or higher-order affordances as *compound invariants*. In other words, the relationships among objects give more information to the perceiver than simply picking up the objects themselves in isolation. Thus, with development, older children learn to abstract higher-order structures of which younger children may remain entirely naïve.

Consider the following example: have you ever watched an infant try to make their way down a small incline, say a very short staircase? This situation was studied by Karen Adolph and her colleagues (Adolph, Eppler, & Gibson, 1993). They had two groups of infants try to negotiate a series of ramps which varied in slope. Infants were placed on the top of the ramp and encouraged to descend by their mother who waited at the bottom. Adolph's subjects were a group of 8 month-old infants who were crawling but not walking, and a group of 14 month-old infants who had learned to walk. On the basis of Gibsonian theory, you would expect the older infants to recognize that gentle slopes afforded walking whereas steeper slopes required a different strategy. In contrast, 8 month-olds will not have had enough locomotor experience to have encountered many inclines and hence will not have developed much in the way of a strategies for dealing with these. This is in fact what Adolph and her colleagues found: 14 month-olds walked down gentle slopes but approached the steeper slopes by sitting down and sliding (usually after a good deal of searching for an alternative method). By way of contrast, the 8 month-olds simply approached each ramp the same way, by crawling down head first. On the steep ramps this often led to the infant sliding down in an uncontrolled manner. The results of this study supported a Gibsonian account of perceptual development. Older infants, with appropriate experience, could perceive the affordances offered to them by the different ramps, and adjusted their strategy for descending accordingly. Younger infants were unable to perceive the affordances for walking vs. sliding and tended to approach each ramp in the same way.

Ways of Studying Perceptual Development in Infants

Given that much of the research on perceptual development is conducted with infants in an effort to understand what perceptual abilities they come equipped with and how these change with age, it is important to briefly examine the particular methods which are used to study what infants know and what they can do. Studying infant development is particularly challenging because of the methodological difficulties entailed; that is, you cannot simply ask babies questions about what they see and what they do not (well you can, but you should not expect particularly good answers). In short, we need to find other methods of testing that will allow us to learn which aspects of the world infants can perceive.

One of the most common and simple techniques employed by researchers examining perceptual development is to make use of an infant's perceptual *preferences* (Fantz, 1961). That is, we try to figure out what it is that infants prefer to look at in a display by measuring such behaviours as looking time (how much they look at a particular stimulus in relation to another). Using measures such as looking time may reveal that the infant prefers to look at one stimulus over another, a fact which gives rise to the name of these methods: *preferential looking techniques* (Miller, 1998).

Generally, the strategy researchers using these techniques take is to observe changes in naturally occurring behaviours, such as *gaze* at an object or display. A researcher will introduce some stimulus to the infant and then look for changes in the *rate*, *duration* or *intensity* of gazing (or some other behaviour). Importantly, these changes can serve as an index of whether or not the baby has perceived the stimulus. Using a preferential looking technique, the researcher can infer that because the infant prefers to look at one stimulus relevant to another, the infant *perceives a difference* between two sets of stimuli. In addition, infants' preferences tell us two significant things about their perceptual systems. First, they tell us what sorts of stimuli the infant's perceptual system can distinguish or discriminate. That is, an organism cannot systematically attend to, or prefer, one thing over another unless it can somehow perceptually discriminate one from the other. For example, if an infant prefers to look at a pattern in fine back and white stripes rather than a plain grey pattern (which are equal in total brightness), that preference tells us that the infant has the ability to see the stripes.

Second, the infant's preferences tell us something about the nature of their perceptual systems; that is, we can observe what the infant is more and less inclined to attend to, which in turn tells us about the design of the infant's perceptual, attentional and related psychological systems. For example, infants may prefer to look more at an object when it is in motion than at the same object when it is stationary. This suggests that the infant's perceptual system is constructed to be more attentive to movement than to non-movement. Preferential looking methods can thereby provide researchers with a powerful method for examining several aspects of perceptual development.

Habituation studies are similar to preferential looking studies, and are used in many studies of infant cognition, perception and emotion (Miller, 1998). Habituation studies involve the use of two simple concepts: *boredom* and *novelty*. In general, psychological research has shown that humans prefer novelty; that is, we are designed to look at or attend to things that are new. Once some stimulus display becomes familiar (i.e. it loses its novelty), we become bored of it and stop attending to the display. In psychological terms, we say we have *habituated* to the display. Physiological changes, including a reduction in heart rate, respiration rate and looking, typically all decline. Finally, when we see something new or the stimulus display alters in such a way as to become novel, we show a *release from habituation*, that is, we once again attend to the stimulus. In infant research, habituation paradigms provide us with a tool for learning about infant development. They allow us to contrast various sorts of stimulus conditions and see whether the infant detects changes in these, measured by the amount of time they attend to the stimuli. Interestingly, 2 month-old infants take longer to habituate than younger and older infants (Colombo, 2002), perhaps due to the concurrent visual system gains (which we will examine shortly) achieved at this age.

As good as these methods are for studying infant development, they have some limitations, for example preferential looking methods. It is possible that an infant may, in fact, be able to perceptually discriminate between two stimuli but perhaps not show any preference for one stimulus over the other. As a result, their ability to discriminate between the stimuli would go undetected. In other words, preferences imply discrimination, but discrimination does not imply preference. Whatever limitations might accompany preferential looking and habituation techniques, these methods represent an important advance in the ability to examine perceptual development from the earliest point in the life span.

Can you think of any other possible limitations of the preferential looking and habituation techniques? In considering your answer, perhaps it might be worth re-reading the section on observation in Chapter 3.

The Development of the Senses

Touch

Our sense of touch is an extremely important sense. The sense organ which allows us to discriminate touch is of course the skin. The skin is our largest organ, covering our entire body. Nerve endings, located under our skin, mediate our sense of touch, responding to sensations on the skin.

These same nerve endings also respond to dimensions such as temperature. Our sense of touch is also mediated by nerve endings in other specialized surfaces, such as the lips.

We know that newborn infants are sensitive to touch. The **rooting reflex**, the tendency for infants to search for objects which touch them on the cheek (which helps them locate their mother's nipple for feeding), is a sign that the infant is sensitive to touch. Similarly, the **Babinski reflex**, a splaying of the toes and foot, is elicited in newborn infants by lightly stroking the bottom of the infant's foot, from heel to toe. This reflex is useful in detecting early damage to the nervous system as it is absent in infants with spinal cord defects. A study by Reisman (1987) showed that 1 day-old infants are also sensitive to temperature. In this study, infants reacted negatively to having a cold glass tube placed on their cheek, turning their heads to avoid it. In contrast, infants turned their head towards a warm glass tube. In general, newborn infants are sensitive to any stimuli that are colder than their body temperature (Humphrey, 1978).

There is widespread agreement that our sense of touch is operative at birth. In fact, according to Field (2001), our sense of touch may be active well before we are born, and there is evidence to suggest it may be the first sense to develop. Infants in the womb are surrounded by fluid and are in contact with the mother's tissues. It would seem likely that these factors stimulate an infant's sense of touch before they are born.

Before the end of their first year, infants can learn to discriminate objects solely on the basis of touch (Streri & Pecheux, 1986). For example, a study by Gibson and Walker (1984) gave 1 month-old infants one of two stimuli to suck on: either a plastic rod or a soft sponge made into the same shape as the plastic rod. Then infants watched an experimental display where two rods were shown moving around. One rod remained rigid and did not bend as it was moved about whereas the other rod was shown to bend and flex with movement. The experimenters measured infants looking times at the two stimuli. The findings revealed that infants looked longer at the type of object they had previously sucked on. If the infants had sucked on the sponge rod, they tended to look more at the rod in the display which bent as it moved. These findings strongly suggest that infants discriminated the rods on the basis of their oral contact with them. In other words, they could remember the feel of the rods by having spent time mouthing them. More recent research suggests that babies as young as 2 days-old can discriminate on the basis of touch (Streri, Lhote, & Dutilleul, 2000). Objects were placed in the hands of 2 day-old infants. They quickly habituated to the objects, indicated by holding time. To control for the possibility that the infants grew fatigued rather than habituated, the researchers placed new objects in the infants' hands and holding time increased again. The findings suggested that even very young infants use touch to understand their world.

Infants' use of touch to explore the world of objects increases as soon as they can successfully grasp them. Babies are frequently observed to mouth objects and, as parents know, one needs to be especially vigilant to make certain that the wrong sorts of objects do not end up in their mouths. The use of mouthing to explore objects reaches its zenith by about 6 months of age, after which it declines steadily in favour of more complex exploration using the new-found ability to reach for and grasp objects so they can be examined in a multitude of ways (Ruff, Saltarelli, Cappazoli, & Dubiner, 1992).

At one time, it was believed that infants did not experience pain and, as a result, many medical procedures were carried out without administering the infant any pain-relieving medications.

Table 6.2   Milestones in children's perceptual development

Age	Milestone
1 to 3 months	A clear preference for human faces is in evidence by 3 months old.
	Sense of touch is operative.
	Newborns can distinguish tastes such as salty and sweet.
	Newborns are able to distinguish their own mother based on her smell. Newborns react to noxious smells but learning which smells are noxious takes some time.
	Newborns' hearing is much less sensitive (by about 17db) than adults'. Most sensitive to sounds within the typical range of the human voice.
	Visual acuity in newborns is very poor. Improves dramatically over the first year. Visual accommodation reaches adult levels by 2 months old.
	Newborns are unable to discriminate objects on the basis of colour. Colour vision develops by about 2 to 3 months old.
	Size and shape constancy are present at birth but refined into the early childhood years.
	1 month-olds show evidence of intermodal perception in that they can match visual and tactile cues.
3 to 6 months	Exploration of objects through touch. Reaches its zenith by 6 months.
	Can distinguish between a range of musical sounds.
	Can use sounds to help locate objects in a darkened room.
	Infants show a preference for increasingly complex visual patterns.
6 to 12 months	Can distinguish objects on the basis of touch alone.
	Can distinguish between simple melodic patterns.
	Ability to use sounds to locate object improves dramatically.
	Can recognize human forms from point light displays.
	Infants can perceive depth; they show a reluctance to cross the visual cliff.
12 months and beyond	Ability to discriminate pitch develops to adult levels by 2 years old.
	Visual acuity improves; reaches adult levels by about 5 years old.
	Refinement of perceptual skill as a function of increasing experience in a domain (i.e. development of expertise).

For example, male infants were routinely circumcised without an anaesthetic to relieve their pain. The findings we have reviewed on the newborn infant's sensitivity to touch have led to new ways of thinking about pain. One source of evidence that suggests infants do, in fact, experience pain during such procedures is the release of the stress hormone cortisol into the bloodstream. Male infants have been found to show significantly higher levels of cortisol in their bloodstream (when compared to a pre-procedure cortisol measure) after a circumcision (Gunnar, Malone, Vance, & Fisch, 1985).

While concerns about the safety of pain-relieving drugs with infants have typically meant that their use with infants is limited, newer drugs are being developed which may prove safe for infants. In addition, other methods are being developed to help relieve infant discomfort, such as the use of an artificial nipple which delivers a sweet solution to the infant during the procedure. The sweet solution helps induce calm in the infants, and even produces a reduction in their heart rate (Blass & Ciaramitaro, 1994).

Taste

Are infants sensitive to different tastes such as *sweet*, *salty* and *bitter*? Research with new-born infants suggests that they are indeed sensitive to taste. Blass and Ciaramitaro (1994) have shown that, like adults, newborns prefer sweet tastes. Rosenstein and Oster (1988) performed an experiment wherein newborn infants, only 2 hours old, were given sweet, sour, bitter and salty substances. The infants produced distinct facial expressions in response to each. Infants tended to purse their lips in response to sour tastes and produced a reaction of disgust (an arched mouth and narrowed eyes) to the bitter substances. Infants showed a relaxed response to the sweet substance. Other research has shown that when sucking on a nipple which produces a sweet fluid, infants' sucking changes, showing fewer pauses between each suck (Crook & Lipsitt, 1976). Such findings tend to suggest that taste preferences may be innate. However, work by Menella and Beauchamp (1996) has shown that infant taste preferences can be modified by early experience. As explored in Research Example 6.1, infant taste preferences have a robust effect on the development of long-term taste preferences.

Research Example 6.1

Long-term Effects of Exposure to Salt in Food

In a recent study from the Monell Chemical Senses Centre, researchers examined the long-term effect of feeding starchy table foods – including bread, breakfast cereals and crackers which often contain added salt – to 6 month-old infants (Stein, Cowart, & Beauchamp, 2012). The study was important because excess sodium intake has been linked to a range of health problems later in life.

The salt preferences of 61 infants were tested at 2 and 6 months of age, and a sub-set of the children were examined again at 36–48 months. During the infant testing period, infants were allowed to drink from three bottles for two minutes. One bottled contained water, another a moderate amount of salt, and the third contained a relatively high concentration of salt (even by adult standards). Preference for salt was calculated as a solution intake to water ratio. Mothers also reported on their child's intake of salty foods (measured as simply 'yes' or 'no'). Similar comparisons were calculated for exposure to fruit. Salt

(Continued)

preference at 36–48 months was measured by mother-reported questionnaires asking about the child's food preferences: in addition, children were presented with salty and non-salty foods, asked to taste the foods, and then categorize them as 'like' versus 'dislike'. Liking was indicated by sharing the food with a doll representing a well-known children's character, such as Big Bird, whereas disliked foods were given to a grumpy character such as Oscar the Grouch 'to throw away'.

Results indicated a relationship between previous exposure to salty foods and consumption of the salty solution at 6 months of age. Fruit exposure was not related to consumption of the salty fluid. Moreover, by the time they were of preschool age, the infants fed starchy foods early on were more likely to lick salt from the surface of foods and tended to be more likely to eat plain salt. The findings demonstrate the significant role of early dietary experience in shaping food preferences later in life. Unlike preference for sweet foods and dislike of bitter foods, which seem to be present at birth, response to salty taste develops postnatally. The study is one of the latest in a mounting evidence base showing that the first few months of life represent a sensitive period for shaping flavour preferences.

Questions: What are the implications of this research in terms of preventing health problems later in life, such as obesity?

What are the study design issues that do not allow us to make definitive statements about cause and effect?

Is there a more accurate or revealing way we could measure an infant's intake of salty food?

Smell

As we noted earlier, the development of the senses is important in that it provides part of the foundation for later social interaction. In particular, the sense of smell plays a key role in helping infants to distinguish the key people in their world. Smell helps animals to identify their offspring, providing them with more protection against predators. Human mothers can similarly identify their own babies by smell, although here our sense is less well developed than that of other species. Is a newborn similarly able to identify their own mother through smell? In a classic study, MacFarlane (1975) showed that 6 day-old infants could distinguish their mother from other females on the basis of smell. MacFarlane used the breast pads which absorb leaking breast milk as the source of the mother's smell. She also used pads from other women who were breast feeding. Infants were placed on their backs on a table with a pad from their mother on one side and a pad from a strange female on the other. Infants turned more to the pad from their mother than to the other pad, suggesting that they recognized their mother's scent. Whether infants are breast-fed or bottle-fed, they still learn to recognize the distinctive scent of their own mother, although this process may take somewhat longer for bottle-fed infants (Cernoch & Porter, 1985; Porter, Makin, Davis, & Christensen, 1992).

Their sense of smell also provides infants with a measure protection against odours which may emanate from toxic substances. Rieser, Yonas and Wilkner (1976) found that newborns would quickly turn their head away from a noxious smell like ammonia. Infants' preferences for smells are not unlike those of adults. For example, they prefer smells such as bananas, honey and chocolate, and reject smells such as rotten eggs (Maurer & Maurer, 1988; Steiner, 1979). Are infants' preferences for certain smells innate? Research has suggested that, while newborns do seem to have an innate preference for certain smells and are quickly able to learn to distinguish particular scents such as that of their mother, some learning about what 'smells good' still occurs. One study exploring the learning of odour preferences in newborns found that babies of mothers who had consumed anise responded to an anise smell quite positively. In contrast, babies of mothers who had never consumed anise often turned way from the smell, and displayed negative facial expressions such as grimacing (Schaal, Marlier, & Soussignan, 2000). Studies have shown that preschool children can also learn odour preferences; they do not respond in the same way as adults when exposed to many odours which adults naturally find unpleasant (Crook, 1987). Even into adulthood we may continue to learn to discriminate on the basis of smell, for example, learning to distinguish different varieties of wine.

Hearing

So far, we have seen that an infant's sensory abilities are quite well developed at birth. Perhaps not surprisingly, then, hearing is no exception to this trend. Tests given to babies shortly after birth reveal that newborns have advanced hearing ability (Saffran, Werker, & Werner, 2006). However, this does not mean that infants hear as well as adults. One dimension on which infants' hearing does not match that of adults is *auditory sensitivity*. Adults can hear much softer, quieter sounds than can newborn infants. A sound must be approximately 10 to 17 decibels louder for an infant to hear it than for an adult (a *decibel* is the measure of the loudness of a sound) (Hecox, 1975). According to Maurer and Maurer (1988), infants' auditory sensitivity improves steadily through infancy and reaches its height by the time children are ready for school.

The sounds to which infants are most sensitive are those which come within the typical frequency range of a human voice (Aslin, Jusczyk, & Pisoni, 1998). A number of researchers have studied infant speech perception, as it seems that babies have especially sensitive hearing when it comes to human language. Habituation studies have found that newborn infants prefer human speech over non-speech sounds which are structurally similar (Vouloumanos & Werker, 2004). Other habituation studies have found that infants can discriminate between many speech sounds, including 'ba' and 'ga'. In fact, it seems that an infant's ability to discriminate between sounds is more fine-tuned than an adult's (Aldridge, Stillman, & Bower, 2001). However, infants are also less sensitive to low-pitched sounds. This fact may explain why people often use a higher pitch when speaking to young infants. Research has further shown that infants are much more attentive to speech uttered with a higher pitch (Cooper & Aslin, 1990; Fernald, 1985). While newborns may have difficulty discriminating sounds that are low in pitch, infants quickly reach adult levels of pitch discrimination, usually by 2 years of age (Saffran & Griepentrog, 2001).

Is speech the only type of sound to which infants are attuned? Interestingly, infants seem very well attuned to musical sounds. Newborn infants will increase their rate of sucking if they are rewarded with hearing musical sounds instead of noise. By the time they are a few days old, infants can distinguish patterns of tones in a rising or descending order (Bijeljac-Babic, Bertoncini, & Mehler, 1993). By 2 months they can distinguish a range of musical sounds, and by 6 months of age they can discriminate between simple melodic patterns (Trehub & Trainor, 1993). Such findings have led to the conclusion that, like speech, there seems to be a biological preparedness to perceive music (Kagan & Zetner, 1996).

An important aspect of hearing is its role in infants' exploration of the environment. A variety of research has shown that infants have impressive capabilities locating the source of sounds. Newborns will turn their head in the direction of a sound (Muir & Clifton, 1985; Muir & Field, 1979). Clifton and her colleagues (Clifton et al., 1994) have shown that 4 month-old infants placed in a completely dark room can use auditory cues to help them accurately reach out to an object which emits a sound. Soon afterwards, they can use auditory cues to help them judge whether the object is too far away to reach or not (Clifton, Perris, & Bullinger, 1991). Over the first half year, infants generally become increasingly adept at using sound to locate objects (Morrongiello, Hewitt, & Gotowiec, 1991).

One might ask why infants' hearing is so remarkably good at birth. Have newborn infants had some experience with hearing before birth? The research findings on this question suggest that this is, in fact, the case. Consider a study by DeCasper and Spence (1986) designed to address this question, in which pregnant mothers were asked to read a particular book, *The Cat in the Hat* by Dr Seuss, twice a day to their infants for the last six weeks of their pregnancy. After birth, they used a preferential sucking paradigm to measure infant preferences (i.e. they measured the rates at which infants sucked on an artificial nipple while listening to different stimuli, in this case, stories). The experimenters had the mothers record themselves reading *The Cat in the Hat* and another story. Over several trials, the infants would learn that if they sucked in a particular pattern (e.g. long, slow sucks) they would hear *The Cat in the Hat*, and if they sucked in another pattern, they would hear the other story. The investigators found that infants sucked such that they listened to *The Cat in the Hat* significantly more than to the other story. The findings suggest that the infants discriminated the stories on the basis of familiarity, that is, they preferred the story they had heard previously. While these findings are impressive and indicate that infants can hear in the womb, it is clear that further work remains to be done in order to examine what aspects of the sounds they hear infants can use and how prenatal auditory experience affects the development of the auditory system.

The Development of Vision

It is probably true to say that humans are more reliant on their vision than they are on any of their other senses. Ironically, the visual system is the least developed of any of the five senses in infancy. While newborns can perform impressive visual feats, such as detecting motion in the visual field and tracking moving objects with their eyes (Kellman & Banks, 1998), the 'hardware' which makes up their visual system is not fully developed at birth. One aspect of the visual system which undergoes further development after birth is the **retina**, the membrane that lines the back of the eyes and receives light which is then sent as signals from the eye through the optic nerve to the brain. The cells which make up the retina have not fully matured at birth. Moreover, the pathways this information takes to reach the brain, and indeed the parts of the brain which are responsible for processing this information, also undergo further maturation, a process which may take several years (Kellman & Banks, 1998). Given that selected aspects of the visual system require further maturation, there may be certain classes of information which are either handled poorly by the infant or not handled at all (see the discussion on colour vision below).

The developing brain constructs images of the world from neural activity in many interconnected brain regions that have specialized roles in seeing. Two main aspects of seeing exist – the 'where' and the 'what' (Aamodt & Wang, 2011). We will discuss both aspects below. The 'where' refers to perception of motor and space while the 'what' pathway refers to the evaluation of objects, which includes perception of shape, colour and patterns.

Visual acuity

The term **visual acuity** refers to the quality of a person's vision, measured in terms of the fineness of discriminations which they can make. Good visual acuity allows one to see the fine details of an object or a scene. Psychologists are interested in visual acuity because it helps shed light on the development of the components of the visual system. Visual acuity is usually measured in terms of the distance and size of the object; tests of visual acuity usually involve attempting to discriminate stimulus items such as letters of the alphabet at standardized distances. For example, if you are able to discriminate a letter only at 20 feet away while people with perfect vision can read the same letter at 60 feet, you would have 20/60 vision.

Courage and Adams (1990) used this same index with newborn infants. Typically, infants can see an object at 20 feet as well as adults can at 600 feet (ranging from 200 to 800 feet). Recent research confirms this finding (Slater, 2001). According to Kellman and Banks (1998), infants at this age would be defined as legally blind on the basis of their visual acuity. Anything that is not held quite close to a baby will not be seen by them. Using tests of visual discrimination involving black stripes on a grey field, Maurer and Maurer (1988) found that infants' ability to discriminate the stripes from the background was one-thirtieth that of a normally-sighted adult. In other words, infants could not see stripes that were narrower than .1 of an inch from one foot away. Fortunately, their visual acuity undergoes rapid changes over the first few months of life. By 8 months of age, infants see about one fourth as well as an adult (i.e. stripes of about .01 of an inch wide from one foot away). Visual acuity reaches adult levels by about 5 years of age (Maurer & Maurer, 1988).

Another aspect of the infant's visual system which limits their acuity and impedes their ability to see very close or very distant objects is the relative immaturity of the muscles which guide eye movements. When viewing distant objects, the muscles of the eye actually change the shape of the lens to provide an appropriate focus on the object. This process of changing the shape of the lens is referred to as **visual accommodation** (Bremner, 1994). The eye movements of infants are less accurate than those of adults and can accommodate only minor changes initially. Newborn infants focus best on those objects placed about 10 inches from their face; objects which are much further or much closer will appear blurry to them. Between 2 to 4 months of age, infants become much more practised at visual accommodation and begin to achieve adult levels of performance (Bremner, 1994; Maurer & Maurer, 1988).

In fact, acuity continues to develop and become refined over childhood and seems to be modified by genes and experience. One interesting aspect of our environment that has been identified as important in the development of vision across childhood is time spent outdoors. While genes have been implicated in vision problems, such as myopia, otherwise known as nearsightedness, and resulting in faraway objects appearing blurry, the amount of time a child spends outdoors also plays a key role. Rates of myopia have been increasing exponentially in recent years. Researchers comparing 6 to 7 year-old children of Chinese descent living in Australia to those living in Singapore found vastly increased rates of myopia in the Singapore residents (almost 30% compared to 3% living in Australia) (Rose et al., 2008); this was despite their parents having similar rates of myopia (around 70%) in both countries. Children in Australia spent an average of 14 hours per week outside versus three hours per week outside in Singapore. Explanations remain speculative, but one possible reason for the protective effects of outdoor activity on vision development is exposure to bright light, since our brains evolved in an environment where children spent most of their time outdoors.

Colour vision

One of the most active areas of research in infant perception has been the study of colour vision. The most basic question for much of this research has been 'when can infants distinguish colours on the basis of hue alone?' To answer this question, we first need to define **hue**. Hue refers to the wavelength of light, the primary feature which distinguishes one colour from another. The colour we call red has a different wavelength from that for the colour we call green. We can discriminate hue from **brightness**, the intensity of a colour. This distinction is important because two stimuli with different hues may also differ in terms of their brightness, thus we cannot be certain on which feature infants might distinguish the stimuli. We know from early research on infant perception that newborn infants can distinguish brightness (Maurer & Maurer, 1988) but what about hue? Studies of newborns have generated strong evidence that they do not perceive colours. When brightness is controlled across a pair of stimuli which differ only in terms of hue, infants cannot discriminate between them. The evidence on when exactly infants do perceive colour is mixed. Some researchers have stated that by 2 months of age, infants are able to discriminate colours across the entire spectrum, and by 3 months of age infants are also able to group colours into the basic colour categories such as red, green and blue (Teller, 1997). In other words, by the time they have reached 4 months of age, infants perceive colours in the same way as do adults.

In a review of the literature on visual development, Kellman and Banks (1998) suggest that infants younger than 7 weeks of age probably cannot process colour information. They argue that this limit occurs because of the relatively immature state of the newborn's visual system. The cells which process colour reside in the middle of the eye and are called **cones**. The cones in a newborn infant's eye are not fully developed at birth and it takes some weeks before they begin to function properly (Bremner, 1994; Maurer & Maurer, 1988). It may be that these deficits in colour processing are related to the immature state of the structure of the infant's eye; colour perception only becomes possible when the neural structures in the eye and the visual cortex begin to perform their functions. It may also be the case that infants can perceive colour, but that the methods employed in testing are flawed. It is difficult to design studies that separate hue and brightness, and infants may in fact be able to detect different hues, but remain unresponsive to different levels of brightness.

Pattern perception

Recall the quote by William James on the nature of infants' sensory experience mentioned at the beginning of this chapter, suggesting that their world is a 'confusion' of perceptions. Psychologists working since James have been interested in examining whether this claim is in fact true. Do infants experience the world as confusion or do they experience more meaningful, organized patterns? If they do experience patterns, do they have to learn to construct their sensations into meaningful, organized wholes?

One of the pioneers of research on perceptual development in infancy, Robert Fantz (1961), showed that newborn infants prefer to look at patterned rather than plain stimuli: for example, infants prefer a drawing of a face to a black and white drawing of a circle. As they age, infants seem to prefer increasingly complex visual patterns (Banks & Salapatek, 1983), although the attempt to figure out why infants prefer certain patterns has proven to be a difficult exercise for perceptual researchers. One of the features which seems to govern infants' preferences is called **contrast sensitivity** (Banks & Ginsburg, 1985). This refers to the characteristic changes in brightness across the different regions of a visual pattern, for example, the differences in the black and white squares of a checkerboard pattern. Infants prefer patterns with higher contrasts. Of course the ability to perceive contrasts is related to visual acuity and so very young infants, because of their poor acuity, will prefer the contrasts found in large patterns such as in a checkerboard with very large squares. As their visual acuity increases and they become able to resolve finer patterns, infants will shift their preference to more fine-grained patterns with a high contrast, such as checkerboards with smaller squares (Maurer & Maurer, 1988).

Another aspect of pattern perception which develops is the way in which infants visually scan patterns. When looking at a visual pattern such as a human face, infants will initially focus on the edges and boundaries of that face (Maurer & Salapatek, 1976), but by 2 months of age they will begin to take in features which reside inside the pattern (Kellman & Arterberry, 2006; Kellman & Banks, 1998). By about 3 months of age, infants are almost as able as adults to see a unified pattern in a moving image (Booth, Pinto, & Berthenthal, 2002). While, initially, infants seem to perceive only the isolated aspects of visual patterns, with time and experience they begin to combine these elements so they can perceive more complex, meaningful patterns, such as the ability to perceive a human figure in motion from a *point light display*. This is created by placing dots on a visual image, for example, the joints of a human figure walking. When the image is removed and only the pattern of moving lights remains, you have a point light image. Research by Bertenthal and colleagues has demonstrated that by about 9 months of age infants show a distinct preference for a pattern of lights representing a person in motion as opposed to a pattern of randomly moving lights (Bertenthal, Profitt, & Kramer, 1987).

Object perception

A further development in infants' developing perceptual skills is the ability to perceive the world of objects. Unlike pattern perception, the ability to perceive objects requires perception in three dimensions. Given the fact that learning to perceive and interact with objects is critical to an infant's developing cognitive system, we need to examine the developmental course of the abilities which govern object perception.

One important development in object perception is the ability to perceive an object's size as the same no matter what its distance is from the observer and independent of the size of its retinal image. This ability is known as **size constancy**. Research has suggested that newborn infants come equipped with this ability (Slater, Mattock, & Brown, 1990). The ability to perceive size constancy, while present at birth, develops further as an infant's binocular vision improves due to changes in muscular coordination (refer to our discussion of visual accommodation, above). Indeed, refinements in the perception of size constancy continue to take place until about 11 years of age (Kellman & Banks, 1998).

Another aspect of object perception is the achievement of **shape constancy**. Shape constancy refers to the perception of an object's shape as being consistent even though movement may change the shape of its image on the retina. A study by Slater and Morrison (1985) shows that this ability is also present at birth. Both of these findings on object perception serve to underscore the point that, in contrast to theories such as Piaget's (1954, 1969), infants come remarkably well equipped with perceptual capacities that allow them to organize and interpret their perceptual experiences from birth.

Very young infants seem to distinguish an object from its surrounding by relying on motion. When two objects are touching, infants younger than 4 months will see these as one object. It is only as infants observe objects in motion that they can see extra information such as the object's outlines, colour and texture. This explains why infants tend to be particularly attracted to moving objects and people (Bahrick, Gogate, & Ruiz, 2002).

Face perception

As we saw earlier, infants prefer to look at complex patterns such as faces. In fact, a number of studies have revealed that infants do in fact come with a bias to look at human faces over other sorts of visual patterns. Early work in this field by Fantz (1966) demonstrated that infants prefer to look at schematic illustrations of human faces more so than at other patterns. Fantz showed newborn infants a black and white picture of a schematic human face along with a variety of other visual patterns, such as a bull's-eye or plain colours. His data indicated that newborn infants looked longer at the face than at any of the other stimuli. Further work by Fantz revealed that this preference was difficult to interpret. When he showed infants both scrambled human faces (drawings where the arrangement of parts such as the ears, nose and eyes were mixed up) and normal faces, infants below 2 months showed no clear visual preference (Maurer & Barrera, 1981). These findings tend to suggest that infants younger than 2 months of age do not see faces as structured wholes, but rather as a collection of parts. Research into the features which guide infants to pay attention to faces, whether arranged correctly or scrambled, is ongoing.

However, by about 3 months of age, infants seem to show a clear preference for correctly arranged human faces (Maurer & Maurer, 1988). Work by Dannemiller and Stephens (1988) illustrated this fact rather nicely. They presented two groups of infants aged 1½ and 3 months-old two sets of stimuli, computer-generated faces and computer-generated abstract patterns. Two sets of faces were shown to the infants, a 'normal' face and an 'odd' face (a negative image of the normal face). Similarly, the infants were shown two sets of abstract patterns, a normal image and its reversed image. In addition, both sets of images, faces and shapes were equated for contour density and complexity. Using a preferential looking paradigm, Dannemiller and Stephens found that 1½ month-old infants were no more likely to look at the face stimuli than they were the abstract patterns. In contrast, the 3 month-old infants preferred the schematic faces over the abstract patterns and favoured the 'normal face' over the 'odd face'. Lest you think infants' preference for the normal face was simply because they found the non-reversed image more interesting, Dannemiller and Stephens found that, for the abstract stimuli, there was no such preference: infants were equally likely to look at either the normal or reversed abstract patterns, suggesting they did not simply find the non-reversed images more attractive.

Interestingly, the preference for faces co-occurs with changes in the way infants scan faces. Maurer and Salapatek (1976) showed that at 1 month old infants scan the edges or boundaries of faces but fail to scan the internal features of the face. Consistent with findings described earlier, infants seem to be attracted to the areas of the face which show high contrast, such as the border between the hairline and the forehead. It is not until 2 to 3 months of age that infants begin to scan the interior of the face (Cohen & Salapatek, 1975). Infants as young as 7 weeks tend to be drawn to eyes, but this does not mean they are seeing the face as a whole (Haith, Bergman, & Moore, 1977). Similarly, the finding that newborns prefer their mother's face to a stranger's face does not mean they are 'seeing' her face the same way we do. The preference may be due to the baby's focus on a particular feature. When the mother does something to slightly alter her appearance, such as wear a headscarf, newborns tend to look at her and a stranger equally, suggesting the baby no longer recognizes her (Pascalis De Schonen, Morten, Deruelle, & Fabre-Grenet, 1995).

Depth perception

An important dimension which infants must learn to perceive is depth. After all, an infant lives in a three-dimensional world. When do infants begin to perceive depth? Gibson and Walk (1960) devised a test of depth perception known as the **visual cliff**. The visual cliff is basically two tables with a gap in between them which creates a drop-off or 'cliff'. The tables are covered in a checkerboard pattern which accentuates the drop, making it clear to the infant. However, rather than allow them to plummet over the edge, Gibson and Walk cover the cliff with a sheet of clear Plexiglas, which can easily support an infant should they choose to venture out across the surface. The experimental device creates a very convincing illusion of a cliff. Gibson and Walk arranged the experiment such that infants were placed

Image 6B   In a classic experiment, a 'visual cliff' with an illusory drop is used to test babies' depth perception. Only inexperienced crawlers were enticed by their mothers to venture across the plexiglass covered drop

Source: Dahl, Campos and Anderson (2013)

on one side of the cliff to the mother stood on the other side, with the drop-off in between them. The experimenters asked mothers to try to entice their infants to crawl across the cliff. They found that by 6 months of age, infants were extremely reluctant to cross over, suggesting that, by this age, they perceived the depth and understood its significance to their wellbeing.

Further work using the visual cliff paradigm has added greatly to our understanding of the development of depth perception. In one set of studies, Joseph Campos and his colleagues employed a visual cliff apparatus which had both a 'shallow' side and a 'deep' side. Campos arranged for 1½ month-old infants to be placed directly on the shallow side of the cliff and then on the deep side of the cliff. The infants' heart rates were measured in order to see how they reacted to being placed on the cliff. The results showed that when placed on the shallow side and then on the deep side, infants showed a slowed heart rate, indicating that they were *interested* in the experience (Campos, Langer, & Krowitz, 1970). In contrast, when 7 to 9 month-old infants were placed onto the deep end of the cliff, they showed heart rate acceleration, indicating, once again, that they were afraid, because they perceived the depth and recognized the situation as threatening (Bertenthal & Campos 1987; Campos, Bertenthal, & Kermonian, 1992).

Research using the visual cliff paradigm has also demonstrated that locomotor experience is very important to the development of depth perception. In one study investigating the effects of locomotor experience, Bertenthal, Campos and Kermonian (1994) found that when infants who did not yet crawl were given 30 to 40 hours' worth of experience in infant walkers (wheeled devices which allow the infant to move themselves about a room), they showed fear on the visual cliff. Locomotor experience clearly provides infants with chances to learn about depth perception and the meaning of heights (Bertenthal & Clifton, 1998).

Research Example 6.2

Visual Expectations: Infants' Perception of Object Trajectories

In a series of studies designed to examine how infants visually perceive partially hidden objects, Johnson, Amso and Slemmer (2003) found that the ability to *visually expect* gradually emerges in infancy. To test for this, the experimenters placed a computer screen in front of the infants which showed a series of balls, either moving across the screen or partially hidden by a box as they moved across the screen. Infant interest was measured by timing how long they looked at the screen. Six month-old infants tended to look longer at the discontinuous trajectory, indicating that they were surprised by the balls disappearing behind the box. In contrast, 4 month-old infants tended to look longer at the continuous trajectory. Two month-old infants showed a different pattern of response, not discriminating between the two conditions (not hidden versus partially hidden). Further, when the experimenters narrowed the occlusion gap, i.e. made the ball hidden for less time, the 4 month-old infants behaved similarly to the 6 month-old infants. At 2 months, the infants were still equally interested (or uninterested) in either ball trajectory. These findings indicate that by 6 months of age, infants are able to perceive the continuity of an object's trajectory despite partial occlusion, even when that object is hidden for some time. At 4 months of age visual perception is somewhat developed, and dependent on the length of time an object is hidden. In contrast, infants at 2 months do not appear to have a sufficiently developed visual system to perceive an object's path when it is hidden for even a short amount of time. Overall, the findings show that perceptual continuity gradually emerges a few months after birth and becomes more established by 6 months of age. Can you think of a theory that these findings might have implications for? Return to our section on Piaget (Chapter 6), and more specifically the development of object permanence, and see if you can link these findings to Piaget's theory.

There are a variety of visual cues which give rise to the perception of depth. One set of cues, known as **kinetic depth cues**, come from the motion of objects through our visual field. This movement provides clues as to how close or distant things are from us by the speed with which they pass through our visual field. Nearby objects move past more quickly than more distant objects (Nánez, 1987). Studies suggest that infants are sensitive to kinetic cues by about 3 months of age (Yonas & Owsley, 1987). The fact that we have binocular vision also provides further cues to depth. One such cue which we use to see depth is **retinal disparity**, the fact that each eye receives slightly different images of a given scene. Our brains are sensitive to this disparity between the two retinal images and use this information to create an awareness of depth. Studies that examine this awareness present two overlapping images to infants, who wear special goggles that ensure each eye sees one of the images. If binocular cues are developed, the baby should see a three-dimensional view, otherwise the image looks like a disorganized series of dots. By about 3 months of age infants are able to use retinal disparity to perceive depth, and this ability improves rapidly over the first year of life (Brown & Miracle, 2003). Finally, infants are also able to take advantage of what are called **pictorial depth cues**. These are the kinds of information that artists use to convey depth and perspective in two-dimensional art forms such as drawing. Think of how you might draw railway tracks leading off into the distance. You would probably make the lines which represent the rails move closer together until they vanish at a horizon. This effect suggests distance to the viewer. Research has suggested that infants gradually learn to use this sort of information to perceive depth. By the time they are about 7 months old infants begin to respond to pictorial depth cues (Arterberry, Yonas, & Bensen, 1989; Sen, Yonas, & Knill, 2001), although this development is far from complete (Kellman & Banks, 1998). A sensitivity to pictorial depth cues is one of the last aspects of perception to develop.

Intermodal perception

So far, we have examined each of the senses in isolation. However, it is clearly the case that humans can combine information across the different sensory modalities. It should be obvious from your own experience that you combine or integrate various forms of sensory information, for example, sight and sound, so that you perceive a coherent whole. This integration of sensory information from more than one modality at a time is called **intermodal perception**. Of what use is intermodal perception? Intermodal perception is critical to our ability to make sense of the world. For instance, matching up lip movements and sounds is an example of intermodal perception and, moreover, one that is critical to our ability to understand speech. You might think that intermodal perception sounds like a complicated process in that there must be some work involved to integrate the senses; however, research on the development of intermodal perception suggests that this impression would be somewhat mistaken.

Meltzoff and Borton (1979) performed a classic study on intermodal perception. They looked at infants' ability to integrate tactile and visual information. In this study, two groups of 1 month-old infants were given either a normal, smooth infant pacifier or a specially designed pacifier which was covered in knobs. After some experience sucking on the pacifiers, these were removed. Infants were then shown a display which contained pictures of two pacifiers, the smooth one and the knobbly one. Infants' looking time at the two displays was measured. Findings indicated that infants who had received the smooth pacifier looked more at its corresponding picture; this same finding applied to the group who had received the textured pacifier. The authors suggested that infants were able to grasp the equivalence of the information obtained by touch and sight and that, given the young age of the infants involved in the study, this ability is probably unlearned. This study was replicated by Kaye and Bower (1994) with newborn infants who ranged in age from 13 to 43 hours, a very young sample. Importantly, these infants were all breast-fed and had had no previous experience with pacifiers. As in the Meltzoff and Borton study, the infants in Kaye and Bower's study showed a visual preference for the pacifier on which they had been sucking, even though the amount of time they were given with the pacifier (20 seconds) was very limited. These findings provide support for the nativist position: that intermodal perception is an innate, unlearned ability.

However, infants' ability to perceive correspondences across sensory modalities does not appear to be as easy across all the combinations of modalities. Spelke (1987) found that it is not until 4 months of age that infants learn to match sights and sounds, such as the sound of a voice to a display of faces with moving lips. Such findings have suggested there are rules to be learned which guide the integration of information across sensory modalities and that it takes some time to learn these rules. Moreover, infants require experience with the world before they can be expected to learn to match a sound with an object they have never seen before. Thus what is of interest to developmentalists interested in perception is not so much the issue of *when* an infant learns to perceive a particular sensory combination, but *how* they learn to do so. Further research will be required in order to learn more about the processes that underlie intermodal perception (Haith & Benson, 1998).

Can you think of any ways in which intermodal perception might contribute to other aspects of development?

Perceptual Development across the Life Span

What about perceptual development across the life span? We tend to think of perceptual ability as something that declines with age, for example, the decline in visual acuity throughout adulthood. However, there is an obvious area where we see perceptual development occur at any age: the development of expertise in a given domain. According to some theories, expertise is the development of perceptual skills or the perception of higher-order invariances in the environment (Carey, 1996). At any stage of life, people can become more expert at forms of perceptual discrimination. Avid birdwatchers become more able to identify species of birds and the differences among them. Art lovers can learn to identify a painter by their brushstrokes and discriminate among schools of artists based on combinations of properties such as type of brushstroke and use of colour. Tennis players learn to swing or not swing at a given shot based on how their opponent hits the ball, judging rapidly whether or not a shot will be out of bounds. In fact, some psychologists would argue that developing expertise is a process of being increasingly able to specify the invariances or norms that exist across a set of stimuli. For example, people who become judges at dog shows learn to perceive certain relationships among stimuli such as the shininess of the dog's coat, but they also learn to see relations among various properties (e.g. shininess, stature, and obedience) and can learn to perceive the norms in those properties which allow them to make judgements about individuals and compare or rank individuals. According to Carey (1996), this process is not particularly *developmental* at all, in that it does not derive from general limitations on a person's cognitive abilities but, rather, reflects their *experience* with a class of stimuli. Once again, the question of interest is how experience is utilized.

Summary

As we have seen, perceptual abilities are surprisingly well developed in infancy, although there are many important changes which follow on from these early abilities. An issue which remains unresolved in the field is the extent to which our perceptual abilities are either learned or innate. The study of perceptual development is also worth our attention given the fact that perceptual abilities provide for the ability to interact with the physical and social worlds and, thus, are very relevant to the study of children's cognitive and social development.

Glossary

Affordances are the properties of objects that offer the individual the potential to interact with it in a variety of ways.

Babinski reflex is a splaying of the toes and foot elicited in newborn infants by a light stroking of the bottom of the infant's foot, from heel to toe.

Brightness refers to the intensity of a colour.

Cones are the cells which process colour and reside in the middle of the eye.

Contrast sensitivity refers to the characteristic changes in the brightness across the different regions of a visual pattern.

Direct perception is a theory of perception associated with James and Eleanor Gibson which proposes that our sensory systems simply detect or pick up information which is already available in the structure of the information we receive from the world.

Hue refers to the wavelength of light, the primary feature which distinguishes one colour from another.

Intermodal perception refers to the use of sensory information from more than one sensory modality at a time (e.g. sight and sound) which is combined so that we perceive a coherent whole.

Invariances are aspects of the visual environment which do not change.

Kinetic depth cues arise via the motion of objects through our visual field, providing us with clues as to how close or distant objects are from us.

Neonate refers to a newborn baby.

Perception is the processes by which we make sense of our sensations.

Pictorial depth cues are the kinds of information that convey depth and perspective in two-dimensional art forms such as drawing.

Retina is the membrane that lines the back of the eyes and receives light which is then sent as signals from the eye through the optic nerve to the brain.

Retinal disparity refers to the fact that each eye receives slightly different images of a given scene. These cues help us to perceive depth.

Rooting reflex is the tendency for infants to search for objects which touch them on the cheek (a reflex which helps them locate their mother's nipple for feeding).

Schema are the terms used to describe a knowledge structure which guides our understanding and exploration of the environment.

Sensation refers to the act of detecting a stimulus event via a sensory system.

Shape constancy refers to the perception of an object's shape as being consistent even though movement may change the shape of its image on the retina.

Size constancy is the ability to perceive an object's size as the same no matter what its distance is from the observer.

Visual accommodation refers to the change in the shape of the lens to provide an appropriate focus on a viewed object.

Visual acuity refers to the quality of a person's vision, measured in terms of the fineness of the discriminations they can make.

Visual cliff is an apparatus designed to test infants' depth perception. It uses patterned materials to highlight a deep 'cliff' over which an infant can crawl. This cliff is actually covered in clear Plexiglas to prevent the infant from falling.

TEST YOUR KNOWLEDGE

1. Which of the following is not a reason, according to John Flavell, for our previous underestimation of infant perceptual abilities?

   a) An unwarranted generalization from older children
   b) The assumption that we begin life with very minimal capabilities which are gradually built up through learning

(Continued)

    c) Our primate relatives show poor perceptual skills, as must human infants

    d) A tendency to extrapolate downwards from the findings of poor perceptual skills in years after infancy

2. What kind of theory is Gibson's theory of perceptual development?

    a) Constructivist

    b) Bioecological

    c) Nativist

    d) A combination of nature and nurture

3. What principles do studies using habitation use?

    a) Boredom and novelty

    b) Novelty and disappointment

    c) Expectation and boredom

    d) Boredom, novelty and expectation

4. Which perceptual system takes the longest to emerge in infancy?

    a) Touch

    b) Taste

    c) Hearing

    d) Vision

    e) Olfaction

ANSWERS: 1–C, 2–C, 3–A, 4–D

Suggested Reading

Bremner, G. (2003). Perception, knowledge and action. In A. Slater and G. Bremner (eds), *An Introduction to Developmental Psychology* (pp. 115–140). Oxford: Blackwell.

Kellman, P. J., & Banks, M. S. (1998). Infant visual perception. In W. Damon (gen. ed.), D. Kuhn and R. Siegler (vol. eds), *Handbook of Child Psychology: Vol. 2: Cognition, perception and language* (5th edition, pp. 103–146). New York: Wiley.

Slater, A. M. (1998). *Perceptual Development: Visual, auditory and speech perception in infancy.* Hove: Psychology Press Ltd.

Want to learn more? For links to online resources relevant to this chapter, interactive quizzes and much more, visit the companion website at **https://edge.sagepub.com/keenan3e/**

Theories of Cognitive Development

7

Chapter Outline

LEARNING AIMS

At the end of this chapter you should:

- be able to describe the three theories of cognitive development covered
- understand and be able to define the key concepts of Piagetian theory, including *adaptation, organization, equilibration, and assimilation and accommodation*
- be familiar with the four stages of development described by Piaget
- be aware of evidence both for and against Piaget's theory
- understand and be able to define the key concepts of Vygotskian theory, including *elementary* and *higher mental functions, internalization, zone of proximal development* and *scaffolding*
- be aware of evidence both for and against Vygotsky's theory
- be able to describe the model of the human information processing system covered
- understand and be able to define the key concepts of the information processing approach, including *long-term* and *working memory, encoding, automatization* and *m-space*
- be able to articulate some of the similarities and differences between the three theories

Introduction

Cognition is the study of the thought processes or mental activity by which we acquire and deal with knowledge. The study of human cognition is a vast field, encompassing an extremely wide variety of topics. Examine any cognition textbook and you will find chapters on memory, attention, language, social cognition, reasoning, problem solving, and more. While ideally we would review each of these topics, it is simply impossible to do so in one chapter (especially in a book not devoted entirely to cognitive development). Therefore, in this chapter, we will cover three of the most influential theories of cognitive development – the work of Jean Piaget, Lev Vygotsky – and information processing views on cognitive development. Within the discussion of each theory we will consider some of the key aspects of cognitive development across childhood.

Piaget's Theory of Cognitive Development

Piaget's theory of cognitive development is considered the most important to emerge from the study of human development (Siegler, 1998), although it is perhaps the most controversial theory as well (Beilin, 1992). Piaget's theory and ideas are still at the centre of a debate in developmental psychology. Ultimately, whether you agree or disagree with his position, the student of human development needs to understand Piagetian theory in order to understand the field of cognitive development. Thus, we start the chapter with a survey of Piaget's theory of cognitive development.

According to Siegler (1998), there are a number of reasons for the longevity of Piaget's theory. First, his observations of children provide a remarkable 'feel' for what cognitive development looks like. Second, his theory addresses fundamental questions that are of interest to philosophers and lay people alike. Piaget's theory attempts to provide answers to questions such as 'what is intelligence?' and 'how do we develop knowledge?' Finally, his theory was notable for its breadth, drawing together seemingly unrelated aspects of development under a coherent theory.

However, the fact that Piaget's theory has been influential in the study of cognitive development does not mean it has been accepted uncritically. A number of serious problems with the theory have been identified. We will review some of these at the end of this section, but where the research bears on a specific stage of development, we will review evidence that runs counter to Piagetian theory.

An overview of Piagetian theory: key concepts

In contrast to the assumptions of behaviourist theories, that children developed in reaction to their environment and the rewards and punishments it provided, Piaget argued that children actively explore their world, and their thoughts are ultimately derived from their actions on the world. Piaget believed that children *construct* their reality as they manipulate and explore the world, and what children actually construct are cognitive structures which Piaget termed **schemes**. A scheme is an interrelated set of actions, memories, thoughts or strategies which are employed to predict and understand the environment. Gardner (1973) elaborates on this concept, arguing that a scheme is the aspects of an action or a mental operation which can be repeated with or generalized to a similar action or operation. Schemes form the basis for organizing one's reactions to the environment. As children grow, they develop and refine their schemes.

Piaget's early training was in the field of biology. Central to his theory were two biological concepts, **adaptation** and **organization** (Ginsburg & Opper, 1988). Organization refers to the individual's tendency to organize their cognitive structures or schemes into efficient systems (Lutz & Sternberg, 1999). Organization can take place independently of interaction with the environment. Children naturally begin to link together schemes, creating a more organized and interrelated cognitive system. For example, infants eventually begin to link together schemes developed for reaching, grasping and sucking objects, combining these into more complex structures that can be generalized to other situations and thus further their ability to negotiate the environment. Initially they cannot combine these actions but via the process of organization they are able to do so. This brings us to the concept of adaptation.

Adaptation involves the creation of cognitive structures or schemes through our interactions with the environment, allowing us to adjust to the demands posed by that environment. Adaptation takes place through two complementary processes called **assimilation** and **accommodation** (Piaget, 1952). Assimilation refers to the process of integrating the environment into one's current psychological structures (Lutz & Sternberg, 1999). That is, assimilation uses current schemes to interpret new knowledge. When we assimilate something, we mould it to fit in with our existing structures. Accommodation is the opposite process; it occurs when old schemes are adjusted to better fit with the demands of the environment. Assimilation and accommodation are most often seen to operate simultaneously (Ginsburg & Opper, 1988). Consider the following illustration of how this process works: the infant sees a circular ring and can assimilate this new object into their experience, applying their grasping scheme. Then the infant encounters a much smaller object, such as a plastic token. The child cannot grasp it using their standard grip. They are forced to accommodate to the object, altering their grip so as to be able to pick up the token and continue their exploration.

Piaget believed that development occurred as a result of our predispositions to organize and adapt to new experiences. However, there are times when our cognitive structures tend to remain in one state more than another. At some points in time, we will be able to assimilate most new experiences, whereas at others, we will be forced to accommodate and adapt our structures to the environment. Piaget argued that when we can assimilate changes in the environment we are in a state of cognitive *equilibrium*, a 'steady state' which our system aims for. However, when we are forced to accommodate we enter into a state of cognitive *disequilibrium*. States of disequilibrium force us to modify our cognitive structures so that we can assimilate changes and regain equilibrium. Piaget referred to this continual balance between achieving states of equilibrium and disequilibrium as **equilibration** (Piaget, 1952). The process of equilibration leads to the development of more efficient cognitive structures (Lutz & Sternberg, 1999).

Piaget noted that the organization of cognitive structures occurs in stages. For him, a **stage** of development was a period in which the child's cognitive structures were *qualitatively* similar. Piaget also maintained that stages had two important characteristics. First, they occurred in an *invariant* order in development; that is, stages are not missed and children move through these in a fixed order. Second, stages were *universal*, in that they were applicable to all children and were not affected by cultural or social norms. While children may progress through the stages at different speeds as a function of inherited traits or particular environmental influences (Piaget, 1926), the nature of the stages through which they progress does not change. Piaget postulated four stages of development. We will consider each of these stages in turn.

The sensorimotor stage

The **sensorimotor stage** encompasses the first two years of an infant's life. During the sensorimotor stage of infancy, children move from responding to the environment in a simplistic and reflexive manner to being able to think about the environment using symbols. According to Piaget (1954), the major achievement of the sensorimotor stage is the development of **object permanence**. This is the idea that objects continue to exist independently of our ability to perceive them or act on them. Object permanence is important as it signals the beginnings of the ability to think using representations rather than through actions. In what follows, we consider each of the six substages.

Table 7.1 Piaget's stages of sensorimotor development

Substage	Age	Significant Accomplishments and Limitations
Sensorimotor Stage	0 to 2 years	Infants initially understand the world via action but gradually develop the ability to use symbolic representations.
• Reflexive Schemes	0 to 1 months	Infants gain control over and practice reflex behaviours.
• Primary Circular Reactions	1 to 4 months	Infants repeat chance behaviours that lead to satisfying results (e.g. thumb sucking), and show a limited ability to anticipate events.
• Secondary Circular Reactions	4 to 8 months	Infants can combine single schemes into larger structures (e.g. repeatedly grasping and shaking a rattle). This behaviour is not goal-directed, however.
• Coordination of Secondary Circular Reactions	8 to 12 months	Secondary circular reactions are combined into new actions, and become intentional. For example, infants can coordinate a means and a goal.
• Tertiary Circular Reactions	12 to 18 months	Infants begin to repeat actions and vary them in a deliberately exploratory manner. Can solve the A-not-B task and develop object permanence.
• The Invention of New Means through Mental Combinations	18 to 24 months	Onset of the child's ability to think symbolically and mentally represent reality. Also heralds the beginning of pretend play.

Piaget (1952) argued that the sensorimotor stage of development was comprised of six substages. The first substage, *Reflexive Schemes*, runs from birth to 1 month-old. For Piaget, newborn behaviour consisted of little more than reflex behaviours. Development during this stage consisted of the infant gaining control over these behaviours and practising them. The second substage, *Primary Circular Reactions*, runs from about 1 to 4 months of age. During this stage, infants begin repeating chance behaviours that lead to satisfying results, developing simple motor habits such as sucking their thumbs and opening and closing their hands. Piaget termed these behaviours **primary circular reactions**. Additionally, infants start to vary their newly acquired behaviours in response to environmental demands, as, for example, when they open their mouths differently to a nipple than to a spoon. In other words, they show a limited ability to anticipate events.

Substage 3, *Secondary Circular Reactions*, runs from 4 to 8 months of age. Now infants perform actions that are more definitely oriented towards objects and events outside their own bodies, what Piaget termed **secondary circular reactions**. Using the secondary circular reaction, they try to maintain, through repetition, the interesting effects produced by their own actions, such as creating a sound with a rattle. During this stage, infants move beyond employing one scheme at a time, and begin to combine schemes into larger structures, for example, grasping and shaking. Although they are a great cognitive advance over the previous stage, secondary circular reactions are limited in that they involve undifferentiated connections between actions and objects. Piaget did not view the infant's behaviour as goal-directed or *intentional*; infants simply repeated newly acquired actions with respect to that object.

In substage 4, *Coordination of Secondary Circular Reactions* (which runs from 8 to 12 months of age), previously acquired secondary circular reactions are combined into new action sequences that are intentional and goal-directed. A clear example was provided by Piaget's object-hiding tasks, in which he showed the infant an attractive object which was then hidden under a cloth cover or beneath a cup. By substage 4, infants could set aside the obstacle and retrieve the object, coordinating two schemes: a *means* (pushing aside the cup) and a *goal* (grasping the object). Piaget regarded this means-end behaviour as the first truly intelligent behaviour and the foundation of all later problem solving. As well, the fact that substage 4 infants could retrieve a hidden object indicated that they had achieved some appreciation of object permanence. However, Piaget believed that infants' understanding of object permanence was limited at this stage. He claimed that, if an object were moved to a new location, infants of this level of ability would still search for the object in the place in which it had first been concealed, revealing that they did not view the object as existing independently of their actions on it. Finally, at this stage infants begin to show a tendency to engage in the *imitation* of behaviour.

From 12 to 18 months of age, infants progress through substage 5, *Tertiary Circular Reactions*, in which they begin to repeat actions and vary these in a deliberately exploratory manner. In doing so, infants try to provoke new results, as they quickly habituate to results they are familiar with and are no longer satisfied with them. At this stage, infants can solve the **A-not-B task**. In this task, infants search for hidden objects, but after a set number of trials where they search for an object at one location (the A trials) the object is hidden in a second location (the B trial). Substage 4 infants will continue to search at A on the B trial, whereas substage 5 infants will correctly search for the object at the new location. Another aspect of this stage is that infants can imitate more complex and unfamiliar behaviours. They can also exercise their schemes in play when, for example, they bang blocks together in different ways or drop toys (or food) from their highchair on purpose. Finally, infants will begin to distinguish themselves and their own actions from the world around them, showing the first signs of a developing sense of *self* (demonstrated through performance on the *rouge test*; see Chapter 11).

Infants typically reach substage 6, *The Invention of New Means through Mental Combinations*, at 18 months (lasting through to 2 years of age). Substage 6 marks the onset of a child's ability to think symbolically, that is to use mental representations of reality. Thus, at substage 6, the infant can think 'in their heads' before they act. In other words, they are able to combine symbols or representations in their heads rather than being tied to acting them out in sensorimotor behaviour, as in the previous stages. At substage 6, infants engage in *deferred imitation*, copying the *past* behaviour of models. Thus, it is not uncommon for children during this substage to repeat a word they have heard a day or even a week ago, almost as if the word springs to mind from nowhere. In addition, infants can pass *invisible displacement tasks*, a more advanced version of the A-not-B task. Invisible displacement tasks involve an investigator hiding an object out of the child's sight, and at this stage children can successfully find the object. Finally, at substage 6, infants engage for the first time in **pretend play**, where they act out imaginary activities and use real objects to stand for imagined objects.

Although research has supported the existence of Piaget's substages, other studies indicate that young children have more advanced cognitive abilities than he gave them credit for. Due to the development of new research paradigms, including the use of habituation to test for infant interest, we know that even young infants are aware of physical reality and the existence of objects outside their sight (Baillargeon & DeVos, 1991). We will examine this research in detail below. Newborn babies are also capable of exploring and controlling their worlds. Young infants when presented with a nipple that provides reinforcement in the form of interesting sights and sounds will vigorously suck to produce these stimuli. This kind of behaviour is consistent with secondary circular reactions, which Piaget believed did not develop until 4 to 8 months old.

Early understanding of object permanence

Renee Baillargeon and her colleagues have found results which stand in sharp contrast to Piaget's findings. In one study, Baillargeon and DeVos (1991) used a violation-of-expectation paradigm to examine the understanding of object permanence in 3½ month-old infants. This study involved two phases: in the first phase, infants watched as two carrots were moved along a track from a position on one side of a screen and travelled behind it (out of the infant's sight) to appear on the opposite side of the screen. Infants watched two types of event in this phase, the first involving a short carrot and the second a tall carrot. After the infants were habituated to these two displays, they entered into the second phase of the experiment. In this phase, the short and tall carrots moved behind a screen which had a 'window' cut out in the middle. The window was designed to be high enough so that the tall carrot would be seen when passing behind the screen while the short carrot would not appear in the window, remaining invisible while behind the screen. Infants watched two further events in the second phase, a *possible event* and an *impossible event*. In the possible event, a short carrot moved behind the screen in the same fashion as before, not appearing in the window. In the impossible event, the tall carrot moved behind the screen and appeared on the other side in the usual fashion, but also did not appear in the window. Baillargeon and deVos measured infants' looking times for these two events. Infants did not look any longer at the possible event than they did at the short carrot in the first phase of the experiment, indicating

Habituation Events

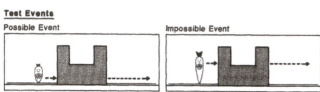

Image 7A   Baillargeon and DeVos' (1991) violation-of-expectation paradigm to examine the understanding of object permanence in 3½ month-old infants

Source: Baillargeon and DeVos (1991). Reprinted with permission.

they remained habituated to the possible event. However, infants dishabituated to the impossible event looked at this event much longer than they did in the first phase of the study. This finding indicates that the infants recognized that the tall carrot should have appeared in the window while behind the screen, suggesting that these very young infants had an understanding of object permanence. That is, they understood the tall carrot continued to exist when occluded by the screen and therefore should have remained in view when passing the window.

The findings of this study and many others (Baillargeon, 1987, 1991; Baillargeon & Graber, 1988; Spelke, Breinlinger, Macomber, & Jacobson, 1992) have shown that infants have a great deal of knowledge about objects and their properties. Moreover, this research has shown that infants seem to come equipped with a rich understanding of the physical world. According to Piaget, this is knowledge infants should not possess until they are much older and able to engage in means-end reasoning. How can we reconcile these results? Researchers have suggested that the knowledge tapped by object permanence tasks which employ looking as the measure of understanding may reveal a different type of knowledge from tasks like Piaget's A-not-B task which require infants to manually search for the hidden object (Ahmed & Ruffman, 1998; Bremner & Mareschal, 2004). They distinguish between **implicit knowledge** and **explicit knowledge**. Roughly speaking, explicit knowledge is knowledge which is accessible to consciousness (that is, you can reflect on it) whereas implicit knowledge is knowledge which is not accessible to consciousness but still plays a role in guiding behaviour. Baillargeon et al.'s impossible event paradigms may reveal implicit knowledge. In contrast, Piaget's A-not-B task focused on the development of explicit knowledge. The findings may also reveal that babies have a preference for novelty rather than reveal their understanding of object permanence (Haith, 1999).

Some attempts to replicate Baillargeon's research have failed to find similar results (e.g. Bogartz, Shinskey, & Schilling, 2000). You may also recall from the research example in the previous chapter that infants only grasp that the motion of an object disappearing behind a box shows a continuous trajectory by the time they are 4 to 6 months old. On the whole, the findings suggest that infants may have a concept of object permanence before Piaget thought, although young infants (i.e. a few months old) only show a weak grasp of this. Further research by Baillargeon has revealed that object permanence shows décalage similar to Piaget's horizontal décalage, which we will describe in the next section. Specifically, infants appear to acquire object permanence in different stages depending on the manner in which objects are occluded. Thus, 4½ month-old infants are surprised when a tall object becomes almost fully hidden behind but not inside a short container. Similarly, 9 month-old infants are surprised when a tall object becomes hidden inside a short container, but not when the short container is turned upside down and lowered over the tall object (Wang, Baillargeon, & Patterson, 2005). These findings suggest that infants do not respond to all object permanence tasks in the same way, and their accuracy is related to the qualities of the objects. Some tasks are relatively easy even for young infants, but other conditions rely on more advanced knowledge about spatial and object properties.

The preoperational stage

The preoperational stage of development characterizes children's thinking between 2 and 7 years of age. The major change observed in children's thinking during this period of development is in the growth of representational abilities. Children make great strides in their use of language, number, pictorial representation, spatial representations and pretend play. Rather than cover development within each of these areas, we focus instead on some key characteristics of children's thinking during the preoperational stage of development.

While children do make much progress in their ability to use representational thought, Piaget focused more on the *limitations* of a preoperational child's thought than on what they accomplished during this stage of development (Beilin, 1992). One of the limitations Piaget focused upon was what he referred to as egocentrism. This refers to the child's tendency to think only from their own perspective; egocentric thinking fails to consider other viewpoints. According to Piaget, the preoperational child's thought is egocentric in nature. To demonstrate this quality of preoperational children's thinking, he employed a task called the 'three mountains task' (Piaget & Inhelder, 1956). In this task, the child sits on one side of a table upon which is a three-dimensional model of a number of mountains and some distinctive landmarks such as a cross and a house. Importantly, some landmarks can only be seen from certain perspectives and children were allowed to experience this for themselves by walking around the entire table. The child was then seated on one side of the table and a doll was placed on the opposite side. The child's task was to choose from a set of photographs which best described what the doll could see. Before the age of 6 or 7, children have great difficulties with this task and often respond by picking the photograph which is consistent with their own point of view.

According to Piaget (1926), another aspect of preoperational children's thinking is that it is animistic. Animistic thinking refers to the tendency to attribute lifelike qualities to inanimate objects such as plants, rocks or the moon. For example, young children may believe that the moon follows them while driving or that picking a flower might hurt it. In Piaget's view, animistic thinking was a consequence of the child's tendency to think egocentrically. Animistic thinking declines during the preoperational stage as children acquire a better understanding of the world.

Another important limitation in preoperational children's thinking is the inability to employ mental operations. An operation is a procedure that can be carried out on some mental content. For example, preoperational children fail to understand a simple operation like *reversibility*, the idea that a transformation can be reversed by carrying out a second transformation which negates the first. For example, if you have no apples and are given two apples, you can reverse the transformation by subtracting two apples to get back to the original state.

Piaget tested children's ability to employ operations using the **conservation task**. This tests children's understanding that the physical characteristics of an object or substance or quantity remain the same even though their physical appearance may change. A classic demonstration of the conservation task uses three glasses. Children are presented with two identical glasses, tall and thin in shape, each of which contains an identical amount of water. The experimenter takes one of these glasses and empties it into a third glass which is short and wide. The child is then asked which glass has more water, less water, or the same amount of water as the water remaining in the original tall thin glass. In this example, the preoperational child will usually answer that the tall thin glass has more water. They recognize that no water was taken away from or added by the experimenter, yet they insist that the amount of water has changed. Children's failure on this task illustrates a number of the characteristics of preoperational thought. First, the preoperational child's thinking is bound by the perceptual characteristics of the task; that is to say, they focus on appearances rather than on the nature of what occurs. A related characteristic is what Piaget called **centration**. Centration in the preoperational child's thinking leads them to focus on only one characteristic of the task. In our example, the child centres on the *height* of the water in the glass, a perceptual characteristic. Most importantly, children's failure on the task illustrates their inability to reverse the transformation which created the situation; the failure to understand the reversibility of the transformation leads them to mistakenly infer the quantity of water in the glass has changed. Only with the ability to carry out mental operations such as reversibility do children pass the conservation task.

Much like his work on sensorimotor development, Piaget's thoughts on the preoperational stage have also been criticized. For example, using a simplified version of the three mountains task, Borke (1975) showed that Piaget exaggerated children's difficulty with the task, suggesting that they are less egocentric than he may have thought. Research on children's developing social cognition – that is, their *theory of mind* (see Chapter 11) – supports this view, showing that by the preschool years, children are quite adept at perspective taking, recognizing, for example, that people can hold different beliefs about a situation or that a person's belief might differ from reality (Wimmer & Perner, 1983). Similarly, Piaget may have overestimated how much animistic thinking children engage in. By kindergarten, few children attribute the characteristics of living things to inanimate objects (Carey, 1985). Children as young as 2½ years give psychological explanations for people and animals, but rarely for objects (Hickling & Wellman, 2001). Thus you will hear a 2 year-old say 'he wants' in reference to a person or a pet but not for a table. Children's incorrect responses tend to result from their lack of knowledge about living things and suggest that they have a theory of what 'alive' means that is different in some respects from the adult norm. Finally, research has suggested that preoperational children can be trained to understand concepts such as conservation (Beilin, 1978), suggesting that Piaget's belief that the development of operational thought is absent in one stage and present at another is incorrect. In summary, research on preoperational thinking has suggested that children's thought is far more complex than Piaget believed.

The concrete operational stage

The hallmark of children's entry into the concrete operational stage is the ability to think using mental operations. Operations are mental representations of both the static and the dynamic aspects of the environment (Siegler, 1998). At this stage, the child can now represent transformations carried out mentally. For example, in the conservation problem, children acquire the ability to mentally represent the transformation that helps them realize that the quantity of water in the glasses was not changed, that only its appearance was altered. An interesting aspect of children's development of the concept of conservation is that, once learned, this is not necessarily applied to all types of conservation problem. The liquid conservation problem we looked at in our example is not the only type of conservation problem. Children must also learn to conserve number, for example, recognizing that rearranging a fixed number of jelly beans does not alter how many jelly beans one has. Similarly, if you take a ball of bread dough and roll it into another shape, the amount of dough does not change. Children presented with different types of conservation problem – number, length, mass, liquid and area – usually pass the tasks in this order (Brainerd, 1978). You may recognize that this fact does not fit well with Piaget's theory. Remember that he argued that each stage is a qualitatively new level of understanding. The logical competencies which underlie a stage should apply to all tasks that are structurally similar. However, the fact that conservation tasks are acquired in a particular order contradicts this assertion. Evidence has accumulated that children at a given stage do not always show only stage-appropriate levels of performance (Case, 1992; Lutz & Sternberg, 1999), occasionally children's familiarity or lack of familiarity with the task materials may lead them to show performance above or below what should be expected of them. Piaget recognized this fact and coined the term **horizontal décalage** to describe this unevenness in the mastery of a concept. The existence of horizontal décalage has been pointed to as a failing of Piaget's theory and evidence that cognitive development may not be as stage-like as he suggested.

Conservation is one of the most important achievements of the concrete operational stage; however, it is not the only accomplishment. During this stage, children develop the mental skills which will allow them to understand classification hierarchies. For example, the child who collects sports cards can now sort them by team, by the players' positions, or in a multitude of other ways. This understanding of classification hierarchies allows children to solve the **class inclusion problem**. In this task, children are presented with a picture of a bunch of flowers consisting of some white roses and a larger number of red tulips. Children asked the question 'are there more tulips or more flowers?' correctly answer that there are, indeed, more flowers; that is, they recognize the tulips are a class by themselves as well as members of the larger class of flowers and, therefore, that there must be more flowers. In contrast, preoperational children will routinely fail this question. Concrete operational children also pass *transitive inference* problems. For example, given the information that *John is bigger than Bob, and Bob is bigger than Allan*, they can correctly infer that John is bigger than Allan.

More recent research on these tasks has questioned Piaget's findings. Class inclusion problems have been criticized for the wording of the test question. Donaldson (1978) simplified the question and found that much younger children were able to pass the task. Similarly, Bryant and Trabasso (1971) argued that preoperational children could pass transitive inference tasks when the memory requirements of the task were reduced. These and other findings suggest that, once again, Piaget's estimates of when children can pass these tasks were incorrect. They also call into question his assumptions regarding the discontinuity of cognitive development, suggesting that development may in fact be more continuous than he believed. Cultural differences have also been noted, as described in Research Example 7.1

Research Example 7.1

Context in the Concrete Operational Stage

In a study of 9 year-olds in Harare, Zimbabwe, a researcher named Gustav Jahoda found evidence for cross-cultural differences in children's performance on Piagetian concrete operations tasks (Jahoda, 1983). At the time, most Piagetian studies with non-European children had found a cultural lag in the achievement of concrete operations. Jahoda set out to test whether this lag was simply a function of lack of familiarity with the types of concept being tested, as well as the testing context and materials that researchers typically used during the tasks. In this experiment, Jahoda attempted to find a context that would actually have the non-European children at a greater experiential advantage.

Participants included 107 4th to 6th grade African children in Harare. The children had varying experience of parental or personal involvement in small trading. Children's understanding of the concept of profit was assessed during a role-playing procedure. The task involved a shopkeeper-type game in which a mock shop was set up. Findings indicated that the African children had a more advanced understanding of economic principles than similarly aged British children. The African children were able to accurately explain the concept of profit and demonstrated advanced understanding of various strategies for trading. However, the British children struggled with even the basic elements of the task such as that a shopkeeper buys for less than they sell at. The African children were involved in their parents' small businesses and hence had greater familiarity with the task, as well as a likely motivation to understand the principles of profit and loss. The study was an important step in demonstrating that context does affect children's cognitive development and, moreover, that many of Piaget's tasks favour the kind of experience and knowledge that children from industrialized nations are familiar with, but that with some fine-tuning and sensitivity to the child's context, Piagetian-type tasks can assess children's understanding in a variety of cultures.

Questions: What other aspects of Piagetian testing, apart from the familiarity of the context, may affect non-western children's performance on Piagetian tasks?

What are some implications of Jahoda's findings for educating children from varied cultural backgrounds?

The formal operational stage

Whereas the concrete operational child can solve a variety of logical problems, such as conservation tasks, transitive inference problems and class inclusion problems, they still fail to understand logical problems when they are required to go beyond the concrete and consider the abstract or the hypothetical. Around 11 years of age, children reach the **formal operational stage** which, in Piaget's view, was the endpoint of cognitive development. By the formal operational stage, children become capable of reasoning in propositional, abstract and hypothetical ways (Inhelder &

Piaget, 1958). Formal operational children reason in a specific way, using what has been called **hypothetico-deductive reasoning**. When trying to solve a difficult problem, adolescents start with a general theory of all of the factors which might impact on the outcome of the problem and then try to deduce specific hypotheses in light of these factors. Next, they test their hypotheses and if necessary, revise their theory. This type of reasoning represents the hypothetical and abstract nature of adolescent thinking. According to Keating (1990), these characteristics of adolescent thinking, namely hypothesis testing and hypothetical thinking, are what truly distinguish formal operational thought from the previous stage.

Table 7.2 Piaget's stages – the preoperational, concrete operational and formal operational

Stage	Age	Description
Preoperational Stage	2 to 7 years	The growth of representational abilities: • Egocentrism: the child at this stage has a tendency to think only from their own perspective. • Animistic thinking: the child attributes lifelike qualities to inanimate objects. • Inability to employ mental operations, such as reversibility and conservation tasks. • Centration: child only focuses on one aspect of a problem.
Concrete Operations	7 to 11 years	The ability to think using mental operations: • Conversation: understanding that the physical characteristics of an object or substance or quantity remain the same even if their physical appearance may change. • Classification hierarchies: flexible grouping of objects into classes and subclasses; allows children to solve class inclusion problems. • Transitive inference: given two statements, such as John is bigger than Bob, and Bob is bigger than Allen, can infer that John is bigger than Allen.
Formal Operations	11+ years	Endpoint of cognitive development. Reasoning in propositional, abstract and hypothetical ways. • Hypothetico-deductive reasoning: the ability to start with a general theory of all the factors involved in a problem, the deduction of specific hypotheses considering these factors, and a testing and possible revision of the hypothesis. • Propositional thinking: reasoning based on the logical properties of a set of statements rather than requiring concrete examples.

Adolescents also think in a propositional manner; that is, they can reason based on the logical properties of a set of statements rather than requiring concrete examples. Osherson and Markman (1975) conducted a study in which they gave adolescents and younger, concrete-operational children two types of problem. The participants were shown a pile of poker chips of different colours and were told that they were going to hear statements about the chips and that they should try to state whether these were true or false. In one condition, the experimenter concealed a chip in their hand and said, *'Either the chip in my hand is green or it is not green'* or *'The chip in my hand is green and it is not green'*. In this case only adolescents were able to state that the first statement was true and the second false. In another condition the experimenter made the same types of statement about a different chip but held that chip in plain view. In this case, both groups were able to correctly state whether the statements were true or false. The concrete operational children were able to pass the task when they could match the statement to a concrete property of the chips: when they were unable to do this, they failed the tasks. In contrast, adolescents used the logic of the statements themselves: 'and' statements were always incorrect since a chip could not be one colour and another at the same time and 'either-or' statements were always true.

Criticisms focusing on the idea of a formal operational stage concentrated on two main issues: first, whether all individuals reach the formal operational stage and, second, whether children might develop the ability to test hypotheses and think abstractly earlier than Piaget suggested. In regard to the first issue, research has shown that, contrary to Piaget's belief that formal operation is universally attained by all normally developing adolescents, a significant number of individuals fail to attain formal operational reasoning. In one study, Keating (1979) showed that between 40 and 60% of college students failed Piagetian formal operations tasks. Research has also shown that in many cases, adults do not reason at the level of formal operations (Neimark, 1975). In addition, cross-cultural evidence suggests that in many cases, formal operational reasoning is not naturally achieved in other cultures. While the literature on adolescent reasoning clearly supports a distinction in the nature of reasoning exhibited by adolescents and younger children (Keating, 1990; Moshman, 1998), it seems there is considerable variation in the attainment of formal operations, possibly as an effect of schooling practices in literate societies which emphasize logical thinking and problem solving.

To address the question of whether children might show abstract thinking and reasoning abilities earlier than Piaget suggested, we can turn to a study by Ruffman, Perner, Olson and Doherty (1993). Ruffman et al. showed that 6 year-olds were able to understand the relationship between hypotheses and evidence, recognizing that one needed appropriate evidence to confirm or reject a hypothesis. They also recognized that hypotheses would constrain a person's predictions about future events. However, children were only able to come to this recognition for very simple sets of variables and relationships. The results from Ruffman et al.'s study (see also Sodian, Zaitchik, & Carey, 1991) suggested that under the appropriate conditions, even quite young children can show some ability to think in an abstract, hypothesis-driven fashion.

Finally, some theorists have advocated the addition of a fifth stage of cognitive development to Piaget's model, a stage at which people begin to recognize that thinking occurs in a continuous and increasingly complex manner (Riegel, 1973). Whether cognitive development continues beyond adolescence, however, is still an open question (Moshman, 1998).

Criticisms of Piagetian theory

A good theory should be able to integrate a wide array of information and stimulate new research: Piaget's theory does well on both counts. He integrated a great number of diverse facts about children's cognitive development under a coherent theory. Moreover, his theory incorporated development in domains as diverse as *time*, *space*, *number* and *physics*, showing how development in each of these areas is related to the child's acquisition of an increasingly powerful mental logic. Piagetian theory has also stimulated a great deal of new research, evident in the vast number of studies influenced by his work since the 1960s when this first became widely known in North America. Importantly, although the bulk of this research has suggested that Piaget's ideas about cognitive development were incorrect on a variety of points, the inspiration for much of this research was his theory. Even though he may have underestimated children's knowledge in many domains, Piaget was responsible for pushing the field of cognitive development forward.

While his theory has important strengths, it has also been heavily criticized, as shown earlier in this chapter. Piaget's erroneous conclusions regarding children's cognitive ability stemmed partly from his reliance on verbal interview methods. New developments in methodology have allowed for a better understanding of emerging abilities. Piagetian theory has also been criticized for its adherence to a conception of development as occurring in stages. Development is not necessarily stage-like (Brainerd, 1978). Today, most researchers would agree that children's cognitive abilities are a good deal more continuous than Piaget's stages suggest (Flavell, Miller, & Miller, 2002). As Siegler (1998) has argued, whether development appears stage-like or more continuous depends in large part on the level of analysis one chooses. If you assess children's competence every few months, then sudden changes in their level of reasoning will appear abrupt and stage-like. If you assess development on a smaller timescale, their development may look more continuous.

Piaget's stage theory has also been criticized for its proposed universality. As we have seen, the sequence of stages might not proceed in as orderly a fashion as he suggested. Some stages may not occur across cultures and their development may be heavily dependent on cultural and social factors (Rogoff, 1998). There is substantial research to suggest that not all people develop an understanding of the world. In fact, cultural influences play a large role in children's understanding of the concepts that Piaget described. For example, in many tribal societies, formal operational tasks are not achieved (Cole, 1990). When given a propositional statement, people in non-literate societies tend not to want to answer, believing that unless they have first-hand experience of a situation or proposition, they should not pass judgement. This is not to say that people from other cultures are incapable of formal operational thought; they may simply have a different view of many of the tasks used to measure development.

Other criticisms levelled at Piaget include the complaint that concepts such as *assimilation* and *accommodation* are too vague to be of any use (Brainerd, 1978). Finally, it is possible that development may not occur in an across-the-board or *domain general* fashion as Piaget suggested. Recent research in cognitive development has increasingly focused on *domain-specific* developments, that is, development within specific domains of knowledge such as biology and physics (Gopnik & Wellman, 1994). The focus of much of this research has been on how the acquisition of knowledge leads to development within a given domain.

Educational applications of Piaget's theory

Despite the criticisms of Piaget's theory, it has nonetheless been very influential in shaping views about education, particularly in the early years, and the early educational curricula in many countries

Image 7B Piaget's contributions to education include active and child-lead learning, since he saw children as active explorers, constructing knowledge through their explorations and interactions with the world

© Olesia Bilkei/Shutterstock

can be seen to embrace Piagetian ideas. Many early educational curricula specify the importance of active learning and child-led activities in the classroom. For example, in the curricula in the various regions of the United Kingdom, there is an explicit requirement for teachers to use such approaches to facilitate learning in the classroom. This ties in with Piaget's view of children as active explorers of their worlds and constructing knowledge through their explorations and interactions with their physical and social worlds.

Piaget's view that children pass through the various stages at their own pace is also implicit in Early Years educational curricula, which also place a strong emphasis and the individual observation and reporting of children's progress and teachers planning specific activities for children based on their abilities at a given time. Related to this is the application of Piaget's notion of the schema in Early Years education. This has been developed further as an approach to identifying children's *schematic behaviours* in the classroom (see for example Athey, 2007; Atherton & Nutbrown, 2013). In this context, schemas are defined as 'persistent patterns which underlie children's spontaneous behaviours' (Atherton & Nutbrown, 2013: 13). When careful observations are made of young children in a care or classroom setting, it is often possible to identify patterns that underpin several behaviours that would otherwise appear unconnected and these patterns or 'schemas' can inform us about a child's current thinking and understanding. So, for example, a young child in a nursery who engages in behaviours such as putting crayons in a box, rolling themselves up in a blanket or putting spoons into a teacup is not just simply flitting from one activity to another. Instead these behaviours can be seen as their using an 'enveloping and containing' schema, a particular way of thinking about the world that informs their actions. Once a child's schema has been identified, an Early Years teacher can then plan for a variety of activities across the curriculum in the classroom to capitalize on that schema, and in this way extend a child's understanding of the world.

Vygotsky's Sociocultural Theory of Cognitive Development

In their review of the wide variety of theoretical positions which guide the study of human development, Dixon and Lerner (1998) identified the work of Lev Vygotsky and his emphasis on the cultural contexts in which human development occurs as one of the main forces behind the spread of the family of theories which they label as *contextualist* theories. Like Piaget, Vygotsky was strongly committed to the idea that children were active explorers of their world who tested their ideas against reality, seeking to expand their knowledge. However, unlike Piaget, who viewed children essentially as solitary figures involved in the construction of knowledge, Vygotsky believed that the child's social environment was an active force in their development, working to mould children's growing knowledge in ways that were adaptive to the wider culture in which they grew up. Vygotsky's perspective on development is often referred to as a **sociocultural theory** because of his emphasis on the child's culture and the social environment as forces which shape development. Because of his rejection of an individualistic view and his focus on the developing child in the context of society, Vygotsky has received acclaim (Tudge & Scrimsher, 2003).

According to Wertsch (1991), there are three main themes which encapsulate Vygotsky's view of cognitive development. First, Vygotsky maintained that the study of development must rely on 'genetic analyses'. This sounds misleading as, like Piaget, Vygotsky used the term 'genetic' to refer to the idea of development and *not* to our biological endowment. His idea was that understanding a mental process was only possible through an examination of the origins and transformations that the process undergoes from its immature to its mature form. In other words, the study of development is, in a very real sense, an historical process. Thus, Vygotsky was a strong advocate of the developmental method, focusing on the origins of mental processes and the transformations which these undergo.

Second, as mentioned above, Vygotsky was adamant in his belief that an individual's cognitive development was largely a social process, and not an individualistic construction, as Piaget believed. For Vygotsky, cognitive development occurred as a function of the child's interactions with partners who were more highly skilled than the child. These others interacted with the child, and through the instruction and assistance they provided to the child, promoted cognitive development (Vygotsky, 1935/1978). Vygotsky did believe that a child was equipped with a set of innate abilities, but he maintained that these developed only to a limited extent without the intervention of other members of the child's community. Vygotsky referred to the abilities with which the child is naturally endowed, specifically attention, memory and perception, as the **elementary mental functions**. He contrasted these with the same functions once they were transformed by social interactions with other, more experienced members of the culture. These **higher mental functions** are the socially transformed products of the child's initial endowment. An important aspect of the higher mental functions is that they are *mediated* processes; they rely on 'mediators' or psychological tools such as language or the number system.

The third major aspect of Vygotsky's theory centres on this notion of mediation. Vygotsky argued that all human cognitive activity, both social and individual, was mediated by the use of symbolic 'tools' such as language, art, numbers, and other culturally derived products. Vygotsky believed that our natural development and our cultural development followed separate lines (Wertsch, 1991); that is to say, the abilities with which we come innately endowed develop to a point without the need for social intervention, following a maturationally-based timetable, but then plateau. This halt in the natural line of development comes about because of the child's acquisition of mediators like language. Once children have developed the symbolic capabilities which allow them to interact with other members of their culture, they enter into a dialogue which transforms their innate abilities into the uniquely human, higher mental functions (Vygotsky, 1981).

It is necessary to note here the patterning of development according to Vygotsky's view. He stated that 'Any function in the child's cultural development appears twice, or on two planes. First, it appears on the social plane, and then on the psychological plane' (Vygotsky, 1981). In this statement, Vygotsky argued that development resulted from processes which occurred first *between* people and then *within* the individual. He referred to this process of functions moving from the interpersonal to the intrapersonal as *internalization*. The development of all higher mental functions occurs, in large part, as the result of the internalization. This does not mean that cognitive development is a simple process of copying social processes (Wertsch, 1991). Internalization does involve transformations of social processes by the individual, however Vygotsky advocated that our cognition was strongly grounded in social processes.

The zone of proximal development

Vygotsky (1978) believed that the interactions between parents and children which led to intellectual development took place in a specific way. He proposed the concept of the **zone of proximal development** (ZPD) as a means of illustrating how social interactions between experienced members of the culture and less experienced children led to development. He defined the zone of proximal development as 'the difference between the child's actual developmental level as determined by independent problem solving' and their 'potential development as determined through problem solving under adult guidance or in collaboration with more capable peers' (Vygotsky, 1978: 86). There are two aspects of the concept which are important to note (Cole, 1985). First, the zone of proximal development represents a specific way in which more capable members of the culture assist the child's development. This is achieved by working with the child at a level slightly beyond that child's own capabilities. We will examine this aspect further below. Second, the zone of proximal development highlights his concern with how intellectual functioning is measured. Vygotsky felt it was critical to measure the child's *potential* for learning under adult guidance; such a measure of intelligence had a greater utility according to Vygotsky than a simple assessment of what the child was capable of doing alone. Given his belief in the study of developmental processes rather than endpoints, Vygotsky's emphasis on the child's potential as the state we should be concerned with in assessment is extremely appealing.

The zone of proximal development has had a great influence on the study of cognitive development. One way in which it has had an influence is on how developmentalists think about the quality of instruction children receive from others. Vygotsky did not specify how adults and children worked within the zone of proximal development, but later researchers, looking more carefully at the processes involved, came up with the term **scaffolding** (Bruner, 1983; Wood, Bruner, & Ross, 1976) to describe the processes involved. Scaffolding is an interactive process in which adults adjust both the amount and type of support they offer to a child, leading to eventual mastery of the skill being taught. When adults provide effective scaffolding for a child, they initially try to encourage them to operate at the limit of their ability. If the child does not respond, the adult will use more specific behaviours to direct them, and, in addition, they may vary the type of instruction offered. As the child begins to experience success, the adult intervenes in more indirect ways, reducing their level of instruction and encouraging the child to move forward.

The key to effective scaffolding is sensitivity to the child's level of development (Rogoff, 1998; Wood & Middleton, 1975). Research has shown that when mothers are more effective at scaffolding their children's behaviours in the context of a problem-solving task, children are more likely to act successfully on their own in a similar task (Berk & Spuhl, 1995).

Another important way that social interaction leads to cognitive development is through intersubjectivity, which occurs when two participants beginning a task with different understandings come to a shared understanding. Communication is facilitated in this way, as each member of the interaction adjusts and shares their views. For example, an adult may try to figure out how to translate ideas so that a child can understand. In a reciprocal way, the child's mental capabilities are exercised as they try to understand what the adult is saying. Children also create intersubjectivity for each other. Between the ages of 3 and 5 children start to create dialogues with each other, and enjoy expressing and listening to each others' viewpoints (Berk, 2001).

Language and play

A key question we need to ask is whether or not there is any evidence for Vygotsky's idea that development proceeds from the social plane to the individual? One phenomenon which Vygotsky cited as evidence for this progression was children's speech to themselves. You may have noticed that preschool children often talk to themselves while performing problem-solving tasks or while carrying out everyday activities. For example, while playing with toy blocks young children can often be heard uttering things such as 'now I need a blue one' or 'that doesn't go here'. Jean Piaget noticed this tendency as well. He referred to this as **egocentric speech**, believing that because of the preschool child's inability to think from another's perspective, their communications were often profoundly egocentric, that is, not adapted to another's viewpoint. Vygotsky took exception to Piaget's classification of children's speech as egocentric. In contrast to Piaget, Vygotsky (1934/1986) believed children's speech to themselves was a powerful means of regulating their own behaviour. Language gives children the means to reflect on their own behaviour, organize behaviour, and control their behaviour. Children's speech to themselves reflects the fact that their thought is organized in the form of dialogues with others, and because thought is dialogic, the language which supports it gets expressed. As children become more competent with cognitive tasks, these dialogues become internalized and their speech to themselves declines in frequency. Research has consistently supported Vygotsky's view, and children's inner speech is now referred to as *private speech*, rather than Piaget's term, egocentric speech (Berk, 2003). Furthermore, in accord with Vygotsky's view, children who use private speech show greater improvement on problem-solving tasks than their peers who do not use (or use less) private speech. Also as Vygotsky predicted, as children get older private speech changes in form to become whispers and silent lip movements (Winsler & Naglieri, 2003).

Like Piaget, Vygotsky (1978) also took notice of young children's tendency to engage in pretend play, and he pointed to an interesting fact about it. Vygotsky noted that children's pretend play tended to occur at a level beyond their stage in life; that is, sometimes when they pretend, children take on roles such as *parent* or *doctor* rather than roles that are appropriate to children. Through pretend play, children place themselves in a zone of proximal development, where they play at a level which is in advance of their real capabilities. Pretend play has the ability to stimulate development in a variety of ways. One way has to do with the child's use of their imagination. In pretend play, children learn that the objects they use can be separated from their normal referents, and that these can stand for other things. Thus a child can play with a banana as if it were a telephone. In addition, pretend play tends to be based on rules. The child who pretends to be a baby has to follow the rules and go to sleep when their pretend Mummy tells them to, and the child who pretends to be Daddy may have to pretend to cut the lawn. In other words, children's play is constrained by the rules which guide behaviour in these roles, and because of this they learn about the social norms that are expected of people. Vygotsky believed that pretend play was an important context in which children learned about the social world. Research exists to back this view: preschool children who play according to complex sociodramatic rules are more likely to follow classroom rules when they enter a formal educational setting (Elias & Berk, 2002).

Although it is popular to contrast the theories of Piaget and Vygotsky, their respective ideas can actually be thought of as complementary (Cole & Wertsch, 2000; Shayer, 2003). While Piaget often focused on children's words as a window into their cognitive development, Vygotsky often chose to examine children's actions. Together, their two perspectives give us a rich understanding of children's words and deeds. Rather than promoting conflicting views of the child, Vygotsky and Piaget may have provided different pieces of the same developmental puzzle. Indeed, it has been argued that the two psychologists have at times suggested very similar ideas, so much so that many developmental psychologists cannot differentiate between statements that Piaget and Vygotsky made (Smith, 1996).

The implications of Vygotsky's theory for education

Vygotsky's theory has had a major impact on education in recent years, largely because of his stress on the importance of social interactions with more experienced others as a force which drives learning. Vygotsky's belief was not simply that education was a process of refining cognitive structures which the child has already acquired; instead, he maintained that education was a fundamental aspect of human development. Social interactions with more experienced others are essential to our education.

Vygotsky's theory has much to say about how education might best take place. Peer collaboration is a key concept in the Vygotskian approach to education. One educational device that has been developed on the basis of his theory is called **reciprocal teaching**. Reciprocal teaching is a method of using peers to foster dialogues about a subject matter such that they provide a level which is beyond the individual child's capability but within their zone of proximal development (Brown & Palinscar, 1982; Palinscar & Brown, 1984). The method was designed to improve the reading ability of children who were designated as having academic difficulties, but it has been extended into other subject areas, such as science. The reciprocal teaching method involves the student in a group with several other students and a teacher. The aim of the group is to engage in collaborative learning, that is, to make certain that the entire group works through and learns a topic. Within the group, students take turns at leading discussions on a particular text. The leader of the group discussion is responsible for ensuring that all the students take part in all phases of the discussion. There are four activities that are required of students within the group: questioning, summarizing, clarifying and predicting. In a reciprocal teaching group, the leader of a discussion begins the learning process by asking questions about the content of the text. In this phase, group members answer questions, elaborate on others' statements, try to resolve disagreements (by re-reading if necessary) and raise questions of their own. This is followed up by the leader's summary of the text and a period of clarification where group members who have trouble grasping certain ideas try to work through these with the group. Finally, the group is asked to use their understanding to predict the future content of the text. The idea of reciprocal teaching is to make the processes which a skilled reader engages in automatically more *explicit* so that group members who have problems with these skills can internalize them. As you can see, the practices engaged in by students in reciprocal teaching are very consistent with Vygotsky's theory.

Another way in which Vygotsky's theory is employed in the classroom is through **cooperative learning**. This is a technique in which the child's learning environment is structured into small groups of peers who work together towards a common learning goal. Unlike reciprocal teaching, a teacher is not used to guide each group. Instead, groups are formed from combinations of more and less knowledgeable peers. Cooperative learning environments work best when children truly adopt and share common goals (Forman & McPhail, 1993) and when the group consists of children who are truly accomplished at the particular task and can provide expert instruction for others who are less skilled (Azmitia, 1988; Rogoff, 1998).

Criticisms of Vygotsky's theory

Vygotsky's theory has proven very influential in recent years and has inspired a great deal of research and speculation regarding the role of culture and social interaction in human development (Rogoff, 1998). However, the relatively recent entry of Vygotsky's theory into the study of human development means the theory has not yet received the same level of critical analysis that more established theories, such as Piaget's, have received (Miller, 1993). One aspect of Vygotsky's work which has been heavily criticized is his almost exclusive focus on the cultural aspects of development. Recall that Vygotsky distinguished between the *natural* line of development and the *cultural* line; however, his theory tells us almost nothing about the natural line of development. Consequently, it is not possible to understand within the confines of Vygotskian theory how exactly the elementary processes, such as attention and memory, contribute to the development of symbolically mediated forms of cognition (Wertsch & Tulviste, 1992). Importantly, children's cognitive abilities are used as indicators of the kinds of social experiences which will be made available to them. Vygotsky's theory has little to say about how children's developmental level serves to constrain or enhance their opportunities for participation in various contexts. Other issues which are raised as challenges for Vygotskian and other contextualist theories include: the examination of how people determine the goals of their collaborative efforts and the means by which these are carried out; how children and adults collaborate outside the context of experimental settings; the dynamics of groups larger than two persons; and the nature of interactions in cultures other than middle-class, North American and European groups (Rogoff, 1998). Vygotsky has also been criticized for his almost exclusive reliance on language as communication. In some cultures, verbal interaction is but one manner of skilled communication.

For example, adults in Yucatec Mayan society in Mexico place more emphasis on showing children the rules of social behaviour; verbal communication takes second place to observation and participation (Rogoff, 2003). Rogoff has pointed out that, given the typical emphasis in developmental research on the *individual* as the unit of study, it is not surprising that we have little information on some of these questions. The current interest in Vygotskian and other sociocultural theories suggests it is only a matter of time before these and other critical issues begin to be addressed.

Can you suggest how Piagetian and Vygotskyan perspectives might inform the use of play as a means of facilitating development?

Information Processing Theories

The **information processing approach** to cognitive development is based on an analogy between the digital computer and the human mind. Most information processing theorists share the view that the mind is a system which manipulates symbols according to a set of rules. Like computers, our minds encode information received from the environment, cast it into a symbolic form which the mind can process and, through a variety of operations, process this information to produce useful output such as the solution to a problem. There are other parallels between human cognition and computers that have been explored by information processing theorists. Like computers, we also have finite resources, such as memory, which place limits on our cognitive performance, and just as computers 'develop' in terms of the sophistication of their hardware, so too does the human brain develop, leading to the growth of more powerful thought processes. However, as Klahr and MacWhinney (1998) caution, information processing theorists do not literally believe that the mind is a computer. Rather, they see the computer as a tool for testing models of cognitive development. In essence, the goal is to test whether a theory of intelligent behaviour can be accounted for by a computational system, whether the computations are run in a brain or on a computer.

While there are a large number of information processing theories, all approaches share three basic assumptions (Siegler, 1998). The first belief is that *thinking is information processing*; that is, any thought process, such as remembering or perceiving, involves the processing of information. Second, information processing theories emphasize the need to study the *change mechanisms* that move development from one state to the next. Third, development within information processing systems is driven by *self-modification*; that is, earlier knowledge and strategies can modify thinking and thus lead to higher levels of development.

The information processing system

According to Siegler (1998), information processing theories focus on the organization of the information processing system, or what he calls the *structural characteristics* and the *processes* that provide the means for cognition to adapt to the changing demands of the environment. We examine these two aspects of the information processing system in turn.

The structural characteristics of the information processing system are believed to be universal in that all children share the same basic organization of cognitive structures. Springing from the work of cognitive psychologists (e.g. Atkinson & Shiffrin, 1968, 1971), most theories of information processing are based on a three-part model (known as the 'store' model) which consists of a **sensory register**, **working memory** and **long-term memory**. In this store model, information is believed to flow into the cognitive system through the sensory register. The sensory register is a memory store which allows us to briefly store large amounts of sensory information (e.g. visual images and sounds) for a very short duration, somewhere around one second (Sperling, 1960). If you look closely at something, close your eyes and monitor your experience, you will notice that a visual image of the scene will last for a brief time. From the sensory register, information flows into working memory (also referred to as short-term memory).

Working memory is the area of the system where thinking occurs. That is, working memory allows us a space from which to operate on incoming information, combining it with long-term memory or transforming it in various ways. A critical point regarding working memory is that it is a limited resource. First, working memory is of limited *capacity*; that is, we can only store so much information in working memory at one time. Estimates of working memory capacity suggest that it can hold approximately seven units of information (Miller, 1956). Second, information can only be held in working memory for a brief period, somewhere in the order of 15 to 30 seconds (Siegler, 1998). Thus, working memory provides a bottleneck in the system because of this limited capacity. Incoming information pushes information out of working memory such that it is either forgotten or it is moved into long-term memory. An important aspect of working memory is that its capacity can be increased through the application of strategies such as **chunking**, where information held in working memory is organized into more meaningful units. For example, instead of treating the first three digits of a phone number as three separate units of information, you can chunk them into a single unit, remembering '388' instead of '3', '8' and '8'. Chunking allows us to increase our working memory capacity and thus to form more complex mental representations.

Information from working memory can move into long-term memory. Long-term memory is the part of the cognitive system that contains our permanent knowledge base. It is a storehouse of information which seems to have no limit, in terms of either its capacity or in how long information can reside here. Many theorists believe that long-term memory is organized as an *associative network* in that to retrieve information we need to have cues that allow us to find the stored information (Atkinson & Shiffrin, 1968; Broadbent, 1984). The more associations we form between an item and cues which help us retrieve it, the more likely it is we will remember the item, that is, bring it from long-term to working memory.

As noted above, there are a number of processes which may operate on information held in the three memory stores. Unlike the architecture of the information processing system, these processes show considerable development over time; that is, children gain greater expertise with these strategies, leading to the more efficient handling of information within the cognitive system. One important process is **encoding**. Given the finite capacity of our sensory register and working memory, we are limited in the amount of information that we can manage to transform into mental representations. Encoding is the process by which we pick out significant features of an object or event so that we can form a representation. Efficient encoding processes allow us to quickly focus on the relevant features that are important to our thinking. In contrast, inefficient encoding processes can lead to the loss of information, producing limitations in the usefulness of the representations children form. Another critical process is **automatization**. Cognitive psychologists (Shiffrin & Schneider, 1977) distinguish between *controlled* processes, that is, processes which require conscious attention, and *automatic processes*, processes which require little or no conscious attention. The more controlled a process is, the more working memory capacity it requires. Thus, the processes that lead to the automatization of some task are generally beneficial in that they free up mental resources that can be allocated in other ways. Consider a child learning to solve simple arithmetic problems such as 'What is 5 + 3?' At first the child may count off five fingers and then count off a further three fingers, and from there count up the total number of fingers which are raised (Siegler, 1998). However, with practice children will begin to memorize the solutions to these simple problems. That is, they have automatized the answer and can simply recall the product of the addition without counting it out. The automatization of a skill leads to increases in the speed of the child's ability to execute it, as well as leaving more free working memory capacity so that the child can monitor their cognitive performance and, perhaps, learn to further improve their abilities through the application of strategies.

The store model has been used to understand the development of the child's cognitive system in two ways. First, the basic capacity of the store, most notably working memory, increases with age. Second, children's ability to use strategies to increase information storage and retrieval increases with age. The work described in Research Example 7.2 illustrates these phenomena. This knowledge has led to the kind of neo-Piagetian theorizing described below.

Research Example 7.2

Short-term Memory Increases with Age

A group of researchers (Cowan et al., 1999) set out to address whether the capacity of the human memory system expanded as children mature. By capacity, the researchers meant the basic amount of information that can be held in mind (similar to Robbie Case's m-space), without applying strategies to assist with memory. First- and fourth-grade children as well as adults were presented with two sets of lists of numbers to remember. This kind of task is generally considered a working memory test, as it assesses the maximum amount of information that can be recalled. Children of 2 years old can generally recall two bits of information: this capacity increases to four or five bits of information at 7 years old, and then six to seven pieces of information in adolescence (does this remind you of chunking?)

The lists of numbers that participants were given involved two different conditions: in the first condition, children and adults simply listened to the numbers and, when cued, recalled as many of them as they could in the original order. In a second 'interference' condition, participants listened to the numbers while simultaneously playing a computer game. This distraction meant that participants were unlikely to be able to use strategies to help them remember the numbers. The results of the study revealed that working memory steadily increased across age-groups, such that first grade children showed slightly less recall than fourth grade children, who showed less recall than adults. Interestingly, the results were similar for the distraction condition. Gains in working memory across age applied even when memory strategies were prevented, although recall was less accurate than in the non-distraction condition. Overall, the findings indicated that gains in basic working memory capacity occur with age, and the opportunity to use memory strategies enhances this basic capacity.

A neo-Piagetian theory of cognitive development

One of the many information processing theories of cognitive development is that of Robbie Case (1985, 1992). Case's theory of cognitive development is similar to Piaget's in that it postulates broad, qualitative changes in cognitive development; however, Case differs from Piaget in that he believes the shifts in cognitive development result from increases in a child's information processing capacity (i.e. working memory). In his theory, Case refers to the growth of information processing capacity as **m-space** and argues that these increases in capacity represent the child's ability to use their limited capacity more efficiently. Case attributes the growth of information processing capacity as stemming from three processes. First, the maturation of the brain leads to increases in information processing capacity through increases in the speed with which mental operations can be carried out. A neural process called myelinization speeds up the transmission of electrical impulses through the brain and thereby increases speed. In turn, speed increases capacity by utilizing working memory more efficiently. Second, the development of cognitive strategies also frees up capacity, speeding up the process of automatization. Finally, automatization of knowledge and schemes leads to the development of *central conceptual structures*. These are networks of concepts and relations between concepts which allow the child to think about some situations in more advanced ways. Case and Griffin (1990) argued that because central conceptual structures lead to the development of more efficient means of thinking about situations, they too free up information processing capacity.

One of the great strengths of Case's theory is its ability to account for the transition from one stage of thought to another. Case argues that the increases in m-space lead to the child moving from one stage to the next; that is, when the child acquires enough m-space to represent a situation in a more complex way, they have progressed to a new level of thinking. In support of this idea, Case has conducted a great deal of research which shows strong correlations between measures of m-space and cognitive performance: the greater one's m-space, the higher the level of cognitive development. Case's theory represents an important step beyond Piaget, combining concepts from information processing theory with Piaget's ideas and providing us with a more comprehensive and testable account of cognitive development. Case's theory provides further benefit to children's education. Children who lag behind on conceptual development can usually be given training that translates to academic tasks (Case, Griffin, & Kelly, 2001). Case's theory can therefore be used to help children who are not performing as well as they could be academically.

Connectionism

The field of developmental cognitive neuroscience has asked new questions about what actually occurs in children's brains as they develop. Researchers in this area are using computers to answer these questions; specifically, **connectionist** or artificial neural network models are used. These connectionist models basically simulate information processing that takes place in neurons and the connections between neurons. An artificial neural network is devised that looks like the brain's neurological structure, typically involving many layers from input to output. The connections between the layers are programmed to change according to experience; the simulated system therefore has a powerful capacity to learn. The system also receives feedback about its responses, promoting further learning. Researchers then compare the learning of the computer with that for children and adults to determine whether the simulation is an apt model of human learning. Connectionists generally believe that the human cognitive system gradually attains knowledge as a result of learning opportunities (Thelen & Bates, 2003), thereby disagreeing with the idea that babies are born with innate learning systems that unfold as a matter of course. However, connectionist models have been criticized as being too simplistic. Children may behave like computers in some respects, but they are also capable of choices that defy the expected. Children modify their responses after they make errors but, unlike a computer, also after their successes.

Summary

Our survey of the theories of Piaget, Vygotsky and the information processing tradition captures some of the differences in opinion which exist in how to tackle the study of children's cognitive development. Each theory emphasizes different factors as being important to an understanding of cognition. The Piagetian tradition focuses on the nature of children's interactions with their physical environment, whereas Vygotskian theory stresses that social interactions between children and more skilled members of their culture are critical to cognitive development. In contrast to both of these positions, the information processing theorists emphasize the importance of studying the mechanisms which lead to developmental change. As was noted at the outset, covering the whole field of cognition is beyond the scope of this book, but armed with knowledge of these theories, you should be in a position to understand much of the research in this field.

Glossary

Accommodation is the process of adjusting old schemes to better fit with the demands of the environment (the complement of assimilation).

Adaptation involves the creation of cognitive structures or schemes through our interactions with the environment, allowing us to adjust to the demands posed by the environment.

An important aspect of the higher mental functions is that they are **mediated** processes, relying on systems such as language or the numerical system.

Animistic thinking refers to the tendency to attribute lifelike qualities to inanimate objects such as plants or rocks.

A-not-B task is a task in which infants search for hidden objects, first at one location (the A trials) and then later at a second location (the B trials). Used by Piaget to test for object permanence.

Assimilation refers to the process of integrating the environment into one's current psychological structures, using current schemes to interpret new knowledge (the complement of accommodation).

Automatization is the process by which behaviours that require conscious, controlled attention are transformed so that they require little or no conscious attention.

Centration refers to the quality of a child's thinking which leads them to focus on only one characteristic or dimension of a task or problem.

Chunking is a process whereby the information held in working memory is organized into a smaller number of more meaningful units.

Class inclusion problem is a problem designed by Piaget to test children's understanding of classification hierarchies.

Connectionism is an information processing model based on neural networks and often uses computer simulation.

Conservation task is Piaget's task which tests children's understanding that the physical characteristics of an object, substance or quantity remain the same even though their physical appearance may change.

Cooperative learning is a technique in which the child's learning environment is structured into small groups of peers who work together towards a common learning goal.

Egocentric speech is communications that are not adapted to another's viewpoint.

Egocentrism refers to the child's tendency to think only from their own perspective, failing to consider other possible viewpoints.

Elementary mental functions are, in Vygotsky's view, the abilities with which the child is naturally endowed, such as attention, memory and perception.

Encoding is the process by which we pick out the important features of an object or event so we can form a mental representation.

Equilibration is Piaget's term for the striving of the cognitive system to maintain a state of equilibrium.

Explicit knowledge is knowledge which is accessible to consciousness.

Formal operational stage is the stage of cognitive development where adolescents become capable of reasoning in propositional, abstract and hypothetical ways. In Piaget's view, this is the endpoint of cognitive development.

Higher mental functions are, in Vygotsky's view, cognitive functions that have been transformed by social interactions with other, more experienced members of the culture.

Horizontal décalage is used to describe the unevenness in children's mastery of the different forms of a concept such as conservation.

Hypothetico-deductive reasoning is a form of reasoning where a child starts with a general theory of all of the factors which might impact on the outcome of a problem and then tries to deduce specific hypotheses in light of these factors. Next, they test their hypotheses and, if necessary, revise their theory.

Implicit knowledge is knowledge which is not accessible to consciousness but still plays a role in guiding behaviour.

Information processing approach is an approach to the study of cognitive development which focuses on how information is encoded from the environment, cast into a symbolic form which the mind can process, and processed through a variety of mental operations to create useful output, such as the solution to a problem.

Long-term memory is the part of the cognitive system that contains our permanent knowledge base. It is a storehouse of information which seems to have no limit, in terms of either its capacity or in how long information can reside here.

m-space refers to a child's capacity to hold information actively in mind. This is believed to increase with their development through to adolescence.

Object permanence refers to the concept that objects continue to exist independently of our ability to perceive or act on them.

Operations refer to procedures that can be carried out on some mental content.

Organization refers to the individual's tendency to organize their cognitive structures or schemes into efficient systems.

Pretend play is play where children act out imaginary activities and use real objects to stand for imagined objects.

Primary circular reactions is Piaget's term for simple motor habits seen in infants, such as thumb sucking, that can be repeated and which are pleasurable.

Reciprocal teaching is a method of using small groups of peers to create dialogues about a subject matter, providing a level of instruction which is beyond the individual child's capability but within their zone of proximal development. It emphasizes four cognitive processes: predicting, questioning, summarizing and clarifying.

Scaffolding is an interactive process in which adults adjust both the amount and the type of support they offer to the child, leading to the eventual mastery of the skill being taught.

Schemes is the term used by Piaget to refer to an interrelated set of actions, memories, thoughts or strategies which are employed to predict and understand the environment.

Secondary circular reactions are behaviours focused on the environment which produce interesting reactions which the infant attempts to maintain through repetition.

Sensorimotor stage refers to the first two years of an infant's life during which the infant moves from responding to the environment in a simplistic, reflexive manner to being able to think in symbolic forms and in a goal-directed manner.

Sensory register is a memory store which allows us to briefly store large amounts of sensory information for a very short duration.

Sociocultural theory refers to Vygotsky's perspective on development which places a strong emphasis on the child's culture and the social environment as forces which shape development.

Stage is a period of development in which the child's cognitive structures are qualitatively similar.

Store model is a model of the flow of information through the cognitive system which posits a variety of information stores including the sensory register, short-term memory, and long-term memory.

Working memory is a mental space from which we operate on incoming information, combining it with long-term memory or transforming it in various ways.

Zone of proximal development is the difference between the child's independently determined developmental level and their potential level of development determined when problem solving under adult guidance or in collaboration with more capable peers.

TEST YOUR KNOWLEDGE

1. Which of the following is not one of Piaget's stages?

   a) Sensorimotor
   b) Equilibration
   c) Preoperational
   d) Concrete operations
   e) Formal operations

2. How do assimilation and accommodation differ?

   a) Assimilation uses existing schemes whereas accommodation requires changes to existing schemes
   b) Assimilation requires changes to existing schemes whereas accommodation uses existing schemes

(Continued)

    c) They are the same thing

    d) Assimilation occurs when we are forced into a state of cognitive disequilibrium

3. Why did Vygotsky believe play was important to children's development?

    a) Because it fosters creativity

    b) Because it provides an opportunity for children to forge social bonds

    c) Because it allows children a brief freedom away from adults and their restrictions

    d) Because it gives children insight and experience into the rules that guide behaviour for future social roles

4. Why do information processing theorists liken the human mind to a computer?

    a) Both are complex and experience unexplained blips on occasion

    b) They both use intelligence to make decisions

    c) They encode and retrieve information in a similar manner

    d) They have similar levels of power and memory

ANSWERS: 1–B, 2–A, 3–D, 4–C

Suggested Reading

Bornstein, M., & Lamb, M. (1999). *Developmental Psychology: An advanced textbook* (4th edition, pp. 3–46). Mahwah, NJ: Erlbaum.

Siegler, R. S. (1998). *Children's Thinking* (3rd edition). Upper Saddle River, NJ: Prentice-Hall.

Want to learn more? For links to online resources relevant to this chapter, interactive quizzes and much more, visit the companion website at **https://edge.sagepub.com/keenan3e/**

Cognitive Processes

Chapter Outline

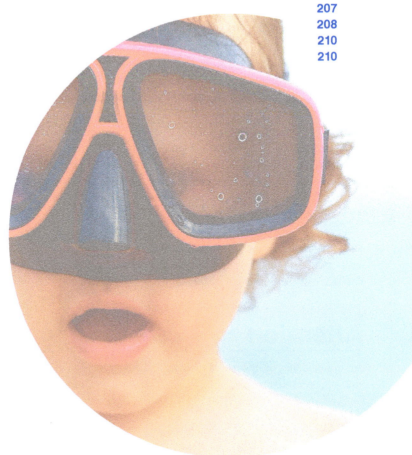

LEARNING AIMS

At the end of this chapter you should:

- be familiar with the various aspects of attention, including sustained, selective and flexible attention, attention strategies including planning and; attention as a cognitive resource
- understand memory processes, including memory retrieval and memory strategies
- be able to describe metacognition, including the adaptive choice strategy model and the possible adaptive function of children's limitations in thinking about thinking
- be able to articulate gains in problem solving, early manifestations of means-end behaviour, rules, tool use and reasoning

Introduction

While we have discussed some general ideas about cognition, here we take a more detailed examination of specific cognitive processes, such as attention, memory, metacognition and problem solving. Attention is required to gather and work on information, so that it can be stored in the memory system in order that we may retrieve it when needed. Without attention, we would likely never get the information we need into memory. However, the challenge of information processing is not over at this point. Depending on how we store information in memory, we may have an easier or more difficult time calling upon it. Although much of our discussion stems from the information processing model, other models, such as Vygotsky's sociocultural theory and Piaget's cognitive theory, have been used to provide a richer and more integrated view of these cognitive processes. For example, as we will discuss, children learn about attention and planning strategies in a cultural context. The evolutionary perspective has also been particularly useful in shedding light on the development of metacognition and how children's selection of successful metacognitive strategies might be understood as a process of selection, adaptation and survival. One fact that will become apparent over the course of this chapter is that research on cognitive processes such as attention and memory is becoming increasingly integrated, bridging the gaps between various theoretical perspectives as a means to allow us to best capitalize on our knowledge of the developing child.

Attention

Attention is the cornerstone of most forms of cognition, as in order to think about something we must first pay attention to relevant and necessary information. Young children are easily distracted and often only pay attention to limited information; however, children develop increasingly sophisticated attention resources and can eventually pay attention in class and keep track of necessary information in order to complete a given task. During early- and middle-childhood, corresponding with the start of formal schooling, children's attention becomes more selective, flexible and sustained.

Aspects of attention

Controlling concentration through **sustained attention** is necessary if we are to see a complex task through to completion. Early on, infants can only sustain attention for short periods of time before finding something else of interest to focus on. By 9 months of age, however, infants are able to control their attention sufficiently to solve problems such as retrieving toys from behind a partition (Willatts, 1990). Sustained attention tends to increase over time in a linear fashion, particularly once children have started preschool. Sustained attention appears to be related to an increasing ability to ignore social distractions (Lopez, Menez, & Hernandez-Guzman, 2005), suggesting that children's ability to focus for longer periods of time tends to co-occur with their ability to ignore competing information, a process otherwise known as selective attention.

Selective attention is important because very often we must ignore irrelevant information and focus on the relevant information pertaining to a task. One way that researchers examine children's developing selective attention is by observing their responses and errors on computer games. In one study, children were shown a stream of numbers on a computer screen and told to hit a button only when a particular combination of numbers appeared. Sharp improvements were found in their ability to select the correct information between 6 and 10 years of age (Goldberg, Maurer, & Lewis, 2001). Another study examined the differences in second- and fifth-graders on performance and attention strategies on a popular computer game. Older children, who were – not surprisingly – better at the game, reported using specific attentional strategies to ensure success, whereas younger children tended to think more about how they did on the task and seemed to be caught up in these global evaluations so that they failed to consider specific attention strategies for doing well (Blumberg, 1998). Even into late adulthood we can continue to develop our ability to select relevant information and pay attention (Levy, Jennings, & Langer, 2001).

Flexible attention can be described as being adaptable or shifting one's focus. One method for assessing attentional flexibility is to ask children to sort cards on the basis of one category (such as colour) and then mid-way through the task ask them to switch to a different category (such as shape). Children around 5 years old are able to do this quite effectively, whereas younger children tend to perseverate, or engage in the same sorting strategy even though it is incorrect (Brooks, Hanauere, Padowska, & Rosman, 2003).

Attention strategies

One of the earliest ways that children lean about attention is through *joint attention*, which occurs when children attend to the same object, event or person as another individual. This shared attention contributes to children's understanding of attention as a mental state. Caregivers often encourage joint attention in infants. Holding a toy up and shaking it to increase the likelihood of children sharing interest, or verbal expressions such as 'doesn't this look exciting', encourage children to focus along with their caregiver. Research has found that adults generally arouse children's joint attention through a summons (e.g. 'look at this'): the infant then responds, showing interest by looking or vocalizing, and the adult may further engage the baby's interest with additional language and gestures as a means to keep their attention (Estigarribia & Clark, 2007). Joint attention, in turn, has been associated with a range of positive outcomes in infancy and later childhood, including increased sustained attention and more advanced language and social skills (Van Hecke, Vaughan, Mundy, Acra, Block, et al., 2007). Early joint attention skills seem to influence later language development, but not the other way around (Beuker et al., 2013). These results are not surprising when considering that social interaction generally involves setting up common ground, which requires joint attention. A recent study with infants and mothers from low socioeconomic backgrounds in Chile found that mothers scaffold joint attention through the use of maintaining a specific strategy a mother uses in following and reinforcing the infant's focus of attention. Moreover, mothers used this strategy approximately 50% of the time in the observation period, indicating the presence of positive interactive strategies within a low-SES group (Mendive, Bornstein, & Sebastián, 2013). Research Example 8.1 illustrates further recent research highlighting sociocultural factors in the development of joint attention.

Children must also engage in **cognitive inhibition** if they are to attend to relevant information. Cognitive inhibition ensures that working memory, which is limited (as we saw in the previous chapter), is protected from becoming cluttered with unnecessary information. An unencumbered working memory further leads to more efficient and effective information processing skills (Handley, Capon, Beveridge, Dennis, & Evans, 2004). Cognitive inhibition also helps children deal with social situations by keeping impulses and hostile emotions and actions at bay. By the preschool years, children are vastly better at inhibiting untoward or unwanted thoughts and behaviour. For example, children show steady improvements with age in performing a stroop task in which they are asked to say the colour of a word that is printed in a different colour. A game such as 'Simon Says' also involves inhibiting incorrect responses. Cognitive inhibition generally corresponds with cortical brain activation and growth, particularly in the frontal lobes, an area associated with planning and higher level functions (Rubia, Smith, Woolley, Nosarti, Heyman et al., 2006).

Research Example 8.1

Culture Impacts on the Development of Joint Attention Strategies

In a recent study of sociocultural influences in infant gestures signalling joint attention, researchers from the Netherlands examined the daily activities of 48 infants aged 8 to 15 months to test for the presence and frequency of joint actions in three different cultures: Yucatec-Mayans (Mexico), Dutch

(Netherlands) and Shanghai-Chinese (China). The researchers were interested in understanding whether infants' gestures emerged independently of social interaction or whether their gestures emerged through social–interactional experiences. Gesture use is a way that communicators, including infants and parents, can engage the other person's joint attention. In this instance, gesturing was related to calling attention to an object. It was unknown whether caregivers gestured in response to infants' otherwise independently developing gestures, or whether caregivers' interactions led infants to gesture.

The researchers hypothesized differences between the children based on common cultural child-rearing practices. In the Netherlands (thought to reflect wider western parenting practices), caregivers provide attention for the child, but within the limits of caregivers' availability, and with the intention that children play by themselves (Harkness, Super, & Tijen, 2000). In Mayan culture, it is believed that young children learn independently of caregivers' interactions, and parents rarely engage in joint object play with their infants (Gaskins, 1996). In contrast, Shanghai Chinese infants are commonly the centre of attention (Goh & Kuczynski, 2009). The infant's intention to jointly engage with the caregiver was measured using index finger-pointing. All infants were matched on age. Infants and caregivers/other family members were videotaped interacting in their own homes over four sessions. The frequency of infant finger-pointing to elicit joint attention from the caregiver was recorded and indexed.

Results confirmed that infants did indeed gesture more and at an earlier age depending on the amount of joint action infants were exposed to: Mayan infants spent less time in jointly attending to an object (such as a toy or book) with their caregivers/family members compared to Dutch infants, who in turn spent less time than Chinese infants. However, an important take-home point was that despite showing differences in the frequency of these behaviours, all infants – regardless of their cultural backgrounds – engaged in joint attention and gesturing. The authors interpreted the findings as providing evidence of the universality of joint action, with clear evidence for the influence of caregivers' actions upon the development of joint attention behaviours and communication.

Questions: What other factors, apart from culturally-specific parenting beliefs, may have impacted on the findings (hint: think possible environmental and non-environmental factors)?

What other behaviours, indicative of joint attention, could the researchers have measured?

Which cognitive theory (you might want to revisit the previous chapter) do the findings support?

Planning is perhaps one of the more complex cognitive processes, involving the ability to think ahead and use attention appropriately to achieve a set of goals. One test of children's planning involves generating a 'shopping' list that children are told to use in a play supermarket. A study examining the performance of 5 to 9 year-olds given such a list found that older children were more likely to look over the store and pause after each item before moving onto the next – indicating more planning – and they consequently took less time to acquire all the items than did the younger children (Szepkouski, Gauvain, & Carberry, 1994). A recent version of the task with preschoolers of high and moderate intellectual ability found that both groups of children performed equally well at planning their shopping trip (Nellis & Gridley, 2000), suggesting that planning within this context may be more about social experience and age rather than superior cognitive abilities.

Attention as a cognitive resource

Taken together, findings on planning and various aspects of attention indicate the multifaceted nature of attention. Attention likely involves cognitive, socioemotional, and motivational systems (Chang & Burns, 2005). While we still consider attention primarily under the domain of cognitive processes, it is a pertinent example of the overlapping nature of cognitive, physical and emotional/social aspects of development.

Psychologists working from a Vygotskian perspective have suggested that the development of attention needs to take into consideration the importance of the social and cultural contexts where learning to be attentive and planful occurs. Children learn about attention and planning from active members of the culture they live within. Children also learn attention strategies once they enter school, and attention can be used as a cognitive resource in facilitating learning. A recent study examined individual differences in 5 year-olds' cognitive resources and found that quality of the child-rearing environment was related to attention and memory. In particular, the quality of the family environment, including stimulating and sensitive care, played a large role in the development of children's cognitive resources, followed by the quality of child care and the quality of children's schooling (NICHD Early Child Care Research Network, 2005).

Image 8A Children's games, such as 'Simon Says', provide an opportunity for children to refine important cognitive skills, such as sustained attention and impulse inhibition

© monkeybusinessimages/iStock/Thinkstock

The importance of attention as a cognitive resource is perhaps nowhere more apparent than the case of children with Attention Deficit and/or Hyperactivity Disorder (ADHD). We will discuss this disorder more fully in the Chapter 13, but the difficulties these children encounter with many tasks is worth noting here. ADHD can manifest in a number of ways, but the hallmark of this condition is difficulty concentrating on a task that requires mental effort for more than a few minutes. Children with ADHD may have difficulty paying attention in class, lose things, forget instructions, and often seem to act impulsively. As a result, children with ADHD may experience deficits in many aspects of their lives, including social, school and home activities.

Can you think of ways in which children's interactions with adults might promote the development of attention and planning?

Memory

The study of memory is of great interest to researchers and the public alike. If you consider that almost everything you know about yourself, other people and the world around you is rooted in memory, it's no surprise that many of us are interested in how memory works. What allows us to remember information and how do we retrieve this information when we need it? These sorts of questions are especially relevant to students, teachers and information processing theorists. Child development specialists recognize that children make incredible leaps in their ability to use their memory, and this is the topic of our next section.

Even young babies are capable of remembering. A number of studies have found that 3 month-olds can remember how to make a mobile move by kicking it one week after receiving training. By 6 months babies can remember the task two weeks later (Rovee-Collier & Bhatt, 1993). However, memory is relatively limited at first. Expanding on the example above, when babies are tested in a different crib that presents different visual cues, they can no longer remember how to make the mobile move, even after short delays (Boller, Grabelle, & Rovee-Collier, 1995). In addition, as outlined in Research Example 8.2, many of us do not form lasting memories of childhood events. Clear memory strategies generally do not develop until the preschool years, and it is only in middle childhood that memory strategies truly start to become elaborate and effective (Schneider, 2002). The way that children of different ages retrieve information from their memory systems also changes and becomes more sophisticated.

Research Example 8.2

Infantile Amnesia

How do we reconcile research showing that infants and toddlers clearly have memory for events and people, yet most of us do not have memories of our very early childhood? *Infantile amnesia* is the term that has been given to the observation that very few people have memories for events before the age of 2 or 3. A number of theories exist to explain this phenomenon. One invokes changes in frontal lobe growth that allow for explicit or conscious memories (Bauer, 2008). Another explanation is based on the finding that our autobiographical memory of events corresponds to our linguistic development, which suggests that it may be difficult to form memories without language; our increasing ability to encode

(Continued)

events verbally may lead to greater accessibility of memories for those events (Hayne, 2004). Emotion knowledge, or having schemes for how we feel after certain kinds of situations, may also play an integral role in the formation of our autobiographical memory in childhood.

In a recent longitudinal study, 140 Canadian children aged 4 to 13 years were asked to recall their three earliest memories. Two years later they were again asked about their earliest memories. The children were also asked to estimate how old they were at the time of each memory. Parents provided confirmation about the accuracy of the events and the child's age at the time of the event. Younger children aged 4 to 7 were more likely to change their earliest memories over time than were older children aged 10 to 13, who showed greater consistency in retelling their earliest memories (Peterson, Warren, & Short, 2011). The younger children's memories seemed to be replaced with memories from older ages.

One longitudinal study found that children's emotion knowledge uniquely predicted their autobiographical memory ability across groups and time points and independent of language skills (Wang, 2008). Emotion knowledge, which generally does not flourish until the preschool years, may be integral in allowing children to understand and remember autobiographical events, and to keep these memories consistent. The findings also provide support for the notion that different aspects of development, such as cognitive and social/emotional systems, work together to move development forward.

Question: Given that we seem to lose memories from our early years, replacing them with memories of a later age, would you agree with the authors of the Canadian study who indicate that 'our psychological childhoods begin much later than our real childhood'?

Retrieving memory

Once information enters the realm of long-term memory, we must somehow recover it in order to make use of it. Sometimes information has been attended to, entered the working memory, and even passed to long-term memory, yet we still have difficulty retrieving it. Many of us are familiar with the 'tip of the tongue' phenomenon which demonstrates our difficulty with memory retrieval. This is when we are sure we know a particular name or word (such as the capital city of Tahiti) but can't, despite any amount of forehead tapping, coax the word from our mind (the answer, is Papeete). Memory retrieval occurs in two main ways: through recall and recognition.

Recall involves creating a mental representation of stimuli that are no longer present. Recall seems to be present as early as 1 year of age, evidenced by research showing infants are able to find hidden objects and imitate the actions and facial expressions of others they have seen even after a delay of hours or days (Herbert & Hayne, 2000). While long-term recall is evident in the first year of life, it becomes much more reliable and efficient during the second year

(Bauer, 2002). However, infants' and young children's ability remains somewhat limited and generally requires a number of cues or hints. In addition, how much information young children can recall is limited. At 2 years old children can usually only recall one or two items; their ability increases slightly so they may recall three or four pieces of information when they reach 4 years of age (Perlmutter, 1984). In comparison to older children and adults, toddlers and pre-school-aged children's recall appears deficient. Young children with good recall abilities tend to also have superior linguistic skills, suggesting that language may be important for generating mental representations about information that happened in the past (Simcock & Hayne, 2003). Long-term recall is contingent upon the development of multiple connections between regions of the brain. During the second year these circuits become highly established (Nelson, 1977), making recall more likely after this point.

A distinction also needs to be made between different forms of memory that can be recalled. *Declarative memory* is recall of a fact or an episode from the past. Declarative memory requires the hippocampus and the neocortex and continues to improve throughout childhood. Evidence of declarative memory tends to hinge upon language (such as when a preschooler relates which animals they saw at the zoo that morning). However, it can also be noted by nonverbal behaviour, including experiments where toddlers can learn to navigate with the help of shaped objects as landmarks to remind them of where to go (Wang, Hermer, & Spelke, 1999). In contrast, non-declarative memory involves a wide range of nonverbal memories, associations, skills and habits. Even very young infants demonstrate evidence of nondeclarative associative memory, such as when a mother strokes her infant's head during feeding, and eventually the mere act of stroking the infant's head calms the child when hungry. Another type of nondeclarative memory is procedural learning, such as learning to tie one's shoelaces or ride a bike. Simple procedures are typically learned around the first birthday. Both declarative and procedural memories appear to be consolidated during sleep (a tried and tested tip for studying for exams is to get a good night's sleep after a study session).

Recognition is an even more basic form of memory retrieval, and involves identifying that a stimulus is identical or similar to a previously experienced stimulus. Recognition tells us a great deal about retrieval over development as even young infants are capable of successfully recognizing information. Unlike recall, where information must be plucked from memory with limited or no clues, during recognition the information to be remembered is available the entire time. For obvious reasons, asking infants to recall information from their memory is impossible. Assessing recognition and associated signals of recognition such as habituation behaviour allows researchers to circumvent infants' verbal and cognitive imitations. Thus, a researcher may show infants a set of pictures. After a short delay, the babies are shown the items again. If looking time is markedly less than for a set of items the infant hasn't seen before, the researcher can conclude that the infant remembers the initial set. Such research indicates that infant recognition memory is robust and quite resistant to decay and interference (Rose, Feldman, & Jankowski, 2004). A similar task with older children might involve asking them to point to those items they had been shown before. A common test of recognition memory in middle childhood and beyond is the multiple choice test. Like recall, recognition memory increases with age. Older children are increasingly able to apply memory strategies during storage that assists with recognizing the information later on (Mandler & Robinson, 1978). We now turn our discussion to such strategies.

We saw in Chapter 6 that habituation methods can be used to study perception in infants. Do you think that this technique might also be useful for studying infant memory?

Memory strategies

Rehearsal involves repeating information over and over again. Thus, children learning to spell 'cat' may repeat 'c-a-t' many times until they remember the correct order of the letters. Rehearsal is the most basic memory strategy we can use, and tends to be the first method adopted by children when they begin school. Rehearsal increases spontaneously with age, such that older children seem to naturally adopt this style of remembering (Flavell, Beach, & Chinsky, 1966). Children often do not master rehearsal until the middle childhood years, perhaps due to limitations in working memory. Older children seem to chunk information (as we discussed in Chapter 7, this involves organizing information into more meaningful units) together more effectively when performing rehearsal (Ornstein, Naus, & Liberty, 1975). Younger children also tend to repeat information only once or twice, perhaps overestimating their ability to remember from just a small number of repetitions (Naus, 1982). However, even young children can use rehearsal effectively when trained or instructed how to do so. Moreover, it seems that overestimating memory ability is associated with greater recall performance in early school-aged children, suggesting an extra dose of confidence may be an adaptive function (HyeEun, Bjorklund, & Beck, 2007).

Organization is a more effective way of remembering information, as this is reformed in a way that makes it more meaningful and thus easier to remember. Organization often involves forming hierarchical relationships between the information. Therefore, if a child was asked to remember a list such as *parrot*, *dinosaur*, *bus*, *dog*, and *car*, organizing the list into two categories, 'animals' and 'vehicles', would allow for much more efficient storage than simply repeating the list over and over again. Effective use of organization occurs later than rehearsal, usually at around age 9 or 10 (Bjorklund, 2005). That is not to say younger children cannot use organization to help them remember; in fact, children as young as 2 or 3 can use basic categories to learn and remember (Waxman, Shipley, & Shepperson, 1991), although younger children often need to actively learn this strategy in order to use it effectively. Older children tend to combine memory strategies by rehearsing and organizing together, to best effect (Coyle & Bjorklund, 1997).

Elaboration is perhaps the most sophisticated and effective memory strategy. In elaboration, we add to the information we need to remember in order to increase its meaningfulness. In this way, it is more likely to enter our long-term memory. Elaboration can involve making the information bizarre or humorous, or using a memorable visualization of the words. We can also use multiple sensory modalities in addition to the mental image, such as feeling, hearing and smelling, to increase its meaningful and hence transfer it to our long-term memory. An example from a research study that used a story elaboration strategy involved giving fourth and fifth graders a list of 14 words. Stories were created that inserted the words, such as 'the grey *cat* jumped over the *log* and crossed the *street* to find the *bowl* of cold *milk* under the *chair*'. Recall of the words was better when such elaboration strategies were used compared to repetitively learning the words (Levin & Rohwer, 1968). Many such studies using a variety of elaborative strategies have found this method greatly enhances children's memory. Given the increasing cognitive complexity of this strategy, elaboration generally occurs in older children (Schneider & Pressley, 1997).

The **knowledge base**, although not strictly a memory strategy, nevertheless helps us store information. It refers to what we have learned previously and our knowledge of the world in general. The more we know, the more we are likely to remember. Facts that we already know act as anchor points for remembering new information. The more anchor points we have, the more meaning we can bring to new information, and the more likely we are to remember it. A classic study illustrating the power of the knowledge base is the work of Michelene Chi (1978) with children expert in chess. In this study, child chess experts and a group of adults who only had a basic understanding were tested on their recall of chess-piece positions and a series of numbers. The third and eighth grade children did not perform as well as the adults on the number memory task, yet far surpassed the adults when it came to remembering chess positions. It seemed a child's knowledge base for chess affected their performance on the task. Having prior knowledge of chess allowed the children to process and store new chess information in a much more effective and efficient manner than adults who did not have the same kind of knowledge base. Overall, the use of memory strategies together with an existing knowledge base likely interact to enhance memory.

Metacognition

Metacognition is thinking about thinking. To work well, the information processing system must be able to reflect upon itself. Any time you thought to yourself 'I must write that address down or I'll forget it' you were engaging in metacognition, which allows you to remember and access information more effectively. Children increasingly develop the capacity to reflect on their own abilities and cognitive processes. A child who is able to recognize that they know their brother's favourite cupcake flavour and helps to find a recipe that accommodates his likes is displaying metacognition. Knowing that it might be different from their own favourite cupcake can also be considered a form of metacognition. Such understanding of people as mental beings or 'mind reading' is specifically referred to as *theory of mind*, a topic we discuss in more detail in the following chapter, and is an example of how children use metacognition in a social context.

Metacognition appears to encompass a number of reflective abilities. A broad definition of metacognition that has been offered includes: (1) conceptual information about the mind; (2) cognitive monitoring, or the ability to read one's own mental states and accurately assess how present and future performance on mental tasks will be affected by that state; and (3) strategy regulation, or the ability to use metacognitive knowledge to achieve goals (Alexander & Schwanenflugel, 1996). The relationship between metacognition and strategy use is likely to be circular, in that information during a task feeds back into the metacognitive system, which culminates in a more effective strategy system and greater metacognitive knowledge (Bjorklund, 2005). Children gradually develop metacognitive abilities. Yet it has been argued that children's limited metacognitive knowledge at first has adaptive features (Bjorklund, 1997). Thus, a preschooler's limitations in attention and memory may actually facilitate their understanding of language, as not processing everything said to them may in fact assist comprehension. If we consider that immaturity is sometimes adaptive to the developing child, we are able to view children's seeming incompetence in a different light, and perhaps even see efficiency in deficiency.

Other research that has linked the development of strategies to metacognition has been described by Siegler's *model of adaptive strategy choice* (Siegler, 1996). This model states that when presented with a problem, children think about a number of different strategies for solving the problem. With experience, children select specific strategies which over time emerge as their preferred strategies, as these appear to work most efficiently. The idea, rooted in evolutionary theory, is that we first begin with variation, which over time evolves into selected mental strategies which have adaptive problem-solving capacities. The microgenetic research design has become synonymous with Siegler's work. As you may recall from our chapter on research methods, microgenetic research involves giving children a variety of problems over a certain period of time and observing or measuring their responses repeatedly over that period. Using this design, Siegler found that children evidenced strategies that displayed an overlapping-waves pattern. With arithmetic problems, for example, children tried a variety of strategies which over time waxed and waned similar to waves (depicting frequency of use that rises and then falls) that overlap (multiple strategies might be used at any one time). Ultimately, only the most effective strategies increase in occurrence. Recent work has found that teaching strategies can streamline this process, as, when taught an effective strategy, children are more likely to abandon other less effective strategies in favour of the one taught (Siegler & Booth, 2004). Even so, given their still-developing memory and attention systems, children may take some time before wholeheartedly taking on board a newly-learned adaptive strategy. Siegler's research demonstrates that not all children will respond to problems in the same way, and indeed, one child may respond differently to the same problem on two occasions.

Problem Solving

Advances in problem solving and reasoning are evident across childhood. Some researchers argue that **means-end behaviour** is evident from birth. A variety of behaviours, such as looking, sucking, and early imitation, are likely to involve the infant anticipating future events and actions in anticipation of those events (Cox & Smitsman, 2006). By 8 to 12 months of age, infants engage in intentional or means-end behaviour, such as looking for hidden objects as in the object permanence task. Not long afterwards, children create and follow *rules*. One example of advances in rule following that applies to children's everyday behaviour is their ability to engage in make-believe play which increases after the end of the second year. During make-believe play children are compelled to follow the rules of play, which often involve inhibiting impulses that might get in the way of play (Duncan & Tarulli, 2003). For example, a child pretending to be 'the mother' must conform to the rules of parental behaviour. Engaging in such problem-solving behaviour assists not only with children's cognitive understanding but also with their social competence. Research has found that increased complex sociodramatic play during the preschool years is associated with an increased ability to follow classroom rules (Elias & Berk, 2002). In fact, rule following is likely to be important for many aspects of children's lives, including their cognitive and social functioning

Another area that appears to involve a development of reasoning skill is children's *tool use*. A tool can be defined as any implement used to assist with a goal-directed activity. Eating utensils, telephones and hairbrushes – almost any objects you can think of – can be used as tools. In order to effectively use tools to assist activity, children must engage in multi-step problem solving involving at least two coupled phases of activity. Children have to determine what the problem is and how the given tool can be used to assist them. A recent study that examined 2 and 3 year-olds' hand use in picking up and using a tool (either a stick or a cane) to move an object to a specified goal location found changes in both aspects of tool use with age (Cox & Smitsman, 2006). Thus, older children displayed advances in goal-related information and tool-related information in order to successfully complete the task.

More complex problem solving includes children's analogical and syllogistic or formal reasoning. **Analogical thinking** involves an inference from one particular to another particular, and includes language use such as similes and allegories. The format for analogical thinking generally takes the form of presenting two items 'A and B', and a third item 'C' which then requires generating 'D' which has the same relation to C as B has to A. For example, a question such as 'Finger is to hand as toe is to ___?' would assess analogical reasoning (the correct answer is 'foot' if you are wondering). Simpler versions of this reasoning have been generated using picture

books presented as a game and simpler analogies that children may be familiar with, such as 'playdough is to cut playdough as apple is to cut apple'. When presented in this fashion, children as young as 4 years old demonstrated their knowledge of analogical reasoning (Goswami & Brown, 1990). **Syllogistic reasoning** is more complex and involves evaluating whether a conclusion logically follows on from two premises. A syllogism consists of three parts: the major premise, the minor premise and the conclusion. For example, All humans are mortal (major premise); I am human (minor premise); therefore I am mortal (conclusion). Generally, school-aged children find syllogistic reasoning quite difficult, and make a number of common errors. Not until adolescence do most children recognize that the accuracy of conclusions

Image 8B Make-believe play provides a valuable means for children to develop cognitive and social competence, including problem-solving and rule following

© oliveromg/Shutterstock

drawn from premises relies on the rules of logic, and not their own experiences. If given an example that defies usual experience, such as 'If dogs are bigger than elephants and elephants are bigger than mice, then dogs are bigger than mice', children younger than 10 say this is incorrect, even though the conclusion satisfies both the major and minor premises. Children find this kind of syllogism difficult partly because it stands in the face of their real-world experience with these animals and they must inhibit this information if they are to answer correctly (Moshman & Franks, 1986). Recent work has confirmed that inhibitory control is necessary when children reason about syllogisms where prior belief and logic interfere (Moutier, Plagne-Cayeux, Melot, & Houde, 2006).

How would Piaget's theory account for the difficulty experienced by children younger than 10 with syllogistic reasoning problems that are not in accordance with their real-world experience?

Summary

In all, we can see that children make great leaps in their ability to process information over childhood. Most begin with relatively immature attention, memory and reasoning systems to emerge as highly evolved thinkers capable of complex syllogistic reasoning by early adolescence.

Glossary

Analogical thinking involves an inference from one particular to another, often in the form of presenting two items 'A and B', a third item 'C', and the generation of 'D' which has the same relation to C as B has to A.

Cognitive inhibition is the ability to control internal and external distracting stimuli in order to carry out the required or desired operation.

Elaboration is a memory strategy in which one adds to information to be memorized to increase its meaningfulness.

Flexible attention is demonstrated by shifting one's focus from one source of information to another.

Knowledge base is the sum total of one's knowledge of the world or a specific topic.

Means-end behaviour is shown by action taken in anticipation of a specific outcome.

Metacognition is conscious reflection on thought processes, or 'thinking about thinking'.

Organization is a memory strategy which involves reforming information in a meaningful manner.

Planning is the ability to think ahead and use attention in an appropriate manner to achieve a set of goals.

Recall is a type of memory retrieval wherein one creates a mental representation of stimuli no longer present (e.g. an open-ended answer test).

Recognition is a type of memory retrieval in which one identifies that a stimulus is similar to a previously experienced stimulus (e.g. a multiple choice test).

Rehearsal is a memory strategy which consists of repeating information.

Selective attention involves focusing on relevant information and simultaneously ignoring irrelevant information.

Sustained attention is focusing concentration for an extended period of time.

Syllogistic reasoning is the evaluation of whether a conclusion follows on from two premises.

TEST YOUR KNOWLEDGE

1. Which of the following is not typically involved in attention?

   a) Flexibility of thought
   b) Cognitive inhibition
   c) Planning
   d) Tool use

2. Which memory strategy is associated with the greatest memory storage and retrieval?

   a) Elaboration
   b) Rote learning
   c) Rehearsal
   d) Organization

3. Metacognition is which of the following?

   a) Being able to understand another's mental state, including beliefs, desires, goals
   b) Cognitive inhibition
   c) Reflection on thought processes
   d) The combined effect of attention and memory

(Continued)

4. Nine month-old Kelly lifts a blanket to reveal the toy her brother, Reid, hid beneath it. Which form of reasoning is she showing signs of?

   a) Rule following
   b) Means-end behaviour
   c) Tool use
   d) Analogical thinking

ANSWERS: 1–D, 2–A, 3–C, 4–B

Suggested Reading

Fivush, R., & Haden, C. A. (2003). *Autobiographical Memory and the Construction of a Narrative Self: Developmental and cultural perspectives* (pp. 49–69). Mahwah, NJ: Erlbaum

Forrest-Pressley, D. L., MacKinnon, G. E., & Waller, T. G. (eds) (1985). *Metacognition, Cognition, and Human Performance, Vol. 1: Theoretical perspectives.* Orlando, FL: Academic.

McGonigle-Chambers, M. (2014). *Understanding Cognitive Development.* London: Sage.

Want to learn more? For links to online resources relevant to this chapter, interactive quizzes and much more, visit the companion website at **https://edge.sagepub.com/keenan3e/**

The Development of Language and Communication

9

Chapter Outline

LEARNING AIMS

At the end of this chapter you should:

- understand the different facets involved in the study of human language
- be able to articulate the essential points of learning, nativist, and interactionist accounts of language
- be aware of evidence for and against each of the three theoretical accounts
- be able to describe the key concepts involved in phonological development
- be able to describe the course of semantic development, including concepts such as *fast mapping* and the constraints which support the development of children's word learning
- be able to describe the course of grammatical development, including concepts such as *syntactic bootstrapping*
- be able to describe the developmental course of pragmatic knowledge and key concepts such as *speech registers*, *conversational implicature* and the *cooperative principle*

Introduction

When we communicate successfully, we do so because we are able to do at least four different things. First, we need to be able to produce the sounds that make up a language and convey meanings to other people. Second, we need to know what the words of a language mean. Third, we need to know how to put these words together in grammatically appropriate ways such that others will understand us. Finally, we also need to know how to effectively *use* our language to communicate with others. Psychologists who study language refer to these four processes by separate names. How we produce meaningful sounds is the study of **phonology**. The study of **semantics** refers to the developing knowledge of word meanings and how we acquire a vocabulary. The study of **grammar** refers to how we learn the grammar of our language, that is, the rules for combining words into meaningful sentences. Finally, **pragmatics** refers to the study of how we use language to achieve our communicative goals. If you want to be *polite*, make a *promise*, or speak in a *sarcastic* way, you need to know more than simply how to string words together.

Note that in what follows, we focus on the development of spoken language. While there are other topics which could be considered, such as the development of written language or nonverbal communication, these will not be addressed in a systematic way in this chapter.

Theories of Language Development

Two approaches have dominated the study of language. The first of these theories of language were accounts based on the behaviourist approach to psychology, so influential in the 1940s and 1950s. These behaviourist-inspired theories of language fell out of favour after a devastating review of learning theory accounts of language published by Noam Chomsky (1959). With Chomsky's review, a new theory of language based on nativist ideas emerged. Simply put, Chomsky and his followers believed that we do not learn a language; indeed, Chomsky argued that it makes little sense to use the word 'learn' in connection with how we acquire a language. Instead, he claimed that language quite naturally developed as we matured. Until recently, Chomskian accounts have dominated work on language development, however, a variety of learning accounts have been put forward which stress the importance of environmental influences on language learning. In what follows, we will review each of these positions.

Learning theory

Learning theory accounts of language development are distinguished from more contemporary theories of language by their adherence to the traditional principles of learning theory, that is, reinforcement and punishment. Learning theory views of language range from the radical behaviourism of B. F. Skinner (1957) to the social learning theory of Albert Bandura (1989) with its emphasis on cognitive processes. Skinner's theory of language was put forth in his 1957 book *Verbal Behavior*. Skinner argued that language is like any other form of behaviour in that it is acquired through operant conditioning. That is, parents selectively reinforce their child's linguistic behaviours, rewarding only those behaviours which they recognize as words or as appropriate grammatically correct utterances. In Skinner's view, children gradually begin to use only those words or utterances for which they have been reinforced. Through the use of reinforcement, parents gradually shape their children's linguistic behaviour until, over time, it begins to sound like adult speech. Essentially, then, Skinner's theory was a way to describe how children chain together words to produce grammatically correct speech. These days his theory of verbal behaviour has very few adherents, although some psychologists continue to work within this framework (Moerk, 1992).

More commonly observed in the research on language is the influence of Bandura's social learning theory. Bandura (1989) argued that children's learning took place primarily through observational learning or *imitation*; that is, the child picks up words by overhearing other people and imitating their behaviour. Imitation is an especially important process for describing how a child might learn more complex phrases and longer utterances. According to this view, through processes such as reinforcement and generalization children apply what they have learned to new situations and through feedback about the appropriateness of their speech they learn to use language in an increasingly mature fashion.

Learning theory accounts of language have been criticized on a number of counts (see Pinker, 1994); however, here we consider only three major arguments. First, critics have pointed out that it is simply not possible for parents to reinforce all of the possible utterances a child will use. The amount of time required would amount to a lifetime, yet children come to master most aspects of their language by the end of their preschool years. Second, studies of parent–child interactions (Brown & Hanlon, 1970) have shown that parents do not reward only grammatically correct speech. They are just as likely to reward utterances which are grammatically incorrect but truthful. Parents simply do not provide the kind of corrective feedback which learning theory suggests is the main mechanism behind language learning. Third, Chomsky (1957) directed our attention to the nature of the language that children actually hear, highlighting what he called the **poverty of the stimulus**. Analyses of the linguistic data that children actually receive show that it contains too few examples of the complex structures they eventually acquire to suppose that learning accounts could provide a correct model for children's language learning. Only by positing an innate set of specifications can we explain how children actually learn language so quickly.

In the view of many theorists, then, learning a language cannot take place *exclusively* through processes such as reinforcement and imitation. It is clear that imitation and reinforcement are important processes in language acquisition (and are perhaps more important to particular processes, such as word learning), but on their own, they are unable to explain complex developments such as the acquisition of grammar (Chomsky, 1959; Pinker, 1994). So does learning theory have any useful contribution to make to the study of human language? The answer to this question is 'yes': a variety of programmes designed to help language-delayed children catch up with their peers have successfully incorporated learning principles (Ratner, 1993; Zelazo, Kearsley, & Ungerer, 1984).

Nativist theory

The nativist view of language development is traced back to the work of Noam Chomsky (1957, 1968). In contrast to the perspective offered by learning theory, Chomsky argued that language was the product of an unlearned, biologically-based, internal mental structure. He reasoned that the rules which govern the proper use of a language were too complex to be acquired by children in the few short years it took them to learn a language. Therefore, some aspects of language must be *innately specified*, meaning that these aspects of our language are not learned but are, in fact, a part of our biological heritage.

All nativist theories of language development share certain elements. First, they assume that certain grammatical concepts are common to all languages and are therefore innate. For example, the fact that all human languages contain concepts such as *subject* (what the sentence is about), *verb* (what the subject does) and *object* (the object of the subject's actions) is consistent with this view. Second, nativist views propose that children are biologically predisposed to learn language. Finally, all children come to the task of acquiring a language with a set of innate *hypotheses* which guide their attempts to abstract the principles that govern their language. These hypotheses constrain the hypotheses children will form about the rules which underlie the language they hear, helping to reduce the complexity of learning a language.

Table 9.1 Theories of language development

Learning Theory	
Skinner	Focus on operant conditioning, with the development of language occurring through parental selective reinforcement of 'appropriate' linguistic behaviours.
Bandura	Focus on observational learning, with imitation of others resulting in the learning of complex and lengthy utterances. The reinforcement of such imitation and its generalization allows the application of newly learnt language to new situations, and feedback helps children understand the appropriateness of such.
Criticisms of the theory	Given the rapid nature of language learning and the long period of time over which principles of operant conditioning and observational learning influence behaviours, it appears unlikely that the latter can be applied to the former. Positive parental feedback is not limited to the grammar of children's language, but rather to its truth. The language children are exposed to rarely includes instances of complex structures, and this stimulus poverty means that it would be difficult, if not impossible, for children to adequately learn how to accurately apply such complex structures in their own language.
Nativist Theory	
Shared assumptions	Certain grammatical concepts are common to all languages and are thus innate; children have a biological predisposition to language learning; children's innate hypotheses regarding language allow the extraction of principles which govern language.
Chomsky	The innate mental structure responsible for language is the language acquisition device (LAD). It contains the common grammatical concepts, or universal grammar, which allows its operation with reference to any language. Once the principles of the specific relevant language are extracted by the LAD, these principles are built into the LAD in order to allow interpretation of further speech.
Criticisms of the theory	What kind of universal grammar is common to all languages? The lengthy time period over which understanding of grammatical rules emerges suggests that if knowledge is innate, it must be more limited than that proposed by most nativist theorists. There is little neurological evidence for a biological predisposition to language learning, such as the LAD.
Interactionist Theory	
Bruner	The social support and social context of instruction in language acquisition are as important as biological factors. Scaffolding, motherese, and expansion and recast all facilitate the effective operation of the strong biological predisposition towards language acquisition. This collection of strategies has been termed the language acquisition support system (LASS).
Criticisms of the theory	Direct feedback on the appropriateness of language is rare and cannot be regarded as an essential element of any LASS. Language acquisition appears to occur at the same rate across cultures, even though not all cultures utilize the techniques that are elements of the LASS.

Chomsky (1968) proposed that children come equipped with an innate mental structure which makes the task of learning language feasible. He called this structure the **language acquisition device (LAD)**. According to Chomsky, this contains a set of features common to all languages, which he termed a **universal grammar**. This refers to the entire set of rules or linguistic parameters which specify all possible human languages. The learning of grammar occurs when the LAD operates on speech to abstract out the linguistic parameters which underlie the particular language used in the child's environment. Chomsky termed this process of determining the parameters or rules of one's native language **parameter setting**. Parameter setting is akin to flipping a switch – once the LAD abstracts out a rule or parameter, the parameter is fixed, and the newly learned rule is now used to interpret further speech. For example, one parameter that needs to be set is the word order of the language. In the English language, the basic order of words is Subject – Verb – Object, whereas in German, the word order is Subject – Object – Verb. In this view, learning grammar is much like a game of 20 questions, where children are given data and gradually refine their guesses until they have determined the answer, except they are acquiring something much more complex: the set of rules which comprise their language.

In support of nativist accounts of language development, nativists would point to the ease and rapidity with which children acquired some very complex sets of rules (Maratsos, 1998; Pinker, 1994). Given the *poverty of the stimulus* argument described by Chomsky, it is certainly an impressive accomplishment that we acquire so complex a system of rules by the early pre-school years. The rapidity with which we acquire language despite poor examples from which to learn provides support for the theory that much of what we learn is innately specified. In addition, nativists have also argued that there is a *critical period* for language learning (Hoff-Ginsburg, 1997), that is, a period during which children are particularly sensitive to language but after which it is difficult or perhaps impossible to acquire language normally. For example, case studies (such as the heart-breaking story of Genie mentioned earlier in the book) have revealed that people who have suffered extreme neglect by being locked away from social contact during their childhood have great difficulty learning language beyond puberty. Similarly, brain damage to the areas responsible for language production and comprehension can be recovered from if the damage occurs before puberty; after this time, however, recovery is incomplete and usually quite poor (Lennenberg, 1967). Imaging studies have shown that, consistent with Chomsky's view, the left side of the brain appears to be specialized for language. These patterns are consistent across most individuals. Damage to the frontal lobe usually results in deficits in language production, whereas damage to other lobes results in comprehension problems (Dick, Dronkers, Pizzamiglio, Saygin, Small, & Wilson, 2004).

Nativist views have also been criticized on a number of counts. One issue with Chomsky's theory in particular is that linguists have failed to specify the universal grammar or set of parameters that could specify all possible human languages. Some critics of Chomsky have doubted whether one set of rules can explain all grammatical variations (Tomasello, 2003). Another criticism of the nativist position is that grammar is not acquired as rapidly as might be expected if a great deal of innate knowledge is specified. Such criticisms suggest that more general learning mechanisms might be required to learn language than are typically specified in nativist theories. Learning grammar, for instance, is not quickly attained in childhood, as Chomsky suggests. Rather, certain forms of grammar, such as the passive voice, are not mastered until late childhood (Tager-Flusberg, 2005) and this implies that language mastery is more of a slow and involved process than Chomsky believed. Finally, although Chomsky proposes the existence of a biologically-based LAD, there is little neurological evidence to support the existence of such a device (Bates & MacWhinney, 1989). Whereas some parts of the brain have been clearly identified as supporting linguistic functions, no complete picture of how these and other parts of the brain which are involved in processing language has emerged. Nevertheless, thanks to Chomsky it is now widely recognized that we have an innate, biologically-based ability to learn language.

Which aspects of language development do you think are best accounted for by nativist approaches? Which aspects are best accounted for by learning theory?

Interactionist views

A variety of theories have arisen in recent years which attempt to reconcile the roles of biology and environment in children's language learning. These *interactionist theories* are concerned with the interplay between environmental and biological factors in the process of acquiring language. Interactionists tend to view children as having a strong biological predisposition to acquire a language; however, in contrast to nativists, interactionists stress the importance of both the social support that parents provide the young language learner and the social contexts in which a language-learning child is instructed (Bloom, 1998; Bohannon, 1993; Bruner, 1983). Proponents of the interactionist view also stress that language development is not separate from other areas of development (Bloom & Tinker, 2001). For example, children's desire to learn language must be viewed within the context of their willingness to interact with others or their social development.

According to Bruner (1983), one advocate of an interactionist position, parents provide their children not with an LAD but with a *language acquisition support system* or ***LASS*** (notice the parody of Chomsky's view here). According to Bruner, LASS is simply a collection of strategies which parents employ to facilitate their children's acquisition of language. One of these strategies involves scaffolding, the deliberate use of language pitched at a level that is slightly beyond what children can comprehend at a given point in time. With support from the parent, scaffolding leads the child to acquire complex language more quickly than they might on their own. Bruner also pointed out that parents provide support for their children's learning by introducing names for things in the context of play, by carefully monitoring their children's understanding, and by finding new ways to convey rules when children fail to grasp a particular instance. Another method which parents use to teach support language is **infant-directed speech**, or what has often been referred to as **motherese**. When using infant-directed speech, parents speak in a higher pitch, stress important words, and talk more slowly to their infants (Fernald & Kuhl, 1987). Research has shown that very young infants show a clear preference for infant-directed speech, whether it is employed by women or men (Pegg, Werker, & McLeod, 1992). Such techniques both gain an infant's attention and increase the chances of their understanding the message. Finally, we consider a pair of techniques that adults employ known as **expansion** and **recast** (Bohannon & Stanowicz, 1988).

Image 9A Interactionist theories of language development recognize that language is acquired as a result of biological and social factors

© Zsolt Nyulaszi/Hemera/Thinkstock

Expansion occurs when an adult takes a child's utterance and expands on the complexity of it. For example, when a child might utter something like '*Felix eated*', the parent might expand on the complexity, adding, '*yes, that's right, Felix ate his dinner*'. Notice here that the parent, while increasing the complexity of the utterance, has also corrected the child's grammar, changing *eated* to its appropriate past tense form, *ate*. When parents expand, as in this example, they often *recast* the child's utterance as well, correcting the grammatical form of the utterance. Through such methods, adults offer subtle, indirect feedback about the child's language. Children often imitate the expansions and recasts of their parents, and while doing so gain valuable experience with more complex forms of speech. You may recall from Chapter 2 that this is just the sort of learning that Vygotsky espoused.

A variety of criticisms of interactionist theories have been made. For example, deVillers and deVillers (1992) argued that parents rarely offer their children *direct* feedback on the appropriateness of their grammar. Other critics have pointed out that practices regarding linguistic and social interactions between parents and children vary widely across cultures, and some cultures do not use any of the practices described above, yet their children still learn language at similar rates to children in cultures that do employ these practices (Hoff-Ginsburg, 1997). At the same time, it is clear that social interaction has an important influence on language development: German children learn to speak German and Italian children learn to speak Italian not because of any biological differences but because of social interactions between parents, children and other members of the culture. It seems clear that further studies of the effects of social interaction on language development are required before any firm conclusions about how specific types of interaction affect the growth of linguistic skill can be drawn.

Preverbal Communication

While the development of language is an extremely impressive achievement, there are a number of nonverbal precursors to language development which are important phases in children's acquisition of a language (Adamson, 1995). For example, Fogel (1993) has illustrated the ways in which infants' first communicative exchanges take place with their parents. Parents and infants often engage in a kind of dialogue which includes sounds, movement, touch and a variety of facial expressions. Schaffer (1996) has argued that while these exchanges may appear to take the form of 'conversations', they are really under the control of the parent who maintains the interaction, serving as a lesson in communication and conversation for the infant. However, an alternative view of such interactions comes from research by Colwyn Trevarthen and colleagues (see for example Malloch and Trevarthen, 2009). Based on their observations of interactions between mothers and infants, Malloch and Trevarthen argue that such interactions are reciprocal in nature and the infant will often actively seek out such interactions. They argue that these display a quality they refer to as 'communicative musicality'. Essentially, the mother's voice has a distinct 'musical' quality with distinctive patterns of rhythm and intonation and the infant mirrors these qualities in response to the mother. By about 12 months of age, infants have become much

Image 9B   Gestures, such as pointing, are important preverbal methods of communication. This 11-month-old is using protodeclarative pointing to gain his mother's attention.

Photo credit: Nalina Kaufman

more active participants in this process, taking over a greater share of the responsibility for maintaining the interaction (Schaffer, 1979). These early interactions help the child develop the skills required to become a good communicative partner later in life.

Smiles are one of the earliest preverbal forms of communication, helping infants to learn how to string together vocalizations and provide an indication of how they are feeling (Yale, Messinger, Cobo-Lewis, & Delgado, 2003). Another important early nonverbal behaviour is the child's ability to use gestures as a method of communication. By the end of their first year, infants begin to communicate by pointing at objects (Adamson, 1995). These gestures are communicative in that they are used to influence the behaviour of the person the infant is gesturing to. Infants' pointing tends to take two forms (Bates, 1976). **Protodeclarative pointing** occurs when the infant uses pointing gestures to bring an object to another's attention. The infant may point to an object or hold it up to someone, while at the same time monitoring the other's attention to make sure they have seen the object. Infants seem to use protodeclarative pointing to make statements about things that interest them and share these things with other people. However, sometimes infants use pointing to get another to do something for them, such as pointing to the cookie jar or an object that has been placed out of their reach. This form of pointing has been called **protoimperative pointing**. Further developments in gestural communication occur when children begin to use gestures to represent or stand for things they want to communicate (Acredolo & Goodwyn, 1990). For example, a child may use flapping gestures to mimic a bird or may stretch their arms above their head to convey the notion of height. By using gesture in this way, children learn that meanings can be symbolized and shared with others, an insight that they will apply to their use of spoken language. See Research Example 8.1 in the previous chapter for a discussion of how cultural experience impacts on the development of gesturing in infants.

Phonological Development

Most of us are familiar with the ways in which infants pronounce (or often *mis*pronounce) their first words. A classic example of children's early mispronunciation is *nana* for *banana*. Another comes from the first author's own niece who called him *unk*, meaning *uncle*. Phonological development, the process of learning to hear and make the sounds of one's language, is a complex and challenging process for young children. Every language has its own set of speech sounds, some of which are unique, and some of which are shared with other languages. The sounds which make up a specific language are called **phonemes**. Phonological development requires the child to attend to and separate out the sounds they hear in the speech around them, to learn to create these sounds for themselves, and to string these sounds together in meaningful units. Not surprisingly, this process takes some time. Between the end of the first year and the beginning of their fourth year children make considerable strides in this.

Categorical speech perception

As early as 1 month of age, infants can distinguish a variety of speech sounds. Infants are first able to distinguish consonants such as *d* and *n*. Slightly later, at about 2 months of age, they begin to distinguish vowel sounds such as *a* and *i* from one another. An interesting aspect of infants' speech perception abilities is that infants perceive the sound of some consonants in a categorical way, that is, as one sound or another. They do not hear shades of sound that lie in between. This phenomenon has been referred to as **categorical speech perception** (Hoff-Ginsburg, 1997). Findings such as this tend to suggest that infants may be born with an innate mechanism for perceiving the sounds of their language, that is, they do not have to learn these discriminations. However, further research has shown that infants may naturally search for categories for all sounds and not just for speech (Aslin, 1987). Moreover, some authors have suggested that the ability to perceive sounds in a categorical way is simply a product of our aural system, a property which language may have evolved to exploit (Hoff-Ginsburg, 1997).

While very young infants can distinguish between sets of phonemes when presented in isolation, it takes a greater amount of time for them to pick these sounds out of naturally occurring speech and for them to recognize more *meaningful* units of speech, that is, *words*. Segmenting the words of a speaker's utterance is critical in learning to comprehend language. Research suggests that figuring out the boundaries between the words in a sample of fluent speech requires considerable experience with language: deVillers and deVillers (1979) argued that the evidence on phonological perception suggested that it was not until about 24 months of age that children are able to readily accomplish this task. However, a more recent examination of the literature on phonological perception suggests that by the start of their first year infants are able to segment naturally occurring speech such that they can begin to pick out individual words. To do this, infants use cues such as the rhythmic properties of speech (Jusczyk et al., 1993), pauses, pitch and the stresses of particular syllables. Each of these cues helps them to pick out the boundaries between words in fluent speech.

Of course, more than just the ability to perceive and comprehend speech occurs during the first year (Ingram, 1986). From birth, infants are creating their own sounds. Crying is the first of these sounds to be employed. Infants' cries signal their distress but soon come to be modulated to serve a communicative function. By about 1 month of age, infants begin *cooing*, which involves the production of vowel sounds such as *oo*. By 6 months of age, infants begin the process of **babbling**. Babbling occurs when infants begin to string consonants and vowels together. A third development in the early production of speech occurs when infants begin to engage in **patterned speech**. Around the end of their first year, infants begin to string the phonemes of their language together in combinations which at first hearing may sound like meaningful words but, on closer inspection, turn out to be simple strings of sounds with no meaning. Across cultures, these three stages of phonological development tend to occur in the same sequence, suggesting that these changes may be a function of the maturation of the motor cortex (the part of the brain that controls the production of speech) and the vocal tract.

Finally, children begin to utter their first words. Children's first words are usually of the form *consonant-vowel* (Ingram, 1986). Examples include *mama*, *dada*, and *bye-bye*. Interestingly, the words for *mama* and *dada* in most languages are sounds which the young language learner can readily pronounce. In fact, the first words children learn in so many languages seem to have the developing child's phonological limitations in mind. Parents also seem to recognize their children's phonological limitations and choose simplified versions of words (e.g. *tum-tum* for *tummy*) to communicate with their children.

Phonological development does not end with the child's use of their first words. Another aspect of phonological development which extends into the school years is what has been termed **phonological awareness**. This is the ability to be aware of and analyze speech sounds. One method for measuring phonological awareness is by asking children questions such as name a word that rhymes with *blame*, the word that would remain if you took the last sound off of the word *gump*, or what the first sound is in the word *phonology*. Greater phonological awareness is associated with better spelling and reading ability, and training in phonological awareness has been shown to improve reading ability in children labelled as poor readers (Ehri et al., 2001; Wimmer, Landerl, & Schneider, 1994).

Table 9.2 Milestones in children's language development

Age	Milestone
Birth	Infants show a preference for human voices. Cries initially used to signal distress but are quickly modulated to serve communicative functions.
1 to 6 months	Infants begin to distinguish consonant sounds. Slightly later, they learn to distinguish vowel sounds. Infants begin cooing, which quickly turns into babbling. Infants respond to motherese (child-directed speech).
6 to 12 months	Emergence of patterned speech in babbling. Babbling begins to resemble speech. Infants show an increasing preference for their speech in their native language. Infants become increasingly adept at speech perception.
12 to 18 months	Emergence of first words. These usually take a consonant-vowel form (e.g. mama, dada). Gesturing is used to refer to objects or the child's desires. This is often combined with first words. First use of one-word sentences.
18 to 24 months	The naming explosion begins. Children learn new words at a very rapid rate. First appearance of two-word sentences, often referred to as telegraphic speech. Children show the correct use of word order but often drop important grammatical function words.
24 to 36 months	Two year-olds use fast mapping to learn new words. Errors in word learning include overextension and underextension. Beginning of the grammar explosion. First use of three-word sentences and increasing facility with grammatical morphemes. Children show evidence of pragmatic knowledge in early conversational skills.
36 to 48 months	Construction of more complex linguistic constructions such as combined sentences, embedding of clauses and complex question forms. Use of appropriate speech registers. Increasing understanding of pragmatics. Sensitivity to conversational maxims.
Beyond 5 years	By adolescence, children's vocabulary reaches about 30,000 words. Use of more complex grammatical constructions such as passives. More sophisticated understanding of pronoun reference. Increasing sensitivity to verbal ambiguity, the say-mean distinction and development of metalinguistic knowledge. Comprehension for nonliteral forms of speech, such as sarcasm and metaphor.

Semantic Development

For most adults, learning the meaning of a new word is a simple process: we may easily look the word up in a dictionary and commit its meaning to memory. However, we take for granted the host of other developments that have made this achievement possible: for example, a rich network of other concepts, the ability to read, and so on. For young children, the process would seem to be far less simple. Children often hear a word spoken at the same time that a variety of other events occur. Sometimes they hear words spoken about things that are not present in their immediate environment or about past events. Even in seemingly straightforward cases, closer inspection reveals hidden complexity. Consider the parent who points in the direction of the family dog and says 'What's that? That's a dog.' How does the child know which aspect of the situation the word 'dog' refers to? Does *dog* specify the fact that the object is four-legged, that it is furry, or that it is an animal? The philosopher Quine (1960) called this problem the *gavagai* problem, and illustrated just how difficult it was for philosophers, let alone children, to solve. Even with these and other difficulties, children do learn words, beginning slowly and doing so in an increasingly rapid fashion throughout childhood.

First words

Children's first words are generally believed to occur sometime between 10 to 13 months of age. It is often very difficult to pick up on children's very first words and distinguish these from their everyday babbling. Across cultures, the first words that children learn are remarkably similar; they refer to important people in their lives as well as familiar objects and actions (Nelson, 1973). In addition, some of an infant's new words, such as '*all gone*' or '*uh oh*', are linked to cognitive achievements, such as the understanding of object permanence (Gopnik & Meltzoff, 1987).

Reznick and Goldfield (1992) argue that in the period from 12 to 18 months of age, infants are learning approximately three new words per month. However, by about 18 months of age, children are acquiring words much more quickly. This growth spurt in word learning has been called the **naming explosion** (Fenson et al., 1994). Research suggests that, by this age, children have a vocabulary of approximately 22 words and they begin to add from 10 to 20 words per week to their vocabularies (Reznick & Goldfield, 1992). By the time children reach 6 years of age, they have a vocabulary of approximately 10,000 words (Anglin, 1993), suggesting that they acquire approximately five new words each day.

When considering semantic development, it is important to distinguish between two kinds of comprehension that children can show. Research has shown that children's *comprehension*, the words for which they understand the meaning, develops ahead of their *productive vocabulary*, the words which they actually use in their speech. In early word learning, there is a five-month gap between the time when they comprehend 50 words (at about 13 months of age) and the time when they can produce 50 words (Menyuk, Liebergott, & Schultz, 1995). Producing a word is clearly the more difficult task and depends on the state of children's phonological development. Comprehending a word depends more on recognition memory (Kuczaj, 1986).

First words generally refer to important people ('Mama' and 'Dada'), animals ('cow'), food ('milk' is a common one for obvious reasons), everyday actions ('bye-bye'), consequences of familiar actions ('hot') and objects that move ('ball'). Children's first 50 words generally involve exciting people and things; toddlers move on to inanimate objects later. We may also note that most of children's first words are nouns, as it seems that these are more easily learned than verbs (Childers & Tomasello, 2002).

Theories of semantic development

One question raised by the naming explosion is *how* children can begin to learn new words so quickly? For example, 2 year-olds can learn a new word after only a single, brief exposure to it, a process which Carey (1978) referred to as **fast-mapping**. What sorts of information might children use in order to infer the meaning of a new word? That is, how do children solve the *gavagai* problem?

Research on children's word learning (Markman, 1989, 1992) has suggested that children never consider the full range of hypotheses about what a given word could mean; instead, they narrow the range of possible meanings for a word based on built-in *constraints*. In Markman's view, these constraints are innate processes that force the child to consider only certain relevant cues when trying to map a new word onto an object. By narrowing the range of possible hypotheses for a word's meaning, the constraints make the *gavagai* problem a solvable one. Markman proposed three constraints on word meaning: the **whole-object constraint**, the **taxonomic constraint**, and the **mutual-exclusivity constraint**. These are best described by illustrating how they work.

When children see an adult point at an object and name it, they almost never assume the word refers to some part of the object; instead, they assume the person is naming the *whole* object, thus the name *whole-object constraint* (Markman, 1989). The whole-object constraint describes a bias in which children focus on object properties such as boundaries and shape, leading them to consider that names often refer to whole objects. Similarly, the *taxonomic constraint* narrows children's guesses about word meaning by helping them to figure out the level of generality for which an object name is intended (Markman, 1989). In other words, the taxonomic constraint points children to the fact that a new word refers to a known *class* of things: *dog* refers to all members of the class of dogs and not to this particular dog. Finally, consider the case where a child encounters two objects, one for which they already know a word, and is told to 'show me the *bik*' (a nonsense word which avoids the problem of different vocabulary levels across children in the study). In this case, children generally assume that the novel word applies to the object for which they do not already know a name (Markman, 1989). In other words, the fact that an object already has a name means that it is less likely that the new word will apply to it – in other words, names for things are *mutually exclusive*.

Notice that Markman's constraints are geared towards understanding how children learn *nouns*; they have little to say about how children learn verbs. Gleitman and her co-workers

(1990; Landau & Gleitman, 1985) have addressed this problem. Gleitman proposed a theory of how children learn verbs, called **syntactic bootstrapping**. According to Gleitman, children also gain information about the referent of a word from syntactic information, that is, from how the word is used in a sentence. For example, some verbs only require two noun phrases to complete a sentence, whereas other verbs may require three noun phrases. Consider the verb *to see*. Seeing requires only a subject (the observer) and an object (the thing observed). In contrast, the verb *give* requires a subject, an object and a receiver. Such syntactic clues can help the child who hears a verb occur in context figure out what action it refers to. Syntactic information is yet another very useful constraint on the induction of a word's meaning (deVillers & deVillers, 1992).

Critics of Markman's nativist position, such as Nelson (1988), have suggested that Markman is incorrect in assuming such built-in constraints. Nelson argues that much could be learned by attending instead to the social and communicative contexts in which children learn words. The use of the word constraint suggests that these principles operate in an 'all or none' fashion, yet the data on word learning show that this is not the case (deVillers & deVillers, 1992). Moreover, research has found that parents influence their children's vocabulary growth, which is at odds with a nativist position (Huttenlocher, Haight, Bryk, Seltzer, & Lyons, 1991). A compromise position acknowledges that these constraints are important but only work within the context of the social and communicative experiences provided by parents and others who interact with the child (Hoff-Ginsburg, 1997).

Errors in early semantic development

Even with the constraints on word learning and the social support provided by parents, children's first attempts to learn words are not always successful; children do, in fact, make a number of errors. Here we will consider two of the most common errors they make. Of particular interest is what these errors tell us about the processes behind children's word learning.

Two of the most characteristic errors in semantic development are **overextension** and **underextension**. Underextensions, where children use a particular word in a highly restricted way, occur much less frequently than errors which take the form of overextensions. In underextension, a child might use the word *doggie* to refer only to his dog and not to other dogs that he encounters (Bloom, 1998). In contrast, overextension occurs when a child uses a single word to label a variety of different objects. Overextensions occur almost exclusively in the production of speech; they rarely occur in children's comprehension (Naigles & Gelman, 1995). A classic example of an overextension is the use of the word *doggie* to cover everything from dogs to cows. Overextension is a particularly common error; about one-third of children's words become overextended at some point (Rescorla, 1980). Overextensions are often based on perceptual similarity: the child may extend the use of the word *doggie* to animals with four legs and a tail, or *ball* to anything which is round, such as a clock or the moon. As children's vocabularies and conceptual categories develop, overextensions become increasingly rare (deVillers & deVillers, 1992).

The presence of both of these errors suggests that children's word learning is an active process in which they attempt to learn words based on their hypotheses about the relations between objects and their labels.

Semantic development beyond the preschool years

Semantic development does indeed occur beyond the preschool years, although children's accomplishments are generally less salient to parents. Children typically add about 20,000 words to their vocabulary during their school years and, by adolescence, know some 30,000 words. Moreover, older children can acquire words simply by reading the definition of a word in a dictionary; they no longer directly experience the referent of a particular word. As with earlier ages, children benefit from conversation with more expert speakers, especially when parents or peers explain complex words (Weizman & Snow, 2001). During the school years, children also begin to acquire an appreciation of the ambiguity of word meaning, recognizing that one word can mean different things. For example, the word *bank* can refer to either a river bank or a financial institution. This burgeoning recognition of ambiguity allows children to appreciate humour based on it. Thus, in the school years children begin to enjoy riddles, puns and jokes (McGhee, 1979). Try presenting a joke such as, '*what has four wheels and flies?*' (answer: *a garbage truck*) to a preschool child and a school-aged child. Most young children will fail to appreciate the humour, whereas the older children will usually find the joke funny. To grasp this joke, the child needs to recognize that the word *flies* has two meanings: *to fly* and *an insect that likes garbage*.

Finally, school-aged children begin to appreciate nonliteral speech such as *metaphor* (Winner, 1988). Metaphor requires comprehension of the fact that one thing can be described as another. For example, Shakespeare's metaphor, *Juliet is the sun*, compares Juliet to the sun, using one concept to help clarify another. Understanding metaphor requires both an understanding that a speaker can say one thing to mean another (Olson, 1988) and an appropriately-developed knowledge base (Winner, 1988). Throughout childhood, the understanding of metaphor develops as children gain both a broader knowledge base and the ability to gauge communicative intentions.

The Development of Syntax/Grammar

A number of issues are apparent within the study of the child's acquisition of grammar. According to deVillers and deVillers (1992), some of these issues are: to what extent is children's grammar a function of development in other cognitive abilities?; does experience with language play a role in the development of grammar?; and are there biases or constraints which play a role in the ability to learn a grammar? As we shall see, research has not yet offered a definitive answer to any of these questions.

As identified in Research Example 9.1, it is clear that children possess a lag in their understanding versus the production of correct grammar.

Research Example 9.1

Even Toddlers can Understand Complex Grammar

Researchers in the UK have discovered that children as young as 2 years of age can understand complex grammar before they have learned to speak in full sentences (Noble, Rowland, & Pine, 2011). In order to understand the meaning of a sentence, children must put together a number of complex pieces of information, including the grammatical cues that lead to meaning that are specific to their language. For example, in English, the cause and the target of an event are denoted by the order of the words in a sentence. Children can then use this knowledge to understand the meaning of new words. The question of how early in development children are able to do this has been vigorously debated.

In this study, 82 English-learning 2, 3 and 4 year-olds were presented with a short cartoon of a rabbit and duck. All the children were given the option of being accompanied by a familiar adult, who sat at the child's side and interacted minimally. The child was told they were going to play a pointing game. One cartoon involved the rabbit acting on the duck, such as lifting the duck's leg, and the other was a cartoon of the animals acting independently, such as swinging a leg. The researchers then played sentences with made-up verbs, such as 'the rabbit is glorping the duck', over a loudspeaker and asked the children to point to the correct picture. Even the youngest children in the study were able to identify the correct image that matched the sentence more often than would be expected by chance (which means *statistical significance* was demonstrated). This occurs at an age when most children are only able to string together two words. Averages for the three ages showed that performance only slightly improved with age.

The study suggests that young children know more about language structure than they can express, and at an earlier age than was initially believed. The study also supports the notion that children use the syntax of a sentence to understand new words. Children can use the grammar of a sentence to help them narrow down the possible meaning of words, augmenting their learning of language.

Questions: Considering the results presented in Research Example 9.1, what are the sociocultural limitations of this study?

How might the results have been affected if children were unfamiliar with the animals in the cartoon?

Do the study's findings say anything about each of the three main language theories?

First sentences

Around 18 to 27 months of age, children typically begin to utter their first combinations of words (deVillers & deVillers, 1992). These first sentences often use correct word order but they tend to omit many of the important grammatical function words. Thus, their speech appears sparse, as if they are trying to conserve words, leading to the dubbing of such speech as **telegraphic speech** (Reich, 1986). Examples of such speech include *Daddy read*, *Give juice*, and *More shoe*. Features of telegraphic speech are that it omits the marking of tense (e.g. past tense or future tense), infrequently includes articles (e.g. *a* or *the*) and does not employ a special syntax to mark *questions*. However, at this stage children do not omit all function words. In particular, they are likely to include pronouns such as *me* and *you* and possessive adjectives such as *mine* and *yours*, demonstrative pronouns such as *this* and *that*, and verb particles such as *put down* or *take off* (Reich, 1986). Despite its limitations, telegraphic speech allows children to communicate a great deal to others because of our ability to infer their communicative intent, that is, the meaning they are trying to get across to the listener. In other words, adults 'read into' the utterances of young children and base their responses on what a child intended to say (deVillers & deVillers, 1992).

Between 27 and 36 months of age, there is a very rapid development of grammar appearing in children's speech, leading some to refer to this period as the 'grammar explosion', which makes reference to the similar period in children's semantic development (deVillers & deVillers, 1992). At this time, three-word sentences make their first appearance, with the extra content being comprised of grammatical terms. Children begin to use *modal verbs*, such as *I will do it* or *Daddy can read*; they learn to use negations, such as *I won't do it*; and they begin to apply *tense markings* to words, for example, *Mommy liked my picture* or *I goes to the game*. Research by Roger Brown (1973) suggests that children learn to add **grammatical morphemes** – the small changes to a word which change the meaning of the sentence – to their utterances, and that they do so in a very particular order. Brown suggested that this ordering comes about because of two factors which have to do with the complexity of the grammatical morphemes and how much change is required. For example, some changes only require the child to make a small change to a word, such as adding *ing* to a verb to indicate the present tense (as in *He is dancing*). Other grammatical morphemes require more complex changes, such as making the subject and the object of a sentence agree (as in *I am dancing* versus *He is dancing*). Brown's findings on grammatical development have been confirmed by other investigators (Maratsos, 1998). Children also show their developing understanding of grammatical morphemes in the errors that they make. *Overregularizations* become common, in which children treat all words as regular words, for example '*he runned home*', '*I see two sheeps*'. These errors often persist into the school years (Maratsos, 2000). Interestingly, children may initially apply grammatical morphemes correctly before the first overregularization errors appear (Marcus et al., 1992). The appearance of these errors thus demonstrates that children have learned a new rule about language with regard to forming tenses or plurals.

At around 30 to 48 months of age children begin building more complex linguistic constructions, combining sentences, embedding clauses within other clauses, and producing complex questions. In each of these attempts, children are sometimes successful and sometimes not. In part, this is because they encounter words which prove to be exceptions to the rules they have learned and which they need to take into account. Another reason is that they encounter words which have special properties, for example, the verb *to promise* (deVillers & deVillers, 1992: 380). In the sentence, *John promised Mary to mow the lawn*, unless Mary is a slave who can be lent out, John is the person who will mow the lawn. That is, the subject makes the promise and must carry out the action promised. Similarly, the verb *to promise* requires that the subject actually be able to carry out the action promised: promising that the weather will be perfect tomorrow is an incorrect usage of the verb because one cannot control the weather and thus ensure the conditions of the promise are fulfilled. Astington (1988) showed that learning the specialized conditions of promising takes children some years to master; in fact, they usually do not grasp these before 9 years of age.

Other grammatical achievements that extend well into the school years include understanding *passive* constructions and coping with **pronoun reference**. Most often we use linguistic constructions such as '*The boy kicked the ball*' to express ourselves. However, we could also legitimately say '*The ball was kicked by the boy*', using a construction which linguists call the *passive voice*. In the passive voice, a speaker changes the subject–verb–object structure of the language, reversing the position of the object and the subject. According to Horgan (1978), passive sentence are rarely uttered by children until after age 6, and even then are used in a restricted way. The development of the passive structure (deVillers & deVillers, 1992) involves the gradual application of this form to a wider variety of subject matter and an increasing use of the full passive form (seen in the example above). *Pronoun reference* involves understanding the rules which govern to whom or to what a pronoun refers. Consider an example from Smyth (1995) which illustrates how difficult this can be: in the sentence '*Batman told Superman that he liked Wonderwoman*', the pronoun *he* refers to Batman; however, in the sentence '*Batman told Superman that Wonderwoman liked him*', the pronoun *him* refers to Superman. Confused? Perhaps, not surprisingly, it takes young children some time to learn these rules. This developing ability to understand the complexity of pronoun reference is partly a function of development in perspective-taking skill (Smyth, 1995).

In summary, then, grammatical development in the school years is linked to the child's developing knowledge base, experience with the language and new cognitive achievements. While the most fundamental grammatical forms are in place by approximately 5 years of age, specific aspects of grammatical development continue into the school years (Maratsos, 1998). One group of theorists adopting connectionist models (see Chapter 6) explained how grammatical development takes place. They argued that children master grammar by observing the structure of their language. Children note where words appear in sentences, which words 'go' together and how words are linked (e.g. Tomasello, 2003). Theorists have tested this using connectionist models with computers: artificial neural networks are exposed to the same kind of language that children are exposed to and are tested to see if they show similar grammatical outcomes as them.

The Development of Pragmatics

As we noted at the outset of this chapter, language is a social behaviour: it is one of the things that we *do* to communicate with other people. To be effective communicators, children have to learn more than the phonology, semantics and grammar of their language; they must also learn how language is used within their culture. Among other things, they need to know how to engage in conversations with other people, how to select the right language for a situation and how to interpret a speaker who is deliberately not telling the truth. This knowledge about the social conventions of language use which lead to effective communication is called pragmatics (O'Neill, 1996). When we examine the development of pragmatic knowledge, we shift the focus from the study of meaning and syntax to the study of how language is used to communicate with others. (See Research Example 9.2 for more on how emotion can play a role in becoming a communicator.)

Becoming an effective communicator

One of the earliest skills that children must acquire in order to communicate effectively is the ability to maintain a conversation with another person. There are a number of components to conversational skill which we will examine in turn. Two requirements for effective conversation are the abilities to engage a listener's attention and to respond appropriately to the feedback provided by a listener. A study by Wellman and Lempers (1977) showed that by 2 years of age, children clearly demonstrated these skills. For example, if they received no response from a listener, 2 year-olds would repeat the message. If the listener showed signs that they did not comprehend, such as a puzzled facial expression, children made further attempts to communicate. Based on their findings, Wellman and Lempers suggested that 2 year-olds were quite effective at the rudiments of conversation. By the time they reach preschool, children are able to take turns in conversations, make eye contact and respond appropriately to their conversational partner's remarks (Garvey, 1974). Children also adjust their speech depending on their conversational partner, such as when speaking to a younger child. Children adjust their speech, exaggerating and simplifying it, so as to engage and hold their attention and ensure comprehension (Dunn, 1988; Shatz & Gelman, 1973).

Preschool-aged children are not consummate communicators; while they are able to maintain a conversation, conversational skills do continue to develop. For example, preschoolers are better at communicating in one-to-one situations than they are at communicating with a group. Ervin-Tripp (1979) showed that preschoolers are more likely to interrupt others and to be interrupted when speaking in the context of a group than when speaking to one other person. The ability to converse with groups continues to develop through to adolescence and perhaps beyond. Another aspect of language use which progresses throughout childhood is children's ability to use **speech registers**. Speech registers are the adaptations that occur when we adjust the level of our speech to our audience. For example, a child might talk to her teacher in a certain tone of voice and choose a particular style of language. In contrast, when speaking to friends, these aspects of language use will change. When speaking to a younger child, the school-aged child will provide more redundant information in their communication, attempting to ensure that their message is comprehensible (Sonnenschein, 1988).

Clearly, children do attempt to take their listener into account in their speech, but how good are they at doing so? According to Reich (1986), many of the problems young children have in communicating information to another have to do with children's relative inexperience and skill. In his view, this ability develops slowly and continuously throughout childhood. One of the means used to measure the growth of this skill is the **referential communication task**. In a referential communication task, children are given a set of stimuli, for example a series of complex geometric shapes, printed on blocks. They are told that their partner, seated opposite them but separated by a screen, has an identical set of shapes presented in a scrambled order. Their job is to describe the shapes to the listener so that the latter can arrange their blocks in the same order. According to Glucksberg, Krauss and Weissberg (1966), when preschoolers were presented with pictures of animals they could perform this task easily. However, when the stimuli were random geometric shapes, their performance was dismal: the preschool children failed to provide the listener with enough information in order to be able to accurately pick out the block to which they were referring, and in fact many of their utterances were ambiguous, failing to distinguish one block from another. Older children are better able to provide the listener with some unambiguous clues as to the block they intend for the listener to pick. In further research using the referential communication task, Glucksberg and Krauss (1967) showed that it is not until they reach early adolescence that ability on the task reaches an adult level.

Another aspect of pragmatic understanding which develops during the school years is the ability to distinguish between what a speaker *says* and what the speaker really *means*, termed the **say-mean distinction** (Olson, 1994; Torrance & Olson, 1987). Everyday speech is often marked by a discrepancy between what people say and what they mean; for example, a sarcastic speaker usually says one thing but means the opposite. In order to communicate effectively, children must learn to recognize that their own or another person's intentions may not always be clearly articulated. Adults are relatively good at recognizing that a message may not convey the intended meaning. In contrast, young children's understanding of the very possibility of a distinction between what was said (what is called the *literal meaning* of the message) and what was meant (the *intended meaning*, i.e. what the speaker tried to convey) remains somewhat tenuous (Beal & Flavell, 1984; Bonitatibus, 1988; Robinson, Goelman, & Olson, 1983).

Consider the following study by Robinson et al. (1983), who presented a child speaker and a listener with identical arrays of pictures of differently coloured flowers. The speaker picked the red flower from his array and then requested the listener to select a matching flower, but instead of providing a complete unambiguous description, such as the 'red flower', the speaker's utterance was ambiguous, telling the listener to pick the 'flower'. When they were asked what the speaker had told the listener to choose, 5 to 7 year-old children tended to accept as correct a phrase which described the speaker's intended meaning (e.g. 'red flower') rather than what had actually been said. Robinson et al. argued that children equated the literal meaning of the message (what was said) with the intended meaning (what was meant). Further research by Bonitatibus (1988) has since replicated these findings. The ability to distinguish between the literal meaning of a sentence and the speaker's intended meaning is an important development which is strongly tied to the child's developing theory of mind (Olson, 1994; see Chapter 11 for a description of *theory of mind*).

In summary, we find that while children's pragmatic ability is sufficient to allow some advanced communication from an early age, there are skills which require further development – a process which lasts until late childhood or early adolescence. Some of these achievements are tied to other cognitive developments, such as in the say-mean distinction, while other areas only require further experience and opportunity for children to refine their skills.

Can you think of ways in which a child's cognitive development might contribute to the development of various language skills? In considering your answer to this question, you might want to revisit the theories of cognitive development covered in Chapter 7.

Research Example 9.2

Emotion and Children's Speech Production

As with any area of children's development, language and communication abilities can be compromised early on. One aspect of language development that can suffer is children's speech production, resulting, for example, in stuttering. Since communication, social and emotional development are all closely linked, Karrass and colleagues (Karrass, Walden, Conture, Graham, Arnold, et al., 2006) sought to examine some of the emotional correlates of stuttering in children. Study participants included 65 preschool children who stuttered and a control group of 65 preschool children who did not stutter. Parents completed a questionnaire measuring temperament, emotional reactivity and emotion regulation. Findings showed that when compared to fluent-speaking children in the control group, children who stuttered displayed a range of emotion reactions: they were more reactive, less able to regulate their emotions and less able to regulate their attention. Children who displayed reactivity were more likely to respond to people and situations in a 'highly-strung' manner.

The authors interpreted the findings to indicate that problems with emotion regulation and reactivity may contribute to the language difficulties of children who stutter. It is not surprising to imagine that if a child feels anxious in a situation, and has difficulty controlling their arousal, the ability to produce words will be compromised, especially if speech production is already difficult or stressful for the child. It is important to bear in mind that this study employed a correlational design. Recall from Chapter 3 that correlational research designs do not allow us to draw firm conclusions about causality. Therefore, the findings of the Karrass et al. (2006) study may just as readily indicate that children with language problems develop emotional difficulties due to embarrassment or stress in response to stuttering. It is likely that speech and emotion difficulties are mutually influential, with exacerbations in either causing a corresponding problem in the other.

Regardless of which conclusion is more likely, the study has important implications for children with speech production difficulties. This study also demonstrates the close link between language and emotional development; disruption in one area can have wide-reaching effects. The findings are not simply limited to a language–emotion connection. It is likely that emotion affects social development as well. Research does indeed show that children who are less able to understand and control their emotions have more difficulties interacting with peers. For example, in a recent study toddlers with more developed language skills were better able to manage frustration and were less likely to express anger at age 3 to 4 than toddlers with less developed language skills (Roben, Cole, & Armstrong, 2013). Language skills may help children to verbalize their needs, rather than use emotions to demonstrate what they want.

Question: What is a third explanation linking emotion and speech problems (you may wish to revisit the section on correlations)?

Speech act theory

One of the many ways of understanding pragmatics that has come to guide research within pragmatics is **speech act theory** (Austin, 1962; Searle, 1969). Speech act theory holds that language is a form of *action*. Speech act theorists recognize the essentially social and cooperative nature of communication and stress the importance of considering the intentions and beliefs of speakers and listeners. Austin (1962) proposed that the act of saying something, which he called the **locutionary act**, can be subdivided into two further components: the way in which an utterance is expressed, or the **illocutionary force** of an utterance, and the effect an utterance has on its audience, or the **perlocutionary effect**. Austin's analysis of speech acts focuses on the types of speech act that we can perform and the effects these acts are intended to cause. Examples of speech acts are *promises*, *assertions*, *denials* and *warnings*. Each act has a distinct tone or force and is used in different ways. Moreover, as we saw earlier in the chapter in our discussion of the verb *to promise* (Astington, 1988), children gradually acquire this knowledge throughout the school years.

You will notice that speech act theory focuses on the uses or *functions* of language (Halliday, 1975). Proponents of speech act theory argue that we cannot understand language development without understanding the various functions of language. While not all researchers agree on how to best to classify the functions of children's communications (O'Neill, 1996), they do agree on the fact that people perform a variety of different functions with language. For example, recall the earlier discussion of protodeclarative and protoimperative pointing: even prelinguistic children use gestures for a variety of functions. By distinguishing the illocutionary and perlocutionary aspects of language, Austin provides us with a useful framework for understanding the development of effective communication.

Conversational implicature

One of the fundamentals of the study of pragmatics is the recognition that comprehension and usage of language are strongly influenced by the contexts in which language occurs, contexts which may have little or nothing to do with the actual wording of a sentence (O'Neill, 1996). This recognition was exploited by the philosopher of language H. P. Grice (1975), who formulated a theory about how people use such contextual information to make inferences about what a speaker really means. Grice called this **conversational implicature**. Conversational implicature works by exploiting a principle which guides communicative exchanges, the idea that in conversation we typically cooperate with our conversational partners. Grice (1975) referred to this as the **cooperative principle**. This states that participants in a communicative exchange are expected to make contributions to a conversation as required, keeping in mind the mutually accepted purpose or direction of the exchange. The cooperative principle is represented by four further *maxims* which Grice termed the maxims of *quantity*, *quality*, *relation* and *manner*. These maxims are outlined in Table 9.3.

You will probably notice at this point that there will have been many occasions on which you have violated these maxims, and occasionally may have done so deliberately. It was Grice's belief that when a speaker deliberately violates one or more of the maxims, they invite the listener to make inferences about *why* they may have done so, that is, to generate a conversational implicature. The generation of conversational implicature allows the listener to go beyond the semantic content of the words in the message and to infer what the speaker really meant.

Consider the following example of conversational implicature in action. Your flatmate comes in from a date. Being friendly, you inquire, '*How was your date?*' Your flatmate responds, '*He had nice shoes*'. How should you take this response? If you take her at face value, you might wonder whether she misunderstood you or whether she has recently become delirious. However, if you assume the remark was made deliberately, then a variety of possibilities present themselves. Notice that your flatmate has flouted the maxim of *relation*, in that she has seemingly made a response which is not relevant to the current exchange. Assuming that she intended you to recognize this violation as intentional, her response might communicate *I had a bad time with him* or *It was a rotten night*. Your flatmate's response can be taken as sarcastic in that she expresses a critical attitude towards the situation but does so in a nonliteral way. Now imagine you are a young child. How would you expect a child to take such an utterance? Would they view it as sarcastic? A good start would be to examine whether or not young children are sensitive to the conversational maxims which Grice (1975) identifies as crucial to the process of communication. Conti and Camras (1984) have produced data to suggest that children as young as 6 have some understanding of when Gricean conversational maxims are violated. More recently, Perner and Leekam (1986) have shown that children as young as 3 have the ability to adjust the content of their responses in accordance with the maxim of quantity. Also, as noted earlier, by 2 to 3 years-old children are relatively adept at minding the maxim of relation, keeping their contributions to a conversation in line with the agreed-upon topic (Wellman & Lempers, 1977). In short, these results suggest that by the time they reach preschool, young children seem to adhere to the cooperative principle and its attendant maxims. Given that even young children are relatively adept at recognizing violations of Grice's conversational maxims, can they go on to infer a speaker's meaning? In what follows, we briefly consider some of the work on children's comprehension of nonliteral language.

Table 9.3 The conversational maxims

Conversational Maxim	Description
Quantity	Make your contribution as informative (but not more informative) as is required for the current purpose of the exchange.
Quality	Try to make your contribution one that is true; do not say that which you believe to be false or for which you have no evidence.
Relation	Make your contribution relevant to the current exchange.
Manner	Try to avoid obscurity and ambiguity in your language.

Nonliteral language

Consider this curious fact: in a great deal of our everyday speech we fail to say exactly what we mean. For example, we often use *indirect speech*. If we want someone to close a window, we might simply ask, '*Is the window open?*' in the hope that the listener might close it. In this example, rather than ask directly, the speaker is indirect, and asks the listener to infer what it is they mean or want. Another form of nonliteral language is *idiomatic speech*. In the case where a friend has made public some secret, we might ask '*Why did you spill the beans?*' As we noted above, we also have *sarcasm*, where the speaker says one thing to mean the opposite. Each of these is a common form of **nonliteral language**, language where the speaker does not say what they mean. Let's consider the case of sarcasm as an example of some of the issues involved in the development of nonliteral language.

Comprehension of sarcasm requires a child to appreciate that speakers can say one thing but intend this to be taken in a different way – as meaning the opposite of what they say.

What kinds of processes are required for a listener to grasp sarcasm? First, children must detect the *incongruity* of the utterance, that is, the inconsistency between what the speaker says and what the speaker means. In other words, children need to make the say-mean distinction (described above). Second, the listener must infer the speaker's **communicative intent**, that is, how did the speaker want to be understood? Children's goal here is to ascertain whether the speaker's purpose was to be sarcastic or to be taken in some other way. Notice that the two steps are successive: if children fail to note the incongruity of an utterance, they are unlikely to see a need for inferring the speaker's communicative intent. In other words, inferences about the speaker's meaning are made only when this discrepancy is perceived by the listener.

Ackerman (1981) found that, by around age 6, children have some ability to recognize both sarcastic utterances and lies as deliberately false. In spite of this achievement, it is not until age 12 that children were able to correctly infer a sarcastic speaker's communicative intention. Using a simplified procedure that relied less on children's productive language skills, Winner and Leekam (1991) showed that by age 6 children could recognize that a sarcastic speaker wanted to be understood as meaning the opposite of what they said. Demorest, Silberstein, Gardner and Winner (1983) studied sarcasm comprehension in children aged 6 to 11. They found that children made two types of comprehension error: they made literal interpretations of the statement, indicating a failure to recognize the incongruity of the remark, or they correctly perceived the incongruity of the sarcastic remark but failed to identify the speaker's communicative purpose. Only the oldest children were very adept at correctly stating the speaker's communicative intention. Finally, Keenan and Quigley (1999) have shown that children make great strides in their ability to comprehend simple instances of sarcasm at around 8 to 10 years of age. They demonstrated that features of the utterance, such as an exaggerated mocking or nasal intonation, can help a child recognize when someone is being sarcastic. Older children, however, are much less reliant on such features and were able to use more subtle linguistic cues to detect the speaker's true meaning. In sum, these findings suggest that the comprehension of sarcasm can take some time to fully develop, but by the time they reach adolescence most people are very adept at sarcasm.

Metalinguistic ability

Another linguistic ability that emerges as children get older is their **metalinguistic awareness**, which is an awareness of language itself, including the understanding that language is a rule-based system of communication. Children who have achieved this awareness realize they know language and can think and talk about language. The beginning of this realization develops in early childhood: 4 year-olds know that an object could be called another word in another language, and by age 5 children have a decent concept of what 'word' means (Karmiloff-Smith et al., 1996). Thus, when children are asked to repeat the last word in a story they have just been told, they are able to correctly do so, such that they know the last word is 'bed' rather than 'under-the-bed', for example. Metalinguistic awareness is ongoing, and children gradually acquire the ability to reflect on word sounds, grammatical correctness and rhyming words. Early attainment of metalinguistic ability has been associated with later reading ability and language skills (Goswami & Bryant, 1990), indicating that thinking about language is an important precursor to knowing language.

Summary

The growth of language skills is one of the most noticeable aspects of children's development. Within a very short period of time, we move from babbling infants to competent native speakers. Researchers investigating the development of language are striving to understand how exactly these changes come about: as the result of general-purpose learning mechanisms, a specific language faculty, or some combination of social influences and biological predispositions. The evidence for each of these positions is by no means complete, and psychologists continue to examine children's language learning.

Glossary

Babbling occurs when infants begin to string consonants and vowels together.

Categorical speech perception refers to the tendency of infants to perceive the sound of some consonants in a categorical way, that is, as one sound or another.

Communicative intent refers to the speaker's intention in communicating something to another; for example, how the speaker wants to be understood by the listener.

Conversational implicature refers to Grice's notions regarding how people use context to understand a speaker's meaning.

Cooperative principle is a principle which Grice believed to underlie conversations. It states that participants in a communicative exchange are expected to make contributions to the conversation that are in keeping with the accepted purpose or direction of the exchange.

Expansion is a technique in which adults take a child's utterance and expand it, usually increasing the complexity of the original statement.

Fast-mapping refers to children's ability to learn a new word after only a single, brief exposure to it.

Grammatical morphemes are the smallest changes to a word which can change the meaning of a sentence.

Illocutionary force refers to the way in which an utterance is said.

Infant-directed speech (or **motherese**) is a simplified style of speech in which parents speak to the infant using a higher pitch, repetition, stressing important words, and talking more slowly to their infants.

Language acquisition device (LAD) is an innate mental structure that Chomsky proposed that children come equipped with which makes the task of learning language feasible.

Locutionary act is the act of saying something.

Metalinguistic awareness is the ability to think about language, including the rules, nuances and properties of language, and monitoring words as they are being used.

Mutual exclusivity constraint is a word-learning constraint in which children generally assume that a novel word applies to the object for which they do not already know a name.

Naming explosion is the spurt in vocabulary growth occurring around 18 months of age.

Negative evidence refers to the evidence parents provide to children about what is *not* correct about their utterances.

Nonliteral language refers to forms of language where the speaker does not say what they mean, such as sarcasm, metaphor, idiomatic speech and indirect speech.

Overextension refers to instances where children use a single word to label a variety of different objects.

Parameter setting refers to the process of determining the parameters or rules of one's native language.

Patterned speech refers to pseudospeech wherein infants begin to string the phonemes of their language together in combinations that initially sound like meaningful words.

Perlocutionary effect refers to the effect an utterance has on its audience.

Phonemes are the set of speech sounds which make up the phonetic system of a language; the smallest units of speech which can affect meaning.

Phonological awareness is the ability to be aware of and analyze speech sounds.

Phonology refers to the system of sounds that make up a language.

Poverty of the stimulus refers to Chomsky's argument that the linguistic data that children actually receive is inadequate for them learn syntax.

Pragmatics refers to the study of the rules which govern how we use our language in particular social contexts and achieve particular communicative goals.

Pronoun reference involves understanding the rules which govern to whom or to what a pronoun refers.

Protodeclarative pointing is when the infant uses pointing gestures to bring an object to another's attention.

Protoimperative pointing is pointing that an infant engages in to get another to do something for them.

Recast is a technique wherein adults restate the child's utterance while correcting its grammatical form.

Say-mean distinction refers to the ability to distinguish what a speaker says from what they actually mean.

Semantics refers to the study of word meanings and how they are acquired.

Speech act theory holds that language is a form of action and that a consideration of the intentions and beliefs of speakers and listeners is critical to understanding communication.

Speech registers are the adaptations that occur when we adjust the level of our speech to our audience.

Syntactic bootstrapping is a theory of how children learn the meaning of verbs. According to Gleitman, children gain information about the referent of a verb from how the word is used in a sentence.

Syntax refers to the study of the rules for combining words into meaningful phrases and sentences (also known as **grammar**).

Taxonomic constraint is a word-learning constraint that points children to the fact that a new word refers to a known class of things and not just to a particular instance.

Telegraphic speech describes how children's first sentences often omit all but the most essential words required to convey their meaning, leading to speech which sounds sparse, as if they are trying to conserve words.

Underextension refers to instances where children use a particular word in a highly restricted way.

Universal grammar refers to the entire set of rules or linguistic parameters which specify all possible human languages.

Whole-object constraint is a word-learning constraint in which children focus on object properties such as boundaries and shape, leading them to consider that names often refer to whole objects.

TEST YOUR KNOWLEDGE

1. Which of the following is not one of the main theories of language development?

    a) Nativist
    b) Interactionist
    c) Sociocultural
    d) Learning

2. What is the language acquisition device?

    a) The area of the brain associated with language development
    b) In connectionist theories, the system of the computer that simulates human language production
    c) The innate human mental structure which makes the task of learning language feasible
    d) Interactions between mother and child that stimulate language production in the child

3. What are phonemes?

    a) Grammatical rules
    b) The sounds which make up a specific language
    c) A technique in which adults take a child's utterance and expand it, usually increasing the complexity of the original statement
    d) The study of the rules which govern how we use our language in particular social contexts and to achieve particular communicative goals

4. What does speech act theory refer to?

    a) Children and adults generally act according to what they say
    b) The close connections in the brain between speech and action
    c) The active reinforcement that children receive from their parents in response to their speech efforts
    d) Language is a form of *action*; communication is a social and cooperative skill meaning that the intentions and beliefs of speakers and listeners should be attended to

ANSWERS: 1–C, 2–C, 3–B, 4–D

Suggested Reading

Kennison, S.M. (2014). *Introduction to Language Development*. Thousand Oaks, CA: Sage.

Pinker, S. (1994). *The Language Instinct: How the mind creates language*. New York: William Morrow.

Saxton, M. (2010). *Child Language: Acquisition and development.* London: Sage.

Tomasello, M., & Bates, E. (2001). *Language Development: The essential readings*. Malden, MA: Blackwell.

Yip, V., & Matthews, S. (2007). *The Bilingual Child: Early development and language contact*. Cambridge: Cambridge University Press.

Want to learn more? For links to online resources relevant to this chapter, interactive quizzes and much more, visit the companion website at **https://edge.sagepub.com/keenan3e/**

IV

EMOTIONAL, SOCIAL AND MORAL DEVELOPMENT

Emotional Development

10

Chapter Outline

At the end of this chapter you should:

- be able to describe the developmental course of emotion expression, emotion understanding and emotion regulation
- be familiar with the concept of emotional intelligence and the issues surrounding its measurement
- be able to explain key concepts such as *social referencing*, *basic emotions* and *emotional display rules*
- understand the important aspects of attachment theory, know the four phases of attachment, and be able to describe the differences between securely and insecurely attached children
- understand and be able to define the concept of temperament and key concepts such as *goodness of fit*
- be able to comment on evidence for and against the stability of temperament

Introduction

Emotions are one of the most salient aspects of our experiences and it is not surprising that the study of emotion has captured the attention of developmental researchers of nearly all theoretical persuasions. Emotions play a vital role in our behaviour, a role to which psychologists have only recently become aware. The study of emotion has recently been undergoing a series of dramatic changes (Saarni, Mumme, & Campos, 1998). While there are a variety of theoretical perspectives that guide the study of emotion, the most important theory to emerge is the *functionalist* approach. At the most basic level, functionalist approaches see emotions as stimulating a person to act in a way that helps them to attain goals (Campos, Frankel, & Camras, 2004). This applies to everything from avoiding a detested vegetable to greeting an old friend you haven't seen in a while. Functionalist theories stress that emotions are adaptive processes which organize functioning in a variety of domains of human development, including the social, cognitive and perceptual (Barrett & Campos, 1987; Campos et al., 1983). While emotions may interfere with or undermine an individual's functioning, emotion can also guide and motivate adaptive processes (Halle, 2003). In most current work on emotional development, emotion is viewed as a regulator of both social and cognitive behaviour.

Taking a functionalist approach in their review of the study of emotional development, Saarni et al. (1998: 238) defined emotion as '*the person's readiness to establish, maintain, or change the relation between the person and the environment on matters of significance to that person*'. The authors note that this definition may strike the reader as odd because of its lack of emphasis on what are seen as the traditional components of emotion, such as internal states, feelings and facial expressions. Instead, functionalist theories emphasize the relevance of emotions to a person's goals, the close ties between emotion and actions, and the consequences of emotional states. In the following review of emotional development, functionalist views on emotion dominate much of the research.

The Development of Emotional Expressions

Early emotions

A number of researchers have argued through the years that infants are born with a set of readily observable and discrete emotions. The belief that infants enter into the world with the ability to experience and communicate a set of emotions within the first few weeks of life is a belief in the presence of a set of *basic emotions*. The basic emotions which most psychologists seem to agree on are *disgust, happiness, fear, anger, sadness, interest and surprise* (Campos et al., 1983). The evidence for basic emotions is the presence of facial expressions corresponding to the hypothesized emotional states and, somewhat later, the correspondence between facial expressions, gaze, tone of voice and the relation between emotions and

situations. The argument for the presence of basic emotions is controversial, but most psychologists would agree that by 6 months of age, most of these emotions have made their appearance (e.g. Izard, 1994; Sroufe, 1996). According to Izard (1994; Izard & Malatesta, 1987), the first emotional expressions to appear in the infant's repertoire are *startle, disgust* and *distress*. Around the third month, infants begin to display facial expressions of *anger, interest, surprise* and *sadness. Fear* develops at around 7 months of age (Camras, Malatesta, & Izard, 1991). Sroufe (1996) has described a developmental progression of emotional expression which is very similar to that proposed by Izard and his colleagues. Let's briefly consider the development of some emotions appearing early in infancy.

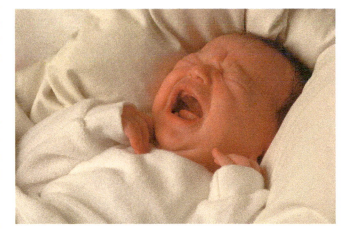

Image 10A Distress is one of the first human emotions to appear. At first, little differentiation exists between negative emotions, with subtleties in anger, surprise and sadness only appearing from 3 months onwards

© iStock.com/Kemter

Why, from an evolutionary point of view, might it be advantageous for an infant to be born equipped with a set of basic emotions?

Expressions of happiness are often observed when infants master a new problem or develop a new skill. They also have the positive effect of creating stronger ties between the infant and other people. *Smiles* and *laughter* generate similar responses in the caregiver, creating feelings of warmth and increasing the strength of the bond between parent and infant. Initially, an infant's smiles do not occur in reaction to external stimulation. In fact, very young infants will often smile mysteriously in their sleep. However, by 6 to 10 weeks infants smile in response to social exchanges, such as smiling human faces, and to interesting events that capture their attention. Infants increasingly smile around other people rather than when they are alone (LaFreniere, 2000). By 3 months an infant's smiles are elicited most often by a responsive person who interacts contingently with the infant (Ellsworth, Muir, & Hains, 1993). In the first 6 months of infancy repeated exposure to a stimulus may be required to generate a smile or other positive response, but after 6 months emotional reactions are more immediate (Camras et al., 1992; Sroufe, 1996). Laughter appears first around 3 to 4 months of age and reflects the infant's increased cognitive ability to perceive discrepancies, such as changes from their normal experience, for example, Daddy talking in a funny voice or making a face (Sroufe & Wunsch, 1972). By the beginning of their first year and throughout their second year, infants laugh increasingly in response to their own activities and actions; by the preschool years, laughter becomes more and more of a social event, occurring in the presence of others.

Of course, the infant's emotional expressions are not all positive. In the first 6 months expressions of *anger* and *fear* are evident in the infant's emotional repertoire. Perhaps the most salient of these expressions (much to the chagrin of many parents) is the fear aroused in an infant by strangers. Through their interactions with the world, infants naturally start to differentiate the familiar from the unfamiliar and, as a result, infants' reactions to unfamiliar people change over time. Whereas a 3 month-old will smile indiscriminately at strangers and parents alike, a 4 month-old infant will begin to smile preferentially at caregivers and show some *wariness* to unfamiliar people (Sroufe, 1996). However, somewhere in between the age of 7 to 9 months, infants begin to show a genuine fear of strangers, what has been termed **stranger distress** (Sroufe, 1996). Typically, stranger distress lasts for two to three months and may continue into their second year (Emde, Gaensbauer, & Harmon, 1976; Waters, Matas, & Sroufe, 1975). Stranger distress has all the aspects of a true fear reaction, including crying and whimpering, avoidance reactions such as pulling away from a stranger, and general wariness of strangers. As Sroufe, Waters and Matas (1974) point out, it is not simply *novelty* which engenders stranger distress from an infant, as mothers can perform novel actions (such as approaching the infant while wearing a mask) which do not upset them. Contextual factors such as whether the infant meets the stranger in their own home or in unfamiliar surroundings make an important difference to whether or not distress is elicited (Sroufe et al., 1974). The characteristics of the stranger also play a key role in eliciting distress: infants are less afraid of young children than they are of adults (Lewis & Brooks, 1974) and they react poorly to strangers who are sober and quiet as opposed to strangers who smile, gesture and interact in an active, friendly manner. Significantly, each of these points show that infants react not simply to the occurrence of an event but, rather, on the basis of its meaning; that is, they evaluate situations and appraise the threats they pose.

Table 10.1   Milestones in the development of emotional expression and understanding

Age	Emotional Expressions	Emotional Understanding
0 to 3 months	Startle, disgust, distress, the social smile	
3 to 6 months	Laughter, anger, interest, surprise, sadness	
7 months	Fear	
7 to 9 months	Stranger distress	
12 months		Social referencing
18 to 24 months	Shame, pride	
2 to 3 years	Envy, guilt, embarrassment	
3 to 5 years		Emotional display rules
6 to 8 years		Awareness that two emotions can occur in sequence
9 years and beyond		Awareness that emotions of the same valence can occur simultaneously
11 years		Awareness that one event can elicit a range of feelings

Emotional development beyond infancy

The development of emotional expression clearly extends beyond infancy, and, in fact, continues well into adolescence. Emotions such as shame, guilt, pride and envy are first seen in toddlers (Campos et al., 1983). These developments seem to go hand-in-hand with developments in their cognitive abilities. Of course, many changes in emotional expression have little to do with cognitive changes but instead reflect the **socialization** attempts of people in the child's life, such as parents, siblings, peers and others. Work on mother–infant interactions has shown that mothers selectively reinforce their infant's emotional expressions, rewarding expressions of positive affect and not responding to negative expressions (Malatesta & Haviland, 1982). Research has also shown that the amount of time a mother engages her baby affects how successful the baby is in recognizing emotions in others (Montague & Walker-Andrews, 2002). Parents also shape emotional expressions differently for boys and girls. Mothers tend to reinforce a wider range of emotional expression in female infants than they do in male infants (Malatesta & Haviland, 1985). Emotion socialization is a powerful means of shaping the growing child's emotional expressions and adults use a wide variety of means to accomplish this.

As we will discuss later in this chapter, one of the child's major challenges with respect to emotional development is the process of learning how to control their emotional expression and experience (Saarni, 1990). Much of the early development in the control of emotion is due to adults' attempts at emotion socialization in children. During the preschool years, children begin to learn to control their emotional expressions, adopting these to fit with what is expected of them. In essence, children learn a series of 'rules' about emotional expression, what we call **emotional display rules**. Simply put, these are rules which dictate which emotions are appropriate to express in a given circumstance (Saarni et al., 1998). For example, toddlers learn to substitute one emotional expression (e.g. pouting) for another more appropriate expression (e.g. crying). Later on, children gain a deeper understanding of display rules as they come to learn the social norms of their culture. They come to understand situations where it is inappropriate to laugh or to cry. Moreover, they learn to feign a variety of emotional expressions to accomplish certain ends, such as deceiving a sibling. Learning to follow display rules is an important accomplishment for the developing child. Research suggests that preschool children who are able to control their negative emotions are less likely to be disruptive in kindergarten and school (Gilliom, Shaw, Beck, Schonberg, & Lukon, 2002).

As we have seen, children put display rules into use early on, but they have little understanding of the gap between what they feel and what they actually express (Harris, 1989). Somewhat later, children learn to separate their true feelings from the emotions they express. In one study, Gross and Harris (1988) showed that 6 year-olds were able to distinguish between how a story character would look and how that same character would really feel. In contrast, 4 year-olds were unable to make this distinction, conflating how the character would really feel with how they looked. In other words, the children failed to distinguish between real and apparent emotions. These data support Harris's conclusion that preschool children can employ display rules but have little understanding of them.

The Development of Emotional Understanding

Using emotional information: social referencing

It is not only the range of emotional expressions that infants are capable of expressing which develops throughout infancy and early childhood, but also their *understanding* of emotion. One of the first examples of a developing understanding of emotion is a phenomenon which has been labelled **social referencing**. Social referencing, simply put, is the use of another's emotional expressions as a source of information, allowing a person to interpret events or situations that are either ambiguous or too difficult to grasp (Sorce, Emde, Campos, & Klinnert, 1985). Before we explore this phenomenon in infants and young children, think about your own experience with respect to social referencing. Many people have found themselves in a situation where, for example, someone makes what appears to be a joke and you are not sure whether laughter is appropriate. What do you do? One common strategy is to look to other people's behaviour. Are they laughing or smiling? Other people's emotional expressions can provide us with a valuable source of information for making sense of such situations and deciding on the appropriate course of behaviour. Recall our discussion of functionalism for a moment; one of the important functions of emotion is their ability to serve as a signalling system about our own and other people's internal states. Social referencing exploits this fact about emotion.

Social referencing is first observed at about 12 months of age. One tool used to study how infants employ social referencing is the experimental paradigm known as the visual cliff (see Chapter 6). In this work by Sorce et al. (1985), 12 month-old infants were placed at the top of the visual cliff, on the shallow side of the apparatus. Infants' mothers stood on the opposite side of the cliff and were asked to pose either *happy* or *frightened* emotional expressions at the time when their infants approached the edge of the cliff (remember the cliff was covered by glass so the infants were in no actual danger). The results of the study showed an effect of the emotional expression: when mothers posed happy expressions, most of the infants crossed the cliff. In contrast, when mothers posed frightened expressions, most infants refused to cross. Other studies have shown that mothers' facial expressions can affect how their infants react to new toys or new people (Klinnert et al., 1986).

Social referencing involves more than simply reading another person's emotional expressions. Recent research confirms that the expression conveyed in tone of voice can play an even larger social referencing cue than facial expressions (Vaish & Striano, 2004).

The development of complex emotions

Of course, emotions continue to develop after infancy. Another development in the nature of the emotions that we experience is the appearance of what is sometimes called **self-conscious emotion** (Barrett, 1997; Campos et al., 1983; Lewis, Sullivan, Stanger, & Weiss, 1989). This term is used to describe emotions such as *guilt*, *shame*, *envy*, *embarrassment* and *pride*, emotions which typically emerge in the second half of the second year. What makes these emotions different from others, such as anger or happiness, is that they emerge out of the child's developing sense of self-awareness, that is, their sense of having a unique self which is different from the world around them. Moreover, they require the child to consider multiple factors which may influence a given situation, for example, integrating or differentiating more than one perspective. This can be made clear by considering a specific example of a self-conscious emotion – embarrassment. Think of what goes on when you are embarrassed: typically you feel embarrassed when you have done something which you think others may judge to be silly, wrong, or at a level which does not suit you. You evaluate your behaviour against a social standard or a perceived point of view and find your behaviour wanting in some way. Other self-conscious emotions, such as envy, occur when a child evaluates themself against particular others. Pride occurs when children feel good about their accomplishments, comparing their performance to specific others or perceived standards. The developing understanding of emotions such as pride also goes hand-in-hand with cognitive development in other areas. Children's conceptions of pride, for example, are closely tied to their ability to evaluate the difficulty of an activity. By 3 years of age, children know that they are more likely to feel pride if they solve a difficult task as opposed to an easy task (Lewis, Alessandri, & Sullivan, 1992).

Understanding multiple emotions

Throughout childhood and into early adolescence, children gradually become aware that people can experience multiple emotions at the same time (Harter & Buddin, 1987; Wintre & Vallance, 1994). Whereas toddlers and young children clearly *experience* conflicting emotions or blends of emotions, the ability to *understand* these multiple emotions in one's self and others lags well behind. According to Harter and Buddin (1987), there are five stages in the development of multiple emotions. Between 4 and 6 years of age, children can conceive a person holding only one emotion at a time. They can imagine situations that will arouse one emotion but see it as impossible to provoke two simultaneous emotions. From about 6 to 8 years, children begin to grasp that people can hold two emotions, but see these as occurring in sequence rather than simultaneously. Around 8 to 9 children can describe another as holding two different emotions simultaneously as long as they are of the same valence (e.g. 'If she hit me I'd be *angry* and *upset*') or if they arise in response to two different situations (e.g. 'I would be happy if I did well but proud if I won'). At age 10, children start describing opposing feelings in response to different aspects of a single situation, and finally, by age 11, children are able to understand that a single event can cause very different sets of feelings. Harter and Buddin's work shows a clear developmental progression in the complexity of children's emotional understanding, the development of which is not complete until early adolescence.

Emotion scripts

As we have seen, children's understanding of emotional experience undergoes significant developments between infancy and adolescence. Similar developments are observed in the meaning of emotion-specific words and the typical situations that evoke these emotions. This development can be viewed as the child's acquisition of emotion-specific knowledge which takes the form of scripts (Lewis, 1989), that is, knowledge of what kinds of emotions a particular event or situation might arouse. Research by Borke (1971) showed that even 3 to 4 year-old children were able to match possible emotional reactions (using depictions of facial expressions printed on cards) to particular stories about events such as a birthday party or an argument. Children can also work backwards, specifying the types of situation that might arouse particular emotions, such as *happiness*, *surprise* or *anger* (Trabasso, Stein, & Johnson, 1981). Of course, as they mature, children's emotional scripts increase in complexity (Harris, 1989) to the point where eventually adolescents are able to attribute emotions to others even when there are no obvious behavioural manifestations, such as facial expressions.

Children also learn that emotions are intimately tied to a person's *desires*, *intentions* and *beliefs* (Harris, 1989). For example, in a study by Harris and his colleagues (Harris, Johnson, Hutton, Andrews & Cook, 1989) 4 and 6 year-old children watched as the investigator acted out a story with two puppets. For example, in one story, they are shown a puppet called Ellie the Elephant with a carton of milk and are told that Ellie only likes to drink milk. While Ellie is temporarily absent, another puppet, Mickey the Monkey, comes along and pours Ellie's milk out and fills the carton with orange juice. Children at both ages were accurate at predicting how Ellie would feel when she took a drink and found juice. However, when children were asked to state how Ellie would feel *before* she took a drink, 4 year-olds failed to take Ellie's mistaken belief into account and predicted she would be sad on being presented with the deceptive milk carton. Only by age 6 were children able to take Ellie's mistaken belief into account, recognizing that she would feel happy on seeing the milk carton because she was unaware of the true contents. Harris (1989) argues that understanding and predicting another's emotions requires the child to do more than simply acquire script-like knowledge; they must also view emotions as psychological states which depend on a consideration of their desires and beliefs. Work by Ruffman and Keenan (1996) has examined children's understanding of *surprise* and has confirmed that the ability to predict and understand the conditions under which another will be surprised follows a similar developmental course to that described by Harris.

Emotion Regulation

Recall that, on functionalist accounts of emotional development, emotions have the potential to organize or disrupt functioning. The extent to which emotions can organize or interfere with functioning on a given task is mostly governed by the individual's capacity to *regulate* their emotions. The disruptive effects of negative effect such as *anxiety* on cognitive performance have been well documented. You can probably recall a time when anxiety has interfered with your ability to think clearly about a problem, for example, during an exam. However, positive emotions can have similar effects. Try to recall a time when excitement has led to someone you know behaving in unacceptable ways, for example, the child who gets too excited on Christmas morning and cannot sleep. Clearly, emotions, both positive and negative, need to be maintained within certain limits. **Emotion regulation** – the processes by which an individual's emotional arousal is maintained within their capacity to cope – is defined by Thompson (1991: 271) as 'the extrinsic and intrinsic processes responsible for monitoring, evaluating, and modifying emotional reactions, especially their intensive and temporal features'. Every time you take a deep breath at the thought of an upcoming exam, remind yourself that it will soon be over, or count sheep to get to sleep, you are engaging in emotion regulation.

Thompson argues that the study of emotion regulation is critical to an understanding of emotional development in that it provides a window into the growth of personality and social functioning. One key aspect of self-regulation is the presence of both extrinsic and intrinsic pro-cesses. By intrinsic processes, Thompson refers to developments within the individual which allow for the ability to engage in the voluntary and effortful management of emotions. You may have noticed that many forms of self-regulation require the individual to make a clear decision about how to act in the face of stress. Internal developments allow for this, such as growth in the nervous system and brain, changes in cognitive abilities and the growth of linguistic abilities. These intrinsic processes gradually develop and correspond with the development of the fron-tal lobes of the brain (Fox & Calkins, 2003). You may recall that the frontal brain plays a role in higher order processes such as planning and attention, skills clearly needed when trying to divert one's mind away from unwanted emotion. Extrinsic processes are also involved and these refer to factors which stem from outside the individual. The soothing and comforting provided to an infant in distress by its parents, the chance to talk about one's feelings to a close friend, or the cultural prescriptions for how one should feel in a given situation are examples of extrinsic processes by which emotion is regulated. As Thompson (1991) notes, the extrinsic regulation of emotion continues throughout the life span, but is most prevalent during infancy. Infants are initially highly dependent on their caregivers to regulate their emotions but become increasingly able to take over the regulation of their affect.

At birth, the nervous system is far from mature. Therefore, the ability to exert control over the emotional processes is still immature. A baby may be able to turn their head away from an uncomfortable stimulus or suck their thumb when their feelings become too upsetting, but control over the myriad internal and external stimuli is limited. Developing brain capacity and sensitive parental stimulation result in an increase in tolerance of stimulation (Kopp & Neufeld, 2003). A sensitive adult can regulate the baby's arousal level – which very young infants can't do for them-selves – by responding to the infant's cues, such as turning towards the baby when they indicate a desire for interaction, or calmly toning down the level of stimulation when they seem fussy or overstimulated. However, even sensitive parents frequently misinterpret cues, and this appears to be a normal part of synchrony, which refers to the back-and-forth mutually rewarding interactions that healthy parents and infants engage in (Feldman, 2007).

Prolonged missed cues and asynchrony between the infant and caregiver can result in sig-nificant distress in the baby. Young babies become very upset if their parent stops responding to them. Studies have demonstrated behavioural and physiological stress, including increased heart rate and stress hormones, in babies when their caregiver stops their usual interaction and is instructed to freeze. In fact, a lack of response is more upsetting to infants than physical sep-aration from the mother or if she turns away to talk to someone else (Mesman, van IJzendoorn, & Bakermans-Kranenburg, 2009). Long-term lack of parental effort to regulate the baby's stress seems to result in a range of problems: for example, brain structures that buffer stress may not develop sufficiently and the infant may grow up to be anxious and emotionally explosive (Nelson & Bosquet, 2000). Problems affecting either the parent or the child can lead to asynchronous behaviour. For example, depressed mothers are less sensitive to their babies cues, respond more slowly and show less positive emotions than nondepressed mothers (Feldman, 2007), behaviour that has a range of negative effects upon attachment security, development of self-control and, later, empathy. Similarly, premature babies may not respond in a synchronous manner to their parents' efforts, and are often more irritable and provide less clear cues about their needs, which can lead to the parent failing to respond appropriately, despite their best attempts.

With the help of their parents, babies increasingly have control over their reactions; infants can, for example, suppress a desire to cry or change the tone of a cry to attract the caregiver's attention. Self-regulation further becomes controlled by the infant; around their first birthday infants are able to crawl or walk away or towards stimuli. The role of the parent in children's emotion regulation remains important and reciprocal. For example, early negative parenting – including expression of negative emotions – during the infant's first 6 months of age can set up a long-term cycle of child anger and parent hostility and conflict that persists across childhood (Lorber & Egeland, 2011).

Changes in the child's cognitive functioning also lead to new developments in the ability to modulate emotional processes. The development of the child's representational abilities, occurring during the preschool years, allows them to evoke memories in order to alter emotional responses. For example, the child experiencing separation anxiety when briefly removed from their caregiver can think about that person in order to soothe themselves and reduce their anxiety (Miller & Green, 1985; Thompson, 1990). Older children can use their cognitive processes in even more sophisticated ways. Whereas preschool children understand that their emotions can be altered by simply avoiding thinking about something, by redirecting their thought processes, or by refocusing their attention (1994), older children understand that a situation or event which makes them feel a particular way can be reframed and thought about in an entirely differently way (Band & Weisz, 1988). Thus, older children learn that they can choose to reinterpret a situation as a method to alter their feelings.

The relationship between emotion regulation and cognition works both ways. Changes in emotion regulation allow for greater cognitive processing demands: the ability to control negative emotions and keep attention on a goal is involved in cognitive performance. A study examining 9 month-olds' performance on an object permanence task found that unsuccessful searching for a hidden toy was predicted by negative affect and low attention (Keenan, 2002). Thus, babies who could not overcome the negative emotion of not finding the toy in a previous task were more likely to fail future tasks.

Changes in language ability also play an important role in emotion regulation. Language allows us to conceptualize and convey our emotional experiences to others. As a consequence of this, we can encourage extrinsic forms of regulation by discussing our feelings with others. Verbal interactions around emotion can effect changes in emotion regulation in several ways (Thompson, 1991). First, parents can direct their children's regulatory processes through commands (e.g. 'don't get so excited' or 'please stop crying'). Second, parent–child talk about emotion can also suggest to the child new ways of thinking about their feelings, allowing them to better manage them. Finally, parents can suggest emotion regulation strategies directly to the child, such as getting them to think about a comfortable image, rethink their goals, or engage in some sort of self-soothing behaviour.

By adolescence, the developments in self-understanding which have occurred lay the groundwork for the development of what Thompson (1991) referred to as a **theory of personal emotion**.

A theory of personal emotion is essentially a coherent network of beliefs about one's own emotional processes. For example, an adolescent may recognize that they naturally shy away from social interaction and realize that in order to be accepted by their peers, they need to find ways in which to overcome this tendency, such as expressing more positive affect to others and making a conscious effort to smile and make eye contact. In middle childhood, children begin to appreciate the fact that their emotional experiences may differ from those of others, and they start to acquire general knowledge about their own emotional processes, such as the particular idiosyncrasies that may characterize their own emotional experiences. In addition, as they grow children acquire more refined knowledge about coping strategies and, more specifically, which coping strategies work best for them depending on the situation. However, it is during adolescence that the theory of personal emotion acquires its coherence. As adolescents develop a progressively more complex network of self-referential beliefs, their theory of personal emotion is incorporated into their conception of themselves.

Research Example 10.1

Boys may need Sensitive Handling of Negative Emotions

Many young children do not have sufficient behavioural inhibition and control to deal with their frequently strong emotions, including fear and anger. Research has examined the future consequences of parental responses to toddlers' displays of negative emotionality. Part of a larger study on children's social and emotional development and parent–child relationships, 107 children and their parents were observed at various points across early development (Engle & McElwain, 2011). Mothers and fathers independently completed questionnaires assessing parental reactions to their child's negative emotions (including fear and sadness) and child negative emotionality (including how often their child had displayed anger or social fearfulness in the last month) at Time 1 (33 months) and child behaviour problems at Time 2 (39 months). During Time 1, parents also reported on how they would respond to the child's negative emotions in a series of hypothetical situations (for example, '*If my child is afraid of going to the doctor or of getting shots and becomes quite shaky and teary, I would ...*'). Two types of parental reaction to the child's negative emotions were examined. One type was to minimize the child's emotions (for example, a response such as 'stop behaving like a baby'). The second type included punishing the child for the emotion (for example, a parent might take away a toy or privilege for crying). At Time 2, parents answered questions about their child's current behaviour.

First, findings revealed that child negative emotionality was significantly related to greater internalizing and externalizing behaviour, such as anxiety, depression and acting out, at Time 2. Second, mothers and fathers who punished their children when they showed fear or frustration at Time 1 were more likely *to* have children with higher levels of anxious and depressive behaviours at Time 2. This finding only held for boys with high levels of negative emotionality.

The results suggest that when parents punish their toddlers for becoming angry or scared, children learn to hide their emotions, which may lead to anxiety when they have these feelings because they know they will be punished. This may be the case particularly for boys. The authors advise that when children are upset, it may be most appropriate to talk with them and help them work through their emotions. Young children, especially boys who are prone to feeling negative emotions intensely, may need comfort and support when their emotions threaten to overwhelm them. Experts tend to agree that responding flexibly and appropriately to individual episodes of negative behaviour may be the most effective strategy.

Questions: What are some of the study limitations?

Can you think of possible reasons why the findings were more applicable to boys than girls? What are some of the social norms surrounding boys and men expressing negative emotions, including fear?

Emotional intelligence

The ability to understand emotions in ourselves and others and regulate our emotional experiences is very important for social functioning. Numerous studies have indicated that young children who show a good understanding of emotions are also rated highly by adult observers for social competence and enjoy positive relations with their peers (see for example, Denham et al., 2003). Indeed, it has been suggested that the ability to understand and regulate emotional experiences is a skill that varies between individuals and can be measured. This notion of 'emotional intelligence' (EI) has its roots in Gardner's (1983) proposal of multiple forms of intelligence, and in particular his identification of interpersonal and intrapersonal intelligence, which refers to the ability to understand emotions in the self and others. The concept of emotional intelligence was developed further by Salovey and Mayer (for example, Mayer & Salovey, 1993; Salovey & Mayer, 1990), who identified five domains of emotional intelligence: (1) Knowing one's feelings; (2) The ability to use and manage feelings in a manner appropriate to a given situation; (3) Self-motivation, the ability to make conscious decisions regarding our goals and behaving in a manner appropriate to achieving that goal; (4) Recognizing emotions in others; (5) Building and maintaining positive relationships with others.

More recently, there has been much debate about the nature of emotional intelligence and how it should be measured. Salovey and Mayer argue that emotional intelligence should be regarded as an ability that can be measured through the use of 'maximum performance' tests in much the same way as intelligence and other cognitive skills. Proponents of this view of EI (known as ability EI) measure this ability using tasks such as recognizing facial expressions in pictures and answering questions about strategies for managing emotions. Salovey and Mayer took this view of EI and developed an ability EI measure known as the Mayer Salovey Caruso Emotional Intelligence test (MSCEIT) (Mayer, Caruso, & Salovey, 2000). However, other researchers are critical of this approach, arguing that the subjective nature of emotional experiences makes them very difficult to measure in the same way that one would measure intelligence. For example, when presented with a question regarding how to manage emotions in a given situation, it is not always clear what might constitute a 'correct', emotionally intelligent response (Mavroveli, Petrides, Shove, & Whitehead, 2008). Instead, Mavroveli et al. argue that EI should be seen more as a personality trait. Proponents of the trait EI viewpoint argue that this should be measured using self-report methods, such as presenting children with statements (for example, 'I can control my anger when I want to') and asking them to indicate the extent to which they agree or disagree with them. Petrides and colleagues (see for example, Mavroveli et al., 2008; Petrides & Furnham, 2001) took this view of EI and developed a test known as the Trait Emotional Intelligence Questionnaire (TEIQue). Versions of this test have also been devised for children aged 8 to11 (TEIQue-CF) and adolescents (TEIQue-ASF). Research by Mavroveli et al. (2008) has found a link between trait EI and a number of different measures of social functioning in children. Children who were low in trait EI had higher rates of unauthorized absences from school and were also more likely to show signs of peer difficulties, conduct problems, emotional symptoms and hyperactivity.

More recently, there has been much interest in devising interventions to improve emotional intelligence in children and a variety of programmes have been devised to help children identify and understand their feelings and understand the links between the way they feel and their relationships with others. In general, such programmes appear to have positive results. One study by Durlak et al. (2011) analyzed the outcomes of 213 school-based Social and Emotional Learning (SEL) programmes in the USA. The results of this study indicated that compared to control participants, children and adolescents who participated in SEL programmes showed marked gains in social and emotional skills, positive behaviour and school achievement. Overall these findings indicate that emotional intelligence is indeed vital for effective functioning in everyday life and promoting the development of these skills in children and young people is as important as the promotion of traditional academic skills.

Culture and emotion

Emotional development takes place in a cultural context. While parents, peers and siblings all have a role in the infant's understanding, expression and control of emotion, wider social forces are also at play. Different cultures have varying standards for the appropriate expression of emotion, and thus we find large differences in emotion socialization across cultures. Even the emergence of smiling shows distinct patterns across cultures and countries. Although it is common for girls of all ages to smile more than boys (LaFrance, Hecht, & Paluck, 2003), it seems this disparity is greater in certain countries. Girls from the United States and Canada are more likely to smile than boys, but this sex difference is less apparent in Great Britain (LaFrance et al., 2003). Similarly, white American boys and girls are more dissimilar in their smiling than African American boys and girls. Socialization is the probable force behind these findings: in European American families, girls are more likely to be encouraged to smile than boys (Saarni, 1999) whereas children of other ethnicities may be equally encouraged to smile. Other emotional display rules and emotion regulation also show cultural differences. One study compared the emotional reactions of Buddhist and Hindu children from Nepal in response to emotion-provoking stories (e.g. of unjust parental punishment) (Cole & Tamang, 1998). Children's behaviour was consistent with their culture: Buddhist children interpreted the stories so they did not feel anger, whereas Hindu children were more likely to respond that they would feel angry, but they would try to hide this anger. Self-reports from Hindu mothers revealed that they were indeed more likely to encourage emotional control. In contrast, a follow-up study involving children from the USA found that North American children were more likely to express their anger (Cole, Bruschi, & Tamang, 2002), which seems highly consistent with a Western emphasis on personal rights and expression.

The Development of Attachment

Bowlby's theory of attachment

Like the young of many species, human infants are relatively helpless at birth and for the first few months thereafter. We are born with very limited sensory abilities, little in the way of physical motor skills and few cognitive abilities. This fact means that human infants are vulnerable at birth and for some time thereafter. While it is unlikely that in these modern times an infant is likely to be carried off by a predator, our situation was not always so secure. During one point in our evolutionary history, conditions were such that this threat was a very real one. Thus, it is not surprising that we have developed behaviours which help us adapt to such conditions.

The study of bonding between parents and infants owes much to the pioneering work of John Bowlby (1958, 1960). Bowlby formulated a theory of the relationship between the caregiver and the infant – what he called an **attachment relationship** – drawing largely from work in *psychoanalytic theory*, *ethological theory* and work in *cognitive* and *developmental psychology* (Ainsworth, Blehar, Waters, & Wall, 1978). Attachment theory focuses on both the processes which lead to the bonding of parents and children and the impact of this relationship on psychological development. Furthermore, attachment theory focuses our attention on the development of affectional ties between the caregiver and infant, and on the behaviours and cognitive structures by which these ties are maintained over time.

In contrast to Sigmund Freud, who believed that an infant's affectional tie to their caregiver was developed on the basis of being fed by the caregiver, Bowlby believed that selection pressures acting over the course of human evolution led to infants having an innate set of behaviours which caused them to seek an appropriate level of *proximity* to the caregiver. Proximity refers to the physical distance between the infant and the caregiver. By staying close to a caregiver who can protect them against dangers such as predators, an infant has a better chance of survival. Thus, these behaviours are passed on from generation to generation. Human infants also come equipped with a communicative system of cries and facial expressions which allows them to signal for the caregiver to increase their proximity. In other words, we can initiate proximity through means such as crying or smiling. Bowlby argued that both affectional ties and the behaviours that promote proximity to one's caregiver have an evolutionary basis (Campos et al., 1983) in that they are unlearned and instinctive, that is, a part of our biological heritage.

Of course, the effectiveness of the infant's communicative signals depends on the ability of the adult to receive and interpret them, thus, human adults must also have a complementary system by which to interpret these signals (e.g. Frodi & Lamb, 1978). Attachment is a two-way process, a relationship between two people: it is *not* simply a set of learned behaviours emitted by infants or adults (Ainsworth et al., 1978; Sroufe, 1996). The effectiveness of the infant's signals depends on the ability of the caregiver to understand and react appropriately to these. In an important way, attachment theory extends the study of emotional development into the social realm, breaking down traditional barriers that focus solely on the individual as opposed to the individual as situated in relationships with other people.

Bowlby's attachment theory was also influenced by work in control-systems theory (Ainsworth et al., 1978). According to control-systems theory, behaviours which serve a common function are grouped together with the purpose of achieving a particular goal. The behaviours are activated to achieve the goal of the system: if the goal changes, the behaviours are altered to achieve the new goal. Consider the example of an infant which is placed in an unfamiliar room. Given the unfamiliar surroundings, the initial goal of the control system will be to maintain proximity to the caregiver. After some time, as the infant begins to feel comfortable, the goal of the system is altered and the need to maintain proximity is relaxed, freeing the infant to move about and explore. This move away from the mother may be interrupted by the entrance of a stranger. If the infant interprets the stranger as threatening, the need for proximity will be reasserted and the infant will seek out the caregiver. If the infant feels secure with the stranger, exploration will continue and no increase in proximity will be called for.

Another major contributor to attachment theory, Mary Ainsworth (1973), noted that infants use adults both as a *safe haven* and as a *secure base*; that is, infants organize their attachment behaviours such that they use the adult as a refuge and source of comfort when they are distressed, but also as a safe vantage point from which to explore their environment. One of Ainsworth's major contributions to attachment theory was the study of how infants' secure base behaviour can be used to inform us about the quality of an infant's attachment relationship with its caregiver, a topic explored in the next section.

Much of the research in attachment focuses on the attachment between mothers and infants. However, Bowlby recognized that infants form attachments to other people as well. Infants form attachment relationships with fathers, grandparents, siblings and peers, among others (Lamb, 1981; Lewis, 1987; Schaffer, 1996). These attachments differ in important ways across individuals, yet at the same time, Bowlby argued that the nature of an infant's attachment to its primary caregiver has a profound effect on its other relationships. Bowlby claimed that this influence is exerted by the development of what has been called an **internal working model** (Bowlby, 1973). This is a mental representation or 'mental model' of the infant's experiences with their primary attachment figure. Internal working models are relatively stable over time; however, Bowlby chose the term *working model* to highlight that they are updated on the basis of experience. Importantly, internal working models serve to combine cognitive representations of the infant's relationship with their caregiver with an affective component, that is, how the infant *feels* about the attachment relationship. Bowlby believed that the child's attachment relationship with their primary caregiver influenced all of that child's subsequent relationships. A child who is not securely attached to their primary caregiver is more likely to have difficulty in forming and maintaining other relationships.

The development of the attachment relationship

Attachment relationships do not occur suddenly but instead emerge gradually throughout the first two years of life. There are four phases in the development of attachment (Ainsworth et al., 1978; Schaffer, 1996). Initially, infants show little preference for particular others: their social behaviours are indiscriminately directed towards others. This phase, called *preattachment*, encompasses the first two months of the life span. In the second phase, *attachment-in-the-making*, which runs from 2 to 7 months of age, infants begin to discriminate familiar from unfamiliar people and show a distinct preference for the attachment figure. At about 7 months of age, the third phase, *clear-cut attachment*, begins. At this time, infants develop marked attachments to

particular people with whom they have regular contact, such as their mother and father, grandparents, and day-care workers. Infants actively seek out these people and often protest or show upset when they leave. The final phase of attachment, which begins at 2 years of age, is called a *goal-corrected partnership*. In this phase, the child begins to take into account the feelings and plans of the attachment figure when planning their own actions. The responsibility for the attachment relationship begins to shift from the mother to the child as the child develops the ability to communicate their thoughts and feelings through language. The child has truly become a partner in maintaining the relationship between themselves and their caregiver. At this final phase, the attachment relationship between caregiver and child has reached a new level of sophistication (Ainsworth et al., 1978).

Although attachment theory has traditionally focused on the mother's role, it is now recognized that children form a number of important attachment relationships throughout their lives. Fathers, in particular, are a key attachment figure in many children's lives. Fathers who take an interest in their babies early on are just as likely as mothers to hold, kiss and talk to their babies, and are likely to have an attachment relationship with their child that is similar to the relationship between mother and child (Parke, 1996). In many cultures fathers also have an additional role to play,

Image 10B   Attachment theory now recognizes that when fathers such as this stay-at-home dad take an interest in their babies, holding, kissing and caring for them, babies develop strong attachments similar to the mother–child bond

that of the playmate. While mothers tend to engage with their babies verbally and play less boisterous games like peek-a-boo, fathers tend to engage in much more rough and tumble play. Infants seem to like this unpredictable and energetic play, reacting more positively to father play than mother play (Parke, 2002). Moreover, when fathers respond with enthusiasm and sensitivity to infants' attempts at play, children are more likely to have a secure internal working model of attachment (Grossman, Grossman, & Kindler, 2005).

Quality of attachment and the strange situation

Ideally, the attachment relationship serves as a source of affection and nurturance. The attachment relationship allows an infant to feel confident and secure while exploring and learning about the world. Ainsworth was among the first to highlight the importance of parenting in fostering the development of a secure attachment in children (Ainsworth & Bell, 1974). The caregivers of securely attached infants usually show a high degree of **sensitivity**. That is, these parents are generally responsive to their infant's needs and engage in consistent patterns of behaviour (Cassidy & Berlin, 1994). Their care giving allows the infant to play a role in these daily interactions. Ainsworth et al. (1978) argued that when mothers are *insensitive* to their infant's needs, either by being overly *intrusive* or by *neglecting* them, the infant can develop an **insecure attachment**. Insecure attachments are attachment relationships which fail to provide the infant with a sense of confidence and security. Interestingly, the suggestion has been made that the various forms of insecure attachment may actually be *adaptive* solutions for these infants, in that they allow the infant to make sense of a difficult relationship (e.g. Cassidy, 1994; Main & Solomon, 1990). For example, an avoidant attachment relationship helps to minimize the importance of the caregiver for the infant and allows the infant to avoid the negative affect associated with being rejected or neglected by their caregiver.

The quality of an infant's attachment to its caregiver can be measured using a testing paradigm known as the **strange situation** (Ainsworth et al., 1978; Waters, Vaughn, Posada, & Kondo-Ikemura, 1995). Briefly, in the strange situation, the infant is separated from its mother, exposed to a stranger, and then reunited with the mother. Use of the strange situation allows the experimenter to examine differences in attachment behaviour which differ as a function of the infant's quality of attachment to the caregiver. Using a classification system designed by Ainsworth and her colleagues (Ainsworth et al., 1978), infants' attachment relationships with the caregiver can be described as falling into one of three categories. Most commonly observed in a sample of normal children is a **secure attachment**. Securely attached infants are only minimally disturbed by separations from the caregiver, continue to explore the environment while the caregiver is present, and show positive affect on the caregiver's return after separation. In contrast, infants classified as showing an **insecure-avoidant** attachment tended to show little distress on separation from the caregiver. However, they are clearly upset by her departure, as a study by Spangler and Grossman (1993), which measured infant heart rate, revealed. In addition, when the caregiver returns, insecure-avoidant infants typically pay no attention to her and actively *avoid* contact with her. A third type of insecure attachment is the **insecure-resistant** type (this type is sometimes labelled **insecure-ambivalent**). These infants are most often extremely distressed by separation from the caregiver, showing high levels of crying and upset. However, when the caregiver returns insecure-resistant children show a pattern of alternately seeking contact with her and then resisting contact or pushing away from the caregiver. Ainsworth's research with the strange situation showed that for American samples, some 60 to 65% of infants were classified as secure, 20% as insecure-avoidant, and some 10 to 15% as insecure-resistant. Work by Main and Solomon (1990) revealed a fourth type of insecure attachment which they called **insecure-disorganized**. Insecure-disorganized infants display extremely peculiar behaviours in the strange situation: they often engage in repetitive movements such as rocking, show a tendency to freeze (i.e. remain extremely immobile) in the middle of a movement, and in general seem confused or disoriented during their reunion with the mother. Sadly, researchers have found that insecure-disorganized attachments often co-occur with child mistreatment (Carlson et al., 1989; Lyons-Ruth et al., 1990) and maternal depression (Field, 1990). In the study by Carlson et al., 82% of a sample of mistreated infants developed insecure-disorganized attachments whereas only 19% of children who were not mistreated showed this pattern. Unfortunately for these infants, insecure-disorganized attachment has been associated with negative developmental outcomes (Main & Solomon, 1990).

Although the strange situation is a well-established method for studying attachment security, it is not without its critics. Can you think of any limitations of this technique?

The stability of attachment

An aspect of attachment theory suggested by Bowlby and confirmed by many researchers is the assertion that the quality of attachment relationships is stable over time. Waters (1978) studied the stability of attachment classifications in children from 12 to 18 months of age. He found a near-perfect consistency in the classifications across this time-span. Similarly, Main and Cassidy (1988) studied a sample of infants who were seen in the strange situation at 12 months and were then observed again aged 6. In the latter group, the children were given a measure of attachment security used with older children. Main and Cassidy found a high level of consistency for attachment classifications from infancy to age 6. These and other findings suggest that attachment is highly stable across time (Sroufe, 1979; Vaughn et al., 1979).

Such early studies have been criticized on a number of grounds, one of these being that early research on the stability of attachment tended to use largely middle-class samples in hope of reducing factors such as stressful life events which might impact on the consistency of attachment classifications. What happens when researchers take into account the effects of stressful life events such as changes in employment (e.g. becoming unemployed or being forced into a lower paying job) or changes in marital status (e.g. divorce or separation)? When such factors are examined, the results provide less evidence for stability in attachment classifications over time. Studies have found that stressful life events, as reported by parents, were associated with changes in attachment classifications in their children (Thompson et al., 1982; Vaughn et al., 1979). In families that experience poverty, limited social support and parental psychological difficulties, attachment seems to swing from secure to insecure or from one insecure style to another (Vondra, Shaw, Swearingen, Cohen, & Owens, 2001). Interestingly, changes in attachment classifications are bi-directional, that is, they can move from secure to insecure or vice versa. Thus, improvements in family life can lead to the development of secure attachments. Thompson (1998) and Sroufe (1996) have suggested that attachment relationships continue to develop over time and that change in the stability of a child's attachment relationship is a function of their environment. Stable environments will tend to lead to stable attachment relationships.

The consequences of attachment relationships

Many attachment theorists, including Bowlby, argued that the quality of an infant's attachment to their caregiver has important consequences for development. One such theory is that the quality of the attachment relationship will act as an organizer for further development (Erikson, 1963), namely that attachment security is associated with different developmental pathways: securely attached children will tend to follow certain pathways through life whereas insecurely attached infants will follow different paths. According to Sroufe (1979), secure attachments are the foundation of healthy psychological development. Infants who form secure attachments should develop into competent, healthy children who are able to form satisfying relationships with others, whereas infants with insecure attachments will have a basic distrust of themselves and their social world, feelings of anxiety and guilt, and difficulties in forming relationships (Bowlby, 1969). A fundamental prediction of attachment theory is that our early social experience has a profound effect on our later development in the social, emotional and cognitive domains.

One of the first studies to demonstrate the effects of secure attachments on later outcomes was carried out by Matas, Arend and Sroufe (1978). In this study, a sample of toddlers was seen at 18 months of age and their attachment quality to their mother was assessed. These same children were then observed at 24 months of age and asked to engage in a series of problem-solving tasks and a play task. In general, securely attached children were less negative, cried and whined less often, and showed less aggression during the tasks than did insecurely attached children. Securely attached children were more enthusiastic on the problem-solving tasks, were frustrated less easily, and were more persistent in trying to find a solution than insecurely attached infants. Securely attached infants also tended to engage in more symbolic play than did insecurely attached children. Finally, securely attached children were more compliant: when their mother made suggestions for solving the tasks, securely attached children were more likely to make use of these suggestions than were insecure children.

Further research showed that these same benefits associated with a secure attachment relationship held into the preschool years, with preschool teachers rating securely attached children as less aggressive towards their peers, less dependent on help from the teacher, and more competent than insecurely attached children (LaFreniere & Sroufe, 1985; Waters, Wippman, & Sroufe, 1979). Work by Elizabeth Meins (Meins, Russell, Fernyhough, & Clark-Carter, 1998) showed that securely attached children did better on theory of mind tasks at age 4; these children were more likely to pass the false belief task (see Chapter 11) than insecurely attached children.

Finally, Lyons-Ruth et al. (1997) found that infants who were judged to be securely attached at 18 months of age were highly likely to be functioning well in interpersonal contexts at school when measured at age 7. In contrast, children assessed as showing disorganized attachments at 18 months were likely to develop *externalizing behaviours* such as hostility towards their peers, and acting out in class. Children whose attachment relationships were classified as avoidant were likely to show *internalizing behaviours* at age 7, such as depression, anxiety and self-criticism. (Internalizing and externalizing behaviours are discussed in greater detail in Chapter 13.) In general, the research by Matas and her colleagues, as well as a host of studies by other researchers, have demonstrated several important benefits to emotional, cognitive and social development, following the formation of a secure attachment relationship.

Recently, Grazyna Kochanska and her colleagues have demonstrated that to reap the benefits of early parent–infant bonding and secure attachments upon later social and emotional health, children may only need to feel secure with one parent (Kochanska & Kim, 2013a). Infants who were securely attached to both parents did not seem to have additional mental and emotional advantages later in childhood, compared to those who had been close to just one parent. It seems that a warm, secure and positive bond with at least one primary caregiver may be enough to meet the child's need for security and provide a solid foundation for development. Moreover, being securely attached to a father provided just as many benefits as being securely attached to a mother. The study is reassuring for single mothers and stay-at-home fathers. It is not known whether the findings are applicable to day-care providers, and further research in this area is warranted.

Attachment and culture

Infant attachment behaviours are not universal, and should be considered in the context of the culture in which the child is raised. Most of what we know about attachment has been built on research conducted with babies from Caucasian American middle-class families. However, differences exist even between European babies and American babies of European ancestry. Thus, German infants show significantly more avoidant attachment, due to a corresponding parenting culture of raising independent children (Grossman et al., 2005). In contrast, mothers of the Dogon people in Mali tend to hold their infants close a great deal and promptly respond to their slightest need. As a result, infants in this culture rarely show avoidant attachment behaviours (True, Pisani, & Oumar, 2001). Despite such differences in the rates of attachment security, secure attachment still appears to be the most common attachment category across cultures.

Temperament

Defining temperament

Early studies of children (e.g. Gesell, 1928) noted that there were striking individual differences between children in terms of their 'core of personality' (Shirley, 1933). Importantly, these researchers recognized that these differences in infants' traits were not fixed and often showed considerable change over time, yet they seemed to be constant enough in most cases that one could plausibly argue that these traits were constitutionally based, that is, rooted in the child's biological makeup. Another aspect of this early research was the examination of how these differences across children led to a variety of possible developmental outcomes. For example, Gesell described how particular traits, such as sociability, might predispose one towards generally positive outcomes later in life. Much of this early work on what we now call **temperament** has been confirmed by current research. These early observations of individual differences in infants and children highlight three issues central to the study of temperament today: temperamental traits are inherent, constitutionally-based characteristics that make up the core of personality; although stability is a feature of many temperamental traits, it is widely recognized that stability greatly depends on the social context in which the child grows; temperament is related to a variety of possible long-term outcomes, such as the quality of relationships with peers, psychological adjustment and psychopathology.

What is temperament then? Temperament involves the study of individual differences in the basic psychological processes that constitute 'the affective, activational, and attentional core of personality and its development' (Rothbart & Bates, 1998: 108). Temperament is strongly tied to emotion, hence its inclusion in this chapter. For example, Allport (1961: 34) described temperament as the characteristics of an individual's emotional nature, such as their susceptibility to emotional stimulation, the nature of their typical emotional responses, and the quality of their prevailing mood. Most recently, temperament has been defined as involving reactivity and self-regulation (Rothbart, 2004). Reactivity refers to the speed and intensity of attention, arousal and motor action – essentially how quickly we respond to stimuli and how intensely we react. For example, news that the boss has suddenly cut all overtime pay may be met with anger by some workers, while others shrug their shoulders and look for a new job. Self-regulatory processes are those processes which serve to modulate our reactivity. For example, when distressed by a particular thought, you can consciously distract yourself by thinking about other more pleasant thoughts, such as focusing on the vacation time you have accrued and how you might spend it. As research has shown, differences in self-regulatory behaviour seem to have a constitutional basis and show a degree of stability which has led many researchers to view these as fundamental aspects of temperament.

Temperament is considered central to an individual's emerging personality and indeed, there is a great deal of overlap between the characteristics identified as being related to temperament and those related to personality. However, it is important to note that temperament and personality are not identical. Although researchers have identified links between early temperament and later personality (e.g. Caspi & Silva, 1995), much work remains to establish exactly how these are linked (Rothbart & Bates, 1998).

Most, if not all, theories of temperament argue that the individual differences which are central to the study of temperament are genetically or biologically rooted (see Chapter 5 for further discussion on the genetic and biological basis of behaviour), attested to by the focus on 'constitutionally based' in the above definitions (Kagan, 1998). A number of twin and adoption studies have shown that individual differences in child temperament are influenced by genetics. However, recent work in the behavioural genetics field has shown some interesting interactions between nature and nurture for children's temperament (Saudino, 2005); this is not surprising given that genetic and biological predispositions are strongly influenced by maturation and experience (Bates, 1989; Goldsmith et al., 1987). Research shows that specific genes lie behind the development of specific temperament characteristics. Non-shared environmental factors which include everything from peer groups to accidents, illnesses and birth order also play a role (Saudino, 2005). It is thought that between 20% and 60% of variability in personality is due to genetic factors while the remaining 40% to 80% is accounted for by environmental factors. Research Example 10.2 shows examples of the kinds of studies that are undertaken to determine these figures. In particular, changes in environment, such as moving schools, can cause changes in temperament. Thus, all temperamental effects on behaviour represent a combination of biological and environmental effects and are best characterized as *interactions* of the two factors. It is important to keep this fact in mind as we discuss research on temperament and its role in emotional and social development.

Research Example 10.2

Attachment Security and Temperament: The role of genetics and environment

Although the basic distinction in the nature–nurture debate is between the varied roles of genetics and environment in understanding development and behaviour, we can make a further distinction between different forms of environmental influences. Shared environment factors can be distinguished from non-shared environmental factors. Environmental influences that are shared by family members include everything from neighbourhoods, family socioeconomic status and family religion. They result in behavioural similarities between family members. In contrast, non-shared environmental influences are specific to an individual and include peers, birth order, differential parental treatment and any non-normative life events like accidents or deaths (Saudino, 2005).

A behaviour genetics study examined the influence of these kinds of environmental influences and genetic influences on infant attachment and temperament (Bokhorst, Bakermans-Kranenburg, Fearon, van IJzendoorn, Fonagy, & Schuengel, 2003). The study involved 157 pairs of monozygotic and dizygotic twins from the Netherlands and London. Infants were placed in the *strange situation* to measure mother–infant attachment and mothers completed a questionnaire on the child's temperament. Cross-tabulations of attachment classifications within the pairs of twins revealed that genetic contributions were relatively small. For monozygotic twins, the concordance for secure attachment was 42%, while for dizygotic twins, the concordance was 41%. This result was striking in that both types of twin showed comparable rates of genetic similarity, even though monozygotic twins have identical genotypes (compared to the 50% genetic similarity between dizygotic twins).

(Continued)

After completing some complex modelling that accounted for genetics, shared and non-shared factors, the authors found that shared and non-shared environments were strong predictors of secure versus insecure attachment (the role of genetics was negligible). For temperament, the findings were slightly different. The difference in concordance between monozygotic and dizygotic twins was greater, and pointed to more of a genetic component. Results from statistical modelling revealed that 77% of temperamental differences were explained by genes, while the remaining 23% were explained by non-shared environmental factors.

Together, these findings indicate a strong role for environmental factors in attachment security; and in particular, non-shared environments. Parenting has been considered an important influence in whether children display secure attachments, and these findings support this. It is likely that parenting can be either a shared or a non-shared influence, as although parents may have an underlying parenting philosophy, they often parent differently with different children, resulting in non-shared influence as well. In contrast, the role of genetics is stronger in the development of temperament. It seems that infants are born with at least part of their tendency to react to and regulate emotion, and their individual experiences in the world explain the rest.

Initial work on temperament in infancy by Thomas and Chess (1977) identified nine dimensions of temperament. These are: *activity level* (the frequency and tempo of an infant's motor activity); *rhythmicity* (the extent to which activities such as sleeping and eating are regular or predictable); *approach/withdrawal* (how the infant reacts to new situations); *adaptability* (how easily a response is modified to fit a new situation); *intensity* (how energetic the infant's typical reactions are); *threshold* (how strong a response needs to be before the infant reacts); *mood* (the general quality of the infant's mood); *distractibility* (ease with which the infant's activities can be interrupted); and *attention span/persistence* (the extent to which an infant remains engaged in activity). Recent research has gone beyond these descriptive categories of behaviour to focus on additional qualities such as the ability to regulate one's own behaviour (Rothbart, 1989), and makes finer subdivisions between the variability within the broad dimensions identified by Thomas and Chess (1977) and other researchers (Rothbart & Bates, 1988).

Based on their analysis of these dimensions, Thomas and Chess (1986) proposed a typology of temperament that has gained wide acceptance, perhaps largely due to its intuitive appeal. Under their scheme, infants can be classified as *easy*, *difficult*, or *slow-to-warm*. Easy infants are sociable, happy, rhythmic and adaptable. In contrast, difficult infants are easily upset by novelty, tend to fuss and cry often, and are low on rhythmicity, having difficulty sleeping and eating regularly. Slow-to-warm infants fall in between easy and difficult. These infants tend to initially respond to novel experiences poorly, but over time or repeated contact show a pattern of gradually warming to and accepting the experience. Thomas and Chess found that easy children

Table 10.2 Temperamental dimensions and types

Dimension	Description
Activity level	The frequency and tempo of an infant's motor activity
Rhythmicity	The extent to which activities (like sleeping) are regular
Approach/withdrawal	How the infant reacts to novel situations
Adaptability	How easily a response is modified to fit a new situation
Intensity	How energetic the infant's usual reactions are
Threshold	How intense stimulation needs to be before the infant reacts
Mood	The general quality of the infant's mood (e.g. friendly and cheerful vs. unfriendly behaviour)
Distractibility	How easily the infant's activities can be interrupted
Attention span/persistence	How long the infant remains engaged in an activity
Typology	
Easy	Cheerful, rhythmic and adaptable
Difficult	Low on rhythmicity, easily upset by novelty, cries often
Slow-to-warm	Adjusts slowly to new experiences, negative mood and inactive

constituted approximately 40% of their sample while difficult and slow-to-warm infants made up 10% and 50% of the remainder.

The measurement of temperament

A wide variety of methods have been developed to measure temperament. These include: caregiver reports for infants and young children; teacher reports for the preschool and school-aged child; self-reports for older children and adolescents; naturalistic or observational assessments; and laboratory procedures. Not surprisingly, each methodology has its own benefits and limitations. For example, parent reports of temperament provide a unique insight from the people who spend the most time with the child, yet they are also open to bias as the parent's report is a function of their own characteristics. Parents tend to have quite set ideas about their children's behaviour, which may affect their reports. A consistent finding in twin studies, for example, is that parents exaggerate the similarities between monozygotic twins and play down the similarities between dizygotic twins (Saudino, 2005). Laboratory assessments get around this issue of bias by subjecting children to standard procedures. However, they suffer from particular limitations, such as carryover effects from repeated testing and the constraints placed on the types of response children can give. It is difficult for researchers to capture the full range of children's behaviour in an artificial environment, and the laboratory may place extra strain on some stress-prone children who have acquired methods to cope with stress in their own environments but are unable to use these strategies in a lab setting (Wachs & Bates, 2001).

Recent studies have used psychophysiological measures such as heart rate, hormone levels and EEG brain waves to understand temperament. Particularly inhibited or shy children and uninhibited or sociable children tend to show quite different results on these measures. There is some evidence that the amygdala, a brain structure associated with memory of emotion and fear, contributes to temperament (Kagan, 2003). In shy children, stimuli easily activate the amygdala, preparing the body for a fight-or-flight response, whereas in sociable children the same stimulation barely registers. Results using fMRI provide support for the role of the amygdala in shy versus uninhibited temperaments (Schwartz, Wright, Shin, Kagan, & Raugh, 2003). However, as our discussion above highlighted, biology isn't the only explanation behind who develops what kind of temperament. Thus, measures of temperament are best conducted using a variety of strategies that account for biological and environmental correlates of temperamental differences.

The continuity of temperament

Research evaluating the continuity of temperament over time has produced mixed assessments. While most early research in the field emphasized the stability of temperament across assessments (e.g. Buss & Plomin, 1975), more recent work has suggested that temperament develops throughout childhood and is thus modified over time (Goldsmith, 1996). The course of this development reveals that initial individual differences in motor activity and emotionality are modified as developing self-regulatory systems 'come online' (Rothbart & Bates, 1998). The stability of temperamental classifications also varies depending on the temperamental dimension being measured and the time periods across which it is measured. For example, research with a sample of New Zealand children (Caspi & Silva, 1995) reported that 3 year-olds rated as shy and subdued tended to describe themselves at age 18 (using a personality inventory) as shy or reserved. In contrast, work on the temperamental dimension of *distress proneness* showed little stability for distress measured over the first three months of life (Worobey & Lewis, 1989). Rothbart (1986) showed that positive and negative affect measured at 3 months of age were not correlated with the same measures at 9 months of age. However, distress measured later in infancy tended to show stability well into the school years, at age 6 to 7 (Rothbart, Derryberry, & Hershey, 1995). In a sample of 5 and 6 year-old Australian children (Pedlow, Sanson, Prior, & Oberklaid, 1993), those who were difficult to soothe showed the same characteristics later in childhood. Clearly, research on this question has produced mixed results.

The attempt to show stability in temperament is hampered in at least two ways. First, measures of temperament appropriate for one age group (e.g. infants) are not necessarily appropriate for another (e.g. school-age children). For example, infants show their distress by crying while school-aged children are much more likely to demonstrate distress in a wide variety of ways. This means the temperament researcher needs to develop different measures for different age groups. And using different measures for different age groups means there is a possibility that somewhat different things are being measured, and thus it remains uncertain how much change is a function of development and how much is associated with measurement error. Second, a variety of developmental phenomena may interfere with attempts to show stability. For example, during the period between 1 and 3 months infants find it extremely difficult to disengage their attention from a location, and as a consequence tend to show a high degree of irritability. Measures of temperamental dimensions (such as *mood*) given during this time, when infants are naturally irritable, may not present an accurate picture of their core temperament, but rather, reflect a perfectly natural state in the infant's development (Johnson, Posner, & Rothbart, 1991). For these and other reasons, further research remains to be done on the question of whether temperament remains stable over time.

Goodness of fit

An important aspect of theories of temperament is the idea that temperament is rooted in our biology. As we have discussed above, behavioural genetic research suggests that temperament is not fixed but, rather, is modified by experience. Therefore, it is not the case that a difficult infant will necessarily remain a difficult infant, although temperament is often stable and resistant to change. A difficult temperament can be modified over time with the provision of appropriate care giving. Thomas and Chess (1986) introduced the concept goodness of fit to the study of temperament in order to explain how temperament can change. By goodness of fit, Thomas and Chess referred to the fit between a child's temperament and their parents' expectations and behaviours towards the child. For example, parents who had strong expectations for a quiet, sociable and happy child may have difficulty adapting to their difficult infant. They may lack the resources (e.g. coping skills, social support) to deal with a difficult infant and may behave towards their infant in ways that do little to promote change in the baby's behaviours. As a consequence, their behaviours may reinforce the undesirable aspects of that infant's temperament. In contrast, the same child, when born into a family where the parents are able to respond calmly, positively and warmly to the child's temperamental traits, will be more likely to have its temperament altered. As Thomas and Chess point out, with patience and care, parents can help their child to make the most of their traits.

To date, research on the goodness of fit hypothesis has been mixed. The idea itself seems intuitively appealing and provides a useful explanatory tool for developmentalists interested in temperament and behaviour, but researchers have found it a difficult hypothesis to confirm (e.g. Crockenberg, 1986). Further work remains to be done in this area.

Can you think of some reasons why the goodness of fit hypothesis might be difficult to confirm?

Temperament and adjustment

As we noted earlier, since the earliest research on temperament, psychologists have attempted to examine exactly how early temperament leads to later behavioural outcomes. That is, are the observed individual differences in *adjustment* among children predictable as a function of their temperamental classification? Studies of the developmental outcomes associated with temperamental classifications vary in their assessments of whether there are demonstrable relationships between early measures of temperament and later measures of children's level of adjustment. For example, in work based on the Dunedin Longitudinal Study in New Zealand, Caspi and Silva (1995) showed that children who were rated as inhibited at age 3 were more likely to score low on *aggression* and low on *social potency* (a measure of how effective one is in social situations) at 18. In a study of temperament and social behaviour in 6 and 7 year-olds, Rothbart, Ahadi and Hershey (1994) found that negative affectivity measured using parent reports was associated with particular social traits, such as aggressiveness. They also found that a small sub-sample of the children in this study who had been through a laboratory assessment of temperament as infants showed a similar pattern: infant measures of negative affectivity were associated with higher levels of aggressiveness and help-seeking at 6 to 7 years of age. Eisenberg et al. (1996) showed that school children identified by teachers' reports as showing low self-regulation were more likely to show behaviour problems such as acting out in class. In regard to the relationship between temperament and positive behaviours, Kochanska (1995) provided evidence that temperament was also related to children's moral development.

One review of temperament and social development indicates that there are a number of strong links between temperament traits and problem behaviours in a social setting (Sanson, Hemphill, & Smart, 2004). These include relationships between: negative reactivity (such as irritability and negative mood) and externalizing behaviour (such as acting out and aggression); inhibition or shyness and internalizing problems (such as depression and anxiety); and attention regulation and school functioning. In terms of more positive relationships, high regulation (being able to control attention and emotions) is related to sympathy and social skills in general (Eisenberg, 2000). As discussed in Chapter 1, very recent work suggests that the relationship between temperament and future outcomes may be more complex. According to proponents of the differential susceptibility hypothesis (Belsky & Pluess, 2009), difficult temperament features may be indicative of sensitivity, such that children with difficult temperaments early on are particularly susceptive to both negative and positive environmental influences, and those receiving positive influences, including warm, supportive parenting, may in fact go on to have better outcomes than children with easier temperaments receiving the same level of warmth and nurturing. Research into individual differences in temperament and future outcomes is still ongoing.

Summary

It should be clear to you that the study of emotional development takes in a wide variety of topics, from the study of changes in emotional expressions to understanding how we learn to control our emotions. Also current in the study of emotional development are the topics of attachment and temperament, constructs which emphasize the importance of our emotional nature to growth in other areas. You should recognize that the study of emotional development is intimately tied to developments in cognition and social understanding. In many ways, these overlaps between areas such as cognition and emotion are among the most interesting areas of study in child development.

Glossary

Attachment relationship is the emotional bond which is formed between an infant and a caregiver.

Emotion regulation refers to the processes by which an individual's emotional arousal is maintained within their capacity to cope.

Emotional display rules are the rules which dictate which emotions are appropriate to express in a given circumstance.

Functionalist theory of emotion stresses that emotions are adaptive processes which organize functioning in a variety of domains of human development.

Goodness of fit refers to the fit between a child's temperament and parents' expectations and behaviours towards the child.

Insecure attachments are attachment relationships which fail to provide the infant with a sense of confidence and security and comprise three subtypes: infants who show an **insecure-avoidant** attachment typically avoid contact with the mother during reunion; infants who show an **insecure-resistant** attachment show a pattern of alternately seeking and resisting contact with the caregiver; infants who show an **insecure-disorganized** attachment seem confused or disoriented during the reunion with the mother.

Internal working model is a mental representation of the infant's relationship with their primary caregiver.

Scripts are a form of mental representation which includes knowledge of what kinds of behaviours and emotions are appropriate to a particular event or situation.

Secure attachment Securely attached infants show only minimal disruption during separations from the caregiver and positive affect on reunion with the caregiver.

Secure base refers to the function of the caregiver as a refuge and source of comfort from which to explore their environment.

Self-conscious emotion is the term given to emotions such as guilt, shame, envy, embarrassment and pride.

Sensitivity refers to the parental behaviour that is consistent and responsive to the infant's needs.

Social referencing is the use of another's emotional expressions as a source of information, allowing the child to interpret the meaning of events and situations.

Socialization refers to the processes by which parents, siblings, peers and others work to shape children's behaviour.

Strange situation A situation for testing attachment wherein the infant is separated from the caregiver mother, exposed to a stranger, and then reunited with the mother in order to assess the quality of the attachment relationship.

Stranger distress is a fear of strangers shown by infants that first emerges around 7 to 9 months.

Temperament refers to constitutionally-based, individual differences in emotional, motor and attentional reactivity and self-regulation.

Theory of personal emotion is a coherent network of beliefs about one's own emotional processes.

TEST YOUR KNOWLEDGE

1. The basic emotions that infants enter the world being able to communicate and experience are which of the following?

   a) Fear and anger
   b) Disgust, happiness, fear, anger, sadness, interest, and surprise
   c) Disgust, happiness, fear, anger, sadness, interest, surprise and empathy
   d) All emotions are innate

2. The different kinds of attachment as measured by the strange situation are which of the following?

   a) Secure, avoidant, insecure and disorganized
   b) Secure and insecure
   c) Secure, avoidant, resistant and disorganized
   d) The strange situation does not measure attachment

3. At what age is social referencing first seen?

   a) 12 months
   b) 12 years

c) 6 months
d) The first few weeks of life

4. Which processes is temperament thought to consist of?

a) Reactivity and attachment
b) Self-regulation and emotion regulation
c) Slow-to-warm, easy and difficult
d) Reactivity and self-regulation

ANSWERS: 1–B, 2–C, 3–A, 4–D

Suggested Reading

Baumeister, R. F., & Vohs, K. D. (2004). *Handbook of Self-regulation: Research, theory, and applications*. New York: Guilford.

LaFreniere, P. J. (2000). *Emotional Development: A biosocial perspective*. Belmont, CA: Wadsworth.

Tronick, E. (2007). *The Neurobehavioral and Social Emotional Development of Infants and Children*. New York: Norton.

Want to learn more? For links to online resources relevant to this chapter, interactive quizzes and much more, visit the companion website at
https://edge.sagepub.com/keenan3e/

Social Development

Chapter Outline

LEARNING AIMS

At the end of this chapter you should:

- be familiar with the major theoretical contributions to the study of socialization, including group socialization theory
- understand the role of play in social development, the functions associated with play and the different types of play
- be able to describe the developmental course of peer interaction and define key concepts such as *dominance hierarchies*, *cliques* and *crowds*
- understand the importance of peer acceptance for social development and the consequences of low peer status, and describe the various categories of peer acceptance based on *sociometric techniques*
- be familiar with the processes of friendship formation and the development of conceptions of friendship across childhood
- be able to define *theory of mind* and describe the course of theory-of-mind development
- development of a sense of self and explain the importance of the *rouge test*
- understand Selman's model of the development of perspective taking

Introduction

The study of social development has a rich history within developmental psychology. Developmental research in the 1920s and 1930s focused heavily on children's groups as important agents of socialization, and researchers developed a number of new and influential methodologies by which to study children's social development. This early work focused largely on individual differences in sociability, assertiveness, aggression, leadership, group dynamics, peer acceptance, and the correlates of individual differences in social skills (Rubin & Coplan, 1992). The focus on children was put aside briefly during World War II but was more permanently ousted during the cognitive revolution and the discovery of Piaget in the United States. Piagetian theory characterized young children as *egocentric*, and thus as incapable of understanding others until middle childhood, a characterization which effectively put a halt to most of the research in social development. However, a growing recognition of the key role of social development to children's cognitive achievements has forced a reconsideration of the importance of studying children's social development. For example, research has shown that one of the best predictors of academic failure is rejection by the peer group. In addition to the relationship between social and cognitive development, there is a growing list of the important functions which friendship and peer relations serve in children's development. In the following chapter we will examine these and other issues.

Theories of Social Development

A number of theories have been used to understand the typical course of social development and, more specifically, the importance of friendships in social development. Piaget (1932) argued that children's relationships with adults were qualitatively different from their relationships with other children. He believed that children's relations with adults were structured along what we could call a **vertical dimension**. That is, relations with adults are asymmetrical and fall along a vertical dimension of power assertion and dominance, with children falling below adults. In contrast, children's relationships with other children are somewhat more balanced and egalitarian, and thus are structured on a more **horizontal** plane. Piaget believed it was on this plane, where children's relationships are more or less equal, that they could explore conflicting ideas and perspectives and learn to generate compromises. Piaget's ideas have influenced many researchers interested in social development (Rubin & Coplan, 1992).

Another early theorist who influenced many current researchers was Harry Stack Sullivan (1953). Sullivan emphasized the role of friendships in children's development and the special functions which friendship served for the child. In his view, children were initially insensitive to peers but eventually move towards entering into complex, reciprocal relationships with those peers. He also held that children's early relationships helped to shape their personality and the later relationships they would go on to form in adolescence and adulthood.

Ethological theories have also proven important to current research within the domain of social development. These are concerned with the biological and evolutionary bases of behaviour. An important aspect of ethological theory for the study of social development is the methodologies developed by ethologists for the observation of animal behaviour. The methods employed by ethologists, such as naturalistic observation, are key elements in the study of social development. Ethological theorists argue that all behaviours are 'limited by the biological constraints related to their adaptive evolutionary function' (Rubin, Bukowski, & Parker, 1998: 632). According to Tinbergen (1951), when an ethologist observes a particular behaviour of interest they must ask: (1) Why did the individual demonstrate the behaviour at that particular point in time?; (2) How did the individual produce the behaviour?; and (3) What is the function or survival value of the behaviour? Asking such questions focuses the developmentalist on how we learn a behaviour, the developmental course of the behaviour, what biological constraints guide its emergence, and its adaptive significance.

Social learning theorists have also been concerned with peer relations, arguing that children learn about their social world and how to behave within it through their interactions with peers (Bandura & Walters, 1963). This learning can take place either *directly*, through children teaching one another concepts and behaviours, or it can take place *indirectly*, through the child's observation of their peers' behaviours. From a social learning perspective, children are viewed as agents of behavioural control who positively reinforce and punish those behaviours which they regard as appropriate or inappropriate. Social learning theories have been very influential in the study of peer relationships and children's social behaviours (Hartup, 1983).

Research into children's learning of social behaviour has shown a developmental progression in how children copy the actions of those around them to achieve similar outcomes. In one study, children at 12, 18 and 24 months of age observed a model opening a series of boxes to obtain a desirable toy (Nielson, 2006). The younger infants tended not to copy the model's specific actions, and opened the boxes any way they could. In contrast, the older children copied the model's object use, and were especially inclined to do so when the model was behaving sociably. The findings show that social learning takes place, but a child's receptiveness to learning depends on the communicative cues of a model, and the child's age. Thus, children become increasingly receptive to adopting the specific 'rules' of behaviour. It has been argued by social learning theorists that acquiring the conventions and rules of a culture involves a similar kind of social learning, by children observing the way that other people in their lives interact with objects (Tomasello, 1999). Studying how children learn to use objects has therefore been argued as providing leading cues in understanding how they learn about culture.

A child's cultural context is important in understanding socialization. Not only are children socialized to conform to the rules of their society, but a child's culture also shapes their relationships with others. Peer interactions in western countries, which emphasize individualism and independence are quite different from peer interactions in collectivist societies which value cooperation and group harmony. For example, children in India tend to play quite different games involving high levels of cooperation and uniformity compared to children in western nations (Roopnarine, Johnson, & Hooper, 1994). In cultures where children assume responsibility and chores early, the kind of make-believe and sociodramatic play that you might see in preschools in the USA or Britain is rare; instead, children are encouraged to watch and learn the work of adults around them. Even though these children spend little time playing, they are nevertheless socially competent (Gaskins, 2000). Children appear to learn the kind of social skills that are consistent with the culture in which they live.

One relatively recent contribution to theory has been **group socialization theory**, proposed by Judith Harris (1998). In this theory, children are viewed as learning largely from groups of their peers, rather than from their parents. According to Harris, children's interactions with the larger peer culture are what explain their socialization. One-on-one interactions with a parent, teacher or friend are not considered to have lasting influences into adulthood and are thought to be situation-specific. That is, what a child learns at home from a parent does not generalize to their life outside the home. Parents may be strong socialization models for infants (whose life for the time being is essentially the parent), but *group* socialization – or non-shared environmental factors – that the child encounters away from parents has lasting effects on personality and behaviour. In support for her theory, Harris calls on the kind of research we outlined in the previous chapter on the influence of non-shared environmental factors. Group socialization theory is not without its critics (e.g. Vandell, 2000), who stress that a parent's role is important in socialization, and that it is a mistake to relegate a parent's role to a shared environment influence as even children from within the same family may receive quite different parenting (hence, it can be considered a non-shared influence).

It is likely that socialization results from a number of forces, including peers and family members. Much of the following chapter examines the influential role of peers in socialization. As you will see, Harris is astute in recognizing the significance of children's peer groups. However, the research suggests that children first develop their social skills with parents, such as when they provide playmates for children, monitor the child's interactions, use parenting strategies, and even play with the child (Ladd & Pettit, 2002). Siblings also influence social development. Older siblings, in particular, often play a role in teaching younger brothers or sisters the rules of socialization. Older siblings can provide negative influences,

Image 11A Group socialization theory stresses that children's interactions with the larger peer culture are primary socialization agents for social development

by encouraging drug use and association with delinquent peers (Garcia et al., 2000), or provide positive, prosocial and responsible role models. As we will explore in Research Example 11.1, a child's birth order or placement in the family can also have an impact on how the child comes to see themselves.

Research Example 11.1

Siblings as Socialization

Psychologists and the general public have long been fascinated with the notion that birth order affects personality. First-borns are traditionally thought to be the most responsible and high-achieving children in families, while younger children are considered more sociable and risk taking. While some observations confirm these stereotypes, such that first-borns are overrepresented in politics and science (Hudson, 1990), the research is not always consistent and most often studies merely note correlations. Many studies find differences on certain personality traits, such as conscientiousness (with elder children scoring higher), but birth order differences in other personality dimensions, such as extraversion, are contentious. It is

(Continued)

thought that first-borns tend to be bigger and stronger than their younger siblings, which results in first-borns becoming more assertive, but also more eager to please adults to ensure they receive first dibs on parental resources. In contrast, younger siblings are likely to become agreeable and sociable to prevent any threatening confrontations with the eldest child in the family (Sulloway, 2001). However, research exploring these ideas has thus far been mixed.

A recent study attempted to get around the problems of earlier studies, which have traditionally used between-family designs, examining siblings of different birth orders in different families. This study, conducted with undergraduate and graduate students from a university in London, examined siblings born within the same family, thus comparing a first-born with a younger sibling, rather than a younger sibling from another family (Beck, Burnet, & Vosper, 2006). The researchers did indeed find that birth-order affected social development. First-borns rated themselves as more dominant than younger siblings, while later-borns were rated as more sociable. It seems that how a child's parent and siblings relate to them early on has a lasting effect on personality and socialization. However, it is worth noting that such studies generally ask about personality in the context of the family, and it is possible that these birth-order tendencies do not extend to other situations. Thus, later-born children may be quite sociable in comparison to their older sibling within their family, yet have an average social life at work.

Question: How would you go about designing the ideal study (within ethical boundaries) to test the effects of birth-order on personality and sociability?

Types of Play and Their Functions

On the basis of an observational study of preschool children during their play periods, Parten (1932) observed six different types of play that preschoolers engaged in. She also measured the frequency of each type of play and how that frequency changed as a function of age. Parten argued that the different types of play she observed involved differing levels of complexity. In the following, we begin with the most complex form of play and work our way downwards. *Cooperative play* was the most complex form of play Parten observed. Cooperative play includes behaviours like playing formal games, social pretend play where children take on pretend roles, and constructive play, where children build things together, such as models out of Lego blocks. Parten found the cooperative play was rare before age 3. *Associative play* occurs when children talk to one another and share the same materials in their play, but do not take on different roles within the same imaginary context or work towards completing a joint project. Associative play was found to be the most common form of play among 4 year-old children. *Parallel play* occurs when children play *beside* other children rather than *with* other children, using the same toys and materials but not interacting. Parallel play was the most common form of play observed among 2 year-olds and was almost as common among 4 year-olds as associative play (Parten, 1932). Parten also defined three categories which are non-social and reflect an absence of play. *Onlooker behaviour* occurs when the child is watching other children play but is not joining in. *Unoccupied play* occurs when the child does not play with anything but simply watches whatever interests them. *Solitary play* is when children play by themselves in a way that is different from those around them. Subsequent research has provided additional evidence for the validity of these categories, although researchers typically draw quite different conclusions from those of Parten (Hartup, 1983; Rubin, Fein, & Vandenburg, 1983). Whereas Parten's focus on play was on the level of children's *social interactions*, modern researchers have also examined the *cognitive* complexity of children's play (Piaget, 1962). Her categories do not capture all of the variations in children's play, but her data are important in demonstrating significant changes in the nature of peer interactions through the preschool years.

While Parten's research focused on the levels of social interaction in children's play, more recent research has focused on the different *types* of play in which children engage, the emergence of these types of play and how they might contribute to development. There are many different types of play that can be identified, but the areas that have been the focus of most research include *physical* or *locomotor play*, *rough and tumble play*, *play with objects*, *pretend play* and *sociodramatic play*. Physical play consists of whole and part body movements that are performed by infants and children because they are enjoyable in themselves. Infants spend much of their time engaged in this type of play and much play in the early years consists of physical activity, with the incidence of such play behaviours eventually declining with increasing

Table 11.1 Types of play

Play Type	Description
Cooperative play	Cooperative play includes behaviours like playing formal games, social pretend play (where children take on pretend roles), and constructive play (where children build things together, such as block models). Cooperative play is rare before age 3.
Associative play	Associative play occurs when children talk to one another and share the same materials in their play, but do not take on different roles within the same imaginary context or work towards completing a joint project.
Parallel play	Parallel play occurs when children play *beside* other children rather than *with* other children. They use the same toys and materials but do not interact with each other.
Onlooker	Onlooker behaviour occurs when a child watches other children play but does not join in.
Unoccupied play	Unoccupied play occurs when the child does not play with anything but simply watches other interactions, events and objects that are of interest.
Solitary play	Solitary play is when children play by themselves in a way which is noticeably different from those around them.

age (Pellegrini, 2011). Rough and tumble play becomes common during the school years and consists of behaviours such as play fighting and chasing. Smiles and laughter indicate the non-hostile nature of such activities, although very occasionally play fights can develop into real fights, usually as a result of temperamentally aggressive children misinterpreting the signals or as a result of 'mistakes' in which a child gets hurt (Smith, 1997). Play with objects appears from around the age of 5 months and seems to follow a distinct course of development (Hughes, 2010). Initially infants will explore objects by feeling them or putting them in their mouths. Gradually, however, they become more interested in what can be done with the objects, such as banging or shaking them to make noise. Toddlers start to play with two or more objects at the same time and also come to the realization that objects have specific uses, such as throwing a ball or stacking blocks. Eventually toddlers begin incorporating objects in pretend play, such as using a cloth as a 'blanket' for a doll. Pretend play appears around 12 to 15 months (Fein, 1981) and seems to develop in three sequences (Hughes, 2010). First, there is *decentration*, in which the child draws others into pretend activities, and these can include parents but also objects such as stuffed toys and dolls. This is followed by *decontextualisation*, in which the child can use one object to represent another, such as using a stick as a sword. Initially children rely on real objects or realistic substitutes (such as using a cloth as a blanket) but by age 3, they can also use objects removed from reality (such as pretending a wooden block is a cake and pretending to 'eat' it). Finally, there is *integration*, which refers to individual acts of pretend play becoming 'joined up' into patterns of connected activities (such as making a doll run, climb up a tower of blocks and jump off). *Sociodramatic* play refers to pretend play with other people and this also appears around 12 months of age and increases markedly in frequency during the preschool and school years (Rubin, Fein, & Vandenburg, 1983).

A wide variety of functions have been attributed to play (e.g. Hughes, 2010; Smith, 2010). Classical theories of play saw it as a means of *exercising skills* that will be required later in life. In essence, play is an instinctive way of acquiring and rehearsing future skills. Many aspects of children's play, such as the rough and tumble play of middle childhood, resemble the play of our primate ancestors, which suggests that children practise skills which are adaptive for survival (Biben & Suomi, 1993). Other theories of play focus instead on the *content* of play. Piagetian theorists believe that the social interactions which occur within the context of play are essential for driving cognitive development. Vygotskian theorists suggest that play builds mental structures through the child's use of tools acquired from the culture around them, such as language and number. For example, a child playing at being a shopkeeper utilizes several concepts, such as buying and selling and the role of money in commercial transactions. Play also allows children to explore their social world by adopting various roles and interaction patterns, thereby promoting social development. In some theories, play promotes the development of social competence (Haight & Miller, 1993). Social play seems to be especially prominent in animals that show a great deal of behavioural plasticity, including humans, suggesting that play serves an important higher-level function, likely providing a survival advantage (Aamodt & Wang, 2011).

A number of areas of children's development seem to benefit from the opportunity to play, including problem solving, creativity, theory of mind and self-control (which will be discussed further in the next chapter). Object play has been related to skills in problem solving. A number of experiments have been carried out using a *lure retrieval* procedure (see Smith, 2010 and Smith and Simon, 1984 for a review of such studies). In this type of study, children are presented with a set of sticks which can be joined up to form a rake which can then be used to retrieve an out-of-reach toy. Such experiments have typically compared the performance of children who were allowed to play with the sticks beforehand against that of children who observed an experimenter join the sticks together or children who neither played with nor observed the use of the sticks. In most of these studies, children allowed to play with the sticks solved the problem more quickly and were more persistent in their efforts compared to the observation and no treatment groups. Another set of studies has linked object play to creativity. In these studies of 'associative fluency', children have been presented with an everyday object and asked to suggest as many uses as possible (standard or non-standard) for that object. The typical finding here is that children allowed to play with the object beforehand are able to suggest more non-standard uses for the object than those exposed to non-play experiences with the objects (Smith, 2010; Smith & Simon, 1984). Sociodramatic play has been linked to the development of theory of

Image 11B Physical play can be immensely enjoyable to children, and is associated with benefits such as decreased stress hormones like cortisol

mind. For example, in an Australian study reported by Dockett (1998), 4 year-old children were split into two groups – one received sociodramatic play training for three weeks, the other received the regular curriculum. The play training group showed significant improvement, relative to the control group, on measures of group pretence and theory of mind. As discussed in the coming chapter, play therapy has also been used to improve self-control and social functioning (Blair & Diamond, 2008). An additional benefit is that play may serve a necessary stress release function. Although yet to be replicated in humans, young squirrel monkeys who engage in high amounts of play have less circulating stress hormones (Biben, 1999), possibly indicating that play reduces stress.

Play is valued highly by professionals who work with children and is regarded by many as essential for healthy development. This can be seen in the Early Years educational curricula in many countries, which emphasize the use of play as a means of facilitating learning in the classroom. There are also many occupations that use play in everyday work with children, such as playworkers, hospital play specialists and occupational therapists. The right of children to play is also enshrined in the United Nations Convention on the Rights of the Child, with Article 31 stating that 'every child has the right to relax, play and take part in a wide range of cultural and artistic activities' (UNICEF UK, 2013: 1). The research evidence cited in the previous paragraph would perhaps be seen as providing a justification for these views. However, one leading play researcher, Peter Smith, has cautioned against adopting what he refers to as the **play ethos** (Smith, 2010), the viewpoint that play is *essential* for all aspects of development. Even though there are many research studies that have linked play to positive developmental outcomes, there are often limitations with these studies. For example, Smith (2010) and Smith and Simon (1984) have highlighted various methodological flaws in experimental studies using the lure retrieval and associative fluency approaches, including experimenter effects, a lack of double-blind procedures and suitable control groups, and general concerns about the ability of such brief experimental studies to capture the real-life benefits of play. In some of these studies, it has been found that children also perform effectively in non-play conditions such as observation and structured training. There are also many correlational studies linking levels of play with other developmental outcomes, such as theory of mind performance, but Smith (2010) has noted that often the correlations obtained in these studies, while statistically significant, are still quite modest. Smith (2010) argues that the play ethos is not really based on the research evidence but instead can be seen as a well-intentioned reaction to the materialistic and achievement-oriented culture that is prevalent in western society, and fears that opportunities for children to play are threatened by developments such as school league tables and concerns over the costs of providing and maintaining play areas for children. However, Smith argues that play should not be seen as *essential* but *useful* for development. It is an enjoyable and harmless activity for children that should be valued in its own right, and even though flaws and limitations can be identified in the experimental literature on play and development, he argues that overall 'play comes out well on the balance sheet' (Smith, 2010: 216), with children subjected to play experiences generally performing as well or better than children subjected to other experiences, such as observation and structured training. However, he also points out that while play is useful, children benefit from other types of experiences, such as observation, direct instruction and structured training. He argues that approaches blending play with these other types of experiences are best for promoting development.

The Developmental Course of Peer Interaction

Infancy (birth to 1 year)

Early researchers who examined social interaction in infancy regarded infants as having some significant 'social shortcomings' (Rubin, Bukowski, & Parker, 1998: 633). Early researchers (Bühler, 1935) held that until about 6 months old an infant was unaware of the presence of another infant. While it is clear that infants do have some significant social limitations, it is also true that careful and detailed observation of infants reveals that they do show an interest

Table 11.2 Milestones in children's social development

Age	Milestone
Birth to 6 months	By 6 months of age, infants are aware of and take an interest in other infants.
	Increase in rates of vocalization and smiling around peers.
6 to 12 months	Infants show a clear interest in their peers.
	Displays emotional expressions to peers and responds to peers in a contingent fashion.
12 to 24 months	Mainly engages in *parallel play*.
	Social interactions increase in length and complexity and involve the use of language.
	Development of *self-understanding* around 18 months, as evidenced by success on the *rouge test*.
	Understanding of the rules of social exchange.
	First evidence of *prosocial behaviours* such as *empathy*.
	Child operates according to a *desire* psychology.
3 years	Begins to engage in *cooperative* play.
	Child operates according to a *belief-desire psychology*.
	Dominance hierarchies observed in children's peer groups.
4 years	Most commonly observed in *associative play*.
	Has acquired a *representational theory of mind* indicated by performance on the *false belief task*.
	Conflict is observed in children's relationships.
6 years	Sharp increase in time spent with peers. Peer groups increase in size. Peer interactions take place in a wider range of settings and are less under the control of adults.
	The goal of friendships is typically defined by *shared interests* and the maintenance of coordinated and successful play.
	Child can understand *second-order mental states*.
7 to 9 years	The goal of friendships is gaining peer *acceptance*.
Early adolescence	Friendships are centred on *intimacy* and *self-disclosure*.
	Peer groups become organized around *cliques* and *crowds*.
	First appearance of *adolescent egocentrism*.
Late adolescence	Friends are increasingly seen as a source of emotional and social support.
	Adolescent egocentrism declines.

in social exchanges with other infants. At 2 months old, infants will gaze at one another (Rubin et al., 1998). At 6 months old infants are aware of and take an interest in other infants (Rubin & Coplan, 1992), indicated by the increased rates of smiling, vocalizations and gaze in the presence of other infants. By their ninth month, infants are showing a clear interest in peers, challenging the widespread belief that infants are not social. By the end of their first year, infants have consolidated several important behaviours: they intentionally display smiles, frowns and other gestures to their interaction partners, they attend carefully to their play partners' behaviours, and they respond in a contingent fashion to their interaction partners' behaviours. Of course, infants' interactions are very rudimentary and limited by their cognitive, motoric and linguistic capabilities. However, their interactions with significant adults play a role in how young children relate to one another: parents and other adults who interact sensitively with children pave the way for later skills with other children (Trevarthen, 2003).

 Consider the various ways in which children's early interactions with parents might facilitate the development of skills that will allow them to interact successfully with other children. In answering this question, you might also consider some of the findings covered in Chapter 9 (on the development of language and communication) and Chapter 10 (on emotional development)

Early childhood (2 to 5 years)

By the second year of life, new forms of social interactions are made possible by an infant's increased locomotor and physical abilities as well as by a toddler's developing cognitive and language skills. Using words to communicate with an interaction partner opens up a whole new dimension for interacting. Social interactions become more complex, more reciprocal, and the interactive sequences are sustained over significantly longer periods of time than in infancy (Ross & Conant, 1992).

Rubin and Coplan (1992) note that many researchers believe that there also seems to be an elementary understanding of the rules of social exchange demonstrated during the second year, mainly in the form of the games toddlers play. Toddlers show an understanding of turn taking and tend to coordinate their play with a partner. They imitate behaviours displayed by others and recognize when others are imitating their behaviours (Eckerman, 1993). The emergence of pretend play in individual children is seen in the second year but by their third year, young children are much more likely to share in pretend play. Moreover, during that third year the first signs of prosocial behaviour, such as sharing and helping, emerge (Radke-Yarrow, Zahn-Waxler, & Chapman, 1983). Children share symbolic meanings with each other and assign imaginary roles in their pretend play (e.g. Astington & Jenkins, 1995; Howes, 1987). These developments reflect the preschooler's evolving ability to take another's perspective, reflecting what is termed their theory of mind (Astington, 1994; Wellman, 1990). In early childhood the emergence of conflict is noted (Rubin et al., 1998). Interestingly, sociable toddlers are the most likely children to enter into conflicts. Finally, toddlers develop relationships, that is, reciprocal relations with another child over a succession of encounters (essentially, a shared history of interactions) which involve both positive and negative exchanges. In the early years, children's relationships do not equal true friendships, although by the end of the early childhood period, children do go on to form true friendships.

Also of interest to social development is the emergence of social dominance hierarchies during the preschool years (Rubin & Coplan, 1992). **Dominance hierarchies** are rankings of individuals in terms of their dominance (i.e. their *toughness* and *assertiveness*) within the group. Although there is some evidence for the emergence of pecking orders in groups of toddlers, with girls often maintaining a dominant position over boys (Hawley & Little, 1999), dominance hierarchies become more fully formed after the age of 3, with boys typically asserting themselves more. Research examining dominance hierarchies in preschoolers has consistently revealed that more dominant children are the winners of conflicts and less dominant children tend to lose conflicts (e.g. Strayer & Strayer, 1976). Children who are dominant are also more likely to elicit conforming behaviours in lower-status children (Rubin, Wojslawowicz, Rose-Krasnor, Booth-LaForce, & Burgess, 2006). However, the preschool child is not aware of these dominance relations, often nominating themself as the most dominant individual. Dominance hierarchies can serve a number of different functions. They can reduce aggression within groups since high-ranking children tend to keep the other members of the group in line. Research has found that aggression is rare in groups with established hierarchies (Hawley & Little, 1999). Hierarchies also determine the allocation of resources and provide tasks for different members of the group. Thus, in a preschool-aged group, you may see a 'king' or 'queen' ruling over their worker bees.

In summary, by the end of the early childhood period, children have learned skills which comprise the ability to coordinate their play with that of another, to imitate and recognize that they are being imitated, and to take turns. However, it is also important to note that in the early childhood years children's opportunities for social participation are largely controlled by their parents. Their parents determine who they will see, when they will see them, what kinds of friends they will have, and so on. In addition, various aspects of a child's social ecology will control the formation of peer relationships: for example, the nature of the child's community (e.g. rural versus urban, violent versus safe), religious participation and ethnic background can have a marked effect on the kinds of opportunities for social participation that children are exposed to.

Middle to late childhood (6 to 12 years)

According to their review of the social development literature, Rubin et al. (1998) suggest that a simple indication of the changing nature of children's social interactions can be found in examining *who* is involved in children's interactions. The developmental trend is towards increasing contact with peers as children age. For 2 year-olds, approximately 10% of the time spent in social interactions is with peers whereas in middle childhood this figure rises dramatically to around 30%. In addition, the preference for interacting with peers rises sharply (Ellis, Rogoff, & Cromer, 1981). Children's peer groups become larger and more diverse as children are brought into contact with new groups of peers. In addition, children's groups become less supervised. Much of this change is a function of the onset of formal schooling and the other group activities (e.g. sports, band and cultural activities) that children enter into. Thus, the settings for their social interactions change from the home and preschool settings to reflect a wider variety of locations and institutions. Verbal aggression becomes more prominent in middle and late childhood, replacing earlier forms of physical aggression, and play tends to take the form of games with rules. Social dominance hierarchies also tend to become more stable in middle childhood (Strayer & Strayer, 1976) and most children are able to agree on which individuals in a group are dominant.

Adolescence (12 to 18 years)

Peer relationships in adolescence continue the trend towards increased time spent with peers. As an adolescent's relationships with family are restructured, peer relationships multiply and become more intense as new demands and social expectations are made apparent to the adolescent by their peer group. While the overall number of friends decreases in adolescence, peer relationships often surpass parents as the adolescent's primary sources of social support (Adler & Furman, 1988). Friendships take on new significance in adolescence and are centred on *intimacy* and *self-disclosure* (Buhrmester, 1996; Parker & Gottman, 1989). In addition, sexuality adds a new dimension to the adolescent's social life as dating begins and new possibilities for intimacy develop.

Adolescent social life is organized around two primary social structures, the clique and the crowd (Dunphy, 1963). **Cliques** are close-knit groups of friends ranging in size from three to nine people who are held together by mutual acceptance and common interests. Cliques generally contain same-sex members, although initially same-sex cliques may build strong ties to opposite-sex cliques, affording new types of social activity (Dunphy, 1963). Eventually, towards the end of adolescence, these cliques dissolve into smaller, more tightly knit groups when members 'pair off' in dating relationships. Clique membership comprises an important part of adolescents' psychological wellbeing. Dunphy formulated his ideas regarding crowds and cliques based on observations of adolescent cliques conducted in Sydney, Australia. Research has found that membership of a clique enhances children's psychological wellbeing and adaptive coping abilities (Rubin et al., 2006). This is likely due to the protective qualities of social acceptance, which tends to preclude loneliness.

Another important social structure for adolescents is **crowds**. These are groups of adolescents who organize on the basis of reputation, are comprised of similarly stereotyped individuals, and are defined on the basis of the attitudes held by the members (Rubin et al., 1993). Examples of the sorts of groups pointed to as crowds by adolescents include *jocks*, *punks*, *brains* and *druggies*. Crowds are less cohesive than cliques but have the function of bringing together a more extended set of adolescents. Initially adolescents describe the members of crowds in terms of their behaviours, but through adolescence there is a shift to describing crowds in terms of the dispositions and values of their members. These changes in the perception of crowds seem to reflect the importance of crowds in adolescents' social lives. Crowds have the function of exposing the adolescent to a wider range of activities, such as parties and other social functions, and serve to introduce members of same-sex cliques into an environment where they can meet members of opposite-sex cliques (Dunphy, 1963).

Determinants of Peer Acceptance

Children's social skills are important determinants of their acceptance by peers. Children's judgements of their peers, however, are not simply made on the basis of social skills and other personal characteristics but on the basis of less rational qualities over which children themselves have very little control. One such surface characteristic on which children base their impressions of others is *names*. Names are an important factor in children's judgements about each other. Children with unfamiliar names are likely to be poorly regarded by their peers (Rubin et al., 1999). Of course, the familiarity of names varies from culture to culture and across time, so it is difficult to give examples here that are universally unfamiliar to children. Yet it is the case that unfamiliar names will often generate an adverse response from children, especially if there are other factors that set a child apart from their peers.

Another factor on which children base their judgements of the acceptability of peers is *physical attractiveness* or beauty. Beauty may only be skin deep; however, for children who are judged to be physically attractive, the benefits of their beauty are many. Both children and adults are likely to attribute more desirable characteristics to attractive people than to unattractive people (Langlois, 1985). Children who are viewed as less physically attractive are judged to be aggressive, antisocial and mean, while children viewed as physically attractive are seen as independent, pleasant, honest, fearless and friendly. Physical attractiveness seems to be more important to girls' popularity than it is to boys' popularity (Vaughn & Langlois, 1983). Langlois and Downs (1979) examined the social behaviour of 3 year-old and 5 year-old children judged to be attractive and unattractive. Whereas there were no differences in the social behaviour of the 3 year-olds, unattractive 5 year-olds were more likely to aggress against other children. The authors interpreted the results to suggest that the age trend in the data, that is, the difference between the two groups, revealed the existence of a self-fulfilling prophecy at work. The 5 year-olds' aggressive behaviour may be a result of peers' and adults' negative perceptions of them; their bad behaviour is caused, in part, by the characteristics that are attributed to them and the expectations that others hold for them.

Children's perceptions of physical attractiveness also extend to body size; overweight children are rated as less friendly, more aggressive and less liked than their thinner counterparts. What's more, these negative attitudes begin very early. One study examining the attitudes of preschool children towards body size found that children as young as 3 years of age expressed the opinion that 'fat is bad' (Cramer & Steinwert, 1998). Stigmatization of a larger body size was prevalent across genders and children who were themselves overweight demonstrated the strongest negative attitudes towards story characters who were overweight. Negative attitudes towards obesity continue through childhood and adulthood. As a result, obese children often face a gamut of psychological and social problems, including social isolation (Strauss & Pollack, 2003).

Two other factors are important determinants of peer acceptance, *sex* and *age*. Children generally prefer to play with peers who are the same sex as they are. This is especially evident after age 7. Before this time, children will play with both boys and girls, although they tend to prefer playing with same-sex partners. However, the tendency to choose same-sex partners increases throughout the school years (Maccoby, 1990). Maccoby and Jacklin (1987) suggest that one reason for the preference for same-sex play has to do with personality differences between boys and girls. Boys tend to be more aggressive, having higher activity levels and engaging in more rough and tumble play (Humphreys & Smith, 1987). With the onset of adolescence, more cross-sex mixing occurs. Age may also be an important factor in who children choose to play with, although across cultures there are wide differences in this trend. The majority of children in western cultures spend most of their time playing with children who are the same age as they are (Ellis et al., 1981), while in many other cultures, older children will play with children much younger than they are. You may have noticed that there is a commonality to many of these factors, namely, *similarity*. On the whole, we tend to accept and like people who are similar to us. Berndt (1988) argues that the similarity of another person to themselves is the key factor behind many of children's judgements.

Peer status

Adults, such as coaches or teachers, who are familiar with a group of children, generally have good insights into issues such as which children are well liked by their peers or which children are popular. It may surprise you to learn that even very young children have a good understanding of which children in a group are popular and which children are unpopular. Researchers interested in social development have been able to exploit this knowledge using **sociometric techniques**. These involve asking children to nominate a specific number of their peers who fit some criterion. For example, *name three classmates who you really like*. The number of times that children are nominated by other classmates can give the researcher a picture of the relative status of an individual within the group. Sociometric nominations have a number of strengths. First, peers are likely to have information about other children that adults are simply unable to access. Second, peers tend to have a broader range of experiences with other children in a group. Third, peer nominations and ratings represent a group perspective which is not reliant on the ratings of a single source, such as a teacher.

The use of sociometric nominations allows a researcher to classify children into one of a number of sociometric categories. One such system described by Rubin and Coplan (1992) and which is popular among researchers uses five categories. *Popular* children are children who are rated highly on a dimension of *most liked* and rated low on a dimension of *least liked*. Popular children are good at *initiating* new relationships and at *maintaining* the relationships they have built. They tend to be viewed as socially competent. In general, their status within the groups is clear-cut. *Controversial* children are those individuals who are rated high on *most liked* and high on *least liked*; simply put, controversial children are both liked and disliked. *Neglected* children are children who score low on *liked most* and low on *liked least*. Neglected children are friendless children but, importantly, are not usually actively disliked. *Average* children fit somewhere in the middle, receiving some positive and some negative evaluations; they are not as popular as popular children and not as disliked as neglected children. *Rejected* children score low on *liked most* and high on *liked least* and tend to cluster into two subcategories (French, 1988, 1990). *Aggressive rejected* children have high levels of behaviour problems, poor self-control and show high levels of aggression. *Nonaggressive rejected* children are rejected by their peers for different reasons from those for aggressive rejected children, in large part because they are socially unskilled, withdrawn and socially anxious. Extremely anxious withdrawn children are noted by their peers as socially deviant and are rejected on these grounds. Rejected children report feeling lonelier and more isolated than their popular peers (Asher, Parkhurst, Hymel, & Williams, 1990).

A number of researchers have shown that the categorizations *popular* and *rejected* are extremely stable over time. Popular and rejected children tend to remain popular or rejected children (Coie & Dodge, 1983). When changes do occur they tend to be to closely related categories: popular children may become average children but only rarely do popular children become rejected (Rubin & Coplan, 1992).

Recently, a new way of measuring popularity has emerged within the field of sociometric status. Now, psychologists make a distinction between sociometric popularity (how much students are liked, and not disliked, by classmates) and *perceived popularity*, a measure of social visibility, where children are asked not about who they like, but who they think is the most popular with classmates. There is some overlap between the measures, although perceived popularity often picks up other aspects of social interaction that sociometric popularity does not, such as social dominance, leaderships and sometimes aggression in high-status cliques (Cillessen & Mayeux, 2004).

Consequences of low peer status

What are the consequences of being unpopular or disliked by one's peers? Many of the consequences that researchers have focused on are developmental outcomes related to academic matters, such as academic difficulties, truancy and dropout (Rubin & Coplan, 1992). This connection is not particularly surprising. Clearly, school is less pleasant when a child has serious troubles with their peers, perhaps even becoming the target of their hostility. Outcomes such as truancy may seem adaptive when faced with such difficulties. In one study by Wentzel and Asher (1995), children rated as *rejected* by their peers were shown to be perceived by teachers and peers as weak students. *Rejected aggressive* children (relative to *average* children and *rejected withdrawn* children) showed low interest in school and were viewed by their teachers as noncompliant, troublesome and disruptive. Parker and Asher (1987) reported that children who were unaccepted by their peers were significantly more likely than their accepted peers to drop out of school. Finally, Kupersmidt and Coie (1990) reported that children identified as *rejected* were twice as likely as the rest of the sample to engage in delinquent acts in adolescence.

Unpopular children also tend to feel social dissatisfaction and loneliness as a consequence of their lack of peer acceptance. Rejected children are especially likely to feel lonely, with nonaggressive rejected children feeling the loneliest of all (Parkhurst & Asher, 1992).

Image 11B   Children rejected by their peers are more likely to experience persistent loneliness and school difficulties than accepted peers, highlighting the importance of reducing bullying in schools

© SpeedKingz/Shutterstock

In a study of the consequences of peer rejection in Australian schoolchildren, Renshaw and Brown (1993) followed groups of third and sixth grade children for one year. They found that children who moved towards being less accepted by their peers were more likely to have lost friends and to report that they were poor at developing friendships. In general, nonaggressive rejected children feel more poorly about their own social competence and their difficulties with social skills and peer relationships (Rubin, 1985).

As we have just seen, peer rejection is associated with a variety of adverse outcomes. However, we have also seen that some children are classified as 'neglected'. What would you expect to be the outcomes associated with this peer status? Would you expect these to be worse, better or similar to those for rejected children?

Some recent evidence suggests that for children identified as rejected by their peers, even one quality friendship can act as a buffer against the negative effects of their social status (Parker & Asher, 1993). This finding suggests that friendship quality is an important variable to consider when measuring children's social networks. Interestingly, other research has suggested the opposite. Studies by Hoza, Molina, Bukowski and Sippola (1995) and Kupersmidt, Burchinal and Patterson (1995) showed that the presence of a best friend increased the severity of negative outcomes for children identified as *rejected aggressive*. One explanation for these findings is that the friendship networks of rejected aggressive children are likely to comprise other aggressive children, as suggested by Patterson, DeBaryshe, and Ramsey (1989) in their model of the developmental progression of antisocial behaviour. The involvement in a deviant peer group comprised of other children with behaviour problems reinforces and supports the rejected aggressive child's inappropriate behaviours. Research Example 11.2 highlights some interesting and unexpected research about possible therapeutic avenues for increasing social adaptation.

Research Example 11.2

Unexpected Benefits of Drama

It is commonly believed that music lessons lead to a host of capabilities in children. However, most studies have used a correlation research design, showing that kids who take music classes tend to have advanced skills in a number of areas, including mathematical ability. It is impossible to say whether musically experienced children who took part in these studies were brighter to begin with. A Canadian psychologist, E.Glenn Schellenberg, set out to examine whether this claim was true by using a randomized controlled trial research design (Schellenberg, 2004).

A sample of 144 6 year olds was recruited through community-placed advertisements offering free art lessons. The children were randomly assigned to four different groups: to two music classes (keyboard or voice), or two control groups (drama classes or a one-year waiting list). The drama and waitlist groups were designed to be the control conditions to which the two music classes were compared. Music and drama lessons were given at a prestigious school, Toronto's Royal Conservatory of Music. Classes were taught weekly for 36 weeks and each class had a maximum of six children. IQ was measured before and after the classes in addition to a number of other measures, including social functioning and psychological health.

All four groups had significant increases in IQ, which were likely a result of the children entering grade school. The two music classes had similar increases in IQ, which were significantly higher than those for the control groups. The aspects of IQ that improved included resistance to distractibility, processing speed, verbal comprehension and mathematical computation. On average, children receiving music scored better on the IQ test than 62% of the control children. This finding translates as a small but real link between music lessons and certain aspects of IQ.

However, perhaps the most notable finding came from the drama group, which you may recall, was merely designed as a comparison group and was not expected to result in any specific advantages. Yet children undertaking drama showed marked improvement on scales assessing adaptability and other social skills. The effect size was relatively large, such that the average child receiving drama scored higher than 72% of children in the nondrama groups (including the two music groups). This would result in a more noticeable effect than the music–IQ link.

Possible mechanisms explaining the drama class results include neurodevelopmental changes in areas of the brain associated with daily social interaction augmented by inhabiting the character of another person, and essentially having to step into another person's shoes for a time. Pretend play has more generally been associated with advances in theory of mind and other aspects of social development, so perhaps the drama classes provided additional, dedicated time for children to explore and practise the kind of imaginative play that is essential for social development.

Question: What were the strengths of the study that allowed for conclusions about cause and effect? Are there any other classes you imagine would result in similar improvements in social development?

Friendship

Friendship formation

Friendship can be defined as a relationship between two (more or less) equals which involves *commitment* to one another and *reciprocity* (Hartup, 1989; Shantz, 1983). *Liking* is an important part of friendships, but it is not a sufficient condition for the development of friendship (Shantz, 1983). The simple question, '*How do children become friends?*', has proven to be a difficult problem for psychologists interested in the development of peer relations and social processes to untangle. However, many inroads have been made into the processes involved in the development of friendships.

John Gottman (1983) set out to examine this question in a series of studies. In the first, Gottman tape-recorded the conversations of children aged 3 to 9 who played either with a stranger or with their best friend. One of the central findings of this study was the identification of a set of social processes which were related to friendship formation, and which distinguished between the play patterns of children with their best friends or with the strangers. The processes identified were: connectedness in communication (i.e. making communicative exchanges clear and relevant to the topic at hand); exchanging information; establishing common ground (e.g. exploring similarities and differences and working jointly); successfully resolving conflicts; showing positive reciprocity (e.g. responding to another's behaviours and comments in a positive manner); and self-disclosure (e.g. sharing information about one's own feelings). Best friends were more likely than strangers to score highly on these six dimensions. Moreover, in a second study, Gottman showed that when children were introduced to a same-aged stranger for a series of play sessions, those children who got along well were more likely to score highly on these six dimensions than children who did not get on well.

Parker and Gottman (1989; Gottman & Mettetal, 1986) argued that the focus of friendships changes with age. In early childhood, around 3 to 7 years of age, the goal of peer interaction is to achieve successful, coordinated play. The social processes employed to achieve this goal are those centred on play. Around 8 to 12 years of age, the goal of children's friendships changes, with the gaining of acceptance from one's peers taking precedence. At this stage, children are concerned with figuring out which behaviours will lead to acceptance by their peer group and which behaviours will lead to rejection. Finally, around adolescence (13 years of age onwards), the goal of friendships changes to developing a better understanding of the self, and adolescent friendships show a corresponding increase in the focus on self-disclosure.

Conceptions of friendship

These changes in the focus of friendships correspond closely with children's developing conceptions of friendship, that is, what characterizes a friendship. Damon (1977) interviewed children about their knowledge of friendship and found evidence for three levels of friendship. At Level 1 (ages 5 to 7 years), friends are seen in a momentary or transient way and are defined by how the child interacts with them. Friends are *playmates*, people who *share* toys and other things, and are *fun*. At Level 2 (8 to 10 years), children's conceptions of friends are focused on issues surrounding *trust* in one another and on the *dispositions* or *traits* which one likes about another person. At Level 3 (age 11 and beyond) conceptions of friendships are centred on *intimacy*, revealed in disclosure and the sharing of thoughts, feelings and attitudes and the development of *mutual understanding* (Youniss, 1980). A number of other 'stage theories' of friendship show similar developmental patterns in children's conceptions of friendship (Selman, 1981; Youniss & Volpe, 1978), although Berndt (1981) maintains that children's conceptions of friendship do *not* develop in a stage-like manner. Rather, their conceptions represent an accumulation of dimensions such as commonalities in favoured modes of play and an increasing interest in intimacy and self-disclosure. Further research on these issues is required in order to sort out exactly how such development in children's conceptions of friendship takes place (Rubin & Coplan, 1992).

The maintenance of friendships

Children's early friendships are often fragile bonds which can be quickly formed and just as easily terminated. As children grow older, their friendships become more stable and enduring as the characteristics on which the friendships are based evolve. In a study of fourth- and eighth-grade children (approximately 9 and 13 year of age, respectively) in the United States, Berndt, Hawkins and Hoyle (1986) found that over two-thirds of children who reported that they were close friends at the beginning of the school year were still close friends at the end of the year. The friendships which endured the year were characterized by the children as involving frequent interaction and a high degree of mutual liking. Unstable friendships were characterized by a lack of intimacy. Children's friendships do not differ from their lesser relationships or acquaintanceships in terms of conflict experienced with the relationship, but friends are more likely to be concerned with resolving conflict than are acquaintances (Newcomb & Bagwell, 1995).

The functions of friendship

Friendships have a number of important functions in children's development. According to Sullivan (1953), friendships in childhood serve to offer consensual validation of one's feelings and interests; to bolster the child's feelings of self-worth and importance; to provide affection; to provide opportunities for intimacy and disclosure; to promote the growth of interpersonal sensitivity; to offer prototypes for later relationships. According to Rubin and Coplan (1992), a number of other functions for friendship have been suggested, from providing companionship and offering a context for transmitting social norms, to promoting a sense of loyalty and alliance. Friendships also offer a 'secure base' (Ainsworth et al., 1978) outside the family. As Parker and Gottman (1989) suggest, friendships are at the heart of the development of social and emotional competence.

What are the ways in which friendships might be considered to be similar to attachment relationships with significant adults? (In answering this question you might want to refer to the relevant section in Chapter 10.)

Social Cognitive Development

Piaget's focus was on cognitive development, and as a result he had little to say about the child's developing social awareness. However, Piaget's theory was the inspiration for a great deal of research which attempted to examine whether the changes in children's cognitive development he identified could explain the development of their social understanding and behaviour, particularly, their understanding of themselves and others (Hart & Damon, 1992). This focus on children's social cognition has become a major area of research, with many facets (Flavell & Miller, 1998). Here we examine work in two areas: the child's developing 'theory of mind' and the development of a sense of self and other.

The child's 'theory of mind'

Consider the following scenario adapted from Simon Baron-Cohen (1995): John walks into the kitchen, looks around, and then leaves. How do we explain John's behaviour? According to Baron-Cohen, we effortlessly generate explanations for John's behaviour based on his mental states, that is, internal states such as *beliefs, desires, intentions* and *emotions* which exist in the mind. For example, we might say that *John came to the kitchen because he **wanted** something, but he **forgot** what it was so he left*. Alternatively, we might argue *John was **looking** for something but could not find it*. Both explanations seem natural and plausible. However, consider an explanation such as *John walks into the kitchen everyday, looks around, and then leaves*. Such explanations sound odd and do not seem to really explain the facts. As Baron-Cohen argues, it is hard for us to make sense of behaviour in any other way than via the attribution of mental states to others. We engage in such processes automatically and often unconsciously, and they form an important piece of the puzzle in our understanding of the social world.

The attribution of mental states to others is a kind of commonsense psychology that we all employ. Developmental psychologists interested in this area have used the term **theory of mind** to describe the attribution of mental states to explain behaviour in both ourselves and other people (Astington, Harris, & Olson, 1988; Perner, 1991; Wellman, 1990). This ability to infer the existence of mental states and to use them as explanatory devices for human behaviour is an important step in the child's developing understanding of the social world. Holding a theory of mind allows us to easily understand both our own and other's actions and to predict and control their behaviour by manipulating their mental states. Thus, the child who has acquired a theory of mind is in a good position to *deceive* someone by making them think something that is false or to *empathize* with someone in order to comfort them. Holding a theory of mind is a crucial step in the child's participation in the social world. As you will recall, we briefly discussed the development of a theory of mind in Chapter 6. In this chapter we will examine how a theory of mind is related to children's social cognitive development, that is, their thinking about social interactions.

Why call it a 'theory' of mind?

Before we go on, let us consider an important question we have not yet addressed. Why do researchers call the child's developing knowledge of mental states a 'theory' of mind? There are at least three reasons for doing so. First, as with all scientific theories, the concepts that make up a child's theory of mind – beliefs, desires, intentions and emotions – are defined in relation to one another. Thus, *beliefs* are mental states which can be true or false, while desires are states which are either satisfied or not. Second, like any scientific theory, the child's theory of mind applies to a particular domain – the domain of mental states, a domain which is quite different from, say, the world of objects which the infant is so concerned with. Third, like scientific theories, the child's theory of mind is used to predict and control phenomena in the world, in this case, people's behaviour.

According to Gopnik (Gopnik, 1996; Gopnik & Meltzoff, 1996), one of the pioneers of theory of mind research, children act like young scientists, *forming* theories about people's behaviour, actively *evaluating* the evidence for their theory, and *revising* or *discarding* their theory when they encounter evidence that the theory cannot adequately explain. Gopnik and many others (e.g. Carey, 1985; Wellman, 1990) believe that the child's development of ever more complex theories is explained by the same basic processes of theory change which characterize how scientists work; in other words, by the construction and revision of theories. Of course, children's theories are different in that they are not explicitly held as scientific theories are. However, the comparison of children and scientists has led to some important findings regarding children's developing understanding of the mind.

Desires and beliefs

Around age 2, children begin to talk about their mental states. Bartsch and Wellman (1995) analyzed a database of linguistic transcripts providing daily samples of preschool children's talk. Bartsch and Wellman found that around this age children's everyday speech is littered with examples of mental state talk, in particular, talk about their *desires* and their *intentions*. Young children are notoriously good at making clear what it is they want. According to Wellman (1990), the child's first theory of mind can be called **desire psychology** because 2 year-old children understand that people have internal states which correspond to desires, and furthermore they understand that people's actions and emotional reactions can be predicted on the basis of those states. Knowing that someone wants an apple, it is easy to predict that they are likely to go to the kitchen and get an apple as opposed to going to the playground. A 2 year-old recognizes that people act to satisfy their desires. Wellman suggests that while that 2 year-old's understanding of desire is still not exactly the same as an adult's conception, it is very similar and allows the child to make many of the same predictions as an adult.

By age 3, children have elaborated their basic theory to include an understanding of *beliefs*. Wellman calls this theory a **belief-desire psychology** since it incorporates both concepts. The child who is equipped with a belief-desire psychology can make much more complex predictions about behaviour; they explain behaviour using the concepts of belief and desire (Wellman, 1990). In other words, children show an ability to relate a person's actions to their beliefs and desires. Bartsch and Wellman (1989) performed a series of experiments that showed 3 year-old children readily engage in this sort of reasoning, sharing at least the rudiments of an adult theory of mind. Moreover, with a belief-desire psychology, a 3 year-old child can understand that two people could have the same desire, but might act in different ways, in accordance with their beliefs.

This sort of phenomenon would be extremely difficult for a child equipped only with a simple desire psychology to accommodate. Thus, by age 3 the child reasons about their own and other's behaviour in a way that is very similar to an adult's. There is, however, one crucial difference between 3 year-olds and adults, a fact about mental representations which 3 year-olds have not yet grasped: the notion that one's beliefs are not always true of the world, that is, that beliefs can be *false*.

Understanding misrepresentation: the case of false beliefs

Around age 4, children begin to conceive of the fact that beliefs can be false, that a person's mental states can *misrepresent* a situation. As children get older, they begin to appreciate that people's beliefs depend on their perceptions and are not direct copies of the environment (Carpendale & Chandler, 1996; Keenan, Ruffman, & Olson, 1994). In other words, we act on the basis of our representations of reality and not on the basis of reality itself. The 4 year-old has developed a much more sophisticated theory of mind, a theory which includes the idea that our beliefs, desires and intentions are mental representations, and that these representations can differ in their relation to reality. Furthermore, 4 year-olds begin to understand that people act on the basis of their beliefs and not simply on the basis of reality. Many psychologists refer to this level of understanding as a **representational theory of mind** (Perner, 1991; Wellman, 1990).

How do developmentalists test whether or not a child holds a representational theory of mind? Wimmer and Perner (1983) devised a task known as the **false belief task** which has become the litmus test for demonstrating that children understand that people act on the basis of their representations of the world. In the false belief task, a child watches as one of two puppets places an object like a piece of candy in a distinct location, say a red box. This puppet then leaves the scene. In the next part of the story, a second puppet takes the object from the red box and places it in a second location, a green box. Finally, the first puppet returns and the child subject is asked 'Where will puppet look for her candy?' or 'Where will she think her candy is?' Wimmer and Perner (1983) found that most 3 year-olds failed the false belief task, incorrectly claiming that the puppet would look where the chocolate really is. These children erred on the task because their theory predicted that people's beliefs tend to directly reflect reality, so the person acting in accord with their beliefs will search for the object where it is really located. On the other hand, most 4 year-olds correctly understood that the puppet would look for her candy in the location where she originally put it. These older children understand that the puppet would hold a false belief, and, moreover, would act on the basis of that false belief and not based on the actual situation.

The use of the false belief task as a test for the presence of theory of mind in young children has its critics, however, and some researchers (see, for example, Bloom & German, 2000) argue that children younger than 4 fail this task, not because of the absence of a theory of mind but simply because the task is linguistically and attentionally too complex for young children. More recently, studies using an alternative approach have suggested that a basic understanding of other people's beliefs is present in children as young as 15 months of age. A study by Onishi and Baillargeon (2005) used a 'violation of expectation' paradigm to study understanding of false beliefs in infants. We saw in Chapter 7 that studies using this technique by Baillargeon and colleagues (e.g. Baillargeon & DeVos, 1991) have also shed light on the age at which infants acquire an understanding of object permanence. In Onishi and Baillargeon's study, infants watched an actor with a false belief about the location of a toy search for that toy. They found that when an actor with a false belief about the location searched in the 'correct' box, infants spent longer looking at that location, indicating that this was surprising to them and they had expected the actor to look in the 'wrong' location based on her belief. This type of finding has also been replicated in studies by Onishi, Baillargeon and Leslie (2007) and Surian, Caldi and Sperber (2007), indicating that a basic understanding of other people's beliefs is present in infants long before they can respond verbally to such tasks.

Early social experience and the development of theory of mind

There are a number of factors in children's early social interactions which help them take steps towards the acquisition of a theory of mind. One line of research has examined the role of family structures in children's acquisition of a theory of mind. Perner and his colleagues (Perner, Ruffman, & Leekam, 1994) showed that the age at which children passed the false belief task was positively correlated with the number of siblings which the child had: 3 year-old children with older siblings were as likely to pass a false belief task as 4 year-old children with no siblings. On Perner et al.'s account, having an older sibling seems to be worth about a year's experience. Presumably, children in larger families receive more 'exposure' to theory of mind through the kinds of talk and social interchanges which take place in sibling interactions). Recent work has shown that the age of siblings is more important than the presence of siblings. Children with a non-twin sibling perform better on tasks assessing theory of mind than children who have a twin and no other siblings (Wright, Shaw, Brown, & Perkins, 2005). It seems that for early theory of mind development, children must be exposed to more sophisticated talk about thoughts and beliefs than a sibling of their own age or younger can provide. Adults also provide opportunities for children to acquire a theory of mind, thus only-children and twins are not entirely disadvantaged (Lewis, Freeman, Kyriakidou, Maridaki-Kassotaki, & Berridge, 1996).

Work by Meins, Fernyhough, Russell and Clark-Carter (1998) has examined how parents may play a role in the child's acquisition of a theory of mind. Meins et al. found that children who passed the false belief task at an early age tended to have parents who were what she called *mind-minded*, that is, who often spoke to children of mental states or used mental state terms in their speech to children. Ruffman, Perner and Parkin (1998) showed a similar finding. In their study, mothers of 2 year-olds were asked to imagine what they would say to their child after some transgression, such as hitting another child. Mothers wrote their responses and these were coded for whether they showed evidence of mental state talk. Ruffman et al. found that children whose mothers used mental state terms in their responses, for example, saying things like, '*Imagine how that child feels. Would you like to be hit?*', were more likely to pass the false belief task at age 3 than children whose mothers talked to their child in other ways such as '*You shouldn't do that*' or

'*Was that a nice thing to do?*' In another study conducted by Dunn, Brown, Slomkowski, Tesla and Youngblade (1991), family discourse about feelings measured when they were 43 months of age predicted children's later performance on both false belief and affective perspective-taking tasks (measured seven months later). The authors of this study argue that talk about the social world mediates children's social cognitive development. Clearly, parents' socialization efforts with their children can have a profound effect on the nature of their children's development; in this case, when their children acquire an understanding of a fundamental aspect of the social world.

While the relationship between parental mental state language and later theory of mind performance in their children is well established, can you think of any other reasons for this relationship? How might you investigate the various explanations for this relationship?

Theory of mind and later social development

A final question which we will consider in relation to the child's developing understanding of the mind is how it relates to other developmental achievements. Keenan and Harvey (1998) have suggested that a child's theory of mind acts as a **developmental organizer** for subsequent social development. That is, aspects of theory-of-mind development, such as whether children acquire the concepts relatively early or relatively late, can play a role in shaping later development. In other words, when children develop a theory of mind might affect aspects of later social development, such as children's ability to form friendships. Thus, theory of mind organizes the nature and course of later development. What evidence is there that the acquisition of a theory of mind really does lead to a reorganization of how children understand the social world?

Work by Watson and her colleagues has addressed this question. Watson et al. (1999) showed that 3 to 5 year-old children's performance on a false belief task was positively correlated with their peer social skills, as assessed by the children's teacher. This relationship held even when the researchers controlled for the effects of individual differences in language development across children. In a second study, Capage and Watson (in press) showed that performance on a false belief task was negatively correlated with children's level of aggression and positively correlated with social competence. Thus, the results of both studies show a significant relation between the development of a theory of mind and social behaviour. However, given the correlational nature of the studies, it is impossible to do more than speculate on whether an understanding of false belief causes changes in social behaviour or vice versa. Further longitudinal work on this issue is required.

Perner (1988: 271) argued that 'the social significance of human interactions depends on the mental states of the interacting parties, particularly their higher-order mental states'. By 'higher-order mental states' Perner refers to what psychologists call **second-order mental states**. These are simply embedded mental state expressions such as *Jill wants Jack to believe that there is someone behind him*. You can see from this example that Jill has a *desire* to create a particular *belief* in Jack. The acquisition of an understanding of second-order mental states typically lags behind the understanding of false belief, as children do not typically understand second-order mental states until about age 6.

An understanding of second-order mental states is particularly important in understanding non-literal language (speech where someone doesn't say what they mean). For example, when a story character (Jill) tells another character (Jack) a lie such as *I had a really nice day*, the child who watches the interaction needs to recognize that Jill wants Jack to believe what she says (that she had a nice day). This is because Jill wants to influence Jack's beliefs, that is, to create in him the false belief that Jill had a nice day. When the child acquires this level of understanding, they are in a position to understand quite complex social interactions (Harris, 1989). Imagine, for example, that Jill had a car accident, lost her wallet, and missed an important appointment. Jack asks how Jill's day was and she replies *I had a really nice day*. The child who understands second-order mental states is in a position to recognize that Jill's utterance was meant *sarcastically*. Jill does not want Jack to think she had a good day but instead wants the opposite – for him to recognize she had a horrible day. Notice that in both cases the speaker makes the same remark but can mean quite different things by it depending on how they intend the listener to understand them. The child observer of such interactions needs to appreciate second-order mental states in order to dif-ferentiate between speech acts such as *lies* and *sarcasm* (Keenan & Quigley, 1999; Perner, 1988). The complex quality of linguistic interactions is but one of many possible examples of where a child's theory of mind plays an important role in their developing social understanding.

LaLonde and Chandler (1995: 182) have argued that once children acquire an understanding of the mind and its role in behaviour, they may then begin to frame their social judgements. Children may put their newly acquired understanding to use in tasks such as choosing friends, manipulating other people, making interpersonal comparisons. LaLonde and Chandler argue that what is required to evaluate this claim is longitudinal research which tracks the consequences of acquiring a representational theory of mind. It is a certainty that future work on theory of mind and social development will undertake this challenge.

The development of self and the differentiation of self from others

At some point in our development, we begin to differentiate ourselves from others. In the view of many, a notion of *self* cannot develop without a notion of *other* (Damon & Hart, 1992). At the same time, the concepts of self and other are distinct and independent categories which serve distinct functions (Neisser, 1988). In other words, our understanding of self is different from our understanding of other. Developing a sense of self is a central process in the development of social cognition (Harter, 1998). How, then, does the development of a sense of self take place and what is its developmental course?

The differentiation of self from other begins in infancy. This is illustrated in a clever study by Murray and Trevarthen (1985). These researchers devised a procedure using a closed-circuit television where 2 to 4 month-old infants could interact with their mothers via the television (the infants saw the mothers on a screen at the same time as the mothers, in another room, saw the infants on their screen). For a few minutes, interactions went on normally and the infants reacted with pleasure and interest to their mothers. However, after a few minutes, Murray and Trevarthen interrupted the live interaction and instead played a videotape to the infants of the mother during her first minute of interaction. Infants became quite distressed by this. According to the authors of the study, this was because of the lack of *contingency* in the interaction between infant and mother; the mother's actions were no longer tied to their infant's and were thus unsynchronized. According to Damon and Hart (1992), these findings show that even very young infants are both aware of their own actions and sensitive to the presence of others.

Using a test of self-awareness, researchers have been able to show that a true sense of self develops sometime between 18 and 24 months of age (Amsterdam, 1972; Bertenthal & Fischer, 1978; Lewis & Brooks-Gunn, 1978). This is done using the **rouge test**. In this test, an experimenter carefully marks an infant's face with rouge (or in variants of the task, places a bright yellow sticker in the child's hair) in such a way that the child does not feel this act occur. Then the infant is seated in front of a mirror and their behaviours are recorded. If the infant moves to explore or try to remove the spot, they are credited with having a sense of self because the infant who removes the mark recognizes that their face looks different now from how it had looked in the past. In a study by Amsterdam (1972), it was found that infants younger than 20 months of age rarely tried to remove the spot. Note the parallel between the development of self and when children acquire a concept of object permanence; developing a concept of object permanence may be a prerequisite for the development of a sense of self.

Throughout the rest of childhood, there are changes in the development of the sense of self and the sense of other. Preschool-aged children describe themselves largely in terms of physical attributes or preferences (e.g. *I am 5 years-old*; *I am tall*; *I like to play with my dog*). As they move past early childhood, their self-descriptions become more complex, involving more descriptions of psychological characteristics (e.g. *I am an outgoing person*; *Sometimes I feel shy*) and values (e.g. *I am an honest person*) and the first use of trait labels such as *smart*, *lazy* and *mean* (Harter, 1998; Lively & Bromley, 1973). Children at this stage of their development are creating a description of their personality, trying to integrate their various characteristics into a meaningful whole, that is, a theory of their own personality (Damon & Hart, 1992). By adolescence, the growth of cognitive abilities which allow the adolescent to think abstractly supports them in their attempts to forge a more coherent view of the self which integrates their various characteristics (Harter, 1998). Adolescents develop an explicit theory of the self which aids them in the task of better understanding themselves and their own thoughts, feelings and behaviours.

Understanding others' perspectives

An important aspect of learning to interact with others is the ability to take another person's perspective, what has often been referred to in the literature as **role taking**. This is the ability to reason from another person's perspective or, in other words, to refrain from thinking egocentrically. The theory of mind literature attests to the fact that children become less egocentric in their thinking about other people by the preschool years, and it also provides important information about the understanding of representation which makes this feat possible. However, theory of mind has relatively little to say about the development of social cognition beyond the preschool years. As we have seen already, in middle childhood, the use of psychological statements about the self increases dramatically; this also applies to the way children think about others (Livesly & Bromley, 1973).

Selman (1981) has proposed a five-stage model of the development of role-taking ability. In this model, Selman describes how children learn to differentiate between their own and other people's perspectives. At stage 0, the child does not distinguish between their perspective and another's; that is, they reason egocentrically. At stage 1, the child can recognize that they and another may have different perspectives, but they have difficulty describing what the other's perspective might be like. At stage 2, children can see themselves from another's perspective and they know that others are similarly capable. By stage 3, the child recognizes how a third person might view both their perspective and another's on a situation. Finally, at stage 4, children understand that there exists a network of perspectives which binds individuals into a social system. Selman's research has shown that there is a steady progression in role-taking ability through to adolescence. Other research has shown that the development of role-taking ability is associated with other sorts of social behaviours, such as children's tendency to engage in altruistic or unselfish acts (Eisenberg & Fabes, 1998).

Finally, we consider an aspect of adolescent social cognition, a kind of side-effect of their developing ability to think abstractly. Elkind (1967) described an aspect of adolescent cognition that was termed **adolescent egocentrism**. Adolescent egocentrism is the emerging recognition that one may be the focus of another's attention. Adolescents tend to overgeneralize this new understanding, leading to a high degree of self-consciousness because of the mistaken belief that their behaviours are constantly the focus of others' thoughts. The available evidence suggests that egocentrism decreases as adolescence progresses (Elkind & Bowen, 1979) and beliefs about others' perspectives of one become more realistic. This development is important because an excessive preoccupation with the self may interfere with giving the necessary attention to others' perspectives, which underlies social competence.

Summary

The study of social development is one of the busiest areas of research in child development at present, particularly because the task of understanding how children get on in a highly social environment is so important to their overall wellbeing. Social development is strongly tied to changes in cognitive development, although the issue of cause and effect (i.e. do changes in cognition underlie social developments or vice versa?) is still unresolved. The development of friendships and peer relationships are examples of topics which are relevant to other areas of study, such as developmental psychopathology and emotional development, where researchers are often interested in trying to better understand the processes by which people negotiate a very complex social environment.

Glossary

Adolescent egocentrism is the recognition that one may be the focus of another's attention, which leads to a high degree of self-consciousness.

Belief-desire psychology refers to Wellman's term for the child's theory of mind at age 3. Children understand that people act to satisfy their desires in light of their beliefs; however, they do not yet understand that beliefs can be false.

Cliques are close-knit groups of friends, ranging in size from three to nine members, who are held together by mutual acceptance and common interests.

Crowds are groups of adolescents who organize on the basis of reputation and are defined on the basis of the attitudes held by their members.

Desire psychology refers to Wellman's description of the 2 year-old child's theory of mind. Two year-olds understand that people have internal states which correspond to desires and, furthermore, they understand that people's actions and emotional reactions can be predicted on the basis of those states.

Developmental organizer refers to the notion that some developmental changes have a significant impact on subsequent changes and functioning in that they organize later development.

Dominance hierarchies are rankings of individuals in terms of their dominance within a group.

False belief task is a test of children's understanding that people act on the basis of their representations of the world. In the false belief task, a child watches as one of two puppets places an object like a piece of candy in a distinct location, say a red box. This puppet then leaves the scene. In the next part of the story, a second puppet takes the object from the red box and places it in a second location, a green box. Finally, the first puppet returns and the child subject is asked 'Where will puppet look for her candy?' or 'Where will she think her candy is?'

Group socialization theory is the idea that children's socialization results from association with peer groups rather than parents or one-on-one interactions.

Horizontal dimension refers to children's relationships with other children because of their balanced and egalitarian nature.

Play ethos refers to the viewpoint taken by some researchers and educationalists that play is *essential* for normal development. Other researchers argue that this view overstates the case for play.

Representational theory of mind refers to a theory of mind which includes an understanding of the mind as a representational medium. When children recognize the possibility of false beliefs, they are said to hold a representational theory of mind.

Role taking is the ability to reason from another person's perspective or, in other words, to refrain from thinking egocentrically.

Rouge test is an experimental task used to test for self-recognition. The infant is surreptitiously marked with a sticker, seated in front of a mirror, and their behaviours are recorded. If the infant explores or tries to remove the sticker, they are credited with having a sense of self.

Second-order mental states are simply embedded mental state expressions such as *Jill wants Jack to believe that there is someone behind him.*

Sociometric techniques are procedures for measuring children's status within their peer group. Sociometric techniques involve asking children to nominate a specific number of their peers who fit some criterion, such as friends.

Theory of mind refers to the child's developing knowledge of the mind and its role in behaviour. A theory of mind is an organized set of concepts, namely, mental states, which are used to predict and explain other people's behaviour.

Vertical dimension refers to children's relationships with adults because of their asymmetrical nature.

TEST YOUR KNOWLEDGE

1. How did Piaget's views influence the study of infant social development?

   a) He saw infants as egocentric, and thus not capable of real social interactions; studying social development was therefore not useful
   b) Piaget was keen on social development; the zone of proximal development is a socializing force, after all
   c) He was undecided whether social development was worthwhile to understand
   d) He saw infants as egocentric and in need of social learning, making the study of social development very worthwhile to pursue

2. What functions do dominance hierarchies serve?

   a) Increase aggression and resources for high-status members
   b) Provide the opportunity for children to play
   c) Reduce aggression, allocation of resources, provide tasks for members of the group
   d) Reduce aggression and provide an environment for role taking

(Continued)

3. Which of the following factors facilitate a child's chances of being socially accepted?

   a) Having an unusual name
   b) Being attractive
   c) Being a boy
   d) Being the oldest in the group

4. At what age do children typically pass the false belief task?

   a) 6 months old
   b) 3 years old
   c) 4 years old
   d) 6 years old

ANSWERS: 1–A, 2–C, 3–B, 4–C

Suggested Reading

Ding, S., & Littleton, K. (2005). *Children's Personal and Social Development*. London: Wiley Blackwell.

Riley, D., San Juan, R., & Klinker, J. (2008). *Social and Emotional Development: Connecting science and practice in early childhood settings*. Washington, DC: Redleaf.

Underwood, M., & Rosen, L. (2013). *Social Development*. New York: Guilford Publications.

Want to learn more? For links to online resources relevant to this chapter, interactive quizzes and much more, visit the companion website at **https://edge.sagepub.com/keenan3e/**

Moral Development

12

Chapter Outline

LEARNING AIMS

At the end of this chapter you should:

- understand the cognitive, affective and behavioural components of moral development
- be familiar with the major theories of moral development
- be able to identify the emotional aspects of morality, including guilt and empathy, and recognize the importance of self-regulation and self-control
- be able to appreciate the determinants of prosocial development, including biological and environmental influences
- understand the current theories explaining the development of aggression in children

Introduction

Morality operates at both societal and individual levels. Culture determines what is regarded as moral or proper behaviour, specifying codes of conduct that we must all abide by. At the same time, morality is an individual quality that is embedded in our personal psychology. **Moral understanding** is thought to reflect cognitive, emotional and behavioural components, so this chapter is structured around these distinctions. First, we consider a variety of theories that have been offered as explanations of moral development. Many psychologists are interested in what we think about morality and such cognitive theorists examine how children's understanding of morality changes with their developing cognitive abilities (Killen & Smetana, 2006). Next, we examine the relationship between emotion and moral development. Morality depends in large part on our emotions, for example, our ability to experience feelings of empathy, which involves the ability to experience the same emotion as another person, and this often affects how we treat others (Cimbora & McIntosh, 2005). Of course, our cognitions and emotions are only visible to others through our behaviour (both moral and immoral), making the study of moral behaviour an important component in the study of moral development. Finally, we will consider the development of aggression, which in many cases, is the opposite of moral behaviour.

Until recently, the various facets of moral development were studied separately, but psychologists are becoming aware that thought, emotion and behaviour related to morality are interconnected. In passing on standards of morality, society and parents expect children to acquire this at a cognitive level as well as to feel and act on that morality. It is therefore often fruitful to consider how the various elements of morality are related. Initially, a child's morality is controlled by parents or other significant adults, who regulate the child's behaviour. As children develop, they are expected to internalize this morality and take on 'good' behaviour standards as their own. It is argued that this process of **internalization**, or of knowing right from wrong in the absence of a parent or other external force telling the child so, is essential to the development of morality. Indeed, many of our ideas about responsible, mature behaviour depend on an individual's ability to monitor their own behaviour; parents can tell a child how to behave for only so long. We will discuss the significance of self-control for many aspects of children's development.

Finally, we will examine both the development of behaviours negatively associated with morality, such as aggression and deceit, as well as concepts that relate positively to morality, such as empathy, altruism and prosocial behaviour

Theories of Moral Development

Over the years, a variety of theories of moral development have been proposed. These range from approaches based on learning theory, to cognitive theories of moral development emphasizing moral reasoning, to more contextual and cross-cultural approaches that draw on both social learning theory and cognitive approaches. The most prominent cognitive theories of moral development are Jean Piaget's and Lawrence Kohlberg's developmental theories of morality, both of which are based on Piaget's theory of cognitive development. In this chapter, we consider the strengths and weaknesses of these various theoretical approaches to moral development.

Learning theory and social learning theory

Learning theorists see morality as developing like any other behaviour in childhood, through the processes of learning described in Chapter 2: namely, operant conditioning; reinforcement and punishment; and observation, modelling and imitation. Operant conditioning can be used to help teach children moral behaviour (Skinner, 1953, 1971). Skinner proposed that consequences teach children to obey the moral rules set down by their parents, teachers and other adult figures in their lives (Susky, 1979). When children engage in behaviour that is considered 'good', parents will often show the child approval in the form of affection and other rewards like star charts. In contrast, as a method of discouraging children's 'bad' behaviour (such as hitting, lying or stealing), some parents will also use various forms of discipline, such as 'time outs' or the withdrawal of privileges. As a consequence of such techniques, Skinner believed the frequency of children's good behaviour should increase and their unacceptable behaviour should decrease.

Mild forms of punishment, such as warnings and disapproval, can be used successfully to supplement a parent's instructions (Grusec & Goodnow, 1994). Time out and withdrawal of privileges may also lead children to think about the consequences of their actions. Such discipline is most effective if it is done within the context of a warm parent–child relationship, consistent, and followed up with explanations for why a behaviour is not acceptable (Canadian Psychological Association, 2004). However, excessive or forceful punishment is far less successful, and may actually harm the child in a number of ways. Children who are insulted or hit may be less inclined to internalize social rules and may learn to hit or insult other children; they are also more likely to suffer various problems, including depression and antisocial behaviour (Kochanska, Aksan, & Nichols, 2003).

Effective parents tend to use a strategy known as **inductive discipline** to discipline their children. Inductive discipline combines some disciplinary action with an explanation by the parents of why the punished behaviour is considered wrong (Hoffman, 1970, 1988). Inductive discipline is especially useful in helping younger children to gain control of their behaviour and see the effects of their behaviour from another child's perspective, thus increasing their empathy for other children who may have been the victims of their poor behaviour. Children whose parents use more power-assertive forms of control, such as physical punishment, often have children who show lower levels of self-control than the children of parents who use inductive discipline (Kochanska, Murray, Jacques, Koenig, & Vandergeest, 1996). However, as Kochanska (1997) points out, inductive discipline may not work effectively for children of all temperaments, particularly those with difficult temperaments. These children do seem to benefit more from firm discipline and less from inductive strategies. In short, parents may need to mould their disciplinary strategies to their child's nature.

As common as parents' efforts to control children's behaviour through reinforcement are, social learning theorists suggest that these methods are not as powerful as modelling for teaching morality (Bandura, 1989). Moral behaviour is especially likely to develop when parents serve as models of caring and when children are given an opportunity to try such caring behaviour for themselves (Eisenberg, Fabes, & Spinrad, 2006). A number of characteristics of the model can increase the likelihood of the child imitating the model's behaviour, including warmth, competence and consistency. Thus, children are more likely to copy another person's behaviour if the model is warm and responsive and if the child admires the model (Yarrow, Scott, & Waxler, 1973). Of course, once moral behaviour has been learned through modelling, positive reinforcement can increase the frequency with which it occurs. When a child has learned the conventions about caring for others through watching their parents demonstrate such caring, parents can effectively cement this learning by responding to the child's caring behaviour with praise. Models appear to have the most effect during the preschool years. After that, many moral acts seem to be internalized, with children behaving according to the morality they have been taught regardless of whether their parents or other socializing forces are present (Mussen & Eisenberg-Berg, 1977).

Most parents recognize that there are times when children may disregard what would otherwise seem to be moral behaviour, for example, running across the street in order to help a younger child. The fact that children sometimes behave in ways that are at odds with their parents' or social convention, but may actually be more caring or prosocial in the long run, suggests that morality is more than simply learned social conventions. Recognizing this fact, cognitive-developmental theorists such as Piaget (1965) and Kohlberg (1969) argued that moral development occurs when children actively construct definitions of moral behaviour, such as justice and caring. As their cognitive abilities develop, children's definitions of morality become increasingly sophisticated and context-dependent. Consistent with Piaget's stage-like views of cognitive development, moral reasoning is seen as unfolding through important changes in moral understanding.

Piaget's Theory of Moral Development

Piaget's (1965) theory of moral development is heavily based on his more general ideas about cognitive development. He had earlier proposed a two-stage theory of moral development (Piaget, 1932). From birth through early childhood, children are essentially in a **premoral stage**. At this time, children do not yet understand the concept of rules, and they have very little idea of morality. The first real stage of moral development is what Piaget termed the **moral realism stage** and this runs from about 5 to 9 years of age. At this stage, children become quite enamoured of rules, viewing them as unchanging, inflexible, and handed down by adults (Piaget, 1965). Children at this stage equate wrongdoing with *consequences* rather than the *intentions* of an actor. As a result, the moral realist child may argue that a child who accidentally broke a cup should be punished, since they broke a cup (regardless of whether they meant to). Piaget believed that egocentricism was behind much of the rigidity in morality that children of this age display.

The second stage in Piaget's theory of moral development is the **moral relativism stage**, in which children around the ages of 8 to 12 begin to understand that social rules can be arbitrary, should sometimes be changed, and can be changed with social agreement (Piaget, 1965). The moral relativist child can see that obedience to authority is not always desirable, such as when an adult asks you to do something 'bad'. Children also begin to distinguish clearly between accidents and acts that are committed intentionally, taking into account an actor's intentions. Thus, the moral relativist will distinguish between a child who rushes out of a store and accidentally takes a candy bar without paying, and a child who took the candy and deliberately left the store without paying. The 8 year-old would likely argue that both children should return and pay for the candy but that the child who deliberately took the candy should be punished. Thus, by age 8, the child begins to give more weight to intentions than to consequences, reversing the earlier priority they assigned to consequences.

Piaget's ideas on morality have not gone unchallenged. His research on moral understanding has been criticized for relying too heavily on clinical interviews and stories that may have allowed children's limited cognitive capacities to mask their moral understanding (Chandler, Greenspan, & Barenboim, 1973). Despite these criticisms, it is generally accepted that moral knowledge proceeds in the general direction that Piaget described (Zelazo et al., 1996).

Kohlberg's Theory of Moral Development

Lawrence Kohlberg's theory of moral development (1969, 1985) has had a very powerful impact on the field (Colby, Kohlberg, Gibbs, & Lieberman, 1983). Kohlberg started with Piaget's assumptions that children develop moral understanding in a stage-like manner and progression though these stages is determined by the child's cognitive abilities. Kohlberg used the **moral judgement interview** to test his theory. Children were presented with stories that involved conflicts between two moral values and had to justify their decisions. Children essentially had to choose between obeying rules or ignoring these rules and instead focusing on the welfare of another person. To illustrate, we'll look at one of the better known of these stories, the Heinz Dilemma.

There was once a woman who was near dying from cancer. Her husband, who was named Heinz, was trying to save her life. He discovered that there was a drug that could save her life, but it was very expensive and he could not afford to buy it. The pharmacist in the town was charging a great deal of money for the drug; in fact, ten times what it cost him to make it. Heinz went to everyone he knew to try to borrow the money to save his dying wife, but he could only get half of the money the pharmacist was asking for the drug. The pharmacist refused to sell the drug to Heinz for less, or even let Heinz pay the rest of the money later. Heinz must now decide what to do. Should he break into the store to steal the drug for his wife?

Heinz is faced with a difficult dilemma. Should he obey the rules of society or violate them and save his wife's life? Kohlberg devised a methodology for evaluating children's moral reasoning in response to the dilemmas he set them. As you can see from Table 12.1, answers can be either pro- or anti-stealing; it is the child's justification for their decision that Kohlberg used to judge their level of morality.

Based on his findings, Kohlberg developed a model of moral development which consists of three levels of moral development, each level being made up of two substages. As you can see in Table 12.1, the answers to the Heinz dilemma become increasingly sophisticated at higher stages. The first overall level is **preconventional morality**, which consists of two substages: *punishment and obedience orientation* and *instrumental orientation*. Here, morality is externally managed, children are accepting of rules, and the consequences of actions are what matters. The second level is **conventional morality**, where children continue to think that conforming to rules is important, but they are less focused on the individual's self-interest and more on the wellbeing of society. The norms of the group to which the individual belongs (e.g. family, peer group, church, nation) become the basis of moral judgements. The two stages are: *good boy-good girl morality* and *maintenance of social order*. The third and final level is **postconventional morality**, which is characterized by moving beyond conforming to rules and involves actively questioning society's laws; individuals who have attained this level think in terms of abstract moral principles. The two stages are *social-contract orientation* and *universal ethical principle orientation*.

Research has supported a number of aspects of Kohlberg's theory. Progress through the stages has been consistently related to age (Colby et al., 1983) and most children move through the stages as Kohlberg predicted (Rest, 1986). The development of moral reasoning is slow and gradual, with changes that take place across childhood, adolescence, and even late into adulthood. Few children operate beyond Stage 1 or 2 and most adolescents are found to reason at Stages 2 and 3 (Walker, de Vries, & Trevathan, 1987). By adulthood, moral reasoning is generally at Stages 3 and 4 (Colby et al., 1983; Gibson, 1990). Few people at any age reason at the postconventional level (Stages 5 & 6). Another aspect of Kohlberg's theory that has received support is the link between moral maturity and IQ, perspective-taking and cognitive performance (Walker & Hennig, 1997). Kohlberg believed that each level of morality could not be attained without a corresponding increase in cognitive maturity, and the research seems to support this.

A significant problem with Kohlberg's ideas has been identified by Carol Gilligan (1982), who argues that Kohlberg did not account for the morality of girls and women, as his interviews took place entirely with males. Gilligan points out that women have a different sense of morality from men, in that they are more likely to focus on the ethic of care which would only be accounted for in Stage 3 or 4. The higher stages are abstract and more suited to the moral reasoning of men. According to Gilligan, women's morality is different from – not less than – the patterns of male reasoning on which Kohlberg based his theory. Some studies have found that girls do tend to stress empathy and boys stress justice (Jaffe & Hyde, 2000), although recent research shows that girls reason at the same level as boys (Turiel, 2006), indicating that Kohlberg's theory accounts for both kinds of values. Another criticism of Kohlberg's theory relates to its lack of consideration for culture. Some argue that he focused on individual rights, and his theory undervalues the collectivist ideals of morality held in other cultures (Kahn, 1997).

Table 12.1 Kohlberg's Theory of Moral Development

	Description	Possible Answer to the Heinz Dilemma
Level I Preconventional Morality		
Stage 1: Punishment and obedience orientation	The child abides by parental rules unquestioningly; these must be obeyed to prevent punishment.	'Heinz is wrong to steal the drug because it's bad to steal. He'll go to jail.'
Stage 2: Instrumental orientation	Children recognize that people can have different views, but correct behaviour comes from self-interest.	'Heinz might steal the drug if he wants his wife to live, but maybe he wants to marry someone else.'
Level II Conventional Morality		
Stage 1: Good boy-good girl morality	Morality is more than an exchange; people should live up to expectations of family and society. The child is concerned with doing good, but out of a desire for approval rather than fear of parental power.	'Heinz is right to steal the drug because he is a good man for saving the life of a loved one.'
Stage 2: Maintenance of social order	The individual takes into account the larger social law perspective. A kind of 'law and order' morality, where rules are considered essential for natural order. Many people never go beyond this stage.	'It's natural for Heinz to want to steal the drug, but it's still his duty to obey the law. If everyone starts breaking the law, there'd be no civilization.'
Level III Postconventional Morality		

Table 12.1   (Continued)

	Description	Possible Answer to the Heinz Dilemma
Stage 1: Social-contract orientation	Rules are regarded as flexible and for promoting human wellbeing. Laws are social contracts that can be modified when members of a society decide it is advantageous for everyone's wellbeing.	'It is Heinz's duty to save his wife. Her life being in danger transcends every other moral standard. Life is more important than property.'
Stage 2: Universal ethical principle orientation	Morality involves social standards and internalized ideals, or a conscience. Decisions are based on principles such as justice, compassion and equality. Morality is based on respect for others, which might at times conflict with the prevailing rules.	'If Heinz does not do everything in his power to save his wife then he values life less than material things. People could still live without money and objects, making respect for human life the absolute.'

A final critique of Kohlberg's work is his tendency to conflate morality with **social convention**. Social convention refers to any rules, norms or customs that are generally agreed upon by a society. According to Turiel (1998), even young children understand that there is a difference between morality (e.g. people should not steal) and social conventions (e.g. people should make their beds in the morning). Thus, while convention relates to customs and rules that may change according to the situation, morality relates to fairness and justice applying across situations. Turiel suggests that children begin to understand this distinction through their own experiences. Thus, when a child engages in immoral behaviour such as hitting or lying, they observe how others react: typically with hurt, outrage, and often with the message 'how would you feel?' Peers and adults do not usually respond to violating a social convention in the same manner. These messages teach children early on that moral and social convention transgressions are quite different. Research supports Turiel's view. Even 3 and 4 year-old children identify that moral violations are worse than disregarded conventions, and that moral violations are not acceptable in other settings, cultures, or even if an adult said so (Smetana, 1995).

We have just provided an overview of moral development from the perspective of learning theory and cognitive developmental theory. Do you think that any of the other theories of development might be relevant to understanding the development of moral behaviour? Consider the possible applicability of approaches such as psychodynamics, ethology and Vygotsky's sociocultural theory. You might want to revisit the broad overviews of these approaches provided in Chapter 2.

Emotion and Morality

Children and adults don't just think about moral behaviour; feelings also play an important role in morality. Even young children will tend to feel guilt or shame or embarrassment when breaking a rule. Most of us are also able to sympathize or empathize with the distress of others. All of these emotions come into play in our understanding and display of morality.

Guilt, shame and embarrassment

Guilt, shame and embarrassment have been termed the 'self-conscious' moral emotions (Eisenberg, 2000). The term 'self-conscious' refers to the fact that the experience of these emotions depends on the child being able to understand and evaluate themself. Although guilt, shame and embarrassment are related in that each involves a sense of hurt directed at the self, they involve subtle distinctions. Embarrassment is thought to be the least negative and serious, involving less anger at oneself. It is considered an emotion less about moral transgressions than an accidental transgression of social conventions. Embarrassment is thought to play a role in morality in that it serves to mollify others when an accidental act is committed (Keltner, 1995). Thus, signs of embarrassment, like blushing and gaze aversion, may lessen the impact of a child's mistake, such as wetting the bed, that may otherwise be considered 'bad' behaviour.

Shame and guilt, on the other hand, play much more significant roles in morality. In this context, guilt is often defined as regret about wrongdoing (Eisenberg, 2000) and serves to make the offending person take responsibility for their actions and either make amends for the wrongdoing or punish the self (Ferguson & Stegge, 1998). Shame involves more self-hate than guilt, and involves feeling exposed and degraded. Shame is concerned with opinions of oneself whereas guilt is more about behaviour that is not necessarily an attack on the self (Ferguson, Stegge, & Damhuis, 1991). It is thought that guilt is the most morally-relevant emotion; as guilt is directed at behaviour rather than the self, it is easier for people to accept responsibility and change the offending behaviour. Guilt is thought to motivate apologies and making right (Tangey, 1998).

Whereas shame is negatively correlated with empathy, guilt is positively related to feelings for others (Tangey, 1991). Children who show early signs of guilt are also more likely to be concerned with rules and morality (Kochanska, 2002). Many parents seem to instinctively recognize the role of guilt in morality, and use *empathy-based guilt* in guiding children's moral development. This involves getting the child to accept responsibility for actions and encouraging a show of regret (e.g. 'I'm sorry I hurt your feelings'). Such empathy-based guilt responses are related to caring and moral behaviour (Baumeister, 1998). Conversely, excessive punishment leads children to experience less guilt and less caring behaviour (Hetherington et al., 2006). However, this is not to say that all experiences of guilt are a good thing. Chronic guilt has also been associated with childhood problems, including aggression and sadness (Ferguson, Stegge, Miller, & Olsen, 1999; Zahn-Waxler & Robinson, 1995). It is seems that inducing moderate levels of guilt that relate to how another person is feeling promotes moral development in children, but excessive guilt and shame can hinder moral development.

Sympathy, empathy and perspective taking

The ability to understand another person's point of view is important to the child's developing sense of morality. Although they are related, **sympathy** differs from **empathy** in its emotional content. Empathy denotes an understanding of the plight of another and the experience of a similar emotion. In this sense, it can be thought of as self-related emotion (Eisenberg, 2000). Sympathy is more cognitively sophisticated in that it involves a similar comprehension of another's emotional state but involves concern for the other person, and in this sense is more other-directed (Eisenberg, 2000). Despite these proposed differences, the terms 'empathy' and 'sympathy' are often used interchangeably, and can be generally understood as a sense of feeling for the plight of others.

Perspective taking is an important correlate of empathy. Children who are able to understand the perspective of others are more likely to show **altruism**, a form of morality in which an individual helps another at no benefit to themself (Eisenberg et al., 2006). This sense of 'standing in another's shoes' allows children to understand not only how a person might be feeling in an immediate situation, but over the course of late childhood and adolescence, the young person may also begin to feel for other people's general life situations, such as the challenges faced by the poor, underprivileged and homeless (Hoffman, 2000). Perspective taking seems to work in conjunction with sympathy to truly produce a sense of morality (Denham, 1998).

Parents and other adults who are significant to children, such as teachers, can have an impact on children's moral emotions. The use of inductive discipline strategies often promotes the development of empathy (Kerr, Lopez, Olson, & Sameroff, 2004). For example, it is not uncommon for toddlers and preschoolers to 'borrow' a toy from another child right in the middle of the toy owner's game. An adult using inductive discipline might say to the borrower, 'Look at Penny. She is crying because you took her toy'. As the child gets older, the adult can use more cognitively advanced versions of this technique, referring to psychological explanations, such as 'Penny was really proud of the game she made up all by herself. Now her feelings are hurt because you interrupted her game and took her toy away' (Hoffman, 2000). As long as the instructions match the child's cognitive level and are given in a warm but firm manner, inductive discipline appears to promote sympathy and even physical displays of affection, including hugs and handing over toys to other children (Zahn-Waxler, Radke-Yarrow, & King, 1979). It is also possible to provide

Image 12A   This teacher uses induction to explain to these fighting children the impact of their behaviour on others. Inductive discipline supports moral development through increasing empathy, clarifying parental and teacher expectations for how the child should behave, and providing an opportunity for the transgressing child to make up

© iStock.com/MachineHeadz

situations in which children can learn how to understand others. Research has found that inducing people to experience sympathy for members of a stigmatized group results in at least short-term changes, with the trained individuals continuing to view the stigmatized group with more understanding (Batson, Polycarpou, Harmon-Jones, Imhoff et al., 1997).

Moral Reasoning and Moral Behaviour

Thinking about and even feeling a sense of concern for others do not always translate into moral behaviour. Children may experience a sense of how another feels but resist actively helping them in a prosocial fashion. For example, a child may empathize with a victim of bullying but fail to come to that victim's assistance. Similarly, a child might know everyone should get the same-sized piece of cookie, but still divide the treat so that they end up with the largest piece. Finally, moral behaviour sometimes requires the ability to resist temptation, for example, following instructions not to take a luscious chocolate chip cookie when Mum is out of sight. Children who seem to possess advanced moral cognitions do not always make congruent behavioural choices, and this especially applies to young children whose behaviour is often impulsive (Batson & Thompson, 2001; Blasi, 1983).

Prosocial behaviour

Recent research provides clues as to the specific relationship between moral emotion and behaviour. It seems that emotions such as gratitude, guilt and love mediate the relationship between prosocial thought and behaviour. Such emotions serve to make us think that engaging prosocially is 'worth it' (Bartlett & DeSteno, 2006). **Prosocial behaviour** can be defined as actions which are intended to help another person (Eisenberg et al., 2006). This includes showing concern for a particular individual, such as displays of sympathy, talking through difficulties and helping solve problems, as well as acting kindly and generously towards groups of people, such as when children in a school raise money for victims of war. Altruistic behaviour is similar in that it involves helping others, but the motivation behind altruism is unselfish. Thus, a child is acting prosocially if he hears another child crying and responds by passing that child a toy for comfort (but expects a 'thank you' and prompt return of the toy), whereas an altruistic act would involve no such expectation of reward or gratitude. Altruistic behaviour is motivated by internalized values and self-rewards that do not carry any anticipated social rewards (Eisenberg et al., 2006). Altruism sometimes even involves a risk to the welfare of the person acting. The beginnings of prosocial behaviour are evident in young infants, such as when babies smile or laugh or give toys to others, but altruism is generally only seen later on in development (Eisenberg, 2000).

Studies examining the developmental course of prosocial behaviour reveal that as children grow older, many aspects of their prosocial responding increase, including empathy and perspective taking (Eisenberg, Cumberland, Guthrie, Murphy, & Shepard, 2005). Prosocial behaviour increases consistently across the preschool and school years, peaking in adolescence. Prosocial behaviour also tends to be stable over time; children who are helpful and considerate at age 6 are more likely to be rated that way at age 12 (Cote, Tremblay, Nagin, Zoccolillo, & Vitaro, 2002), suggesting that prosocial behaviour early in childhood is a strong predictor of prosocial behaviour in the future (Eisenberg et al., 2006). As we will explore, there are a number of individual, parental and cultural influences that can affect the timing, emergence and stability of prosocial behaviour.

A number of factors are involved in the development of prosocial behaviour. Increases in prosocial behaviour are tied to advances in cognitive development (Hoffman, 2000) and emotional understanding (Denham, 1998). Prosocial behaviour also appears to be influenced by both the child's environment and their genes. A recent twin design study examining stability and change in prosocial behaviour found that genetic effects account for both change and stability in prosocial behaviour while nonshared environment was associated with change in prosocial behaviour (Knafo & Plomin, 2006). The influence of shared environmental effects steadily decreased over childhood. These findings are not surprising given that genes are present at birth, hence contributing to prosocial stability, but the effects of genes are also seen in areas of change, such as increasing cognitive development, hence their effect on prosocial changes. Nonshared environmental factors mostly change as the child gets older, contributing to change in prosocial behaviour. Peers and teachers change, favourite television shows are replaced. Genes and nonshared environmental factors clearly continue to be important in prosocial behaviour over childhood. Conversely, the influence of shared environmental factors lessens as the child develops. The contributions of genes and environment to prosocial behaviour interact in complex ways.

The consequences of prosocial behaviour are not only advantageous for societies and individual families, but recent research has identified that positive social behaviour also has direct benefits for the child. Researchers using a Canadian sample of 9 to 11 year-old children reported that those who performed acts of kindness were in fact happier and more accepted by their peers than children who weren't particularly kind (Layous et al., 2012). It is likely that the findings can be extended to the prevention of bullying. The authors of the study concluded that by simply asking students to think about how they could act kindly towards those around them, teachers can create a sense of connectedness in the classroom and reduce the likelihood of bullying.

Self-control and delay of gratification

Being able to control one's behaviour, or self-regulation, is essential to moral action. Self-regulation involves having exercise of control over one's inner states or responses, including thoughts, feelings, impulses, desires and attention (Carver & Scheier, 2011). By definition, children who are self-regulated, displaying self-control, do not require parents or other adults to control their behaviour, and are able to motivate themselves. Self-control has been identified as a remarkably strong predictor of future success, whether success is measured as academic achievement, financial stability or the quality and stability of future relationships. Self-discipline (most often demonstrated though inhibition on tests) predicts more improvement on academic measures than does IQ (Duckworth & Seligman, 2005). Conversely, behavioural dysregulation is related to adverse outcomes. For example, in a recent longitudinal study with Dutch children, dysregulation in childhood was associated with risk of anxiety, depression, disruptive behaviour and substance abuse in adulthood (Althoff et al., 2010). Another longitudinal study, this time from New Zealand, followed 1,000 children from birth to age 32 and found that 3 year-olds who had poor self-control (including low frustration tolerance, ability to stick with a task and ability to wait for a turn) were more likely to have problems with their health – including obesity, high cholesterol and blood pressure – as well as more substance abuse, financial problems and criminality at age 32. The results held even after controlling for the effects of IQ and socioeconomic status (Moffitt et al., 2011).

While parents initially take on the role of controlling young children's behaviour, it becomes increasingly essential that children learn to do this on their own. To perform moral or prosocial actions, children must sometimes inhibit the tendency to respond in nonmoral ways, as in the cookie example used above. In short, children must learn how to cope with **delay of gratification** in order to behave morally. Delay of gratification refers to the ability to refrain from engaging in a pleasurable activity until a later time. Every time a child is able to save her Easter eggs for another day's feast, or refrain from opening her Christmas presents even though she knows where they are hidden, she is engaging in delay of gratification.

Delay of gratification often happens naturally as children mature. In a classic study, Vaughn, Kopp and Krakow (1984) placed children aged 18, 24 and 30 months-old in front of some attractive objects. The children were told not to touch the objects. Not surprisingly, the 18 month-olds waited an average of 20 seconds before reaching for the forbidden objects, while the 30 month-olds were able to wait for an average of 100 seconds. Despite this general progression of self-control, some children develop self-regulation and control much earlier than other children. Some of the characteristics of early self-regulators include superior language skills (Vaughn, Kopp, & Krakow, 1984), endorsing parental values (Kochanska, 2002), and possessing a temperament that is moderately fearful and inhibited (Rothbart, Ahadi, & Evans, 2000). Parenting can also have an impact on children's self-control. Parents who adjust their discipline to coincide with the child's cognitive development and increasingly rely on verbal explanations have children with higher levels of control (Kopp, 2002).

Delay of gratification has long-term influences on children's moral and responsible behaviour. The ability to delay gratification is associated with correctly interpreting social information; when children have the patience to understand the messages behind other people's vocalizations and actions they are more likely to have social success (Gronau & Waas, 1997). Moreover, success at delaying gratification in the preschool years has been associated with planning, concentration and coping abilities in adolescence, as well as with self-understanding (Mischel, Shoda, & Peake, 1988). This kind of moral self-regulation, having insight into one's behaviour and being able to change one's conduct depending on what is situationally appropriate (Bandura, 1991), is vital for interacting with and caring for others. Thankfully, even if a child's temperament or circumstances mean that self-control and delay of gratification do not come easily, self-regulation skills can be taught and practised throughout childhood, beginning in the preschool years (see Research Example 12.1 below).

Research Example 12.1

Tools of the Mind

When engaged in imaginative play, children must follow rules. Whether children are playing as a baby, mother, father, or rubbish collector, they must inhibit impulses and act like the character they are playing. Following these rules means children must control their behaviour to achieve a desired goal. Imaginative play provides one of the earliest experiences of self-control.

Tools of the Mind, a preschool play-based programme based on Vygotsky's teachings, has proven to be successful in using play to teach disadvantaged children how to regulate their behaviour (Diamond, Barnett, Thomas, & Munro, 2007). At the core of Tools of the Mind is a curriculum of 40 self-regulation-promoting activities, including telling oneself out loud what one should do ('self-regulatory private speech'), dramatic play and aids to facilitate memory and attention. The activities are woven into daily activities. For example, children may be asked how they wish to spend their play time and are then encouraged to stick to that plan. Within the activity, teachers help children to regulate turn taking. The goal of the programme is to help children develop the ability to control their own behaviour, and move beyond simply following rules to receive rewards or avoid punishments.

Teachers in the intervention were regular preschool teachers trained in these activities. To assess the programme, researcher Adele Diamond and her colleagues randomly assigned teachers and children to two curricula: Tools of the Mind (in which teachers spent approximately 80% of the classroom day using the self-regulation tasks described above) and a standard curriculum. All classrooms received exactly the same resources and the same amounts of teacher training and support. Participants included 147 preschoolers (85 in the Tools programme) from the same low-income neighbourhood, who participated in the programmes for one or two years.

Longitudinal data are still being collected, but at the first round of assessments children in the Tools programme demonstrated improved self-regulation skills, including performance on rule-following tasks involving attention, memory and inhibition. In fact, educators in one school were so impressed with the initial results that they halted the study after one year. The findings have been replicated in other schools and with other teachers and children in the USA.

Questions: How might parents use these strategies within their imaginative play at home with preschoolers?

What are some areas you imagine these improvements may generalize to? How might you test for these outcomes in a study?

The study was conducted with children from low-income backgrounds. Would you expect the results to generalize to other populations?

What are the implications of the finding that self-regulation can be taught so early in development, in a relatively easy, cost-effective manner (especially considering that self-discipline seems to be more important than IQ for academic performance)?

Distributive justice

Distributive justice refers to children's beliefs about how to divide goods fairly (Deutsch, 1975; Zajac, 1995). A child's understanding of distributive justice is reflected every time they decide how to divide a cookie between themself and a sibling, how many pieces of a block of chocolate each member of a group of friends should receive, or how to allocate rewards to members of a group based on the efforts they made. William Damon (1977) tracked the development of children's conceptions of justice across early and middle childhood and provided some of the most telling research in this area. Damon's typical research paradigm involved presenting children with a story about children who completed a hypothetical task together. The participating children were then asked about the best way to distribute the resources between the children in the story, and from this to provide a rationale for why the money should be divided up as they saw fit (McGillicuddy-De Lisi, Watkins, & Vinchur, 1994).

Damon (1977) described three broad stages in the development of distributive justice. In Stage 1, preschool children (aged 4 to 5) tend to base judgements of distributive justice on *desire* and *irrelevant facts* (e.g. 'give more money to the older child'). By Stage 2 (aged 6 to 8), children base their conceptions first on *equality* ('all children should be given the same amount of money') and, slightly later, on the basis of *equity* ('the child who worked hardest on the art should be awarded the most money'). At Stage 3 (aged 8 and above), *need* and *circumstance* tend to be considered in determining distributive equations ('the poorest child should be given the most'). Research tends to support this stage-like reasoning about distributive justice (e.g. Freeman & Daly, 1984). Recent work by Fraser, Kemp and Keenan (2007) found that 5 to 9 year-old children from Indonesia and New Zealand reasoned about allocating rewards in a guessing game as predicted by Damon's theory. Whereas 5 year-olds tended to act in their own interests, using neither the principles of equity or equality, most 7 and 9 year-olds used the equality principle. Moreover, Fraser et al. showed that children's hypothetical distributions (i.e. what they would do) were actually reasonably consistent with the allocation rules they applied when given a behavioural task where they had to make distributions of real chocolates to themselves and another child.

Other research on distributive justice indicates that older children consider a wider range of factors in determining justice. For example, older children will use the equality principle when distributing the money if the characters are friends and the equity principle when the characters are strangers (McGillicuddy-De Lisi et al., 1994). Recent cross-cultural research has shown that preschool-aged children from Hong Kong also tend to consider contextual information in decisions on fairness (Wong & Nunes, 2003). In terms of the long-term consequences of reasoning about fairness, it has been found that advanced reasoning about distributive justice is associated with well-developed social skills and prosocial behaviour (Blotner & Bearison, 1984).

Aggression

We will now look at the development of aggression, which is commonly thought of as the opposite of moral behaviour. Although many behaviours may come to mind when you think about aggression, including hitting others and calling names in childhood, and perhaps cheating or stealing; within developmental psychology **aggression** is specifically defined as any behaviour that causes intentional harm, pain or injury to another. We can see from this definition that while the outcome is important in determining if behaviour is aggressive, the person's intention is even more important. What's more, we can further classify aggression into **instrumental aggression**, in which children attack another person who is in the way of a desired object or space and **hostile aggression**, which is when children simply hurt others. Hostile aggression may involve any of three forms of injury: *physical*, such as hitting or punching; *verbal*, such as teasing; and *relational* aggression, which is designed to damage another person's social standing through behaviours such as gossiping, spreading rumours and social exclusion (Murray-Close, Crick, & Galotti, 2006).

Aggression across development

While all children engage in aggressive acts occasionally, aggressive behaviour shows an initial peak as children's interactions with peers and siblings increase (Tremblay, 2002).

The form of aggressive behaviour also changes over time. Preschool children are more likely to engage in instrumental aggression, since they will often fight over favoured toys or playing space, while school-aged children are more likely to show hostile aggression, and name-calling in particular (Dodge, Coie, & Tremblay, 2006). Physical aggression also gradually gives way to an increase in verbal aggression (Tremblay, Japel, Perusse, Boivin, Zoccolillo, Montplaisir, & McDuff, 1999), which is likely due to the child's corresponding language development as well as changes in adults' expectations. Adults often view physical aggression in a toddler with more lenience than in an 8 year-old, and older children soon learn to find other ways to express their anger and hostility.

As children learn to solve problems using their increasingly sophisticated verbal and emotional skills, aggression lessens throughout childhood. Despite this general decline, individual children still show great stability in their use of aggression (Dodge, Coie, & Tremblay, 2006). Thus, if a child is considered an aggressive preschooler, they are more likely to be rated as aggressive through school and even into adolescence. However, this does not mean that all aggressive children grow up to be aggressive teenagers and adults. Estimates suggest that about 12.5% of aggressive 5 year-olds continue to be highly aggressive in adolescence (Hagin & Tremblay, 1999).

Gender differences

The development of aggression in boys and girls is markedly different. Aggression shows few sex differences in infancy, but by the time children reach the preschool years, boys are far more likely to be involved in aggressive acts than girls (Maccoby, 1998). This gender disparity increases across the school years and into adolescence. Although the gender gap is becoming less apparent, teenage boys are still far more likely to engage in delinquent and aggressive acts than are teenage girls (Moffitt, Caspi, Rutter, & Silva, 2001). Girls, even in childhood, are more likely to resolve conflict and verbally negotiate a compromise before a quarrel becomes a full-blown fight (Eisenberg, Fabes, Nyman, Bernzweig, & Pinuelas, 1994). This does not mean girls' behaviour is squeaky clean, in fact they seem to display more underhanded forms of aggression than boys. Girls are much more likely to engage in relational aggression by damaging personal relationships (Underwood, 2003). Thus they will often try to hurt their opponents through gossip and exclusion from the main peer group or clique. Even though such relational aggression tends to be quite covert, it still does not go unnoticed. Girls, even though they are more likely to use it, view relational aggression as hurtful (Underwood, 2003). In contrast, boys view physical aggression as more hurtful than relational aggression, perhaps because this is the form of aggression they are most familiar with. Boys tend to physically aggress, and are much more likely to retaliate to a threat than girls (Darvill & Cheyne, 1981). They are also more likely to approve of aggression than are girls (Huesmann & Guerra, 1997).

Causes of aggression

The presence of gender differences in aggression points to environmental and social causes of aggression, as there are few such differences at birth. However, aggression may also result from biological differences in hormones and personality. We will now examine what research has revealed about how aggression arises, including the way social cognitions are processed.

Kenneth Dodge and his colleagues have proposed a model suggesting that some children are *inaccurate* in understanding other people's intentions, and respond to even innocuous situations with aggression (Crick & Dodge, 1994; Dodge, 1986). Under the **social information processing model**, aggressive children tend to interpret ambiguous situations as aggressive and respond with aggression in kind. To illustrate, let's take a situation that many children encounter on the playground – being hit by a stray ball. Children who are adept at reading social information tend not to jump to the conclusion that it was a deliberate act meant to hurt them. Conversely, aggressive children with social information processing difficulties are likely to think 'That hurt! Whoever threw that ball meant to hit me! I'll get them back!', and then hunt down the ball's owner to hit them back. The theory suggests that aggressive children see the world in a way that is different from that of nonaggressive children, that is, through a hostile and aggressive filter. Unfortunately, research has found that some of these biases may actually be based in reality. Thus, aggressive boys tend not only to be more aggressive, but they are also more likely to be the targets of aggressive actions compared to nonaggressive boys (Dodge & Frame, 1982). What's more, aggressive children are likely to experience more toxic social environments than nonaggressive boys, where injustice and uncaring are rife, undermining empathy and resulting in such children lashing out at their hostile world (Arsenio & Gold, 2006).

Another way that aggressive children show biases in social cognition is in their evaluation of themselves. Aggressive children tend to show inflated self-esteem and a belief that they are superior to others, despite the fact they are often failing both in school and in their relationships with others. When the behaviours or words of others undermine their self-assuredness, such children react with anger and violence as if to say 'how dare you make me feel bad about myself?' (Baumeister, Smart, & Boden, 1996). Aggressive children also tend to indulge in a 'blame the victim' attitude, to prevent them from empathizing with victims and ensuring their sense of self-esteem remains intact (Liau, Barriga, & Gibbs, 1998).

There is also strong evidence for a biological basis to aggressive behaviour. Adolescent violent offenders tend to have higher levels of testosterone than non-violent offenders (Brooks & Reddon, 1996). Another study found that boys who had high levels of testosterone were more likely to respond to threats with aggression and were also more likely to be irritable, which may predispose them to react aggressively (Olweus, Mattison, Schaling, & Low, 1988). However, the relationship between aggression and hormones may actually be bidirectional. Thus, winning fights leads to increases in testosterone (Schaal, Tremblay, Soussignan, & Susman, 1996).

One of the most significant environmental contexts in which children develop aggressive behaviour is the family. Parents who use negative comments, physical punishment and inconsistent discipline often set the stage for children to become antisocial and aggressive (e.g. Rubin, Burgess, Dwyer, & Hastings, 2003). Negative interactions between parents and children tend to form a cycle of discord (Patterson, 2002) such that children will use aversive strategies, including whining or even violence, in order to get their way. Parents will then respond with physical punishment and other forms of negative parenting. These responses will further increase the child's bad behaviour as, very often, parents end up giving in to children, thus reinforcing the aggression and furthering the cycle. Siblings can also play a role in this process. Younger siblings are particularly at risk of developing aggressive behaviour if older siblings pair up to create discord (Slomkowski, Rende, Conger, Sinous, & Conger, 2001). Taken together, these findings suggest that aggressive children, parents and siblings all engage in cycles of aggression, with each member of the family influencing the others.

Children's experiences outside the home also influence their behaviour. Association with peers, in particular, can provide reinforcement for delinquent behaviour. Research suggests that children who befriend disruptive peers are more likely to themselves engage in delinquent behaviour (Thornberry, Krohn, Lizotte, Smith, & Tobin, 2003). Instances where negative family and peer factors combine can promote especially problematic behaviour.

Therefore, children in families that provide minimal supervision of youngsters and little monitoring of their child's friends may be particularly at risk, while antisocial behaviour is lower in children who spend ample, enjoyable time with their parents (Laird, Pettit, Dodge, & Bates, 2003).

Suppose you were tasked with designing an intervention for changing the behaviour of aggressive children. What strategies might you include in this intervention? In considering your answer, think of some relevant theories you have encountered that might inform your approach (e.g. social learning theory). Should the intervention focus purely on the child or involve other people in the child's life?

Research Example 12.2

Friendship Groups for At-risk Children

Many interventions exist to teach children who have difficulties interacting with others to learn more effective ways of relating. A group of researchers examined how the friendship group component of a multi-component preventive intervention programme called Fast Track impacted on children's social outcomes (Lavallee, Bierman, Nix, and the Conduct Problems Prevention Research Group, 2005). The study was primarily interested in seeing whether associating with other aggressive children in the friendship groups led to more aggression in children. The Fast Track programme was designed to place at-risk children in a social skills training environment designed to prevent further aggressive and disruptive behaviour. The friendship group component of this programme involved five or six children meeting once a week to learn new social cognitions, prosocial behaviour and how to reduce aggression. The friendship groups were run by trained adults. A total of 266 children aged 6 to 7 were placed in a friendship group (56% belonged to a minority group, 29% were female). The authors reported a number of interesting findings:

- Children placed in the friendship groups were significantly more likely than children in control groups to show improvements in moral behaviour.
- Children's pre-intervention positive and negative behaviour was related to their post-intervention behaviour such that children who started off aggressive were more likely to remain aggressive.
- Children who received encouragement from other members of the group for 'naughty' behaviour were less likely to show improvements in their behaviour.
- Simply being in the presence of other disruptive or well-behaved children did not significantly impact on children's post-intervention behaviour.
- The presence of girls in the friendship groups led to significantly better behaviour in all members.

These results have a number of important implications for interventions designed to increase children's moral actions. Specifically, children's own typical behaviour is likely to affect training success more than the influence of other members of the group. Children don't seem to learn disruptive behaviour from others unless the peer group encourages a child's existing disruptive behaviour. Girls appear to have a prosocial strengthening effect, which the authors suggest could reflect that girls promote more acceptance and cohesion in friendship groups. Perhaps every future Fast Track programme should include at least one girl.

Summary

Moral development consists of cognitive, emotional and behavioural components. Perspectives such as Kohlberg's theory of moral development account for children's moral cognitions; evolutionary psychology sheds light on why emotions are important in moral development; social learning theory can be used to understand how children begin to learn their culture's moral behaviour. Moral action can be expressed through empathy and prosocial behaviour while aggression typically involves immoral behaviour. The characteristics of the individual, the family and the wider social context should all be considered when trying to understand how empathy, prosocial behaviour and aggression develop.

Glossary

Aggression is behaviour designed to cause harm, pain or injury to another.

Altruism is unselfish concern for the wellbeing of other people.

Conventional morality is Kohlberg's second level of moral understanding, in which children's behaviour is consistent with others' approval. The child unquestioningly accepts parental and societal rules for good behaviour.

Delay of gratification is the ability to refrain from pleasure until a later time, often for the reward of greater pleasure.

Distributive justice is children's understanding and behaviour regarding how to fairly divide resources among a number of people or how to allocate rewards based on the various contributions of individuals.

Embarrassment is considered the least damaging of the self-conscious emotions; it involves accidental transgressions and minimal anger at oneself.

Empathy is the ability to experience the same emotion as another person, such as distress or suffering.

Guilt is a self-conscious emotion which involves regret about wrongdoing.

Hostile aggression is behaviour designed to hurt another for no apparent purpose.

Inductive discipline is a strategy used to help children gain control of their behaviour, and which may promote the development of empathy. It involves combining discipline with an explanation of why the punished behaviour was wrong.

Instrumental aggression is children's attacking behaviour to gain a coveted object or space.

Moral judgement interview is a technique that Kohlberg used to assess children's moral understanding. Stories which involve a moral dilemma are presented to children, who are asked to justify their moral decisions.

Moral realism stage is the second of Piaget's stages of moral development, in which children show a great deal of respect for rules.

Moral relativism stage is the third of Piaget's stages of moral development, in which children both understand that rules can be questioned and believe in justice for everyone.

Moral understanding is an individual and social acceptance of what constitutes appropriate or correct behaviour. It has cognitive, emotional and behavioural aspects.

Perspective taking is the ability to understand another person's viewpoint. It is related to empathy.

Postconventional morality is Kohlberg's theory's third level of moral development, in which the individual's morality is controlled by an internalized sense of justice that is above the approval and disapproval of others.

Preconventional morality is Kohlberg's theory's first level of moral development, in which children's behaviour is based on avoiding punishment and attracting rewards.

Premoral stage is the first stage of Piaget's theory of moral development, in which children show minimal concern for rules.

Prosocial behaviour is action that is designed to help others.

Shame is a self-conscious emotion which involves self-hate.

Social conventions are the unwritten rules, norms or customs that are generally agreed upon by a society.

Social information processing model suggests aggressive children have an information processing bias that leads them to see all intentions, including ambiguous ones, as aggressive in nature.

Sympathy is feeling concern or sadness for a person in distress, pain or need.

TEST YOUR KNOWLEDGE

1. What are the three levels of Kohlberg's theory of moral development?

   a) Preconventional, conventional and postconventional morality
   b) Good-boy morality, postconventional morality and the development of a conscience
   c) Premoral, moral realism and morality of reciprocity
   d) Trick question: there are six levels in Kohlberg's theory

2. What does the Heinz dilemma test?

   a) Piaget's theory about morality
   b) Kohlberg's moral judgements

(Continued)

    c) The only way to assess children's moral cognitions, emotions and behavioural responses

    d) Children's understanding of sympathy

3. Which of the following is not considered a moral emotion?

    a) Sympathy

    b) Empathy

    c) Embarrassment

    d) Distributive justice

4. How might delay of gratification be tested?

    a) Children are given a moral judgement interview

    b) Children are asked to resist touching an attractive toy

    c) Children are asked to look for an object they saw the experimenter hide

    d) Children are taught to think of fluffy white clouds every time they think of chocolate

ANSWERS: 1–A, 2–B, 3–D, 4–B

Suggested Reading

Damon, W. (1990). *Moral Child: Nurturing children's natural moral growth.* New York: The Free Press.

Damon, W., Lerner, R. M., & Eisenberg, N. (2006). *Handbook of Child Psychology: Vol. 3: Social, emotional, and personality development.* Hoboken, NJ: Wiley.

Langford, P. (1995). *Approaches to the Development of Moral Reasoning.* Hove, East Sussex: Erlbaum.

Want to learn more? For links to online resources relevant to this chapter, interactive quizzes and much more, visit the companion website at **https://edge.sagepub.com/keenan3e/**

V

APPLIED HUMAN DEVELOPMENT

Developmental Psychopathology

13

Chapter Outline

LEARNING AIMS

At the end of this chapter you should:

- be able to describe the importance of a developmental approach to the study of psychopathology
- be familiar with the issues surrounding the measurement of psychopathology in childhood and some of the instruments used by psychologists
- be able to describe some common forms of psychopathology, including *depression*, *anxiety disorders*, *Attention Deficit/Hyperactivity Disorder*, *conduct disorder* and *autism*
- be able to explain the concepts of *risk* and *resilience* and *protective mechanisms*
- understand the issues involved in the prevention and treatment of childhood psychopathology

Introduction

Thus far we have traced the development of the typical child, but what about children who do not follow the norm? This chapter is concerned with children whose development shows signs of psychopathology. **Developmental psychopathology** is the study of childhood disorders and can be thought of as non-typical development (Kerig & Wenar, 2006). Researchers in this area commonly examine disorders such as depression and anxiety, and ask questions about who develops such disorders and why.

Psychologists who adopt the developmental psychopathology framework stress that it is important to look at a range of functioning to understand children's problem behaviours, including the child's biology, environment and wider social context (Cicchetti, 1993: 473). This might remind you of Bronfenbrenner's bioecological approach which we examined in Chapter 2. The **biopsychosocial theory**, which is concerned with interactions between the mind, the body and the environment, has been used to understand mental and physical illness in children and adults (Ogden, 2007).

Psychologists adopting a developmental psychopathology approach to the study of mental disorders assume a continuum of behaviour with 'normal' behaviour at one end of the scale and non-typical behaviour at the other end. Under this model, developmental principles are important to both typical and psychopathological behaviour as the same life-course principles apply along the continuum. Take the development of attachment: becoming securely attached to a primary caregiver in infancy provides a base for the child's future wellbeing and healthy exploration of the world. However, becoming overly attached may lead to high separation anxiety and difficulties with starting school and forming relationships away from the primary attachment figure. This kind of anxiety may disrupt the child's social development. Thus, the same mechanism that leads to healthy development is also involved in sub-optimal functioning.

Can you think of some other processes involved in normal development that might also contribute to the development of psychopathology? In considering this question, perhaps it might be worth revisiting Chapter 2 (Theories of Development) to remind yourself of the different perspectives on development.

Understanding typical development is important in understanding psychopathology, and likewise, knowledge about psychopathology leads to knowledge about normal functioning (Cicchetti, 1990). Cicchetti (1993) has further pointed out that to understand normal development is to be as interested in the children who are at risk of developing a disorder and do not as in those who do actually develop a disorder. These concerns relate to the study of risk and resilience, which we will examine later in this chapter.

There are four main reasons why developmental principles are important in understanding childhood psychopathology (Cicchetti & Toth, 2006; Rutter & Garmezy, 1983). First, the child's developmental level, or age, is central to understanding the onset, significance and course of psychopathology. The age at which a behaviour becomes manifest is crucial: to illustrate, *enuresis* (bed-wetting) takes on very different meanings depending on whether the individual is 2, 10, or 20 years of age. A related point is that susceptibility to stress or risk of psychopathology is linked to the child's age, such that individuals are more vulnerable at different times in their lives. The second major tenet is that the development of a disorder, such as depression, is often based on experiences at an earlier point in development, which calls for a life-span approach. Third, individual differences are important. Researchers may examine many different paths that lead to general dysfunctional behaviour, or to specific disorders. The fourth tenet is concerned with the continuity and discontinuity of behaviour. Problems in childhood often continue through to adulthood. Some children who experience peer rejection become involved with other antisocial children and go on to commit self-destructive and antisocial acts such as drug abuse, stealing and violence (Gelfand & Drew, 2003); however, this is not the case for all children. A significant issue in the study of developmental psychopathology is therefore discovering which factors promote or prevent a childhood disorder from continuing or reoccurring, because some children seem to 'outgrow' their problems.

Related to continuity/discontinuity are the concepts of equifinality and multifinality. **Equifinality** refers to the idea that there are many different ways that children come to manifest disturbed behaviour (Cicchetti & Rogers, 1996). For example, a child who is physically abused may, in turn, act out their aggression on others, while a child who is neglected may also experience frustration and be aggressive. Different origins may produce similar behaviour. A related idea is **multifinality**, which means that a particular risk factor can have a number of different developmental outcomes depending on the characteristics of the individual, previous experiences and the environment. Some children who are physically abused may act this out in aggression or, conversely, become withdrawn and depressed.

The Measurement of Psychopathology

The primary issue in the diagnosis of psychopathology is the achievement of an effective and accurate working definition. In the introduction we saw that typical and psychopathological behaviour can be conceptualized as based along a continuum. However, this model leaves open the question of where normality ends and psychopathology begins. Indeed, there is no one definition of psychopathology that is universally accepted. Depending on a person's personal, cultural, religious, social or historical influences, what may be considered 'normal' changes?

A number of classification systems have sprung up to try to more clearly define psychopathology, and generally these centre on behaviour that is dangerous or causes distress. As we will see, each definition focuses on slightly different criteria depending on whether developmental considerations are addressed. We will look at three of the better known diagnostic systems: the Diagnostic and Statistical Manual of Mental Disorders (DSM), the Child Behaviour Checklist (CBCL) and the Strengths and Difficulties Questionnaire (SDQ). Bear in mind that we are limited to a short review here, and there are many other ways of identifying psychopathology.

First, it is important to note that the classification of disorders is not straightforward, and diagnosing children is often complex. **Co-morbidity**, or the presence of two or more disorders at once, is quite common in children displaying problem behaviour, meaning that multiple diagnoses are often required. Thus, it is not uncommon for a child to suffer from depression as well as anxiety (Nilzon & Palmerus, 1997), although different classification systems deal with this issue in different ways.

The most common and widely used form of diagnosing psychopathology is the **Diagnostic and Statistical Manual of Mental Disorders**, which is now in its fifth edition (American Psychiatric Association, 2013). The proper use of the DSM is dependent on a clinician's skills in determining whether a client's symptoms match those listed in order to diagnose a particular disorder or syndrome. The DSM is not concerned with classifying people, but focuses on behaviour. You will not see reference made to a 'juvenile delinquent', but rather to a 'child with conduct disorder'. This focus on behaviour helps to remove the negative stigma of certain terms, such as 'alcoholic' and 'delinquent', which are sometimes used to label people. The DSM-5 is an attempt to provide an objective diagnostic tool to be used by all kinds of clinicians whether they are psychiatrists or psychologists, and it is therefore guided by empirical work and not grounded in any one model or theory.

A number of aspects of people's functioning are targeted in the DSM-5, through a multiaxial classification system. Axis I is concerned with the *classification of specific disorders*, such as depression, which is the most well-known role of the DSM-5. Axis II deals with the *personality disorders* and *mental retardation*, as these have a pervasive, often life-long impact on the individual's behaviour. In Axis III, the clinician notes any *medical conditions* that could potentially have an effect on the person's functioning, such as a physical injury. The individual's *psychosocial and environmental problems*, such as insufficient social support, are the focus of Axis IV. Finally, Axis V is concerned with a *global assessment of functioning*, which is a score based on the clinician's judgement of an overall level of functioning, ranging from 1 (the lowest) to 100 (the highest).

One advantage of the DSM system is that it acknowledges *cross-cultural norms* and expectations in the diagnosis of individuals. Beliefs about what constitutes psychopathology, and the causes of psychopathology, can vary between cultures. For example, hearing voices is likely to mean psychopathology in many western countries, but could be a symptom of *zar*, or spirit possession, in North Africa (Kerig, Ludlow, & Wenar, 2012). A list of culturally-specific syndromes is provided in the DSM, and enables clinicians to bring a wider context and meaning to the child's symptoms and potential diagnosis. Other ways in which the DSM tries to address multicultural considerations include cautions about labelling culturally sanctioned behaviour as symptoms of a disorder. For example, if a certain culture deems children should be shy and withdrawn, then withdrawn behaviours should not be considered symptoms of a disorder. As we discussed in Chapter 1, cross-cultural research has taught us that different behaviours may be viewed differentially by parents across cultures. Thus, if there is a poor fit between the child's behaviour, for example an inability to sit still and be quiet for extended periods of time, and the cultural expectations of where that child lives, the child may be at risk of being labelled as hyperactive. In contrast, in a culture where activity and a certain amount of inattentiveness are a normal part of childhood, the same child is less likely to be viewed as problematic by their parents and teachers and is less likely to receive a diagnosis (Kerig et al., 2012). Despite these cultural considerations, the DSM system remains a western creation, and it is questionable whether the diagnostic categories are universally valid.

Questions also exist as to whether the DSM-5 deals with important issues, including the child's developmental level. There is no provision for changes in the behaviour underlying a disorder which may occur as a function of age. Research has shown that as children develop, their symptoms of a disorder tend to change. For example, younger children with Attention Deficit/Hyperactivity Disorder (which we will look at in the next section) show more hyperactivity or physical disturbance, whereas older children are more inattentive (Hart et al., 1995). Despite the many strengths of the DSM system, it seems that this diagnostic system does not adequately classify children's and adolescents' changing behaviour. The *reliability* and *validity* of the DSM have also been questioned (Beutler & Malik, 2002). You may remember these terms from Chapter 3; they refer here to the finding that not all clinicians arrive at the same diagnosis when using the DSM (Keller et al., 1995), which brings its reliability into question. It is thus worth making note of other diagnostic approaches, in particular, the **Child Behaviour Checklist (CBCL)**.

While the DSM-5 uses categories to classify behaviour – an individual either has a disorder or not – the CBCL is dimensional and thus provides information about the extent to which that individual shows disturbance. This approach fits more neatly with the definition of psychopathology outlined in the introduction, where deviation was viewed as continuous from normality. The CBCL, as devised by Thomas Achenbach (1995, 1997), is comprised of 118 items which create a profile of eight *narrow-band* and two *wide-band* factors. The narrow-band factors include withdrawal, physical (or *somatic*) complaints, anxiety/depression, social problems, thought problems, attention problems, delinquent behaviour and aggressive behaviour. The more general wide-band factors, which encompass the narrow-band factors, are the *internalizing* and *externalizing* scales. These two terms have actually been adopted in a general way in developmental psychopathology.

Internalizing disorders refer to an inward form of suffering or distress and include disorders such as anxiety and depression. **Externalizing disorders** are a more outward or 'acting out' form of distress and include aggression and delinquent behaviour. It is possible, and actually common, for children to behave in a way that would be considered both internalizing and externalizing. A child may, for instance, be sulky and aggressive at the same time.

Norms that differ by age and gender are available for the CBCL, so that comparisons can be made with an individual's scores. Based on this comparison, a clinician can determine how close to normality an individual's behaviour is and thereby classify the extent of their psychopathology. Three different forms of the CBCL are available, including the self-report, parent report and teacher report. All can be used to gather information about a child. There are often important differences between these sources: parents and teachers will often provide more reliable reports of a child's externalizing behaviour, while the child tends to provide a more accurate report of their internalizing behaviour (Cantwell, 1996). However, reporter characteristics can affect how the child is viewed. For example, a depressed or abusive mother may perceive her child's behaviour to be worse than it really is (Azar, 2002; Cicchetti & Toth, 1996).

A significant problem with the CBCL is that it does not include some of the major childhood disorders, such as autism, learning disabilities and eating disorders (Kerig & Wenar, 2006), all of which are covered in the DSM-5. The CBCL is concerned with degrees of normality, and it is likely that certain disorders, such as autism, do not have a 'normal' endpoint on a continuum. Such disorders are thus best dealt with by the DSM-5, which is able to provide information about the severity of a disorder, but assumes that that disorder is distinct from non-pathological behaviour. The DSM-5, Axis I, and the CBCL will be used to examine some developmental disorders in the next section, so that disorders which are clearly a continuum of normal behaviour will be represented as well as those which are not. Many disorders exist, but we will limit our analysis to a few of the more well-known or common childhood disorders.

Another instrument for assessing psychopathology that has become popular in recent years is the **Strengths and Difficulties Questionnaire (SDQ)**, which was developed by Goodman (1997). This is a brief behavioural screening instrument that can be used for children and adolescents. Like the CBCL, it is a dimensional measure and is concerned with the extent to which behaviour can be seen as normal or pathological. It consists of 25 items divided into five subscales: emotional symptoms, conduct problems, hyperactivity/inattention, peer relationship problems and prosocial behaviour. Scores from the first four of these scales can be added up to obtain a total 'difficulties' score for the child. Scores in the region of 0–13 are regarded as 'normal', scores in the region of 14–16 are regarded as 'borderline', and scores from 17–40 are regarded as 'abnormal'. There are different versions of the SDQ available, including an informant version that is completed by parents and a self-report version than can be completed by older children and adolescents.

One of the main advantages of the SDQ is its brevity compared to instruments such as the CBCL. This makes it quick and easy to administer, and yet this brevity does not seem to have an adverse effect on its reliability and validity. A study by Goodman and Scott (1999), in which mothers completed both the CBCL and SDQ about their children, indicated that the SDQ was more effective than the CBCL at detecting inattention and hyperactivity, and at least as effective as the

CBCL in identifying internalizing and externalizing problems. Mothers also preferred completing the SDQ, which is probably unsurprising given its brevity in comparison to the 69-item CBCL.

However, there are also some limitations to the SDQ. As with the CBCL, there can also be differences in reports between different informants. A study by Van der Meer, Dixon and Rose (2008) collected a large sample of parent and child self-reports using the SDQ and while the reports were often correlated, they also found some cases of discrepancies: children were more likely to report mood disorders while parents were more likely to identify conduct problems. There were often disagreements between parents and children regarding the extent to which behaviours were problematic, with some parents regarding their children's problems as clinically significant when their children did not, and a small sample of children self-reported problems which were not endorsed by their parents. Research by Dave, Nazareth, Senior and Sherr (2008) also noted that there could sometimes be disagreements between mothers and fathers concerning their children's problems. Fathers tended to give higher scores than mothers for externalizing problems and were more likely to report hyperactivity in boys than in girls. Fathers' tendencies to report problems in their children were also related to other factors, such as their use of alcohol and the quality of their relationship with the mother. Given the possibility of discrepancies between different informants, the general advice to clinicians is to combine reports from different sources to maximize the utility of this questionnaire in clinical settings.

Can you think of any other issues that may need to be kept in mind when relying on parental reports or children and adolescent self-reports of problem behaviours using instruments such as the CBCL or SDQ?

Childhood Disorders

Intellectual disability

While strictly not a disorder in the same way that depression or autism are disorders of childhood, we consider intellectual disability as our first specific childhood problem to explore since it is so pervasive. In fact, intellectual disability (ID) is coded as a DSM Axis II problem since it has such a significant impact on the individual's functioning, and may affect the presence and diagnosis of other disorders. On the one hand, ID does not seem appropriately placed next to, say, anxiety or conduct disorder, as the child with intellectual disability may not show troubling behaviour, but instead is simply cognitively more challenged than other children. However, children with ID are three to four times more likely to develop a host of psychological problems compared to typically developing children (Kerig et al., 2012), including Attention Deficit/Hyperactivity Disorder, aggression, schizophrenia, autism, depression and anxiety.

Traditionally, ID was defined in terms of below-average intelligence, as measured by an intelligence quotient (IQ) test. However, ID is currently defined in terms of functioning, such that if a child's intellectual limitations do not affect functioning, then the child would not be considered to have an ID (Foreman, 2003). If the child is able to cope well in the community without special support services, then they are not considered to have a disability, even if they display a low IQ score. Using this definition, an ID can be outgrown, not in the traditional sense that a child may outgrow their low IQ (IQ scores tend to remain fairly stable), but if the child's environment changes, they may no longer be at a functional disadvantage. For example, a child with ID who requires a number of support services to function in school may find a niche in the working world once he or she leaves school that allows for independence of living. That individual would no longer be considered to have an ID.

Intellectual disability occurs in around 1–3% of the population, depending on how the disability is defined (Maulik et al., 2011). Regardless of definition issues, it is a relatively common condition affecting many children worldwide. Intellectual disability is often only detected once a child reaches school, where their academic performance provides a benchmark for their functioning compared to that of their peers. Consequently, the prevalence rate tends to be highest during the school years. A gender imbalance exists, with as many as three times more boys being affected than girls, which may reflect that genetically linked disorders tend to affect males more than females. Intellectual disabilities, particularly mild forms, are also more common in socioeconomically disadvantaged groups, probably due to a number of reasons, including a link between poverty and low IQ in parents, as well as an association between poverty and chronic understimulation in the home environment (Turkheimer et al., 2003).

Any factor occurring before, during or after birth that leads to brain damage can cause ID. Such factors may include exposure to teratogens during pregnancy, complications during birth, malnutrition, trauma and understimulation during the early years. Genetic disorders are another common cause, with hundreds of genetic anomalies resulting in ID. Of the genetic, biological conditions underlying ID, perhaps the most well known is Down syndrome. Children with this disorder have an extra number 21 chromosome. Physical characteristics include disproportionate eyes, ears, hands and feet in addition to intellectual impairment. Children with Down syndrome also typically have a host of medical problems, including congenital heart defects, liver problems and respiratory issues.

Image 13A   Early intervention, often delivered by a team of special educators, speech therapists, occupational therapists, physical therapists, and social workers, significantly improves outcomes for children with Down syndrome

© Denis Kuvaev/Shutterstock

Intervention efforts to address intellectual disability focus on three levels. Through primary intervention, effort is made to prevent cases of ID in the first case. Such efforts include the provision of quality prenatal care, preventing accidents and preventing maternal use of drugs and alcohol during pregnancy. Secondary interventions involve changing situations that may lead to ID, which may occur in utero, such as when a pregnant woman receives an amniocentesis to screen for birth defects, or during childhood, such as the provision of services, like Head Start, to prevent developmental delays. Lastly, tertiary prevention involves treatment of existing ID, and often includes efforts to treat associated medical complications, such as heart surgery for a child with Down syndrome who has a heart defect.

Depression

The criteria in the DSM for depressive disorders are the same, or very similar, for children and adults. Yet there are some important differences in the ways children of varying ages manifest these disorders, making a developmental perspective highly relevant.

Feeling depressed is fairly common. Most people will feel down in the dumps every now and then. To be diagnosed with a *depressive disorder*, or what is otherwise known as **clinical depression**, the normal depressive symptoms that many of us experience on occasion, such as sadness, fatigue and self-pity, have to be marked and severe. As with most disorders, the hallmark of clinical depression is an impairment of day-to-day functioning and/or the presence of significant distress. Thus, an individual suffering from depression may have the above symptoms, as well as recurrent thoughts of death, an obvious decrease in interest and pleasure, and a loss of appetite. Depression exists in varying levels of severity and the above description is based on the criteria for *major depression*, which is a debilitating form of depression marked by a single episode or multiple episodes. Very often children with depression will also experience **somatic complaints**, which are internal distress manifested as physical complaints such as headaches or stomach aches (Gelfand & Drew, 2003).

Although it has been noted that the symptoms of depression in childhood are very similar to those seen in adulthood (Cicchetti & Toth, 1998), there are some important developmental differences. For example, in infancy and toddlerhood, depression may be distinguished by a loss of developmentally appropriate behaviour, such as toilet training and intellectual functioning. During the preschool years, equivalent symptoms may include a sad appearance, a return to earlier stages of development, such as intense separation anxiety, and sleep problems. School-aged children are better able to vocalize their distress, and therefore their depression may be more in line with adult symptoms. Eating and sleep disturbances are often present, although unlike in adulthood, such disturbances are so common in childhood it can be difficult to distinguish when the behaviour is a symptom of depression. Another developmental difference in depression is crying, the meaning and incidence of which will change dramatically from childhood to adulthood (Goodman & Gotlib, 2002).

There are also important gender differences in the development of depression. In childhood depression affects boys and girls almost equally. However, at the onset of puberty females experience more severe and frequent episodes of depression, and this pattern persists into adulthood such that nearly twice as many women as men suffer from depression (Goodman & Gotlib, 2002). Reasons for this gender difference include: a tendency for girls to internalize their stress; increased negative life events for females, such as sexual abuse; more intense family and peer control and expectancies than boys are subject to (Nolen-Hoeksema, 1994). It also seems likely that the biological and, specifically, hormonal differences between boys and girls play a role: hence the sudden gender difference in depression rates around puberty.

What about the long-term consequences for depression in childhood? Depression ratings taken during the early school years have been found to predict the presence of depressive disorders up to six years later for both males and females (Achenbach, Howell, McConaughy & Stanger, 1995). It has further been reported that depressed children who no longer show signs of that particular type of depression in adolescence and adulthood very often develop another form of depression later (Harrington, Rutter, & Fombonne, 1996).

There are many theories surrounding the causes of depression. The finding that adults who are clinically depressed are more likely to have children who are depressed (Cicchetti & Toth, 2006) raises the nature/nurture debate. *Biological* theories suggest that an individual's neurochemical makeup, partly due to genetics, can determine who becomes depressed. Although much research

Table 13.1 The development of some significant childhood disorders

Disorder	Common Features	Gender Differences	Outcomes in Adulthood
Depression	Sadness, fatigue, self-pity, recurrent thoughts of death, decrease in interest and pleasure, and a loss of appetite.	Childhood: equal rates Puberty: females > males	Depression is a fairly stable disorder (although the *form* of depression may change with age).
Anxiety	Intense fear or worry; may be towards a situation (e.g. social phobia) or thing (e.g. specific phobia) which is maladaptive, persistent and beyond the individual's voluntary control.	Depends on the anxiety disorder, e.g. for obsessive-compulsive disorder, boys > girls, but for panic disorder, girls > boys.	Anxiety in childhood often predisposes the individual to either anxiety in adulthood or other forms of psychopathology.
Attention Deficit/ Hyperactivity Disorder	Inattention and/or hyperactivity and impulsivity that is frequent and severe. Impairment is often seen in social, academic or occupational functioning.	Males > females Females experience greater distress	The disorder persists into adulthood for many children. Later antisocial problems and drug abuse may also be associated.
Conduct Disorder	A pattern of antisocial behaviour which is persistent and repetitive, e.g. aggression towards people and animals, destruction of property, deceitfulness and theft, and a serious violation of rules.	Males > females	Childhood onset CD is often associated with problems, such as Antisocial Personality Disorder, criminal behaviour and drug and alcohol abuse later in life.
Autism	A disturbance in social interactions, a host of unusual behaviours and problems with communication, e.g. the child may not engage in eye contact, may be mute, and engage in repetitive behaviours. The disorder has a very early onset (infancy).	Males > females. Females with autism are more likely to display intellectual disability.	The disorder is most often life-long, and over half of children affected continue to be completely dependent on caregivers in adulthood.

has documented the role of neurochemicals such as serotonin in adult depression, the findings are less clear for children (Karponai & Vetro, 2008). *Psychological* theories examine a range of cognitive and emotional factors. Although very young children are unlikely to have the cognitive skills to fully contemplate their helplessness, they are still capable of acting upon their worlds, and developing a sense of self-efficacy. Children who are not given ample opportunity to explore their environments and learn key skills may become depressed. Another example of a psychological theory derives from the attachment perspective, which suggests that insecure attachment leads to depression in infants, children and adolescents (Cicchetti & Toth, 1998). Insecure attachment causes the individual to feel unworthy and that others are unloving. These feelings, in turn, make the individual vulnerable to thoughts of their own worthlessness and hopelessness. *Social* and environmental theories call on research suggesting that ineffective social support and peer rejection are linked to depression in children (Pederson, Vitaro, Barker, & Borge, 2007). The number of stressful life events, such as a death or loss in the family, has also been linked to depression in children (Williamson, Birmaher, Dahl, & Ryan, 2005). It would seem that the best way to understand the development of depression is to combine key aspects of these theories. A biopsychosocial approach which seeks to understand the various ways that hormones, neurochemicals, cognitions, life events and environmental factors interact may be the most effective way of understanding the aetiology of child depression.

Anxiety

A condition that often accompanies depression in both childhood and adulthood is **anxiety**. Anxiety may be the most common psychological disorder of childhood (Cartwright-Hatton, 2006). There are a number of different types of anxiety disorder listed in the DSM, including *specific phobias* (as in a fear of heights, for example), *separation anxiety disorder*, *obsessive-compulsive disorder*, *social anxiety disorder* and *panic disorder*. All of these have commonalities, namely the presence of intense fear, which is maladaptive, persistent and beyond the individual's voluntary control.

Like some of the depressive symptoms, being fearful is a common feeling that visits most of us from time to time. You may be all too familiar with that feeling of a sick stomach and racing heart right before an exam, for example. However, when an individual's normal and adaptive functioning is severely impaired, fear becomes an anxiety disorder. When a sinking stomach and beating heart become so intense that a person is unable to attend school, or even leave the house, a psychologist is likely to classify the behaviour as a symptom of an anxiety disorder. Using the continuum model for psychopathology outlined at the beginning of the chapter, anxiety disorders are situated at the extreme end of the fear spectrum.

Although the developmental course of each of the anxiety disorders differs, it is generally the case that anxiety increases with age. For example, Vasey and colleagues (Vasey, Crnic, & Carter, 1994) examined anxiety in children aged between 5 and 12. The presence of worrisome thoughts was more prevalent in children aged 8 and older. In particular, the 11 to 12 year-olds displayed significantly more evidence of anxiety than the younger children did. It is likely that these increases in anxiety may be related to increases in the capacity for abstract thinking in older

Image 13B Through the process of social referencing, children may acquire anxiety by observing their parent's fear

children. As children get older they have an increased ability to think about the future and also to use *counterfactual thinking* (what might have happened in a given situation) which may in turn exacerbate their anxieties (Kertz and Woodruff-Borden, 2011). This again illustrates the point made earlier in the chapter that the mechanisms underlying healthy development can also contribute in some cases to sub-optimal functioning.

Both heredity and environment are likely to play a role in anxiety disorders. Toddlers who appear shy and have inherited an inhibited temperament are at increased risk for social anxiety disorder later (Hirshfeld-Becker, Biederman, Henin, Faraone, Davis et al., 2007). An important aside here is that not all shy children will be anxious. Brain imaging studies have also shown that social anxiety disorder is associated with increased activity in the amygdala, a brain area involved in fear, especially in response to social cues such as faces (Stein, Goldin, Sareen, Zorrilla, & Brown, 2002). Overprotective parenting, an environmental influence, is also associated with social anxiety disorder, although it is questionable whether hypercritical parenting causes or results from children's anxiety. Again, it is likely that the interplay of inherited temperamental factors and the manner in which the child is treated form anxiety. For example, if parents protect a child with a low toleration for novelty from minor stresses, this may make it harder for the child to cope with such stresses in the future. Another suggestion is that children acquire anxieties by watching their own parent's anxious reactions to feared objects or situations. We saw in Chapter 10 that infants can use social referencing to understand how to react in a given situation and there is some evidence that anxiety can also be transmitted in this manner (Murray, Cresswell and Cooper, 2009).

Some researchers have pointed out that there is much overlap between the symptoms of anxiety and depression and that these commonly co-occur. Under such a unifying model, it is thought that anxiety and depression both have an underlying common factor. For example, the personality trait of neuroticism, which, broadly defined, involves strong negative emotional reactions to stress, may underlie both symptoms of anxiety and depression. Rather than being treated as separate disorders, the most successful strategy for dealing with anxiety and depression may involve treating the underlying negative emotionality (Brown & Barlow, 2009). It is not yet clear whether such a trans-diagnostic model is useful in treatment of the symptoms of anxiety and depression in children and, at this time, the DSM still uses a disorder-specific criteria set and classifies anxiety and depression as separate disorders.

Some children with mood disorders outgrow them, but in many circumstances early susceptibility to anxiety problems continues in later life. In a longitudinal study on the outcome of children diagnosed with an anxiety disorder, many no longer had the disorder after a four-year follow-up, and up to 30% of the children had developed another psychiatric disorder, which demonstrates evidence for the overlap of disorders (Last et al., 1996). Internalizing problems such as mood and anxiety disorders are also associated with later problems, such as substance abuse (Compton, Burns, Helen, & Robertson, 2002). However, alcohol and drug abuse are traditionally linked to externalizing problems, such as conduct disorder, which we will examine next.

Conduct disorder

In contrast to the internalizing disorders of depression and anxiety, conduct disorder and **Attention Deficit/Hyperactivity Disorder (ADHD)** (to be discussed in the next section) are externalizing forms of maladjustment. Conduct disorder (CD) is defined in the DSM as 'a repetitive and persistent pattern of behaviour in which the basic rights of others or major age-appropriate societal norms or rules are violated' (American Psychiatric Association, 2013). Antisocial behaviour thus defined refers to the extreme end of relatively common childhood behaviours like stealing, lying and fighting. The activities of children with CD constitute a serious and severe deviation that affects many aspects of the individual's life. Estimates for the prevalence of CD in the community range between 2% and 6%, and the disorder affects boys in the range of three to four times more than girls (Kazdin, 1997; Moffitt et al., 2001). Reasons for this gender disparity include differences in predispositions to acting aggressively, and parent–child socialization differences that encourage boys to be active and girls to be passive, boys to freely express their anger and girls to feel empathy and guilt (Zahn-Waxler, Cole, & Barrett, 1991).

There are a number of main criteria that the DSM lists to guide the clinician's diagnosis of conduct disorder. Included are: *aggression to people and animals*, such as bullying, and *destruction of property*, like fire-setting. Antisocial activity varies in degrees of severity as we can see with the merging of 'normal' and 'naughty' behaviour in most children. Likewise, there are various levels of conduct disorder that the clinician can identify, ranging from mild, through to moderate and severe. Conduct disorder can also be defined in terms of childhood onset (before age 10) and adolescent onset (absence of CD before age 10). This distinction appears to have important implications for the outcomes for children with conduct disorder.

Childhood-onset CD seems to constitute a more serious and pervasive form of the disorder, as these children are more likely than the adolescent-onset youths to persist in aggressive and criminal behaviour and continue dysfunctional behaviour into adulthood. In order to meet a diagnosis of Antisocial Personality Disorder (an adult disorder that constitutes an Axis II diagnosis and is characterized by unlawful, aggressive, deceitful and generally severe antisocial behaviour), conduct disorder must have been present in youth. Longitudinal studies have shown that conduct disorder in childhood predicts similar levels of deviance up to thirty years later (Farrington, 1991). Recent work has revealed that the continuity of conduct problems is especially pronounced in families suffering from economic hardship (Lahey, Loeber, Burke, & Applegate, 2005).

Not all children with CD continue with antisocial behaviour in adolescence and adulthood. 'Life-course persistent' delinquency has been contrasted with 'adolescent-limited' delinquency, a less serious and more transitory form of antisocial behaviour afflicting many teenagers (Moffitt, 1993). In a classic study, Robins (1978) found that less than 50% of children displaying conduct disorder carried on with their antisocial behaviour into adulthood. While some children may escape a protracted course of conduct disorder, they are still at risk of developing a range of other disorders later in life. It was once thought that adolescent-limited delinquency resolved itself completely; it is now known that even temporary conduct problems are associated with hardship (including internalizing symptoms and life stress) later on (Aguilar et al., 2000). Similarly, Kazdin (1997) has identified a range of difficulties that individuals with a history of CD are prone to, including: *psychiatric problems*, such as anxiety and alcohol abuse; *criminal behaviour*; *occupational problems*, such as difficulty getting and keeping jobs; *marital problems*, characterized by high divorce rates; and *physical illness*, in the form of higher early mortality rates and hospitalization for physical problems. Although conduct disorder is associated with less serious consequences for some children, a closer look reveals that even the children who seem to emerge unscathed may still carry the scars of their early psychopathology.

 Can you think of some reasons why individuals with 'adolescent-limited' conduct disorder may continue to experience a range of difficulties in later life, even if they are no longer engaging in delinquent behaviour?

As with most other forms of psychopathology, determining what causes conduct disorder is a complex question. One line of interesting work has examined the cognitions of aggressive children. As we saw earlier, Kenneth Dodge and his colleagues (e.g. Crick & Dodge, 1994) have studied the role of social-information processing in aggressive behaviour. They have shown that hostile attribution bias, or the tendency to misinterpret other people's motivations as hostile, is common in children who react with aggression. It is likely that such faulty social-information processing arises from a range of parental, temperamental and environmental influences.

A recent study has identified that the development of delinquent and criminal behaviour may be subject to a sensitive period. You may recall from Chapter 5 that sensitive periods are important windows in development when the brain may be particularly susceptive to positive versus maladaptive experiences. In this study, using data from the Minnesota Longitudinal Study of Risk and Adaptation, low socioeconomic status (SES) and unpredictability (including such variables as frequent changes in job status of parents, residential changes, and parental transitions such as divorce) experienced in early childhood (age 0–5) versus in later childhood (age 6–16) were examined in relation to risky behaviour at age 23. The authors found that the strongest predictor of later delinquent behaviour was an unpredictable environment between the ages of 0 and 5. In contrast, an unpredictable environment during ages 6–16 was, for the most part, not significantly related to risky outcomes at age 23. These findings indicate that children may have sensitive periods in their development where they are more or less susceptible to environmental risk factors for the future development of conduct-type problems.

Attention Deficit/Hyperactivity Disorder

The core features of ADHD can be inferred from its name: the disorder involves the ongoing presence of *inattention*, *hyperactivity* and/or *impulsivity* that is both more frequent and more severe than can be accounted for by developmentally appropriate behaviour. To constitute a diagnosis of ADHD some symptoms must have been evident before a child is 7 years old, impairment must cross contexts so that, for example, behaviour at school and at home is affected, and there must be sufficient evidence of significant impairment in social, academic or occupational functioning (American Psychiatric Association, 2013).

As is the case with many disorders, a relatively common range of behaviours must clearly cross the boundary from typical to psychopathological in order to reach a diagnosis of ADHD. Thus, an inability to sit still for long periods of time is common, and indeed expected, during the preschool years (and has been known to follow many of us into adulthood), but for children with ADHD, inattention and/or hyperactivity affects multiple areas of functioning, including school, interpersonal and home life. Another important distinction between the activity levels of children with and without ADHD is the quality of activity. Children given free play may show signs of hyperactivity, but it is in the structured, controlled environment of a classroom, for example, that the hyperactivity of children with ADHD becomes apparent (Campbell, 2000).

Psychologists often refer to the different symptoms of ADHD: inattention, hyperactivity and impulsivity. The *inattention* type of ADHD reflects the behaviour of children who have great difficulty keeping their attention on tasks, compared to those with age-appropriate levels of concentration. Thus, such children may be described as easily distracted, not seeming to listen, as daydreamers, and as continually losing things. Children characterized by *hyperactivity* appear to have boundless levels of energy and are constantly on the move. These children very often fidget or squirm when seated, run and climb at any opportunity, and talk excessively. Children with impulsivity can't seem to hold themselves back, and frequently blurt out answers, can't wait their turn and interrupt other people's conversations or games. It is once again important to note that these behaviours may be common at earlier times in development, but children with ADHD clearly do not display developmentally appropriate levels of attention and/or action-impulse control.

ADHD can be quite difficult to detect during the toddler and preschool years, as a short attention span is characteristic of young children. However, the severity, frequency and chronicity of the child's behaviour are important identifiers of ADHD at this age (Campbell, 1990). The disorder is easier to detect in middle childhood, as standards for self-control and concentration abilities are more perceptible and firmly set. The prevalence of ADHD is thought to be somewhere in the range of 3–5% of the general population of children (Kerig & Wenar, 2006), although recent estimates suggest numbers are growing. Estimates vary for gender differences, but boys appear to be affected more than girls (Gomez, Harvey, Quick et al., 1999). However, research into gender differences in ADHD has identified that girls suffer more psychological distress associated with the disorder than do boys. Rucklidge and Tannock (2001) examined a Canadian sample of children with ADHD and found that girls were more likely to be impaired on measures of anxiety, distress, depression, sense of control and vocabulary. Although boys are more likely to experience ADHD, it seems that girls find it more troubling.

The question of what causes ADHD is still being answered. Again, biology and environment are likely to share key roles. Biological theories suggest that ADHD may result from brain abnormalities. Computer imaging techniques such as magnetic resonance imaging (MRI) have shown that certain areas of the brain, including the frontal lobes, may be impaired in children with ADHD (Kelly, Margilies, & Castellanos, 2007), and in particular these areas appear to be less active and relatively underdeveloped compared to those of typically developing peers. You may recall from Chapter 4 that the frontal lobes are concerned with planning, organization and higher level mental functions, so perhaps it is not surprising that this area of the brain is implicated in ADHD behaviour. Another branch of biological theory posits that ADHD is a genetic disorder. Family, twin and adoption studies have shown that ADHD is a highly heritable disorder (Khan & Faraone, 2006). In terms of environmental influences, a number of early life experiences, including exposure to maternal or second-hand smoke during pregnancy (Liu et al., 2013), and in utero exposure to low levels of oxygen, as can occur during birth complications (Getahum et al., 2012), have been linked to ADHD later in life. A range of family environmental stressors has also been implicated in the manifestation of ADHD, including parents' marital discord, financial stress, inappropriate parenting practices and low levels of parental education (Campbell, 2000). No one factor by itself explains the aetiology of ADHD, and a variety of these environmental and biological causes are likely to be involved.

In terms of what ADHD means for the future lives of sufferers, the news is mixed. It is estimated that 30–50% of children with ADHD continue to have the disorder as adults (Jackson & Farrugia, 1997). Some evidence suggests that adults who experienced hyperactivity as children are not occupationally disadvantaged compared to their peers (Campbell, 2000), perhaps because they find niches that turn their weaknesses into strengths. However, in a recent 33-year longitudinal follow-up study men who were diagnosed with ADHD had significantly worse educational, occupational, economic and social outcomes compared to men without ADHD (Klein et al., 2012). Children with the hyperactive-inattentive type of ADHD may fare the worst. These children are at least seven times more likely than others to have antisocial problems in adulthood (Manuzza et al., 1993). This may stem, at least in part, from a co-morbid antisocial problem in childhood. It may not be surprising to learn that children who can't sit still and frequently disrupt activities and games are less liked by their peers. In fact, 50–60% of children with ADHD are rejected by other children (Whalen & Henker, 1999).

ADHD is often treated with medication and behavioural interventions. While drug therapy, commonly in the form of psychostimulants (which actually have a calming effect on people with ADHD as they are thought to stimulate the areas of the brain involved in attention, planning and impulse control), has proven effective in many cases, parents and physicians have growing concerns about the side-effects and costs of medication. Recent research has revealed that lifestyle changes can improve symptoms, and come without adverse side-effects or costs. For example, even a few minutes of exercise has been linked to better academic performance in children with ADHD (Pontifex et al., 2013). In this study, 40 children (20 with ADHD) aged 8–10 spent 20 minutes either walking briskly on a treadmill or reading while seated. Children then took a brief reading comprehension and mathematics exam, and played a computer game requiring inhibition skills, in which they had to ignore visual stimuli to determine which direction a cartoon fish was swimming. Children performed better on all tasks after exercising, and children with ADHD were able to slow down after making an error on the computer game, displaying a level of inhibition that is often impaired in ADHD. Although the study is small and preliminary, the authors argue that perhaps the first course of action, before prescription of medication, is to increase children's physical activity, particularly during the school day.

Autism

Autism has become an increasingly studied disorder, in part due to its growing prevalence. Autism was once considered a relatively rare disorder (Bailey, Phillips, & Rutter, 1996); however, current estimates suggest that approximately one in every 150 children is affected. Rates are higher for boys, with a recent US survey indicating that one in every 54 boys may be affected (Boyle et al., 2011).

Hallmarks of the disorder are a disturbance in *social interactions*, *problems with communication*, a host of *unusual behaviours*, and *very early onset* (Klin & Volkmar, 1997). Examples of these characteristics include a lack of eye-to-eye contact, difficulty understanding social interactions and language, and engaging in repetitive behaviours such as rocking over and over again. A rare form of the condition is characterized by savant skills, or unusual gifts in specific areas, such as memorizing lists, drawing or music. Many people with autism do have unusual sensory perceptions, such as describing light or touch as painful, while others may not feel pain at all. In reality, the disorder manifests differently from person to person and the disorder can be difficult to classify in high-functioning individuals.

Children with autism have problems with fundamental developmental issues such as emotional, social and cognitive maturity, which allow children to successfully interact with others. In severe cases of autism, it is almost as though the child cannot see those around them as people who are capable of thoughts and feelings. Indeed, there is now fairly concrete evidence to suggest that children with autism have a deficient or non-existent theory of mind (Baron-Cohen, 2004), which cannot be explained by a more general cognitive impairment (Frith & Happé, 1999). As you may recall from Chapter 9, theory of mind refers to the ability to take another's perspective and understand mental states, such as beliefs, desires, intentions and emotions. Children with autism can seem incapable of understanding what others think and feel, a process which non-impaired children develop naturally in the early preschool years.

Another problematic symptom includes sleep difficulties, with 40–70% of individuals failing to achieve sufficient restorative sleep, often displaying insomnia and early rising (Kotagal & Broomall, 2012). Sleep problems may confound the challenges of autism, with research showing that sleep difficulties have a negative effect on daytime behaviour and are strongly related to memory problems as well as internalizing and externalizing behaviour (Sikora et al., 2012). This can present an enormous burden not only for affected children but also for their parents, who may struggle with the cognitive and mood effects of chronic sleep deprivation themselves.

Autism was once classed as a relatively extreme manifestation of the types of behaviour listed above. Related conditions that were considered types of 'high-functioning' autism included Asperger's Disorder and Pervasive Developmental Disorder (not otherwise specified). However, very recently the DSM-5 criteria have changed to dissolve these once separate conditions into one diagnosis called Autistic Spectrum Disorder. According to the American Psychiatric Association, which is charged with producing the DSM, this represents an effort to more accurately diagnose all individuals showing the signs of autism.

Although most children aren't diagnosed until the preschool years, evidence for the disorder usually exists very early in infancy or toddlerhood. Autism is likely congenital (meaning it is present at birth), but the signs can be difficult to identify in infancy. Parents usually become concerned when their toddler fails to reach important developmental milestones, such as talking, and does not seem to enjoy social games like peek-a-boo. In fact, differences in brain development may be evident as early as 6 months of age in children who are later identified as having autism. Children diagnosed as having autism had abnormal development of white matter in the brain (Wolff et al., 2014) (which you may recall reflects the presence of glial cells and myelinated axons). Researchers tracked high-risk children, defined as having a sibling with autism, at 6 months, 1 year and 2 years of age. Children who met criteria for autism at age 2 displayed abnormal connections in many areas of their white brain matter, such that they had increased pathways that connected brain regions at 6 months of age, but then experienced slower development over time. The study suggests that autism does not appear suddenly, but instead develops over an extended period in infancy, and may thus be sensitive to intensive early treatment before the disorder leaves a more permanent mark on brain development.

The question of why there has been such a steep rise in autism rates may have answers in many domains. First, some of the increase is due to the identification of children with autism. Health professionals are increasingly likely to screen for, identify and diagnosis early symptoms. However, increases in autism can only be partially explained by increasing awareness among professionals and parents. Clues as to the reasons for the increase may also be gleaned from research into possible risk factors (see below). For example, maternal obesity is on the rise in most industrialized nations and has been identified as a risk factor for autism.

An early explanation of the cause of autism was that it was related to poor quality parenting, particularly on the part of the mother (known as the 'refrigerator mother' hypothesis). Essentially, autistic symptoms represented the child retreating into their own world in response to a cold, uncaring and emotionally unavailable mother. This view was expressed most forcefully by the psychoanalyst Bruno Bettelheim in his book *The Empty Fortress* (Bettelheim, 1965). Based on this view of autism, Bettelheim advocated long periods of separation of children from their parents as a treatment of the condition. However, this view of the cause of autism has been thoroughly discredited. Many studies have demonstrated that parents of autistic children are no different in their personality characteristics and parenting skills from other parents, and indeed such parents often show great skill in caring for and interacting with their children (Herbert, Sharp, & Gaudiano, 2002; Koegel et al., 1983). Moreover, following his death in 1990, Bettelheim's views were further discredited when it emerged that he had lied about his qualifications in psychoanalysis, and many of the cases he had reportedly 'cured' of autism were in fact fabrications (Herbert, Sharp, & Gaudiano, 2002). The cause of autism is still unknown, although it is likely to result from a complex interaction between genetic and environmental influences. The specific nature of the genetic role has yet to be discovered, although a number of environmental risk factors have been identified (Newschaffer, Croen, Daniels, Giarelli, Grether et al., 2007). Recent environmental factors that have been identified include paternal age, being exposed to high levels of air pollution in utero (Volk et al., 2013), and the mother's health while pregnant, such that obesity, high blood pressure and diabetes during pregnancy have been linked to an elevated risk of autism in babies (Krakowiak et al., 2012). In the past, a great deal of attention was given to the immunization hypothesis, which states that autism, among other developmental disorders, results from the MMR (measles, mumps, rubella) vaccine and the mercury-based preservative used in certain vaccinations (e.g. Wakefield et al., 1998). However, the 1998 'study' that sparked this assertion has now been entirely discredited as a fraud. In a valuable lesson on ethics, the author was found to have misrepresented the study's data and the case has emerged as one of the most damaging medical scares in the history of medicine (Godlee, Smith, & Marcovitch, 2011). Even before the study was debunked, multiple follow-up studies indicated a lack of evidence for a link between vaccinations and the development of autism (DeStefano, 2007). The search is still on to locate its genetic and environmental causes.

The long-term effects of autism are profound, with 60% of children diagnosed as autistic continuing to display significant impairment in adulthood. Many fail to develop friendships (Baron-Cohen, 2004), which is likely to affect their ongoing occupational and personal lives. The transition to young adulthood may be especially difficult for individuals with autism without economic advantages. A recent survey in the USA found that approximately one in three teenagers with autism went on to attend university, but half of the teens surveyed failed to continue their education or find employment within two years of high school (Shattuck et al., 2012). Young adults with autism may demonstrate even more challenges than those with other developmental disabilities. And young adults with autism from economically disadvantaged backgrounds had even fewer opportunities in the survey.

The earlier children with autism receive treatment, the better their emotional, social and cognitive outcomes. It is thought that early intervention does more than show a child how to behave; it may actually change their brain wiring. One early treatment involved an intensive model of 20 hours per week one-on-one interaction with a trained therapist. Parents trained in the technique, a form of structured play, were also required to work with their children. By age 4 children undergoing the treatment displayed a host of improvements, including a higher IQ, higher general functioning, and a less severe autism diagnosis, compared to children receiving the standard treatment for autism (whatever it happened to be in their community) (Rogers et al., 2012). Moreover, the brains of children receiving the treatment changed (Dawson et al., 2012). The brain activity of children without autism shows a specific pattern of activity when looking at pictures of a human face that is not present when they look at inanimate objects. Just the reverse is true of children with autism; their brains light up when looking an inanimate objects but not human faces. After receiving treatment, the brains of children with autism looked much more like a typical 4 year-old's brain. Early intervention clearly has the potential to change not only behavioural outcomes, but also brain development. It is possible that a compensatory mechanism is at play. The authors of the study were careful to conclude that the children had not been 'cured'. They still had autism, but their symptoms had dramatically improved. Another novel treatment for autism is outlined in Research Example 13.1.

Research Example 13.1

Treating Autism with a Love Hormone

Researchers have long theorized that one of the brain mechanisms involved in the social difficulties seen in people with autism stems from a disruption in an important chemical produced in the brain and throughout the body, oxytocin. The hormone is involved in many aspects of reproduction and social bonding. For example, oxytocin is released in women during contraction of the uterus to stimulate labour, during breastfeeding and maternal bonding. In breastfeeding mothers, oxytocin is responsible for the 'let down' of milk, which can occur involuntarily when mothers hear their babies cry. Oxytocin is also involved in social recognition, orgasm and feelings of calmness, and has hence been dubbed the 'love hormone'.

International genetic studies have pointed to a defective oxytocin receptor gene in individuals with autism. Recently, scientists at Yale University tested the use of oxytocin as a treatment for children and adolescents aged 7–18 years with autism and found increased brain function in brain areas involved in processing social information following treatment. The research team conducted a clinical trial using a double-blind, placebo-controlled study in which neither the treating physicians nor patients were aware of which group they were in – the intervention or control group. The intervention group received a single dose of oxytocin in a nasal spray, while the control group received a placebo: fMRIs were used to examine post-intervention brain changes. The group who received oxytocin displayed an almost immediate increased activation in brain regions that are known to process social information. The brain changes were also related to improvements on social information processing tasks that are relevant to understanding other people's intention, thoughts and behaviour.

However, further studies are needed to further understand the precise role of oxytocin in the etiology and treatment of autism.

Questions: Given the findings of this study, and those discussed above related to the success of play therapy, what are your suggestions for the best management of autism going forward?

What might be some of the mechanisms involved in these interventions (hint, think back to Chapter 5 and the topic of neuroplasticity)?

Risk and Resilience

Why do some children emerge from a highly stressful and harmful situation psychologically intact, while others are subject to significantly less adversity and cope much less effectively? These are the kind of questions that research on risk and resilience address. These concepts can be thought of as flipsides of the same coin – research on resilience is usually concerned with the first scenario whereas research on risk looks at the second – but there are also important differences between the two (Rutter, 1987) and we will explore both in turn.

Risk or **vulnerability factors** are fairly enduring characteristics of an individual's external and internal worlds that are likely to lead to maladaptive and negative functioning. Put simply, a risk factor is any factor that increases the chance of an individual developing a psychopathological condition. External factors include the family, social dynamics and, more generally, the environment of the individual. Internal factors relate to influences such as genetics, biology, cognitions and temperament.

Sir Michael Rutter and others (1979, 1985; Rutter & Quinton, 1987) have proposed six significant risk factors that are commonly involved in the development of psychopathology. These are primarily chronic family problems, and are thus extrinsic to the individual. Note that this list is by no means exhaustive, and is simply meant to provide examples of the types of risk which may lead to psychopathology. The factors include: severe marital discord, maternal psychiatric illness; low socioeconomic status; overcrowding or large family size; parental criminality; and the placement of a child out of the family home. Such distal risk factors, which may not directly include the child, are important as they may influence proximal factors that lead to problems more directly. To illustrate, severe marital discord may not in itself cause problems in children. Rather, it is likely that ineffective parenting resulting from discord poses a risk for the development of problem behaviour (Dubow, Roecker, & D'Imperio, 1997). Another example of distal and proximal risk can be seen in recent research conducted on the impact of chronic pain in mothers on their children (Evans, Keenan, & Shipton, 2007). In Research Example 13.2, we'll examine a series of studies that address this topic.

Research Example 13.2

The Effects of Maternal Chronic Pain on Children

It is known that parental mental health can impact children. However, much less is known about the effects of parental physical health. Evans, Shipton and Keenan (2007) set out to examine this question in the city of Christchurch in New Zealand. A group of 39 mothers with chronic pain and their 55 children were compared to a group of 35 control mothers in good health and their 48 children. Mothers in the chronic pain group had conditions such as migraine, arthritis, and neck and back pain that were significantly debilitating. Questionnaires were given to mothers, who reported on their health and parenting, as well as their child's pain and psychosocial behaviour; children reported on their own pain, behaviour and attachment security; fathers or a significant other family member provided information on the child's behaviour; and the child's teacher also reported on the child's pain and psychosocial behaviour. The

(Continued)

study also involved a qualitative interview with mothers and children about what it was like to live with maternal chronic pain.

Analyses revealed that mothers with chronic pain reported significantly more social, physical health and mental health problems than control mothers; they also reported more difficulty in day-to-day parenting tasks, all of which suggests that physical pain may be a risk factor for children's development (Evans, Shipton, & Keenan, 2005). Second, children living with maternal chronic pain were more likely than control-group children to report a range of problems, including their own internalizing and externalizing behaviours, insecure attachment, decreased social skills and increased pain complaints. Reports from children, mothers and fathers were fairly consistent. Teachers didn't report as many problems, but they did note more social problems and pain behaviour in children of mothers with chronic pain than control children (Evans, Keenan, & Shipton, 2007). A third set of analyses that attempted to explain *how* chronic pain in mothers affects children revealed that dysfunctional parenting strategies mediated, or explained, this association. It therefore seems that chronic pain in mothers leads to parenting problems (perhaps due to short-temperedness and an inability to be available both emotionally and physically to children), which in turn lead to problems in children. From these findings we can see that it's not so much the presence of maternal chronic pain that adversely affects children (a distal risk factor) so much as the compromised parenting (a proximal risk factor) that has an impact on children (Evans, Keenan, & Shipton, 2006).

Finally, the qualitative interviews underscored the quantitative results above (Evans & De Souza, 2008). Many children reported feeling anxious and insecure about their mother's pain. Hospitalizations and operations for mothers were frightening for children, and many did not understand their mother's pain. For example, one young child of a mother suffering from chronic migraines reported that he was scared his mother's head was going to explode one day – a quite literal interpretation of her pain descriptions. Mothers also reported that they were worried their pain was going to negatively affect their child's future, and many were concerned that their children were already reporting pain in their own bodies. Mothers also expected their children to take on extra responsibilities around the home and miss out on social activities or fun time when the pain was too much. As you can imagine, children's feelings were mixed; they felt bad for their mothers and tried to help out when they could, but this was tinged with a sense of unfairness and resentment. The findings illustrate that asking mothers and children about their experiences is an important addition to any study of risk and resilience.

Risk factors can also be additive: the sheer number of risk factors that apply to an individual's life may be a more significant determinant of future pathology than specific combinations of risk factors (Garmezy & Masten, 1994). For example, Williams et al. (1990) found that when children experienced fewer than two risk factors from a list similar to that given above, only 7% showed problem behaviour; where children were subject to at least eight such risk factors, that figure rose to 40%. It has similarly been found that the likelihood of an ADHD diagnosis rose as a direct function of the number of family problem risk factors the child was subjected to (Biederman, et al., 1995).

Intrinsic risk factors are equally likely to impact on the child's level of adaptive functioning. This is especially clear in a study of the effects of children's temperament and behaviour (Tschann et al., 1996). Recent research has identified some very specific temperament pathways to psychopathology. Conduct disorder is likely to involve an underlying low fear response and high anger reactivity, while anxiety disorders are likely to involve high negative emotionality (Nigg, 2006). Children with difficult temperaments who lived in families characterized by adversity exhibited more internalizing and externalizing disorders than children who lived in families with a similar level of conflict but who had easy temperaments.

The child's age or developmental level, and thus their intellectual and social-cognitive skills, are core developmental considerations in the assessment of risk. It has, for example, been proposed that older children generally cope with a first case of depression in their parents more effectively than younger children. This is likely to be due to older children's greater level of maturity (Goodman & Gotlib, 1999) and their increased level of competency to effectively cope with the stress (Sroufe & Rutter, 1984). On the other hand, it has been suggested that the very increase in complexity of thought and affect that is achieved in later childhood may cause an increased level of distress for the child, and therefore be associated with higher levels of psychopathology (Cicchetti & Toth, 1998).

Children's behaviour may itself be a risk factor. Gerald Patterson (1996) has made the following notable observation: antisocial children are generally coercive and not very effective in dealing with others. This is, at least in part, a result of poor parental discipline and management of behaviour. However, the child's coercive style and poor social skills feed back into the risk process as provocation for negative parental behaviour, which in turn intensifies the child's existing antisocial behaviour. Patterson's observation makes it clear that models of risk should consider how the complete dynamics of the environment and the individual interact to produce an effect. It is also evident from Patterson's work that we should be careful when making inferences about the causes and effects of behaviour. The determination of cause and effect in the development of psychopathology (or developmental psychology more generally) is a complex task.

This notion of viewing the child's biologically-based risk or diathesis (such as a difficult temperament) as interacting with the child's environment is called a *stress-diathesis model*. Thus a child with a difficult temperament, including high negative emotionality (such as anger) and poor self-regulation, who is exposed to rejecting, harsh or unresponsive parenting, is indeed likely to develop a range of behaviour problems. However, the same child reared with warmth, responsiveness and authoritative parenting is unlikely to experience such behaviour problems (Kim & Kochanska, 2012).

The term 'resilience' refers to an individual's ability to rise above an adverse or stressful situation to function both competently and successfully (Rutter, 1990). It includes the skills, attributes and abilities that allow for this competence (Alvord & Grados, 2005). These qualities are not necessarily exceptional or rare, and may even be as basic as a child's ability to find positive role models in a friend's family. Masten (2001) has argued that resilience is common and stems from

Image 13C   The presence of supportive networks, such as loving and committed elders, represents an important protective factor for children living in at-risk environments

Source: fujidreams/Pixabay.com

normal adaptation. There may be cases when a child comes across a fortuitous change in their environment that protects them, such as a teacher who takes a particular interest in the child's academic progress and nurtures the child's life success, but very often resilience can be found closer to home.

A number of **protective factors** have been identified as contributing to children's resilience, and many of these are qualities inherent in healthy individuals and families across the globe. These have been grouped into three broad sets of factors by Garmezy (1985): *personality features*, such as easy temperament and self-esteem; *family unity* and minimal family conflict; and the *presence of support networks*, such as the emotional availability of peers and elders in the community. However, the presence of such factors is not adequate to explain why certain children display resiliency. Protective factors may not act in the same ways for all children, and they may be differentially significant at each stage of development. For example, the early primary school years are considered to be a sensitive time (Meyer, 1957), when resilient children emerge from the stress of the new environment of school relatively intact compared to less resilient children.

Rutter (1990) has therefore proposed that we look at *protective mechanisms* which go beyond a simple list of factors to help us understand how a child may become resilient. The first mechanism he has identified is *reduction of risk impact*, which applies to children who are buffered from a risky situation. For example, having a caring and trusted older sibling may lessen the negative impact of an emotionally unavailable and distanced parent. The second mechanism is *reduction of negative chain reactions*, which refers to ways in which a vicious cycle can be cut short. For example, a common ring of adversity involves poverty, the presence of deviant peers and criminal behaviour. However, identification with a positive peer group can prevent the link to crime. The third mechanism is the *fostering of self-esteem*, which helps children feel like they can deal with their problems and have the confidence to see that while parts of their lives might not be okay, they themselves are still okay. The fourth and final mechanism is the *emergence of opportunities*. There are turning points in everyone's lives when it is important to take advantage of the opportunities at hand, such as the option to stay at school and receive a higher education as opposed to dropping out and leaving oneself with fewer alternatives.

Another consideration identified by Rutter (1987) is the differential interaction of various risk and protective factors. For example, it has been found that shyness in boys is related to poor social interactions, and may thus be classed as a possible risk factor for problem behaviour. However, the same characteristic in girls is related to positive interactions with others, and consequently is more of a protective factor (Stevenson-Hinde & Hinde, 1986). Therefore, the ways in which children may be protected from, and at risk of, psychopathology are complex and dependent on a number of interacting processes that do not necessarily have the same effect in isolation from each other.

Resiliency is not an all-or-nothing concept covering every aspect of functioning; children may be protected from certain problems in one context, but not in another. For example, children may function poorly at school, but nevertheless be successful in other situations, such as their interactions with peers (Cicchetti & Toth, 1998). This highlights the need in resilience research to make distinctions between functioning in a number of areas, such as behaviour at home, school and peer relationships. A related point is that resilience is not a static concept. Just because an individual is resilient at one stage of their lives does not mean they always will be. If the person's situations alters, so too does their protection from adversity (Rutter, 1987).

It has been documented that children who appear to function well in the face of stressors often internalize their stress, in the form of depression and anxiety (Luthar, 1991). It thus seems that even resilient children may not completely escape negative outcomes, although they are able to inhibit outward expressions of disturbance. Ongoing support may be just as important for resilient children as for individuals who clearly display psychopathological tendencies. Indeed, it is possible that the *continued* availability of help for resilient children is a factor in whether they continue to display resiliency in later life.

In recent years, a novel notion of risk and resilience has emerged. Two researchers in Britain, Jay Belsky and Micheal Pluess, have developed the **differential susceptibility model**, under which genetically at-risk children (such as those with a difficult, anger-prone temperament) may be at further risk when placed in high-adversity environments – consistent with existing notions of risk – but those same children, when placed in supportive environments, are not only protected from adversity, but may actually thrive, even compared to other easier-going children also raised in supportive environments (Belsky & Pleuss, 2009). The differential susceptibility model encompasses the traditional diathesis-stress model outlined above, as well as a plasticity effect, where difficult children who receive positive parenting have better outcomes than easier children also receiving positive parenting. According to this mode, certain potentially problematic traits, such as a difficult temperament, should be viewed not as risk factors, but instead as plastic traits that are highly malleable. The model also assumes that children with a difficult temperament are more sensitive to their environments than easy children, which can be either advantageous or a disadvantage depending on the kind of environment the temperament is paired with. Support for this model has been demonstrated by a number of studies, including a longitudinal examination of the interaction between early reported difficult child temperament and childcare quality on later behaviour problems and social competence. Childcare quality was determined through a number of observational assessments of caregiver–child interactions. The authors found that childcare quality (but not quantity or type of childcare) interacted with infant negativity in predicting behaviour problems and social competence, such that children with early difficult temperaments showed both more behaviour problems when they had experienced low-quality care and fewer problems when experiencing high-quality care than children with easy temperaments (Pleuss & Belsky, 2009). However, the model may not apply to all family ecologies. The high levels of stress and adversity that many economically disadvantaged families experience may impact on interactions between the child's temperament and parenting such that positive parenting may be sufficient to buffer the child from disadvantage (consistent with the stress-diathesis model), but is not sufficient to produce the same kind of flourishing effects on the child seen in more economically advantaged homes (Kochanska & Kim, 2013b).

Developmental principles allow for an examination of contextual factors in the study of risk and resilience. Thus, we now recognize that risk and protection can vary with factors such as history and culture (Cicchetti & Rogosch, 2002). How distress manifests, and how it is interpreted, is contingent on a child's culture. An interesting cross-cultural study revealed that American parents were more likely to view children's behaviour as delinquent than Thai parents, and to predict that the behaviour would be persistent (Weisz, Donenberg, Han, & Kauneckis, 1995). The concept of childhood psychopathology is therefore at least partly nested in culture.

It is largely due to the adoption of a developmental perspective on psychopathology that there is a growing increase in resilience research (Cicchetti & Toth, 1998). Knowledge about both normal and so-called abnormal development is enhanced by understanding how a child may be able to successfully adapt in an otherwise negative environment, and allows for the application of 'resilience-promoting' factors to children's lives. In short, the study of resilient children is very important to the *prevention* and *treatment* of psychopathology. By understanding what has prevented certain children from developing psychopathology in the past, it is possible to develop early intervention efforts to halt psychopathology in the future.

Research Example 13.3

Promoting Resilience through Early Interventions

We have seen throughout this chapter that one major factor that puts children at risk for developing psychopathology is a low socioeconomic status. This is unsurprising considering the stresses encountered by disadvantaged families. Given the link between low socioeconomic status and later psychological and social problems, there has been interest in the possibilities for early interventions that may seek to break this cycle of disadvantage and raise the prospects for children in such families. An example of such an intervention was the High/Scope Perry project. This was a preschool programme implemented in the Ypsilanti School District, Michigan, between 1962 and 1967 and aimed to boost the cognitive, linguistic and social development of children from disadvantaged families and give them skills that they might not acquire from their home environments alone. In this way it was hoped that these children would be better prepared for school entry, which in turn might raise their long-term prospects. The following description draws on the accounts provided by Schweinhart, Barnes, Weikart, Barnett and Epstein (1993), Schweinhart and Weikart (1998) and Weikart (1998).

The High/Scope programme was initiated in 1962 and involved a sample of 123 African-American children aged 3–4 from families living in poverty and whose family characteristics included limited education, low income or welfare dependency, lone parenthood and that the children themselves were assessed as being of high risk of school failure. These children were then randomly assigned to one of two groups: one received the High/Scope preschool programme and the second formed a control group who remained at home with the family. The educational progress of both groups was assessed annually up to the age of 10, with further follow-up assessments at ages 14, 19 and 27.

The High/Scope Perry programme consisted of children attending a three-hour class five days a week and they also received a one-and-a-half-hour home visit from project workers every week. The programme consisted of activities related to language and literacy, social relationships and initiative, numeracy, music and movement. An important feature was the active involvement of the children, and while teachers planned the materials for the sessions, children were encouraged to make choices and suggestions of how to use them.

Interviews were conducted with 95% of the original participants of the study when they reached the age of 27, and clear differences were noted between the programme and comparison groups. Just 7% of the programme group had been arrested five or more times compared to 35% of the control group. Members of the programme group were also more likely to have graduated from high school, had higher earnings and had higher rates of home and car ownership.

Advocates of the High/Scope programme argue that it was the clearly defined curriculum and the child-centred nature of the intervention with its emphasis on planning, social reasoning and other social objectives that underpinned the success of this programme. This conclusion was strengthened by the findings of a second longitudinal study launched in 1967 in which progress of a group of children allocated to the High/Scope programme was compared to that of a group of children exposed to a direct instruction programme focusing purely on academic skills and a traditional nursery educational programme incorporating social objectives and learning through free-play. As with the first study, children were randomly allocated to each group, and the progress of the children was followed up annually until age 10, with assessments taken again at ages 15 and 23.

There did not appear to be significant group differences up to the age of 15; however, when 76% of the original participants were interviewed at age 23, significant group differences did emerge. Members of the direct instruction group had three times as many arrests as the other two groups, and 47% of this group had received treatment for emotional impairments and disturbance during their schooling, compared to just 6% of either of the other two groups.

These findings suggest that while early interventions can indeed raise the long-term prospects for children from disadvantaged families, the nature of the interventions is also important, and interventions that develop social as well as academic skills and involve children's active participation are more likely to be successful.

Questions: Can you think of any ethical issues in the design of the studies investigating the High/Scope Perry programme?

Can you think of any lessons from this programme that might be useful for programmes such as SureStart in the United Kingdom?

Prevention and Treatment

While psychological researchers typically examine the factors explaining psychopathology, it is up to the clinical psychologist or therapist to deal with problems in children hands-on. Prevention and treatment efforts differ according to the theoretical viewpoint of the clinician or therapist. Psychodynamic therapists use techniques such as **play therapy** with children. This is a process in which the therapist observes and interacts with the child in the context of play. As young children can't always talk about their difficulties, therapists often interpret fantasies and behaviour during play as an indication of stresses or problems the child may be experiencing (LeBlanc & Ritchie, 2001). In contrast, the behavioural therapist uses techniques guided by the general principles of behaviour change, such as instructing parents to consistently reward child's desirable behaviours in order to shape the child's behaviour, getting them to use these behaviours more often. Research suggests that behaviour therapy is useful in treating a range of psychopathology (Gelfand & Drew, 2003). Finally, cognitive therapists look to mental processes, rather than overt behaviour, as the focus of their interventions. Thus, the primary goal of cognitive therapy is to change the way disturbed children think. As a consequence, behavioural changes are predicted to follow.

Previously, each of the techniques covered by the various models of psychopathology was argued by their respective proponents to be the best form of treatment. However, in recent years there has been recognition of the strengths and weaknesses of each approach, and a consequently more unified and sophisticated attempt to understand which kinds of therapy are most effective with whom and under what circumstances. Thus, many therapists currently combine techniques borrowed from a number of theoretical positions, including Eastern practices such as meditation, to create a more holistic form of therapy (Walsh & Shapiro, 2006).

Treatment differs according to the disorder or problem that is the focus of intervention. For example, when treating depression, a combination of antidepressant drugs, correcting the child's negative thinking and increasing positive reinforcement (such as praise from the parents) may all be employed (Mufson & Moreau, 1997). In contrast, when helping children with conduct disorder, a predominantly behavioural family intervention, where parents are trained in such areas as child management, problem solving and family communication, may prove to be effective (Woolfenden, Williams, & Peat, 2001).

It is important for the clinician to keep in mind the child's developmental level when considering treatment options. For example, it has been found that cognitive-behaviour therapy is more effective for 11 to 13 year-old children, who are presumably more adept at thinking abstractly, than for younger children. It has been argued that younger children, in the pre-operational and concrete operations stages of cognitive development, do not have the same level of cognitive sophistication needed to benefit from cognitive-behavioural therapy (Durlak, Fuhram, & Lampman, 1991). Thus, methods of treatment requiring less verbal sophistication are needed for younger children. Regardless of the form of treatment, however, it has been found that the outcome for children who receive help is better than for children who do not receive treatment (Shapiro & Shapiro, 1982).

There are a number of general problems that may arise in the treatment of children under stress. Initial access to help may be a difficulty, as children don't usually present themselves for treatment and rely on their parents or teachers to seek help, which does not always happen as quickly as it should. Family breakdowns may also make it difficult for a child to receive help, as the child's problem may fade into the background when the parents or caregivers are facing personal hardships of their own. Once treatment has actually been sought, there are a host of reasons why help can be discontinued, including economic hardship; dropout from treatment tends to be higher in lower socioeconomic status groups (Peters, 2005). Dropout rates for children being treated with CD have been reported to be as high as 50% (Kazdin, 1990). Other reasons for treatment termination include low expectations of treatment, limited skills of the therapist, personal factors like low family and peer support, and environmental factors, such as the unavailability of nearby clinics or centres for treatment (Prinz & Miller, 1991).

Regardless of the types of intervention technique used, there are a number of developmental considerations that may be useful to guide therapy and prevention efforts with children (Kerig & Wenar, 2006). First, an understanding of normal development is important for an accurate distinction between normal and pathological behaviour. Second, treatment and prevention programmes should be tailored to the child's cognitive, emotional and social level of development as we have already seen in the preceding chapters that the differences between a preschool and school-aged child can be profound. Thus, a therapy which is effective at one age may not be quite so useful with children from an earlier or older age group. For example, limits on children's language abilities may limit the usefulness of some types of therapy. Third, knowledge about the various developmental challenges a child of any given age may face can put their behaviour into context and make it more understandable. For example, seeing the conflict between a desire to be autonomous and the constraints presented by their physical limitations can shed light on the cause and seriousness of a 2 year-old's temper tantrums. An understanding of key points in development can provide a guide to the best time for intervention. Thus, an adolescent just starting high school, who is very much aware of the tasks of 'fitting in' and making friends in a new environment, may be vulnerable to the demands of an antisocial peer group and therefore a candidate for preventative interventions.

Summary

As we have seen, the developmental psychopathology approach has made a number of important contributions to the study of non-typical development. Two key aspects of this approach are the emphasis on the study of typical development in relation to the treatment of psychopathology, and the conceptualization of development as taking place on a continuum from normal to typical to problematic.

Glossary

Anxiety refers to disorders which have an intense, maladaptive and persistent fear that is beyond the individual's voluntary control.

Attention Deficit/Hyperactivity Disorder (ADHD) involves the ongoing presence of inattention and/or hyperactivity-impulsivity that is both more frequent and more severe than is appropriate for the child's developmental level.

Autism is an early-onset disorder with a genetic basis which causes disturbance in social interactions, problems with communication and repetitive or stereotyped behaviours.

Biopsychosocial theory examines the child's biological, psychological and wider social influences together in understanding behaviour.

Child Behaviour Checklist (CBCL) is a parent-, teacher- or self-report measure of psychopathology for children and adolescents.

Clinical depression refers to an impairment of day-to-day functioning and/or the presence of significant distress, including pervasive low mood, loss of interest in usual activities and diminished ability to experience pleasure.

Co-morbidity refers to the presence of two or more disorders at one time.

Developmental psychopathology is a discipline which takes a developmental approach to the study of psychopathology, focusing on the course, change and continuity in maladaptive behaviours.

Diagnostic and Statistical Manual of Mental Disorders (DSM-5) is the most common and widely used tool for diagnosing psychopathology.

Equifinality refers to the notion that there are many developmental pathways that can lead to the same outcome.

Externalizing disorders are a more outward or 'acting out' form of distress and include aggression and delinquent behaviour.

Internalizing disorders refer to an inward suffering or distress and include disorders such as anxiety and depression.

Multifinality refers to the notion that a single developmental pathway can lead to multiple outcomes.

Play therapy describes a set of processes by which a therapist observes and interacts with the child in the context of play, using the child's expression of fantasies and behaviours as an indication of the stresses or problems the child may be experiencing.

Protective factors are factors or mechanisms that are identified as contributing to the development of resiliency in children.

Resilience refers to an individual's ability to rise above an adverse or stressful situation, maintaining competent and successful functioning.

Risk or vulnerability factors are enduring characteristics of an individual's disposition or environment that are likely to lead to maladaptive and negative functioning. A risk factor is any factor that increases the chance of an individual developing a psychopathological condition.

Somatic complaint is a form of internal distress that is exhibited externally as a physical health complaint.

TEST YOUR KNOWLEDGE

1. Which is the most accurate definition of developmental psychopathology?

    a) A life-span perspective on how and why certain people become psychopaths
    b) The study of human development from infancy to death
    c) A marriage of developmental psychology and the study of childhood disorders
    d) Odd and unacceptable behaviour such as bed-wetting and aggression

2. Terrie Moffitt has identified two groups of people with anti-social behaviour. These are which of the following?

    a) Those who are at risk of or resilient to delinquency
    b) Adolescent-limited and life-course persistent delinquency
    c) Pot-heads and vandals
    d) Individuals with internalizing and externalizing forms of psychopathology

3. Which of the following is not an internalizing form of psychopathology?

    a) Anxiety
    b) Depression
    c) Autism
    d) Frequent unexplained stomach aches
    e) Recurrent thoughts of death

4. What is the major distinction between a distal and a proximal factor?

    a) Distal factors are not significantly related to an outcome, whereas proximal factors are
    b) They are both the same thing
    c) Distal factors explain risk whereas proximal factors explain resilience
    d) Distal factors are important in that they affect proximal factors which are directly related to an outcome

(continued)

5. Resilience in the context of developmental psychopathology can best be described as which of the following?

   a) A child's ability to use their skills and opportunities to rise above a negative situation to function successfully
   b) The exceptional case where a child gets lucky and can rise above adversity
   c) A reduction of negative chain reactions
   d) When children are faced with a life time of risk

ANSWERS: 1–C, 2–B, 3–C, 4–D, 5–A

Suggested Reading

Cohen, D. J., & Cicchetti, D. (2006). *Developmental Psychopathology: Risk, disorder and adaptation*. Hoboken, NJ: Wiley.

Kerig, P., Ludlow, A., & Wenar, C. (2012). *Developmental Psychopathology: From infancy through adolescence* (6th edition). New York: McGraw-Hill Education.

Want to learn more? For links to online resources relevant to this chapter, interactive quizzes and much more, visit the companion website at **https://edge.sagepub.com/keenan3e/**

References

Aamodt, S. and Wang, S. (2011). *Welcome to Your Child's Brain*. New York: Bloomsbury.

Achenbach, T. (1995). *Bibliography of Published Studies Using the CBCL and Related Materials*. Burlington, VT: University of Vermont Press.

Achenbach, T., Howell, C. T., & Stanger, C. (1995). Six-year predictors of problems in a national sample of children and youths: I. Cross-informant syndromes. *Journal of the American Academy of Child and Adolescent Psychiatry, 34*, 336–347.

Ackerman, B. P. (1981). Young children's understanding of a speaker's intentional use of a false utterance. *Developmental Psychology, 17*, 472–480.

Acredolo, L. P., & Goodwyn, S. W. (1990). Sign language in babies: the significance of symbolic gesturing for understanding language development. In R. Vasta (ed.), *Annals of Child Development* (Vol. 7, pp. 1–42). Greenwich, CT: JAI.

Adamson, L. B. (1995). *Communication Development During Infancy*. Madison, WI: Brown & Benchmark.

Adler, T., & Furman, W. (1988). A model for children's relationships and relationship dysfunctions. In S. W. Duck (ed.), *Handbook of Personal Relationships: Theory, research and interventions* (pp. 211–228). London: Wiley.

Adolph, K. E., Eppler, M. A., & Gibson, E. J. (1993). Crawling versus walking infants' perception of affordances for locomotion over sloping surfaces. Special Section: Developmental biodynamics: Brain, body, behavior connections. *Child Development, 64*, 1158–1174.

Adolph, K. E., Vereijken, B., & Shrout, P. E. (2003). What changes in infant walking and why. *Child Development, 74*, 474–497.

Afeiche, M., Peterson, K. E., Sánchez, B. N., Schnaas, L., Cantonwine, D., Ettinger, A. S., Solano-Gonzalez, M., Hernandez-Avila, M., Hu, H., & Téllez-Rojo, M. M. (2012). Windows of lead exposure sensitivity, attained height, and body mass index at 48 months. *The Journal of Pediatrics, 160*, 1044–1049.

Aguilar, B., Sroufe, L., Egeland, B., & Carlson, E. (2000). Distinguishing the earlyonset/persistent and adolescence-onset antisocial behavior types: from birth to 16 years. *Developmental Psychopathology, 12*, 109–132.

Ahmed, A., & Ruffman, T. (1998). Why do infants make A not B errors in a search task, yet show memory for the location of hidden objects in a nonsearch task? *Developmental Psychology, 34*, 441–453.

Ainsworth, M. D. (1973). The development of infant-mother attachment. In B. Caldwell & H. Ricciuti (eds), *Review of Child Development Research* (Vol. 3). Chicago: University of Chicago Press.

Ainsworth, M. D., Bell, S. M., & Stayton, D. J. (1974). Infant mother attachment and social development: 'socialization' as a product of reciprocal responsiveness to signals. In M. P. M. Richards (ed.), *The Integration of a Child into a Social World* (pp. 91–135). Cambridge: Cambridge University Press.

Ainsworth, M. D., Blehar, M., Waters, E., & Wall, S. (1978). *Patterns of Attachment*. Hillsdale, NJ: Erlbaum.

Aldridge, M. A., Stillman, R. D., & Bower, T. G. R. (2001). Newborn categorization of vowel-like sounds. *Developmental Psychology, 4*, 220–232.

References

Alexander, J. M., & Schwanenflugel, P. J. (1996). Development of metacognitive concepts about thinking in gifted and nongifted children: recent research. *Learning and Individual Differences*, *8*, 305–325.

Allport, G. W. (1961). *Pattern and Growth in Personality*. New York: Holt.

Allsworth, J., Weitzen, S., & Boardman, L. (2005). Early age at menarche and allostatic load: data from the Third National Health and Nutrition Examination Survey. *Annals of Epidemiology*, *15*, 438–444.

Althoff, R. R., Verhulst, F. C., Rettew, D. C., Hudziak, J. J., & van der Ende, J. (2010). Adult outcomes of childhood dysregulation: a 14-year follow-up study. *Journal of the American Academy of Child & Adolescent Psychiatry*, *49*, 1105–1116.

Alvord, M., & Grados, J. (2005). Enhancing resilience in children: a proactive approach. *Professional Psychology: Research and Practice*, *36*, 238–245.

American Psychiatric Association (2013). *Diagnostic and Statistical Manual of Mental Disorders DSM-5-TR* (5th edition). Washington, DC: APA.

Amsterdam, B. K. (1972). Mirror self-image reactions before age two. *Developmental Psychobiology*, 5, 297–305.

Anderson, V., Spencer-Smith, M., & Wood, A. (2011). Do children really recover better? Neurobehavioural plasticity after early brain insult. *Brain*, *103,* 2197–2221.

Anglin, J. M. (1993). Vocabulary development: a morphological analysis. *Monographs of the Society for Research in Child Development*, *58* (10, Serial No. 238), 1–165.

Apgar, V. (1953). Proposal for a new method of evaluation of the newborn infant. *Current Research in Anesthesia and Analgesia*, *92*, 22–25.

Arai, J. A., Li, S., Hartley, D. M., & Feig, L. A. (2009). Transgenerational rescue of a genetic defect in long-term potentiation and memory formation by juvenile enrichment. *The Journal of Neuroscience*, *29*, 1496–1502.

Arsenio, W. F., & Gold, J. (2006). The effects of social injustice on children's moral judgments and behavior: towards a theoretical model. *Cognitive Development*, *21*, 388–400.

Arterberry, M. E., Yonas, A., & Bensen, A. S. (1989). Self-produced locomotion and the development of responsiveness to linear perspective and texture gradients. *Developmental Psychology*, *25*, 976–982.

Asher, S. R., Parkhurst, J. T., Hymel, S., & Williams, G. A. (1990). Peer rejection and loneliness in childhood. In S. R. Asher and J. D. Coie (eds), *Peer Rejection in Childhood* (pp. 253–273). New York: Cambridge University Press.

Aslin, R. N. (1987). Visual and auditory development in infancy. In J. D. Osofsky (ed.), *Handbook of Infant Development* (2nd edition, pp. 5–97). New York: Wiley.

Aslin, R. N., Jusczyk, P. W., & Pisoni, D. B. (1998). Speech and auditory processing during infancy: constraints on and precursors to language. In W. Damon (gen. ed.), D. Kuhn, & R. Siegler (vol. eds), *Handbook of Child Psychology: Vol. 2. Cognition, perception and language* (pp. 147–198). New York: Wiley.

Astington, J. W. (1988). Children's understanding of the speech act of promising. *Journal of Child Language*, *15*, 157–173.

Astington, J. W. (1994). *The Child's Discovery of the Mind*. London: Fontana.

Astington, J. W., & Jenkins, J. (1995). Theory of mind development and social understanding. *Cognition & Emotion*, *9*, 151–166.

Astington, J. W., Harris, P. L., & Olson, D. R. (1988). *Developing Theories of Mind*. New York: Cambridge University Press.

Atherton, F., & Nutbrown, C. (2013). *Understanding Schemas and Young Children: From Birth to Three*. London: Sage.

Athey, C. (2007). *Extending Thought in Young Children: A Parent-Teacher Partnership* (2nd edition). London: Sage.

Atkinson, R. C., & Shiffrin, R. M. (1968). Human memory: a proposed system and its control processes. In K. W. Spence and J. T. Spence (eds), *Advances in the Psychology of Learning and Motivation* (Vol. 2, pp. 90–195). New York: Academic.

Atkinson, R. C., & Shiffrin, R. M. (1971). The control of short-term memory. *Scientific American, 225*, 82–90.

Austin, J. L. (1962). *How To Do Things With Words*. London: Oxford University Press.

Azar, S. T. (2002). Parenting and child maltreatment. In M. H. Bornstein (ed.), *Handbook of Parenting, Vol. 4: Applied Parenting and Social Conditions* (pp. 361–88). Mahwah, NJ: Elrbaum.

Azmitia, M. (1988). Peer interaction and problem solving: when are two heads better than one? *Child Development, 59*, 87–96.

Bagwell, C. L., & Coie, J. D. (2004). The best friendships of aggressive boys: relationship quality, conflict management, and rule-breaking behavior. *Journal of Experimental Child Psychology, 88*, 5–24.

Bahrick, L. E., Gogate, L. J., & Ruiz, I. (2002). Attention and memory for faces and actions in infancy: the salience of actions over faces in dynamic events. *Child Development, 73*, 1629–1643.

Bailey, A., Phillips, W., & Rutter, M. (1996). Autism: towards an integration of clinical, genetic, neuropsychological, and neurobiological perspectives. *Journal of Child Psychology and Psychiatry and Allied Disciplines, 37*, 89–126.

Baillargeon, R. (1987). Object permanence in 3.5- and 4.5-month-old infants. *Developmental Psychology, 23*, 655–664.

Baillargeon, R. (1991). Reasoning about the height and location of a hidden object in 4.5- and 6.5-month-old infants. *Cognition, 38*, 13–42.

Baillargeon, R., & DeVos, J. (1991). Object permanence in young infants: further evidence. *Child Development, 62*, 1227–1246.

Baillargeon, R., DeVos, J., & Graber, M. (1989). Location memory in 8-month-old infants in a non-search AB task: further evidence. *Cognitive Development, 4*, 345–367.

Baillargeon, R., & Graber, M. (1988). Evidence of location memory in 8-month-old infants in a nonsearch AB task. *Developmental Psychology, 24*, 502–511.

Bakeman, R., & Gottman, J. M. (1997). *Observing Interaction: An introduction to sequential analysis* (2nd edition). New York: Cambridge University Press.

Baltes, P. B. (1987). Theoretical propositions of life span developmental psychology: on the dynamics between growth and decline. *Developmental Psychology, 23*, 611–626.

Baltes, P. B., Reese, H. W., & Lipsitt, L. P. (1980). Life-span developmental psychology. *Annual Review of Psychology, 31*, 65–110.

Baltes, P. B., Reuter-Lorenz, P., & Rosler, F. (2006). *Lifespan Development: The perspective of biocultural co-constructivism*. New York: Cambridge University Press.

Baltes, P. B., & Smith, J. (2004). Life span psychology: From developmental contextualism to developmental biocultural coconstructivism. *Research in Human Development, 1*(3), 123–143.

Band, E. B., & Weisz, J. R. (1988). How to feel better when it feels bad: children's perspectives on coping with everyday stress. *Developmental Psychology, 24*, 247–253.

References

Bandura, A. (1977). *Social Learning Theory*. Englewood Cliffs, NJ: Prentice-Hall.

Bandura, A. (1989). Social cognitive theory. In R. Vasta (ed.), *Annals of Child Development: Six theories of child development* (Vol. 6, pp. 1–60). Greenwich, CT: JAI.

Bandura, A. (1991). Social cognitive theory of moral thought and action. *Handbook of Moral Behavior and Development* (Vol. 1, pp. 45–103). Hillsdale, NJ: Erlbaum.

Bandura, A. (1992). Perceived self-efficacy in cognitive development and functioning. *Educational Psychologist*, *28*, 117–148.

Bandura, A., Ross, D., & Ross, S. A. (1961). Transmission of aggression through imitation of aggressive models. *Journal of Abnormal Social Psychology, 63*, 575–582.

Bandura, A., & Walters, R. H. (1963). *Social Learning and Personality Development.* New York: Holt, Rinehart & Winston.

Banish, J. T. (1998). Integration of information between cerebral hemispheres. *Current Directions in Psychological Science, 7*, 32–37.

Banks, M. S., & Ginsburg, A. P. (1985). Early visual preferences: a review and new theoretical treatment. In H. W. Reese (ed.), *Advances in Child Development and Behavior* (Vol. 19, pp. 207–246). New York: Academic.

Banks, M. S., & Salapatek, P. (1983). Infant visual perception. In M. M. Haith and J. J. Campos (eds), *Handbook of Child Psychology: Vol. 2. Infancy and developmental psychobiology* (pp. 435–571). New York: Wiley.

Baranowski, T., Abdelsamad, D., Baranowski, J., O'Connor, T. M., Thompson, D., Barnett, A., Cerin, E., & Chen, T. A. (2012). Impact of an active video game on healthy children's physical activity. *Pediatrics*, *129*, e636–e642.

Barkow, J. H., Cosmides, L., & Tooby, J. (1992). *The Adapted Mind: Evolutionary psychology and the generation of culture.* Oxford: Oxford University Press.

Baron-Cohen, S. (1995). *Mindblindness: An essay on autism and theory of mind.* Cambridge, MA: MIT.

Baron-Cohen, S. (2004). Autism: research into causes and intervention. *Paediatric Rehabilitation*, *7*, 73–78.

Baron-Cohen, S., Ring, H., Moriarty, J., Schmitz, B., Costa, D., & Ell, P. (1994). The brain basis of theory of mind: the role of the orbito-frontal region. *British Journal of Psychiatry*, *165*, 640–649.

Barr, H. M., Steissguth, A. P., Darby, B. L., & Sampson, P. D (1990). Prenatal exposure to alcohol, caffeine, tobacco, and aspirin: effects on fine and gross motor performance in 4-year-old children. *Developmental Psychology*, *26*, 339–348.

Barrett, K. C. (1997). The self and relationship development. In S. Duck (ed.), *Handbook of Personal Relationships*. New York: Wiley.

Barrett, K. C., & Campos, J. J. (1987). Perspectives on emotional development II: a functionalist approach to emotions. In J. D. Osofsky (ed.), *Handbook of Infant Development* (2nd edition, pp. 83–108). New York: Routledge.

Bartlett, M. Y., & DeSteno, D. (2006). Gratitude and prosocial behavior: helping when it costs you. *Psychological Science*, *17*(*4*), 319–325.

Bartsch, K., & Wellman, H. (1989). Young children's attribution of action to beliefs and desires. *Child Development*, *60*, 946–964.

Bartsch, K., & Wellman, H. (1995). *Children Talk about the Mind*. New York: Oxford University Press.

Bates, E. (1976). *Language and Context: The acquisition of pragmatics*. New York: Academic.

Bates, E., & MacWhinney, B. (1989). Functionalism and the competition model. In B. MacWhinney and E. Bates (eds), *The Cross-linguistic Study of Sentence Processing*. New York: Cambridge University Press.

Bates, E., & Roe, K. (2001). Language development in children with unilateral brain injury. In C. A. Nelson and M. Luciana (eds), *Handbook of Developmental Cognitive Neuroscience* (pp. 281–307). Cambridge, MA: MIT.

Bates, J. (2001). Adjustment style in childhood as a product of parenting and temperament. In T. D. Wachs & H. Kohnstamm (eds), *Temperament in Context*. Mahwah, NJ: Erlbaum.

Bates, J. E. (1989). Applications of temperament concepts. In G. A. Kohnstamm, J. E. Bates and M. K. Rothbart (eds), *Temperament in Childhood* (pp. 321–355). New York: Wiley.

Batson, C. D., Polycarpou, M. P., Harmon-Jones, E., Imhoff, H. J., Mitchener, E. C., Bednar, L. L., et al. (1997). Empathy and attitudes: can feeling for a member of a stigmatized group improve feelings toward the group? *Journal of Personality and Social Psychology, 72*, 105–118.

Batson, C. D., & Thompson, E. R. (2001). Why don't moral people act morally? Motivational considerations. *Current Directions in Psychological Science, 10*, 54–57.

Bauer, P. J. (2002). Long-term recall memory: behavioural and neuron-developmental changes in the first 2 years of life. *Current Directions in Psychological Science, 11*, 137–141.

Bauer, P. J. (2008). Toward a neuro-developmental account of the development of declarative memory. *Developmental Psychobiology, 50*, 19–31.

Baumeister, R. F. (1998). Inducing guilt. In J. Bybee (ed.), *Guilt and Children* (pp. 185–213). San Diego, CA: Academic.

Baumeister, R. F., Smart, L., & Boden, J. M. (1996). Relation of threatened egotism to violence and aggression: the dark side of high self-esteem. *Psychology Review, 103*, 5–33.

Bayley, N. (1969). *Bayley Scales of Infant Development*. New York: Psychological Corporation.

Beal, C. R., & Flavell, J. H. (1984). Development of the ability to distinguish communicative intention and literal message meaning. *Child Development, 55*, 60–70.

Beck, E., Burnet, K. L., & Vosper, J. (2006). Birth order effects on facets of extraversion. *Personality and Individual Differences, 40*, 953–959.

Beckett, C., Maughan, B., Rutter, M., Castle, J., Colvert, E., Groothues, C., Kreppner, J., Stevens, S., O'Conner, T., & Sonuga-Barke, E. (2006). Do the effects of early severe deprivation on cognition persist into early adolescence? Findings from the English and Romanian adoptees study. *Child Development, 77*, 696–711.

Beilin, H. (1978). Inducing conservation through training. In G. Steiner (ed.), *Psychology of the Twentieth Century* (Vol. 7, pp. 260–289). Munich: Kindler.

Beilin, H. (1992). Piaget's enduring contribution to developmental psychology. *Developmental Psychology, 28*, 191–204.

Bell, M. A., & Fox, N. A. (1997). Individual differences in object permanence performance at 8 months: locomotor experience and brain electrical activity. *Developmental Psychobiology, 31*, 287–297.

Belsky, J. and Pluess, M. (2009). Beyond diathesis stress: differential susceptibility to environmental influences. *Psychological Bulletin, 135*, 885–908.

Belsky, J., Steinberg, L., & Draper, P. (1991). Childhood experience, interpersonal development, and reproductive strategy: an evolutionary theory of socialization. *Child Development, 62*, 647–670.

Berk, L. E. (2001). *Awakening Children's Minds: How parents and teachers can make a difference*. New York: Oxford University Press.

References

Berk, L. E. (2003). Vygotsky, Lev. *Encyclopedia of Cognitive Science (Vol 6)*. L. Nadel. London: Macmillan.

Berk, L. E. (2006). *Child Development* (7th edition). Boston, MA: Pearson Education.

Berk, L. E., & Spuhl, S. T. (1995). Maternal interaction, private speech, and task performance in preschool children. *Early Childhood Research Quarterly, 10*, 145–169.

Berndt, T. J. (1981). Relations between social cognition, nonsocial cognition, and social behavior: the case of friendship. In J. H. Flavell and L. Ross (eds), *Social Cognitive Development* (pp. 176–199). Cambridge: Cambridge University Press.

Berndt, T. J. (1988). The nature and significance of children's friendships. In R. Vasta (ed.), *Annals of Child Development* (Vol. 5, pp. 155–186). Greenwich, CT: JAI.

Berndt, T. J., Hawkins, J. A., & Hoyle, S. G. (1986). Changes in friendship during a school year: effects on children's and adolescents' impression of friendship and sharing with friends. *Child Development, 57*, 1284–1297.

Bertalanffy, L. von (1968). *General Systems Theory*. New York: Braziller.

Bertenthal, B. I., & Campos, J. J. (1987). New directions in the study of early experience. *Child Development, 58*, 560–567.

Bertenthal, B. I., Campos, J. J., & Kermonian, R. (1994). An epigenetic perspective on the development of self-produced locomotion and its consequences. *Current Directions in Psychological Science, 3*, 140–145.

Bertenthal, B. I., & Clifton, R. K. (1998). Perception and action. In W. Damon (gen. ed.), D. Kuhn and R. Siegler (vol. eds), *Handbook of Child Psychology: Vol. 2. Cognition, perception and language* (pp. 51–102). New York: Wiley.

Bertenthal, B. I., Profitt, D. R., & Kramer, S. J. (1987). The perception of biomechanical motions: implementation of various processing constraints. *Journal of Experimental Psychology: Human perception and performance, 13*, 577–585.

Best, C. T. (1988). The emergence of cerebral asymmetries in early human development: a model. In D. L. Molfese and S. J. Segalowitz (eds), *Brain Lateralization in Children* (pp. 5–35). New York: Guildford.

Bettelheim, B. (1967). *The Empty Fortress*. New York: Free Press.

Beuker, K. T., Rommelse, N. N., Donders, R., & Buitelaar, J. K. (2013). Development of early communication skills in the first two years of life. *Infant Behavior and Development, 36*, 71–83.

Beutler, L. E., & Malik, M. (eds) (2002). *Rethinking the DSM: Psychological Perspectives*. Washington, DC: American Psychological Association.

Biben, M.C., & Champoux, M. (1999). Play and stress: cortisol as a negative correlate of play in Saimiri. In S. Reifel (ed.), *Play & Culture Studies: Play contexts, revisited* (pp. 191–208). Stamford, CT: Greenwood.

Biben, M., & Suomi, S. (1993). Lessons from primate play. In K. MacDonald et al. (eds), *Parent-child Play: Descriptions and implications* (pp. 185–196). Albany, NY: State University of New York Press.

Biederman, J., Milberger, S., Faraone, S., et al. (1995). Family-environment risk factors for attention-deficit hyperactivity disorder. *Archives of General Psychiatry, 52*, 464–470.

Bijeljac-Babic, R., Bertoncini, J., & Mehler, J. (1993). How do 4-day-old infants categorize multisyllable utterances? *Developmental Psychology, 29*, 711–721.

Bjorklund, D. F. (1997). The role of immaturity in human development. *Psychological Bulletin, 122*, 153–169

Bjorklund, D. F. (2005). *Children's Thinking: Cognitive development and individual differences* (4th edition). Belmont, CA: Wadsworth.

Black, J. E., Jones, T. A., Nelson, C. A., & Greenough, W. T. (1998). Neuronal plasticity and the developing brain. In N. E. Alessi, J. T. Coyle, S. I. Harrison and E. Eth (eds), *Handbook of Child and Adolescent Psychiatry* (Vol. 6, pp. 31–53). New York: Wiley.

Blair, C., & Diamond, A. (2008). Biological processes in prevention and intervention: the promotion of self-regulation as a means of preventing school failure. *Development and Psychopathology, 20*, 899–911.

Blasi, A. (1983). Moral cognition and moral action: a theoretical perspective. *Developmental Review, 3*, 178–210.

Blass, E. M., & Ciaramitaro, V. (1994). A new look at some old mechanisms in human newborns: taste and tactile determinants of state, affect, and action. *Monographs of the Society for Research in Child Development, 59* (1, Serial No. 239).

Blatz, W. E. (1938). *The Five Sisters: A study of child psychology*. Toronto: McClelland & Stewart.

Block, N. (1995). How heritability misleads about race. In A. Montagu (ed.), *Race & IQ: Expanded edition* (pp. 444–486). New York: Oxford University Press.

Bloom, L. (1998). Language acquisition in its developmental context. In W. Damon (gen. ed.), D. Kuhn, & R. S. Siegler (vol. eds), *Handbook of Child Psychology: Vol. 2. Cognition, perception, and language* (5th edition, pp. 309–371). New York: Wiley.

Bloom, L., & Tinker, E. (2001). The intentionality model and language acquisition: engagement, effort, and the essential tension. *Monographs of the Society for Research in Child Development, 66* (Serial No. 267).

Bloom, P., & German T. P. (2000). Two reasons to abandon the false-belief task as a test of theory of mind. *Cognition, 77*, 25–31.

Blotner, R., & Bearison, D. J. (1984). Developmental consistencies in sociomoral knowledge: justice reasoning and altruistic behavior. *Merrill-Palmer Quarterly, 30*, 349–367.

Blumberg, F. (1998). Developmental differences as play: children's selective attention and performance in video games. *Journal of Applied Developmental Psychology, 19*, 615–624.

Bogartz, R. S., Shinskey, J. L., & Schilling, T. H. (2000). Object permanence in five-and-a-half-month-old infants. *Infancy, 1*, 403–428.

Bohannon, J. N. III (1993). Theoretical approaches to language acquisition. In J. Berko Gleason (ed.), *The Development of Language* (pp. 239–297). New York: Macmillan.

Bohannon, J. N. III, & Stanowicz, L. (1988). The issue of negative evidence: adult responses to children's language errors. *Developmental Psychology, 24*, 684–689.

Bokhorst, C. L., Bakermans-Kranenburg, M. J., Fearon, P., van Ijzendoorn, M. H., Fonagy, P., & Schuengel, C. (2003). The importance of shared environment in mother-infant attachment: a behavioral genetic study. *Child Development, 74*, 1769–1782.

Boller, K., Grabelle, M., & Rovee-Collier, C. (1995). Effects of postevent information on infants' memory for a central target. *Journal of Experimental Child Psychology, 59*, 372–396.

Bonitatibus, G. (1988). Comprehension monitoring and the apprehension of literal meaning. *Child Development, 59*, 60–70.

Booth, A., Pinto, J., & Bertenthal, B. (2002). Perception of the symmetrical patterning of human gait by infants. *Developmental Psychology, 38*, 554–563.

Borke, H. (1971). Interpersonal perception of young children: egocentrism or empathy? *Developmental Psychology, 5*, 263–269.

Borke, H. (1975). Piaget's mountains revisited: changes in the egocentric landscape. *Developmental Psychology, 11*, 240–243.

Bornstein, M. H. (1989). Sensitive periods in development: structural characteristics and causal interpretations. *Psychological Bulletin, 105*, 179–197.

Bornstein, M. H., & Arterberry, M. E. (1999). Perceptual development. In M. H. Bornstein and M. E. Lamb (eds), *Developmental Psychology: An advanced textbook* (4th edition, pp. 231–274). Mahwah, NJ: Erlbaum.

Bouchard, C. (1994). *The Genetics of Obesity*. Boca Raton, FL: CRC.

Bouchard, T. J. Jr., & McGue, M. (1981). Familial studies of intelligence: a review. *Science, 212*, 1055–1058.

Bower, T. G. R. (1982). *Development in Infancy*. New York: W. H. Freeman.

Bowlby, J. (1958). The nature of the child's tie to his mother. *International Journal of Psychoanalysis, 39*, 350–373.

Bowlby, J. (1960). Grief and mourning in infancy and early childhood. *The Psychoanalytic Study of the Child, 15*.

Bowlby, J. (1969). *Attachment and Loss: Vol. 1. Attachment*. New York: Basic.

Bowlby, J. (1973). *Separation and Loss*. New York: Basic.

Boyce, W. T., & Ellis, B. J. (2005). Biological sensitivity to context: I. An evolutionary-developmental theory of the origins and functions of stress reactivity. *Developmental Psychopathology, 17*, 271–301.

Boyle, C. A., Boulet, S., Schieve, L. A., Cohen, R. A., Blumberg, S. J., Yeargin-Allsopp, M., Visser, S., & Kogan, M. D. (2011). Trends in the prevalence of developmental disabilities in US children, 1997–2008. *Pediatrics, 127*, 1034–1042.

Brainerd, C. J. (1978). The stage question in cognitive developmental theory. *Behavioral and Brain Sciences, 1*, 173–213.

Bremner, A. J., & Mareschal, D. (2004). Reasoning ... what reasoning? *Developmental Science, 7*, 419–421; discussion 422–424.

Bremner, J. G. (1994). *Infancy* (2nd edition). Oxford: Blackwell.

Broadbent, D. (1984). The Maltese cross: a new simplistic model for memory. *Behavioral and Brain Sciences, 7*, 55–94.

Bronfenbrenner, U. (1972). The roots of alienation. In U. Bronfenbrenner (ed.), *Influences on Human Development*. Hinsdale, IL: Dryden.

Bronfenbrenner, U. (1974). Developmental research, public policy, and the ecology of childhood. *Child Development, 45*, 1–5.

Bronfenbrenner, U. (1979). *The Ecology of Human Development: Experiments by nature and by design*. Cambridge, MA: Harvard University Press.

Bronfenbrenner, U. (1989). Ecological systems theory. In R. Vasta (ed.), *Annals of Child Development* (Vol. 6, pp. 187–251). Greenwich, CT: JAI.

Bronfenbrenner, U., & Crouter, A. C. (1983). The evolution of environmental models in developmental research. In P. H. Mussen (series ed.) and W. Kessen (vol. ed.), *Handbook of Child Psychology: Vol. 1 History, theory, and methods* (pp. 357–414). New York: Wiley.

Bronfenbrenner, U., & Evans, G. W. (2000). Developmental science in the 21st century: emerging questions, theoretical models, research designs and empirical findings. *Social Development, 9*, 115–125.

Bronfenbrenner, U., & Morris, P. (1998). The ecology of developmental processes. In W. Damon (gen. ed.) and R. M. Lerner (vol. ed.), *Handbook of Child Psychology: Vol. 1. Theoretical models of human development* (5th edition, pp. 993–1028). New York: Wiley.

Brooks, J. H., & Reddon, J. R. (1996). Serum testosterone in violent and nonviolent young offenders. *Journal of Clinical Psychology, 52*, 475–83.

Brooks, P. J., Hanauer, J., Padowska, B., & Rosman, H. (2003). The role of selective attention in preschoolers' rule use in a novel dimensional card sort. *Cognitive Development*, *18*, 195–215.

Brooks-Gunn, J. (1988). Antecedents and consequences of variations in girls' maturational timing. *Journal of Adolescent Health Care*, *9*, 365–373.

Brown, A. (2011). Media use by children younger than 2 years. *Pediatrics*, *128*, 1040–1045.

Brown, A. L., & Palinscar, A. S. (1982). Inducing strategic learning from texts by means of informed, self-control training. *Topics in Learning and Learning Disabilities*, *2*, 1–17.

Brown, A. M., & Miracle, J. A. (2003). Early binocular vision in human infants: limitations on the generality of the Superposition Hypothesis. *Vision Research*, *43*, 1563–1574.

Brown, R. (1973). *A First Language: The early stages*. Cambridge, MA: Harvard University Press.

Brown, R., & Hanlon, C. (1970). Derivational complexity and order of acquisition in child speech. In J. R. Hayes (ed.), *Cognition and the Development of Language* (pp. 11–53). New York: Wiley.

Brown, T. A., & Barlow, D. H. (2009). A proposal for a dimensional classification system based on the shared features of the DSM-IV anxiety and mood disorders: implications for assessment and treatment. *Psychological Assessment*, *21*, 256.

Bruner, J. (1983). *Child's Talk: Learning to use language*. Oxford: Oxford University Press.

Bryant, P. E., & Trabasso, T. (1971). Transitive inferences and memory in young children. *Nature*, *232*, 456–458.

Bugental, D., & Grusec, J. (2006). Socialization processes. In N. Eisenberg (ed.), *Handbook of Child Psychology* (6th edition). New York: Wiley.

Bühler, C. (1930). *The First Year of Life* (P. Greenberg & R. Riben, trans.). New York: John Day.

Bühler, C. (1935). *From Birth to Maturity: An outline of the psychological development of the child*. London: Routledge & Kegan Paul.

Buhrmester, D. (1996). Need fulfillment, interpersonal competence, and the developmental contexts of friendship. In W. M. Bukowski, A. F. Newcomb and W. W. Hartup (eds), *The Company They Keep: Friendship during childhood and adolescence* (pp. 158–185). New York: Cambridge University Press.

Bushnell, E. W. (1985). The decline of visually guided reaching during infancy. *Infant Behavior and Development*, *8*, 139–155.

Buss, A. H., & Plomin, R. (1975). *A Temperament Theory of Personality Development*. New York: Wiley.

Buss, D. M. (1995). Evolutionary psychology: a new paradigm for psychological science. *Psychological Inquiry*, *6*, 1–30.

Cairns, R. B. (1998). The making of developmental psychology. In R. M. Lerner (ed.), *Handbook of Child Psychology: Vol. 1. Theoretical models of human development* (5th edition, pp. 25–105). New York: Wiley.

Campbell, D. T., & Stanley, J. (1963). *Experimental and Quasi-Experimental Designs for Research*. Boston, MA: Houghton-Mifflin.

Campbell, S. B. (1990). *Behavior Problems in Preschool Children*. New York: Guilford.

Campbell, S. B. (1998). Attention-deficit/hyperactivity disorder: a developmental view. In A. J. Sameroff, M. Lewis and S. M. Miller (eds), The child with attention deficit hyperactivity disorder in family context. *Handbook of Developmental Psychopathology* (2nd edition, pp. 383–389). New York: Kluwer Academic/ Plenum.

Campos, J. J., Barrett, K. C., Lamb, M. E., Goldsmith, H. A., & Stenberg, C. (1983). Socioemotional development. In P. H. Mussen (series ed.), M. M. Haith and J. J. Campos (vol. eds), *Handbook of Child Psychology: Infancy and developmental psychobiology* (4th edition, pp. 783–915). New York: Wiley.

References

Campos, J. J., & Bertenthal, B. I. (1989). Locomotion and psychological development in infancy. In F. Morrisson, C. Lord and D. Keating (eds), *Applied Developmental Psychology* (Vol. 3, pp. 229–258). New York: Academic.

Campos, J. J., Bertenthal, B., & Kermonian, R. (1992). Early experience and emotional development: the emergence of wariness of heights. *Psychological Science, 3*, 61–64.

Campos, J. J., Frankel, C. B., & Camras, L. (2004). On the nature of emotion regulation. *Child Development, 75*, 377–394.

Campos, J. J., Langer, A., & Krowitz, A. (1970). Cardiac responses on the visual cliff in prelocomotor human infants. *Science, 170*, 196–197.

Camras, L. A. (1992). Expressive development and basic emotions. *Cognition and Emotion, 6*, 269–283.

Camras, L. A. (1994). Two aspects of emotional development: expression and elicitation. In P. Ekman and R. J. Davidson (eds), *The Nature of Emotion: Fundamental questions* (pp. 347–351). New York: Oxford.

Camras, L. A., Malatesta, C., & Izard, C. (1991). The development of facial expressions in infancy. In R. Feldman and B. Rime (eds), *Fundamentals of Nonverbal Behavior.* New York: Cambridge University Press.

Camras, L. A., Oster, H., Campos, J. J., Miayke, K., & Bradshaw, D. (1992). Japanese and American infants' responses to arm restraint. *Developmental Psychology, 28*, 578–583.

Canadian Psychological Association (2004). *Policy Statement on Physical Punishment of Children and Youth.* Ottawa, ON. Author. (Retrieved 29 July 2008 from www.cpa. ca/documents/policy.html)

Cantwell, D. P. (1996). Classification of child and adolescent psychopathology. *Journal of Child Psychology and Psychiatry and Allied Disciplines, 37*, 3–12.

Capage, L. & Watson, A. C. (2001). Individual differences in theory of mind, aggressive behavior, and social skills in young children. *Early Education and Development, 12*, 613–628.

Carey, S. (1978). The child as word learner. In M. Halle, G. Miller and J. Bresnan (eds), *Linguistic Theory and Psychological Reality* (pp. 264–293). Cambridge, MA: MIT.

Carey, S. (1985). *Conceptual Change in Childhood.* Cambridge, MA: Bradford/MIT.

Carey, S. (1996). Perceptual classification and expertise. In R. Gelman and T. Kit-Fong Au (eds), *Perceptual and Cognitive Development* (pp. 49–69). New York: Academic.

Carlson, V., Cicchetti, D., Barnett, D., & Braunwald, K. (1989). Disorganized/disoriented attachment relationships in maltreated infants. *Developmental Psychology, 25*, 525–531.

Carpendale, J., & Chandler, M. (1996). On the distinction between false belief understanding and subscribing to an interpretative theory of mind. *Child Development, 67*, 1686–1706.

Cartwright-Hatton, S. (2006). Anxiety of childhood and adolescent: challenges and opportunities. *Clinical Psychology Review, 26*, 813–816.

Carver, C. S., & Scheier, M. F. (2011). Self-regulation of action and affect. In K. D. Vohs and R. F. Baumeister (eds), *Handbook of Self-Regulation* (2nd edition) (pp. 3–21). New York: Guilford.

Case, R. (1985). *Intellectual Development: A systematic reinterpretation.* New York: Academic.

Case, R. (1992a). Neo-Piagetian theories of child development. In R. J. Sternberg and C. A. Berg (eds), *Intellectual Development* (pp. 161–196). New York: Cambridge University Press.

Case, R. (1992b). *The Mind's Staircase.* Hillsdale, NJ: Erlbaum.

Case, R., & Griffin, S. (1990). Child cognitive development: the role of central conceptual structures in the development of scientific and social thought. In C. A. Hauert (ed.), *Developmental Psychology: Cognitive, perceptuo-motor and neuropsychological perspectives* (pp. 193–230). Amsterdam: North Holland.

Case, R., Griffin, S., & Kelly, W. M (2001). Socioeconomic differences in children's early cognitive development and their readiness for schooling. In S. L. Golbeck (ed.), *Psychological Perspectives on Early Education* (pp. 37–63). Mahwah, NJ: Erlbaum.

Caspi, A., & Moffitt, T. E. (1991). Individual differences are accentuated during periods of social change: the sample case of girls at puberty. *Journal of Personality and Social Psychology*, 61, 157–168.

Caspi, A., & Silva, P. A. (1995). Temperamental qualities at age three predict personality traits in young adulthood: longitudinal evidence from a birth cohort. *Child Development*, 66, 486–498.

Cassidy, J. (1994). Emotion regulation: influences of attachment relationships. *Monographs of the Society for Research in Child Development*, 59 (Serial No. 2–3), 228–283.

Cassidy, J., & Berlin, L. J. (1994). The insecure/ambivalent pattern of attachment: theory and research. *Child Development*, 65, 971–991.

Ceglowski, D. (1997). Understanding and building upon children's perceptions of play activities in early childhood. *Journal of Early Childhood Education*, 25, 107–112.

Cernoch, J. M., & Porter, R. H. (1985). Recognition of maternal axillary odors by infants. *Child Development*, 56, 1593–1598.

Chandler, M. J., Greenspan, S., & Barenboim, C. (1973). Judgments of intentionality in response to videotaped and verbally presented moral dilemmas: the medium is the message. *Child Development*, 44, 315–320.

Chang, F., & Burns, B. M. (2005). Attention in preschoolers: associations with effortful control and motivation. *Child Development*, 76, 247–263.

Charlesworth, W. R. (1992). Darwin and developmental psychology: past and present. *Developmental Psychology*, 28, 5–16.

Chen, P., Goldberg, D. E., Kolb, B., Lanser, M., & Benowitz, L. I. (2002). Inosine induces axonal rewiring and improves behavioral outcome after stroke. *Proceedings of the National Academy of Sciences*, 99, 9031–9036.

Chi, M. T. H. (1978). Knowledge structures and memory development. In R. Siegler (ed.), *Children's Thinking: What develops?* (pp. 73–96). Hillsdale, NJ: Erlbaum.

Childers, J. B. & Tomasello, M. (2002). Two-year-olds learn novel nouns, verbs, and conventional actions from massed or distributed exposures. *Developmental Psychology*, 38, 967–978.

Chomsky, N. (1957). *Syntactic Structures*. The Hague: Mouton.

Chomsky, N. (1959). Review of B. F. Skinner's *Verbal Behavior*. *Language*, 35, 26–129.

Chomsky, N. (1968). *Language and Mind*. New York: Harcourt Brace & World.

Cicchetti, D. (1990). An historical perspective on the discipline of developmental psychopathology. In J. Rolf, A. Masten, D. Cicchetti, K. Nuechterlain and S. Weintraub (eds), *Risk and Protective Factors in the Development of Psychopathology* (pp. 2–28). New York: Cambridge University Press.

Cicchetti, D. (1993). Developmental psychopathology: reactions, reflections, projections. *Developmental Review*, 13, 471–502.

Cicchetti, D., & Rogosch, F. (1996). Equifinality and multifinality in developmental psychopathology. *Development and Psychopathology*, 8, 597–600.

Cicchetti, D., & Rogosch, F. (2002). A developmental psychopathology perspective on adolescence. *Journal of Consulting and Clinical Psychology*, 70, 6–20.

Cicchetti, D., & Toth, S. L. (1998). The development of depression in children and adolescents. *American Psychologist*, 53, 221–241.

References

Cicchetti, D., & Toth, S. L. (2006). A developmental psychopathology perspective on preventive interventions with high risk children and families. In A. Renninger and I. Sigel (eds), *Handbook of Child Psychology* (6th edition). New York: Wiley.

Cillessen, A. H., & Mayeux, L. (2004). From censure to reinforcement: developmental changes in the association between aggression and social status. *Child Development*, *75*, 147–163.

Cimbora, D. M., & McIntosh, D. N. (2005). Understanding the link between moral emotions and behavior. In A. Clark (ed.), *Psychology of Moods*. Hauppauge: Nova Science Publishers.

Clifton, R. K., Perris, E., & Bullinger, A. (1991). Infants' perception of auditory space. *Developmental Psychology*, *27*, 161–171.

Clifton, R. K., Rochat, P., Robin, D. J., & Berthier, N. E. (1994). Multimodal perception in the control of infant reaching. *Journal of Experimental Psychology: Human perception and performance*, *20*, 876–886.

Cohen, L. B., & Salapatek, P. (1975). *Infant Perception: From sensation to cognition*. New York: Academic.

Coie, J. D., & Dodge, K. A. (1983). Continuities and changes in children's social status: a five-year longitudinal study. *Merrill-Palmer Quarterly*, *29*, 261–282.

Colby, A., Kohlberg, L., Gibbs, J. C., & Lieberman, M. (1983). A longitudinal study of moral judgment. *Monographs of the Society for Research in Child Development, 48*.

Cole, K. F., & Wertsch, J. V. (2000). Available at www.massey.ac.nz/-Alock/colevyg.htm

Cole, M. (1985). The zone of proximal development: where culture and cognition create each other. In J. V. Wertsch (ed.), *Culture, Communication, and Cognition: Vygotskian perspectives* (pp. 146–161). Cambridge: Cambridge University Press.

Cole, M. (1990). Cognitive development and formal schooling: the evidence from cross-cultural research. In L. C. Moll (ed.), *Vygotsky and Education*. New York: Cambridge University Press.

Cole, P. M., Bruschi, C. J., & Tamang, B. L. (2002). Cultural differences in children's emotional reactions to difficult situations. *Child Development*, *73*, 983–996.

Cole, P. M., & Tamang, B. L. (1998). Nepali children's ideas about emotional displays in hypothetical challenges. *Developmental Psychology*, *34*, 640–646.

Collins, W. A., Maccoby, E. E., Steinberg, L., Hetherington, E. M., & Bornstein, M. H. (2000). Contemporary research on parenting: the case for nature and nurture. *American Psychology*, *55*, 218–232.

Colombo, J. (2002). Infant attention grows up: the emergence of a developmental cognititve neuroscience perspective. *Current Directions in Psychological Science*, *11*, 196–199.

Compton, S. N., Burns, B. J., Helen, L. E., & Robertson, E. (2002). Review of the evidence base for treatment of childhood psychopathology: internalizing disorders. *Journal of Consulting and Clinical Psychology*, *70*, 1240–1266.

Conboy, B. T., & Mills, D. L. (2006). Two languages, one developing brain: event-related potentials to words in bilingual toddlers. *Developmental Science*, *9*, F1–12.

Conti, D., & Camras, L. (1984). Children's understanding of conversational principals. *Journal of Experimental Child Psychology*, *38*, 456–463.

Cooper, R. P., & Aslin, R. N. (1990). Preference for infant-directed speech in the first month after birth. *Child Development*, *61*, 1584–1595.

Cote, S., Tremblay, R. E., Nagin, D. S., Zoccolillo, M., & Vitaro, F. (2002). Childhood behavioral profiles leading to adolescent conduct disorder: risk trajectories for boys and girls. *Journal of American Academy of Child and Adolescent Psychiatry*, *41*, 1086–1094.

Courage, M. L., & Adams, R. J. (1990). Visual acuity assessment from birth to three years using the acuity card procedures: cross-longitudinal samples. *Optometry and Vision Science, 67*, 713–718.

Cowan, N., Nugent, L. D., Elliot, E. M., Ponomarev, I., & Saults, J. S. (1999). The role of attention in the development of short-term memory: age differences in the verbal span of apprehension. *Child Development, 70*, 1082–1097.

Cowley, G. (2001). Generation XXL. In K. L. Frieberg (ed.), *Human Development (*29th edition, pp. 120–121). Guilford, CT: Duskin/McGraw-Hill.

Cox, R. F. A., & Smitsman, A. W. (2006). Action planning in young children's tool use. *Developmental Science, 9*, 628–641.

Coyle, T. R., & Bjorklund, D. F. (1997). Age differences in and consequences of multiple- and variable-strategy use on a multitrial sort-recall task. *Development Psychology, 33,* 372–380.

Crain, W. (2000). *Theories of Development: Concepts and applications.* Upper Saddle River, NJ: Prentice-Hall.

Cramer, P., & Steinwert, T. (1998). Thin is good, fat is bad: how early does it begin? *Journal of Applied Developmental Psychology, 19*, 417–439.

Cramer, S. C., Sur, M., Dobkin, B. H., O'Brien, C., Sanger, T. D., Trojanowski, J. Q., Rumsey, J. M., Hicks, R., Cameron, J., Chen, D., Chen, W. G., Cohen, L. G., deCharms, C., Duffy, C. J., Eden, G. F., Fetz, E. E., Filart, R., Freund, M., Grant, S. J., Haber, S., Kalivas, P. W., Kolb, B., Kramer, A. F., Lynch, M., Mayberg, H. S. McQuillen, P. S., Nitkin, R., Pascual-Leone, A., Reuter-Lorenz, P., Schiff, N., Sharma, A., & Shekim, L., Stryker, M., Sullivan, E.V., & Vinogradov, S. (2011). Harnessing neuroplasticity for clinical applications. *Brain, 134*, 1591–1609.

Crick, N. R., & Dodge, K.A. (1994). A review and reformulation of social information processing mechanisms in children's social adjustment. *Child Development, 66*, 710–722.

Crockenberg, S. (1986). Are temperamental differences in babies associated with predictable differences in care-giving? In J. V. Lerner and R. M. Lerner (eds), *Temperament and Social Interaction in Infants and Children* (pp. 53–74). San Francisco, CA: Jossey-Bass.

Crook, C. (1987). Taste and olfaction. In P. Salapatek and L. Cohen (eds), *Handbook of Infant Perception. Vol. 1. From sensation to perception* (pp. 237–264). Orlando, FL: Academic.

Crook, C., & Lipsitt, L. P. (1976). Neonatal nutritive sucking: effects of taste stimulation upon sucking rhythm and heart rate. *Child Development, 47*, 518–522.

Damon, W. (1977). *The Social World of the Child.* San Francisco, CA: Jossey-Bass.

Damon, W. & Hart, D. (1998). *Self-understanding in Children and Adolescence.* New York: Cambridge University Press.

Dannemiller, J. L., & Stephens, B. R. (1988). A critical test of infant pattern preference models. *Child Development, 59*, 210–216.

Darwin, C. (1877). Biographical sketch of an infant. *Mind, 2,* 285–294.

Davé, S., Nazareth, I., Senior, R., & Sherr, L. (2008). A comparison of father and mother report of child behaviour on the Strengths and Difficulties Questionnaire. *Child Psychiatry and Human Development, 39*, 399–413.

Davidson, R. J. (1994a). Asymmetric brain function, affective style, and psychopathology: the role of early experience and plasticity. *Development and Psychopathology, 6*, 741–758.

Davidson, R. J. (1994b). Temperament, affective style, and frontal lobe asymmetry. In G. Dawson and K. W. Fischer (eds), *Human Behavior and the Developing Brain.* New York: Guilford.

References

Dawson, G., Jones, E. J., Merkle, K., Venema, K., Lowy, R., Faja, S., Kamara, D., Murias, M., Greenson, J., Winter, J., Smith, M., Rogers, S. J., & Webb, S. J. (2012). Early behavioral intervention is associated with normalized brain activity in young children with autism. *Journal of the American Academy of Child & Adolescent Psychiatry*, *51*, 1150–1159.

Deater-Deckard, K., Dodge, K. A., Bates, J. E., & Pettit, G. S. (1996). Physical punishment among African American and European American mothers: links to children's externalizing behaviors. *Developmental Psychology*, *32*, 1065–1072.

DeCasper, A. J., & Spence, M. J. (1986). Prenatal maternal speech influences newborns' perception of speech sounds. *Infant Behavior & Development*, *9*, 133–150.

DeFries, J. C., Plomin, R., & Fulker, D. W. (1994). *Nature and Nurture during Middle Childhood*. Cambridge, MA: Blackwell.

De Haan, M., & Johnson, M. H. (2003). Mechanisms and theories of brain development. In M. de Haan and M. H. Johnson (eds), *The Cognitive Neuroscience of Development*. Hove: Psychology.

Dellarosa Cummins, D., & Cummins, R. (1999). Biological preparedness and evolutionary explanation. *Cognition*, *73*, 37–53.

Demorest, A., Silberstein, L., Gardner, H., & Winner, E. (1983). Telling it as it isn't: children's understanding of figurative language. *British Journal of Developmental Psychology*, *1*, 121–134.

Denham, S. (1998). *Emotional Development in Young Children*. New York: Guilford.

Denham, S. A., Blair, K.A., DeMulder, E., Levitas, J., Sawyer, K., Auerbach-Major, S., & Queenan, P. (2003). Preschool emotional competence: pathway to social competence? *Child Development, 74*, 238–256.

DeStefano, F. (2007). Vaccines and autism: evidence does not support a causal association. *Clinical Pharmacology and Therapeutics*, *82*, 756–759.

deVilliers, P. A., & deVilliers, J. G. (1979). *Early Language*. Cambridge, MA: Harvard University Press.

deVilliers, P. A., & deVilliers, J. G. (1992). Language development. In M. Bornstein and M. Lamb (eds), *Developmental Psychology: An advanced textbook* (3rd edition, pp. 337–418). Hillsdale, NJ: Erlbaum.

Diamond, A., Barnett, W. S., Thomas, J., & Munro, S. (2007). Preschool program improves cognitive control. *Science*, *318*, 1387–1388.

Dick, F., Dronkers, N., Pizzamiglio, L., Saygin, A. P., Small, S. L., & Wilson, S. (2005). Language and the brain. In M. Tomasello and D. I. Slobin (eds), *Beyond Nature-Nurture: Essays in honor of Elizabeth Bates* (pp. 237–260). Mahwah, NJ: Erlbaum.

DiPietro, J. A. (2004). The role of prenatal maternal stress in child development. *Current Directions in Psychological Science*, *13*, 71–74.

Dixon, R. A., & Lerner, R. M. (1998). History and systems in developmental psychology. In M. Bornstein and M. Lamb (eds), *Developmental Psychology: An advanced textbook* (4th edition, pp. 3–46). Mahwah, NJ: Erlbaum.

Dockett, S. (1998). Constructing understandings through play in the early years. *International Journal of Early Years Education*, *6*, 105–116.

Dodge, K., Coie, J., & Tremblay, R. E. (2006). Aggression. In E. W. Damon (ed.), *Handbook of Child Psychology: Vol 3* (6th edition). New York: Wiley.

Dodge, K.A., & Frame, C. L. (1982). Social cognitive biases and deficits in aggressive boys. *Child Development*, *53*, 620–635.

Donaldson, M. (1978). *Children's Minds*. New York: Norton.

Dragonas, T. G. (1992). Greek fathers' participation in labour and care of the infant. *Scandinavian Journal of Caring Sciences*, *6*, 151–159.

Dubow, E., Roecker, C., & D'Imperio, R. (1997). Mental health. In R. Ammerman, M. Hersen et al. (eds), *Handbook of Prevention and Treatment with Children and Adolescents: Interventions in the real world context* (pp. 259–286). New York: Wiley.

Duckworth, A. L., & Seligman, M. E. (2005). Self-discipline outdoes IQ in predicting academic performance of adolescents. *Psychological Science*, *16*, 939–944.

Duncan, R. M. & Tarulli, D. (2003). Play as the leading activity of the preschool period: insights from Vygotsky, Leontyev, and Bakhtin. *Early Education and Development*, *14*, 271–292.

Dunn, J. (1988). *The Beginnings of Social Understanding*. Cambridge, MA: Harvard University Press.

Dunn, J., Brown, J., Slomkowski, C., & Youngblade, L. (1991). Young children's understanding of other people's feelings and beliefs: individual differences and their antecedents. *Child Development*, *62*, 1352–1366.

Dunphy, D. C. (1963). The social structure of urban adolescent peer groups. *Sociometry*, *26*, 230–246.

Durlak, J. A., Fuhrman, P., & Lampman, C. (1991). Effectiveness of cognitive-behavior therapy for maladapting children: a meta-analysis. *Psychological Bulletin*, *110*, 204–214.

Durlak, J.A., Weissberg, R.P., Dymnicki, A.B., Taylor, R. D., & Schellinger, K. B. (2011). The impact of enhancing students' social and emotional learning: a meta-analysis of school-based universal interventions. *Child Development, 82*, 405–432.

Dwairy, M., & Achoui, M. (2010). Parental control: a second cross-cultural research on parenting and psychological adjustment of children. *Journal of Child and Family Studies, 19*, 16–22.

Eberhard, J., & Geissbühler, V. (2000). Influence of alternative birth methods on traditional birth management. *Fetal Diagnosis Therapy*, *15*, 283–290.

Eckerman, C. O. (1993). Imitation and toddlers' achievement of coordinated action with others. In J. Nadel and L. Camaioni (eds), *New Perspectives in Early Communicative Development* (pp. 116–156). New York: Routledge.

Ehri, L. C., Nunes, S. R., Willows, D.M., Schuster, B.V., Yaghoub-Zadeh, Z., & Shanahan, T. (2001). Phonemic instruction helps children learn to read: evidence from the National Reading Panel's meta-analysis. *Reading Research Quarterly, 36*, 250–287.

Eisenberg, N. (2000). Emotion, regulation, and moral development. *Annual Review Psychology*, *51*, 665–697.

Eisenberg, N., & Fabes, R.A. (1998). Prosocial development. In W. Damon (gen. ed.) and N. Eisenberg (vol. ed.), *Handbook of Child Psychology: Vol. 3. Social, emotional, and personality development* (5th edition). New York: Wiley.

Eisenberg, N., Fabes, R. A., Guthrie, I. K., & Murphy, B. C. (1996). The relations of regulation and emotionality to problem behavior in elementary school children. *Development & Psychopathology*, *8*, 141–162.

Eisenberg, N., Fabes, R. A., Nyman, M., Bernzweig, J., & Pinuelas, A. (1994). The relations of emotionality and regulation to children's anger-related reactions. *Child Development*, *65*, 109–128.

Eisenberg, N., Fabes, R. A., Shepard, S., Murphy, B., Guthrie, I., Jones, S., Friedman, J., Poulin, R., & Maszk, P. (1998). Contemporaneous and longitudinal prediction of children's sympathy from dispositional regulation and emotionality. *Developmental Psychology*, *34*, 910–924.

Eisenberg, N., Fabes, R. A., & Spinrad, T. (2006). Prosocial development. In R. M. Damon and N. Eisenberg (eds), *Handbook of Child Psychology Vol 3* (6th edition). New York: Wiley.

References

Eisenberg, N., Sadovsky, A., Spinrad, I. L., Fabes, R. A., Losoya, S. H., & Valiente, C. (2005). The relations of problem behavior status to children's negative emotionality, effortful control, and impulsivity: concurrent relations and prediction of change. *Developmental Psychology*, *41*, 193–211.

Elder, G. H. (1974). *Children of the Great Depression*. Chicago: University of Chicago Press.

Elder, G. H. (1995). Human lives in changing societies: life course and developmental insights. In R. B. Cairns, G. H. Elder and E. J. Costello (eds), *Developmental Science: Multidisciplinary perspectives*. New York: Cambridge University Press.

Elder, G. H. (1998). The life course and human development. In W. Damon (gen. ed.) and R. M. Lerner (vol. ed.), *Handbook of Child Psychology: Vol. 1. Theoretical models of human development* (5th edition, pp. 939–991). New York: Wiley.

Elias, C. L., & Berk, L. E. (2002). Self-regulation in young children: is there a role for sociodramatic play? *Early Childhood Research Quarterly*, *17*, 1–17.

Elkind, D., & Bowen, R. (1979). Imaginary audience behavior in children and adolescence. *Developmental Psychology, 15*, 33–44.

Ellis, B. J., Bates, J. E., Dodge, K. A., Fergusson, D. M., Horwood, J. L., Pettit, G. S., & Woodward, L. (2003). Does father absence place daughters at special risk for early sexual activity and teenage pregnancy? *Child Development*, *74*, 801–821.

Ellis, B. J., Essex, M. J., & Boyce, W. T. (2005). Biological sensitivity to context: II. Empirical explorations of an evolutionary-developmental theory. *Developmental Psychopathology*, *17*, 303–328.

Ellis, B. J., McFayden-Ketchum, S., Dodge, K. A., Petit, G. S., & Bates, J. E. (1999). Quality of early family relationships and individual differences in the timing of pubertal maturation in girls: a longitudinal test of an evolutionary model. *Child Development*, *77*, 387–401.

Ellis, S., Rogoff, B., & Cromer, C. (1981). Age segregation in children's social interactions. *Developmental Psychology*, *17*, 399–407.

Ellsworth, C. P., Muir, D. W., & Hains, S. M. J. (1993). Social competence and person-object differentiation: an analysis of the still face effect. *Developmental Psychology*, *29*, 63–73.

Elman, J. L., Bates, E. A., Johnson, M. J., Karmiloff-Smith, A., Parisi, D., & Plunkett, K. (1996). *Rethinking Innateness: A connectionist perspective on development*. Cambridge, MA: Bradford/MIT.

Emde, R. N., Gaensbauer, T. J., & Harmon, R. J. (1976). Emotional expression in infancy: a biobehavioral study. *Psychological Issues* (Vol. 10, No. 37). New York: International Universities Press.

Engle, J. M., & McElwain, N. L. (2011). Parental reactions to toddlers' negative emotions and child negative emotionality as correlates of problem behavior at the age of three. *Social Development*, *20*, 251–271.

Engle, W. A., & Kominiarek, M. A. (2008). Late preterm infants, early term infants, and timing of elective deliveries. *Clinics in Perinatology*, *35*, 325–341.

Epstein, J. L., & Sanders, M. G. (2002). Family, school, and community partnerships. In M. Bornstein (ed.), *Handbook of Parenting, Vol 5: Practical issues in parenting* (2nd edition) (pp. 407–438). Mahwah, NJ: Lawrence Erlbaum Associates.

Erikson, E. H. (1963). *Childhood and Society* (2nd edition). New York: Norton.

Ervin-Tripp, S. (1979). Children's verbal turn-taking. In E. Ochs and B. Schieffelin (eds), *Developmental Pragmatics* (pp. 391–414). New York: Academic.

Estigarribia, B., & Clark, E. V. (2007). Getting and maintaining attention in talk to young children. *Journal of Child Language*, *34*, 799–814.

Evans, S., & De Souza, L. (2008). Families dealing with chronic pain: giving voice to the experiences of mothers with chronic pain and their children. *Qualitative Health Research*, *18*, 489–500.

Evans, S., Keenan, T. R., & Shipton, E. A. (2006). The relationship between maternal chronic pain and child adjustment: the role of parenting as a mediator. *Journal of Pain*, *7*, 236–243.

Evans, S., Keenan, T. R., & Shipton, E. A. (2007). Psychosocial adjustment and physical health of children living with maternal chronic pain. *Journal of Pediatrics and Child Health*, *43*, 262–270.

Evans, S., Shipton, E. A., & Keenan, T. R. (2005). Psychosocial functioning of mothers with chronic pain: a comparison to pain-free controls. *European Journal of Pain*, *9*, 683–690.

Evans, J., Workman, L., Mayer, P., & Crowley, K. (2002). Differential bilingual laterality: mythical monster found in Wales. *Brain and Language*, *83*, 291–299.

Fancy, S. P., Chan, J. R., Baranzini, S. E., Franklin, R. J., & Rowitch, D. H. (2011). Myelin regeneration: a recapitulation of development? *Annual Review of Neuroscience*, *34*, 21–43.

Fantz, R. L. (1961). The origin of form perception. *Scientific American*, *204*, 66–72.

Fantz, R. L. (1966). Pattern discrimination and selective attention as determinants of perceptual development from birth. In A. H. Kidd and J. L. Rivoire (eds), *Perceptual Development in Children*. New York: International University Press.

Farrington, D. P. (1991). Childhood aggression and adult violence: early precursors and later life outcomes. In D. J. Pepler and K. H. Rubin (eds), *The Development and Treatment of Childhood Aggression* (pp. 5–29). Hillsdale, NJ: Erlbaum.

Fein, G. G. (1981). Pretend play in childhood: an integrative review. *Child Development, 52*, 1095–1118.

Feldman, R. (2007). Parent–infant synchrony and the construction of shared timing; physiological precursors, developmental outcomes, and risk conditions. *Journal of Child Psychology and Psychiatry*, *48*, 329–354.

Fenson, L., Dale, P. S., Reznick, J. S., Bates, E., Thal, D. J., & Pethick, S. J. (1994). Variability in early communicative development. *Monographs of the Society for Research in Child Development*, *59* (5, Serial No. 242).

Ferguson, T. J., & Stegge, H. (1998). Measuring guilt in children: a rose by any other name still has thorns. In J. Bybee (ed.), *Guilt and Children* (pp. 19–74). San Diego, CA: Academic.

Ferguson, T. J., Stegge, H., & Damhuis, I. (1991). Children's understanding of guilt and shame. *Child Development*, *62*, 827–839.

Ferguson, T. J., Stegge, H., Miller, E. R., & Olsen, M. E. (1999). Guilt, shame, and symptoms in children. *Developmental Psychology*, *35*, 347–357.

Fernald, A. (1985). Four-month-old infants prefer to listen to motherese. *Infant Behavior and Development*, *8*, 181–195.

Fernald, A., & Kuhl, P. (1987). Acoustical determinants of infant preference for motherese speech. *Infant Behavior and Development*, *10*, 279–293.

Field, T. M. (1990). *Infancy*. Cambridge, MA: Harvard University Press.

Field, T. M. (2001). *Touch*. Cambridge, MA: Harvard University Press.

Fischer, K. W., & Bidell, T. R. (2006). Dynamic development of action, thought, and emotion. In W. L. Damon and R.M. Lerner (eds), *Handbook of Child Psychology: Theoretical models of human development* (Vol. 1, pp. 313–399). New York: Wiley.

Fischer, K. W., & Rose, S. P. (1994). Dynamic development of coordination of components in brain and behavior: a framework for theory and research. In G. Dawson and K. W. Fischer (eds), *Human Behavior and the Developing Brain* (pp. 3–66). New York: Guilford.

Fischer, K. W., & Rose, S. P. (1995, Fall). Concurrent cycles in the dynamic development of brain and behavior. *SRCD Newsletter*, 3–4, 15–16.

References

Flavell, J. H. (1985). *Cognitive Development* (2nd edition). Englewood Cliffs, NJ: Prentice-Hall.

Flavell, J. H., Beach, D. R., & Chinsky, J. M. (1966). Spontaneous verbal rehearsal in a memory task as a function of age. *Child Development, 37,* 283–299.

Flavell, J. H., & Miller, P. H. (1998). Social cognition. In W. Damon, D. Kuhn and R. S. Siegler (eds), *Handbook of Child Psychology: Vol. 2. Cognition, perception and language.* New York: Wiley.

Flavell, J. H., Miller, P. H., & Miller, S. A. (2002). *Cognitive Development* (4th edition). Upper Saddle River, NJ: Prentice-Hall.

Fogel, A. (1993). *Developing Through Relationships: Origins of communication, self, and culture.* Chicago: University of Chicago Press.

Foreman, P. (2003). Mental retardation: definition, classification and systems of support, 10th edn. American Association on Mental Retardation. Washington, DC. 2002. *Journal of Intellectual and Developmental Disability, 28,* 310–311.

Forman, E. A., & McPhail, J. (1993). Vygotskian perspectives on children's collaborative problem-solving activities. In E. A. Forman, N. Minck and C. A. Stone (eds), *Contexts for Learning* (pp. 323–347). New York: Cambridge University Press.

Fox, N. A., & Calkins, S. D. (2003).The development of self-control of emotion: intrinsic and extrinsic influences. *Motivation and Emotion, 27,* 7–26.

Fox, N. A., Calkins, S. D., & Bell, M. A. (1994). Neural plasticity and development in the first two years of life: evidence from cognitive and socioemotional domains. *Development and Psychopathology, 6,* 677–696.

Fox, N. A. & Card, J. A. (1999). Psychophysiological measures in the study of attachment. In J. Cassidy and P. R. Shaver (eds.), *Handbook of Attachment: Theory, Research and Clinical Applications* (pp. 226–245). New York: Guilford Press.

Fox, N. A., Schmidt, L. A., & Henderson, H. A. (2000). Developmental psychophysiology: conceptual and methodological perspectives. In L. G. Tassinary (ed.), *Handbook of Psychophysiology* (2nd edition). New York: Cambridge University Press.

Fraser, H. P., Kemp, S., & Keenan, T. (2007). Behavioural studies of distributional justice in children. *European Journal of Developmental Psychology, 4,* 198–219.

Freeman, E. B., & Daly, J. (1984). Distributive justice in children: its relationship to immanent justice and egocentricism. *Early Child Development and Care, 16,* 185–194.

French, D. C. (1988). Heterogeneity of peer rejected boys: aggressive and nonaggressive subtypes. *Child Development, 59,* 976–985.

French, D. C. (1990). Heterogeneity of peer rejected girls. *Child Development, 61,* 2028–2031.

Freud, S. (1917). *Lines of Advance in Psychoanalytic Therapy* (Vol. SE xvii). London: Hogarth Press and The Institute of Psychoanalysis.

Fridlund, A. J., Beck, H. P., Goldie, W. D., & Irons, G. (2012). Little Albert: A neurologically impaired child. *History of Psychology, 15,* 302.

Fried, P., Watkinson, B., & Gray, R. (2003). Differential effects on cognitive functioning in 13- to 16-year-olds prenatally exposed to cigarettes and marihuana. *Neurotoxicology Teratology, 25,* 427–436.

Friedler, G. (1996). Paternal exposures: impact on reproductive and developmental outcome: an overview. *Pharmacology, Biochemistry and Behavior, 55,* 691–700.

Frith, U., & Happé, F. (1999). Theory of mind and self-consciousness: what is it like to be autistic? *Mind and Language, 14,* 1–22.

Frith, U., & Happé, F. (2005). Autism spectrum disorder. *Current Biology, 15*, R786–R790.

Frodi, A. M., & Lamb, M. (1978). Sex differences in responsiveness to infants: a developmental study of psychophysiological and behavioral responses. *Child Development, 49*, 1182–1188.

Fronstin, P., Greenberg, D. H., & Robins, P. K. (2005). The labour market consequences of childhood maladjustment. *Social Science Quarterly, 86*, 1170–1195.

Fulhan, J., Collier, S., & Duggan, C. (2003). Update on pediatric nutrition: breast-feeding, infant nutrition and growth. *Current Opinion in Pediatrics, 15*, 323–332.

Gaillard, W. O., Balsamo, L., Ibrahim, Z., Sachs, B. C., & Xu, B. (2003). Developmental aspects of language processing: fMRI of verbal fluency in children and adults. *Human Brain Mapping*, 18, 176–185.

Gallahue, D. L. (1989). *Understanding Motor Development* (2nd edition). Carmel, IN: Benchmark.

Garcia, M. M., Shaw, D. S., Winslow, E. B., & Yaggi, K. E. (2000). Destructive sibling conflict and the development of conduct problems in young boys. *Developmental Psychology, 36*, 44–53.

Gardner, H. (1973). *The Quest for Mind: Piaget, Lévi-Strauss, and the structuralist movement.* Chicago: The University of Chicago Press.

Garmezy, N. (1985). Stress-resistant children: the search for protective factors. In J. E. Stevenson (ed.), Recent research in developmental psychopathology. *Journal of Child Psychology and Psychiatry Book Supplement 4* (pp. 213–233). Oxford: Pergamon.

Garmezy, N., & Masten, A. S. (1994). Chronic adversities. In M. Rutter, E. Taylor and L. Hersov (eds), *Child and Adolescent Psychiatry: Modern approaches* (3rd edition, pp. 191–208). London: Blackwell.

Garvey, C. (1974). Requests and responses in children's speech. *Journal of Child Language, 2*, 41–60.

Gaskins, S. (1996). How Mayan parental theories come into play. In S. Harkness and C. M. Super (eds) *Parents' Cultural Belief Systems: Their origins, expressions, and consequences* (pp. 345–363). New York: Guilford.

Gaskins, S. (2000). Children's daily activities in a Mayan village: a culturally grounded description. *Cross-Cultural Research, 34*, 375–389.

Ge, X., Brody, G. H., Conger, R. D., Simons, R. L., & Murray, V. M. (2002). Contextual amplification of pubertal transition effects on deviant peer affiliation and externalizing behavior among African American children. *Developmental Psychology, 38*, 42–54.

Ge, X., Conger, R., & Elder, G. (2001). The relation between puberty and psychological distress in adolescent boys. *Journal of Research on Adolescence, 11*, 49–70.

Geary, D. C. (2006). Evolutionary developmental psychology: current status and future directions. *Developmental Review, 26*, 113–119.

Geary, D. C., & Bjorklund, D. F. (2000). Evolutionary developmental psychology. *Child Development, 71*, 57–65.

Gelfland, D. M., & Drew, C. J. (2003). *Understanding Children's Behavior Disorders* (4th edition). Belmont, CA: Wadsworth/Thomson Learning.

Gesell, A. L. (1925). *The Mental Growth of the Preschool Child.* New York: Macmillan.

Gesell, A. L. (1928). *Infancy and Human Growth.* New York: Macmillan.

Gesell, A. L., & Thompson, H. (1929). Learning and growth in identical infant twins: an experimental study by the method of co-twin control. *Genetic Psychology Monographs, 6*, 1–24.

Getahun, D., Rhoads, G. G., Demissie, K., Lu, S. E., Quinn, V. P., Fassett, M. J., Quinn, V. P., Fassett, M. J., Wing, D. A., & Jacobsen, S. J. (2012). In utero exposure to ischemic-hypoxic conditions and attention-deficit/hyperactivity disorder. *Pediatrics*, 131, e53–e61.

Gibson, E. J. (1969). *Principles of Perceptual Learning and Development.* New York: Appleton.

Gibson, E. J. (2003). The world is so full of a number of things: on specification and perceptual learning. *Ecological Psychology, 15*, 283–287.

Gibson, E. J., & Walk, R. D. (1960). The 'visual cliff.' *Scientific American, 202*, 64–71.

Gibson, E. J., & Walker, A. S. (1984). Development of knowledge of visual-tactual affordances of substance. *Child Development, 55*, 453–460.

Gibson, J. J. (1979). *The Ecological Approach to Visual Perception.* Boston, MA: Houghton Mifflin.

Gilligan, C. (1982). *In A Different Voice.* Cambridge, MA: Harvard University Press.

Gilliom, M., Shaw, D. S., Beck, J. E., Schonberg, M. A., & Lukon, J. L. (2002) Anger regulation in disadvantaged preschool boys: strategies, antecedents, and the development of self-control. *Developmental Psychology, 38*, 222–235.

Ginsburg, H. P., & Opper, S. (1988). *Piaget's Theory of Intellectual Development* (3rd edition). Englewood Cliffs, NJ: Prentice-Hall.

Gleitman, L. R. (1990). The structural sources of verb meanings. *Language Acquisition, 1*, 3–55.

Glucksberg, S., & Krauss, R. M. (1967). What do people say after they have learned to talk? Studies of the development of referential communication. *Merrill-Palmer Quarterly, 13*, 309–316.

Glucksberg, S., Krauss, R. M., & Weissberg, R. (1966). Referential communication in nursery school children: method and some preliminary findings. *Journal of Experimental Child Psychology, 3*, 333–342.

Godlee, F., Smith, J., & Marcovitch, H. (2011). Wakefield's article linking MMR vaccine and autism was fraudulent. *BMJ, 342*, c7452.

Goh, E. C., & Kuczynski, L. (2009). Agency and power of single children in multi-generational families in urban Xiamen, China. *Culture & Psychology, 15,* 506–532.

Goldberg, M., Maurer, D., & Lewis, T. (2001). Developmental changes in attention: the effects of endogenous cueing and of distractors. *Developmental Science, 4*, 209–219.

Goldberg, S., & DiVitto, B. (2002). Parenting children born preterm. In M. Bornstein (ed.), *Handbook of Parenting, Volume 1, Children and parenting* (2nd edition, pp. 209– 231). Mahwah, NJ: Erlbaum.

Goldsmith, H. H. (1996). Studying temperament via construction of the Toddler Behavior Assessment Questionnaire. *Child Development, 67*, 218–235.

Goldsmith, H. H., Buss, A. H., Plomin, R., Rothbart, M. K., Thomas, A., Chess, S., Hinde, R. W., & McCall, R. B. (1987). Roundtable: what is temperament? Four approaches. *Child Development, 58*, 505–529.

Gomez, R., Harvey, J., Quick, C., Scharer, I., & Harris, G. (1999). DSM-IV AD/HD: confirmatory factor models, prevalence, and gender and age differences based on parent and teacher ratings of Australian primary school children. *Journal of Child Psychology and Psychiatry and Allied Disciplines, 40*, 265–274.

Goodman, R. (1997). The Strengths and Difficulties Questionnaire: A research note. *Journal of Child Psychology and Psychiatry, 38*, 581–586

Goodman, R., & Scott, S. (1999). Comparing the Strengths and Difficulties Questionnaire and the Child Behavior Checklist: Is small beautiful? *Journal of Abnormal Child Psychology, 27*, 17–24

Goodman, S., & Gotlib, I. (1999). Risk for psychopathology in the children of depressed mothers: a developmental model for understanding mechanisms of transmission. *Psychological Review, 106*, 458–490.

Goodman, S., & Gotlib, I. (2002). *Children of Depressed Parents.* Washington, DC: American Psychological Association.

Gopnik, A. (1996). The post-Piaget era. *Psychological Science, 4*, 221–225.

Gopnik, A., & Meltzoff, A. (1987). The development of categorization in the second year and its relation to other cognitive and linguistic developments. *Child Development*, *58*, 1523–1531.

Gopnik, A., & Meltzoff, A. (1996). *Words, Thoughts and Theories*. Cambridge, MA: Bradford/MIT.

Gopnik, A., & Wellman, H. M. (1994). The theory theory. In L.A. Hirschfeld and S.A. Gelman (eds), *Mapping the Mind: Domain specificity in cognition and culture* (pp. 257–293). New York: Cambridge University Press.

Gordon, I., Vander Wyk, B. C., Bennett, R. H., Cordeaux, C., Lucas, M. V., Eilbott, J. A., Zagoory-Sharon, O., Leckman, J. F., Feldman, R., & Pelphrey, K. A. (2013). Oxytocin enhances brain function in children with autism. *Proceedings of the National Academy of Sciences*, *110*, 20953–20958.

Goswami, U., & Brown, A. L. (1990). Higher-order structure and relational reasoning: contrasting analogical and thematic relations. *Cognition*, *36*, 207–226.

Gottesman, I. I. (1963). Genetic aspects of intelligent behavior. In N. Ellis (ed.), *Handbook of Mental Deficiency: Psychological theory and research* (pp. 253–296). New York: McGraw-Hill.

Gottlieb, G. (1991). Experimental canalization of behavioral development: theory. *Developmental Psychology*, *27*, 4–13.

Gottlieb, G., Wahlsten, D., & Lickliter, R. (1998). The significance of biology for human development: a developmental psychobiological systems view. In W. Damon (gen. ed.) and R. M. Lerner (vol. ed.), *Handbook of Child Psychology: Vol. 1. Theoretical models of human development* (pp. 233–273). New York: Wiley.

Gottman, J. M. (1983). How children become friends. *Monographs for the Society for Research in Child Development*, *48* (Serial No. 201).

Gottman, J. M., & Mettetal, G. (1986). Speculations on social and affective development: friendship and acquaintanceship through adolescence. In J. M. Gottman and J. G. Parker (eds), *The Conversations of Friends* (pp. 192–237). New York: Cambridge University Press.

Graber, J. A., Brooks-Gunn, J., & Warren, M. P. (1995). The antecedents of menarcheal age: heredity, family environment, and stressful life events. *Child Development*, *66*, 346–359.

Green, C. D. (2004). The hiring of James Mark Baldwin and James Gibson Hume at the University of Toronto in 1889. *History of Psychology*, *7*, 130–153.

Greenough, W. T., Black, J. E., & Wallace, C. S. (1987). Experience and brain development. *Child Development*, *58*, 539–559.

Grice, H. P. (1975). Logic and conversation. In P. Cole and J. L. Morgan (eds), *Syntax and Semantics, Vol. 3: Speech acts* (pp. 41–58). New York: Academic.

Gronau, R. C., & Waas, G. A. (1997). Delay of gratification and cue utilization: an examination of children's social information processing. *Merrill Palmer Quarterly*, *43*, 305–322.

Gross, D., & Harris, P. L. (1988). False beliefs about emotion: children's understanding of misleading emotional displays. *International Journal of Behavioral Development*, *11*, 368–398.

Grossman, K., Grossman, K. E., & Kindler, H. (2005). Early care and the roots of attachment and partnership representations: the Bielefeld and Regensburg longitudinal studies. In K. E. Grossman, K. Grossman and E. Waters (eds), *Attachment from Infancy to Adulthood: The major longitudinal studies* (pp. 98–136). New York: Guilford.

Grusec, J. E., & Goodnow, I. J. (1994). Impact of parental discipline methods on the child's internalization of values: a conceptualization of current points of view. *Developmental Psychology*, *30*, 4–19.

Gunnar, M., Malone, S. M., Vance, G., & Fisch, R. (1985). Coping with aversive stimulation in the neonatal period: quiet sleep and plasma cortisol levels during recovery from circumcision. *Child Development*, *56*, 824–834.

References

Haight, W., & Miller, P. (1993). *The Ecology and Development of Pretend Play.* Albany: State University of New York Press.

Haith, K. (1999). Some thoughts about claims for innate knowledge and infant physical reasoning. *Developmental Science, 2*, 153–156.

Haith, M., & Benson, J. (1998). Infant cognition. In W. Damon (gen. ed.), D. Kuhn and R. Siegler (vol. eds.), *Handbook of Child Psychology: Vol. 2: Cognition, perception and language* (5th edition, pp. 199–254). New York: Wiley.

Haith, M., Bergman, T., & Moore, M. (1977). Eye contact and face scanning in early infancy. *Science, 198*, 853–855.

Hall, G. S. (1891). *The contents of children's minds on entering school. The Pedagogical Seminary, 1*, 139–173.

Hall, G. S. (1893). *The Contents of Children's Minds on Entering School.* New York: E. L. Kellog.

Hall, G. S. (1904). *Adolescence* (Vols. 1–2). New York: Appleton-Century-Crofts.

Halle, T. (2003). Emotional development and well-being. In M. Bornstein and L. Davidson (eds), *Well-being: Positive development across the life course* (pp. 125–138). Mahwah, NJ: Erlbaum.

Halliday, M. A. K. (1975). *Learning How To Mean: Exploration in the development of language.* London: Arnold.

Halverson, H. M. (1931). An experimental study of prehension in infants by means of systematic cinema records. *Genetic Psychology Monographs, 10*, 107–286.

Handley, S. J., Capon, A., Beveridge, M., Dennis, I., & Evans, J. (2004). Working memory, inhibitory control and the development of children's reasoning. *Thinking & Reasoning, 10*, 175–195.

Harkness, S., Super, C. M., & Tijen, N. V. (2000). Individualism and the "Western mind" reconsidered: American and Dutch parents' ethnotheories of the child. *New Directions for Child and Adolescent Development, 2000*, 23–39.

Harrington, R., Rutter, M., & Fombonne, E. (1996). Developmental pathways in depression: multiple meanings, antecedents, and endpoints. *Development and Psychopathology, 8*, 601–616.

Harris, J. R. (1995). Where is the child's environment? A group socialization theory of development. *Psychological Review, 102*, 458–489.

Harris, J. R. (1998). *The Nurture Assumption: Why children turn out the way they do.* New York: Free Press.

Harris, P. L. (1989). *Children and Emotion.* New York: Blackwell.

Harris, P. L., Johnson, C. N., Hutton, D., Andrews, G., & Cook, T. (1989). Young children's theory of mind and emotion. *Cognition and Emotion, 3*, 379–400.

Hart, E., Lahey, B., Loeber, R., & Applegate, B. (1995). Developmental change in attention-deficit hyperactivity disorder in boys: a four-year longitudinal study. *Journal of Abnormal Child Development, 23*, 729–749.

Harter, S. (1998). The development of self-representations. In W. Damon (gen. ed.) and N. Eisenberg (vol. ed.), *Handbook of Child Psychology: Vol. 3. Social, emotional, and personality development* (5th edition, pp. 177–235). New York: Wiley.

Harter, S., & Buddin, B. J. (1987). Children's understanding of the simultaneity of two emotions: a five-stage developmental acquisition sequence. *Developmental Psychology, 23*, 388–399.

Hartmann, D. P., & George, T. P. (1999). Design, measurement, and analysis in developmental research. In M. Bornstein and M. Lamb (eds), *Developmental Psychology: An advanced textbook* (4th edition, pp. 125–195). Mahwah, NJ: Erlbaum.

Hartup, W. W. (1983). Peer relations. In P. H. Mussen (series ed.) and E. M. Hetherington (vol. ed.), *Handbook of Child Psychology: Vol. 4: Socialization, personality, and social development* (4th edition, pp. 103–196). New York: Wiley.

Hartup, W. W. (1989). Social relationships and their developmental significance. *American Psychologist*, *44*, 120–126.

Haslam, S. and McGarty, C. (2003). *Research Methods and Statistics in Psychology.* Thousand Oaks, CA: Sage.

Havighurst, R. J. (1952). *Developmental Tasks and Education.* New York: McKay.

Hawley, P. H., & Little, T. D. (1999). On winning some and losing some: social dominance in toddlers. *Merrill Palmer Quarterly, 45*, 185–214

Hayne, H. (2004). Infant memory development: implications for childhood amnesia. *Developmental Review*, *24*, 33–73.

Hecox, K. (1975). Electrophysiological correlates of human auditory development. In L. B. Cohen and P. Salapatek (eds), *Infant Perception: From sensation to cognition, Vol. 2*: *perception of space, speech and sound* (pp. 151–191). Orlando, FL: Academic.

Henderson, H. A., Marshall, P. J., Fox, N. A., & Rubin, K. H. (2004). Psychophysiological and behavioral evidence for varying forms and functions of nonsocial behavior in preschoolers. *Child Development*, *75*, 251–263.

Herbert, J., & Hayne, H. (2000). Memory retrieval by 18–30-months-old: age-related changes in representational flexibility. *Developmental Psychology*, *36*, 473–484.

Herbert, J.D., Sharp, I.R., & Gaudiano, B.A. (2002). Separating fact from fiction in the etiology and treatment of autism: a scientific review of the evidence. *Scientific Review of Mental Health Practice, 1*, 23–43.

Hetherington, E. M., Parke, R. D., Gauvain, M., & Locke, V. O. (2006). *Child Development* (6th edition). New York: McGraw-Hill.

Hickling, A. K., & Wellman, H. M. (2001). The emergence of children's causal explanations and theories: evidence from everyday conversation. *Developmental Psychology*, *37*, 668–683.

Hirshfeld-Becker, D. R., Biederman, J., Henin, A., Faraone, S. V., Davis, S., Harrington, K., & Rosenbaum, J. F. (2007). Behavioral inhibition in preschool children at risk is a specific predictor of middle childhood social anxiety: a five-year follow-up. *Journal of Developmental and Behavioral Pediatrics*, *28*, 225–233.

Hoff-Ginsburg, E. (1997). *Language Development.* Pacific Grove, CA: Brooks-Cole.

Hoffman, L. W. (2000). Maternal employment: effects of social context. In M. C. Wang (ed.), *Resilience Across Contexts: Family, work, culture, and community.* Mahwah, NJ: Erlbaum.

Hoffman, M. L. (1975). Moral internalization, parental power, and the nature of parent-child interaction. *Developmental Psychology*, *11*, 228–239.

Hopkins, B., & Westra, T. (1988). Maternal handling and motor development: an intra-cultural study. *Genetic, Social and General Psychology Monographs*, *14*, 377–420.

Horgan, D. (1978). The development of the full passive. *Journal of Child Language*, *5*, 65–80.

Horobin, K., & Acredolo, L. (1986). The role of attentiveness, mobility history, and separation of hiding sites on Stage IV search behavior. *Journal of Experimental Child Psychology*, *41*, 114–127.

Howard, J. (2002). Eliciting young children's perceptions of play, work and learning using the activity apperception story procedure. *Early Child Development and Care, 127*, 489–502.

Howes, C. (1987). Social competence with peers in young children: developmental sequences. *Developmental Review*, *7*, 252–272.

References

Hoza, B., Molina, B., Bukowski, W. M., & Sippola, L. K. (1995). Aggression, withdrawal and measures of popularity and friendship as predictors of internalizing and externalizing problems during adolescence. *Development and Psychopathology*, *7*, 787–802.

Hudson, V. M. (1990). Birth order of world leaders: an exploratory analysis of effects on personality and behavior. *Political Psychology*, *11*, 583–601.

Huesmann, L. R., & Guerra, N. G. (1997). Children's normative beliefs about aggression and aggressive behavior. *Journal of Personality and Social Psychology*, *72*, 408–419.

Hughes, F. P. (2010). *Children, Play and Development* (4th edition). Thousand Oaks, CA: Sage

Humphrey, T. (1978). Function of the nervous system during prenatal life. In U. Stave (ed.), *Perinatal Physiology* (pp. 651–683). New York: Plenum.

Humphreys, A. P., & Smith, P. K. (1987). Rough-and-tumble, friendship, and dominance in school children: evidence for continuity and change with age. *Child Development*, *58*, 210–212.

Huttenlocher, J., Haight, W., Bryk, A., Seltzer, M., & Lyons, T. (1991). Early vocabulary growth: relation to language input and gender. *Developmental Psychology*, *27*, 236–248.

Huttenlocher, P. R. (1990). Morphometric study of human cerebral cortex development. *Neuropsychologia*, *28*, 517–527.

Huttenlocher, P. R. (1994). Synaptogenesis, synapse elimination, and neural plasticity in human cerebral cortex. In C. A. Nelson (ed.), *Threats to Optimal Development*: *The Minnesota symposia on child psychology* (Vol. 27, pp. 35–54). Hillsdale, NJ: Erlbaum.

Huttenlocher, P. R. (2002). *Neural Plasticity: The effects of environment on the development of the cerebral cortex*. Perspectives in Cognitive Neuroscience (Stephen M. Kosslyn, Series Editor). Harvard: Harvard University Press.

Huttenlocher, P. R., & Dabholkar, A. S. (1997). Regional differences in synaptogenesis in human cerebral cortex. *Journal of Comparative Neurology*, *387*, 167–178.

Hyeeun, S., Bjorklund, D. F., & Beck, E. F. (2007). The adaptive nature of children's overestimation in a strategic memory task. *Cognitive Development*, *22*, 197–212.

Hymel, S., Closson, L. M., Caravita, S. C. S., & Vaillancourt, T. (2011). Social status among peers: from sociometric attraction to peer acceptance to perceived popularity. In P. K. Smith and C. H. Hart (eds), *The Wiley-Blackwell Handbook of Childhood Social Development* (2nd edition, pp. 375–392). Oxford: Wiley-Blackwell.

Ingram, D. (1986). Phonological development: production. In P. Fletcher and M. Garman (eds), *Language Acquisition* (2nd edition, pp. 223–239). Cambridge: Cambridge University Press.

Inhelder, B., & Piaget, J. (1958). *The Growth of Logical Thinking from Childhood to Adolescence: An essay on the construction of formal operational structures*. New York: Basic.

Institute of Medicine (2004). *Ethical Conduct of Clinical Research Involving Children*. Washington, DC: National Academic.

Izard, C. E. (1994). Innate and universal facial expressions: evidence from developmental and cross-cultural research. *Psychological Bulletin*, *115*, 288–299.

Izard, C. E., & Malatesta, C. Z. (1987). Perspectives on emotional development I. Differential emotions theory of early emotional development. In J. D. Osofsky (ed.), *Handbook of Infant Development* (2nd edition, pp. 494–554). New York: Wiley.

Jackson, B., & Farrugia, D. (1997). Diagnosis and treatment of adults with ADHD. *Journal of Counseling and Development*, *75*, 312–319.

Jaffe, S. R., & Hyde, J. S. (2000). Gender differences in moral orientation: a meta-analysis. *Psychological Bulletin, 126*, 703–706.

Jahoda, G. (1983). European 'lag' in the development of an economic concept: a study in Zimbabwe. *British Journal of Developmental Psychology, 1*, 113–120.

James, W. (1890). *The Principles of Psychology.* New York: Dover.

Jefferis, J.M.H., Power, C. & Hertzman, C. (2002). Birthweight, childhood socioeconomic environment, and cognitive development in the 1958 British birth cohort study. *British Medical Journal, 325*, 305.

Johnson, J. S., & Newport, E. L. (1989). Critical period effects in second language learning: the influence of maturational state on the acquisition of English as a second language. *Cognitive Psychology, 21*, 60–99.

Johnson, M. H. (2005) *Developmental Cognitive Neuroscience* (2nd edition). Oxford: Blackwell.

Johnson, M. H., Posner, M. I., & Rothbart, M. K. (1991). Components of visual orienting in early infancy: contingency learning, anticipatory looking and disengaging. *Journal of Cognitive Neuroscience, 3*, 335–344.

Johnson, M. J. (1998). The neural basis of cognitive development. In W. Damon (gen. ed.), D. Kuhn and R. Siegler (vol. eds), *Handbook of Child Psychology* (5th edition, pp. 1–49). New York: Wiley.

Johnson, S. P., Amso, D., & Slemmer, J. A. (2003). Development of object concepts in infancy: evidence for early learning in an eye-tracking paradigm. *Proceedings of the National Academy of Sciences, 100*, 10568–10753.

Jones, M. C. (1965). Psychological correlates of somatic development. *Child Development, 36*, 899–911.

Jones, M. C., & Bayley, N. (1950). Physical maturing among boys as related to behavior. *Journal of Educational Psychology, 41*, 129–148.

Jones, M. C., & Mussen, P. H. (1958). Self-conceptions, motivations, and interpersonal attitudes of early-and late-maturing girls. *Child Development, 29*, 491–501.

Jones, P. E. (1995). Contradictions and unanswered questions in the Genie case: a fresh look at the linguistic evidence. *Language & Communication, 15*, 261–280.

Jusczyk, P. W., Friederic, A. D., Wessels, J., Svenkerund, V. Y., & Jusczyk, A. M. (1993). Infants' sensitivity to the sound patterns of native language words. *Journal of Memory and Language, 32*, 402–420.

Kagan, J. (1998). Biology and the child. In W. Damon (gen. ed.) and N. Eisenberg (vol. ed.), *Handbook of Child Psychology: Vol. 3. Social, emotional, and personality development* (5th edition, pp. 177–235). New York: Wiley.

Kagan, J. (2003). Behavioral inhibition as a temperamental category. In R. J. Davidson, K. R. Scherer and H. H. Goldsmith (eds), *Handbook of Affective Science* (pp. 320–331). New York: Oxford University Press.

Kagan, J., & Zetner, M. (1996). Early childhood predictors of adult psychopathology. *Harvard Review of Psychiatry, 3*, 341–350.

Kahn, P. H. (1997). Bayous and jungle rivers: cross-cultural perspectives on children's environmental moral reasoning. In H. D. Saltzstein (ed.), *Culture as a Context for Moral Development* (pp. 23–37). San Francisco, CA: Jossey-Bass.

Kail, R., & Hall, L. K. (1994). Processing speed, naming speed, and reading. *Developmental Psychology, 30*, 949–954.

Kaplan, J. A., Brownell, H. H., Jacobs, J. R., & Gardner, H. (1990). The effects of right hemisphere damage on the pragmatic interpretation of conversational remarks. *Brain and Language, 38*, 315–333.

Karrby, G., (1989). Children's conceptions of their own play. *International Journal of Early Childhood Education, 21*, 49–54.

References

Karmiloff-Smith, A., Grant, J., Jones, M.-C., Sims, K., & Cuckle, P. (1996). Rethinking metalinguistic awareness: representing and accessing what counts as a word. *Cognition, 58*, 197–219.

Karponai, K., & Vetro, A. (2008). Depression in children. *Current Opinion in Psychiatry, 21*, 1–7.

Karrass, J., Walden, T. A., Conture, E. G., Graham, C. G., Arnold, H. S., Hartfield, K. N., & Schwenk, K. A. (2006). Relation of emotional reactivity and regulation to childhood stuttering. *Journal of Communication Disorders, 39*, 402–423.

Kaye, K. L., & Bower, T. G. R. (1994). Learning and intermodal transfer of information in newborns. *Psychological Science, 5*, 286–288.

Kazdin, A. E. (1990). Premature termination from treatment among children referred for antisocial behavior. *Journal of Child Psychology and Psychiatry, 31*, 415–425.

Kazdin, A. E. (1997). Conduct disorder across the life-span. In S. Luthar, J. Burack, D. Cicchetti and J. Weisz (eds), *Developmental Psychopathology: Perspectives on adjustment, risk and disorder* (pp. 248–272). Cambridge: Cambridge University Press.

Keating, D. P. (1979). Adolescent thinking. In J. Adelson (ed.), *Handbook of Adolescent Psychology* (pp. 211–246). New York: Wiley.

Keating, D. P. (1990). Adolescent thinking. In S. S. Feldman and G. Elliott (eds), *At The Threshold: The developing adolescent* (pp. 54–89). Cambridge, MA: Harvard University Press.

Keefer, C. H., Dixon, S., Tronick, E. Z., & Brazelton, T. B. (1991). Cultural mediation between newborn behavior and later development: implications for methodology in cross-cultural research. In J. K. Nugent, B. M. Lester and T. B. Brazelton (eds), *The Cultural Context of Infancy* (pp. 39–61). Norwood, NJ: Ablex.

Keenan, T. (2002). Negative affect predicts performance on an object permanence task. *Developmental Science, 5*, 65–71.

Keenan, T., & Harvey, M. (1998). What's in that child's mind? *New Zealand Science Monthly, 9*, 6–8.

Keenan, T., & Quigley, K. (1999). The role of echoic mention in young children's understanding of sarcasm. *British Journal of Developmental Psychology, 17*, 83–96.

Keenan, T., Ruffman, T., & Olson, D. R. (1994). When do children begin to understand logical inference as a source of knowledge? *Cognitive Development, 9*, 331–353.

Kellman, P. J., & Arterberry, M. E. (2006). Infant visual perception. In D. K. W. Damon and R. Siegler (eds), *Handbook of Child Psychology, Vol. 2*. New York: Wiley.

Kellman, P. J., & Banks, M. S. (1998). Infant visual perception. In W. Damon (gen. ed.), D. Kuhn and R. Siegler (vol. eds), *Handbook of Child Psychology: Vol. 2. Cognition, perception and language* (5th edition, pp. 103–146). New York: Wiley.

Kelly, A. M., Margulies, D. S., & Castellanos, F. X. (2007). Recent advances in structural and functional brain imaging studies of attention-deficit/hyperactivity disorder. *Current Psychiatry Reports, 9*, 401–407.

Keltner, D. (1995). The signs of apeasement: evidence for the distinct displays of embarrassment, amusement and shame. *Journal of Personality and Social Psychology, 68*, 441–454.

Kerig, P., Ludlow, A. & Wenar C. (2012). *Developmental Psychopathology: From Infancy through Adolescence* (6th edition). New York: McGraw-Hill Education.

Kerig, P. K., & Wenar, C. (2006). *Developmental Psychopathology: From infancy through adolescence.* New York: McGraw-Hill.

Kerr, D. C., Lopez, N. L., Olson, S. L., & Sameroff, A. J. (2004). Parental discipline and externalizing behavior problems in early childhood: the roles of moral regulation and child gender. *Journal of Abnormal Psychology, 32*, 369–383.

Kertz, S. J., & Woodruff-Borden, J. (2011). The developmental psychopathology of worry. *Clinical Child and Family Psychology Review*, *14*, 174–197.

Khan, S. A., & Faraone, S. V. (2006). The genetics of ADHD: a literature review of 2005. *Current Psychiatry Reports*, *8*, 393–397.

Killen, M., & Smetana, J. G. (2006). *Handbook of Moral Development*. Mahwah, NJ: Erlbaum.

Kim, S., & Kochanska, G. (2012). Child temperament moderates effects of parent–child mutuality on self-regulation: a relationship-based path for emotionally negative infants. *Child Development*, *83*, 1275–1289.

Kisilevsky, B. S., Hains, S. M., Lee, K., Xie, X., Huang, H., Ye, H. H., Zhang, K., & Wang, Z. (2003). Effects of experience on fetal voice recognition. *Psychological Science*, *14*(3), 220–224.

Klahr, D., & MacWhinney, B. (1998). Information processing. In W. Damon (gen. ed.), D. Kuhn and R. S. Siegler (vol. eds), *Handbook of Child Psychology: Vol. 2. Cognition, perception, and language* (5th edition, pp. 631–678). New York: Wiley.

Klebanoff, M. A., Levine, R. J., Clemens, J. D., & Wilkins, D. G. (2002). Maternal serum caffeine metabolites and small-for-gestational age birth. *American Journal of Epidemiology*, *155*, 32–37.

Klein, M. (1952). On identification. In M. Klein, P. Heimann, S. Isaacs and J. Riviere (eds), *New Directions in Psycho-Analysis* (pp. 292–320). London: Hogarth.

Klein, R. G., Mannuzza, S., Olazagasti, M. A. R., Roizen, E., Hutchison, J. A., Lashua, E. C., & Castellanos, F. X. (2012). Clinical and functional outcome of childhood attention-deficit/hyperactivity disorder 33 years later. *Archives of General Psychiatry*, *69*, 1295–1303.

Klin, A., & Volkmar, F. R. (1997). The pervasive developmental disorders: nosology and profiles of development. In S. Luthar, J. Burack, D. Cicchetti and J. Weisz (eds), *Developmental Psychopathology: Perspectives on adjustment, risk and disorder* (pp. 208– 226). Cambridge: Cambridge University Press.

Klinnert, M. D., Emde, R. N., Butterfield, P., & Campos, J. J. (1986). Social referencing: the infant's use of emotional signals from a friendly adult with mother present. *Developmental Psychology*, *22*, 427–432.

Knafo, A. & Plomin, R. (2006). Prosocial behavior from early to middle childhood: genetic and environmental influences on stability and change. *Developmental Psycholology*, *42*, 771–86.

Kochanska, G. (1995). Children's temperament, mother's discipline, and security of attachment: multiple pathways to emerging internalization. *Child Development*, *66*, 597–615.

Kochanska, G. (2002). Committed compliance, moral self, and internalization: a mediational model. *Developmental Psychology*, 38, 339–351.

Kochanska, G., Aksan, N., & Nichols, K. E. (2003). Maternal power assertion in discipline and moral discourse contexts: commonalities, differences, and implications for children's moral conduct and cognition. *Developmental Psychology*, *39*, 949–963.

Kochanska, G., & Kim, S. (2013a). Early attachment organization with both parents and future behavior problems: From infancy to middle childhood. *Child Development*, *84*, 283–296.

Kochanska, G., & Kim, S. (2013b). Difficult temperament moderates links between maternal responsiveness and children's compliance and behavior problems in low-income families. *Journal of Child Psychology and Psychiatry*, *54*, 323–332.

Kochanska, G., Murray, K., Jacques, T., Koenig, A. L., & Vandegeest, K. (1996). Inhibitory control in young children and its role in emerging internalization. *Child Development*, *67*, 490–507.

References

Koegel, R. L., Schreibman, L., O'Neill, R. E., & Burke, J. C. (1983). The personality and family-interaction characteristics of parents of autistic children. *Journal of Consulting and Clinical Psychology, 15*, 683–692.

Kohlberg, L. (1969). *Stages in Development of Moral Thought and Action.* New York: Holt.

Kohlberg, L. (1985). *The Psychology of Moral Development.* San Francisco, CA: Harper & Row.

Kolb, B., Gorny, G., Li, Y., Samaha, A., & Robinson, T. E. (2003). Amphetamine or cocaine limits the ability of later experience to promote structural plasticity in the neocortex and nucleus acumbens. *Proceedings of the National Academy of Sciences, 100*, 10523–10528.

Kopp, C. B. (2002). Self-regulation in childhood. In N. J. Smelser and P. B. Baltes (eds), *International Encyclopedia of the Social and Behavioral Sciences: Vol 3.* New York: Pergamon.

Kopp, C. B., & Neufeld, S. J. (2003). Emotional development during infancy. In R. J. Davidson, K. R. Scherer and H. H. Goldsmith (eds), *Handbook of Affective Sciences* (pp. 347–374). New York: Oxford University Press.

Kotagal, S., & Broomall, E. (2012). Sleep in children with autism spectrum disorder. *Pediatric Neurology, 47*, 242–251.

Krakowiak, P., Walker, C. K., Bremer, A. A., Baker, A. S., Ozonoff, S., Hansen, R. L., & Hertz-Picciotto, I. (2012). Maternal metabolic conditions and risk for autism and other neurodevelopmental disorders. *Pediatrics, 129*, e1121–e1128.

Kramer, M. S., Aboud, F., Mironova, E., Vanilovich, I., Platt, R., Matush, L., Igumnov, S., Fombonne, E., Bogdanovich, N., Ducruet, T., Collet, J. P., Chalmers, B., Hodnett, E., Davidovsky, S., Skugarevsky, O., Trofimovich, O., Kozlova, L., & Shapiro, S. (2008). Breastfeeding and child cognitive development: new evidence from a large randomized trial. *Archives of General Psychiatry, 65*, 578–584.

Kuczaj, S. A. (1986). Thoughts on the intentional basis of early word description: evidence from comprehension and production. In S. A. Kuczaj and M. D. Barrett (eds), *The Development of Word Meaning* (pp. 99–120). New York: Springer Verlag.

Kuczynski, L. (2003). Beyond bidirectionality. In L. Kuczynski (ed.), *Handbook of Dynamics in Parent-Child Relations* (pp. 3–24). Thousand Oaks, CA: Sage.

Kuhn, D. (1995). Microgenetic study of change: what has it told us? *Psychological Science, 6*, 133–139.

Kupersmidt, J. B., & Coie, J. D. (1990). Preadolescent peer group status, aggression, and social adjustment as predictors of externalizing problems in adolescence. *Child Development, 61*, 1350–1362.

Kupersmidt, J. B., Burchinal, M., & Patterson, C. J. (1995). Developmental patterns of childhood peer relations as predictors of externalizing behavior problems. *Development and Psychopathology, 7*, 649–668.

Labonté, B., Suderman, M., Maussion, G., Navaro, L., Yerko, V., Mahar, I., Bureau, A., Mechawar, N., Szyf, M., Meaney, M. J., & Turecki, G. (2012). Genome-wide epigenetic regulation by early-life trauma. *Archives of General Psychiatry, 69*, 722–731.

Ladd, G. W., & Pettit, G. S. (2002). Parenting and the development of children's peer relationships. In M. H. Bornstein (ed.), *Handbook of Parenting: Vol. 5. Practical issues in parenting* (2nd edition, pp. 269–309). Mahwah, NJ: Erlbaum.

LaFrance, M., Hecht, M., & Paluck, E. L. (2003). The contingent smile: a meta-analysis of sex differences in smiling. *Psychological Bulletin, 129*, 305–334.

LaFreniere, P. J. (2000). *Emotional Development: A biosocial perspective.* New York: Wadsworth.

LaFreniere, P. J., & Sroufe, L. A. (1985). Profiles of peer competence in the preschool: interrelations between measures, influence of social ecology, and relation to attachment history. *Developmental Psychology, 21*, 56–69.

Lahey, B. B., Loeber, R., Burke, J. D., & Applegate, B. (2005). Predicting future antisocial personality disorder in males from a clinical assessment in childhood. *Journal of Consulting and Clinical Psychology*, 73, 389–399.

Laird, R. D., Pettit, G. S., Bates, J. E., & Dodge, K. A. (2003). Parents' monitoring-relevant knowledge and adolescents' delinquent behavior: evidence of correlated developmental changes and reciprocal influences. *Child Development*, 74, 752–768.

LaLonde, C. E., & Chandler, M. (1995). False belief understanding goes to school: on the social-emotional consequences of coming early or late to a first theory of mind. *Cognition and Emotion*, 9, 167–185.

Lamb, M. (1981). Developing trust and perceived effectance in infancy. In L. P. Lipsitt (ed.), *Advances in Infancy Research: Volume 2* (pp. 101–127). Norwood, NJ: Ablex.

Landau, B., & Gleitman, L. R. (1985). *Language and Experience: Evidence from the blind child*. Cambridge, MA: Harvard University Press.

Langlois, J. H. (1985). From the eye of the beholder to behavior reality: the development of social behaviors and social relations as a function of physical attractiveness. In C. P. Herman (ed.), *Physical Appearance, Stigma, and Social Behavior*. Hillsdale, NJ: Erlbaum.

Langlois, J. H., & Downs, C. A. (1979). Peer relations as a function of physical attractiveness: the eye of the beholder or behavioral reality? *Child Development*, 50, 409–418.

Last, C., Perrin, S., Hersen, M., & Kazdin, A. (1997). A prospective study of childhood anxiety disorders. *Journal of the American Academy of Child and Adolescent Psychiatry*, 35, 1502–1510.

Lavallee, K. L., Bierman, K. L., & Nix, R. L. (2005). The impact of first-grade 'friendship group' experiences on child social outcomes in the fast track program. *Journal of Abnormal Child Psychology*, 33, 307–324.

Layous, K., Nelson, S. K., Oberle, E., Schonert-Reichl, K. A., & Lyubomirsky, S. (2012). Kindness counts: prompting prosocial behavior in preadolescents boosts peer acceptance and well-being. *PloS one*, 7(12), e51380.

Lebel, C., & Beaulieu, C. (2011). Longitudinal development of human brain wiring continues from childhood into adulthood. *Journal of Neuroscience*, 31, 10937–10947.

LeBlanc, M., & Ritchie, M. (2001). A meta-analysis of play therapy outcomes. *Counseling Psychology Quarterly*, 14, 149–163.

Lee, H. J., Macbeth, A. H., Pagani, J. H., & Young, W. S. (2009). Oxytocin: the great facilitator of life. *Progress in neurobiology*, 88, 127–151.

Lennenberg, E. (1967). *Biological Foundations of Language*. New York: Wiley.

Lerer, E., Levi, S., Salomon, S., Darvasi, A., Yirmiya, N., & Ebstein, R. P. (2008). Association between the oxytocin receptor (OXTR) gene and autism: relationship to Vineland Adaptive Behavior Scales and cognition. *Molecular Psychiatry*, 13, 980–988.

Levin, J. R., & Rohwer, W. D. (1968). Verbal organization and the facilitation of serial learning. *Journal of Educational Psychology*, 59, 186–191.

Levy, B. R., Jennings, P., & Langer, E. J. (2001). Improving attention in old age. *Behavioral Science*, 8, 1573–3440.

Lewis, C., Freeman, N. H., Kyriakidou, C., Maridaki-Kassotaki, K., & Berridge, D. M. (1996). Social influences on false belief access: specific sibling influences or general apprenticeship?, *Child Development*, 67, 2930–2947.

Lewis, M. (1987). Social development in infancy and early childhood. In J. D. Osofsky (ed.), *Handbook of Infant Development* (pp. 419–493). New York: Wiley.

Lewis, M. (1989). Cultural differences in children's knowledge of emotion scripts. In C. Saarni and P. L. Harris (eds), *Children's Understanding of Emotion*. New York: Cambridge University Press.

Lewis, M., & Brooks, J. (1974). Self, other and fear: infants' reactions to people. In M. Lewis and L. Rosenblum (eds), *The Origins of Fear*. New York: Wiley.

Lewis, M., & Brooks-Gunn, J. (1978). *Social Cognition and the Acquisition of the Self*. New York: Plenum.

Lewis, M., Alessandri, S., & Sullivan, M. W. (1992). Differences in shame and pride as a function of children's gender and task difficulty. *Child Development*, *63*, 630–638.

Lewis, M., Sullivan, M. W., Stanger, C., & Weiss, M. (1989). Self development and self-conscious emotions. *Child Development*, *60*, 146–156.

Liau, A. K., Barriga, A. Q., & Gibbs, J. C. (1998). Relations between self-serving cognitive distortion and overt vs. covert antisocial behavior in adolescents. *Aggressive Behavior*, *24*, 335–346.

Liu, J., Leung, P. W., McCauley, L., Ai, Y., & Pinto-Martin, J. (2013). Mothers' environmental tobacco smoke exposure during pregnancy and externalizing behavior problems in children. *Neurotoxicology*, *34*, 167–174.

Loehlin, J. C. (1992). *Genes and Environment in Personality Development*. Newbury Park, CA: Sage.

Lopez, F., Menez, M., & Hernandez-Guzman, L. (2005). Sustained attention during learning activities: an observational study with pre-school children. *Early Child Development and Care*, *175*, 131–138.

Lorber, M. F., & Egeland, B. (2011). Parenting and infant difficulty: testing a mutual exacerbation hypothesis to predict early onset conduct problems. *Child Development*, *82*, 2006–2020.

Lorenz, K. (1963). *On Aggression*. New York: Harcourt Brace Jovanovich.

Lowes, J., & Tiggemann, M. (2003). Body dissatisfaction, dieting awareness and the impact of parental influence in young children. *British Journal of Health Psychology*, *8*, 135–147.

Lupien, S. J., Parent, S., Evans, A. C., Tremblay, R. E., Zelazo, P. D., Corbo, V., Pruessner, J.C., & Séguin, J. R. (2011). Larger amygdala but no change in hippocampal volume in 10-year-old children exposed to maternal depressive symptomatology since birth. *Proceedings of the National Academy of Sciences*, *108*, 14324–14329.

Luthar, S. S. (1991). Vulnerability and resilience: a study of high-risk adolescents. *Child Development, 62*, 600–616.

Lutz, D. J., & Sternberg, R. J. (1999). Cognitive development. In M. Bornstein and M. Lamb (eds), *Developmental Psychology: An advanced textbook* (4th edition, pp. 275–311). Mahwah, NJ: Erlbaum.

Lyons-Ruth, K., Connell, D. B., Gruenbaum, H. U., & Botein, S. (1990). Infants at social risk: maternal depression and family support services as mediators of infant development and security of attachment. *Child Development*, *61*, 85–98.

Lyons-Ruth, K., Easterbrooks, M. A., & Cibelli, C. D. (1997). Infant attachment strategies, infant mental lag, and maternal depressive symptoms: predictions of internalizing and externalizing problems at age 7. *Developmental Psychology*, *33*, 681–692.

Maccoby, E. E. (1990). Gender and relationships: a developmental account. *American Psychologist*, *45*, 513–521.

Maccoby, E. E. (1998). *The Two Sexes: Growing up apart, coming together*. Cambridge, MA: Belknap/ Harvard University Press.

Maccoby, E. E., & Jacklin, C. N. (1987). Gender segregation in childhood. In H. W. Reese (ed.), *Advances in Child Development and Behavior* (Vol. 20, pp. 239–288). New York: Academic.

MacFarlane, A. (1975). Olfaction in the development of social preferences in the human neonate. *Ciba Foundation Symposium*, *33*, 103–117.

Mackey, M. C. (1995). Women's evaluation of their childbirth performance. *Maternal and Child Nursing Journal, 23,* 57–72.

Maclean, P.D. (1990). *The Triune Brain in Evolution: Role in paleocereberal functions.* New York: Plenum.

Magnusson, D., & Stattin, H. (1998). Person-context interaction theories. In W. Damon and R. M. Lerner (eds), *Handbook of Child Psychology. Vol. 1: Theoretical models of human development* (pp. 685–759). New York: Wiley.

Main, M., & Cassidy, J. (1988). Categories of response to reunion with the parent at age 6: predictable from infant attachment classification and stable over a 1-month period. *Developmental Psychology, 24,* 415–426.

Main, M., & Solomon, J. (1990). Procedures for identifying infants as disorganized/ disoriented during the Ainsworth strange situation. In M. Greenberg, D. Cicchetti and E. M. Cummings (eds), *Attachment in the Preschool Years: Theory, research and intervention* (pp. 121–160). Chicago: University of Chicago Press.

Malatesta, C. Z., & Haviland, J. (1982). Learning display rules: the socialization of emotional expression in infancy. *Child Development, 53,* 991–1003.

Malatesta, C. Z., & Haviland, J. (1985). Signals, symbols, and socialization. In M. Lewis and C. Saarni (eds), *The Socialization of Emotions.* New York: Plenum.

Malina, R. M. (1975). *Growth and Development: The first twenty years in man.* Minneapolis, MN: Burgess.

Malloch, S., & Trevarthen, C. (2009). Musicality: communicating the vital interests of life. In S. Malloch and C. Trevarthen (eds), *Communicative Musicality: Exploring the basis of human companionship* (pp. 1–11). Oxford: Oxford University Press.

Mandler, J. M., & Robinson, C. A. (1978). Developmental differences in picture recognition. *Journal of Experimental Child Psychology, 26,* 122–136.

Mannuzza, S., Klein, R., Bessler, A., & Malloy, P. (1993). Adult outcome of hyperactive boys: educational achievement, occupational rank, and psychiatric status. *Archives of General Psychiatry, 50,* 565–576.

Maratsos, M. (1998). The acquisition of grammar. In W. Damon (gen. ed.), D. Kuhn and R. S. Siegler (vol. eds), *Handbook of Child Psychology: Vol. 2. Cognition, perception, and language* (5th edition, pp. 421–466). New York: Wiley.

Maratsos, M. (2000). More overregularizations after all: new data and discussion on Marcus, Pinker, Ullman, Hollander, Rosen & Xu. *Journal of Child Language, 27,* 183–212.

Marcus, G.F., Pinker, S., Ullman, M., Hollander, M., Rosen, T J., Xu, F., & Clahsen, H. (1992). Overregularization in language acquisition. *Monographs of the Society for Research in Child Development, 57,* 1–178.

Markman, E. M. (1989). *Categorization and Naming in Children.* Cambridge, MA: MIT.

Markman, E. M. (1992). Constraints on word learning: speculations about their nature, origins, and domain specificity. In M. R. Gunnar and M. P. Maratsos (eds), *Minnesota Symposia on Child Psychology* (Vol. 25, pp. 59–101). Hillsdale, NJ: Erlbaum.

Masten, A. (2001). Ordinary magic: resilience processes in development. *American Psychologist, 56,* 227–238.

Matas, L., Arend, R., & Sroufe, L. A. (1978). Continuity of adaptation in the second year: the relationship between quality of attachment and later competence.*Child Development, 49,* 547–556.

Maulik, P. K., Mascarenhas, M. N., Mathers, C. D., Dua, T., & Saxena, S. (2011). Prevalence of intellectual disability: a meta-analysis of population-based studies. *Research in Developmental Disabilities, 32,* 419–436.

References

Maurer, D., & Barrera, M. (1981). Infants' perception of natural and distorted arrangements of a schematic face. *Child Development, 52,* 196–202.

Maurer, D., & Maurer, C. (1988). *The World of the Newborn.* New York: Basic.

Maurer, D., & Salapatek, P. (1976). Developmental changes in the scanning of faces by young infants. *Child Development, 47,* 523–527.

Mavroveli, S., Petrides, K. V., Shove, C., & Whitehead, A. (2008). Investigation of the construct of trait emotional intelligence in children. *European Child and Adolescent Psychiatry, 17,* 516–526.

Mayer, J. D., Caruso, D. R., & Salovey, P. (2000). Emotional intelligence meets the traditional standards for an intelligence. *Intelligence, 27,* 267–298.

Mayer, J. D. & Salovey, P. (1993). The intelligence of emotional intelligence. *Intelligence, 17,* 433–442.

McDougall, J., DeWit, D. J., King, G., Miller, L. T., & Killip, S. (2004). High school-aged youths' attitudes toward their peers with disabilities: the role of school and student interpersonal factors. *International Journal of Disability, Development and Education, 51,* 287–313.

McGhee, P. E. (1979). *Humor: Its origin and development.* San Francisco, CA: Freeman.

McGillicuddy-De Lisi, A. V., Watkins, C., & Vinchur, A. J. (1994). The effect of relationship on children's distributive justice. *Child Development, 65,* 1694–1700.

McGowan, P. O., Sasaki, A., D'Alessio, A. C., Dymov, S., Labonté, B., Szyf, M., Turecki, G., & Meaney, M. J. (2009). Epigenetic regulation of the glucocorticoid receptor in human brain associates with childhood abuse. *Nature Neuroscience, 12,* 342–348.

McGraw, M. B. (1935). *Growth: A study of Johnny and Jimmy.* New York: AppeltonCentury-Crofts.

McMahan, M., Pisani, L., & Oumar, F. (2001). Infant-mother attachment among the Dogon of Mali. *Child Development, 72,* 1451–1466.

Meaney, M. J. (2001). Maternal care, gene expression, and the transmission of individual differences in stress reactivity across generations. *Annual Review of Neuroscience, 24,* 1161–1192.

Meins, E., Fernyhough, C., Russell, J., & Clark-Carter, D. (1998). Security of attachment as a predictor of mentalising abilities: a longitudinal study. *Social Development, 7,* 1–24.

Meltzoff, A. N., & Borton, R. W. (1979). Intermodal matching by human neonates. *Nature, 282,* 403–404.

Mendive, S., Bornstein, M. H., & Sebastián, C. (2013). The role of maternal attention-directing strategies in 9-month-old infants attaining joint engagement. *Infant Behavior and Development, 36,* 115–123.

Menella, J. A., & Beauchamp, G. K. (1996). The effects of repeated exposure to garlic-flavored milk on the nursling's behavior. *Pediatric Research, 34,* 805–808.

Menyuk, P., Liebergott, J. W., & Schultz, M. (1995). *Early Language Development in Full-Term and Premature Infants.* Hillsdale, NJ: Erlbaum.

Mesman, J., van IJzendoorn, M. H., & Bakermans-Kranenburg, M. J. (2009). The many faces of the still-face paradigm: a review and meta-analysis. *Developmental Review, 29,* 120–162.

Meyer, A. (1957). *Psychopathology: A science of man.* Springfield, MA: Thomas.

Miller, G. A. (1956). The magical number seven, plus or minus two: some limits on our capacity for information processing. *Psychological Review, 63,* 81–97.

Miller, P. H. (1993). *Theories of Developmental Psychology* (3rd edition). New York: Freeman.

Miller, P. H. (2002). *Theories of Developmental Psychology* (4th edition). New York: Worth.

Miller, S. A. (1998). *Developmental Research Methods* (2nd edition). Upper Saddle River, NJ: Prentice-Hall.

Miller, S. M., & Green, M. L. (1985). Coping with stress and frustration: origins, nature, and development. In M. Lewis and C. Saarni (eds), *The Socialization of Emotions* (pp. 263–314). New York: Plenum.

Mischel, W., Shoda, Y., & Peake, P. K. (1988). The nature of adolescent competencies predicted by pre-school delay of gratification. *Journal of Personality and Social Psychology, 54*, 687–696.

Moerk, E. L. (1992). *A First Language Taught and Learned*. Baltimore, MD: Paul H. Brookes.

Moffitt, T. E. (1993). Life-course-persistent and adolescence-limited antisocial behavior: a developmental taxonomy. *Psychological Review, 100*, 674–701.

Moffitt, T. E., Arseneault, L., Belsky, D., Dickson, N., Hancox, R. J., Harrington, H., Hours, R., Poulton, R., Roberts, B. W., Ross, S., Sears, M. R., Thomson, W. M., & Caspi, A. (2011). A gradient of child-hood self-control predicts health, wealth, and public safety. *Proceedings of the National Academy of Sciences, 108*, 2693–2698.

Moffitt, T. E., Caspi, A., Belsky, J., & Silva, P. A. (1992). Childhood experience and the onset of menarche: a test of a sociobiological model. *Child Development, 63*, 47–58.

Moffitt, T. E., Caspi, A., Rutter, M., & Silva, P. A. (2001). *Sex Differences in Antisocial Behavior*. Cambridge: Cambridge University Press.

Molfese, D. L., & Molfese, V. J. (1979). Hemisphere and stimulus differences as reflected in the cortical responses of newborn infants to speech stimuli. *Developmental Psychology, 15*, 505–511.

Montague, D. P. F., & Walker-Andrews, A. S. (2001). Peekaboo: a new look at infants' perception of emotion expressions. *Developmental Psychology, 37*, 826–838.

Moore, K. L., & Persaud, T. V. N. (2003). *Before We Are Born* (6th edition). Philadelphia, PA: Saunders.

Morrongiello, B. A., Hewitt, K. L., & Gotowiec, A. (1991). Infant discrimination of relative distance in the auditory modality: approaching versus receding sound sources. *Infant Behavior Development, 14*, 187–208.

Moshman, D. (1998). Cognitive development beyond childhood. In W. Damon (gen. ed.), D. Kuhn and R. S. Siegler (vol. eds), *Handbook of Child Psychology: Vol. 2. Cognition, perception, and language* (5th edition, pp. 947–978). New York: Wiley.

Moshman, D., & Franks, B. A. (1986). Development of the concept of inferential validity. *Child Development, 57*, 153–165.

Moster, D., Lie, R. T., & Markestad, T. (2008). Long-term medical and social consequences of preterm birth. *New England Journal of Medicine, 359*, 262–273.

Moutier, S., Plagne-Cayeux, S., Melot, A., & Houde, O. (2006). Syllogistic reasoning and belief-bias inhibition in school children: evidence from a negative priming paradigm. *Developmental Science, 9*, 166–172.

Mufson, L., & Moreau, D. (1997). Depressive disorders. In R. Ammerman and M. Hersen (eds), *Handbook of Prevention and Treatment with Children and Adolescents* (pp. 403–430). New York: Wiley.

Muir, D., & Clifton, R. (1985). Infants' orientation to the location of sound sources. In G. Gottlieb and N. Krasnegor (eds), *Measurement of Audition and Vision in the First Year of Postnatal Life: A methodological overview* (pp. 171–194). Norwood, NJ: Ablex.

Muir, D., & Field, J. (1979). Newborn infants orient to sounds. *Child Development, 50*, 431–436.

Mulligan, J., Voss, L. D., McCaughey, E. S., Bailey, B. J., & Betts, P. R. (1998). Growth monitoring: testing the new guidelines. *Archives of Disease in Childhood, 79*, 318–322.

Mukherji, P. & Albon, D. (2014). *Research Methods in Early Childhood: An Introductory Guide*. London: Sage.

Murray, L., Cresswell, C., & Cooper, P. J. (2009). The development of anxiety disorders in childhood: an integrative review. *Psychological Medicine, 39*, 1413–1423.

References

Murray, L., & Trevarthen, C. (1985). Emotional regulations of interactions between two-month-olds and their mothers. In T. M. Field and N. A. Fox (eds), *Social Perception in Infants* (pp. 177–197). Norwood, NJ: Ablex.

Murray-Close, D., Crick, N. R., & Galotti, K. M. (2006). Children's moral reasoning regarding physical and relational aggression. *Social Development, 15*, 345–372.

Mussen, P. H., & Eisenberg-Berg, N. (1977). *Roots of Caring, Sharing and Helping.* San Francisco, CA: Freeman.

Naigles, L. G., & Gelman, S. A. (1995). Overextensions in comprehension and production revisited: preferential-looking in a study of dog, cat, and cow. *Journal of Child Language, 22*, 19–46.

Nánez, J., Sr. (1987). Perception of impending collision in 3- to 6-week-old infants. *Infant Behavior and Development, 11*, 447–463.

Naus, M. J. (1982). Memory development in the young reader: the combined effects of knowledge base and memory processing. In W. Otto and S. White (eds), *Reading Expository Text.* New York: Academic.

Neimark, E. D. (1975). Intellectual development during adolescence. In F. D. Horowitz (ed.), *Review of Child Development Research* (Vol. 4, pp. 543–594). Chicago: University of Chicago Press.

Neisser, U. (1976). *Cognition and Reality: Principles and implications of cognitive psychology.* San Francisco, CA: Freeman.

Nellis, L. M., & Gridley, B. E. (2000). Sociocultural problem-solving skills in preschoolers of high-intellectual ability. *Gifted Child Quarterly, 44*, 33–44.

Nelson, C. A., & Bosquet, M. (2000). Neurobiology of fetal and infant development: implications for infant mental health. In C. H. Zeanah (ed.), *Handbook of Infant Mental Health* (2nd edition, pp. 37–59). New York: Guilford.

Nelson, K. (1973). Structure and strategy in learning to talk. *Monographs of the Society for Research in Child Development, 38* (1–2, Serial No. 149).

Nelson, K. (1977). Aspects of language acquisition and form use from age 2 to age 20. *Journal of the American Academy of Child Psychiatry, 16*, 121–132.

Nelson, K. (1988). Constraints on word learning? *Cognitive Development, 3*, 221–246.

Newcomb, A. F., & Bagwell, C. L. (1995). Children's friendship relations: a meta-analytic review. *Psychological Bulletin, 117*, 306–347.

Newschaffer, C. J., Croen, L. A., Daniels, J., Giarelli, E., Grether, J. K., Levy, S. E., Mandell, D. S., Miller, L. A., Pinto-Martin, J., Reaven, J., Reynolds, A. M., Rice, C. E., Schendel, D., & Windham, G. C. (2007). The epidemiology of autism spectrum disorders. *Annual Review Public Health, 28*, 235–258.

NICHD Early Child Care Research Network (2005). Predicting individual differences in attention, memory, and planning in first graders from experiences at home, child care, and school. *Developmental Psychology, 41*, 99–114.

Nielsen, M. (2006). Copying actions and copying outcomes: social learning through the second year. *Developmental Psychology, 42*, 555–565.

Nigg, J. T. (2006). Temperament and developmental psychopathology. *Journal of Child Psychology and Psychiatry, 47*, 395–422.

Nilzon, K. R., & Palmerus, K. (1997). Anxiety in depressed school children. *Social Psychology International, 18*, 165–177.

Noble, C. H., Rowland, C. F., & Pine, J. M. (2011). Comprehension of argument structure and semantic roles: evidence from English-learning children and the Forced-Choice Pointing Paradigm. *Cognitive Science, 35*, 963–982.

Nolen-Hoeksema, S. (1994). An interactive model for the emergence of gender differences in depression in adolescence. *Journal of Research on Adolescence, 4,* 519–534.

O'Connor, M.J., & Paley, B. (2006). Relationship of prenatal alcohol exposure and the postnatal environment to child depressive symptoms. *Journal of Pediatric Psychology, 31,* 50–64.

O'Connor, T. G., Marvin, R. S., Rutter, M., Olrick, J., Britner, P. A., & the ERA Study Team. (2003). Child-parent attachment following early institutional deprivation. *Development and Psychopathology, 15,* 19–38.

Ogden, J. (2007) *Health Psychology: A textbook* (4th edition). Buckingham: McGraw Hill/Open University Press.

Olson, D. R. (1994). *The World on Paper.* Cambridge: Cambridge University Press.

Olson, D. R. (1988). Or what's a metaphor for? *Metaphor and Symbolic Activity, 3,* 215–222.

Olweus, D., Mattison, A., Schalling, D., & Low, H. (1988). Circulating testosterone levels and aggression in adolescent males: a causal analysis. *Psychosomatic Medicine, 50,* 261–272.

O'Neill, D. (1996). Pragmatics and the development of communicative ability. In D. Green et al. (eds), *Cognitive Science: An introduction* (pp. 244–275). Oxford: Blackwell.

Onishi, K. H., & Baillargeon, R. (2005). Do 15-month old infants understand false beliefs? *Science, 308,* 255–258.

Onishi, K.H., Baillargeon, R., & Leslie, A. M. (2007). 15-month old infants detect violations in pretend scenarios. *Acta Psychologica, 124,* 106–128

O'Reilly, M., Dogra, N., & Ronzoni, P.D. (2013). *Research with Children: Theory and practice.* London: Sage.

Ornstein, P. A., Naus, M. J., & Liberty, C. (1975). Rehearsal and organizational processes in children's memory. *Child Development, 46,* 818–830.

Osherson, D., & Markman, E. (1975). Language and the ability to evaluate contradictions and tautologies. *Cognition, 3,* 213–226.

Ostrea, E. M., Ostrea, A. R., & Simpson, P. M. (1997). Mortality within the first 2 years in infants exposed to cocaine, opiate, or cannabinoid during gestation. *Pediatrics, 100,* 79–85.

Palinscar, A. S., & Brown, A. L. (1984). Reciprocal teaching of comprehension-monitoring activities. *Cognition and Instruction, 1,* 117–175.

Parke, R. D. (1996). *Fatherhood.* Cambridge MA: Cambridge University Press.

Parke, R. D. (2002). Fatherhood. In M. Bornstein (ed.), *Handbook of Parenting* (2nd edition). Mahwah, NJ: Erlbaum.

Parker, J. G., & Asher, S. R. (1993). Friendship and friendship quality in middle childhood. *Developmental Psychology, 29,* 611–621.

Parker, J. G., & Gottman, J. M. (1989). Social and emotional development in a relational context: friendship interaction from early childhood to adolescence. In T. J. Berndt and G. W. Ladd (eds), *Peer Relationships in Child Development* (pp. 95–131). New York: Wiley.

Parkhurst, J. T., & Asher, S. R. (1992). Peer rejection in middle school: subgroup differences in behavior, loneliness and interpersonal concerns. *Developmental Psychology, 28,* 231–241.

Parten, M. (1932). Social participation among preschool children. *Journal of Abnormal and Social Psychology, 27,* 243–269.

Pascalis, O., De Schonen, S., Morten, J., Deruelle, C., & Fabre-Grenet, M. (1995). Mother's face recognition by neonates: a replication and extension. *Infant Behavior and Development, 18,* 79–85.

References

Patterson, G. (1996). Some characteristics of a developmental theory for early-onset delinquency. In M. F. Lenzenweger and J. J. Haugaard (eds), *Frontiers of Developmental Psychopathology* (pp. 81–124). New York: Oxford University Press.

Patterson, G. R. (2002). The early development of coercive family processes. In G. R. Reid and J.Snyder (eds), *Antisocial Behavior in Children and Adolescents*. Washington, DC: American Psychological Association.

Patterson, G. R., DeBarshyshe, B., & Ramsey, R. (1989). A developmental perspective on antisocial behavior. *American Psychologist, 44,* 329–335.

Paul, R. (1987). Natural history. In D. Chen, A. Donnelan and R. Paul (eds), *Handbook of Autism and Pervasive Developmental Disorders* (pp. 121–130). New York: Wiley.

Pederson, S., Vitaro, F., Barker, E. D., & Broge, A. I. (2007). The timing of middle-childhood peer rejection and friendship: linking early behavior to early-adolescent adjustment. *Child Development, 78,* 1037–1051.

Pedlow, R., Sanson, A., Prior, M., & Oberklaid, F. (1993). Stability of maternally reported temperament from infancy to 8 years. *Developmental Psychology, 29,* 998–1007.

Pegg, J. E., Werker, J. F., & McLeod, P. J. (1992). Preference for infant-directed over adult-directed speech: evidence from 7-week-old infants. *Infant Behavior and Development, 15,* 325–345.

Pellegrini, A. D. (2011). The development and function of locomotor play. In A. D. Pellegrini (ed.), *The Oxford Handbook of the Development of Play* (pp. 172–184). Oxford: Oxford University Press.

Perlmutter, M. (1984). Continuities and discontinuities in early human memory paradigms, processes, and performance. In R. Kail and N. E. Spear (eds), *Comparative Perspectives on the Development of Memory* (pp. 253–287). Hillsdale, NJ: Erlbaum.

Perner, J. (1988). Higher-order beliefs and intentions in children's understanding of social interaction. In J. W. Astington, P. L. Harris and D. R. Olson (eds), *Developing Theories of Mind* (pp. 271–294). Cambridge: Cambridge University Press.

Perner, J. (1991). *Understanding the Representational Mind.* Cambridge, MA: Bradford/ MIT.

Perner, J., & Leekam, S. R. (1986). Belief and quantity: three-year-olds' adaptation to listener's knowledge. *Journal of Child Language, 13,* 305–315.

Perner, J., Ruffman, T., & Leekam, S. R. (1994). Theory of mind is contagious: you catch it from your sibs. *Child Development, 5,* 1228–1238.

Perry, D. G., & Bussey, K. (1979). The social learning theory of sex differences: imitation is alive and well. *Journal of Personality and Social Psychology, 37,* 1699–1712.

Petanjek, Z., Judaš, M., Šimić, G., Rašin, M. R., Uylings, H. B., Rakic, P., & Kostović, I. (2011). Extraordinary neoteny of synaptic spines in the human prefrontal cortex. *Proceedings of the National Academy of Sciences, 108,* 13281–13286.

Peters, R. D. (2005). A community-based approach to promoting resilience in young children, their families, and their neighbourhoods. In R. D. Peters, B. Leadbeater and R. J. McMahon (eds), *Resilience in Children, Families and Communities: Linking context to practice and policy* (pp. 157–176). New York: Kluwer Academic/Plenum.

Peterson, C., Warren, K. L., & Short, M. M. (2011). Infantile amnesia across the years: a 2-year follow-up of children's earliest memories. *Child Development, 82,* 1092–1105.

Petrides, K.V., & Furnham, A. (2001). Trait emotional intelligence: psychometric investigation with reference to established trait taxonomies. *European Journal of Personality, 15,* 425–448.

Piaget, J. (1926). *The Language and Thought of the Child.* New York: Harcourt, Brace & World.

Piaget, J. (1932). *The Moral Judgement of the Child*. New York: Harcourt Brace.

Piaget, J. (1952). *The Origins of Intelligence in Children*. New York: International Universities Press.

Piaget, J. (1954). *The Construction of Reality in the Child*. New York: Basic.

Piaget, J. (1962). *Play, Dreams and Imitation in Childhood*. New York: Norton.

Piaget, J. (1969). *The Mechanisms of Perception*. New York: Basic.

Piaget, J. (1971). *Biology and Knowledge*. Chicago: University of Chicago Press.

Piaget, J. (1983). Piaget's theory. In P. H. Mussen (series ed.) and W. Kessen (Vol. ed.), *Handbook of Child Psychology: Vol. 1. History, theory, and methods* (pp. 103–128). New York: Wiley.

Piaget, J., & Inhelder, B. (1956). *The Child's Conception of Space*. London: Routledge & Kegan Paul.

Piek, J. P. (2002). The role of variability in early motor development. *Infant Behavior and Development*, *25*, 452–465.

Pinker, S. (1994). *The Language Instinct: How the mind creates language*. New York: William Morrow.

Pisecco, S., Huzinec, C., & Curtis, D. (2001). The effect of child characteristics on teachers' acceptability of classroom-based behavioral strategies and psychostimulant medication for the treatment of ADHD. *Journal of Clinical and Child Psychology*, *30*, 413–421.

Pitcher, J. B., Riley, A. M., Doeltgen, S. H., Kurylowicz, L., Rothwell, J. C., McAllister, S. M., Smith, A. E., Clow, A., Kennaway, D. J., & Ridding, M. C. (2012). Physiological evidence consistent with reduced neuroplasticity in human adolescents born preterm. *Journal of Neuroscience*, *32*, 16410–16416.

Plomin, R., DeFries, J. C., Craig, I. W., & McGuffin, P. (2001). *Behavioral Genetics* (4th edition). New York: Worth.

Plomin, R., DeFries, J. C., McClearn, G. E., & Rutter, M. (1997). *Behavioral Genetics* (3rd edition). New York: Freeman.

Plomin, R., Pederson, N. L., Lichtenstein, P., & McClearn, G. E. (1994). Variability and stability in cognitive abilities are largely genetic later in life. *Behavior Genetics*, *24*, 207–215.

Plomin, R., & Walker, S. O. (2003). Genetics and educational psychology. *British Journal of Educational Psychology*, *73*, 3–14.

Pluess, M., & Belsky, J. (2009). Differential susceptibility to rearing experience: the case of child-care. *Journal of Child Psychology and Psychiatry*,*50*, 396–404.

Pollitt, E. (1994). Poverty and child development: relevance of research in developing countries to the United States. *Child Development*, *65*, 283–295.

Pontifex, M. B., Saliba, B. J., Raine, L. B., Picchietti, D. L., & Hillman, C. H. (2013). Exercise improves behavioral, neurocognitive, and scholastic performance in children with attention-deficit/hyperactivity disorder. *Journal of Pediatrics*, *162*, 543–551.

Porges, S. (1991). Vagal tone: an autonomic mediator of affect. In J. Garber and K. Dodge (eds), *The Development of Emotional Regulation and Dysregulation* (pp. 111–128). Cambridge: Cambridge University Press.

Porter, R. H., Makin, J. W., Davis, L. B., & Christensen, K. M. (1992). Breast-fed infants respond to olfactory cues from their own mother and unfamiliar lactating females. *Infant Behavior and Development*, *15*, 85–93.

Presbie, R. J., & Coiteux, P. F. (1971). Learning to be generous or stingy: imitation of sharing behaviour as a function of model generosity and vicarious reinforcement. *Child Development*, *42*, 1033–1038.

Prinz, R. J., & Miller, G. E. (1991). Issues in understanding and treating childhood conduct problems in disadvantaged populations. *Journal of Clinical Child Psychology*, *20*, 379–385.

Pulaski, M. (1980). *Understanding Piaget: An introduction to children's cognitive development*. New York: Harper & Row.

Purves, D., & Lichtman, J. W. (1980). Elimination of synapses in the developing nervous system. *Science, 210*, 153–157.

Quine, W. V. (1960). *Word and Object*. Cambridge, MA: MIT Press.

Radke-Yarrow, M., Zahn-Waxler, C., & Chapman, M. (1983). Children's prosocial dispositions and behavior. In P. H. Mussen (series ed.) and E. M. Hetherington (vol. ed.), *Handbook of Child Psychology: Vol. 4. Socialization, personality and social development* (pp. 469–545). New York: Wiley.

Rakic, P. (1995). Corticogenesis in human and nonhuman primates. In M. S. Gazzaniga (ed.), *The Cognitive Neurosciences* (pp. 127–145). Cambridge, MA: MIT.

Rakic, P., Bourgeois, J. P., & Goldman-Rakic, P. S. (1994). Synaptic development of the cerebral cortex: implications for learning, memory, and mental illness. In J. van Pelt, M. A. Corner, H. B. M. Uylings and F. H. Lopes da Silva (eds), *The Self-Organizing Brain: From Growth Cones to Functional Networks* (pp. 227–240). New York: Elsevier.

Ratner, N. B. (1993). A typical language development. In J. Berko Gleason (ed.), *The Development of Language* (pp. 325–368). New York: Macmillan.

Reich, P. A. (1986). *Language Development*. Englewood Cliffs, NJ: Prentice-Hall.

Reisman, J. E. (1987). Touch, motion and proprioception. In P. Salapatek and L. Cohen (eds), *Handbook of Infant Perception: Vol. 1. From sensation to perception* (pp. 265–304). Orlando, FL: Academic.

Renshaw, P. D., & Brown, P. J. (1993). Loneliness in middle childhood: concurrent and longitudinal predictors. *Child Development, 64*, 1271–1284.

Rescorla, L.A. (1980). Overextension in early language development. *Journal of Child Language, 7*, 321–335.

Rest, J. R. (1986). *Moral Development: Advances in research and theory*. New York: Praeger.

Restak, R. M. (1984). *The Brain*. New York: Bantam.

Reznick, J. S., & Goldfield, B. A. (1992). Rapid change in lexical development in comprehension and production. *Developmental Psychology, 28*, 406–413.

Riegel, K. F. (1973). Dialectic operations: the final period of cognitive development. *Human Development, 16*, 346–370.

Rieser, J., Yonas, A., & Wilkner, K. (1976). Radial localization of odors by human neonates. *Child Development, 47*, 856–859.

Roben, C. K., Cole, P. M., & Armstrong, L. M. (2013). Longitudinal relations among language skills, anger expression, and regulatory strategies in early childhood. *Child Development, 84*, 891–905.

Robins, L. N. (1978). Sturdy childhood predictors of adult antisocial behavior: replications from longitudinal studies. *Psychological Medicine, 8*, 611–622.

Robinson, E., Goleman, H., & Olson, D. R. (1983). Children's understanding of the relation between expressions (what was said) and intentions (what was meant). *British Journal of Developmental Psychology, 1*, 75–86.

Rogers, S. J., Estes, A., Lord, C., Vismara, L., Winter, J., Fitzpatrick, A., Guo, M., & Dawson, G. (2012). Effects of a brief Early Start Denver Model (ESDM)–based parent intervention on toddlers at risk for autism spectrum disorders: a randomized controlled trial. *Journal of the American Academy of Child & Adolescent Psychiatry, 51*, 1052–1065.

Rogoff, A. (1990). *Apprenticeship in Thinking: Cognitive development in social contexts*. New York: Oxford University Press.

Rogoff, B. (1998). Cognition as a collaborative process. In W. Damon (gen. ed.), D. Kuhn and R. S. Siegler (vol. eds), *Handbook of Child Psychology: Vol. 5. Cognition, perception and language* (5th edition, pp. 679–744). New York: Wiley.

Rogoff, B. (2003). *The Cultural Nature of Human Development*. New York: Oxford University Press.

Rolls, B. J., Engell, D., & Birch, L. L. (2000). Serving portion size influences 5-year-old but not 3-year-old children's food intake. *Journal of American Dietic Association, 100*, 232–234.

Roopnarine, J., Johnson, J. E., & Hooper, H. (1994). *Children's Play in Diverse Cultures*. New York: State University of New York Press.

Rose, K. A., Morgan, I. G., Smith, W., Burlutsky, G., Mitchell, P., & Saw, S. M. (2008). Myopia, lifestyle, and schooling in students of Chinese ethnicity in Singapore and Sydney. *Archives of Ophthalmology, 126*, 527–530.

Rose, S. A., Feldman, J. F., & Jankowski, J. J. (2004). Infant visual recognition memory. *Developmental Review, 24*, 74–100.

Rosenstein, D., & Oster, H. (1988). Differential facial response to four basic tastes in newborns. *Child Development, 59*, 1555–1568.

Rosenthal, R., & Jacobson, L. (1968). Pygmalion in the classroom. *The Urban Review, 3*, 16–20.

Ross, H. S., & Conant, C. L. (1992). The social structure of early conflict: interactions, relationships, and alliances. In C. U. Shantz and W. W. Hartup (eds), *Conflict in Child and Adolescent Development* (pp. 153–185). Cambridge: Cambridge University Press.

Rothbart, M. K. (1986). Longitudinal observation of infant temperament. *Developmental Psychology, 22*, 356–365.

Rothbart, M. K. (1989). Temperament in childhood: a framework. In G. A. Kohnstamm, J. E. Bates and M. K. Rothbart (eds), *Temperament in Childhood* (pp. 59–73). Chichester: Wiley.

Rothbart, M. K. (2004). Commentary: temperament and the pursuit of an integrated developmental psychology. *Merrill-Palmer Quarterly, 50*, 492–505.

Rothbart, M. K., Ahadi, S. A., & Evans, D. E. (2000). Temperament and personality: origins and outcomes. *Journal of Personality and Social Psychology, 78*, 122–135.

Rothbart, M. K., Ahadi, S. A., & Hershey, K. L. (1994). Temperament and social behavior in childhood. *Merrill-Palmer Quarterly, 40*, 21–39.

Rothbart, M. K., & Bates, J. (1998). Temperament. In W. Damon (gen. ed.) and N. Eisenberg (vol. ed.), *Handbook of Child Psychology: Vol. 3. Social and emotional development* (5th edition, pp. 105–176). New York: Wiley.

Rothbart, M. K., Derryberry, D., & Hershey, K. (1995). *Stability of Infant Temperament in Childhood: Laboratory infant assessment to parent report at seven years*. Unpublished manuscript.

Rothbart, M. K., Ziaie, H., & O'Boyle, C. G. (1992). Self-regulation and emotion in infancy. In N. Eisenberg and R. Fabes (eds), *Emotion and its Regulation in Early Development* (pp. 7–23). *New Directions for Child Development, 55*. San Francisco, CA: Jossey-Bass.

Rovee-Collier, C. (1997). Dissociations in infant memory: rethinking the development of implicit and explicit memory. *Psychological Review, 104*, 467–498.

Rovee-Collier, C., & Bhatt, R. (1993). Evidence of long-term memory in infancy. In V. Ross (ed.), *Annals of Child Development* (Vol. 9. pp 1–45). London: Jessica Kingsley.

Rozin, P. (1996). Towards a psychology of food and eating: from motivation to module to model to marker, morality, meaning, and metaphor. *Current Directions in Psychological Science, 5*, 18–24.

Rubia, K., Smith, A. B., Woolley, J., Nosarti, C., Heyman, I., Taylor, E., & Brammer, M. (2006). Progressive increase in frontostriatal brain activation from childhood to adulthood during event-related tasks of cognitive control. *Human Brain Mapping, 27*, 973–993.

Rubin, K. H. (1985). Socially withdrawn children: an 'at risk'population? In B. Schneider, K. H. Rubin and J. Ledingham (eds), *Children's Peer Relations: Issues in assessment and intervention* (pp. 125–139). New York: Springer-Verlag.

Rubin, K. H., Bukowski, W., & Parker, J. G. (1998). Peer interactions, relationships, and groups. In W. Damon (gen. ed.) and N. Eisenberg (vol. ed.), *Handbook of Child Psychology: Vol. 3. Social, emotional, and personality development* (5th edition, pp. 619–700). New York: Wiley.

Rubin, K. H., Burgess, K. B., Dwyer, K., & Hastings, P. D. (2003). Predicting preschoolers' externalizing behaviors from toddler temperament, conflict, and maternal negativity. *Developmental Psychology, 39*, 164–176.

Rubin, K. H., & Coplan, R. (1992). Peer relationships in childhood. In M. Bornstein and M. Lamb (eds), *Developmental Psychology: An advanced textbook* (pp. 519–578). Hillsdale, NJ: Erlbaum.

Rubin, K. H., Coplan, R. J., Nelson, L. J., Cheah, C. S., & Lagace-Seguin, D. G. (1999). Peer relationships in childhood. In M. Bornstein and M. Lamb (eds), *Developmental Psychology: An advanced textbook* (4th edition, pp. 451–501). Mahwah, NJ: Erlbaum.

Rubin, K. H., Fein, G., & Vandenburg, B. (1983). Play. In P. H. Mussen (series ed.) and E. M. Hetherington (vol. ed.), *Handbook of Child Psychology: Vol. 4. Socialization, personality and social development* (pp. 693–774). New York: Wiley.

Rubin, K. H., Wojslawowicz, J. C., Rose-Krasnor, L. R., Booth-LaForce, C., & Burgess, K. B. (2006). The friendships of shy/withdrawn children: prevalence, stability, and relationship quality. *Journal of Abnormal Child Psychology, 34*, 143–157.

Rucklidge, J. J., & Tannock, R. (2001). Psychiatric, psychosocial and cognitive functioning of female adolescents with ADHD. *Journal of the American Academy of Child and Adolescent Psychiatry, 40*, 530–540.

Ruff, H. A., Saltarelli, L. M., Capozzoli, M., & Dubiner, K. (1992). The differentiation of activity in infants' exploration of objects. *Developmental Psychology, 28*, 851–861.

Ruffman, T., & Keenan, T. R. (1996). Children's understanding of surprise: the case for a lag in understanding relative to false belief. *Developmental Psychology, 32*, 40–49.

Ruffman, T., Perner, J., Olson, D. R., & Doherty, M. (1993). Reflecting on scientific thinking: children's understanding of the hypothesis-evidence relation. *Child Development, 64*, 1617–1636.

Ruffman, T., Perner, J., & Parkin, L. (1998). How parenting style affects false belief understanding. *Social Development, 8*, 395–411.

Rutter, M. (1979). Protective factors in children's responses to stress and disadvantage. In W. Kent and J.Rolf (eds), *Primary Prevention in Psychopathology: Social competence in children* (pp. 49–74). Hanover: University of New England Press.

Rutter, M. (1985). Resilience in the face of adversity: protective factors and resistance to psychiatric disorder. *British Journal of Psychiatry, 128*, 493–509.

Rutter, M. (1987). Psychosocial resilience and protective mechanisms. *American Journal of Orthopsychiatry, 57*, 316–331.

Rutter, M. (1990). Psychosocial resilience and protective mechanisms. In J. Rolf, A. S. Masten and D. Cicchetti (eds), *Risk and Protective Factors in the Development of Psychopathology* (pp. 181–214). New York: Cambridge University Press.

Rutter, M. (1998). Developmental catch-up, and deficit, following adoption after severe global early privation. *Journal of Child Psychology and Psychiatry,39*, 465-476.

Rutter, M., & Garmezy, N. (1983). Developmental psychopathology. In P. H. Mussen (series ed.) and E. M. Hetherington (vol. ed.), *Socialization, Personality and Social Development* (4th edition, pp. 775–911). New York: Wiley.

Rutter, M., Kreppner, J., O'Connor, T. G., & the ERA Study Team (2001). Specificity and heterogeneity in children's responses to profound privation. *British Journal of Psychiatry, 179*, 97–103.

Rutter, M., & Quinton, D. (1987). Parental mental illness as a risk factor for psychiatric disorders in childhood. In D. Magnusson and A. Ohman (eds.), *Psychopathology: An interactional perspective* (pp. 199–219). Orlando, FL: Academic.

Rutter, M., & Rutter, M. (1993). *Developing Minds: Challenge and continuity across the lifespan.* New York: Basic.

Saarni, C. (1990). Emotional competence: how emotions and relationships become integrated. In R.A. Thompson (ed.), *Socioemotional Development* (Nebraska Symposium on Motivation, Vol. 36). Lincoln: University of Nebraska Press.

Saarni, C. (1999). *The Development of Emotional Competence.* New York: Guilford.

Saarni, C., Mumme, D. L., & Campos, J. J. (1998). Emotional development: action, communication, and understanding. In W. Damon (gen. ed.) and N. Eisenberg (vol. ed.), *Handbook of Child Psychology: Vol. 3. Social, emotional, and personality development* (pp. 237–310). New York: Wiley.

Saffran, J. R., & Griepentrog, G. J. (2001). Absolute pitch in infant auditory learning: evidence for developmental reorganization. *Developmental Psychology, 37*, 74–85.

Saffran, J. R., Werker, J., & Werner, L. A. (2006). The infant's auditory world. In R. S. D. Kuhn (ed.), *Handbook of Child Development.* New York: Wiley.

Salomo, D., & Liszkowski, U. (2013). Sociocultural settings influence the emergence of prelinguistic deictic gestures. *Child Development, 84*, 1296–1307.

Salovey, P., & Mayer, J. D. (1990). Emotional intelligence. *Imagination, Cognition and Personality, 9*, 185–211.

Sameroff, A. (1983). Developmental systems: contexts and evolution. In P. H. Mussen (series ed.) and W. Kessen (vol. ed.), *Handbook of Child Psychology: Vol. 1. History, theory, and methods* (pp. 237–294). New York: Wiley.

Sampaio, R. C., & Truwit, C. L. (2001). Myelination in the developing brain. In C. A. Nelson and M. Luciana (eds), *Handbook of Developmental Cognitive Neuroscience* (pp. 35–44). Cambridge, MA: MIT.

Sanson, A., Hemphill, S. A., & Smart, D. (2004). Connections between temperament and social development: a review. *Social Development, 13*, 142–170.

Saracho, O. N., & Spodek, B. (1998). A historical overview of theories of play. In O. N. Saracho and B. Spodek (eds), *Multiple Perspectives on Play in Early Childhood Education: Inquiries and insights* (pp. 1–10). Albany, NY: State University of New York Press.

Satcher, D. S. (2001). DHHS blueprint for action on breastfeeding. *Public Health Reports, 116*, 72–73.

Saudino, K. J. (2005). Special article: behavioral genetics and child temperament. *Journal of Developmental & Behavioral Pediatrics, 26*, 214–223.

Scarr, S. (1992). Developmental theories for the 1990s: development and individual differences. *Child Development, 63*, 1–19.

References

Scarr, S. (1996). How people make their own environments: implications for parents and policy makers. *Psychology, Public Policy & Law, 2*, 204–228.

Scarr, S., & McCartney, K. (1983). How people make their own environments: a theory of genotype environment effects. *Child Development, 54*, 424–435.

Schaal, B., Marlier, L., & Soussignan, R. (2000). Human foetuses learn odours from their pregnant mother's diet. *Chemical Senses, 25*, 729–737.

Schaal, B., Tremblay, R. E., Soussignan, R., & Susman, E. (1996). Male testosterone linked to high social dominance but low physical aggression in early adolescence. *Journal of American Academy of Child and Adolescent Psychiatry, 35*, 1322–1330.

Schaffer, H. R. (1979). Acquiring the concept of the dialogue. In M. H. Bornstein and W. Kessen (eds), *Psychological Development from Infancy: Image to intention* (pp. 279–305). Hillsdale, NJ: Erlbaum.

Schaffer, H. R. (1996). *Social Development*. Cambridge, MA: Blackwell.

Schaie, K. W. (1965). A general model for the study of developmental problems. *Psychological Bulletin, 64*, 92–107.

Schellenberg, E. G. (2004). Music lessons enhance IQ. *Psychological Science, 15*, 511–514.

Schneider, W. (2002). Memory development in childhood. In U. Goswami (ed.), *Blackwell Handbook of Childhood Cognitive Development* (pp. 236–256). Malden, MA: Blackwell.

Schneider, W., & Pressley, M. (1997). *Memory Development between Two and Twenty*. Mahwah, NJ: Erlbaum.

Schwartz, C. E., Wright, C. I., Shin, L. M., Kagan, J., & Raugh, S. L. (2003). Inhibited and uninhibited infants 'grown up': adult amygdalar response to novelty. *Science, 300*, 1952–1953.

Schweinhart, L. J., Barnes, H. V., Weikart, D. P., Barnett, W., & Epstein, A. (1993). Significant benefits: the High/Scope Perry Preschool study through age 27. *Monographs of the High/Scope Educational Research Foundation, No.10*. Ypsilanti MI: High/Scope Press.

Schweinhart, L. J., & Weikart, D. P. (1998). Why curriculum matters in early childhood education. *Educational Leadership, 55*, 57–61.

Searle, J. (1969). *Speech Acts: An essay in the philosophy of language.* Cambridge: Cambridge University Press.

Segalowitz, S. J. (1983). *Two Sides of the Brain*. Englewood Cliffs, NJ: Prentice-Hall.

Segalowitz, S. J. (1995). Brain growth and the child's mental development. In K. Covell (ed.), *Readings in Child Development: A Canadian perspective* (pp. 51–71). Toronto: Nelson Canada.

Selman, R. L. (1981). The child as a friendship philosopher. In S. R. Asher and J. M. Gottman (eds), *The Development of Children's Friendships* (pp. 242–272). New York: Cambridge University Press.

Sen, M. G., Yonas, A., & Knill, D. C. (2001). Development of infants' sensitivity to surface contour information for spatial layout. *Perception, 30*, 167–176.

Shantz, C. V. (1983). Social cognitions. In P. H. Mussen (series ed.), J. H. Flavell and E. M. Markman (vol. eds), *Handbook of Child Psychology: Vol. 3. Cognitive development*. New York: Wiley.

Shapiro, D. A., & Shapiro, D. (1982). Meta-analysis of comparative therapy outcome studies: a replication and refinement. *Psychological Bulletin, 92*, 581–604.

Shattuck, P. T., Narendorf, S. C., Cooper, B., Sterzing, P. R., Wagner, M., & Taylor, J. L. (2012). Postsecondary education and employment among youth with an autism spectrum disorder. *Pediatrics, 129*, 1042–1049.

Shatz, M., & Gelman, R. (1973). The development of communication skills: modifications in the speech of young children as a function of the listener. *Monographs of the Society for Research in Child Development, 38* (5, Serial No. 152).

Shaw, P., Greenstein, D., Lerch, J., Clasen, L., Lenroot, R., Gogtay, N., Evans, A., Rapoport, J., & Giedd, J. (2006). Intellectual ability and cortical development in children and adolescents. *Nature, 440*, 676–679.

Shayer, M. (2003). Not just Piaget: not just Vygotsky, and certainly not Vygotsky as alternative to Piaget. *Learning and Instruction, 13*, 465–485.

Shiffrin, R. M., & Schneider, W. (1977). Controlled and automatic human information processing: II. Perceptual learning, automatic attending, and a general theory. *Psychological Review, 84*, 155–171.

Shirley, M. M. (1933). *The First Two Years: A study of 25 babies*. Minneapolis: University of Minnesota Press.

Sidebotham, P., Heron, J., & Golding, J. (2002). Child maltreatment in the 'Children of the Nineties': deprivation, class, and social networks in a UK sample. *Child Abuse and Neglect, 26*, 1243–1259.

Siegal, M. (1991). A clash of conversational worlds: interpreting cognitive development through communication. In L. Resnick, J. Levine and S. Teasley (eds), *Perspectives on Socially Shared Cognition* (pp. 23–40). Washington, DC: American Psychological Association.

Siegal, M., Carrington, J., & Radel, M. (1996). Theory of mind and pragmatic understanding following right hemisphere damage. *Brain and Language, 53*, 40–50.

Siegler, R. S. (1994). Cognitive variability: a key to understanding cognitive development. *Current Directions in Psychological Science, 2*, 1–5.

Siegler, R. S. (1996). *Emerging Minds: The process of change in children's thinking*. New York: Oxford University Press.

Siegler, R. S. (1998). *Children's Thinking* (3rd edition). Upper Saddle River, NJ: Prentice-Hall.

Siegler, R. S. (2000). The rebirth of children's learning. *Child Development, 71*, 26–35.

Siegler, R. S., & Booth, J. L. (2004). Development of numerical estimation in young children. *Child Development, 75*, 428–444.

Siegler, R. S., & Jenkins, E. A. (1989). *How Children Discover New Strategies*. Hillsdale, NJ: Erlbaum.

Sikora, D. M., Johnson, K., Clemons, T., & Katz, T. (2012). The relationship between sleep problems and daytime behavior in children of different ages with autism spectrum disorders. *Pediatrics, 130* (Supplement 2), S83–S90.

Simcock, G., & Hayne, H. (2003). Age-related changes in verbal and nonverbal recall during early childhood. *Developmental Psychology, 39*, 805–814.

Simons, S. H., van Dijk, M., Anand, K. S., Roofthooft, D., van Lingen, R. A., & Tibboel, D. (2003). Do we still hurt newborn babies? A prospective study of procedural pain and analgesia in neonates. *Archives of Pediatric & Adolescent Medicine, 157*, 1058–1064.

Simpson, J. A., Griskevicius, V., Kuo, S. I., Sung, S., & Collins, W. A. (2012). Evolution, stress, and sensitive periods: the influence of unpredictability in early versus late childhood on sex and risky behavior. *Developmental Psychology, 48*, 674.

Skinner, B. F. (1953). *Science and Human Behavior*. New York: Macmillan.

Skinner, B. F. (1957). *Verbal Behavior*. New York: Appelton-Century-Crofts.

Skinner, B. F. (1971). *Beyond Freedom and Dignity*. New York: Knopf.

Slater, A. (2001). Visual perception. In G. B. A. Fogel (ed.), *Blackwell Handbook of Infant Development*. Malden, MA: Blackwell.

Slater, A., Mattock, A., & Brown, E. (1990). Size constancy at birth: newborn infants' responses to retinal and real size. *Journal of Experimental Child Psychology, 49*, 314–322.

Slater, A., & Morrison, V. (1985). Shape constancy and slant perception at birth. *Perception, 14*, 337–344.

References

Slomkowski, C., Rende, R., Conger, K., Simons, R., & Conger, R. (2001). Sisters, brothers, and delinquency: evaluating social influence during early and middle adolescence. *Child Development*, *72*, 271–283.

Smetana, J. G. (1995). Morality in context: abstractions, ambiguities and applications. In R. Vasta (ed.), *Annals of Child Development* (pp. 83–130). Philadelphia, VA: Jessica Kingsley.

Smith, L. (1996). The social construction of rational understanding. *Piaget-Vygotsky: The social genesis of thought*. Hove: Psychology.

Smith, P. K. (1997). Play fighting and real fighting. In A. Schmitt, K. Atzwanger, K. Grammer and K. Schafer (eds), *New Aspects of Human Ethology* (pp.47–64). New York: Springer.

Smith, P. K. (2010). *Children and Play*. Oxford: Wiley-Blackwell.

Smith, P. K., & Simon, T. (1984). Object play, problem-solving and creativity in children. In P.K. Smith (ed.), *Play in Animals and Humans* (pp. 199–216). Oxford: Blackwell.

Smyth, R. (1995). Conceptual perspective-taking and children's interpretation of pronouns in reported speech. *Journal of Child Language*, *22*, 171–187.

Society for Research in Child Development (1993). Ethical standards for research with children. In *Directory of Members* (pp.337–339). Ann Arbor, MI: Author.

Sodian, B., Zaitchik, D., & Carey, S. (1991). Young children's differentiation of hypothetical belief from evidence. *Child Development*, *62*, 753–766.

Sonnenschein, S. (1988). The development of referential communication: speaking to different listeners. *Child Development*, *59*, 694–702.

Sorce, J. F., Emde, R. N., Campos, J. J., & Klinnert, M. D. (1985). Maternal emotional signaling: its effect on the visual cliff behavior of 1-year-olds. *Developmental Psychology*, *21*, 195–200.

Spangler, G., & Grossman, K. E. (1993). Biobehavioral organization in securely and insecurely attached infants. *Child Development*, *64*, 1439–1450.

Spelke, E. S. (1987). The development of intermodal perception. In P. Salapatek and L. Cohen (eds), *Handbook of Infant Perception. Vol. II. From sensation to perception.* (pp. 233–274). Orlando, FL: Academic.

Spelke, E. S., Breinlinger, K., Macomber, J., & Jacobson, K. (1992). Origins of knowledge. *Psychological Review*, *99*, 606–632.

Spencer, J. P., & Schöner, G. (2003). Bridging the representational gap in the dynamic systems approach to development. *Developmental Science, 6*, 392–412.

Sperling, G. (1960). The information available in brief visual presentations. *Psychological Monographs*, *74*, No. 11.

Sprafkin, J.N., Liebert, R.M., & Poulos, R.W. (1975). Effects of prosocial televised example on children's helping. *Journal of Experimental Child Psychology, 20*, 119–126.

Springer, S. P., & Deutsch, G. (1993). *Left Brain, Right Brain*. New York: Freeman.

Sroufe, L. A. (1979). Socioemotional development. In J. D. Osofsky (ed.), *Handbook of Infant Development* (pp. 462–516). New York: Wiley.

Sroufe, L. A. (1996). *Emotional Development: The organization of emotional life in the early years*. New York: Wiley.

Sroufe, L. A., Egeland, B., & Kreutzer, T. (1990). The fate of early experience following developmental change: longitudinal approaches to individual adaptation in childhood. *Child Development*, *61*, 1363–1373.

Sroufe, L. A., & Rutter, M. (1984). The domain of developmental psychopathology. *Child Development*, *55*, 17–29.

Sroufe, L. A., Waters, E., & Matas, L. (1974). Contextual determinants of infant affectional response. In M. Lewis and L. Rosenblum (eds), *Origins of Fear*. New York: Wiley.

Sroufe, L. A., & Wunsch, J. P. (1972). The development of laughter in the first year of life. *Child Development*, *43*, 1326–1344.

Stattin, H., & Magnusson, D. (1990). *Pubertal Maturation in Female Development* (Vol. 2). Hillsdale, NJ: Erlbaum.

Stein, B. E., & Meredith, M. A. (1993). *The Merging of the Senses*. Cambridge, MA: MIT.

Stein, L. J., Cowart, B. J., & Beauchamp, G. K. (2012). The development of salty taste acceptance is related to dietary experience in human infants: a prospective study. *American Journal of Clinical Nutrition*, *95*, 123–129.

Stein, M. B., Goldin, P. R., Sareen, J., Zorrilla, L. T., & Brown, G. G. (2002). Increased amygdala activation to angry and contemptuous faces in generalized social phobia. *Archives of General Psychiatry*, 59, 1027–1034.

Steinberg, L. (1987). Impact of puberty on family relations: effects of pubertal status and pubertal timing. *Developmental Psychology*, *22*, 451–460.

Steinberg, L. (1990). Autonomy, conflict, and harmony in the family relationship. In S.S. Feldman, and G.R. Elliott,. (Ed), *At the Threshold: The Developing Adolescent.* , (pp. 255-276). Cambridge, MA: Harvard University Press.

Steiner, J. E. (1979). Human facial expressions in response to taste and smell stimulation. In H. Reese and L. P. Lipsitt (eds), *Advances in Child Development and Behavior* (Vol. 13, pp. 257–293). New York: Academic.

Sternberg, R., & Okagaki, L. (1989). Continuity and discontinuity in intellectual development are not a matter of 'either-or.' *Human Development*, *32*, 158–166.

Stevenson-Hinde, J., & Hinde, R. A. (1986). Changes in associations between characteristics and interactions. In R. Plomin and J. Dunn (eds), *The Study of Temperament: Changes, Continuities, and Challenges*. Hillsdale, NJ: Erlbaum.

Stiles, J. (2000a). Neural plasticity and cognitive development. *Developmental Neuropsychology*, *18*, 237–272.

Stiles, J. (2000b). Spatial cognitive development following prenatal or perinatal focal brain injury. In H. S. Levin and J. Grafman (eds), *Cerebral Reorganization of Function After Brain Damage* (pp. 201–217). New York: Oxford.

Strauss, R. S., & Pollack, H. A. (2003). Social marginalization of overweight children. *Archives of Pediatric and Adolescent Medicine*, *157*, 746–752.

Strayer, F. F., & Strayer, J. (1976). An ethological analysis of social agonism and dominance relations among preschool children. *Child Development*, *47*, 980–989.

Strazdins, L., George, E., Shipley, M., Sawyer, M., Rodgers, B., & Nicholson, J. (2006). Work, family and children's well-being: which jobs make a difference? International Society for the Study of Behavioural Development conference presentation, Melbourne.

Streri, A., Lhote, M., & Dutilleul, S. (2000). Haptic perception in newborns. *Developmental Science, 3*, 319–327.

Streri, A., & Pecheux, M. (1986). Tactual habituation and discrimination of form in infancy: a comparison with vision. *Child Development*, *57*, 100–104.

Stunkard, A. J., Sørensen, T. I., Hanis, C., Teasdale, T. W., Chakraborty, R., Schull, W. J., & Schulsinger, F. (1986). An adoption study of human obesity. *New England Journal of Medicine*, *314*, 193–198.

Suderman, M., McGowan, P. O., Sasaki, A., Huang, T. C., Hallett, M. T., Meaney, M. J., Turecki, G., & Szyf, M. (2012). Conserved epigenetic sensitivity to early life experience in the rat and human hippocampus. *Proceedings of the National Academy of Sciences*, *109* (Supplement 2), 17266–17272.

Sullivan, H. S. (1953). *The Interpersonal Theory of Psychiatry*. New York: Norton.

Sulloway, F. J. (2001). Birth order, sibling competition, and human behavior. In P. S. Davies and H. R. Holcomb (eds), *Conceptual Challenges in Evolutionary Psychology: Innovative Research Strategies* (pp. 39–83). Dordrecht and Boston: Kluwer.

Super, C. M. (1981). Behavioral development in infancy. In R. H. Monroe, R. L. Monroe and B. B. Whiting (eds), *Handbook of Cross-cultural Development* (pp. 181–270). New York: Garland.

Surian, L., Caldi, S., & Sperber, D. (2007). Attribution of beliefs by 13-month old infants. *Psychological Science, 18*, 580–586.

Susky, J. E. (1979). Compassion and moral development. *Journal of Thought*, 14, 227–234.

Szepkouski, G. M., Gauvain, M., & Carberry, M. (1994). The development of planning skills in children with and without mental retardation. *Journal of Applied Developmental Psychology*, *15*, 187–206.

Tager-Flusberg, H. (2005). What neurodevelopmental disorders can reveal about cognitive architecture: the example of theory of mind. In P. Carruthers, T. Simpson, S. Lawrence and S. Stitch (eds), *The Structure of the Innate Mind* (pp. 3–24). Oxford: Oxford University Press.

Tang, G., Gudsnuk, K., Kuo, S. H., Cotrina, M. L., Rosoklija, G., Sosunov, A., Sonders, M. S., Kanter, E., Castagna, C., Yamamoto, A., Yue, Z., Arancio, O., Peterson, B.S., Champagne, F., Dwork, A.J., Goldman, J., & Sulzer, D. (2014). Loss of mTOR-dependent macroautophagy causes autistic-like synaptic pruning deficits. *Neuron, 83*, 1131–1143.

Tangney, J. P. (1991). Moral affect: the good, the bad, and the ugly. *Journal of Personality and Social Psychology*, *61*, 598–607.

Tangney, J. P. (1998). How does guilt differ from shame? In J. Bybee (ed.), *Guilt and Children*. San Diego, CA: Academic.

Tanner, J. (1990). *Fetus Into Man: Physical growth from conception to maturity*. Cambridge, MA: Harvard University Press.

Teller, D. Y. (1997). First glances: the vision of infants. The Friedenwald Lecture. *Investigative Ophthalmology & Visual Science*, *38*, 2183–2203.

Thatcher, R. W. (1994). Cyclic cortical reorganization: origins of human cognitive development. In G. Dawson and K. W. Fischer (eds), *Human Behavior and the Developing Brain* (pp. 232–266). New York: Guilford.

Thelen, E. (1995). Motor development: a new synthesis. *American Psychologist, 50*, 79–95.

Thelen, E., & Bates, E. (2003). Connectionism and dynamic systems: are they really different? *Developmental Science, 6*, 378–391.

Thelen, E., & Corbetta, D. (2002). Microdevelopment and dynamic systems: applications to infant motor development. In N. P. Granott (ed.), *Microdevelopment: Transition process in development and learning*. New York: Cambridge University Press.

Thelen, E., Corbetta, D., Kamm, K., Spencer, J. P., Schneider, K., & Zernicke, R. F. (1993). The transition to reaching: mapping intention and intrinsic dynamics. *Child Development, 64*, 1058–1098.

Thelen, E., & Fisher, D. M. (1982). Newborn stepping: an explanation for a 'disappearing reflex'. *Developmental Psychology, 18*, 760–770.

Thelen, E., & Smith, L. B. (1994). *A Dynamic Systems Approach to the Development of Cognition and Action*. Cambridge, MA: MIT.

Thelen, E., & Smith, L. B. (1998). Dynamic systems theories. In W. Damon (gen. ed.) and R. M. Lerner (vol. ed.), *Handbook of Child Psychology: Vol. 1. Theoretical models of human development* (5th edition, pp. 563–634). New York: Wiley.

Thelen, E., & Ulrich, B. D. (1991). Hidden skills: a dynamic analysis of treadmill stepping during the first year. *Monographs of the Society for Research in Child Development, 58* (Serial No.223).

Thomas, A., & Chess, S. (1977). *Temperament and Development.* New York: Bruner/Mazel.

Thomas, A., & Chess, S. (1986). The New York Longitudinal Study: From infancy to early adult life. In R. Plomin and J. Dunn (eds), *Changes, Continuities and Challenges.* Hillsdale, NJ: Erlbaum.

Thomas, L., Howard, J., & Miles, G. (2006). The effectiveness of playful practice for learning in the early years. *Psychology of Education Review, 30,* 52–58.

Thompson, R. A. (1990). Vulnerability in research: a developmental perspective on research risk. *Child Development, 61,* 1–16.

Thompson, R. A. (1991). Emotional regulation and emotional development. *Educational Psychology Review, 3,* 269–307.

Thompson, R. A. (1998). Early sociopersonality development. In W. Damon (gen. ed.) and N. Eisenberg (vol. ed.), *Handbook of Child Psychology: Vol. 3. Social, emotional, and personality development* (5th edition, pp. 25–104). New York: Wiley.

Thompson, R. A., Lamb, M. E., & Estes, D. (1982). Stability of infant-mother attachment and its relationship to changing life circumstances in an unselected middle-class sample. *Child Development, 53,* 144–148.

Thompson R. J., Goldstein, R. F.,Oehler, J. M.,Gustafson, K. E.,Catlett, A. T., & Brazy, J. E. (1994). Developmental outcome of very low birthweight infants as a function of biological risk and psychosocial risk. *Journal of Developmental and Behavioral Pediatrics, 15,* 232–238.

Thornberry, T. P., Krohn, M. D., Lizotte, A. J., Smith, C. A., & Tobin, K. (2003). *Gangs and Delinquency in Developmental Perspective.* New York: Cambridge University Press.

Tinbergen, N. (1951). *The Study of Instinct.* Oxford: Oxford University Press.

Todd, L. (2006). Discriminating among levels of college student drinking through an Eriksonian theoretical framework. *Journal of Addictions & Offender Counseling, 27,* 28–45.

Tomasello, M. (1999). *The Cultural Origins of Human Cognition.* Cambridge, MA: Harvard University Press.

Tomasello, M. (2003). Origins of language. In *Constructing a Language: A usage-based theory of language acquisition* (pp. 8–42). Cambridge, MA: Harvard University Press.

Torrance, N., & Olson, D. R. (1987). Development of the metalanguage and the acquisition of literacy. *Interchange, 18,* 136–146.

Tottenham, N., Hare, T. A., Quinn, B. T., McCarry, T. W., Nurse, M., Gilhooly, T., Millner, A., Galvan, A., Davidson, M.C., Eigsti, I. M, Thomas, K. M., Freed, P. J., Booma, E. S., Gunnar, M. R., Altemus, M., Aronson, J., & Casey, B. J. (2010). Prolonged institutional rearing is associated with atypically large amygdala volume and difficulties in emotion regulation. *Developmental Science, 13,* 46–61.

Trabasso, T., Stein, N., & Johnson, L. R. (1981). Children's knowledge of events: a causal analysis of story structure. In G. Bower (ed.), *Learning and Motivation* (Vol. 15). New York: Academic.

Trehub, S. E., & Trainor, L. J. (1993). Listening strategies in infancy: the roots of music and language development. In S. McAdams and E. Bigand (eds), *Thinking in Sound: The cognitive psychology of human audition* (pp. 278–327). New York: Oxford University Press.

Tremblay, R. E. (2002). Prevention of injury by early socialization of aggressive behavior. *Injury Prevention, 8,* 17–21.

Tremblay, R. E., Japel, C., Perusse, D., McDuff, P., Boivin, M., Zoccolillo, M., & Montplaisir, J. (1999). The search for the age of 'onset' of physical aggression: Rousseau and Bandura revisited. *Criminal Behaviour and Mental Health, 9 (1),* 8–23.

Trevarthen, C. (2003). Conversations with a two-month-old. In J. Raphael-Leff (ed.), *Parent-Infant Psychodynamics: Wild things, mirrors and ghosts* (pp. 25–34). Philadelphia: Whurr.

True, M. M., Pisani, L., & Oumar, F. (2001). Infant–mother attachment among the Dogon of Mali. *Child Development, 72,* 1451–1466.

Tsao, J. C. I., Evans, S., Meldrum, M., Altman, T., & Zeltzer, L. K. (2007). A review of CAM for procedural pain in infancy: Part I. Sucrose and nonnutritive sucking. *Evidence-based Complementary and Alternative Medicine.* eCAM Advance Access, published online, 6 November 2007.

Tschann, J. M., Kaiser, P., Chesney, M. A., Alkon, A., & Boyce, W. T. (1996). Resilience and vulnerability among preschool children: family functioning, temperament, and behavior problems. *Journal of American Academy of Child and Adolescent Psychiatry, 35,* 184–192.

Tudge, J. R. H., & Scrimsher, S. (2003). Lev S. Vygotsky on education: a cultural-historical, interpersonal, and individual approach to development. In D. H. Schunu (ed.), *Educational Psychology: A century of contributions* (pp. 207–228). Mahwah, NJ: Erlbaum.

Turiel, E. (1998). The development of morality. In N. Eisenberg (ed.), *Handbook of Child Psychology: Vol 3. Social, emotional and personality development* (pp. 863–932). New York: Wiley.

Turiel, E. (2006). The development of morality. In R. M. Damon (ed.), *Handbook of Child Psychology: Vol 3* (6th edition). New York: Wiley.

Turkheimer, E., Haley, A., Waldron, M., D'Onofrio, B., & Gottesman, I. I. (2003). Socioeconomic status modifies heritability of IQ in young children. *Psychological Science, 14,* 623–628.

Twardosz, S. (2012). Effects of experience on the brain: the role of neuroscience in early development and education. *Early Education & Development, 23,* 96–119.

Underwood, M. K. (2003). *Social Aggression Among Girls.* New York: Guilford.

Vaish, A., & Striano, T. (2004). Is visual reference necessary? Vocal versus facial cues in social referencing. *Developmental Science, 7,* 261–269.

Vandell, D. L. (2000). Parents, peer groups, and other socializing influences. *Developmental Psychology, 26,* 699–710.

Van der Meer, M., Dixon, A., & Rose, D. (2008). Parent and child agreement on reports of problem behaviour obtained from a screening questionnaire, the SDQ. *European Child & Adolescent Psychiatry, 17,* 491–497.

Van Hecke, A., Mundy, P., Acra, C. F., Block, J. J., Delgado, C. E., Parlade, M. V., Meyer, J. A., Neal, A., & Pomares, Y. B. (2007). Infant joint attention, temperament, and social competence in preschool children. *Child Development, 78,* 53–69.

Van Hiel, A., Mervield, I., & De Fruyt, F. (2006). Stagnation and generativity: structure, validity, and differential relationships with adaptive and maladaptive personality. *Journal of Personality, 74,* 543.

Vasey, M., Crnic, K., & Carter, W. (1994). Worry in childhood: a developmental perspective. *Cognitive Therapy and Research, 18,* 529–549.

Vatten, L. J., Mæhle, B. O., Nilsen, T. I., Tretli, S., Hsieh, C. C., Trichopoulos, D., & Stuver, S. O. (2002). Birth weight as a predictor of breast cancer: a case-control study in Norway. *British Journal of Cancer, 86,* 89–91.

Vaughn, B. E., Egeland, B., Waters, E., & Sroufe, L. A. (1979). Individual differences in infant-mother attachment at 12 and 18 months: stability and change in families under stress. *Child Development, 50,* 971–975.

Vaughn, B. E., Kopp, C. B., & Krakow, J. B. (1984). The emergence and consolidation of self-control from eighteen to thirty months of age: normative trends and individual differences. *Child Development*, *55*, 990–1004.

Vaughn, B. E., & Langlois, J. H. (1983). Physical attractiveness as a correlate of peer status and social competence in preschool children. *Developmental Psychology*, *19*, 561–567.

Villar, J., Carroli, G., Zavaleta, N., Donner, A., Wojdyla, D., Faundes, A., Velazco, A., Bataglia, V., Langer, A., Narvaez, A., Valladares, E., Shah, A., Campodonico, L., Romero, M., Reynoso, S., de Padua, K. S., Giordano, D., Kublickas, M., & Acosta, A. (2007) World Health Organization 2005 Global Survey. Maternal and neonatal individual risks and benefits associated with caesarean delivery: multicentre prospective study. *British Medical Journal*, *335*, Epub (7628)1025.

Volk, H. E., Lurmann, F., Penfold, B., Hertz-Picciotto, I., & McConnell, R. (2013). Traffic-related air pollution, particulate matter, and autism. *JAMA psychiatry*, *70*, 71–77.

Vondra, J. I., Shaw, D. S., Swearingen, L., Cohen, M., & Owens, E. B. (2001). Attachment stability and emotional and behavioral regulation from infancy to preschool age. *Development and Psychopathology*, *13*, 13–33.

Vouloumanos, A., &. Werker, J. F. (2004). Tuned to the signal: the privileged status of speech for young infants. *Developmental Science*, *7*, 270–276.

Vygotsky, L. S. (1978). *Mind in Society: The development of higher mental processes*. Cambridge, MA: Harvard University Press.

Vygotsky, L. S. (1981). The genesis of higher mental functions. In J. V. Wertsch (ed.), *The Concept of Activity in Soviet Psychology* (pp. 144–188). Armonk, NY: Sharpe.

Vygotsky, L. S. (1986). *Thought and Language* (A. Kozulin, trans.). Cambridge, MA: MIT.

Wachs T. D. & Bates, J. E. (2001). Temperament. In G. Bremner and A. Fogel, (eds.), *Blackwell Handbook of Infant Development*. (pp. 465-501). Malden: Blackwell Publishing.

Waddington, C. H. (1975). *The Evolution of an Evolutionist*. Ithaca, NY: Cornell University Press.

Walker, L. J., & Henning, K. H. (1997). Moral development in the broader context of personality. In S. Hala (ed.), *The Development of Social Cognition* (pp. 297–327). Hove: Psychology.

Walsh, R., & Shapiro, S. L. (2006). The meeting of meditative disciplines and Western psychology. *American Psychologist*, *61*, 227–239.

Wang, R. F., Hermer, L., & Spelke, E. S. (1999). Mechanisms of reorientation and object localization by children: a comparison with rats. *Behavioral Neuroscience*, *113*, 475.

Wang, Q. (2008). Emotion knowledge and autobiographical memory across the preschool years: a cross-cultural longitudinal investigation. *Cognition*,17 March (Epub).

Wang, S. H., Baillargeon, R., & Patterson, T. (2005). Detecting continuity violations in infancy: a new account and new evidence from covering and tube events. *Cognition*, *95*, 129–173.

Warburton, J., McLaughlin, D., & Pinsker, D. (2006). Generative acts: family and community involvement of older Australians. *International Journal of Aging and Human Development*, *63*, 115–137.

Waschbusch, D. A., Daleiden, E., & Drabman, R. S. (2000). Are parents accurate reporters of their child's cognitive abilities? *Journal of Psychopathology and Behavioral Assessment*, *22*, 61–77.

Waters, E. (1978). The stability of individual differences in infant-mother attachment. *Child Development*, *49*, 484–494.

Waters, E., Matas, L., & Sroufe, L. A. (1975). Infants' reactions to an approaching stranger: description, validation, and functional significance of wariness. *Child Development*, *46*, 348–356.

References

Waters, E., Vaughn, B. E., Posada, G., & Kondo-Ikemura, K. (1995). Caregiving, cultural, and cognitive perspectives on secure-based behavior and working models: new growing points of attachment theory and research. *Monographs of the Society for Research in Child Development, 60* (2–3, Serial No. 244).

Waters, E., Wippman, J., & Sroufe, L. A. (1979). Attachment, positive affect, and competence in the peer group: two studies in construct validation. *Child Development, 50*, 821–829.

Watkins, W. E., & Pollitt, E. (1997). 'Stupidity or worms': do intestinal worms impair mental performance? *Psychological Bulletin, 121*, 171–191.

Watson, A. C., Nixon, C. L., Wilson, A., & Capage, L. (1999). Social interaction skills and theory of mind in young children. *Developmental Psychology, 35*, 386–391.

Watson, J. B. (1928). *Psychological Care of Infant and Child*. New York: Norton.

Watson, J. B. (1930). *Behaviorism*. New York: Norton.

Watson, J. B., & Raynor, R. (1920). Conditioned emotional reactions. *Journal of Experimental Psychology, 3*, 1–14.

Waxman, S. R., Shipley, E. F., & Shepperson, B. (1991). Establishing new subcategories: the role of category labels and existing knowledge. *Child Development, 62*, 127–138.

Weaver, I. C., Cervoni, N., Champagne, F. A., D'Alessio, A. C., Sharma, S., Seckl, J. R., Dymov, S., Szyf, M., & Meaney, M. J. (2004). Epigenetic programming by maternal behavior. *Nature Neuroscience, 7*, 847–854.

Weikart, D. P. (1998). Changing early childhood development through educational intervention. *Preventative Medicine, 27*, 233–237.

Weisz, J. R., Donenberg, G., Han, S., & Kauneckis, D. (1995). Child and adoescent psychotherapy outcomes in experiments versus clinics: Why the disparity? *Journal of Abnormal Child Psychology, 23(1)*, 83–106.

Weizman, Z. O., & Snow, C. E. (2001). Lexical input as related to children's vocabulary acquisition: effects of sophisticated exposure and support for meaning. *Developmental Psychology, 37*, 265–279.

Wellman, H. M. (1990). *The Child's Theory of Mind*. Cambridge: MIT.

Wellman, H. M., & Lempers, J. D. (1977). The naturalistic communicative abilities of two-year-olds. *Child Development, 48*, 1052–1057.

Wentzel, K. R., & Asher, S. R. (1995). The academic lives of neglected, rejected, popular, and controversial children. *Child Development, 66*, 754–763.

Werler, M. M. (2006). Teratogen update: pseudoephedrine. *Birth Defects Research, 76*, 445–452.

Werner, H. (1957). The concept of development from a comparative and organismic point of view. In D. B. Harris (ed.), *The Concept of Development* (pp. 125–148). Minneapolis: University of Minnesota Press.

Wertsch, J. V. (1991). A sociocultural approach to socially shared cognition. In L. B. Resnick, J. M. Levine and S. D. Teasley (eds), *Perspectives on Socially Shared Cognition* (pp. 85–100).Washington, DC: American Psychological Association.

Wertsch, J. V., & Tulviste, P. (1992). Vygotsky and contemporary developmental psychology. *Developmental Psychology, 28*, 548–557.

Whalen, C. K., & Henker, B. (1999). The child with attention-deficit/hyperactivity disorder in family contexts. In H. C. Quay and A. E. Hogan (eds), *Handbook of Disruptive Behavior Disorders* (pp. 139–155). New York: Plenum.

Whiting, B. B., & Edwards, C. P. (1988). *Children of Different Worlds*. Cambridge, MA: Harvard University Press.

Willatts, P. (1999). Development of means-end behaviour in young infants: pulling a support to retrieve a distant object. *Developmental Psychology, 35*, 651–997.

Williams, S., Anderson, J., McGee, R., & Silva, P. A. (1990). Risk factors for behavioral and emotional disorders in preadolescent children. *Journal of the American Academy of Child and Adolescent Psychiatry, 29*, 413–419.

Williamson, D. E., Birmaher, B., Dahl, R. E., & Ryan, N. (2005). Stressful life events in anxious and depressive children. *Journal of Child and Adolescent Psychopharmacology, 15*, 571–580.

Wilson, M. N. (1986). The black extended family: an analytical consideration. *Developmental Psychology, 22*, 246–258.

Wimmer, H., Landerl, K., & Schneider, W. (1994). The role of rhyme awareness in learning to read a regular orthography. *British Journal of Developmental Psychology, 12*, 469–484.

Wimmer, H., & Perner, J. (1983). Beliefs about beliefs: representation and constraining function of wrong beliefs in young children's understanding of deception. *Cognition, 13*, 103–128.

Wing, L. (1993). The definition and prevalence of autism: a review. *European Child and Adolescent Psychiatry, 2*, 61–74.

Winner, E. (1988). *The Point of Words: Children's understanding of metaphor and irony.* Cambridge, MA: Harvard University Press.

Winner, E., & Leekam, S. (1991). Distinguishing irony from deception: understanding the speaker's second-order intention. *British Journal of Developmental Psychology, 9*, 257–270.

Winsler, A., & Naglieri, J. (2003). Overt and covert verbal problem-solving strategies: developmental trends in use, awareness, and relations with task performance in children aged 5 to 17. *Child Development, 74*, 659–678.

Wintre, M. G., & Vallance, D. D. (1994). A developmental sequence in the comprehension of emotions: intensity, multiple emotions and valence. *Developmental Psychology, 30*, 509–514.

Wolff, J. J., Gu, H., Gerig, G., Elison, J. T., Styner, M., Gouttard, S., Botteron, K. N., Dager, S. R., Dawson, G., Estes, A. M., Evans, A. C., Hazlett, H. C., Kostopoulos, P., McKinstry, R. C., Paterson, S. J., Schultz, R.T., Zwaigenbaum, L., Piven, J., & IBIS Network (2014). Differences in white matter fiber tract development present from 6 to 24 months in infants with autism. *American Journal of Psychiatry, 169*, 589–600.

Wong, M., & Nunes, T. (2003). Hong Kong children's concept of distributive justice. *Early Child Development and Care, 173*, 119–129.

Wood, D., Bruner, J., & Ross, G. (1976). The role of tutoring in problem-solving. *Journal of Child Psychology and Psychiatry, 17*, 89–100.

Wood, D., & Middleton, D. (1975). A study of assisted problem-solving. *British Journal of Psychology, 66*, 181–191.

Woolfenden, S. R., Williams, K., & Peat, J. (2001). Family and parenting interventions in children and adolescents with conduct disorder and delinquency aged 10–17. *Cochrane Database of Systematic Reviews*, Issue 2.

Worobey, J., & Lewis, M. (1989). Individual differences in the activity of young infants. *Developmental Psychology, 25*, 663–667.

Wright, C. K., Shaw, F. D., Brown, K., & Perkins, A. (2005). Theory of mind may be contagious, but you don't catch it from your twin. *Child Development, 76*, 97–106.

Yale, M. E., Messinger, D. S., Cobo-Lewis, A. B., & Delgado, C. F. (2003). The temporal coordination of early infant communication. *Developmental Psychology, 39*, 815–824.

References

Yarrow, M. R., Scott, P. M., & Waxler, C. Z. (1973). Learning concern for others. *Developmental Psychology*, *8*, 240–260.

Yonas, A., & Owsley, C. (1987). Development of visual space perception. In P. Salapatek and L. Cohen (eds), *Handbook of Infant Perception. Vol. II. From sensation to perception* (pp. 80–122). Orlando, FL: Academic.

Youniss, J. (1980). *Parents and Peers in Social Development*. Chicago: University of Chicago Press.

Youniss, J., & Volpe, J. (1978). A relational analysis of children's friendships. In W. Damon (ed.), *New Directions for Child Development* (No. 1, pp. 1–22). San Francisco, CA: Jossey-Bass.

Zahn-Waxler, C., Cole, P. M., & Barrett, K. C. (1991). Guilt and empathy: sex differences and implications for the development of depression. In J. Garber and K. A. Dodge (eds), *The Development of Emotion Regulation and Dysregulation* (pp. 243–272). New York: Cambridge University Press.

Zahn-Waxler, C., Radke-Yarrow, M., & King, R. (1979). Child rearing and children's prosocial initiations toward victims of distress. *Child Development*, *50*, 319–330.

Zahn-Waxler, C., & Robinson, J. (1995). Empathy and guilt: early origins of feelings of responsibility. In J. Fischer (ed.), *Self Conscious Emotions* (pp. 143–173). New York: Guilford.

Zambo, D. (2008). Childcare workers' knowledge about the brain and developmentally appropriate practice. *Early Childhood Education Journal*, *35*, 571–577.

Zelazo, P. R., Kearsley, R. B., & Ungerer, J. A. (1984). *Learning to Speak: A manual for parents*. Hillsdale, NJ: Erlbaum.

Zelazo, P. R., Zelazo, N. A., & Kolb, S. (1972). 'Walking' in the newborn. *Science*, *176*, 314–315.

Index

Index

Index